Lecture Notes in Artificial Intelligence   4149

Edited by J. G. Carbonell and J. Siekmann

Subseries of Lecture Notes in Computer Science

Matthias Klusch   Michael Rovatsos
Terry R. Payne (Eds.)

Cooperative Information Agents X

10th International Workshop, CIA 2006
Edinburgh, UK, September 11-13, 2006
Proceedings

 Springer

Series Editors

Jaime G. Carbonell, Carnegie Mellon University, Pittsburgh, PA, USA
Jörg Siekmann, University of Saarland, Saarbrücken, Germany

Volume Editors

Matthias Klusch
German Research Center for Artificial Intelligence
Stuhlsatzenhausweg 3, 66123 Saarbrücken, Germany
E-mail: klusch@dfki.de

Michael Rovatsos
The University of Edingburgh
School of Informatics
Appleton Tower 3.12, Edinburgh, UK
E-mail: mrovatso@inf.ed.ac.uk

Terry R. Payne
University of Southampton
Southampton, SO17 1BJ, UK
E-mail: trp@ecs.soton.ac.uk

Library of Congress Control Number: 2006931573

CR Subject Classification (1998): I.2.11, I.2, H.4, H.3.3, H.2, C.2.4, H.5

LNCS Sublibrary: SL 7 – Artificial Intelligence

ISSN   0302-9743
ISBN-10   3-540-38569-X Springer Berlin Heidelberg New York
ISBN-13   978-3-540-38569-1 Springer Berlin Heidelberg New York

Springer is a part of Springer Science+Business Media

springer.com

© Springer-Verlag Berlin Heidelberg 2006
Printed in Germany

Typesetting: Camera-ready by author, data conversion by Scientific Publishing Services, Chennai, India
Printed on acid-free paper   SPIN: 11839354   06/3142   5 4 3 2 1 0

Preface

These are the proceedings of the Tenth International Workshop on Cooperative Information Agents (CIA 2006), held at the National eScience Centre, Edinburgh, UK, September 11–13, 2006. This year, the annual meeting of the IEEE Computer Society Standards Organisation Committee FIPA on Intelligent and Physical Agents was co-located with CIA 2006.

In today's networked world of linked, heterogeneous, pervasive computer systems, devices, and information landscapes, intelligent coordination and provision of relevant added-value information at any time, anywhere, by means of cooperative information agents becomes increasingly important for a variety of applications. An information agent is a computational software entity that has access to one or multiple heterogeneous and geographically dispersed data and information sources. It pro-actively searches for and maintains information on behalf of its human users or other agents preferably just in time. In other words, it manages and overcomes the difficulties associated with information overload in open, pervasive information and service landscapes. Cooperative information agents may collaborate with each other to accomplish both individual and shared joint goals depending on the actual preferences of their users, budgetary constraints, and resources available. One major challenge of developing agent-based intelligent information systems in open environments is to balance the autonomy of networked data, information, and knowledge sources with the potential payoff of leveraging them by the use of information agents.

The objective of the international workshop series on Cooperative Information Agents (CIA), since its establishment in 1997, has been to provide a small but very distinguished, interdisciplinary forum for researchers and practitioners to get informed about, present, and discuss the state of the art in research and development of agent-based, intelligent, and cooperative information systems and applications for the Internet and Web. Each event in the series offers regular and invited talks of excellence, given by renowned experts in the field, as well as a selected set of system demonstrations, and honors innovative research and development of information agents by means of a best paper award and a system innovation award, respectively. The proceedings of the series are regularly published as volumes of Springer's Lecture Notes in Artificial Intelligence (LNAI) series.

In keeping with its tradition, this year's workshop featured a sequence of regular and invited talks of excellence given by leading researchers covering a broad area of topics of interest, such as agent-based information provision, agents and services, rational cooperation, resource and task allocation, communication and cooperation, agent-based grid computing, and applications. This year's special topic of interest was agent-based semantic grid computing systems and their applications.

CIA 2006 featured 4 invited and 29 regular papers selected from 58 submissions. The result of the peer review of all contributions is included in this volume: a rich collection of papers describing interesting, inspiring, and advanced work on research and development of intelligent information agents worldwide. The proceedings of previous CIA workshops have been published by Springer as Lecture Notes in Artificial Intelligence volumes: 1202 (1997), 1435 (1998), 1652 (1999), 1860 (2000), 2182 (2001), 2446 (2002), 2782 (2003), 3191 (2004), 3550 (2005).

This year the *CIA System Innovation Award* and the *CIA Best Paper Award* were sponsored by Whitestein Technologies AG, Switzerland, and the CIA workshop series, respectively. There has been limited financial support available to a limited number of students as (co-)authors of accepted papers to enable them to present their work at the CIA 2006 workshop; these grants were sponsored by the IEEE FIPA standards committee and the British Society for the Study of Artificial Intelligence and Simulation of Behaviour (AISB).

The CIA 2006 workshop was organized in cooperation with the Association for Computing Machinery (ACM) and the Global Grid Forum (GGF). In addition, we are very much indebted to our sponsors, whose financial support made this event possible. The sponsors of CIA 2006 were:

NATIONAL eSCIENCE CENTRE, UK

CENTRE FOR INTELLIGENT SYSTEMS AND THEIR APPLICATIONS,
THE UNIVERSITY OF EDINBURGH, UK

WHITESTEIN TECHNOLOGIES, SWITZERLAND

BRITISH SOCIETY FOR THE STUDY OF ARTIFICIAL INTELLIGENCE
AND THE SIMULATION OF BEHAVIOUR (AISB)

IEEE COMPUTER SOCIETY STANDARDS ORGANISATION COMMITTEE
FIPA ON INTELLIGENT AND PHYSICAL AGENTS

We are particularly grateful to the authors and invited speakers for contributing their latest and inspiring work to this workshop, as well as to the members of the program committee and the additional reviewers for their critical reviews of submissions. Finally, a deep thanks goes to each of the committed members of the local organization team from the University of Edinburgh and the eScience Institute for their hard work in providing the CIA 2006 event, which marked the tenth anniversary of the series, with a traditionally comfortable, modern, and all-inclusive location and a very nice social program.

We hope you enjoyed CIA 2006 and were inspired for your own work!

September 2006   Matthias Klusch, Michael Rovatsos, Terry Payne

Organization

General Chair

Matthias Klusch   DFKI, Germany

Program Co-chairs

Michael Rovatsos   The University of Edinburgh, UK
Terry Payne   University of Southampton, UK

Program Committee

Karl Aberer	EPF Lausanne, Switzerland
Wolfgang Benn	TU Chemnitz, Germany
Federico Bergenti	U Parma, Italy
Bernard Burg	Panasonic Research, USA
Monique Calisti	Whitestein Technologies, Switzerland
Cristiano Castelfranchi	U Siena, Italy
John Debenham	TU Sydney, Australia
Yves Demazeau	LEIBNIZ/IMAG, France
Boi Faltings	EPF Lausanne, Switzerland
Fausto Giunchiglia	IRST-ITC, Italy
Marie-Pierre Gleizes	IRIT Toulouse, France
Rune Gustavsson	TH Blekinge, Sweden
Heikki Helin	TeliaSonera, Finland/Sweden
Brian Henderson-Sellers	TU Sydney, Australia
Michael Huhns	U South Carolina, USA
Toru Ishida	Kyoto University, Japan
Catholijn Jonker	U Nijmegen, The Netherlands
Hillol Kargupta	UMBC Baltimore, USA
Ewan Klein	U Edinburgh, UK
Christoph Koch	U Saarland, Germany
Manolis Koubarakis	TU Crete, Greece
Sarit Kraus	Bar-Ilan U, Israel
Daniel Kudenko	U York, UK
Maurizio Lenzerini	U Rome, Italy
Victor Lesser	U Massachusetts, USA
Jiming Liu	Hong Kong Baptist U, China
Stefano Lodi	U Bologna, Italy
Aris Ouksel	U Illinois, USA
Sascha Ossowski	U Rey Juan Carlos Madrid, Spain
Paolo Petta	Medical U Vienna, Austria

Alun Preece	U Aberdeen, UK
Omer Rana	U Cardiff, UK
Jeffrey Rosenschein	Hebrew U, Israel
Marie-Christine Rousset	U Paris-Sud, France
Ken Satoh	National Institute for Informatics, Japan
Onn Shehory	IBM Research, Israel
Carles Sierra	CSIC Barcelona, Spain
Steffen Staab	U Koblenz, Germany
Hiroki Suguri	Comtech Sendai, Japan
Katia Sycara	Carnegie Mellon U, USA
Rainer Unland	U Duisburg-Essen, Germany
Gottfried Vossen	U Muenster, Germany

Additional Reviewers

Adam Barker
Alexandra Berger
Valérie Camps
Daniel Dahl
Vasilios Darlagiannis
Esther David
Naoki Fukuta
Dorian Gaertner
Roberto Ghizzioli
Andrea Giovannucci
Pierre Glize
Dominic Greenwood
Koen Hindriks
Marc-Philippe Huget
Tobias John
Sindhu Joseph
Ron Katz
Fabius Klemm
Dimitri Melaye
Eric Platon
Annett Priemel
Giovanni Rimassa
Alex Rogers
Roman Schmidt
Joachim Schwieren
Frank Seifert
Sebastian Stein
Eiji Tokunaga
Dmytro Tykhonov

Table of Contents

Invited Contributions

Agent Based Information Provision

Applications

Agents and Services

Learning

Resource and Task Allocation

Rational Cooperation (1)

Rational Cooperation (2)

Communication and Cooperation

Agent Based Grid Computing

Semantic Web Research Anno 2006: Main Streams, Popular Fallacies, Current Status and Future Challenges

Frank van Harmelen

Vrije Universiteit Amsterdam
Frank.van.Harmelen@cs.vu.nl

Abstract. In this topical[1] paper we try to give an analysis and overview of the current state of Semantic Web research. We point to different interpretations of the Semantic Web as the reason underlying many controversies, we list (and debunk) four false objections which are often raised against the Semantic Web effort. We discuss the current status of the Semantic Web work by reviewing the current answers to four central research questions that need to be answered, and by surveying the uptake of Semantic Web technology in different application areas. Finally, we try to identify the main challenges facing the Semantic Web community.

1 Which Semantic Web?

It has already been pointed out by Marshall and Shipman in [1] that the term "Semantic Web" is used to describe a variety of different goals and methods. They distinguish (1) the Semantic Web as a universal library for human access; (2) as the habitat for automated agents and web-services [2]; and (3) as a method for federating a variety of databases and knowledge bases. And although we in no way share their rather pessimistic analysis of the possibilities for each of these three scenario's (founded as they are on rather strawman versions of each of them), we do agree that it is important to unravel the different ambitions that underly the "Semantic Web" term.

In the current Semantic Web work, we distinguish two main goals. These goals are often unspoken, but the differences between them often account for many debates on design choices, on the applicability of various techniques, and on the feasibility of applications.

---

[1] In the sense of: "of current interest", "concerning contemporary topics of limited validity".

[2] Although Marshall and Shipman do not actually use the term web-services.

M. Klusch, M. Rovatsos, and T. Payne (Eds.): CIA 2006, LNAI 4149, pp. 1–7, 2006.
© Springer-Verlag Berlin Heidelberg 2006

Interpretation 1: The Semantic Web as the Web of Data

In the first interpretation (close to Marshall and Shipman's third option), the main aim of the Semantic Web is to enable the integration of structured and semi-structured data-sources over the Web. The main recipe is to expose datasets on the web in RDF format, to use RDF Schema to express the intended semantics of these data-sets, in order to enable the integration and unexpected re-use of these data-sets.

A typical use-cases for this version of the Semantic Web is the combination of geo-data with a set of consumer ratings for restaurants in order to provide an enriched information source.

Interpretation 2: The Semantic Web as an Enrichment of the Current Web

In the second interpretation, the aim of the Semantic Web is to improve the current World Wide Web. Typical use-cases here are improved search engines, dynamic personalisation of web-sites, and semantic enrichment of existing web-pages.

The source of the required semantic meta-data in this version of the Semantic Web is mostly claimed to come from automatic sources: concept-extraction, named-entity recognition, automatic classification, etc. More recently, the insight is gaining ground that the required semantic markup can also be produced by social mechanisms of in communities that provide large-scale human-produced markup.

Of course there are overlaps between these two versions of the Semantic Web: they both rely on the use of semantic markup, typically in the form of meta-data described by ontology-like schemata. But perhaps more noticeable are the significant differences: different goals, different sources of semantics, different use-cases, different technologies.

2   Four Popular Fallacies

The Semantic Web is subject to a stream of strongly and often polemically voiced criticisms[3]. Unfortunately, not all of these are equally well informed. A closer analysis reveals that many of these polemics attribute a number of false assumptions or claims to the Semantic Web programme. In this section we aim to identify and debunk these fallacies.

Fallacy 1: The Semantic Web Tries to Enforce Meaning from the Top

This fallacy claims that the Semantic Web, enforces meaning on users through its standards OWL and RDF(S). The repost to this fallacy is easy. The only meaning that OWL and RDF(S) enforce is the meaning of the connectives in a

---

[3] e.g. http://www.shirky.com/writings/semantic_syllogism.html and http://www.csdl.tamu.edu/~marshall/mc-semantic-web.html

language that users can use to express their own meaning. The users are free to to choose their own vocabulary, and to assign their own meaning to terms in this vocabulary, to describe whatever domain of their choice. OWL and RDF(S) are entirely neutral in this.

The situation is comparable to HTML: HTML does not enforce the lay-out of web-pages "from the top". All HTML enforces is the language that people can use to describe their own lay-out. And HTML has shown that such an agreement on the use of a standardised language (be it HTML for the lay-out of web-pages, or RDF(S) and OWL for their meaning) is a necessary ingredient for world-wide interoperability.

Fallacy 2: The Semantic Web Requires Everybody to Subscribe to a Single Predefined Meaning for the Terms They Use.

Of course, the meaning of terms cannot be predefined for global use. Of course, meaning is fluid and contextual. The motto of the Semantic Web is not the enforcement of a single ontology. It's motto is rather "let a thousand ontologies blossom". That is exactly the reason why the construction of mappings between ontologies is such a core topic in the Semantic Web community (see [2,3,4] for some surveys). And such mappings are expected to be partial, imperfect and context-dependent.

Fallacy 3: The Semantic Web will Require Users to Understand the Complicated Details of Formalised Knowledge Representation.

Indeed some of the core technology of the Semantic Web relies on intricate details of formalised knowledge representation. The semantics of RDF Schema and OWL, and the layering of the subspecies of OWL are difficult formal matters. The design of good ontologies is a specialised are of Knowledge Engineering. But for most of the users of (current and future) Semantic Web applications, such details will be entirely "under the hood", just as the intricacies of CSS and (X)HTML are under the hood of the current Web. Navigation or personalisation engines can be powered by underlying ontologies, expressed in RDF Schema or OWL, without the user ever being confronted with the ontology, let alone its representation language.

Fallacy 4: The Semantic Web People will Require the Manual Markup of all Existing Web-pages

It's hard enough for most web-site owners to maintain the human-readable content of their site. They will certainly not maintain a second parallel version in which they will have to write a machine-accessible version of the same information in RDF or OWL. If this were the case, that would indeed spell bad news for the Semantic Web. Instead, Semantic Web applications rely on large-scale automation for the extraction of such semantic markup from the sources themselves. This will often be very lightweight semantics, but for many applications, that has shown to be enough.

Notice that this fallacy mostly affects interpretation 2 of the Semantic Web (previous section), since massive markup in the "Web of data" is much easier: the data is already available in (semi-)structured formats, and is often already organised by database schema's that can provide the required semantic interpretation.

3   Current Status

In this section, we will briefly survey the current state of work on the Semantic Work in two ways. First we will try to assess the progress that has been made in answering four key questions on which the success of the Semantic Web relies. Secondly, we will give a quick overview of the main areas in which Semantic Web technology is currently being adopted.

3.1   The Four Main Questions

Question 1: Where does the Meta-data Come from?

As pointed out in our Fallacy No. 4, much of the semantic meta-data will have to come from Natural Language Processing and Machine Learning technology. And indeed, these technologies are delivering this promise. It is now possible with off-the-shelve technology to produce semantic markup for very large corpora of web-pages (millions of pages) by annotating them with terms from very large ontologies (hundreds of thousands of terms), at a sufficiently quality precision and recall to drive semantic navigation interfaces. Our own work on the DOPE prototype is only one of many examples that can be given: 5 million web-pages indexed with an ontology of 235.000 concepts, used for query disambiguation, narrowing, widening and semantic clustering of query results [5].

More recently (and for many in the Semantic Web community somewhat unexpected) is the capability of social communities to do exactly what Fallacy 4 claims is impossible: providing large amounts of human-generated markup. Millions of images, hundreds of millions of manually provided with meta-data tags on some of the most popular "Web 2.0" sites.

Question 2: Where do the ontologies come from?

As pointed out by [6], the term *ontology* as used by the Semantic Web community now covers a wide array of semantic structures, from lightweight hierarchies such as MeSH[4] to heavily axiomatised ontologies such as GALEN[5].

The lesson of a decade worth of Knowledge Engineering and half a decade of Semantic Web research is that indeed the world is full of such "ontologies": companies have product catalogues, organisations have internal glossaries, scientific communities have their public meta-data schemata. These have typically been constructed for other purposes, most often pre-dating the Semantic Web, but very useable as material for Semantic Web applications.

---

[4] http://www.nlm.nih.gov/mesh/
[5] http://www.opengalen.org/

There are also significant advances in the area of ontology-learning, although results there remain mixed: obtaining the concepts of an ontology is feasible given the appropriate circumstances, but placing them in the appropriate hierarchy with the right mutual relationships remains a topic of active research.

Question 3: What to do with Many Ontologies?

As stated in our rebuttal to fallacy No. 2, the Semantic Web crucially relies on the possibility to integrate multiple ontologies. This is known as the problem of ontology alignment, ontology mapping or ontology integration, and is indeed one of the most active areas of research in the Semantic Web community. Excellent surveys of the current state of the art are provided by [2,3,4].

A wide array of techniques is deployed for solving this problem, with ontology mapping techniques based on natural language technology, based on machine-learning, on theorem-proving, on graph-theory, on statistics, etc.

Although encouraging results are obtained, this problem is by no means solved, and automatically obtained results are not yet good enough in terms of recall and precision to drive many of the intended Semantic Web use-cases. Consequently, ontology-mapping is seen by many as the Achilles Heel of the Semantic Web.

Question 4: Wheres the "Web" in the Semantic Web?

The Semantic Web has sometimes been criticised as being too much about "semantic" (i.e. large-scale distributed knowledge-bases), and not enough about "web". This was perhaps true in the early days of Semantic Web developments, where there was a focus on applications in rather circumscribed domains like intranets. This initial emphasis is still visible to a large extent: many of the most successful applications of Semantic Web technology are indeed on company intranets. Of course the main advantage of such intranet-applications are that the ontology-mapping problem can to a large extent be avoided.

Recent years have seen a resurgence in the Web-aspects of Semantic Web applications. A prime example of this is the deployment of FOAF technology[6], and of semantically organised P2P systems (see e.g. the collection of work in [7]).

Of course the Web is more than just textual documents: non-textual media such as images and videos are an integral part of the Web. For the application of Semantic Web technology to such non-textual media we must for the foreseeable future rely on human-generated semantic markup (as discussed above), given the difficulty of automatically generating meaningful markup for such media.

Main Application Areas

It is beyond the scope of this brief paper to give an in-depth and comprehensive overview of all Semantic Web applications. We will limit ourselves to a bird's eye survey.

---

[6] http://www.foaf-project.org/

Looking at industrial events either dedicated events[7] or co-organised with the major international scientific Semantic Web conferences, we observe the following.

A healthy uptake of Semantic Web technologies is beginning to take shape in the following areas:

- knowledge management, mostly in intranets of large corporations
- data-integration (Boeing, Verison and others)
- e-Science, in particular the life-sciences[8]
- convergence with Semantic Grid

If we look at the profiles of companies active in this area, we see a distinct transition from small start-up companies such as Aduna, Ontoprise, Network Inference, Top Quadrant (to name but a few) to large vendors such as IBM (their Snobase ontology Management System[9], HP (with their popular Jena RDF platform[10], Adobe (with their RDF-based based XMP meta-data framework) and Oracle (now lending support for RDF storage and querying in their prime data-base product).

However, besides the application areas listed above, there is also a noticable lack of uptake in some other areas. In particular, promises in the areas of

- personalisation,
- large-scale semantic search (i.e. on the scale of the World Wide Web, not limited to intranets),
- mobility and context-awareness

are largely unfulfilled.

A pattern that seems to emerge between the succes unsuccessfull application areas is that the succesfull areas are all aimed at closed communities (employees of large corporations, scientists in a particular area), while the applications aimed at the general public are still in the laboratory phase at best. The underlying reason for this could well be as discussed above, namely the difficulty of the ontology mapping.

4   Challenges

Many of the challenges that we outlined in an earlier paper [8] are in the meantime active areas of research:

- scale (with inference and storage technology are now scaling to the order of billions of RDF triples,
- ontology evolution and change
- ontology mapping, as outlined above.

---

[7] e.g. http://www.semantic-conference.com/

[8] see e.g. http://www2006.org/speakers/stephens/stephens.ppt for some state-of-the-art industrial work.

[9] http://www.alphaworks.ibm.com/tech/snobase

[10] http://jena.sourceforge.net/

However, a number of items on the research agenda are hardly tackled, but do have a crucial impact on the feasibility of the Semantic Web vision. In particular:

- the mutual interaction between machine-processable representations and the dynamics of social networks of human users
- mechanisms to deal with trust, reputation, integrity and provenance in a semi-automated way
- inference and query facilities that are sufficiently robust to work in the face of limited resources (be it either computation time, network latency, memory or storage-space), and that can make intelligent trace-off decisions between resource use and output-quality

References

1. Marshall, C.C., Shipman, F.M.: Which semantic web? In: HYPERTEXT '03: Proceedings of the fourteenth ACM conference on Hypertext and hypermedia, New York, NY, USA, ACM Press (2003) 57–66
2. Kalfoglou, Y., Schorlemmer, M.: Ontology mapping: the state of the art. The Knowledge Engineering Review Journal (KER) (2003) 1–31
3. Rahm, E., Bernstein, P.: A survey of approaches to automatic schema matching. The VLDB Journal (2001) 334–350
4. Shvaiko, P., Euzenat, J.: A survey of schema-based matching approaches. Journal on Data Semantics (2005) 146–171
5. Stuckenschmidt, H., van Harmelen, F., de Waard, A., Scerri, T., Bhogal, R., van Buel, J., Crowlesmith, I., Fluit, C., Kampman, A., Broekstra, J., van Mulligen, E.: Exploring large document repositories with rdf technology: The dope project. IEEE Intelligent Systems **19** (2004) 34–40
6. Jasper, R., Uschold, M.: A framework for understanding and classifying ontology applications. In: Proceedings 12th Int. Workshop on Knowledge Acquisition, Modelling, and Management KAW. (1999) 4–9
7. Staab, S., Stuckenschmidt, H.: Semantic Web and Peer-to-peer: Decentralized Management and Exchange of Knowledge and Information. Springer (2005)
8. van Harmelen, F.: How the semantic web will change kr: challenges and opportunities for a new research agenda. The Knowledge Engineering Review **17** (2002) 93–96

A Research Agenda for Agent-Based Service-Oriented Architectures

Michael N. Huhns

Department of Computer Science and Engineering
University of South Carolina, Columbia, SC 29208, USA
huhns@sc.edu
http://www.cse.sc.edu/~huhns

Abstract. Web services, especially as fundamental components of service-oriented architectures, are receiving a lot of attention. Their great promise, however, has not yet been realized, and a possible explantion is that significant research and engineering problems remain. We describe the problems, indicate likely directions and approaches for their solution, present an agenda for the deployment of such solutions, and explain the benefits of the resultant deployment. It is our strong expectation that Web services will eventually have an agent basis, which would be needed to address the problems.

1   Introduction

The latest paradigm for structuring large-scale applications is a *service-oriented architecture* (SOA), which involves the linking of small functional services to achieve some larger goal. As the central concept in service-oriented architectures, Web services provide a standardized network-centric approach to making the functionality available in an encapsulated form.

It is worth considering the major benefits of using standardized services. Clearly anything that can be done with services can be done without. So the following are some reasons for using services, especially in standardized form.

- Services provide higher-level abstractions for organizing applications in large-scale, open environments. Even if these were not associated with standards, they would be helpful as we implemented and configured software applications in a manner that improved our productivity and improved the quality of the applications that we developed.
- Moreover, these abstractions are standardized. Standards enable the interoperation of software produced by different programmers. Standards thus improve our productivity for the service use cases described above.
- Standards make it possible to develop general-purpose tools to manage the entire system lifecycle, including design, development, debugging, monitoring, and so on. This proves to be a major practical advantage, because without significant tool support, it would be nearly impossible to create and field robust systems in a feasible manner. Such tools ensure that the components

M. Klusch, M. Rovatsos, and T. Payne (Eds.): CIA 2006, LNAI 4149, pp. 8–22, 2006.

developed are indeed interoperable, because tool vendors can validate their tools and thus shift part of the burden of validation from the application programmer.
– The standards feed other standards. For example the above basic standards enable further standards, e.g., dealing with processes and transactions.

To realize the above advantages, SOAs impose the following requirements:

Loose coupling. No tight transactional properties should generally apply among the components. In general, it would not be appropriate to specify the consistency of data across the information resources that are parts of the various components. However, it would be reasonable to think of the high-level contractual relationships through which the interactions among the components are specified.

Implementation neutrality. The interface is what matters. We cannot depend on the details of the implementations of the interacting components. In particular, the approach cannot be specific to a set of programming languages.

Flexible configurability. The system is configured late and flexibly. In other words, the different components are bound to each other late in the process and the configuration can change dynamically.

Long lifetime. to be useful to external applications, components must have a long lifetime. Morever, since we are dealing with computations among autonomous heterogeneous parties in dynamic environments, we must always be able to handle exceptions. This means that the components must exist long enough to be able to detect any relevant exceptions, to take corrective action, and to respond to the corrective actions taken by others. Components must exist long enough to be discovered, to be relied upon, and to engender trust in their behavior.

Granularity. The participants in an SOA should be understood at a coarse granularity. That is, instead of modeling actions and interactions at a detailed level, it would be better to capture the essential high-level qualities that are (or should be) visible for the purposes of business contracts among the participants. Coarse granularity reduces dependencies among the participants and reduces communications to a few messages of greater significance.

Teams. Instead of framing computations centrally, it would be better to think in terms of how computations are realized by autonomous parties. In other words, instead of a participant commanding its partners, computation in open systems is more a matter of business partners working as a team. That is, instead of an individual, a team of cooperating participants is a better modeling unit. A team-oriented view is a consequence of taking a peer-to-peer architecture seriously.

Web services, viewed as encapsulated and well defined pieces of software functionality accessible to remote applications via a network, are expected to be a fundamental aspect of many future software applications. Many claims have been made about the benefits of Web services for enterprise information systems and next-generation network-based applications, but the widespread availability and adoption of Web services have not yet occurred. The development, deployment, and proliferation of other new computing technologies can be seen as having occurred in stages as developers and users become familiar with the features of the technology and learn how to exploit them. The development of Web services is likely to progress according to the following four stages.

Stage 1. The first stage in the development of Web services, which is the stage that we are in currently, is that a few specific Web services will be available, mostly on intranets. There will be little or no semantics describing them. Because of this, their discovery will occur manually, their invocation will be hardcoded, and their composition with other Web services will be either nonexistent or done manually. There will be no fees for their use. The resultant applications that make use of the Web services will be brittle and static, but large ones can be crafted relatively quickly. There will be some examples of unexpected uses and utilities.

Stage 2. The second stage in the development of Web services will be characterized by many services being available across the Internet. There will be sufficient semantics, via the use of standardized keywords for narrow domains, to enable semi-automatic discovery. Compostion of services will still be arranged manually. There might be some fees for use, but they will be negotiated off-line by humans. The resultant applications might be dynamic via the substitution of Web services that are explicitly mirrored or via the use of alternative equivalents, most likely where the service functionality is common and straightforward. The desirability of this form of dynamism, and its concomitant robustness, might serve as a major motivation for the further proliferation of Web services and for improved semantics to enable dynamic discovery and a limited form of composition. The scope of the dynamic composition would be one-to-one replacement for a malfunctioning component service.

Stage 3. In the third stage, many Web services will be available, each with a rich semantic description of its functionality. The semantics will enable Web services to be discovered and invoked dynamically and on-demand.

Stage 4. During the fourth stage, some of the many available Web services will be *active*, instead of passive, and will have many of the capabilities that characterize software agents. By being active, they will be able to bid for their use in applications, requiring them to be able to negotiate over Quality-of-Service (QoS) and non-functional semantics. This will include negotiation over fees. In some applications, a candidate Web service could be tried and tested for appropriate functionality and QoS. Comparable services could not only substitute for each other, but also be used redundantly for improved robustness. Moreover, services would self-organize, possible on-demand, into service teams to provide aggregate functionality.

The above four stages of development are driven by limitations of current Web services. These can best be described and understood in the context of the well known "Web service triangle," as shown in Figure 1. In a subsequent section, we consider each of the triangle's vertices and edges and point out the desired enhancements, and thus research, needed for advancement to the next stages.

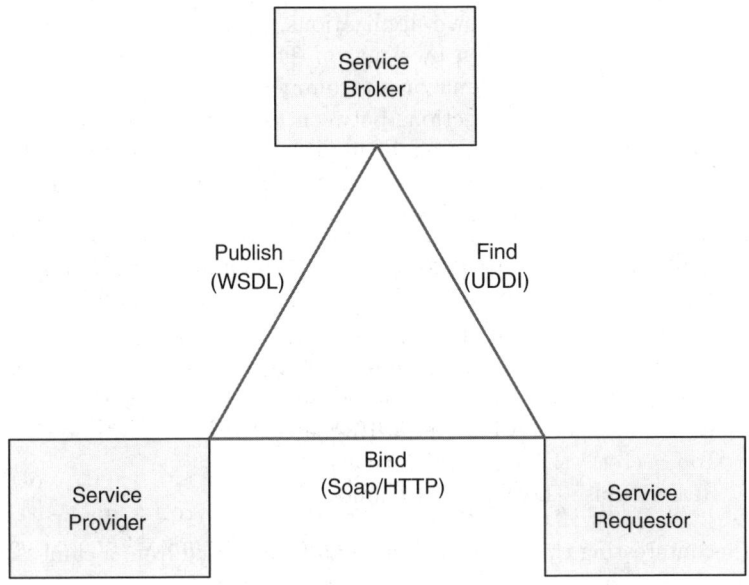

Fig. 1. The familiar Web service triangle. Its limitations can be revealed by considering each of its vertices and edges.

2 An Example of Current SOA Success

To put the above stages in perspective, let's consider a currently successful example of a service-oriented architecture, that of Amazon.com, which serves to explain the great interest in this approach to application development.

Originally, Amazon.com consisted of a large monolithic application that implemented all of the functionality that was made available through its Web site, including the front-end display, back-end database, and business logic [7]. But the monolithic reached a point where it could not be easily scaled to handle the volume of transactions that had to be processed. So, Amazon reengineered it into what became a service-oriented architecture.

Service orientation meant encapsulating the data with the business ligic that operates on it, with the only access through a well defined interface. The services did not share data and did not allow any direct access to the underlying database. The result is hundreds of services and a smaller number of servers that aggregate information from the services. The servers render the Web pages for the Amazon.com application, as well as serve the customer service application, the seller interface, the external interface to Amazon's Web services, and Amazon-hosted third-party applications. When a user visits the Amazon site, over 100 services are typically invoked in constructing the user's personalized Web page.

The end result is that Amazon can build complex applications quickly out of primitive services, and then scale them appropriately. Moreover, third parties can use the services to build their own applications, primarily for e-commerce, but some for applications unforeseen by Amazon. For example, the Web site "The Amazing Baconizer" invokes Amazon's recommendation seervice for entertainment purposes to list the connections between two items. The connections are done by looking at "people who bought item A also bought item B." Here is a sample result for the connection between the book "Surely You're Joking, Mr. Feynman!" and the DVD "Real Genius":

"Surely You're Joking, Mr. Feynman!" $\Longrightarrow$ "Real Genius" (11 hops):

"Surely You're Joking, Mr. Feynman!" – R. Feynman
$\Longrightarrow$ "Genius: The Life and Science of Richard Feynman," – J. Gleick
$\Longrightarrow$ . . .
$\Longrightarrow$ "Weird Science"(DVD) – John Hughes
$\Longrightarrow$ "Top Secret!" (DVD) – Val Kilmer
$\Longrightarrow$ "Real Genius" (DVD) – Val Kilmer

Another interesting third-party service can be accessed from a camera phone. When shopping, a user can take a photo of the bar code for a product, send it to the service, and receive via amazon's services reviews, information on comparable products, and the price.

3   Needed Research for Each Aspect of Web Services

Figure 1 shows the generic architecture for Web services. Although this is a simple picture, it radically alters many of the problems that must be solved in order for the architecture to become viable on a large scale.

- To publish effectively, we must be able to specify services with precision and with greater structure. This is because the service would eventually be invoked by parties that are not from the same administrative space as the provider of the service and differences in assumptions about the semantics of the service could be devastating.
- From the perspective of the registry, it must be able to certify the given providers so that it can endorse the providers to the users of the registry.
- Requestors of services should be able to find a registry that they can trust. This opens up challenges dealing with considerations of trust, reputation, incentives for registries and, most importantly, for the registry to understand the needs of a requestor.

- Once a service has been selected, the requestor and the provider must develop a finer-grained sharing of representations. They must be able to participate in conversations to conduct long-lived, flexible transactions. Related questions are those of how a service level agreement (SLA) can be established and monitored. Success or failure with SLAs feeds into how a service is published and found, and how the reputation of a provider is developed and maintained.

Most of the needed enhancements are related to the scaling of Web services, not only to larger applications but also to more complex environments [1]. That is, there will be a multiplicity of requestors, providers, and registries, whereas the current conception of Web services focuses on just one of each. There will also be more complex interactions than just a simple remote-procedure call to a service: the interactions will be characterized as peer-to-peer, rather than client-server [3].

When there are multiple requestors, then a service provider might be able to share the results of a computation among the requestors, and the requestors might be able to negotiate a "group rate." Of course, this requires the requestors to form a cohesive group and to have a negotiation ability.

Multiple equivalent providers present both a problem and an opportunity. The problem is that a requestor must have and apply a means to choose among them. This would likely require an ability to negotiate over both functional and non-functional attributes (qualities) of the services. The opportunity is that alternatives can yield increased robustness (described more fully below).

Multiple service registries present problems for providers in deciding where to advertise their services and for requestors in deciding where to search for services [4,6]. Also, each registry might employ different semantics and organizations of domain concepts.

Other limitations represented by the current simple model for Web services are

- A Web service knows only about itself—not about its users, clients, or customers
- Web services are not designed to use and reconcile ontologies used by each other or by their clients
- Web services are passive until invoked; they cannot provide alerts or updates when new information becomes available
- Web services do not cooperate with each other or self-organize, although they can be composed by external systems.

Another fundamental problem arises when Web services are composed. Consider the simple example in Figure 2 of one Web service that provides stock quotes in dollars and a second that converts dollars into another currency. Current Web services must be invoked sequentially by a central controller.

A significantly better model is shown in Figure 3, where an interaction protocol under development, WSDL-P, would provide for a continuation by passing a description of an overall workflow through each Web service participating in the workflow. In this way, the composed services would interact directly, rather than through a central intermediary.

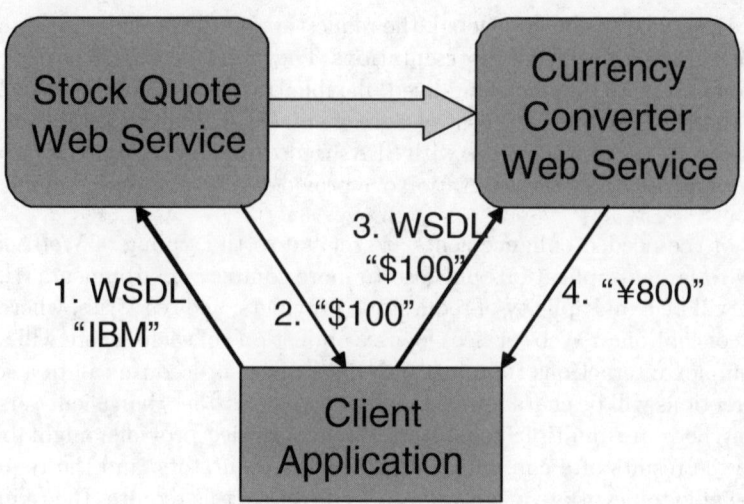

Fig. 2. Composed Web services, which are described traditionally by WSDL

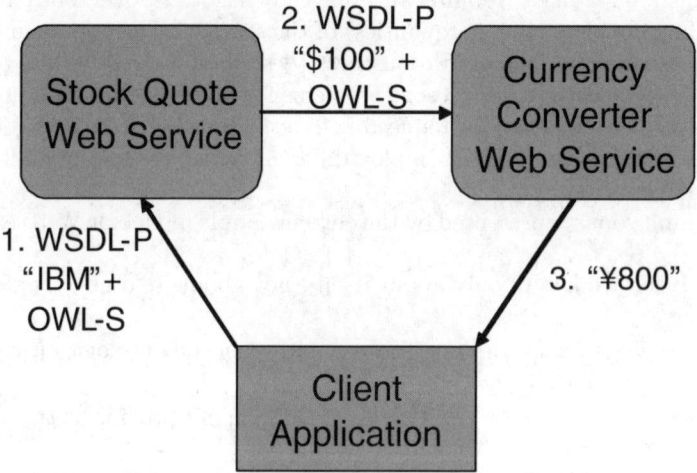

Fig. 3. WSDL-P: Next-Generation Composition. An OWL-S (or BPEL4WS) description of the workflow is communicated through the services

Solutions to the above described problems are under investigation by many research teams. The keys to the next-generation Web are *cooperative services, systemic trust, and understanding based on semantics, coupled with a declarative agent-based infrastructure.* These concepts are elaborated in the next sections, beginning with the notion of commitments as the governing principle for the complex interactions inherent in the later stages of SOA developments.

4   Commitments

For services to apply naturally in open environments, they should be modeled as being autonomous. Autonomy is a natural characteristic of agents, and it is also a characteristic of many envisioned Internet-based services. Among agents, autonomy generally refers to social autonomy, where an agent is aware of its colleagues and is sociable, but nevertheless exercises its independence in certain circumstances. Autonomy is in natural tension with coordination or with the higher-level notion of a commitment. To be coordinated with other agents or to keep its commitments, an agent must relinquish some of its autonomy. However, an agent that is sociable and responsible can still be autonomous. It would attempt to coordinate with others where appropriate and to keep its commitments as much as possible, but it would exercise its autonomy in entering into those commitments in the first place.

The first step to structuring and formalizing interactions among service providers and requestors is to introduce the notion of *directed obligations*, which are obligations directed from one party to another. This is certainly a useful step. Dignum and colleagues describe a temporal deontic logic that helps specify obligations and constraints so that a planner can take deadlines into account while generating plans [2]. However, the approach is based on the notion of obligations, and it does not give operational methods for obligations. Once a deadline has passed and a certain rule has been violated, the logic has nothing to say about the effects on the system. Nevertheless, this approach is semantically rich and detailed in the kinds of deadlines and constraints it allows agents to model. For example, the deadline "as soon as possible," can be modeled.

However, for virtual enterprises and business protocols, it is generally the case that the obligation of one party to another is bounded by the scope of their ongoing interaction. In other words, obligations derived from a virtual enterprise may last no longer than the virtual enterprise in question. Further, there is always the element of conflict, which means that the parties to a contract may be in the need for some adjudication. These considerations suggest that there is an organizational structure to the obligations, which bounds the scopes of the obligations.

The notion of *commitments* (for historical reasons, sometimes referred to as *social commitments*) takes care of the above considerations. Commitments are a legal abstraction, which subsume directed obligations. Importantly, commitments (1) are public, and (2) can thus be used as a basis for compliance. Commitments support the following key properties that make them a useful computational abstraction for service-oriented architectures.

Multiagency. Commitments associate one agent or party with another. The party that "owes" the commitment is called the *debtor* and the other party is called the *creditor*. Each commitment is directed from its debtor to its creditor.

The directionality is simply a representational convenience. In practice, commitments would arise in interrelated sets. For example, a typical business contract would commit one party to pay another party and the second party to deliver goods to the first party.

Scope. Commitments arise within a well-defined scope. This scope functions as the *social context* of the commitment. In other words, the scope is itself modeled as a multiagent system within which the debtor and creditor of the given commitment interact. For example, the parties to a business contract can be understood as forming and acting in a multiagent system in which they create their respective commitments and act on them. The multiagent system may have a short or a long lifetime depending on the requirements of the application. Conceivably, the multiagent system for a one-off interaction would be dissolved immediately, whereas some multiagent systems may even last longer than the specific agents that belong to them.

Manipulability. Commitments can be acted upon and modified. In particular, commitments may be revoked. If we were to prevent modifying or revoking commitments, we would end up ruling out some of the most interesting scenarios where commitments can be applied. For example, irrevocability would be too limiting for the kinds of open applications where service-oriented architectures make sense. Irrevocability would prevent considering errors and exceptions that may occur outside of the administrative domain of the given business partner. For instance, it may simply be impossible for a vendor to deliver the promised goods on time if the vendor's factory burns down or there are difficulties with shipping. However, we must be careful that commitments are not revoked arbitrarily, which would make them worthless. When restrictions (sensitive to a given context) are imposed on the manipulation of commitments, they can support the coherence of computations.

Services, although collaborative, retain their autonomy. They can exercise their local policies for most decisions and can be considered as being constrained only by their commitments.

4.1   A Formalization of Commitments

We write commitments using a predicate C. A commitment has the form

$$C(x, y, p, G)$$

where x is its debtor, y its creditor, p the condition the debtor will bring about, and G a multiagent system, which serves as the organizational context for the given commitment. A commitment has a simple form, e.g., $C(b, s, \text{pay}(b, s, \$10), D)$, where a buyer b commits to pay \$10 to a seller s a seller within the context of a particular business deal D between b and s.

4.2   Operations on Commitments

It helps to treat commitments as an abstract data type. This data type associates a debtor, a creditor, a condition, and a context. The following are then natural for commitments.

- create(x, c) establishes the commitment c in the system. This can only be performed by c's debtor x. For example, x promises to pay \$10 to y.
- cancel(x, c) cancels the commitment c. This can be performed only by c's debtor x, for example, x reneges on its promise to pay \$10. Generally, making another commitment compensates cancellation.
- release(y, c) releases c's debtor x from commitment c. This only can be performed by the creditor y or a higher authority. For example, x decides to waive receiving the \$10, or the government steps in to say that the agreement is null and void.
- assign(y, z, c) replaces y with z as c's creditor. For example, x is now committed to pay \$10 to y's friend z.
- delegate(x, z, c) replaces x with z as the debtor for c. For example, now x's friend is committed to pay \$10 to y.
- discharge(x, c) means that c's debtor x fulfills the commitment. For example, x actually pays \$10 to y or the assigned creditor.

Create and discharge are obvious; delegate and assign add some flexibility to commitments and are also obvious. Cancel and release remove a commitment from being in effect. Cancel is essential to reflect the autonomy of an agent; just because it made a commitment does not mean that the commitment is irrevocable. However, if commitments could be wantonly canceled, there would be no point in having them, so cancellations of commitments must be suitably constrained. Release helps capture various subtleties of relationships among business partners. A partner may decide not to insist that another party discharge its commitments. Alternatively, the organizational context within which the parties interact may find that a commitment should be eliminated. For example, ordinarily a buyer is expected to pay for goods and a pharmacist is expected to ship medicines that are paid for. However, if the goods arrive damaged then the buyer is released from paying for them (but must return them instead); if the medicine prescription turns out to be invalid, the pharmacist is released from the commitment to ship the medications.

5   Robust Services Via Agent-Based Redundancy

A major driver behind an agent basis for Web services is the demand for robustness. All approaches to robustness rely on some form of redundancy, and Web services are a natural source of redundancy for software applications.

Software problems are typically characterized in terms of bugs and errors, which may be either transient or omnipresent. The general approaches for dealing with them are: (1) prediction and estimation, (2) prevention, (3) discovery, (4) repair, and (5) tolerance or exploitation. Bug estimation uses statistical techniques to predict how many flaws might be in a system and how severe their effects might be. Bug prevention is dependent on good software engineering techniques and processes. Good development and run-time tools can aid in bug discovery, whereas repair and tolerance depend on redundancy.

Indeed, redundancy is the basis for most forms of robustness. It can be provided by replication of hardware, software, or information, e.g., by repetition of communication messages. Redundant code cannot be added arbitrarily to a software system, just as steel cannot be added arbitrarily to a bridge. A bridge is made stronger by adding beams that are not identical to ones already there, but that have equivalent functionality. This turns out to be the basis for robustness in service-oriented systems as well: there must be services with equivalent functionality, so that if one fails to perform properly, another can provide what is needed. The challenge is to design service-oriented systems so that they can accommodate the additional services and take advantage of their redundant functionality.

We hypothesize that agents are a convenient level of granularity at which to add redundancy and that the software environment that takes advantage of them is akin to a society of such agents, where there can be multiple agents filling each societal role [8]. Agents by design know how to deal with other agents, so they can accommodate additional or alternative agents naturally.

Fundamentally, the amount of redundancy required is well specified by information theory. If we want a system to provide n functionalities robustly, we must introduce $m \times n$ agents, so that there will be m ways of producing each functionality. Each group of m agents must understand how to detect and correct inconsistencies in each other's behavior, without a fixed leader or centralized controller. If we consider an agent's behavior to be either correct or incorrect (binary), then, based on a notion of Hamming distance for error-correcting codes, $4 \times m$ agents can detect $m - 1$ errors in their behavior and can correct $(m - 1)/2$ errors.

Redundancy must also be balanced with complexity, which is determined by the number and size of the components chosen for building a system. That is, adding more components increases redundancy, but also increases the complexity of the system.

An agent-based system can cope with a growing application domain by increasing the number of agents, each agent's capability, or the computational and infrastructure resources that make the agents more productive. That is, either the agents or their interactions can be enhanced, but to maintain the same redundancy m, they would have to be enhanced by a factor of m.

N-version programming, also called dissimilar software, is a technique for achieving robustness first considered in the 1970s. It consists of N separately developed implementations of the same functionality. Although it has been used to produce several robust systems, it has had limited applicability, because (1) N independent implementations have N times the cost, (2) N implementations based on the same flawed specification might still result in a flawed system, and (3) each change to the specification will have to be made in all N implementations.

Database systems have exploited the idea of transactions: an atomic processing unit that moves a database from one consistent state to another. Consistent transactions are achievable for databases because the types of processing done are regular and limited. Applying this idea to software execution requires that the state of a software system be saved periodically (a checkpoint) so the system can return to that state if an error occurs.

5.1   Architecture and Process

Suppose there are a number of services, each with strengths, weaknesses, and possibly errors. How can the services be combined so that the strengths are exploited and the weaknesses or flaws are compensated or covered?

Three general approaches are evident in Figure 4. First, a preprocessor could choose the best services to perform a task, based on published characteristics of each service. Second, a postprocessor could choose the best result out of several executing services. Third, the services could decide as a group which ones should perform the task.

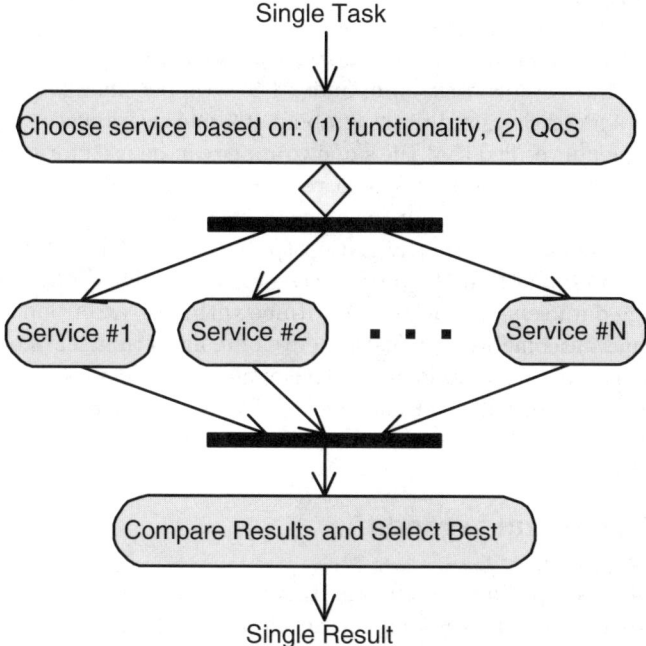

Fig. 4. Improving robustness by combining multiple implementations of a service

The difficulties with the first two approaches are (1) the preprocessor might be flawed, (2) it is difficult to maintain the preprocessor as services are added or changed, and (3) the postprocessor wastes resources, because several services work on the data and their results have to be compared.

The third approach requires distributed decision-making, which is not an ability of conventional Web services. What generic ability could be added to a service to enable it to participate in a distributed decision? The generic capability has the characteristics of an agent, so distributing the centralized functions into the different modules creates a multiagent system. Each agent would have to know its role as well as (1) something about its own service, such as its time and space

complexity, and input and output data structures; (2) the complexity and reliability of other agents; and (3) how to communicate, negotiate, compare results,
and manage reputations and trust.

5.2 Experimental Results

Huhns and colleagues collected one set of 25 algorithms for reversing a dou-
bly linked list and another set for sorting a list. Different novice programmers
wrote each algorithm. For sorting, no specifications were given to the programmers (beyond that the problem was sorting), so the algorithms all have different
data and performance characteristics. For list reversing, the class structure (i.e.,
method signatures) was specified, so the differences among the algorithms are
in performance and correctness.

Each algorithm was converted into an agent, composed of the algorithm written in Java and a wrapper written in Jade. The wrapper knows only about the
signature of its algorithm, and nothing about its inner workings.

Our experiments verified that the same wrapper can be used for both the sorting and list-reversing domains. We also verified our hypothesis that more algorithms give better results than any one alone. Further, we investigated both a distributed preprocessor and a centralized postprocessor for combining the agents'
functionality, and found that the postprocessor is generally better, but performs
worse for large data sets or selected algorithms with long execution times.

The eventual outcome for application development is that service developers
will spend more time on functionality development and less on debugging, because different services will likely have errors in different places and can cover
for each other.

6 Conclusion and Agenda

Service-oriented computing (SOC) represents an emerging class of approaches
with multiagent-like characteristics for developing systems in large-scale open
environments. Indeed, SOC presents several challenges that cannot be tackled
without agent concepts and techniques. Viewed in this light, SOC offer many
ways in which to change the face of computing.

As services become increasingly like agents and their interactions become increasingly dynamic, theyll begin to do more than just manage information in
explicitly programmed ways. In particular, services acting in concert can function
as computational mechanisms in their own right, thus significantly enhancing our
ability to model, design, build, and manage complex software systems. Think of
such MASs as providing a new approach for constructing complex applications
wherein developers concentrate on high-level abstractions, such as overall behavior and key conceptual structures (the active entities, their objectives, and
their interactions), without having to go further into individual agents details or
interactions. This vision becomes more compelling as the target environments
become more

- populous (a monolithic model is intractable, whereas developers can construct an MAS modularly)
- distributed (pulling information to a central location for monitoring and control is prohibitive, whereas techniques based on interaction among agents and the emergence of desired system-level behaviors are much easier to manage)
- dynamic (an MAS can adapt in real time to changes in the target system and the environment in which it is embedded).

Table 1. Reasons for Complex System Development Based on Multiagent Service-Oriented Systems

Multiagent System Properties	Benefits for System Development
Autonomous, objective-oriented behavior; agent-oriented decomposition	Autonomous, active functionality that adapts to the users needs; reuse of whole subsystems and flexible interactions
Dynamic composition and customization	Scalability
Interaction abstractions; statistical or probabilistic protocols	Friction-free software; open systems; interactions among heterogeneous systems; move from sophisticated and learned e-commerce protocols to dynamic selection of protocols
Multiple viewpoints, negotiation, and collaboration	Robustness and reliability
Social abstractions	High-level modeling abstractions

Table 1 shows the ways in which MAS properties can benefit the engineering of complex service-oriented systems. Potential applications and application domains that can also benefit from this approach include meeting scheduling, scientific workflow management, distributed inventory control and supply chains, air and ground traffic control, telecommunications, electric power distribution, water supplies, and weapon systems.

References

1. Mark Burstein, Christoph Bussler, Tim Finin, Michael Huhns, Massimo Paolucci, Amit Sheth, Stuart Williams, and Michael Zaremba, "A Semantic Web Services Architecture," *IEEE Internet Computing*, vol. 9, no. 5, pp. 72–81, September/October 2005.
2. F. Dignum, H. Weigand, and E. Verharen, "Meeting the Deadline: On the Formal Specification of Temporal Deontic Constraints," *Foundations of Intelligent Systems, 9th Intl Symp.*, (ISMIS '96), vol. 1079, Lecture Notes in Computer Science, Springer, 1996, pp. 243–252.
3. A. Eberhart, "Ad-Hoc Invocation of Semantic Web Services," *Proc. IEEE Intl Conf. Web Services*, IEEE CS Press, 2004; www.aifb.uni-karlsruhe.de/WBS/aeb/pubs/icws2004.pdf.

4. K. Sycara et al., "Dynamic Service Matchmaking among Agents in Open Information Environments," *J. ACM SIGMOD Record, Special Issue on Semantic Interoperability in Global Information Systems*, vol. 28, no. 1, 1999, pp. 47–53; http://www-2. cs.cmu.edu/ softagents/papers/ACM99-L.ps.
5. M. Singh and M. Huhns, *Service-Oriented Computing: Semantics, Processes, Agents*, John Wiley & Sons, 2005.
6. K. Sivashanmugam, K. Verma, and A. Sheth, "Discovery of Web Services in a Federated Registry Environment," *Proc. IEEE Intl Conf. Web Services*, IEEE CS Press, 2004; http://lsdis.cs.uga.edu/lib/download/MWSDI-ICWS04- final.pdf.
7. Werner Vogels, "Learning from the Amazon Technology Platform," *ACM Queue*, May 2006, pp. 14–22.
8. R.L. Zavala and M.N. Huhns, "On Building Robust Web Service- Based Applications," in *Extending Web Services Technologies: The Use of Multi-Agent Approaches*, L. Cavedon et al., eds., Kluwer Academic, 2004, pp. 293–310.

The Helpful Environment: Distributed Agents and Services Which Cooperate

Austin Tate

Artificial Intelligence Applications Institute, University of Edinburgh,
Appleton Tower, Crichton Street, Edinburgh EH8 9LE, UK
a.tate@ed.ac.uk

Abstract. Imagine a future environment where networks of agents - people, robots and software agents - interact with sophisticated sensor grids and environmental actuators to provide advice, protection and aid. The systems will be integral to clothing, communications devices, vehicles, transportation systems, buildings, and pervasive in the environment. Vehicles and buildings could assist both their occupants and those around them. Systems would adapt and respond to emergencies whether communication were possible or not. Where feasible, local help would be used, with appropriate calls on shared services facilitated whenever this is both possible and necessary. Through this framework requests for assistance could be validated and brokered to available and appropriate services in a highly distributed fashion. Services would be provided to individuals or communities through this network to add value and give all sorts of assistance beyond emergency response aspects. In emergency situations, the local infrastructure would be augmented by the facilities of the responder teams at any level from local police, ambulance and fire response, all the way up to international response. An emergency zone's own infrastructure could be augmented when necessary by laying down temporary low cost sensor grids and placing specialized devices and robotic responders into the disaster area. These would form the basis for a distributed, adaptable, and resilient "helpful environment" for every individual and organisation at personal, family, business, regional, national and international levels.

Keywords: Intelligent agents, distributed systems, collaborative systems, cooperative systems, sensor grids, emergency response.

1 Introduction

Imagine a future environment where a network of agents - people, robots and software agents - interact with sophisticated sensor grids and environmental actuators to provide advice, protection and aid. The systems will be integral to clothing, communications devices, vehicles, transportation systems, buildings, and pervasive in the environment. These would form the basis for a distributed, adaptable, and resilient "helpful environment" for every individual and organisation at personal, family, business, regional, national and international levels. In natural disaster-prone areas government legislation, building codes and insurance requirements would ensure that

M. Klusch, M. Rovatsos, and T. Payne (Eds.): CIA 2006, LNAI 4149, pp. 23 – 32, 2006.

appropriate sensor/actuator systems were included in future communication devices, vehicles and buildings to assist both their users and those around them. Systems would adapt and respond to emergencies whether communication were possible or not. Where feasible, local help would be used, with appropriate calls on shared services facilitated whenever this is both possible and necessary. Through this framework requests for assistance could be validated and brokered to available and appropriate services in a highly distributed market fashion. Services would be provided to individuals or communities through this network to add value and give all sorts of assistance beyond the emergency response aspects. In emergency situations, the local infrastructure would be augmented by the facilities of the responder teams at any level from local police, ambulance and fire response, all the way up to international response. An emergency zone's own infrastructure could be augmented on demand by laying down temporary low cost sensor grids and placing specialized devices and robotic responders into the disaster area.

2 Emergency Response Challenges

Local or regional governments are often responsible for the event handling, planning, coordination and status reporting involved in responding to an emergency. They must harness capabilities to augment their own by calling on the resources of others when required. The local authority will often have an emergency response centre which, in the event of an emergency, will provide information and support to the public (through emergency phone lines), to the responders and to the decision making authorities.

Across a range of emergency response scenarios, we can identify a common set for which intelligent agents might be of assistance:

- Sensor data management and fusion
- Accurate information gathering
- Correlation and validation
- Relevant and understandable communication
- Contact making
- Requests for assistance and matching to available capabilities
- Use of Standard Operating Procedures and Alarms
- Planning and coordination
- Scale and robustness

But one of the biggest challenges is to help these agents and services and the people using them to communicate and cooperate effectively. There are many instances in which lack of communication and breakdown in coordination has degraded the emergency response and in some cases led to further loss of life and property.

3 AI Challenges

There are many AI challenges to be addressed to give such support and to make the vision a reality. Kitano and Tadokoro (2001) outlined some of this in a 50-year programme of work for future rescue robotics in Japan. They have also introduced the annual RoboCup Rescue Simulation competition held to test systems in a simulation of the 1995 Kobe earthquake. There have been several other proposals for "Grand Challenges" in computing and AI which take as their theme emergency response (Safety.net, 2002; I-Rescue Grand Challenges, 2006). As examples, the UK Advanced Knowledge Technologies (AKT) programme (Aktors, 2005) is addressing emergency response challenge problems, and a European follow-on programme called OpenKnowledge (2006) is using emergency response as one of its challenge problems. The FireGrid project is seeking to link sophisticated and large-scale sensor grids and faster than real-time simulations to emergency response coordination systems.

We can outline a number of core technologies, many having an essential AI component, which need to be developed, matured and integrated with other systems to make this vision of a connected world a reality. Examples of these technologies include:

1. Sensors and Information Gathering
   a. sensor facilities, large-scale sensor grids
   b. human and photographic intelligence gathering
   c. information and knowledge validation and error reduction
   d. Semantic Web and meta-knowledge
   e. simulation and prediction
   f. data interpretation
   g. identification of "need"
2. Emergency Response Capabilities and Availability
   a. robust multi-modal communications
   b. matching needs, brokering and "trading" systems
   c. agent technology for enactment, monitoring and control
3. Hierarchical, distributed, large scale systems
   a. local versus centralized decision making and control
   b. mobile and survivable systems
   c. human and automated mixed-initiative decision making
   d. trust, security
4. Common Operating Methods
   a. shared information and knowledge bases
   b. shared standards and interlingua
   c. shared human-scale self-help web sites and collaboration aids
   d. shared standard operating procedures at levels from local to international
   e. standards for signs, warnings, etc.
5. Public Education
   a. publicity materials
   b. self-help aids
   c. training courses
   d. simulations and exercises

Running through all these is the need for flexible and extendible representations of knowledge with rapidly altering scope, and with changing versions and refinements. There cannot be a single monolithically agreed representation of all the knowledge that will be involved. The science and technology of ontologies and their management will be vital to sustain this knowledge.

The technologies outlined above are drawn from a number of fields, some more mature than others, with each having its own philosophy and assumptions. However, the technological and research advances that are necessary to realize this vision are starting to be made in a number of projects and research programmes which will now be described.

4 I-Rescue

The I-Rescue project (I-Rescue, 2005) is exploring the use of AI planning and collaboration methods in rapidly developing emergency response and rescue situations. The overall aim is the creation and use of task-centric virtual organisations involving people, government and non-governmental organisations, automated systems, grid and web services working alongside intelligent robotic, vehicle, building and environmental systems to respond to very dynamic events on scales from local to global.

The I-X system and I-Plan planner (Tate et. al., 2004) provide a framework for representing, reasoning about, and using plans and processes in collaborative contexts. An underlying ontology, termed <I-N-C-A> (Tate, 2003), is used as the basis of a flexible representation for the issues/questions to address, nodes/activities to be performed, constraints to be maintained and annotations to be kept. The I-X approach to plan representation and use relates activities to their underlying "goal structure" using rich (and enrichable) constraint descriptions which include the impact that the activities are meant to have on the state of the environment. This allows for more precise and useful monitoring of plan execution, allowing plans to be adjusted or repaired as circumstances change. It can make use of the dynamically changing context and status of the agents and products involved (e.g. through emerging geo-location services for people and products). It also provides for the real-time communication of activities and tasks between both human and automated resources.

I-X agents and the underpinning <I-N-C-A> ontology can be used in a range of systems including supportive interfaces for humans and organisations, and potentially in intelligent sensors and robotic devices. It can thus act as a shared mechanism for coordinating these and for providing them with intelligent planning and process support.

I-Rescue and I-X systems aim to be part of a future environment in which there are:

- Multi-level emergency response and aid systems
- Personal, vehicle, home, organisation, district, regional, national, international levels of assistance
- Backbone for progressively more comprehensive aid and emergency response
- Also used for aid-orientated commercial services
- Robust, secure, resilient, distributed system of systems
- Advanced knowledge and collaboration technologies
- Low cost, pervasive sensors, computing and communications
- Changes in building codes, regulations and practices.

5 Coalition Agents Experiment (CoAX)

As recent world events have shown, multi-national Coalitions play an increasingly important role in emergency response operations. The overall aim of is to exploit information better; in Coalitions this requires rapid integration of heterogeneous information handling and command systems, enabling them to inter-operate and share information coherently. However, Coalitions today suffer from labour-intensive information collection and co-ordination, and 'stove-piped' systems with incompatible representations of information.

The Coalition Agents Experiment (CoAX, 2006, Allsop et al., 2003) was an international collaborative research effort involving 30 organisations in four countries. It brought together a wide range of groups exploring agent technologies relevant to multi-national and multi-agency operations in the context of a peace-keeping scenario set in a fictional country – Binni (Rathmell, 1999). The principal research hypothesis was that the software agent technology and principles of the Semantic Web could help to initially construct and then use and maintain loosely coupled systems for complex and very dynamically changing Coalition operations (e.g. as in Wark et al., 2003). CoAX carried out a series of technology demonstrations based on a realistic Coalition scenario. These showed how agents and associated technologies facilitated run-time interoperability across the Coalition, adaptive and agile responses to unexpected events, and selective sharing of information between Coalition partners.

6 Coalition Search and Rescue Task Support (CoSAR-TS)

Search and rescue operations by nature require the kind of rapid dynamic composition of available policy-constrained services making it a good experimental basis for intelligent agent Semantic Web technologies. Semantic Web use within agents in CoAX was taken further in the CoSAR-TS project which also used the CoAX Binni scenario (Rathmell, 1999), and events which immediately followed on from those in the CoAX demonstrations. The KAoS agent domain management framework (Bradshaw et al., 1997) was used to describe the agent domains and the policies under which they interoperate. The project showcases intelligent agents and artificial intelligence planning systems working in a distributed fashion, with dynamic policies originating from various groups and individuals governing who is permitted or obligated to do what. The agents use Semantic Web services to dynamically discover medical information and to find local rescue resources. Semantic Web information access uses the OWL language (2004) and the rescue services are described in OWL-S (2005). I-X (Tate et al., 2002) was used as a task support, planning and execution framework to connect the various participants and services used. In later phases of the work, an exploration of web services composition using I-X's planner (I-Plan) was also included (Uszok et al., 2004).

7 Collaborative Operations for Personnel Recovery (Co-OPR)

Personnel recovery (search and rescue) teams must operate under intense pressure, taking into account not only hard logistics, but also "messy" factors such as the social or political implications of a decision. The "Collaborative Operations for Personnel

Recovery" (Co-OPR) project has developed decision-support for sensemaking in such scenarios, seeking to exploit the complementary strengths of human and machine reasoning. Co-OPR integrates the Compendium (Buckingham-Sum et al., 2006) sensemaking-support tool for real time information and argument mapping, with the I-X (Tate et al., 2002) artificial intelligence planning and execution framework to support group activity and collaboration. Both share a common model for dealing with issues, the refinement of options for the activities to be performed, handling constraints and recording other information. The tools span the spectrum with Compendium being very flexible with few constraints on terminology and content, to the knowledge-based reliance on rich domain models and formal conceptual models (ontologies) of I X. In a personnel recovery experimental simulation of a UN peacekeeping operation, with roles played by military planning staff, the Co-OPR tools were judged by external evaluators to have been very effective.

8   Collaborative Advanced Knowledge Technologies e-Response

The Collaborative Advanced Knowledge Technologies in the Grid (CoAKTinG) project (Buckingham Shum et al., 2002) used technologies from the UK Advanced Knowledge Technologies programme (Aktors, 2006) to support distributed scientific collaboration in an emergency response situation – in particular in a scenario involving the management of an oil spill. Focusing on the interchange between humans in the scenario, CoAKTinG provided tools to assist scientific collaboration by integrating intelligent meeting spaces, ontologically annotated media streams from on-line meetings, decision rationale and group memory capture, meeting facilitation, planning and coordination support, argumentation, and instant messaging/presence.

The focus of AKT as a whole is on the provision of 'next generation' knowledge technologies, particularly in the context of the semantic web as both a medium and a target domain for these technologies.

New work on the AKT project is focused on a challenge problem dealing with the aftermath of a civil cargo aircraft crashing on a large city – an actual scenario for which there are existing contingency plans in place. It looks at how to use the semantic web to assist in making sense of the situation, both to guide emergency responders and to find appropriate specialized rescue and medical capabilities.

9   OpenKnowledge e-Response

OpenKnowledge (OpenKnowledge, 2006) is a European Union project involving Edinburgh, Southampton and the Open Universities in the UK, Amsterdam in The Netherlands, Trento in Italy and Barcelona in Spain. The goal of the project is to provide an open framework for agent interaction and coordination in knowledge-rich environments. It focuses on two challenge problems, one of which is emergency monitoring and management. This domain has been chosen as a testbed because it demands a combination of geographical and geo-presence knowledge alongside active support for collaboration and planning in multi-agent, dynamic situations.

The need to harness electronic communication networks in emergency situations has been recognised as a European research priority. Quoting from the EU "Emergency Response Grid" programme (EU, 2006):

"In times of crisis – be it a natural disaster, terrorist attack or infrastructure failure – mobile workers need to work together in time-critical and dangerous situations. Real-time access to information and knowledge, powered by Grids, will help save lives. Crises are complex situations, with large numbers and varieties of mobile workers – medical and rescue teams, police, fire fighters and other security personnel – appearing on the spot at short notice. These different teams come from different organisations, and generally have incomplete or even contradictory knowledge of the crisis situation."

For OpenKnowledge the challenge of a test bed in this domain is in the rapidity of formation of emergency coalitions – often very intense and opportunistic "communities of practice" where judging the quality of an answer is critical and dynamic. OpenKnowledge involves the exploration of peer-to-peer services such as:

- Network data sources: Sensor data flows need to be coordinated in the large. These data will be classified locally and will need to be made available to different "experts/peers" on the basis of contextual classification schema.
- Collaborative services: to support planning, communication and coordination within the expert peers community.
- Mitigation assessment services: as potential emergency situations are identified, mitigation needs can be determined and prioritized.
- Preparedness services: supporting those activities that prepare for actual emergencies.

10 FireGrid

A broad vision for an emergency response system in the modern built environment is being explored with an integrated and inter-disciplinary approach in FireGrid (Berry et al., 2005; FireGrid, 2006). This is a UK project to address emergency response in the built environment, where sensor grids in large-scale buildings are linked to faster-than-real-time grid-based simulations, and used to assist fire responders to work with the building's internal response systems and occupants to form a team to deal with the emergency.

FireGrid will integrate several core technologies, extending them where necessary:

- High Performance Computing involving fire models and structural models
- Wireless sensors in extreme conditions with adaptive routing algorithms, including input validation and filtering
- Grid computing including sensor-guided computations, mining of data streams for key events and reactive priority-based scheduling
- Command and Control using knowledge-based planning techniques with user guidance

I-X will act as a "front-end" for the emergency response chief to access the various grid and web services which can be called upon to work with the human responders and those in the affected buildings.

11 Helpful Systems and Helpful Organisations

The infrastructure and organisations that would be required to make the vision of the helpful environment possible are being put in place. The Galileo European Satellite Navigation System (Galileo, 2006) and its mobile geo-location and emergency response services programme will be another spur to development. Both commercial and freely provided emergency response facilities are being interwoven to ensure active development and support over a long period.

Examples of the type of 'helpful organisation' that will enact this vision are already starting to emerge. An organisation called the Multinational Planning Augmentation Team (MPAT; Weide, 2006), consisting of 33 nations situated around the Pacific Rim, has been developing shared knowledge and procedures to assist in responses to regional crises. MPAT used computer collaboration aids, and a simple brokering system, during the December 2004 – February 2005 Indian Ocean Tsunami response to help affected countries gain access the specialized capabilities of response organisations more effectively. MPAT is an excellent example of people training and working together to ensure they are ready to respond better to emergencies. It would be a prime beneficiary and exploiter of any future 'helpful environment'.

On a smaller scale the Washington DC area is conducting a programme called Capital Wireless Integrated Network (CapWIN, 2005) led by IBM and the University of Maryland. This programme works with local services to support responses by all agencies to incidents occurring on a single freeway interchange in the DC area. Its aim is to show the potential value of coordinated wireless computing services for integrated and cohesive response across the police, the ambulance service, emergency support teams, the fire brigade, hazardous material units and the military.

12 The Helpful Environment

Imagine in the not too distant future that every citizen, vehicle, package in transit and other "active devices" can be treated as a potential sensor or responder. Individuals or vehicles that need help, as well as local, regional, national and international emergency agencies, could look up specialized capabilities or find local assistance through a much more responsive and effective environment. Systems could inter-operate to enable preventative measures to be taken so that those in imminent danger could be forewarned by their own systems, and by the people, vehicles and buildings around them.

These would support a diverse range of uses, such as:

- Disaster response and evacuation
- Terrorism incident response
- Civil accidents
- Disease control
- Business continuity
- Family emergencies
- Transportation aids
- Help desks
- Procedural assistance

A truly "helpful environment" could be created that is accessible by all.

Acknowledgments. This article is based on evidence given to US and UK government agencies concerned with responses to emergency situations and with "Grand Challenges" for computer science research. A version is included in the IEEE Intelligent Systems special issue on the Future of AI in 2006. Projects mentioned in this paper have been sponsored by a number of organisations. The University of Edinburgh and research sponsors are authorized to reproduce and distribute reprints and on-line copies for their purposes notwithstanding any copyright annotation hereon. The views and conclusions contained herein are those of the author and should not be interpreted as necessarily representing the official policies or endorsements, either expressed or implied, of other parties.

References

1. Aktors (2006) AKT: Advanced Knowledge Technologies.http://aktors.org
2. Allsopp, D.N., Beautement, P., Bradshaw, J.M., Durfee, E.H., Kirton, M., Knoblock, C.A., Suri, N., Tate A., and Thompson, C.W. (2002) Coalition Agents Experiment: Multi-Agent Co-operation in an International Coalition Setting, Special Issue on Knowledge Systems for Coalition Operations (KSCO), IEEE Intelligent Systems, Vol. 17 No. 3 pp. 26-35. May/June 2002.
3. Allsopp, D., Beautement, P., Kirton, M., Tate, A., Bradshaw, J.M., Suri, N. and Burstein, M. (2003) The Coalition Agents Experiment: Network-Enabled Coalition Operations, Special Issue on Network-enabled Capabilities, Journal of Defence Science, Vol. 8, No. 3, pp. 130-141, September 2003.
4. Berry, D., Usmani, A., Terero, J., Tate, A., McLaughlin, S., Potter, S., Trew, A., Baxter, R., Bull, M. and Atkinson, M. (2005) FireGrid: Integrated Emergency Response and Fire Safety Engineering for the Future Built Environment, UK e-Science Programme All Hands Meeting (AHM-2005), 19-22 September 2005, Nottingham, UK. http://www.aiai.ed.ac.uk/project/ix/documents/2005/2005-escience-ahm-firegrid.doc
5. Bradshaw, J M, Dutfield, S, Benoit, P, and Woolley, J D. (1997) KAoS: Toward an industrial-strength open agent architecture. In Software Agents, AAAI Press/MIT Press, Cambridge, Massachusetts, editor J M Bradshaw. Pages 375-418.
6. Buckingham Shum, S., De Roure, D., Eisenstadt, M., Shadbolt, N. and Tate, A. (2002) CoAKTinG: Collaborative Advanced Knowledge Technologies in the Grid, Proceedings of the Second Workshop on Advanced Collaborative Environments, Eleventh IEEE Int. Symposium on High Performance Distributed Computing (HPDC-11), July 24-26, 2002, Edinburgh, Scotland. http://www.aiai.ed.ac.uk/project/ix/documents/2002/2002-wace-coakting.pdf
7. Buckingham Shum, S., Selvin, A., Sierhuis, M., Conklin, J., Haley, C. and Nuseibeh, B. (2006). Hypermedia Support for Argumentation-Based Rationale: 15 Years on from gIBIS and QOC. In: Rationale Management in Software Engineering (Eds.) A.H. Dutoit, R. McCall, I. Mistrik, and B. Paech. Springer-Verlag: Berlin
8. CapWIN (2006) Capital Wireless Integrated Network. http://capwin.org
9. Co-OPR (2006) Coalition Operations for Personnel Recovery. http://www.aiai.ed.ac.uk/project/co-opr/
10. CoSAR-TS (2006) Coalition Search and Rescue Task Support. http://www.aiai.ed.ac.uk/project/cosar-ts/
11. CoAX (2006) Coalition Agents eXperiment http://www.aiai.ed.ac.uk/project/coax/
12. EU (2006) European Union Emergency Response Grid www.cordis.lu/ist/grids/emergencey_response_grid.htm

13. FireGrid (2006) FireGrid: The FireGrid Cluster for Next Generation Emergency Response Systems. http://firegrid.org
14. Galileo (2006) Galileo: European Satellite Navigation System. http://europa.eu.int/comm/dgs/energy_transport/galileo/
15. I-Rescue (2006) I-Rescue: I-X for Emergency Response and Related Grand Challenges. http://i-rescue.org
16. Kitano, H. and Tadokoro, S. (2001) RoboCup Rescue: A Grand Challenge for Multiagent and Intelligent Systems, Artificial Intelligence Magazine, Spring, 2001, American Association of Artificial Intelligence.
17. MPAT (2006) Multinational Planning Augmentation Team Multinational Forces Standing Operating Procedures (MNF SOP) http://www2.apan-info.net/mpat/
18. OpenKnowledge (2006) OpenKnowledge.http://openk.org
19. OWL (2004) Ontology Web Language, World Wide Web Consortium. http://www.w3.org/2004/OWL/
20. OWL-S (2005) Ontology Web Language for Services. http://www.daml.org/services/owl-s/
21. Rathmell, R A. (1999) A Coalition force scenario 'Binni □ gateway to the Golden Bowl of Africa'. In Proceedings of the International Workshop on Knowledge-Based Planning for Coalition Forces, editor A Tate, pages 115-125, Edinburgh, Scotland, May 1999. Available at http://binni.org.
22. Safety Net (2002) Safety.net Grand Challenge Proposal. CRA Conference on "Grand Research Challenges" in Computer Science and Engineering Workshop, June 23-26, 2002, Warrenton, Virginia. http://www.cra.org/Activities/grand.challenges/slides/ubiquitous.pdf
23. Tate, A., Dalton, J., and J. Stader, J. (2002) I-P2- Intelligent Process Panels to Support Coalition Operations. In Proceedings of the Second International Conference on Knowledge Systems for Coalition Operations (KSCO-2002). Toulouse, France, April 2002.
24. Tate, A. (2003) <I-N-C-A>: an Ontology for Mixed-Initiative Synthesis Tasks. In Proceedings of the Workshop on Mixed-Initiative Intelligent Systems (MIIS) at the International Joint Conference on Artificial Intelligence (IJCAI-03), Acapulco, Mexico, August 2003.
25. Tate, A., Dalton, J., Siebra, C., Aitken, S., Bradshaw, J.M. and Uszok, A. (2004) Intelligent Agents for Coalition Search and Rescue Task Support, AAAI-2004 Intelligent Systems Demonstrator, in Proceedings of the Nineteenth National Conference of the American Association of Artificial Intelligence (AAAI-2004), San Jose, CA, USA, July 2004. http://www.aiai.ed.ac.uk/project/ix/documents/2004/2004-aaai-isd-tate-cosarts.pdf
26. Uszok, A., Bradshaw, J.M., Jeffers, R., Johnson, M., Tate, A., Dalton, J. and Aitken, S. (2004) KAoS Policy Management for Semantic Web Services, IEEE Intelligent Systems, pp. 32-41, July/August 2004.
27. Wark, S., Zschorn, A., Perugini, D., Tate, A., Beautement, P., Bradshaw, J.M. and Suri, N. (2003) Dynamic Agent Systems in the CoAX Binni 2002 Experiment, Special Session on Fusion by Distributed Cooperative Agents at the 6th International Conference on Information Fusion (Fusion 2003), Cairns, Australia, July, 2003.
28. Weide, S.A. (2006) Multinational Crisis Response in the Asia-Pacific Region: The Multinational Planning Augmentation Team Model, in "The Liaison", Center of Excellence in Disaster Management & Humanitarian Assistance (COE-DMHA), February 2006. http://www.coe-dmha.org/liaison.htm

Voting in Cooperative Information Agent Scenarios: Use and Abuse

Jeffrey S. Rosenschein and Ariel D. Procaccia

School of Engineering and Computer Science
Hebrew University, Jerusalem, Israel
{jeff, arielpro}@cs.huji.ac.il

Abstract. Social choice theory can serve as an appropriate foundation upon which to build cooperative information agent applications. There is a rich literature on the subject of voting, with important theoretical results, and builders of automated agents can benefit from this work as they engineer systems that reach group consensus.

This paper considers the application of various voting techniques, and examines nuances in their use. In particular, we consider the issue of preference extraction in these systems, with an emphasis on the complexity of manipulating group outcomes. We show that a family of important voting protocols is susceptible to manipulation by coalitions in the average case, when the number of candidates is constant (even though their worst-case manipulations are $\mathcal{NP}$-hard).

1   Introduction

Research on the theory of social choice, and in particular on its computational aspects, has become an important pursuit within computer science (CS). Motivating this work is the belief that social choice theory can have direct implications on the building of systems comprised of multiple automated agents. This paper describes some of that research, so it is a paper about voting and manipulation, but it is also inter alia about how computer science can help scientists and mathematicians see questions in new ways, spurring progress in new theoretical and applied directions.

Computer science occupies a unique position with respect to other fields of scientific endeavor. Its idiosyncratic nature should be celebrated and strengthened; it helps to make computer science in general, and its subfield multiagent systems (MAS), among the most exciting of scientific research areas today.

Computer Science is, at one and the same time:

1. An independent field with its own set of fundamental questions (both theoretical and applied). This distinctive blurring of theoretical and applied research, in both computer science and MAS, can be a great strength. There exist established fields of Applied Physics and Applied Mathematics, but there is no Applied Computer Science. Fundamental research certainly exists in those parts of CS closest to mathematics, but it is hard to conceive of

M. Klusch, M. Rovatsos, and T. Payne (Eds.): CIA 2006, LNAI 4149, pp. 33–50, 2006.
© Springer-Verlag Berlin Heidelberg 2006

a computer scientist, even one who occupies its most mathematical corners, uttering anything analogous to the quote attributed to the mathematician Leonard Eugene Dickson, "Thank God that number theory is unsullied by any application".[1] It's the *aspiration* to be purely theoretical that is absent in computer science.

2. A contributor to other fields of both technological and conceptual enablers; as the much-quoted New York Times article provocatively put it, "All Science is Computer Science" [18]. However, that article was referring mainly to the use of powerful computing in other fields, which is certainly not the core of computer science. One could argue that the more important influence of CS has been in changing how scientists in other fields *view* their problems: computation becomes a basic conceptual model, part of the intellectual toolset of other fields. There have been a number of highly visible examples of this trend, such as in cognitive psychology (e.g., information processing models of memory and attention [11]), attempts to develop computational models of the cell [27], and computational statistical mechanics [17]. The type of work described in this paper has had an influence on political science and sociology.

3. An avid consumer of the results produced by other fields. The interdisciplinary nature of computer science is nowhere more evident than in the area of artificial intelligence (AI), and perhaps nowhere more evident in artificial intelligence than in its subarea of multiagent systems. MAS researchers for the last 20 years have eagerly derived inspiration from fields as diverse as biology, physics, sociology, economics, organization theory, and mathematics. This is appropriate (even necessary), and the field takes a justifiable pride in its interdisciplinary openness.

1.1   Game Theory and Economics in MAS

One of the most exciting trends in computer science (and specifically in MAS) has been the investigation of game theory and economics as tools for automated systems.[2] Beginning with work in the mid-1980s, researchers have turned out a steady drumbeat of results, considering the computational aspects of game theory and economics, and how these fields can be put to appropriate use in the building of automated agents [23,9,29,24,19,15].

In this paper, we explore the use of preference aggregation in multiagent systems. Preference aggregation has deep roots in economics, but what distinguishes the CS work on this issue is the concern for computational issues: how are results arrived at (e.g., equilibrium points)? What is the complexity of the process? Can complexity be used to guard against unwanted phenomena? Does complexity of computation prevent realistic implementation of a technique?

The criteria to be used in evaluating this work (and exploiting its results) needs to take into account the ultimately applied nature of the endeavor. The

---

[1] Of course, number theory eventually provided the basis for the cryptography embedded throughout the internet, so it was not quite as unsullied as all that (eventually).

[2] We use the terms loosely, to encompass related fields and subfields such as decision theory, mechanism design, and general equilibrium theory.

idealized models of classic game theory might fall short when used normatively or descriptively with regard to human behavior, but for the most part that might remain a theoretical concern. *Application* of these models to automated agents quite urgently argued for their adjustment. To take one example, if computing an equilibrium point in a particular interaction is computationally infeasible, what would be the *meaning* of telling an agent to choose one?

Much of what follows first appeared in [21,22,20], and we use that material (particularly from the first of those papers) freely. We present it as a specific example of how preference aggregation can be handled in automated systems, and how computational issues come to the forefront.

1.2   The Theory and Practice of Preference Aggregation

In multiagent environments, it may be the case that different agents have diverse preferences, and it is therefore important to find a way to aggregate agent preferences. Even in situations where the agents are cooperative, there may still be independent motivations, goals, or perspectives that require them to come to a consensus.

A general scheme for preference aggregation is *voting*[3]: the agents reveal their preferences by ranking a set of candidates, and a winner is determined according to a voting protocol. The candidates can be entities of almost any conceivable sort.

For instance, Ghosh et al. [12] designed an automated movie recommendation system, in which the conflicting preferences a user may have about movies were represented as agents, and movies to be suggested were selected according to a voting scheme (in this example there are multiple winners, as several movies are recommended to the user). The candidates in a virtual election could also be items such as beliefs, joint plans [10], or schedules [14]. In fact, to see the generality of the (automated) voting scenario, consider modern web searching. One of the most massive preference aggregation schemes in existence is Google's PageRank algorithm, which can be viewed as a vote among indexed web pages on candidates determined by a user-input search string; winners are ranked (Tennenholtz [26] considers the axiomatic foundations of ranking systems such as this).

Things are made more complicated by the fact that in many automated settings (as in non-virtual environments) the agents are self-interested, or at the very least bring different knowledge/perspectives to the interaction. Such an agent may reveal its preferences untruthfully, if it believes this would make the final outcome of the elections more favorable for it. In fact, well-meaning agents may even lie in an attempt to improve social welfare [20].[4] In any case, whether the agents are acting out of noble or ignoble motives, there may be an undesirable social outcome. Strategic behavior in voting has been of particular interest to AI researchers [3,5,8,21]. This problem is provably acute: it is known [13,25] that, for elections with three or more candidates, in any voting protocol that

---

[3] We use the term in its intuitive sense here, but in the social choice literature, "preference aggregation" and "voting" are basically synonymous.

[4] Though if several do it in parallel there may be unintended negative consequences.

is non-dictatorial,[5] there are elections where an agent is better off by voting untruthfully.

Of course, in some systems, particularly centrally-designed systems, strategic behavior can be effectively banned by fiat. We would argue this covers a distinct minority of multiagent systems.

1.3   Nuances

Different voting protocols will often have different outcomes, as well as different properties. Some protocols may be hard to manipulate; others may skew the preferences of voters in particular ways. Many of these phenomena are well-known in social choice theory, such as the effects of run-off voting on who wins an election (a good heuristic: bring your candidate up for a vote as late as possible in the process). Consider as another example one that comes from a paper in this collection [20]. There we discuss the concepts of *distortion* and *misrepresentation*, two (related, but distinct) measures of how well (or badly) a given candidate represents the desires of a voter.

Quoting from [20]:

> [T]he misrepresentation of a social choice function... can be easily refor-
> mulated as distortion. In fact, similar results can be obtained, but the
> latter formulation favors candidates that are ranked last by few voters,
> whereas the former formulation rewards candidates that are placed first
> by many voters.

So depending on whether distortion or misrepresentation is used, we may be developing a technique that prefers candidates with many first place votes over one that prefers candidates with few last place votes. The choice is in the hands of the designer, and one or the other may be more natural for some specific domain. Continuing from [20]:

> Consider the meeting scheduling problem discussed in [14]: scheduling
> agents schedule meetings on behalf of their associated users, based on
> given user preferences; a winning schedule is decided in an election. Say
> three possible schedules are being voted on. These schedules, being fair,
> conflict with at most two of the requirements specified by any user... In
> this case, having no conflicts at all is vastly superior to having at least
> one conflict, as even one conflict may prevent a user from attending a
> meeting. As noted above, this issue is taken into account in the calcula-
> tion of misrepresentation — emphasis is placed on candidates that were
> often ranked first.

This type of consideration runs throughout our choices of preference aggrega-
tion techniques. The system put into place may have major ramifications on the outcomes. In addition (and this is the main concern of the rest of the paper),

---

[5] In a dictatorial protocol, there is an agent that dictates the outcome regardless of the others' choices.

the resistance of the system to strategic behavior may influence whether agents truthfully reveal their preferences, and whether a socially desirable candidate is elected.

1.4   Complexity to the Rescue

Fortunately, it is reasonable to make the assumption that automated agents are computationally bounded. Therefore, although in principle an agent may be able to manipulate an election, the computation required may be infeasible. This has motivated researchers to study the computational complexity of manipulating voting protocols. It has long been known [2] that there are voting protocols that are $\mathcal{NP}$-hard to manipulate by a single voter. Recent results by Conitzer and Sandholm [6,4] show that some manipulations of common voting protocols are $\mathcal{NP}$-hard, even for a small number of candidates. Moreover, in [7], it is shown that adding a pre-round to some voting protocols can make manipulations hard (even $\mathcal{PSPACE}$-hard in some cases). Elkind and Lipmaa [8] show that the notion of pre-round, together with one-way functions, can be used to construct protocols that are hard to manipulate even by a large minority fraction of the voters.

In computer science, the notion of hardness is usually considered in the sense of worst-case complexity. Not surprisingly, most results on the complexity of manipulation use $\mathcal{NP}$-hardness as the complexity measure. However, it may still be the case that most instances of the problem are easy to manipulate.

A relatively little-known theory of average case complexity exists [28]; that theory introduces the concept of distributional problems, and defines what a reduction between distributional problems is. It is also known that average-case complete problems exist (albeit artificial ones, such as a distributional version of the halting problem).

Sadly, it is very difficult to show that a certain problem is average-case complete, and such results are known only for a handful of problems. Additionally, the goal of the existing theory is to define when a problem is *hard* in the average-case; it does not provide criteria for deciding when a problem is *easy*. A step towards showing that a manipulation is easy on average was made in [8]. It involves an analysis of the plurality protocol with a pre-round, but focuses on a very specific distribution, which does not satisfy some basic desiderata as to what properties an "interesting" distribution should have.

In this paper, we engage in a novel average-case analysis, based on criteria we propose. Coming up with an "interesting" distribution of problem instances with respect to which the average-case complexity is computed is a difficult task, and the solution may be controversial. We analyze problems whose instances are distributed with respect to a *junta distribution*. Such a distribution must satisfy several conditions, which (arguably) guarantee that it focuses on instances that are harder to manipulate. We consider a protocol to be *susceptible* to manipulation when there is a polynomial time algorithm that can usually manipulate it: the probability of failure (when the instances are distributed according to a junta distribution) must be inverse-polynomial. Such an algorithm is known as a *heuristic* polynomial time algorithm.

We use these new methods to show our main result: an important family of protocols, called *scoring* protocols, is susceptible to coalitional manipulation when the number of candidates is constant.[6] Specifically, we contemplate *sensitive* scoring protocols, which include such well-known protocols as Borda and Veto. To accomplish this task, we define a natural distribution μ^* over the instances of a well-defined coalitional manipulation problem, and show that this is a junta distribution. Furthermore, we present the manipulation algorithm GREEDY, and show that it usually succeeds with respect to μ^*.

We also show that all protocols are susceptible to a certain setting of manipulation, where the manipulator is unsure about the others' votes. This result depends upon a basic conjecture regarding junta distributions, but also has implications that transcend our specific definition of these distributions.

In Section 2, we outline some important voting protocols, and properly define the manipulation problems we shall discuss. In Section 3, we formally introduce the tools for our average case analysis: junta distributions, heuristic polynomial time, and susceptibility to manipulations. In Section 4 we present our main result: sensitive scoring protocols are susceptible to coalitional manipulation with few candidates. In Section 5, we discuss the case when a single manipulator is unsure about the other voters' votes. Finally, in Section 6, we present conclusions and directions for future research.

2   Preliminaries

We first describe some common voting protocols and formally define the manipulation problems with which we shall deal. Next, we introduce a useful lemma from probability theory.

2.1   Elections and Manipulations

An election consists of a set C of m candidates, and a set V of n voters, who provide a total order on the candidates. An election also includes a winner determination function from the set of all possible combinations of votes to C. We note that throughout this paper, $m = O(1)$, so the complexity results are in terms of n.

Different voting protocols are distinguished by their winner determination functions. The protocols we shall discuss are:

- *Scoring protocols:* A scoring protocol is defined by vector $\boldsymbol{\alpha} = \langle \alpha_1, \alpha_2, \ldots, \alpha_m \rangle$, such that $\alpha_1 \geq \alpha_2 \geq \ldots \geq \alpha_m$ and $\alpha_i \in \mathbb{N} \cup \{0\}$. A candidate receives α_i points for each voter which ranks it in the i'th place. Examples of scoring protocols are:
  - *Plurality:* $\boldsymbol{\alpha} = \langle 1, 0, \ldots, 0, 0 \rangle$.
  - *Veto:* $\boldsymbol{\alpha} = \langle 1, 1, \ldots, 1, 0 \rangle$.
  - *Borda:* $\boldsymbol{\alpha} = \langle m-1, m-2, \ldots, 1, 0 \rangle$.

---

[6] Proofs can be found in [21].

- *Copeland:* For each possible pair of candidates, simulate an election; a candidate wins such a pairwise election if more voters prefer it over the opponent. A candidate gets 1 point for each pairwise election it wins, and -1 for each pairwise election it loses.
- *Maximin:* A candidate's score in a pairwise election is the number of voters that prefer it over the opponent. The winner is the candidate whose minimum score over all pairwise elections is highest.
- *Single Transferable Vote (STV):* The election proceeds in rounds. In each round, the candidate's score is the number of voters that rank it highest among the remaining candidates; the candidate with the lowest score is eliminated.

Remark 1. We assume that tie-breaking is always adversarial to the manipulator.[7]

In the case of weighted votes, a voter with weight $k \in \mathbb{N}$ is naturally regarded as k voters who vote unanimously. In this paper, we consider weights in $[0, 1]$. This is equivalent, since any set of integer weights in the range $1, \ldots, \text{poly} n$ can be scaled down to weights in the segment $[0, 1]$ with $O(\log n)$ bits of precision.

The main results of the paper focus on scoring protocols. We shall require the following definition:

Definition 1. Let P be a scoring protocol with parameters $\boldsymbol{\alpha} = \langle \alpha_1, \alpha_2, \ldots, \alpha_m \rangle$. We say that P is *sensitive* iff $\alpha_1 \geq \alpha_2 \geq \ldots \geq \alpha_{m-1} > \alpha_m = 0$ (notice the strict inequality on the right).

In particular, Borda and Veto are sensitive scoring protocols.

Remark 2. Generally, from any scoring protocol with $\alpha_{m-1} > \alpha_m$, an equivalent sensitive scoring protocol can be obtained by subtracting α_m on a coordinate-by-coordinate basis from the vector $\boldsymbol{\alpha}$. Moreover, observe that if a protocol is a scoring protocol but is not sensitive, and $\alpha_m = 0$, then $\alpha_{m-1} = 0$. In this case, for three candidates it is equivalent to the plurality protocol, for which most manipulations are tractable even in the worst-case. Therefore, it is sufficient to restrict our results to sensitive scoring protocols.

We next consider some types of manipulations, state the appropriate complexity results, and introduce some notations.

Remark 3. We discuss the constructive cases, where the goal is trying to make a candidate win, as opposed to destructive manipulation, where the goal is to make a candidate lose. Constructive manipulations are always at least as hard (in the worst-case sense) as their destructive counterparts, and in some cases strictly harder (if one is able to determine whether p can be made to win, one can also ask whether any of the other $m - 1$ candidates can be made to win, thus making p lose).

---

[7] This is a standard assumption, also made, for example, in [6,4]. It does, indeed, make it more straightforward to prove certain results.

Definition 2. In the INDIVIDUAL-MANIPULATION problem, we are given all the other votes, and a preferred candidate p. We are asked whether there is a way for the manipulator to cast its vote so that p wins.

Bartholdi and Orlin [2] show that IM is $\mathcal{NP}$-complete in Single Transferable Vote, provided the number of candidates is unbounded. However, the problem is in $\mathcal{P}$ for most voting schemes, and hence will not be studied here.

Definition 3. In the COALITIONAL-WEIGHTED-MANIPULATION (CWM) problem, we are given a set of weighted votes S, the weights of a set of votes T which have not been cast, and a preferred candidate p. We are asked whether there is a way to cast the votes in T so that p wins the election.

We know [6,4] that CWM is $\mathcal{NP}$-complete in Borda, Veto and Single Transferable Vote, even with 3 candidates, and in Maximin and Copeland with at least 4 candidates.

The CWM version that we shall analyze, which is specifically tailored for scoring protocols, is a slightly modified version whose analysis is more straightforward:

Definition 4. In the SCORING-COALITIONAL-WEIGHTED-MANIPULATION (SCWM) problem, we are given an initial score $S[c]$ for each candidate c, the weights of a set of votes T which have not been cast, and a preferred candidate p. We are asked whether there is a way to cast the votes in T so that p wins the election.

$S[c]$ can be interpreted as c's total score from the votes in S. However, we do not require that there exist a combination of votes that actually induces $S[c]$ for all c.

Definition 5. In the UNCERTAIN-VOTES-WEIGHTED-EVALUATION (UVWE) problem, we are given a weight for each voter, a distribution over all the votes, a candidate p, and a number $r \in [0, 1]$. We are asked whether the probability of p winning is greater than r.

Definition 6. In the UNCERTAIN-VOTES-WEIGHTED-MANIPULATION (UVWM) problem, we are given a single manipulative voter with a weight, weights for all other voters, a distribution over all the others' votes, a candidate p, and a number r, where $r \in [0, 1]$. We are asked whether the manipulator can cast its vote so that p wins with probability greater than r.

If CWM is $\mathcal{NP}$-hard in a protocol, then UVWE and UVWM are also $\mathcal{NP}$-hard in it [6]. These problems will be studied in Section 5. We make the assumption that the given distributions over the others' votes can be sampled in polynomial time.

2.2   Chernoff's Bounds

The following lemma will be of much use later on. Informally, it states that the average of independent identically distributed (i.i.d.) random variables is almost always close to the expectation.

Lemma 1 (Chernoff's Bounds). *Let $X_1, \ldots, X_t$ be i.i.d. random variables such that $a \leq X_i \leq b$ and $\mathrm{E}[X_i] = \mu$. Then for any $\epsilon > 0$, it holds that:*

- $\Pr[\frac{1}{t} \sum_{i=1}^{t} X_i \geq \mu + \epsilon] \leq e^{-2t \frac{\epsilon^2}{(b-a)^2}}$
- $\Pr[\frac{1}{t} \sum_{i=1}^{t} X_i \leq \mu - \epsilon] \leq e^{-2t \frac{\epsilon^2}{(b-a)^2}}$

3   Junta Distributions and Susceptible Mechanisms

In this section we lay the mathematical foundations required for an average-case analysis of the complexity of manipulations. All of the definitions are as general as possible; they can be applied to the manipulation of any mechanism, not merely to the manipulation of voting protocols.

We describe a distribution over the instances of a problem as a collection of distributions $\mu_1, \ldots, \mu_n, \ldots$, where μ_n is a distribution over the instances x such that $|x| = n$. We wish to analyze problems whose instances are distributed with respect to a distribution which focuses on hard-to-manipulate instances. Ideally, we would like to insure that if one manages to produce an algorithm which can usually manipulate instances according to this distinguished "difficult" distribution, the algorithm would also usually succeed when the instances are distributed with respect to most other reasonable distributions.

Definition 7. Let $\mu = \{\mu_n\}_{n \in \mathbb{N}}$ be a distribution over the possible instances of an $\mathcal{NP}$-hard manipulation problem M. μ is a *junta* distribution if and only if μ has the following properties:

1. Hardness: The restriction of M to μ is the manipulation problem whose possible instances are only:

$$\bigcup_{n \in \mathbb{N}} \{x : |x| = n \wedge \mu_n(x) > 0\}.$$

   Deciding this restricted problem is still $\mathcal{NP}$-hard.
2. Balance: There exist a constant $c > 1$ and $N \in \mathbb{N}$ such that for all $n \geq N$:

$$\frac{1}{c} \leq \Pr_{x \sim \mu_n}[M(x) = 1] \leq 1 - \frac{1}{c}.$$

3. Dichotomy: for all n and instances x such that $|x| = n$:

$$\mu_n(x) \geq 2^{-\text{poly} n} \vee \mu_n(x) = 0.$$

If M is a voting manipulation problem, we also require the following property:

4. Symmetry: Let v be a voter whose vote is given, let $c_1, c_2 \neq p$ be two candidates, and let $i \in \{1, \ldots, m\}$. The probability that v ranks c_1 in the i'th place is the same as the probability that v ranks c_2 in the i'th place.

If M is a coalitional manipulation problem, we also require the following property:

5. Refinement: Let x be an instance such that $|x| = n$ and $\mu_n(x) > 0$; if all colluders voted identically, then p would not be elected.

The name "junta distribution" comes from the idea that in such a distribution, relatively few "powerful" and difficult instances represent all the other problem instances. Alternatively, our intent is to have a few problematic distributions (the family of junta distributions) convincingly represent all other distributions with respect to the average-case analysis.

The first three properties are basic, and are relevant to problems of manipulating any mechanism. The definition is modular, and additional properties may be added on top of the basic three, in case one wishes to analyze a mechanism which is not a voting protocol.

The exact choice of properties is of extreme importance (and, as we mentioned above, may be arguable). We shall briefly explain our choices. Hardness is meant to insure that the junta distribution contains hard instances. Balance guarantees that a trivial algorithm which always accepts (or always rejects) has a significant chance of failure. The dichotomy property helps in preventing situations where the distribution gives a (positive but) negligible probability to all the hard instances, and a high probability to several easy instances.

We now examine the properties that are specific to manipulation problems. The necessity of symmetry is best explained by an example. Consider CWM in STV with $m \geq 3$. One could design a distribution where p wins if and only if a distinguished candidate loses the first round. Such a distribution could be tailored to satisfy the other conditions, but misses many of the hard instances. In the context of SCWM, we interpret symmetry in the following way: for every two candidates $c_1, c_2 \neq p$ and $y \in \mathbb{R}$,

$$\Pr_{x \sim \mu_n} [S[c_1] = y] = \Pr_{x \sim \mu_n} [S[c_2] = y].$$

Refinement is less important than the other four properties, but seems to help in concentrating the probability on hard instances. Observe that refinement is only relevant to coalitional manipulation; we believe that in the analysis of individual voting manipulation problems, the first four properties are sufficient.

Definition 8. [28] A *distributional problem* is a pair $\langle L, \mu \rangle$ where L is a decision problem and μ is a distribution over the set $\{0, 1\}^*$ of possible inputs.

Informally, an algorithm is a heuristic polynomial time algorithm for a distributional problem if it runs in polynomial time, and fails only on a small fraction of the inputs. We now give a formal definition; this definition is inspired by [28] (there the same name is used for a somewhat different definition).

Definition 9. Let M be a manipulation problem and let $\langle M, \mu \rangle$ be a distributional problem.

1. An algorithm A is a *deterministic heuristic polynomial time* algorithm for the distributional manipulation problem $\langle M, \mu \rangle$ if A always runs in polynomial time, and there exists a polynomial p and $N \in \mathbb{N}$ such that for all $n \geq N$:

$$\Pr_{x \sim \mu^n} [A(x) \neq M(x)] < \frac{1}{p(n)}. \tag{1}$$

2. Let A be a probabilistic algorithm, which uses a random string s. A is a *probabilistic heuristic polynomial time* algorithm for the distributional manipulation problem $\langle M, \mu \rangle$ if A always runs in polynomial time, and there exists a polynomial p and $N \in \mathbb{N}$ such that for all $n \geq N$:

$$\Pr_{x \sim \mu^n, s} [A(x) \neq M(x)] < \frac{1}{p(n)}. \tag{2}$$

Probabilistic algorithms have two potential sources of failure: an unfortunate choice of input, or an unfortunate choice of random string s. The success or failure of deterministic algorithms depends only on the choice of input.

We now combine all the definitions introduced in this section in an attempt to establish when a mechanism is susceptible to manipulation in the average case. The following definition abuses notation a bit: M is both used to refer to the manipulation itself, and the corresponding decision problem.

Definition 10. We say that a mechanism is *susceptible* to a manipulation M if there exists a junta distribution μ, such that there exists a deterministic/probabilistic heuristic polynomial time algorithm for $\langle M, \mu \rangle$.

4   Susceptibility to SCWM

Recall [6,4] that in Borda and Veto, CWM is $\mathcal{NP}$-hard, even with 3 candidates. Since Borda and Veto are examples of sensitive scoring protocols, we would like to know how resistant this family of protocols really is with respect to coalitional manipulation. In this section we use the methods from the previous section to present our main result:

Theorem 1. *Let P be a sensitive scoring protocol. Then P, with candidates $C = \{p, c_1, \ldots, c_m\}$, $m = O(1)$, is susceptible to SCWM.*

Intuitively, the instances of CWM (or SCWM) which are hard are those that require a very specific partitioning of the voters in T to subsets, where each subset votes unanimously. These instances are rare in any reasonable distribution; this insight will ultimately yield the theorem.

The following proposition generalizes Theorem 1 of [6] and Theorem 2 of [4], and justifies our focus on the family of sensitive scoring protocols. A stronger version of Proposition 1 has been independently proven in [16].

Proposition 1. *Let P be a sensitive scoring protocol. Then CWM in P is $\mathcal{NP}$-hard, even with 3 candidates.*

Definition 11. In the PARTITION problem, we are given a set of integers $\{k_i\}_{i\in[t]}$, summing to $2K$, and are asked whether a subset of these integers sum to K.

It is well-known that PARTITION is $\mathcal{NP}$-complete.

Proof (of Proposition 1). All proofs in the paper are omitted, but can be seen in [21].

Since an instance of CWM can be translated to an instance of SCWM in the obvious way, we have:

Corollary 1. *Let P be a sensitive scoring protocol. It holds that SCWM in P is $\mathcal{NP}$-hard, even with 3 candidates.*

4.1　A Junta Distribution

Let $w(v)$ denote the weight of voter v, and let W denote the total weight of the votes in T; P is a sensitive scoring protocol. We denote $|T| = n$: the size of T is the size of the instance.

Consider a distribution $\mu^* = \{\mu_n^*\}_{n\in\mathbb{N}}$ over the instances of CWM in P, with $m+1$ candidates $p, c_1, \ldots, c_m$, where each μ_n^* is induced by the following sampling algorithm:

1. $\forall v \in T$: Randomly and independently choose $w(v) \in [0,1]$ (up to $O(\log n)$ bits of precision).
2. $\forall i \in \{1, \ldots, m\}$: Randomly and independently choose $S[c_i] \in [(\alpha_1 - \alpha_2)W, \alpha_1 W]$ (up to $O(\log n)$ bits of precision).

We assume that $S[p] = 0$, i.e., all voters in S rank p last. This assumption is not a restriction. If it holds for a candidate c that $S[c] \leq S[p]$, then candidate c will surely lose, since the colluders all rank p first. Therefore, if $S[p] > 0$, we may simply normalize the scores by subtracting $S[p]$ from the scores of all candidates. This is equivalent to our assumption.

Remark 4. We believe that μ^* is the most natural distribution with respect to which coalitional manipulation in scoring protocols should be studied. Even if one disagrees with the exact definition of junta distribution, μ^* should satisfy many reasonable conditions one could produce.

We shall, of course, (presently) show that the distribution possesses the properties of a junta distribution.

Proposition 2. *Let P be a sensitive scoring protocol. Then μ^* is a junta distribution for SCWM in P with $C = \{p, c_1, \ldots, c_m\}$, and $m = O(1)$.*

4.2　A Heuristic Polynomial Time Algorithm

We now present our algorithm GREEDY for SCWM, given as Algorithm 1. $\boldsymbol{w}$ denotes the vector of the weights of voters in $T = \{t_1, \ldots, t_n\}$.

Algorithm 1. Decides SCWM

1: **procedure** GREEDY$(S, \boldsymbol{w}, p)$
2:     **for all** $c \in C$ **do**   ▷ Initialization
3:         $S_0[c] \leftarrow S[c]$
4:     **end for**
5:     **for** $i = 1$ to n **do**   ▷ All voters in T
6:         Let $j_1, j_2, \ldots, j_m$ s.t. $\forall l,\ S_{i-1}[c_{j_{l-1}}] \leq S_{i-1}[c_{j_l}]$
7:         Voter t_i votes $p \succ c_{j_1} \succ c_{j_2} \succ \ldots \succ c_{j_m}$
8:         **for** $l = 1$ to m **do**   ▷ Update score
9:             $S_i[c_{j_l}] \leftarrow S_{i-1}[c_{j_l}] + w(t_i)\alpha_{l+1}$
10:        **end for**
11:        $S_i[p] \leftarrow S_{i-1}[p] + w(t_i)\alpha_1$
12:    **end for**
13:    **if** $\mathrm{argmax}_{c \in C} S_n[c] = \{p\}$ **then**   ▷ p wins
14:        **return true**
15:    **else**
16:        **return false**
17:    **end if**
18: **end procedure**

The voters in T, according to some order, each rank p first, and the rest of the candidates by their current score: the candidate with the lowest current score is ranked highest. GREEDY accepts if and only if p wins this election.

This algorithm, designed specifically for scoring protocols, is a realization of an abstract greedy algorithm: at each stage, voter t_i ranks the undesirable candidates in an order that minimizes the highest score that any undesirable candidate obtains after the current vote. If there is a tie between several permutations, the voter chooses the option such that the second highest score is as low as possible, etc. In any case, every colluder always ranks p first.

Remark 5. This abstract scheme might also be appropriate for protocols such as Maximin and Copeland. Similarly to scoring protocols, in these two protocols the colluders are always better off by ranking p first. In addition, the abstract greedy algorithm can be applied to Maximin and Copeland since the result of an election is based on the score each candidate has (unlike STV, for example).

In the following lemmas, a *stage* in the execution of the algorithm is an iteration of the for loop.

Lemma 2. *If there exists a stage i_0 during the execution of* GREEDY, *and two candidates $a, b \neq p$, such that*

$$|S_{i_0}[a] - S_{i_0}[b]| \leq \alpha_2, \tag{3}$$

then for all $i \geq i_0$ it holds that $|S_i[a] - S_i[b]| \leq \alpha_2$.

Lemma 3. *Let $p \neq a, b \in C$, and suppose that there exists a stage i_0 such that $S_{i_0}[a] \geq S_{i_0}[b]$, and a stage $i_1 \geq i_0$ such that $S_{i_1}[b] \geq S_{i_1}[a]$. Then for all $i \geq i_1$ it holds that $|S_i[a] - S_i[b]| \leq \alpha_2$.*

Lemma 4. *Let P be a sensitive scoring protocol, and assume GREEDY errs on an instance of SCWM in P which has a successful manipulation. Then there is $d \in \{2, 3, \ldots, m\}$, and a subset of candidates $D = \{c_{j_1}, \ldots, c_{j_d}\}$, such that:*

$$\sum_{i=1}^{d} (\alpha_1 W - S[c_{j_i}]) - \sum_{i=1}^{d-1} (i \cdot \alpha_2) \leq W \sum_{i=1}^{d} \alpha_{m+2-i}$$

$$\leq \sum_{i=1}^{d} (\alpha_1 W - S[c_{j_i}]).$$

(4)

Lemma 5. *Let M be SCWM in a sensitive scoring protocol P with $C = \{p, c_1, \ldots, c_m\}$, $m = O(1)$. Then GREEDY is a deterministic heuristic polynomial time algorithm for $\langle M, \mu^* \rangle$.*

Clearly, Theorem 1 directly follows.

5   Susceptibility to UVWM

In this section we shall show:

Theorem 2. *Let P be a voting protocol such that there exists a junta distribution μ^P over the instances of UVWM in P, with the following property: r is uniformly distributed in $[0, 1]$. Then P, with candidates $C = \{p, c_1, \ldots, c_m\}$, $m = O(1)$, is susceptible to UVWM.*

The existence of a junta distribution with r uniformly distributed is a very weak requirement (it is even quite natural to have r uniformly distributed). In fact, the following claim is very likely to be true:

Conjecture 1. Let P be a voting protocol. Then there exists a junta distribution μ^P over the instances of UVWM in P, with r uniformly distributed in $[0, 1]$.

If this conjecture is indeed true, we have that all voting protocols are susceptible to UVWM. If for some reason the conjecture is not true with respect to our definition of junta distributions, then perhaps the definition is too restrictive and should be modified accordingly.

To prove Theorem 2, we require a procedure named SAMPLE, which decides UVWE. SAMPLE samples the given distribution on the votes n^3 times, and calculates the winner of the election each time. If p won more than an r-fraction of the elections then the procedure accepts, otherwise it rejects. We omit the details of the procedure.

Algorithm 2. Decides UVWM

1: **procedure** SAMPLE-AND-MANIPULATE(w, ν, p, r)
2:    **for all** permutations of the $m + 1$ candidates **do**
3:        $\pi \leftarrow$ next permutation
4:        $\nu^* \leftarrow$ the manipulator votes π
5:                                      ▷ others' votes are always distributed w.r.t. ν
6:        **if** SAMPLE(w, ν^*, p, r) **then**
7:            **return true**
8:        **end if**
9:    **end for**
10:   **return false**
11: **end procedure**

Lemma 6. *Let P be a voting protocol, and E be UVWE in P with $C = \{p, c_1, \ldots, c_m\}$. Furthermore, let μ be a distribution over the instances of E, with r uniformly distributed in $[0, 1]$. Then there exists N such that for all $n \geq N$:*

$$\Pr_{x \sim \mu_n} [\text{SAMPLE}(x) \neq E(x)] \leq \frac{1}{\text{poly} n}.$$

We now present an algorithm, SAMPLE-AND-MANIPULATE that decides UVWM; it is given as Algorithm 2. Here, w denotes the weights of all voters including the manipulator, and ν is the given distribution over the others' votes.

Given an instance of UVWM, SAMPLE-AND-MANIPULATE generates $(m+1)!$ instances of the UVWE problem, one for each of the manipulator's possible votes, and executes SAMPLE on each instance. SAMPLE-AND-MANIPULATE accepts if and only if SAMPLE accepts one of the instances.

Lemma 7. *Let P be a voting protocol, and M be UVWM in P with $C = \{p, c_1, \ldots, c_m\}$, $m = O(1)$. Furthermore, let μ be a distribution over the instances of UVWM, with r uniformly distributed in $[0, 1]$. It holds that SAMPLE-AND-MANIPULATE is a probabilistic heuristic polynomial time algorithm for $\langle M, \mu \rangle$.*

6   Future Research

The issue of resistance of mechanisms to manipulation is important, particularly in the context of voting protocols. Most results on this issue use $\mathcal{NP}$-hardness as the complexity measure. One of this paper's main contributions has been introducing tools that can be utilized in showing that manipulating mechanisms is *easy* in the average case. We were concerned with the likely case of coalitional manipulation, and showed that sensitive scoring protocols are susceptible to such manipulation when the number of candidates is constant.

These results suggest that scoring protocols cannot be safely employed. More importantly, this paper should be seen as a starting point for studying the average case complexity of other types of manipulations, in other protocols. In addition, the definitions in Section 3 are deliberately general, and can be applied to manipulations of mechanisms that are not voting mechanisms. One such mechanism of which we are aware, whose manipulation is $\mathcal{NP}$-hard, is presented in [1].

There is still room for debate as to the exact definition of a junta distribution, especially if Conjecture 1 turns out to be false. It may also be the case that there are "unconvincing" distributions that satisfy all of the (current) conditions of a junta distribution. It might prove especially fruitful to show that a heuristic polynomial time algorithm with respect to a junta distribution also has the same property with respect to some easy distributions, such as the uniform distribution.

An issue of great importance is coming up with natural criteria to decide when a manipulation problem is *hard* in the average-case. The traditional definition of average-case completeness is very difficult to work with in general; is there a satisfying definition that applies specifically to the case of manipulations? Once the subject is more fully understood, this understanding can be used to design mechanisms that are hard to manipulate in the average-case.

Acknowledgment

This work was partially supported by grant #039-7582 from the Israel Science Foundation.

References

1. Yoram Bachrach and Jeffrey S. Rosenschein. Achieving allocatively-efficient and strongly budget-balanced mechanisms in the network flow domain for bounded-rational agents. In *The Nineteenth International Joint Conference on Artificial Intelligence*, pages 1653–1654, Edinburgh, Scotland, August 2005. Full version published in The Seventh International Workshop on Agent-Mediated Electronic Commerce: Designing Mechanisms and Systems (AMEC 2005), Utrecht, The Netherlands, July 2005.
2. J. Bartholdi and J. Orlin. Single transferable vote resists strategic voting. *Social Choice and Welfare*, 8(4):341–354, 1991.
3. J. Bartholdi, C. A. Tovey, and M. A. Trick. How hard is it to control an election. *Mathematical and Computer Modelling*, 16:27–40, 1992.
4. V. Conitzer, J. Lang, and T. Sandholm. How many candidates are needed to make elections hard to manipulate? In *Proceedings of the International Conference on Theoretical Aspects of Reasoning about Knowledge*, pages 201–214, Bloomington, Indiana, 2003.
5. V. Conitzer and T. Sandholm. Complexity of manipulating elections with few candidates. In *Proceedings of the National Conference on Artificial Intelligence*, pages 314–319, Edmonton, Canada, July 2002.
6. V. Conitzer and T. Sandholm. Complexity of manipulating elections with few candidates. In *Proceedings of the National Conference on Artificial Intelligence*, pages 314–319, Edmonton, Canada, July 2002.
7. V. Conitzer and T. Sandholm. Universal voting protocol tweaks to make manipulation hard. In *Proceedings of the International Joint Conference on Artificial Intelligence*, pages 781–788, Acapulco, Mexico, August 2003.

8. E. Elkind and H. Lipmaa. Small coalitions cannot manipulate voting. In *International Conference on Financial Cryptography*, Lecture Notes in Computer Science. Springer-Verlag, Roseau, The Commonwealth of Dominica, 2005.
9. Eithan Ephrati and Jeffrey S. Rosenschein. The Clarke Tax as a consensus mechanism among automated agents. In *Proceedings of the Ninth National Conference on Artificial Intelligence*, pages 173–178, Anaheim, California, July 1991.
10. Eithan Ephrati and Jeffrey S. Rosenschein. A heuristic technique for multiagent planning. *Annals of Mathematics and Artificial Intelligence*, 20:13–67, Spring 1997.
11. Robert M. Gagné and Karen L. Medsker. *The Conditions of Learning Training Applications*. Harcourt Brace & Company, 1996.
12. S. Ghosh, M. Mundhe, K. Hernandez, and S. Sen. Voting for movies: the anatomy of a recommender system. In *Proceedings of the Third Annual Conference on Autonomous Agents*, pages 434–435, 1999.
13. A. Gibbard. Manipulation of voting schemes. *Econometrica*, 41:587–602, 1973.
14. T. Haynes, S. Sen, N. Arora, and R. Nadella. An automated meeting scheduling system that utilizes user preferences. In *Proceedings of the First International Conference on Autonomous Agents*, pages 308–315, 1997.
15. E. Hemaspaandra, L. Hemaspaandra, and J. Rothe. Anyone but him: The complexity of precluding an alternative. In *Proceedings of the 20th National Conference on Artificial Intelligence*, Pittsburgh, July 2005.
16. E. Hemaspaandra and L. A. Hemaspaandra. Dichotomy for voting systems. University of Rochester Department of Computer Science Technical Report 861, 2005.
17. William G. Hoover. *Computational Statistical Mechanics*. Elsevier, 1991.
18. George Johnson. All science is computer science, 25 March 2001. The New York Times, Week in Review, pages 1, 5.
19. Noam Nisan and Amir Ronen. Algorithmic mechanism design. *Games and Economic Behavior*, 35:166–196, 2001.
20. Ariel D. Procaccia and Jeffrey S. Rosenschein. The distortion of cardinal preferences in voting. In *The Tenth International Workshop on Cooperative Information Agents (CIA 2006)*, Edinburgh, September 2006.
21. Ariel D. Procaccia and Jeffrey S. Rosenschein. Junta distributions and the average-case complexity of manipulating elections. In *The Fifth International Joint Conference on Autonomous Agents and Multiagent Systems*, pages 497–504, Hakodate, Japan, May 2006.
22. Ariel D. Procaccia, Jeffrey S. Rosenschein, and Aviv Zohar. Multi-winner elections: Complexity of manipulation, control and winner-determination. In *The Eighth International Workshop on Agent-Mediated Electronic Commerce (AMEC 2006)*, pages 15–28, Hakodate, Japan, May 2006.
23. Jeffrey S. Rosenschein and Michael R. Genesereth. Deals among rational agents. In *Proceedings of the Ninth International Joint Conference on Artificial Intelligence*, pages 91–99, Los Angeles, California, August 1985.
24. T. Sandholm and V. Lesser. Issues in automated negotiation and electronic commerce: Extending the contract net framework. In *Proceedings of the First International Conference on Multiagent Systems (ICMAS-95)*, pages 328–335, San Francisco, 1995.
25. M. Satterthwaite. Strategy-proofness and Arrow's conditions: Existence and correspondence theorems for voting procedures and social welfare functions. *Journal of Economic Theory*, 10:187–217, 1975.
26. Moshe Tennenholtz and Alon Altman. On the axiomatic foundations of ranking systems. In *Proceedings of the Nineteenth International Joint Conference on Artificial Intelligence (IJCAI'05)*, pages 917–922, Edinburgh, August 2005.

27. Jeffrey D. Thomas, Taesik Lee, and Nam P. Suh. A function-based framework for understanding biological systems. *Annual Review of Biophysics and Biomolecular Structure*, 33:75–93, 2004.
28. L. Trevisan. Lecture notes on computational complexity. Available from http://www.cs.berkeley.edu/~luca/notes/complexitynotes02.pdf, 2002. Lecture 12.
29. Michael P. Wellman. The economic approach to artificial intelligence. *ACM Computing Surveys*, 27:360–362, 1995.

Agents for Information-Rich Environments

John Debenham and Simeon Simoff

University of Technology, Sydney, Australia
{debenham, simeon}@it.uts.edu.au

Abstract. Information-rich environments, such as electronic markets, or even more generally the World Wide Web, require agents that can assimilate and use real-time information flows wisely. A new breed of "information-based" agents aim to meet this requirement. They are founded on concepts from information theory, and are designed to operate with information flows of varying and questionable integrity. These agents are part of a larger project that aims to make informed automated trading, in applications such as eProcurement, a reality.

1   Introduction

Electronic trading environments are awash with information, including information drawn from general resources such as the World Wide Web using smart retrieval technology [1]. Powerful agent architectures that are capable of flexible, autonomous action are well known [2]. However there has been little work on architectures for intelligent agents that are designed the survive and thrive in these information rich environments. This is the question addressed here. This paper describes a data mining system and an agent architecture that have been designed to operate in tandem. These are two components in our e-Market Framework that is available on the World Wide Web[1]. This framework aims to make informed automated trading a reality, and develops further the "Curious Negotiator" framework [3]. This work does not address all of the issues in automated trading. For example, the work relies on developments in: XML and semantic web, secure data exchange, value chain management and financial services. Further the design of marketplaces is not described here. We are presently constructing a "virtual institution" system[1] in a collaborative research project with "Institut d'Investigacio en Intel.ligencia Artificial[2]", Spanish Scientific Research Council, UAB, Barcelona, Spain.

The data mining system is described in Sec. 2. The associated intelligent agents, designed specifically to handle real-time information flows, are described in Sec. 3. The way in which these agents manage the dynamic information flows is described in Sec. 4. The interaction of more than one of these agents engaging in competitive negotiation is described in Sec. 5. Sec. 6 concludes.

---

[1] http://e-markets.org.au
[2] http://www.iiia.csic.es/

M. Klusch, M. Rovatsos, and T. Payne (Eds.): CIA 2006, LNAI 4149, pp. 51–65, 2006.

2 Data Mining

We have designed information discovery and delivery agents that utilise text and network data mining for supporting real-time negotiation. This work has addressed the central issues of extracting relevant information from different on-line repositories with different formats, with possible duplicative and erroneous data. That is, we

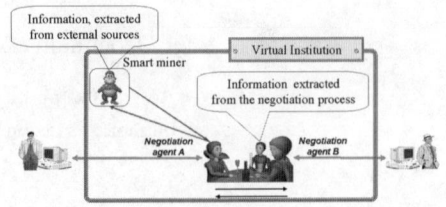

Fig. 1. Information impacts trading

have addressed the central issues in extracting information from the World Wide Web. Our mining agents understand the influence that extracted information has on the subject of negotiation and takes that in account.

Real-time embedded data mining is an essential component of the proposed framework. In this framework the trading agents make their informed decisions, based on utilising two types of information (as illustrated in Figure 1):

- information extracted from the negotiation process (i.e. from the exchange of offers), and;
- information from external sources, extracted and provided in condensed form.

The embedded data mining system provides the information extracted from the external sources. The system complements and services the information-based architecture developed in [4] and [5]. The information request and the information delivery format is defined by the interaction ontology.

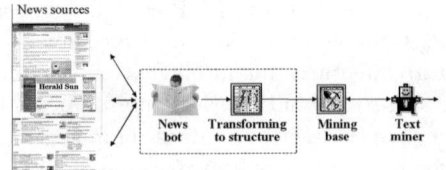

Fig. 2. Pipeline for "focused" data sets

As these agents operate with negotiation parameters with a discrete set of feasible values, the information request is formulated in terms of these values. As agents proceed with negotiation they have a topic of negotiation and a shared ontology that describes that topic. For example, if the topic of negotiation is buying a number of digital cameras for a University, the shared ontology will include the product model of the camera, and some characteristics, like "product reputation" (which on their own can be a list of parameters), that are usually derived from additional sources (for example, from different opinions in a professional community of photographers or digital artists). As the information-based architecture assumes that negotiation parameters are discrete, the information request can be formulated as a subset of the range of values for a negotiation parameter. For example, if the negotiator is interested in cameras with 8 megapixel resolution, and the brand is a negotiation parameter, the information request can be formulated as a set of camera models, e.g. { "Canon Power Shot

Pro 1", "Sony f828", "Nikon Coolpix 8400", "Olympus C-8080"} and a *preference estimate* based on the information in the different articles available. The
collection of parameter sets of the negotiation topic constitutes the input to the
data mining system. Continuous numerical values are replaced by finite number
of ranges of interest.

The data mining system initially constructs data sets that are "focused" on
requested information, as illustrated in Figure 2. From the vast amount of information available in electronic form, we need to filter the information that
is relevant to the information request. In our example, this will be the news,
opinions, comments, white papers related to the five models of digital cameras.
Technically, the automatic retrieval of the information pieces utilises the universal news bot architecture presented in [1]. Developed originally for news sites
only, the approach is currently being extended to discussion boards and company
white papers.

The "focused" data set
is dynamically constructed
in an iterative process. The
data mining agent constructs
the news data set accord-
ing to the concepts in the
query. Each concept is represented as a cluster of key
terms (a term can include
one or more words), defined
by the proximity position
of the frequent key terms.
On each iteration the most
frequent (terms) from the
retrieved data set are extracted and considered to be

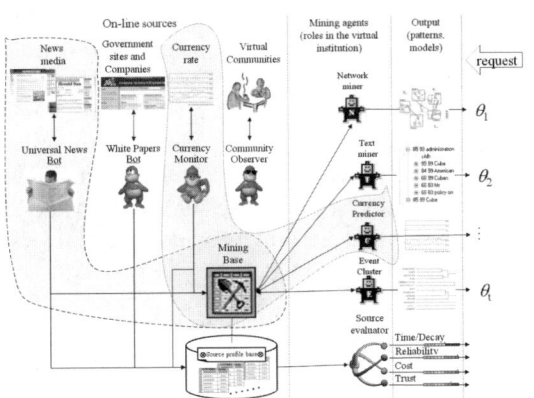

Fig. 3. Architecture of data mining system

related to the same concept. The extracted keywords are resubmitted to the
search engine. The process of query submission, data retrieval and keyword extraction is repeated until the search results start to derail from the given topic.

The set of topics in the original request is used as a set of class labels. In our
example we are interested in the evidence in support of each particular model
camera model. A simple solution is for each model to introduce two labels —
positive opinion and negative opinion, ending with ten labels. In the constructed
"focused" data set, each news article is labelled with one of the values from
this set of labels. An automated approach reported in [1] extends the tree-based
approach proposed in [6].

The data sets required further automatic pre-processing, related to possible
redundancies in the information encoded in the set that can bias the analysis
algorithms. For example, identifying a set of opinions about the camera that
most likely comes from the same author, though it has been retrieved from
different "opinion boards" on the Internet.

Once the set is constructed, building the "advising model" is reduced to a classification data mining problem. As the model is communicated back to the information-based agent architecture, the classifier output should include all the possible class labels with an attached probability estimates for each class. Hence, we use probabilistic classifiers (e.g. Naïve Bayes, Bayesian Network classifiers) [7] without the min-max selection of the class output [e.g., in a classifier based on Naïve Bayes algorithm], we calculate the posterior probability $\mathbb{P}_p(i)$ of each class $c(i)$ with respect to combinations of key terms and then return the tuples $< c(i), \mathbb{P}_p(i) >$ for all classes, not just the one with maximum $\mathbb{P}_p(i)$. In the case when we deal with range variables the data mining system returns the range within which is the estimated value. For example, the response to a request for an estimate of the rate of change between two currencies over specified period of time will be done in three steps: (i) the relative focused news data set will be updated for the specified period; (ii) the model that takes these news in account is updated, and; (iii) the output of the model is compared with requested ranges and the matching one is returned. The details of this part of the data mining system are presented in [8]. The currently used model is a modified linear model with an additional term that incorporates a news index Inews, which reflects the news effect on exchange rate. The current architecture of the data mining system in the e-market environment is shown in Figure 3. The $\{\theta_1, \ldots, \theta_t\}$ denote the output of the system to the information-based agent architecture. In addition, the data mining system provides parameters that define the "quality of the information", including:

- the time span of the "focused" data set, (defined by the eldest and the latest information unit);
- estimates of the characteristics of the information sources, including reliability, trust and cost, that then are used by the information-based agent architecture.

Overall the parameters that will be estimated by the mining algorithms and provided to the negotiating agents are expected to allow information-based agents to devise more effective and better informed situated strategies. In addition to the data coming from external sources, the data mining component of the project will develop techniques for analysing agent behaviourist data with respect to the electronic institution set-up.

3   Information-Based Agents

We have designed a new agent architecture founded on information theory. These "information-based" agents operate in real-time in response to market information flows. We have addressed the central issues of trust in the execution of contracts, and the reliability of information [5]. Our agents understand the value of building business relationships as a foundation for reliable trade. An inherent difficulty in automated trading — including e-procurement — is that it is generally multi-issue. Even a simple trade, such as a quantity of steel, may involve:

delivery date, settlement terms, as well as price and the quality of the steel. The "information-based" agent's reasoning is based on a first-order logic world model that manages multi-issue negotiation as easily as single-issue.

Most of the work on multi-issue negotiation has focussed on one-to-one bargaining — for example [9]. There has been rather less interest in one-to-many, multi-issue auctions — despite the size of the e-procurement market which typically attempts to extend single-issue, reverse auctions to the multi-issue case by post-auction haggling. There has been even less interest in many-to-many, multi-issue exchanges.

The generic architecture of our "information-based" agents is presented in Sec. 3.1. The agent's reasoning employs entropy-based inference and is described in Sec. 3.2. The integrity of the agent's information is in a permanent state of decay, Sec. 4 describes the agent's machinery for managing this decay leading to a characterisation of the "value" of information.

3.1   Agent Architecture

This section describes the essence of "information-based agency". An agent observes events in its environment including what other agents actually do. It chooses to represent some of those observations in its world model as beliefs. As time passes, an agent may not be prepared to accept such beliefs as being "true", and qualifies those representations with epistemic probabilities. Those qualified representations of prior observations are the agent's *information*. This information is primitive — it is the agent's representation of its beliefs about prior events in the environment and about the other agents prior actions. It is independent of what the agent is trying to achieve, or what the agent believes the other agents are trying to achieve. Given this information, an agent may then choose to adopt goals and strategies. Those strategies may be based on game theory, for example. To enable the agent's strategies to make good use of its information, tools from information theory are applied to summarise and process that information. Such an agent is called *information-based*.

An agent called Π is the subject of this discussion. Π engages in multi-issue negotiation with a set of other agents: $\{\Omega_1, \cdots, \Omega_o\}$. The foundation for Π's operation is the information that is generated both by and because of its negotiation exchanges. Any message from one agent to another reveals information about the sender. Π also acquires information from the environment — including general information sources — to support its actions. Π uses ideas from information theory to process and summarise its information. Π's aim may not be "utility optimisation" — it may not be aware of a utility function. If Π *does* know its utility function *and* if it aims to optimise its utility *then* Π may apply the principles of game theory to achieve its aim. The information-based approach does not reject utility optimisation — in general, the selection of a goal and strategy is secondary to the processing and summarising of the information.

In addition to the information derived from its opponents, Π has access to a set of information sources $\{\Theta_1, \cdots, \Theta_t\}$ that may include the marketplace in which trading takes place, and general information sources such as news-feeds accessed via the Internet. Together, Π, $\{\Omega_1, \cdots, \Omega_o\}$ and $\{\Theta_1, \cdots, \Theta_t\}$ make up a multiagent system. The integrity of Π's information, including information extracted from the Internet, will decay in time. The way in which this decay occurs will depend on the type of information, and on the source from which it was drawn. Little appears to be known about how the integrity of real information, such as news-feeds, decays, although its validity can often be checked — "Is company X taking over company Y?" — by proactive action given a co-operative information source Θ_j. So Π has to consider how and when to refresh its decaying information.

Π has two languages: $\mathcal{C}$ and $\mathcal{L}$. $\mathcal{C}$ is an illocutionary-based language for communication. $\mathcal{L}$ is a first-order language for internal representation — precisely it is a first-order language with sentence probabilities optionally attached to each sentence representing Π's epistemic belief in the truth of that sentence. Fig. 4 shows a high-level view of how Π operates. Messages expressed in $\mathcal{C}$ from $\{\Theta_i\}$ and $\{\Omega_i\}$ are received, time-stamped, source-stamped and placed in an *in-box* $\mathcal{X}$. The messages in $\mathcal{X}$ are then translated using an *import function* I into sentences expressed in $\mathcal{L}$ that have integrity decay functions (usually of time) attached to each sentence, they are stored in a *repository* $\mathcal{Y}^t$. And that is all that happens until Π triggers a goal.

Π triggers a goal, $g \in \mathcal{G}$, in two ways: first in response to a message received from an opponent $\{\Omega_i\}$ "I offer you €1 in exchange for an apple", and second in response to some need, $\nu \in \mathcal{N}$, "goodness, we've run out of coffee". In either case, Π is motivated by a need — either a need to strike a deal with a particular feature (such as acquiring coffee) or a general need to trade. Π's goals could be short-term such as obtaining information "what is the time?", medium-term such as striking a deal with one of its opponents, or, rather longer-term such as building a (business) relationship with one of its opponents. So Π has a trigger mechanism T where: $T : \{\mathcal{X} \cup \mathcal{N}\} \to \mathcal{G}$.

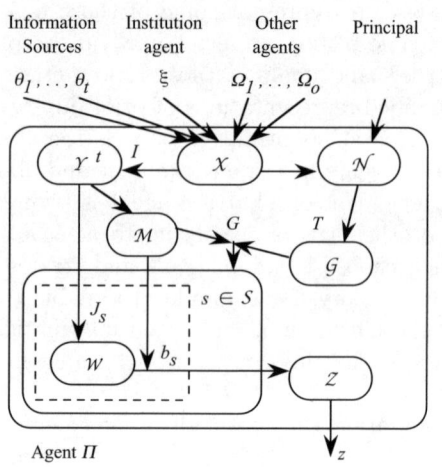

Fig. 4. Architecture of agent Π

For each goal that Π commits to, it has a mechanism, G, for selecting a strategy to achieve it where $G : \mathcal{G} \times \mathcal{M} \to \mathcal{S}$ where $\mathcal{S}$ is the strategy library. A *strategy* s maps an information base into an action, $s(\mathcal{Y}^t) = z \in \mathcal{Z}$. Given a goal, g, and the current state of the social model m^t, a strategy: $s = G(g, m^t)$. Each strategy, s, consists of a *plan*, b_s and a *world model* (construction and revision) *function*, J_s, that constructs, and maintains the currency of, the strategy's *world model* W_s^t that consists of a set of probability distributions. A *plan* derives the agent's next action, z, on the basis of the agent's world model for that strategy and the current state of the social model: $z = b_s(W_s^t, m^t)$, and $z = s(\mathcal{Y}^t)$. J_s employs two forms of entropy-based inference:

- Maximum entropy inference, J_s^+, first constructs an *information base* $\mathcal{I}_s^t$ as a set of sentences expressed in $\mathcal{L}$ derived from $\mathcal{Y}^t$, and then from $\mathcal{I}_s^t$ constructs the world model, W_s^t, as a set of complete probability distributions.
- Given a prior world model, W_s^u, where $u < t$, minimum relative entropy inference, J_s^-, first constructs the incremental information base $\mathcal{I}_s^{(u,t)}$ of sentences derived from those in $\mathcal{Y}^t$ that were received between time u and time t, and then from W_s^u and $\mathcal{I}_s^{(u,t)}$ constructs a new world model, W_s^t.

3.2 Π's Reasoning

Once Π has selected a plan $a \in \mathcal{A}$ it uses maximum entropy inference to derive the $\{D_i^s\}_{i=1}^n$ [see Fig. 4] and minimum relative entropy inference to update those distributions as new data becomes available. *Entropy*, $\mathbb{H}$, is a measure of uncertainty [10] in a probability distribution for a discrete random variable X: $\mathbb{H}(X) \triangleq -\sum_i p(x_i) \log p(x_i)$ where $p(x_i) = \mathbb{P}(X = x_i)$. Maximum entropy inference is used to derive sentence probabilities for that which is not known by constructing the "maximally noncommittal" probability distribution, and is chosen for its ability to generate complete distributions from sparse data.

Let $\mathcal{G}$ be the set of all positive ground literals that can be constructed using Π's language $\mathcal{L}$. A *possible world*, v, is a valuation function: $\mathcal{G} \to \{\top, \bot\}$. $\mathcal{V}|\mathcal{K}^s = \{v_i\}$ is the set of all possible worlds that are consistent with Π's knowledge base $\mathcal{K}^s$ that contains statements which Π believes are true. A *random world* for $\mathcal{K}^s$, $W|\mathcal{K}^s = \{p_i\}$ is a probability distribution over $\mathcal{V}|\mathcal{K}^s = \{v_i\}$, where p_i expresses Π's degree of belief that each of the possible worlds, v_i, is the actual world. The *derived sentence probability* of any $\sigma \in \mathcal{L}$, *with respect to* a random world $W|\mathcal{K}^s$ is:

$$(\forall \sigma \in \mathcal{L})\mathbb{P}_{\{W|\mathcal{K}^s\}}(\sigma) \triangleq \sum_n \{\, p_n \; : \; \sigma \text{ is } \top \text{ in } v_n \,\} \tag{1}$$

The agent's *belief set* $\mathcal{B}_t^s = \{\Omega_j\}_{j=1}^M$ contains statements to which Π attaches a *given sentence probability* $\mathbb{B}(.)$. A random world $W|\mathcal{K}^s$ is *consistent* with $\mathcal{B}_t^s$ if: $(\forall \Omega \in \mathcal{B}_t^s)(\mathbb{B}(\Omega) = \mathbb{P}_{\{W|\mathcal{K}^s\}}(\Omega))$. Let $\{p_i\} = \{\overline{W}|\mathcal{K}^s, \mathcal{B}_t^s\}$ be the "maximum entropy probability distribution over $\mathcal{V}|\mathcal{K}^s$ that is consistent with $\mathcal{B}_t^s$". Given an agent with $\mathcal{K}^s$ and $\mathcal{B}_t^s$, *maximum entropy inference* states that the *derived sentence probability* for any sentence, $\sigma \in \mathcal{L}$, is:

$$(\forall \sigma \in \mathcal{L})\mathbb{P}_{\{\overline{W}|\mathcal{K}^s, \mathcal{B}_t^s\}}(\sigma) \triangleq \sum_n \{\, p_n \; : \; \sigma \text{ is } \top \text{ in } v_n \,\} \tag{2}$$

From Eqn. 2, each belief imposes a linear constraint on the $\{p_i\}$. The maximum entropy distribution: $\arg\max_p \mathbb{H}(\underline{p})$, $\underline{p} = (p_1, \ldots, p_N)$, subject to $M + 1$ linear constraints:

$$g_j(\underline{p}) = \sum_{i=1}^N c_{ji}p_i - \mathbb{B}(\Omega_j) = 0, \quad j = 1, \ldots, M. \qquad g_0(\underline{p}) = \sum_{i=1}^N p_i - 1 = 0$$

where $c_{ji} = 1$ if Ω_j is $\top$ in v_i and 0 otherwise, and $p_i \geq 0, i = 1, \ldots, N$, is found by introducing Lagrange multipliers, and then obtaining a numerical solution using the multivariate Newton-Raphson method. In the subsequent subsections we'll see how an agent updates the sentence probabilities depending on the type of information used in the update.

Given a prior probability distribution $\underline{q} = (q_i)_{i=1}^n$ and a set of constraints C, the *principle of minimum relative entropy* chooses the posterior probability distribution $\underline{p} = (p_i)_{i=1}^n$ that has the least *relative entropy*[3] with respect to $\underline{q}$:

$$\{\underline{W}|\underline{q}, C\} \triangleq \arg\min_{\underline{p}} \sum_{i=1}^n p_i \log \frac{p_i}{q_i}$$

and that satisfies the constraints. This may be found by introducing Lagrange multipliers as above. Given a prior distribution $\underline{q}$ over $\{v_i\}$ — the set of all possible worlds, and a set of constraints C (that could have been derived as above from a set of new beliefs) *minimum relative entropy inference* states that the derived sentence probability for any sentence, $\sigma \in \mathcal{L}$, is:

$$(\forall \sigma \in \mathcal{L})\mathbb{P}_{\{\underline{W}|\underline{q},C\}}(\sigma) \triangleq \sum_n \{ p_n : \sigma \text{ is } \top \text{ in } v_n \} \tag{3}$$

where $\{p_i\} = \{\underline{W}|\underline{q}, C\}$. The principle of minimum relative entropy is a generalisation of the principle of maximum entropy. If the prior distribution $\underline{q}$ is uniform, then the relative entropy of $\underline{p}$ with respect to $\underline{q}$, $\underline{p}\|\underline{q}$, differs from $-\overline{\mathbb{H}}(\underline{p})$ only by a constant. So the principle of maximum entropy is equivalent to the principle of minimum relative entropy with a uniform prior distribution.

4　Managing Dynamic Information Flows

The illocutions in the communication language $\mathcal{C}$ include information, $[info]$. The information received from general information sources will be expressed in terms defined by Π's ontology. We assume that Π makes at least part of that ontology public so that the other agents $\{\Omega_1, \ldots, \Omega_o\}$ may communicate $[info]$ that Π can understand. Ω's *reliability* is an estimate of the extent to which this $[info]$ is correct. For example, Ω may send Π the $[info]$ that "the price of fish will go up by 10% next week", and it may actually go up by 9%.

The only restriction on incoming $[info]$ is that it is expressed in terms of the ontology — this is very general. However, the way in which $[info]$ is used is completely specific — it will be represented as a set of linear constraints on one or more probability distributions. A chunk of $[info]$ may not be directly related to one of Π's chosen distributions or may not be expressed naturally as constraints, and so some inference machinery is required to derive these constraints — this inference is performed by model building functions, J_s, that have been activated by a plan s chosen by Π. $J_s^D([info])$ denotes the set of constraints on distribution D derived by J_s from $[info]$.

---

[3] Otherwise called *cross entropy* or the *Kullback-Leibler* distance between the two probability distributions.

4.1   Updating the World Model with [*info*]

The procedure for updating the world model as [*info*] is received follows. If at time u, Π receives a message containing [*info*] it is time-stamped and source-stamped [*info*]$_{(\Omega,\Pi,u)}$, and placed in a repository $\mathcal{Y}^t$. If Π has an active plan, s, with model building function, J_s, then J_s is applied to [*info*]$_{(\Omega,\Pi,u)}$ to derive constraints on some, or none, of Π's distributions. The extent to which those constraints are permitted to effect the distributions is determined by a value for the *reliability* of Ω, $R^t(\Pi,\Omega,O([info]))$, where $O([info])$ is the ontological context of [*info*].

An agent may have models of integrity decay for some particular distributions, but general models of integrity decay for, say, a chunk of information taken at random from the World Wide Web are generally unknown. However the values to which decaying integrity should tend in time *are* often known. For example, a prior value for the truth of the proposition that a "22 year-old male will default on credit card repayment" is well known to banks. If Π attaches such prior values to a distribution D they are called the *decay limit distribution* for D, $(d_i^D)_{i=1}^n$. No matter how integrity of [*info*] decays, in the absence of any other relevant information it should decay to the decay limit distribution. If a distribution with n values has no decay limit distribution then integrity decays to the maximum entropy value $\frac{1}{n}$. In other words, the maximum entropy distribution is the default decay limit distribution.

In the absence of new [*info*] the integrity of distributions decays. If $D = (q_i)_{i=1}^n$ then we use a geometric model of decay:

$$q_i^{t+1} = (1 - \rho^D) \times d_i^D + \rho^D \times q_i^t, \text{ for } i = 1,\ldots,n \tag{4}$$

where $\rho^D \in (0,1)$ is the decay rate. This raises the question of how to determine ρ^D. Just as an agent may know the decay limit distribution it may also know something about ρ^D. In the case of an information-overfed agent there is no harm in conservatively setting ρ^D "a bit on the low side" as the continually arriving [*info*] will sustain the estimate for D.

We now describe how new [*info*] is imported to the distributions. A single chunk of [*info*] may effect a number of distributions. Suppose that a chunk of [*info*] is received from Ω and that Π attaches the epistemic belief probability $R^t(\Pi,\Omega,O([info]))$ to it. Each distribution models a facet of the world. Given a distribution $D^t = (q_i^t)_{i=1}^n$, q_i^t is the probability that the possible world ω_i for D is the true world for D. The effect that a chunk [*info*] has on distribution D is to enforce the set of linear constraints on D, $J_s^D([info])$. If the constraints $J_s^D([info])$ are taken by Π as valid then Π could update D to the posterior distribution $(p_i^{[info]})_{i=1}^n$ that is the distribution with least relative entropy with respect to $(q_i^t)_{i=1}^n$ satisfying the constraint:

$$\sum_i \{p_i^{[info]} \ : \ J_s^D([info]) \text{ are all } \top \text{ in } \omega_i\} = 1. \tag{5}$$

But $R^t(\Pi,\Omega,O([info])) = r \in [0,1]$ and Π should only treat the $J_s^D([info])$ as valid if $r = 1$. In general r determines the extent to which the effect of [*info*] on

D is closer to $(p_i^{[info]})_{i=1}^n$ or to the prior $(q_i^t)_{i=1}^n$ distribution by:

$$p_i^t = r \times p_i^{[info]} + (1 - r) \times q_i^t \tag{6}$$

But, we should only permit a new chunk of [*info*] to influence D if doing so gives us new information. For example, if 5 minutes ago a trusted agent advises Π that the interest rate will go up by 1%, and 1 minute ago a very unreliable agent advises Π that the interest rate may go up by 0.5%, then the second unreliable chunk should not be permitted to 'overwrite' the first. We capture this by only permitting a new chunk of [*info*] to be imported if the resulting distribution has more information *relative to* the decay limit distribution than the existing distribution has. Precisely, this is measured using the Kullback-Leibler distance measure — this is just one criterion for determining whether the [*info*] should be used — and [*info*] is only used if:

$$\sum_{i=1}^n p_i^t \log \frac{p_i^t}{d_i^D} > \sum_{i=1}^n q_i^t \log \frac{q_i^t}{d_i^D} \tag{7}$$

In addition, we have described in Eqn. 4 how the integrity of each distribution D will decay in time. Combining these two into one result, distribution D is revised to:

$$q_i^{t+1} = \begin{cases} (1 - \rho^D) \times d_i^D + \rho^D \times p_i^t & \text{if usable [info] is received at time } t \\ (1 - \rho^D) \times d_i^D + \rho^D \times q_i^t & \text{otherwise} \end{cases}$$

for $i = 1, \cdots, n$, and decay rate ρ^D as before.

4.2   Information Reliability

We estimate $R^t(\Pi, \Omega, O([info]))$ by measuring the error in information. Π's plans will have constructed a set of distributions. We measure the 'error' in information as the error in the effect that information has on each of Π's distributions. Suppose that a chunk of [*info*] is received from agent Ω at time s and is verified at some later time t. For example, a chunk of information could be "the interest rate will rise by 0.5% next week", and suppose that the interest rate actually rises by 0.25% — call that correct information [*fact*]. What does all this tell agent Π about agent Ω's reliability? Consider one of Π's distributions D that is $\{q_i^s\}$ at time s. Let $(p_i^{[info]})_{i=1}^n$ be the minimum relative entropy distribution given that [*info*] has been received as calculated in Eqn. 5, and let $(p_i^{[fact]})_{i=1}^n$ be that distribution if [*fact*] had been received instead. Suppose that the reliability estimate for distribution D was R_D^s. This section is concerned with what R_D^s should have been in the light of knowing *now*, at time t, that [*info*] should have been [*fact*], and how that knowledge effects our current reliability estimate for D, $R^t(\Pi, \Omega, O([info]))$.

The idea of Eqn. 6, is that the current value of r should be such that, *on average*, $(p_i^s)_{i=1}^n$ will be seen to be "close to" $(p_i^{[fact]})_{i=1}^n$ when we eventually discover [fact] — no matter whether or not [info] was used to update D, as determined by the acceptability test in Eqn. 7 at time s. That is, given [info], [fact] and the prior $(q_i^s)_{i=1}^n$, calculate $(p_i^{[info]})_{i=1}^n$ and $(p_i^{[fact]})_{i=1}^n$ using Eqn. 5. Then the *observed reliability* for distribution D, $R_D^{([info]|[fact])}$, on the basis of the verification of [info] with [fact] is the value of r that minimises the Kullback-Leibler distance between $(p_i^s)_{i=1}^n$ and $(p_i^{[fact]})_{i=1}^n$:

$$\arg\min_r \sum_{i=1}^n (r \cdot p_i^{[info]} + (1-r) \cdot q_i^s) \log \frac{r \cdot p_i^{[info]} + (1-r) \cdot q_i^s}{p_i^{[fact]}}$$

If $E^{[info]}$ is the set of distributions that [info] effects, then the overall *observed reliability* on the basis of the verification of [info] with [fact] is: $R^{([info]|[fact])} = 1 - (\max_{D \in E^{[info]}} |1 - R_D^{([info]|[fact])}|)$. Then for each ontological context o_j, at time t when, perhaps, a chunk of [info], with $O([info]) = o_k$, may have been verified with [fact]:

$$R^{t+1}(\Pi, \Omega, o_j) = (1 - \rho) \times R^t(\Pi, \Omega, o_j) + \rho \times R^{([info]|[fact])} \times \text{Sem}(o_j, o_k)$$

where $\text{Sem}(\cdot, \cdot) : O \times O \to [0,1]$ measures the semantic distance between two sections of the ontology, and ρ is the learning rate. Over time, Π notes the ontological context of the various chunks of [info] received from Ω and over the various ontological contexts calculates the relative frequency, $P^t(o_j)$, of these contexts, $o_j = O([info])$. This leads to a overall expectation of the *reliability* that agent Π has for agent Ω: $R^t(\Pi, \Omega) = \sum_j P^t(o_j) \times R^t(\Pi, \Omega, o_j)$.

5   Negotiation

For illustration Π's communication language [11] is restricted to the illocutions: Offer($\cdot$), Accept($\cdot$), Reject($\cdot$) and Withdraw($\cdot$). The simple strategies that we will describe all use the same world model function, J_s, that maintains the following two probability distributions as their world model:

- $\mathbb{P}^t(\Pi \text{Acc}(\Pi, \Omega, \nu, \delta))$ — the strength of belief that Π has in the proposition that she should accept the proposal $\delta = (a, b)$ from agent Ω in satisfaction of need ν at time t, where a is Π's commitment and b is Ω's commitment. $\mathbb{P}^t(\Pi \text{Acc}(\Pi, \Omega, \nu, \delta))$ is estimated from:
  1. $\mathbb{P}^t(\text{Satisfy}(\Pi, \Omega, \nu, \delta))$ a subjective evaluation (the strength of belief that Π has in the proposition that the expected outcome of accepting the proposal will satisfy some of her needs).
  2. $\mathbb{P}^t(\text{Fair}(\delta))$ an objective evaluation (the strength of belief that Π has in the proposition that the proposal is a "fair deal" in the open market.
  3. $\mathbb{P}^t(\Pi \text{CanDo}(a)$ an estimate of whether Π will be able to meet her commitment a at contract execution time.
  These three arrays of probabilities are estimated by importing relevant information, [info], as described in Sec. 4.

– $\mathbb{P}^t(\Omega\mathrm{Acc}(\beta, \alpha, \delta))$ — the strength of belief that Π has in the proposition that Ω would accept the proposal δ from agent Π at time t. Every time that Ω submits a proposal she is revealing information about what she is prepared to accept, and every time she rejects a proposal she is revealing information about what she is *not* prepared to accept. Eg: having received the stamped illocution $\mathrm{Offer}(\Omega, \Pi, \delta)_{(\Omega, \Pi, u)}$, at time $t > u$, Π may believe that $\mathbb{P}^t(\Omega\mathrm{Acc}(\Omega, \Pi, \delta)) = \kappa$ this is used as a constraint on $\mathbb{P}^{t+1}(\Omega\mathrm{Acc}(\cdot))$ which is calculated using Eqn. 3.

Negotiation is an information revelation process. The agents described in Sec. 3 are primarily concerned with the integrity of their information, and then when they have acquired sufficient information to reduce their uncertainty to an acceptable level they are concerned with acting strategically within the surrounding uncertainty. A basic conundrum in any offer-exchange bargaining is: it is impossible to force your opponent to reveal information about their position without revealing information about your own position. Further, by revealing information about your own position you may change your opponents position — and so on.[4] This infinite regress, of speculation and counter-speculation, is avoided here by ignoring the internals of the opponent and by focussing on what is known for certain — that is: *what* information is contained in the signals received and *when* did those signals arrive.

5.1   Utility-Based Strategies

An agent's strategy s is a function of the information $\mathcal{Y}^t$ that it has at time t. Four simple strategies make offers only on the basis of $\mathbb{P}^t(\Pi\mathrm{Acc}(\Pi, \Omega, \nu, \delta))$, Π's acceptability threshold γ, and $\mathbb{P}^t(\Omega\mathrm{Acc}(\Omega, \Pi, \delta))$. The greedy strategy s^+ chooses:

$$\arg\max_{\delta}\{\mathbb{P}^t(\Pi\mathrm{Acc}(\Pi, \Omega, \nu, \delta)) \mid \mathbb{P}^t(\Omega\mathrm{Acc}(\Omega, \Pi, \delta)) \gg 0\},$$

it is appropriate when Π believes Ω is desperate to trade.

The *expected-acceptability-to-Π-optimising strategy* s^* chooses:

$$\arg\max_{\delta}\{\mathbb{P}^t(\Omega\mathrm{Acc}(\Omega, \Pi, \delta)) \times \mathbb{P}^t(\Pi\mathrm{Acc}(\Pi, \Omega, \nu, \delta)) \mid \mathbb{P}^t(\Pi\mathrm{Acc}(\Pi, \Omega, \nu, \delta)) \geq \gamma\}$$

when Π is confident and not desperate to trade. The strategy s^- chooses:

$$\arg\max_{\delta}\{\mathbb{P}^t(\Omega\mathrm{Acc}(\Omega, \Pi, \delta)) \mid \mathbb{P}^t(\Pi\mathrm{Acc}(\Pi, \Omega, \nu, \delta)) \geq \gamma\}$$

it optimises the likelihood of trade — when Π is keen to trade without compromising its own standards of acceptability.

An approach to issue-tradeoffs is described in [9]. The bargaining strategy described there attempts to make an acceptable offer by "walking round" the

---

[4] This a reminiscent of Werner Heisenberg's indeterminacy relation, or *unbestimmtheitsrelationen*: "you can't measure one feature of an object without changing another" — with apologies.

iso-curve of Π's previous offer δ' (that has, say, an acceptability of $\gamma_{\delta'} \geq \gamma$) towards Ω's subsequent counter offer. In terms of the machinery described here, an analogue is to use the strategy s^-:

$$\arg\max_{\delta}\{\mathbb{P}^t(\Omega\mathrm{Acc}(\Omega, \Pi, \delta)) \mid \mathbb{P}^t(\Pi\mathrm{Acc}(\Pi, \Omega, \nu, \delta)) \geq \gamma_{\delta'}\}$$

with $\gamma = \gamma_{\delta'}$. This is reasonable for an agent that is attempting to be accommodating without compromising its own interests. The complexity of the strategy in [9] is linear with the number of issues. The strategy described here does not have that property, but it benefits from using $\mathbb{P}^t(\Omega\mathrm{Acc}(\Omega, \Pi, \delta))$ that contains foot prints of the prior offer sequence — estimated by repeated use of Eqn. 3 — in that distribution more recent data gives estimates with greater certainty.

5.2   Information-Based Strategies

Π's *negotiation strategy* is a function $s : \mathcal{Y}^t \rightarrow \mathcal{Z}$ where $\mathcal{Z}$ is the set of actions [see Fig. 4] that send *Offer(.)*, *Accept(.)*, *Reject(.)* and *Quit(.)* messages to Ω. If Π sends *Offer(.)*, *Accept(.)* or *Reject(.)* messages to Ω then she is giving Ω information about herself. In an infinite-horizon bargaining game where there is no incentive to trade now rather than later, a self-interested agent will "sit and wait", and do nothing except, perhaps, to ask for information. The well known bargaining response to an approach by an interested party "Well make me an offer" illustrates how a shrewd bargainer may behave in this situation.

An agent may be motivated to act for various reasons — three are mentioned. First, if there are costs involved in the bargaining process due *either* to changes in the value of the negotiation object with time *or* to the intrinsic cost of conducting the negotiation itself. Second, if there is a risk of breakdown caused by the opponent walking away from the bargaining table. Third, if the agent is concerned with establishing a sense of trust [12] with the opponent —this could be the case in the establishment of a business relationship. Of these three reasons the last two are addressed here. The risk of breakdown may be reduced, and a sense of trust may be established, if the agent appears to its opponent to be "approaching the negotiation in an even-handed manner". One dimension of "appearing to be even-handed" is to be equitable with the value of information given to the opponent. Various bargaining strategies, both with and without breakdown, are described in [4], but they do not address this issue. A bargaining strategy is described here that is founded on a principle of "equitable information gain". That is, Π attempts to respond to Ω's messages so that Ω's expected information gain similar to that which Π has received.

Π models Ω by observing her actions, and by representing beliefs about her future actions in the probability distribution $\mathbb{P}(\Omega Acc(\cdot))$. Π measures the value of information that it receives from Ω by the change in the entropy of this distribution as a result of representing that information in $\mathbb{P}(\Omega Acc(\cdot))$. More generally, Π measures the value of information received in a message, μ, by the change in the entropy in its entire representation, $\bigcup_s W_s^t$, as a result of the receipt of that message; this is denoted by: $\Delta_\mu|W^t|$, where $|W^t|$ denotes the value of the uncertainty (as negative entropy) in Π's information in W^t. Although both Π and Ω will build their models of each other using the same data — the messages exchanged — the observed information gain will depend on the way in which each agent has represented this information as discussed in [4]. It is "not unreasonable to suggest" that these two representations should be similar. To support Π's attempts to achieve "equitable information gain" she assumes that Ω's reasoning apparatus mirrors her own, and so is able to estimate the change in Ω's entropy as a result of sending a message μ to Ω: $\Delta_\mu|W_\Omega^t|$. Suppose that Π receives a message $\mu = \textit{Offer}(.)$ from Ω and observes an information gain of $\Delta_\mu|W^t|$. Suppose that Π wishes to reject this offer by sending a counter-offer, $\textit{Offer}(\delta)$, that will give Ω expected "equitable information gain".

$$\delta = \{\arg\max_\delta \mathbb{P}(\Pi Acc(\delta) \mid \mathcal{Y}^t) \geq \alpha \mid (\Delta_{\textit{Offer}(\delta)}|W_\Omega^t| \approx \Delta_\mu|W^t|)\}.$$

That is Π chooses the most acceptable deal to herself that gives her opponent expected "equitable information gain" provided that there is such a deal. If there is not then Π chooses the best available compromise

$$\delta = \{\arg\max_\delta(\Delta_{\textit{Offer}(\delta)}|W_\Omega^t|) \mid \mathbb{P}(\Pi Acc(\delta) \mid \mathcal{Y}^t) \geq \alpha\}$$

provided there is such a deal — this strategy is rather generous, it rates information gain ahead of personal acceptability. If there is not then Π does nothing.

The "equitable information gain" strategy generalises the simple-minded alternating offers strategy. Suppose that Π is trying to buy something from Ω with bilateral bargaining in which all offers and responses stand — ie: there is no decay of offer integrity. Suppose that Π has offered \$1 and Ω has refused, and Ω has asked \$10 and Π has refused. If amounts are limited to whole dollars only then the deal set $\mathcal{D} = \{1, \cdots, 10\}$. Π models Ω with the distribution $\mathbb{P}(\Omega Acc(.))$, and knows that $\mathbb{P}(\Omega Acc(1)) = 0$ and $\mathbb{P}(\Omega Acc(10)) = 1$. The remaining eight values in this distribution are provided by the inference procedure — see Sec. 3.2 — and the entropy of the resulting distribution is 2.2020. To apply the "equitable information gain" strategy Π assumes that Ω's decision-making machinery mirrors its own. In which case Ω is assumed to have constructed a mirror-image distribution to model Π that will have the same entropy. At this stage, time $t = 0$, calibrate the amount of information held by each agent at zero — ie: $|W^0| = |W_\Omega^0| = 0$. Now if, at time $t = 1$, Ω asks Π for \$9 then Ω gives information to Π and $|W^1| = 0.2548$. If Π rejects this offer then she gives information to Ω and $|W_\Omega^1| = 0.2548$. Suppose that Π wishes to counter with an "equitable information gain" offer. If, at time $t = 2$, Π offers Ω \$2 then $|W_\Omega^2| = 0.2548 + 0.2559$. Alternatively, if Π offers Ω \$3 then $|W_\Omega^2| = 0.2548 + 0.5136$. And so \$2 is a near "equitable information gain" response by Π at time $t = 2$. Entropy-based inference operates naturally with multi-issue offers where this calculation becomes considerably more interesting.

6   Conclusions

Electronic marketplaces are awash with dynamic information flows including hard market data and soft textual data such as news feeds. Structured and unstructured data mining methods identify, analyse, condense and deliver signals from this data whose integrity may be questionable. An 'information-based' agent architecture has been described, that is founded on ideas from information theory, and has been developed specifically to operate with the data mining system. It is part of our eMarket platform[1] that also includes a "virtual institution" system in a collaborative research project with "Institut d'Investigacio en Intel.ligencia Artificial", Spanish Scientific Research Council, UAB, Barcelona.

References

1. Zhang, D., Simoff, S.: Informing the Curious Negotiator: Automatic news extraction from the Internet. In Williams, G., Simoff, S., eds.: Data Mining: Theory, Methodology, Techniques, and Applications. Springer-Verlag: Heidelberg, Germany (2006) 176 – 191
2. Wooldridge, M.: Multiagent Systems. Wiley (2002)
3. Simoff, S., Debenham, J.: Curious negotiator. In M. Klusch, S.O., Shehory, O., eds.: Proceedings 6th International Workshop Cooperative Information Agents VI CIA2002, Madrid, Spain, Springer-Verlag: Heidelberg, Germany (2002) 104–111
4. Debenham, J.: Bargaining with information. In Jennings, N., Sierra, C., Sonenberg, L., Tambe, M., eds.: Proceedings Third International Conference on Autonomous Agents and Multi Agent Systems AAMAS-2004, ACM Press, New York (2004) 664 – 671
5. Sierra, C., Debenham, J.: An information-based model for trust. In Dignum, F., Dignum, V., Koenig, S., Kraus, S., Singh, M., Wooldridge, M., eds.: Proceedings Fourth International Conference on Autonomous Agents and Multi Agent Systems AAMAS-2005, Utrecht, The Netherlands, ACM Press, New York (2005) 497 – 504
6. Reis, D., Golgher, P.B., Silva, A., Laender, A.: Automatic web news extraction using tree edit distance. In: Proceedings of the 13th International Conference on the World Wide Web, New York (2004) 502–511
7. Ramoni, M., Sebastiani, P.: Bayesian methods. In: Intelligent Data Analysis. Springer-Verlag: Heidelberg, Germany (2003) 132–168
8. Zhang, D., Simoff, S., Debenham, J.: Exchange rate modelling using news articles and economic data. In: Proceedings of The 18th Australian Joint Conference on Artificial Intelligence, Sydney, Australia, Springer-Verlag: Heidelberg, Germany (2005)
9. Faratin, P., Sierra, C., Jennings, N.: Using similarity criteria to make issue trade-offs in automated negotiation. Journal of Artificial Intelligence **142** (2003) 205–237
10. MacKay, D.: Information Theory, Inference and Learning Algorithms. Cambridge University Press (2003)
11. Jennings, N., Faratin, P., Lomuscio, A., Parsons, S., Sierra, C., Wooldridge, M.: Automated negotiation: Prospects, methods and challenges. International Journal of Group Decision and Negotiation **10** (2001) 199–215
12. Ramchurn, S., Jennings, N., Sierra, C., Godo, L.: A computational trust model for multi-agent interactions based on confidence and reputation. In: Proceedings 5th Int. Workshop on Deception, Fraud and Trust in Agent Societies. (2003)

Information Agents for Optimal Repurposing and Personalization of Web Contents in Semantics-Aware Ubiquitous and Mobile Computing Environments

Fernando Alonso, Sonia Frutos, Miguel Jiménez, and Javier Soriano

School of Computer Science, Universidad Politécnica de Madrid
28660 - Boadilla del Monte, Madrid, Spain
{falonso, sfrutos, jsoriano}@fi.upm.es,
mjimenez@pegaso.ls.fi.upm.es

Abstract. Web contents repurposing and personalization is becoming crucial for enabling ubiquitous Web access from a wide range of mobile devices under varying conditions that may depend on device capabilities, network connectivity, navigation context, user preferences, user disabilities and existing social conventions. Semantic annotations can provide additional information so that a content adaptation engine, based on the holistic integration of both Information Agents and Semantic Web technologies, can make better decisions, leading to optimal results in terms of legibility and usability. Bearing this in mind, this paper presents the rationale behind MorfeoSMC: an open source mobility platform that enables the development of semantics-aware mobile applications and services in order to provide improved Web accessibility and increase social inclusion. In particular, the paper focuses on how MorfeoSMC information agents tackle the use of semantic markup in the information rendered for users through the mobility platform and as part of a user-interest profile-aware and navigation context-aware Web content adaptation process. It also presents an innovative semantic matching framework that is at the core of this semantics-aware Web content adaptation process.

1 Introduction

With the advent of emerging personal computing paradigms, such as ubiquitous and mobile computing, Web contents are becoming accessible from a wide and evolving range of Web-enabled mobile devices, ranging from WAP-enabled phones, through PDAs, to in-car navigation devices. All of these devices have different rendering capabilities than traditional desktop computers and a range of settings, functionality and rendering options that place heavy demands on both interoperability and accessibility. This means that Web contents need to be (a) *repurposed* for transparent access from a variety of client agents, and (b) *personalized*, enabling real-time context-aware delivery of content specific to and/or of interest to the individual or machine visiting a website. Furthermore,

M. Klusch, M. Rovatsos, and T. Payne (Eds.): CIA 2006, LNAI 4149, pp. 66–80, 2006.

Web content repurposing and personalization (e.g. filtering, reformatting, priorizing, rearranging etc.) is useful not only in mobility environments, but also for improving information access for disabled people, especially if they are using mobile devices, which have severe accessibility constraints. This content adaptation is thus crucial for universal Web access under a variety of conditions that may depend on device capabilities, network connectivity, navigation context, user preferences, user disabilities and even existing social conventions.

There are now mechanisms (e.g. [1]) and commercial solutions (e.g. [2]) for automatically adapting Web contents within mobility, commonly termed *transcoding* [3]. The problem with the existing approaches is that they are based exclusively on page syntax and not on the specific meaning of the concepts addressed on these pages or on the semantics associated with the user-interest profile (including both preferences and disabilities) and with the navigation context (e.g. time, location, connectivity, device capabilities, etc.). Therefore, current page transcoders for mobile devices only select and transform the content to be displayed to the user on the basis of the tags that define the page rendering, leading to suboptimal results in terms of legibility and usability.

Of the available technologies, those associated with the autonomous agent-based computation paradigm [4,5] are precisely the ones that are better accepted for dealing with issues associated with ubiquitous and mobile computing, helping to conceive new models, techniques and applications for developing solutions with a higher level of automation, greater potential for interoperability within open environments and better capabilities of cooperation and adaptation. In this respect, intelligent agent technology and, particularly, *information agents* provide a series of new and exciting possibilities in the field of mobile and ubiquitous Web access [6]. These include Web content repurposing, and Web content personalization.

For our purposes, an information agent (i.e. an intelligent agent for the Internet [7]) is supposed to deal with the difficulties associated with the information overload of the user it represents, and on behalf of whom it pro-actively acquires, mediates, and maintains relevant information. Their ability to semantically broker information by resolving the information impedance of both information consumers and providers, and offering value-added information services and products to the user is therefore implicit. An approach to Web content repurposing and personalization that takes into account, among others, semantics-aware preferences in the user-interest profile preferences and substantive aspects related to the navigation context for optimal mobile Web access is a prominent example of such ability in ubiquitous and mobile environments.

Moreover, the success of the process of incorporating information agents, capable of repurposing and personalizing Web contents for optimal use across the evolving range of Web-enabled mobile devices in ubiquitous and mobile environments largely depends on the use of Semantic Web technology. Semantic annotations can provide additional information not only about Web contents, but also about user profiles [8], navigation contexts [9], and policies representing social conventions [10] so that a content adaptation engine, based on Semantic Web technologies, can make better decisions on content repurposing and personalization. Nevertheless this sets new challenges for semantic markup and reasoning in such specific Semantic Web technologies application areas, all of which have direct ramifications on the emerging ubiquitous and mobile computing paradigms: user profile-awareness, navigation context-awareness and policy modeling and enforcement [6].

In the light of the advances achieved by the international research community in both the intelligent agents and the Semantic Web fields, the strategy followed for building the existing Web content adaptation engines should be reconsidered, and the possibility of including a holistic integration of information agents and Semantic Web technologies in the Web content repurposing and personalization process should be examined, as should the benefits of such a decision.

With this in mind, this paper presents the rationale behind an advanced components platform, called Morfeo Semantic Mobility Channel (MorfeoSMC), that enables the development of mobility applications and services and takes into account the above-mentioned points.

The remainder of the paper is organized as follows. Section 2 presents the rationale behind the proposed Agent-based architecture. Section 3 reviews the Morfeo open source mobility platform (MorfeoMC) on which the proposal is based. Then section 4 describes the MorfeoSMC approach to incorporating semantic annotations about the renderings delivered by mobile applications and services developed based on this platform. Section 5 introduces the MorfeoSMC approach to semantics-aware adaptation (i.e. repurposing and personalization) of such Web contents derived from the notion of *user profile-awareness*. It then goes on to present an innovative semantic matching framework based on the proposed conceptualization of the user profile and gives an example of how it is used to match user preferences against trade services descriptions delivered in MorfeoSMC. Section 6 goes a step further by introducing the MorfeoSMC approach to *navigation context-awareness* to improve the Web content adaptation process. To prove the value of the work, section 7 describes how MorfeoSMC is being used to give such a widespread application as TPIs Yellow Pages mobility, as well as aiming to offer search results with semantic information. Finally, we conclude this paper in section 8.

2   Agent-Based Architecture Overview

Separating the structure from the rendering will assist the migration to the Semantic Web, where agents will not only be able to glean information, but will also be capable of filtering and selecting relevant content for devices with lower bandwidth or requiring different navigation approaches, taking into account user interests and the navigation context, thereby providing improved access and increasing social inclusion.

Following ideas from [11], the semantic annotation of a Web application offered on MorfeoSMC is done as two separate processes, as shown in Fig. 1. Each process focuses on a separate semantic annotation process for the Web contents and for the view components in a device-independent rendering. The annotation process A (see Fig. 1) makes this point and offers a supervised description of the view components making up the Web applications in MorfeoSMC. The annotation process B shows the process of semantically describing the contents that will feed the Web applications. Their annotation is also a supervised process performed by a knowledge engineer. These contents are annotated depending on their specific domain and a change of contents domain influences the ontologies used to annotate the view. In the example shown in Fig. 1 contents concerning *Trade Services* (section 5.1) are annotated. Therefore, the ontologies describing the *trade services* are also used to describe the view rendering these services.

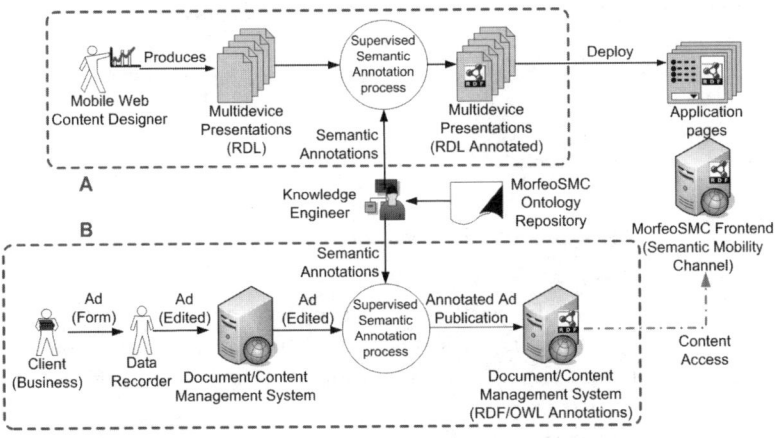

Fig. 1. Semantic Annotation Process in MorfeoSMC

To cope with the huge amount of available information and the constrained capabilities of mobile devices, the MorfeoSMC architecture is populated with a number of semantics-aware information agents, each one acting on the behalf of a user for the purpose of filtering and selecting relevant mobile Web contents offered over the platform. These agents take the semantic description of the Web contents available in the MorfeoSMC contents managers to modify, filter or rearrange the contents depending on their knowledge of the actual user (user-interest profile) or the context in which the data are requested (navigation context).

The personalization of contents will be all the more effective the more knowledge the agent has about the user. However, this server-side approach has a big disadvantage as regards user privacy and security, which calls for a trade-off between privacy and personalization. With the aim of optimizing this trade-off, this paper suggests separating the tasks that are performed by agents on the MorfeoSMC server from those that are implemented as client device plug-ins. Heavy-weight or data bandwidth-intensive tasks are carried out by server-side information agents (e.g. restaurant list prioritizing and page rearranging according to user preferences and geographic nearness), whereas light-weight tasks or tasks requiring more precise knowledge about the user are performed by client-side information agents (e.g. personal information form filling), always keeping more sensitive personal information inside the client device.

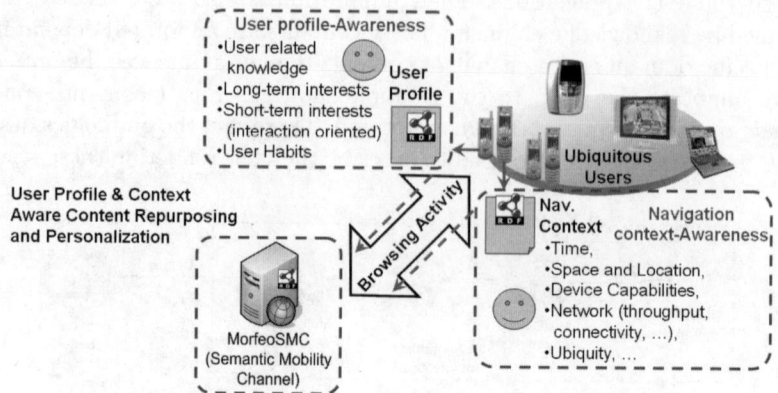

Fig. 2. Information Agents on the Client Device

Two pairs of agents take part in any user-server interaction: (a) two user-interest profile related agents (the client-side information agent handles the user-interest profile and the information about it that it shares with its server-side peer), and (b) two navigation context-aware information agents perform the client- and server-side navigation context-based personalization tasks. The following sections describe in detail how these agents do their jobs and what knowledge they use to complete their tasks.

3 Foundations of the Morfeo Mobility Channel Platform

The MorfeoSMC platform is based on an earlier release of an open source mobility platform called Mobility Channel (MorfeoMC)[1] [13], formerly TIDMobile, which has proven to be useful for rapidly developing applications and services that can be used to create comprehensive and integrated mobile solutions while concealing the complexity involved in managing multiple devices. MorfeoMC performs all multi-device programming tasks, such as identifying the device, adapting the page and contents to fit device technology, markup language and capabilities, and managing sessions using the technology available on each device.

This platform is based on a *channel model* supported by the principles of Service Oriented Architecture (SOA). This means that the *channel adapter*, which has been developed to give access to mobile devices, is run on the front-end,

---

[1] Both MorfeoSMC and MorfeoMC are being developed in the context of the Morfeo open source development community [12], led by Telefónica R & D and undertaken in collaboration with a number of universities.

and does not affect the back-end business logic that it is based on. The contact points between the mobile applications and the business logic are called *Application Operatons* (AOs). These AOs are invoked from the mobile application to access the back-end services and are, thus, the nexus points between the front-end channel adapter and the back-end business logic core.

The mobile applications and services are composed of *Rendering Operations* (ROs). An RO is a set of *renderings* or screens that are designed to perform a *use case*. The renderings are defined in an XML-based grammar called Rendering Definition Language (RDL), as is the flow between ROs and calls to any AOs needed to implement the application. The renderings defined in RDL are made up of high-level visual controls that will be converted to the markup language supported by each specific client device.

RDL Visual controls are similar to HTML tags, but their behavior depends on the capabilities of the target markup language to which they will be translated. Representative examples of these are *head, body, title, menu, table, list*, etc. An example of visual control is given below. It defines a *table* containing the name, address and telephone number of restaurants. *${lrest}* references an object in the server *context*, which is a data warehouse for the mobile application used by the visual controls to pick up their data.

```
<table id="restaurants" optionsbind="${lrest}" keymember="id">
  <th>   <td>Name</td> <td>Address</td> <td>Telephone</td>   </th>
  <tr>   <td member="name"></td>
         <td member="address"></td>
         <td member="telephone"></td> </tr> </table>
```

The page style is defined using W-CSS style sheets. A more detailed description of RDL is given in [13]. Fig. 3 shows the result of applying the same RDL rendering description in three different devices. The illustrated rendering is part of the "partner search" use case in a prototype enterprise mobile service.

Fig. 3. Three different screenshots for the same RDL

A key component of MorfeoMC is the *Code Generation Tool* (CGT). This component is responsible for generating the JSP-based servers that will cater for the client device. The devices are organized according to the supported markup language or technology, and the CGT outputs as many servers as families are supported by MorfeoMC. If MorfeoMC is to support a new technology, a new server should be generated based on that technology. However, some Web content adaption is done at runtime. Runtime content adaption involves data extraction from databases or Content Management Systems, large content pagination or media documents adaptation.

This approach to Web content adaptation has been proven to be better, in terms of performance and resource consumption, than others based on run-time transcoding. It has also been proven to be more flexible than XSLT sheets-based transcoding techniques. MorfeoMC source code is distributed under GPL license and is available from the Morfeo project forge [14].

4 Incorporation of Semantic Annotations About Mobile Web Contents

Semantic annotations provide additional information about Web contents so that MorfeoSMC Semantic Web technologies-based content adaptation engine, based on Semantic Web technologies, can make better decisions on content repurposing and personalization than its predecesor in MorfeoMC. This, in turn, (along with the semantic characterization of both the user-interest profile and the navigation context discussed later) leverage the automation of tasks and processes, leading to an added value for mobile applications and services. This includes automatically filling in personal particulars on forms, rearranging lists/tables of elements according to their relevance for the user, filtering search results that are irrelevant with respect to the user particulars or context, etc.

The mobile contents that are generated by the Mobility Channel are defined in RDL. Therefore, RDL has been extended in MorfeoSMC to contain semantic annotations with the aim of describing those mobile contents. It is our aim, however, to preserve the semantics defined in RDL during the content generation and adaptation process (the contents are stored in structured data warehouses, such as databases or content management systems), as well as to incorporate this process into the final semantic annotations. Hence, the RDL language has been extended with content descriptions, called *semantic bindings*, that describe the content that will be finally sent to the client device.

Therefore, the semantic description of the contents associated with the visual controls in RDL can be defined in two ways: (1) writing down the semantic descriptions about the contents to be sent to the client, or (2) defining the source for the annotations of the contents that will be included in the visual control. In both cases the semantic annotations can describe the actual contents that will be displayed to the user and any additional contents that, although not displayed on screen, are useful for adding to the description of the contents displayed in the rendering (e.g. as part of a later layout optimization process as explained in Section 5).

4.1   Semantic Extensions to RDL

The RDL grammar is semantically extended by describing the data in any visual control that can contain information in this language. These extensions are based on a fixed set of attributes aimed at specifying the semantic information that will be generated together with the visual control with which they are associated:

- **about-resid**: specifies what identifier one or more resources will take.
- **about-class**: refers to the identifier of the class to which a concept belongs.
- **about-prop**: refers to the identifier of a property, whose value is the data item represented in the visual control.
- **about-obj-datatype**: defines the data type of an RDF literal, making use of XML-Schema types. It makes sense when the object is a literal.
- **about-link-prop**: references the identifier of a property with a link to the class that contains the data item to be displayed in a column. It is useful for the *table* visual control.

A semantic annotation method has been developed for each visual control that can contain data. In this paper, however, only the *Table* control, as a representative example of the RDL set of visual controls, and its annotation method will be explained for illustrative purposes. See [15] for a full description of the semantic extensions made to RDL.

The RDL *Table* visual control, used to represent tabular data structures, has been semantically extended with all the semantic attributes described above as follows. The main concept on which the table is based is referenced by the *about-class* attribute, and the resource identifiers for the instances are specified using the *about-resid* attribute. Each concept attribute expressed in a table column is described by means of: (a) an *about-prop* attribute if it references an attribute of the main concept of the table, or (b) an *about-link-prop* attribute if it references an attribute of a different concept.

Below we show the same example as proposed earlier, now including the proposed semantic annotations and the set of RDF triplets that will be generated as a result of the described annotation method.

```
<table id="restaurants"optionsbind="${lrest}" keymember="id"
   about-class="travel:restaurant"
   about-resid="myapp:restaurants:${lrest.id}">
  <th>  <td about-prop="travel:restaurant:name">Name</td>
        <td about-prop="location:street" about-class="location:address"
            about-link-prop="travel:restaurant:address"
            about-resid="myapp:locations:${lrest.address.id}">Address</td>
        <td about-prop="travel:restaurant:tlfn">Telephone</td> </th>
  <tr>  <td member="name"></td>
        <td member="address"></td>
        <td member="telephone"></td> </tr> </table>
```

As the example shows, the notation can concatenate namespace URIs with *context* data (e.g. *about-resid="myapp:restaurants:${lrest.id}"*). The above table definition automatically generates the following RDF triplets:

```
(myapp:restaurants/Id1, rdf:type, travel:restaurant)
(myapp:restaurants/Id1, travel:restaurant:name, "Chistu")
(myapp:restaurants/Id1, travel:restaurant:address, myapp:locations:00596)
(myapp:locations:00596, rdf:type, location:address)
(myapp:locations:00596, location:street, "Highland St.")
(myapp:restaurants/Id1, travel:restaurant:tlfn, "912345678")
(myapp:restaurants/Id1, xpath_ont:reference,"...table[n]/tr[m]")
...[more items]...
```

Note that the last RDF triplet acts as a bridge between the semantic information about an item in the data table and a row in the markup table. This enables the visual elements that are described in the semantic information received together with the markup to be associated on the client side.

5   Enabling User-Interest Profile-Awareness

A *semantic user-interest profile* captures all the information about the user that the system can use to output the contents that are more relevant to him or her. This information includes both the user's personal particulars and interests.

The user's personal particulars are modeled using relations –or *roles* in Description Logic (DL)– according to a defined ontological vocabulary (OWL-DL is also used, but OWL definitions are omitted for brevity). This information together with its semantic description defined on the basis of an ontology can be exploited by semantics-aware Web applications or services. For example, a mobile device would be able to automatically fill in some fields in a form, such as the user's date of birth, if the form is semantically annotated and the device has described the user's respective personal particulars semantically. This feature will be all the more effective the more information the agent has about the user.

The *semantic user-interest profile* also contains information about the user's interests [8], including long-term interests, consisting of likes and dislikes, and short-term interests [16], which are what the user intends to pursue during one particular interaction with the system. For the sake of simplicity and for reasons of space, this paper only covers long-term interests, although short-term interests are dealt with similarly.

The proposed simplification of the *semantic user-interest profile* is as follows:

$$Profile \equiv \sqcap_i \exists hasCharacteristic.Characteristic_i$$
$$\sqcap_j \exists hasInterest.Interest_j$$
$$\sqcap_k \forall hasInterest.(\neg Disinterest_k)$$
$$\sqcap_l \exists demands.Thing$$

where the role *hasCharacteristic* is a super-role of the different relations expressing the user's personal particulars, the role *hasInterest* is used to indicate the concepts in which the user is interested, covered by the $Interest_i$ group, and the concepts in which the user is not interested, expressed by $Disinterest_j$, and *demands* is a super-role of a hierarchy of roles expressing different ways of demanding something, such as *purchasing, swapping*, etc.

For example, the profile of a user who is interested in *Rioja* wines but not in *Ribera del Duero* wines would be as follows:

$$User1 \equiv \exists hasInterest.(Wine \sqcap (\exists hasRegion.Rioja)) \sqcap$$
$$\forall hasInterest.(\neg Wine \sqcup \neg(\exists hasRegion.RiberaDuero))$$

One of the key features of this approach is that the concepts used in the user-interest profile can be refined as much as you like to express the inherent complexity of the user preferences.

5.1 User-Interest Profile-Compatible Description of Semantic Trade Services

To give a clearer idea about how the semantic personalization of Web content works, this section focuses on trade services[2] offered by enterprises and businesses, and considers how well the user preferences are satisfied by the trade service, prioritizing the businesses that offer trade services that better satisfy user interests.

Trade services are concepts of the following form:

$$TradeService \equiv \exists provides.Thing$$

This definition confines a trade service to being anything that provides *Things* (goods and products), and also serves as a definition for the *Trade Service* concept. This simple expression does not explicitly specify the definition of the special characteristics of the services, which can be defined as features of the offered *Things*. The following example makes this point.

$$RestSrvc1 \equiv \exists offers.(RedWine \sqcap (\exists hasRegion.Rioja))$$
$$RestSrvc2 \equiv \exists offers.(Wine \sqcap (\exists hasRegion.Rioja))$$
$$RestSrvc3 \equiv \exists offers.(RedWine \sqcap (\exists hasRegion.RiberaDuero))$$

This example shows a simplification of the trade services offered by several restaurants, which is, however, expressive enough to convey the potential of the description.

The semantic information can be gathered during the content adaptation process, when the semantic annotations related to the visual controls are generated, as explained in Section 4.

5.2 Semantic Matching for Web Content Adaptation

The semantic annotation of the Web contents delivered by the MorfeoSMC platform and the semantic definition of the user-interest profile are of no use without a procedure that can determine whether the Web contents fit the profile. This is done by semantic matching between the concepts expressed in the user-interest profile and the Web contents. In this paper we present a semantic matching between user preferences and trade services to determine whether the user-interest

---

[2] This section refers to the semantic description of trade services, which is not the same thing as the semantic descriptions of Web Services that are dealt with by different approaches such as OWL-S or WSMO and have a different goal.

profile is semantically compatible with a particular trade service and, if so, how well the two match. The use of trade services is for illustrative purposes only, but the framework is applicable for any other sort of Web content delivered by the MorfeoSMC platform.

In terms of ontologies, the concepts describing a user's likes and dislikes have to be compared to the concepts supplied by a trade service:

$$UsersInterest \equiv \exists hasInterest^-.Profile$$
$$ServiceOffer \equiv \exists offers^-.Service$$

The match between *UserInterest* and *ServiceOffer* is a measure of how well the services supplied satisfy the user's preferences, and needs to be calculated for every $< user, offeredservice >$ pair. To determine the degree of match we use the levels proposed in [17], which are listed from best to worst:

– **Exact** if UserInterest is equivalent to ServiceOffer.
– **PlugIn** if UserInterest is a sub-concept of ServiceOffer.
– **Subsume** if UserInterest is a super-concept of ServiceOffer.
– **Intersection** if the intersection between UserInterest and ServiceOffer is satisfiable.
– **Disjoint** if UserInterest and ServiceOffer are completely incompatible.

This procedure scores the elements to be displayed according to their relevance for the user. Therefore, it provides valuable information that can be used to arrange the elements on screen, placing the most relevant items at the top.

According to the proposed semantic matching process, the restaurants shown above would be rearranged as follows: {RestSrvc2, RestSrvc1, RestSrvc3}.

6   Enabling Navigation Context-Awareness

Web browsing is a context-dependent activity, meaning that it is influenced by the user environment. Given the definition in [18], the environment-related information can be referred to as a user's *navigation context*. The *Navigation Context* defines *geographical information* (e.g. the city from where the user is accessing a service), *timing information* (e.g. the expiry time of a request) and *social information* (e.g. information about the position or role the user is playing).

The following are prominent examples of customization needs in the context of a *tourist guide*, highlighting the need for navigation context-awareness in ubiquitous and mobile Web applications:

Time. Display the night-bus schedule or the subway schedule depending on *current time.*
Location. Display a map related to the actual position (*lattitude*, *longitude*) of the user.
Network. Render pictures depending on the *network throughput.*

Display. Depending on the device, display full details about an item, or abbreviation of first name for WAP.

Ubiquity. Rendering all mayor sights as a list (index) for the Web and as a guided tour for WAP.

The *navigation context* can be further described as a set of *attributes* and a *goal* that helps to determine what attributes are relevant any one time. The *goal* is the objective for which the context is used at any particular time, the focus of the ongoing browsing activity. The *goal* can be viewed as being the information that is the most interesting for the user at any one time. For example, selecting an event and filling a form are all goals that determine the way the user will act.

Context-awareness is not a new idea. There are several conceptual representations of context, each of which has strengths and weaknesses as far as our needs are concerned. Our proposal is based on ideas from [19] and uses ontologies to explicitly represent the navigation context and to support reasoning on its different properties.

In our proposal, a context attribute designates the information defining one context element, e.g. "availability" or "connectivity" for network, "capability" for device, "position" for business, "country" or "city" for location, or "currentTime" for time. Each context attribute has at least one value at any one time, but will be multivalued (e.g. "supportedFormats"). Moreover, an attribute will have a hierarchical structure of subattributes. For example "display" and "markup" are subattributes of the the "capability" attribute. The subattributes of the "display" attribute include "resolutionWidth", "rows", and "maxImageWidth" whereas the "markup" attribute includes "preferredMarkup" and "wml.1.2support", as defined in the WURFL standard [20] [3]. V_a denotes the definition domain of a, i.e. all the possible values for a (example: $V_{time} = [0, 24]$).

We can therefore associate an instantiation function, called *valueOf*, with each context value. *ValueOf* is defined for a context attribute as a function from AxP_a to $\wp(V_a)$, where A is the set of all attributes, $\wp(V_a)$ is the power set of V_a, and P_a is the set of parameters needed to compute the value of a.

Not all attributes are relevant for a goal. If *isRelevant*(a, g) is a predicate stating that attribute a is relevant for the goal g, the subset of A that defines the *Relevant Attribute Set* (RAS) for the goal g will be expressed as:

$$RAS(g) = \{a \in A \mid isRelevant(a, g) = true\}$$

An *instantiation of context attribute* $a \in A$ will be denoted as a pair (a, v) where v is the set of values $v \in P(V_a)$ of a at any one time. For instance, (maxRows,2), (maxImageWidth, 60), (supportedFormats, wml.1.2, wml.1.3)) are the instantiation of the respective context attributes Day and *supportedFormats*. The set I of instantiated context attributes is denoted as:

$$I = \{(a, v) \mid a \in A \wedge valueOf(a) = v\}$$

---

[3] Among others for time, location, etc., MorfeoSMC uses a WURFL-based ontology developed by the authors for conceptualizing and reasoning on device capabilities.

Let *Instantiated Relevant Attribute Set* of a goal g, denoted $IRAS(g)$, be the set of instantiated context attributes relevant to goal g:

$$IRAS(g) = \{(a, v) \mid a \in RAS(g) \land (a, v) \in I\}$$

The notion of *navigation context* is what we define as the $IRAS$, as usually understood in related work.

What is said to be *navigation context* is represented using ontologies as a set of *context attributes* defined as *concepts*, which are then regrouped with a number of *properties* or *roles* describing all of the information required to define and instantiate a particular *context attribute*. Consequently, more complex context attributes can be represented than would be possible using mere properties.

For this purpose, we define a class *ContextAttribute* that specifies the following information for a particular attribute: the name of the attribute, the type of needed parameters for the instantiation, the values domain V_a, and whether the attribute can have more than one value, e.g. the *PositionInGroup* attribute will need a *group* parameter and will give a *role* when instantiated. Each attribute is represented as a subclass of *ContextAttribute*, with constraints on each property, in order to have a clear description of the specified attribute.

The following are prominent examples of context attributes:

$$PositionInGroup : (Group) \rightarrow Role,$$
$$TimeZone : (time) \rightarrow zone(zone = \{GMT, GMT + 1, \dots\}),$$
$$DayOfWeek : (time) \rightarrow day(day = \{sunday, monday, \dots\}),$$
$$CurrentTime : () \rightarrow time, Location : (IP) :\rightarrow city$$

Context-awareness is based on two main processes: *selection* of relevant attributes for a certain goal g $(RAS(g))$ and *decision* based on instantiated attributes $(IRAS(g))$. For example, TimeZone and Location are relevant attributes for a goal related to deciding whether to present an item in the list of suggested restaurants, but PositionInGroup could be irrelevant.

The decision-making process knows when to include or exclude an item from the Web page based on the IRAS output from the respective RAS instantiation. For example, if the cinema is near to the user (same city) as inferred from the IP and the showing begins one hour from $currentTime$, the decision-making process will decide to include the cinema and the showing in the list of suggestions.

7   Application Example

The MorfeoSMC is being used to give such a widespread application as TPIs Yellow Pages [21] mobility, as well as aiming to offer search results with semantic information based on location, services and products ontologies. The objective is twofold. On the one hand, the aim is to extend service accessibility to the whole range of mobile devices, which is in line with the philosophy of any yellow pages service, where mobility services and activities search can account for a large proportion of accesses to this application. On the other hand, it aims to take this service further, by sending the results with associated semantic information. In this way, the user is not the only consumer of this information, but his or her device is able to interpret it, integrate this knowledge with other applications accessible in the device thereby maximizing the potential for TPI use, or be proactive and suggest what different actions should be taken in relation to the concepts handled in navigation. On this point, it is worth highlighting the potential offered by Semantic Web Services in conjunction with the semantic information obtained from navigation, integrating access to the SWS in actual navigation.

8   Conclusions

The problem with existing approaches to the automatic adaptation of Web contents within mobile environments is that they are based exclusively on page syntax and not on the specific meaning of the concepts addressed on these pages or on the matching between these concepts and both the user interests and his or her navigation context. This paper takes a step forward by presenting an innovative *semantics-, user-interest profile- and navigation context-aware Web content annotation and adaptation process within mobile environments*, founded on an innovative architecture based on the holistic integration of both Information Agents and Semantic Web technologies. We have stated how, on the basis of these ideas, a content adaptation engine can make better decisions on content repurposing and personalization, therefore improving Web accessibility and increasing social inclusion. It is worth mentioning that the proposed architecture adopts the principles of the W3C Web Accessibility Recommendations [11] and therefore (a) provides metadata as semantic markup, (b) separates structure from presentation both at syntactic and a semantic level, and (c) accomplishes with the provision of device independence in the generated renderings.

Acknowledgements. This work is being supported by the CAM Education Council and the European Social Fund under their Research Personnel Training program, and by the Spanish Ministry of Industry, Tourism and Commerce under its National Program of Service Technologies for the Information Society (contract FIT-350110-2005-73).

References

1. M. Hori, G. Kondoh, K. Ono, S. Hirose, and S. Singhal. Annotation-based web content transcoding. In Proc of the 9th Int World Wide Web Conference (WWW9), Amsterdam, 2000. Available at http://www9.org/.
2. IBM Corporation. WebSphere Transcoding Publisher, 2001. Available at http://www.ibm.com/software/webservers/transcoding/.
3. K. H. Britton, Y. Li, R. Case, C. Seekamp, A. Citron, B. Topol, R. Floyd, and K. Tracey. Transcoding: Extending e-business to new environments. IBM Systems Journal, 40(1):153–178, 2001.

4. Weiss, G. Multi-Agent Systems: A Modern Approach to Distributed Artificial Intelligence, MIT Press, Cambridge, MA, 1999.

5. D'Inverno, M., and Luck, M. Understanding Agent Systems, Springer-Verlag, Heidelberg, Berlin, 2002.

6. O. Lassila. Using the semantic web in ubiquitous and mobile computing (keynote talk). IASW 2005, Jyvaskyl, Finland, August 2005.

7. M. Klusch. Information Agent Technology for the Internet: A Survey. Journal on Data and Knowledge Engineering, Special Issue on Intelligent Information Integration, D. Fensel (Ed.). Elsevier Science, 36(3), 2001.

8. A. Cali, D. Calvanese, S. Colucci, T. D. Noia, and F. M. Donini. A description logic based approach for matching user profiles. In Proc. of the 2004 Description Logic Workshop, Whistler, British Columbia, Canada, June 2004.

9. A. Dey et al. Towards a better understanding of context and context-awareness. GVU Tech. Report GIT-GVU-00-18, Georgia Institute of Technology, 1999.

10. V. Kolovski, Y. Katz, J. Hendler, D. Weitzner and T. Berners-Lee. Towards a Policy-Aware Web. Procs. of the Semantic Web and Policy Workshop, Galway, Ireland, 2005.

11. Developing a Web Accessibility Business Case for Your Organization, S.L. Henry, ed. World Wide Web Consortium (MIT, ERCIM, Keio), August 2005. http://www.w3.org/WAI/bcase/

12. Morfeo project: Open Source Community for Software Platforms and Services Development. Available at http://www.morfeo-project.org/index.php?lang=en.

13. J. M. Cantera, J. J. Hierro, M. Jiménez, and J. Soriano. Delivering Mobile Enterprise Services on MorfeoMC Open Source Platform. In proceedings of the 1st Int. Workshop on Tools and Applications for Mobile Contents (TAMC'06), at the 7th IEEE/ACM International Conference MDM'06, 2006.

14. Morfeo Mobility Channel Source Code. Morfeo's Project Forge. http://forge.morfeo-project.org/projects/mobchannel/.

15. J. Soriano et al. Semantic Web Content Adaptation and Services Delivery on MorfeoSMC. In proceedings of the Int. Workshop on Mobile Services and Ontologies (MoSO'06), at the 7th IEEE/ACM International Conference MDM'06, 2006.

16. A. Hessling, T. Kleemann, and A. Sinner. Semantic User Profiles and their Applications in a Movile environment. In AIMS workshop Ubicomp Conference 2004, Nottingham, England, September 2004.

17. L. Li and I. Horrocks. A software framework for matchmaking based on semantic web technology. In Proceedings of the Twelfth International World Wide Web Conference (WWW 2003), Budapest, Hungary, May 2003.

18. M. Abe and M. Hori. Visual composition of xpath expressions for external metadata authoring, rt-0406. Technical report, IBM Research Laboratory, Tokyo, 2001.

19. Beaune, P., Boissier, O., Bucur, O., 2002. Representing Context in an Agent Architecture for Context-Based Decision Making. International Workshop on Context Representation and Reasoning CCR-05, Paris (France), July 5-8, 2005.

20. WURFL: Wireless Universal Resource File Language. http://wurfl.sourceforge.net/.

21. TPI Yellow Pages service, Telefónica. http://www.tpi.es/.

Turn Taking for Artificial Conversational Agents

Fredrik Kronlid

Graduate School of Language Technology
&
Department of Linguistics
Göteborg University
Box 200
S-405 30 Göteborg
kronlid@ling.gu.se

Abstract. In this paper we describe the design of a turn manager for deployment in artificial conversational agents, using the Harel statechart formalism. We show that the formalism's support for concurrent interrelated processes allows a modular design, producing three smaller statecharts responsible for the turn taking logic. The logic of the turn manager is inspired by a well-known turn management model for human-human conversation.

1 Introduction

This work is motivated by our overall aim to build artificial conversational agents capable of working in a multi-party setting. By an artificial conversational agent we mean a software agent (possibly with embodiment, personality etc.), capable of engaging in conversation with other conversational agents (human or artificial). By a multi-party setting we mean that more than two agents are engaged in the communication or dialogue.

We imagine an environment where a user interacts with a *collective* of conversational agents, some of which are artificial, some of which are human, perhaps in games (where the agents are in-game characters or player characters), perhaps in an information service (where every agent acts as a representative for one company, institution or domain). Such agents can collaborate and compete with each other, using natural language as their communication protocol.

One reason for avoiding a specialized inter-agent communication protocol is the plug-and-play aspect – as long as an agent has appropriate linguistic coverage of its domain combined with some basic linguistic-pragmatic (for instance turn taking) skills it can be plugged into the agent community. Another reason is increased transparency – a user in this setting can, for example, monitor the inter-agent communication and interrupt it or provide additional information if required. Ricordel et al. (in [8]) argue in favour of using a less formal language for inter-agent communication by stating that formal agent-languages constrain the agent model, and that cognitive agents should have a cognitive (as opposed to reactive) interaction model, using their knowledge and beliefs to interpret messages.

M. Klusch, M. Rovatsos, and T. Payne (Eds.): CIA 2006, LNAI 4149, pp. 81–95, 2006.

An agent in an two-participant setup can (almost) safely assume that all user utterances are directed to it, and when the user has finished speaking (or released a push-to-talk button), the floor is free for the agent to make any contribution to the dialogue that it wants (see for instance [2] for a state-based two-party turn management model). In contrast, an agent in a multi-party setting cannot assume that all user utterances are directed to it, since there are other dialogue participants present. Still, it is assumed by the other parties that the agent tries to follow the conversation.

Since the inter-agent communication turns into a natural language conversation, in which users can participate, it is important that the artificial agents handle turn management analogous to the human agents. Below are listed a few informally stated guidelines for agent behavior in this setting, in no particular order.

– Try to speak when you can make a relevant contribution
– Do not try to speak when you have nothing to say
– (but) Speak when you are requested to speak.
– Do not speak when someone else is requested to speak.
– Do not speak when someone else is speaking.

These guidelines for an communicative agent touch on two domains of dialogue system research – Turn Management and Dialogue Management. Turn Management is concerned with who has the right to speak at a certain point in time in a dialogue. Dialogue Management deals with information flow in dialogue – what information is available to a dialogue participant and how it can be used to interpret or generate linguistic behavior, etc.

This paper will focus on the parts related to Turn management. The work on dialogue management will be found in [6].

2   Background

2.1   Turn Taking

An influential and widely accepted model for how turns are managed in human-human conversation is the so called SSJ^1 model [9]. The essence of the model is as follows: A Turn Constructional Unit (TCU) is a phrase, clause, sentence or word with a predictable end (predictability will be described in section 5.1). A TCU corresponds more or less to an utterance[2]. The first possible completion of a TCU constitutes a Transition Relevance Place (TRP) - a place where speaker-change is possible (or preferred). The turn transitions are governed by the following two rules:

1. For any turn, at the first TRP of the first TCU
   (a) The speaker may select the next speaker. In this case, the person selected is the only one with the right and obligation to speak.

---

[1] SSJ because of the first letters in the authors last names - **S**acks **S**chegloff **J**efferson.
[2] The original definition is more complex, but for our purposes this definition suffices.

(b) Else, the next speaker may self-select. The first person to speak acquires the right to a turn.

(c) Else, the current speaker may, but need not continue.

2. Rules 1 (a–c) apply for each next TRP of this TCU until transfer is effected.

Also repair mechanisms are included in the model, for instance overlap resolution and clarification of selection problems.

The Ethernet communication model serves as the blueprint for the turn taking protocol used in [8]. Even though the Ethernet model has been inspired by human-human conversation turn management, the collision resolution mechanism is incompatible with its human counterpart. Since we want to include both artificial and human agents in our conversations, the Ethernet model used in [8] will not be considered for this paper.

The aim of the present paper is to build a turn manager based on the principles of the SSJ model. In order to do this we will use Harel statecharts described in the following section.

2.2 Harel Statecharts

D. Harel describes a tool for modeling and visualizing abstract control, called Harel statecharts, in [4]. The tool is an extension and generalization of ordinary finite state machines. Some of the important extensions and features are:

- Events – the transitions are mostly event driven. Events are either external, coming from sources outside the chart, or internal, generated by transitions or by entering and leaving states. Technically, events are communicated from and to the states in the chart via an event queue.
- Hierarchy – states can contain states, which means good support for modularization. Any state can be seen as a statechart of its own.
- Orthogonality – there can be parallel states, meaning that the machine can be in multiple states at the same time. Any parallel state can generate events that can be read by other states.
- Actions – upon entering or leaving states, or at the time of transitions between states, actions (outside the statechart) may be carried out. Generating an event is considered to be an action.
- Conditions – boolean conditions as well as events may trigger or restrict transitions. It is possible to state as a transition condition that an orthogonal statechart should be in a certain state.

W3C have decided to include Harel statecharts in the next major release of VoiceXML, a markup language to define audio dialogues ([7]). It is not clear what role it will have in VoiceXML, but there is a preliminary specification of an XML implementation available at the W3C web site ([1]). We hope that this extension of VoiceXML will make it possible to use this work in combination with VoiceXML systems.

The major reasons for choosing Harel statecharts as a formalism are that they have good support for modularization of complex systems and for modeling concurrent interrelated processes. In this paper, we will show the usefulness of these features when designing a turn manager.

3   The Agent Architecture

We are interested in an environment where more than one (artificial) agent is present. A group of agents can be modeled as one single state chart, or divided up over several statecharts distributed over several machines. If we make the event queue known at all machines, the distributed agents can still be seen as one single statechart.

Each agent can be seen as a statechart. The Agent statechart will, in our model, contain at least states for turn and dialogue management. Typically, statecharts for parsing, speech recognition, database access, etc. will also be present.

4   Turn Manager Requirements

We assume that there is an entity, somewhere in the agent, which signals certain events in the dialogue to the turn manager. These events are shown in table 1.

Table 1. Events expected from the dialogue manager or other entity

startSpeaking(X)	speaker X starts speaking
stopSpeaking(X)	speaker X stops speaking
trp(X D)	speaker X will (with probably) stop speaking in D units
addressing(X)	speaker X is addressed, meaning that X has been selected as the next speaker by some other DP

In the rest of this paper, when we describe the turn manager for a conversational agent, we will make the description from the perspective of the agent, and we will therefore use a first-person perspective in the descriptions. "I" and "me" will denote the agent for which we are designing the turn manager.

The requirements on a turn manager is that it should signal (to the other components of the agent)

- if I am the only DP (Dialogue Participant, or Dialogue Partner) with the right and obligation to speak at this TRP
- if an agent other than me is the only DP with the right and obligation to speak at this TRP
- if anyone (including myself) may self-select at this TRP
- if the TRP has been cancelled (i.e. someone, with or without the right, has started speaking)
- if my current contribution is overlapping someone else's
- when the abovementioned overlapping has been resolved.

The list could be longer, including support for more repair mechanisms than overlaps etc., but for a prototype, the list is of the right size.

The SSJ model does allow for brief overlaps, but specifies that when two parties start to speak simultaneously, this must be resolved. The SSJ resolution to simultaneous starts (or pseudo-simultaneous starts, rather) is that "first starter goes". Interruptions are another type of overlap that also needs to be resolved. In this paper, when building our turn manager, we will not be concerned with how to resolve such conflicts – we just want to know when there is one and when it has been resolved.

5   Design of a Turn Manager

The list of events in the last section, will be mapped to the events listed in table 2, and will be emitted by our statechart turn manager.

Table 2. Events expected from the Turn manager

`freeTRP`	anyone may self-select
`myTRP`	I am selected as the next speaker
`othersTRP`	Someone else is selected as the next speaker
`noTRP`	TRP canceled
`overlap`	speech is currently overlapping someone else's
`overlapResolved`	speech is no more overlapping.

We identify three building blocks in our turn manager. One block deals with the other participants states – are they speaking or are they silent? – which we call the Outside chart. The second block deals with the relation between the other agents and and myself (the agent whose perspective we are taking). We will call the chart the Inside chart. The last chart deals with identifying TRPs and signaling them. We call this chart the TRP chart. The hierarchical nature of the formalism chosen, together with the concurrency support (orthogonality) allows us to easily model the three components inside one single statechart.

5.1   The Outside Chart

The Outside chart is supposed to keep track of "the world outside", i.e. if the other DPs are speaking or if they are silent. Let us start with a simpler implementation of the Outside chart, where we disregard the predictions of TCUs (and hence TRPs), and assume that only the startSpeaking(X), stopSpeaking(X) and addressing(X) events are received.

A Simpler Outside Chart. The simplest solution to the problem would be to have $N + 1$ states (N = number of DPs): othersSilent, 1Speaking, 2Speaking, ..., N+1Speaking. This would be impractical, since we then would need to grow or to shrink the state chart to keep track of the changes in the dialogue (DPs joining or leaving). Instead, we will use an abstraction - we will have one state `othersSilent` and one state `othersSpeaking`, since these are the crucial states for our purposes. We will use an external data structure (a set) to keep track of how many of the DPs are actually speaking at a given point in time. DPs are added to the set `Speakers` when they start speaking and removed from it when they stop speaking.

The initial state is the `othersSilent` state. If someone (except me) starts speaking, we will need to make a transition to the `othersSpeaking` state. We will also need to add the speaker to the `Speakers` set. If someone starts speaking in the `othersSpeaking` state, we will remain there, but as we need to add the speaker to the `othersSpeaking` set, we will need a transition, labeled `startSpeaking(X) [X != me] / Speakers.add(X)` (the label format being `event [condition] / action`). Since the action will be the same, wherever we are in the machine, we add a superstate that encapsulates the two states. We then add a transition from that superstate to `othersSpeaking`, labeled as described above. This means that in whatever state (encapsulated by the superstate) we are when the event/label combination occurs, we will make the transition to the `othersSpeaking` state.

When some other agent stops speaking, we will remove that agent from the `Speakers` set, and when the set is empty, we will make the transition to the `othersSilent` state. Therefore we add a transition with starting and ending points in the `othersSpeaking` state labeled `stopSpeaking(X) [X != me] / Speakers.remove(X)`, and a second transition from `othersSpeaking` to `othersSilent`, labeled `[Speakers.isEmpty()]`. Now we have a machine that handles the event subset of `startSpeaking(X)`, `stopSpeaking(X)` and `addressing(X)`. The Outside chart can be seen in Figure 1.

Introducing Predictions. An important part of the SSJ model is that TCUs must be syntactically constructed to be predictable[3] in such a way that non-speakers can predict the end of the TCU with a fairly high precision (also with the help of intonation and other phonological clues). The existence of the predictability feature can be explained by the fact that that there are often brief overlaps (or very short pauses) when speaker-change occurs, but that (longer) pauses and long overlaps are rare, suggesting that speakers-to-be are aware of when the utterance will be completed before it actually is. This means that our agents need

1. a mechanism that predicts TRPs
2. a mechanism for deciding how close to a predicted TRP an agent must be to start speaking – in other words how long before the (predicted) TRP actually occurs shall we report it
3. a way of handling the predictions
4. a way of handling mispredictions.

The TRP Predictor. We will not try to build a TRP predictor, but merely state that we need one, describe it from a black-box perspective and give some ideas of how it can be constructed. The TCU predictor is a device that, given a

---

[3] [9] use the term "projection" instead of "prediction".

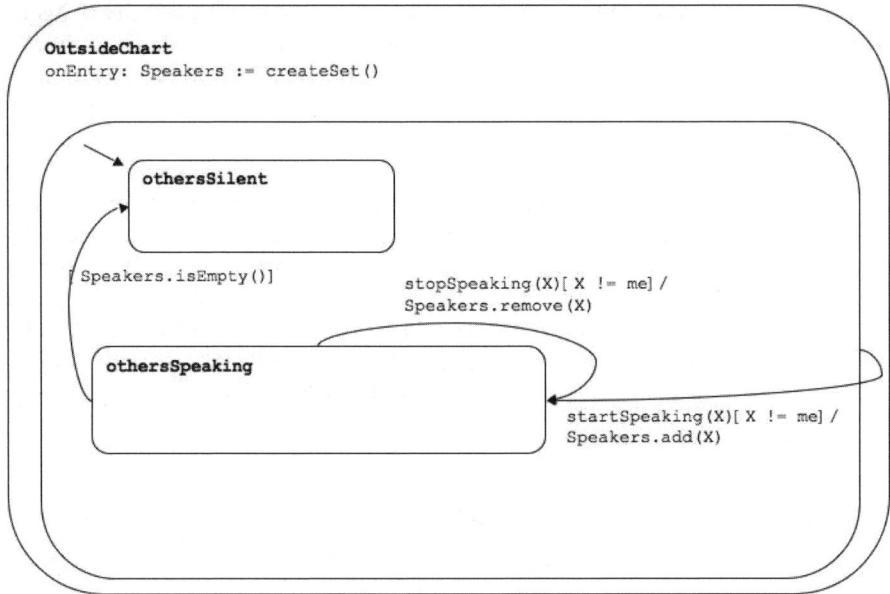

Fig. 1. The Outside Statechart without predictions

description of a language, possibly a dialogue history and an initial chunk of an utterance, calculates how far away in some unit (time, words, syllables, 'beats' [10]) the TCU endpoint (TRP) is. The output is a distance and a prediction of the utterance, and is regularly updated.

The simplest form of TCU predictor, which presupposes a very small language, uses a language model in the form of a list of strings which enumerates all valid sentences in the language. The TCU/TRP are then calculated by comparing the (so far) perceived utterance to the sentences in the language model. The approach, which we have used when experimenting with our agents, is described in [5].

The /nailon/ application for turn endpoint detection [3] takes a more advanced approach and uses prosodic cues. It does not output the predictions of the current TCU. One can imagine other approaches to the task such as statistical or rule-based machine learning applied to speech signal, string of words etc. But, as stated earlier, we are satisfied with the potential existence of such a device, and will not attempt to build one.

The Decision Mechanism. When am I, as an agent, close enough to the TRP to start speaking, and when can I be certain that the predicted TCU (and thus the TRP distance) is correct? The authors of [5] use the following model. A variable *TalkFactor* is available for all agents. *TalkFactor* can take a value between 0 and 1, and is to be seen as the agent's general urgency to start speaking. If $U = \text{TalkFactor}/(1.0 + \text{distanceToNearestTRP}^2)$ then the agent will start speaking with a probability of U. This means that the closer we get to the projected TRP, the higher is the probability that we actually start speaking.

In [5] it is unclear whether the *TalkFactor* is constant over time for each agent, but there is no mention of any action altering the value. However, by altering the *TalkFactor* as the dialogue evolves, or by deriving *TalkFactor* from other values, we may potentially model the status, self-confidence etc. of each agent in a simple and straightforward way.

Now, assume that we get events `trp(X D)` from a TCU predictor, meaning that with a certain probability speaker X will reach a TRP in D units. By adding a single-state statechart DecisionMaker with a single transition (loop) we may introduce the decision making functionality of [5]. The `DecisionMaker` state is without actions. The transition is labeled with the event `trp(X D)` and with the condition `[X!=me && TrueWProb(TalkFactor/(1.0+distanceToNearestTRP`^{2}`))]`. If the transition is carried out, an event `projTRP(X)` is sent, which is to be handled by the overlap statechart. The decision maker is depicted in Figure 2.

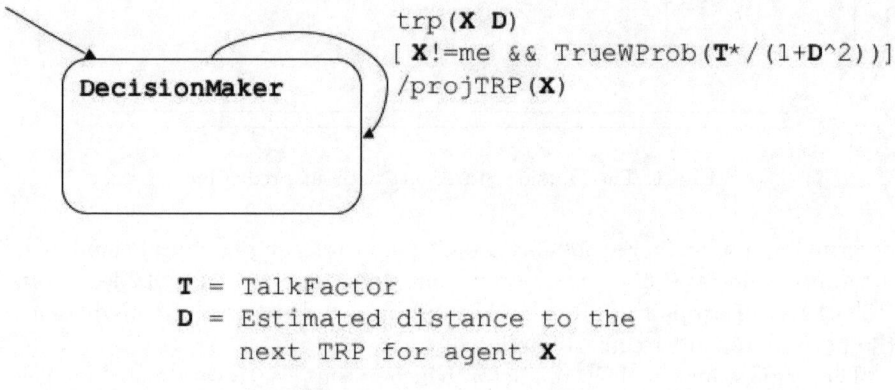

```
T = TalkFactor
D = Estimated distance to the
    next TRP for agent X
```

Fig. 2. The Decision Maker Chart

The Full Outside Chart. We will now extend the predictionless implementation to handle turn-end predictions. The event that we have not considered until now, `projTRP(X)`, requires a number of changes in the implementation. First, we need to keep track of the speakers who are about to stop speaking (signaled with the `projTRP(X)` event). We use a set, `SoonToStop`, where speakers who are about to stop are added. Speakers are removed when it is confirmed that they have stopped speaking or when we believe that the prediction that they were about to stop speaking was wrong (a timeout).

The number of transitions between the states is starting to grow, and therefore it is time to sort out what it means for us to receive a certain event in a certain state. The table 3 shows the meanings of the events in our two states. Table 4 shows the appropriate actions corresponding to the meanings in table 3. Italics indicate actions that are not already in the Outside Chart, or parts of actions that need to be added. We use the `remove(X)` operation in the sense `removeIfMember(X)`.

Table 3. Meaning of events in `othersSilent` and `speaking`

State/Event	othersSilent	othersSpeaking
startSpeaking(X)	Someone who was not speaking, not member of any of the sets, started speaking.	Someone who was not speaking, not member of any of the sets, started speaking.
stopSpeaking(X)	A member of SoonToStop stopped speaking.	Someone, member of one of the sets, stopped speaking.
addressing(X)	none	none
projTRP(X)	A member of SoonToStop will soon stop speaking	Someone, possibly a member of Speakers, will soon stop speaking

Table 4. Actions when reading events in `othersSilent` and `othersSpeaking`

State/Event	othersSilent	othersSpeaking
startSpeaking(X)	Unless X is me, move to the othersSpeaking state and add X to the Speaker set.	Unless X is me, move to the othersSpeaking state and add X to the Speaker set.
stopSpeaking(X)	*Unless X is me, remain in the othersSilent state and remove X from the SoonToStop set.*	Unless X is me, remain in the othersSpeaking state and remove X from the Speakers set *and from the SoonToStop set.*
addressing(X)	none	none
projTRP(X)	N/A	*Unless X is me, remain in othersSpeaking state, make sure that X is removed from the Speakers set, add X to the SoonToStop set and set a timer to emit the event timeOut(X) in D time units.*

We will add the missing actions to our statechart as follows (going top-down left-right in table 4. We add a transition with starting and ending points in `othersSilent`, labeled `stopSpeaking(X)[X != me]/SoonToStop.remove(X)`.

We alter the loop transition from/to `othersSpeaking` by adding the action `SoonToStop.remove(X)`. Finally we add a loop transition from/to the `othersSpeaking` state. The label consists of the event `projTRP(X)`, the condition `[X != me]` and the action `/timer(D, timeOut(X))`.

The event `timeOut`, introduced in the last paragraph, needs to be handled appropriately. The meaning of reading the event `timeOut` is that someone recently was reported to be in the process of stopping to speak, and that the speaker should be silent by now. If he did stop speaking, he is not a member of any set, and we should not do anything. If he did not stop speaking, he is a member of the set `SoonToStop`. What we want to do when reading this event, is to check if X is a member of `SoonToStop`. In that case, we should remove

X from the SoonToStop set and add X to the Speakers set, since this means that the speaker did not stop speaking. In whatever state we are in at the moment, we should move to the othersSpeaking state. Hence, the transition should go from the enclosing superstate to the othersSpeaking state and the label should be timeOut(X) [SoonToStop.contains(X)] / Speakers.add(X), SoonToStop.remove(X), trpTimeOut. The trpTimeOut at the end of the label means that we are generating an event trpTimeOut in order for other machines (the TRP chart) to know that a speaker that we believed was about to stop speaking did not, and therefore possibly canceled a TRP. The complete Outside chart can be seen in Figure 3.

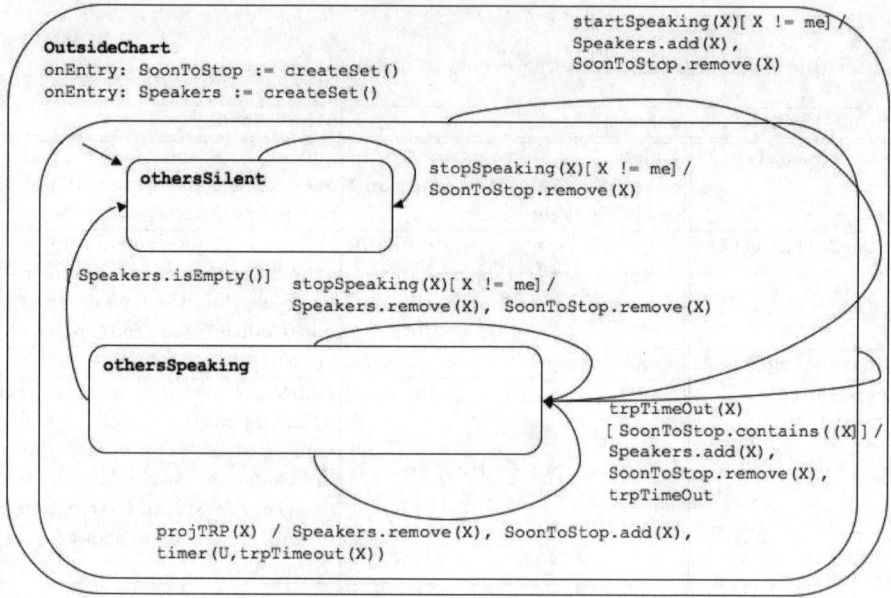

Fig. 3. The Outside Statechart

5.2   The Inside Chart

A parallel Harel statechart can, as mentioned earlier, listen to events coming from the outside and to events emanating from other orthogonal states in the chart. What the Inside Chart needs to do is to signal (to relevant components in the agent) when there is an overlap and when an overlap has been resolved. The overlaps that are interesting are the ones where I am involved, which means that this machine should signal when I am speaking at the same time as someone else.

Since the state we are interested in cannot be reached if I am silent, we start out with the two states iAmSilent and iAmSpeaking. We add transitions between the states labeled with the events startSpeaking(X) and stopSpeaking(X) respectively and the condition that X evaluates to be my (the agent's) name, in the

obvious directions. As embedded states in iAmSpeaking we add nonOverlap and
overlap. Optimistically, we indicate nonOverlap as the initial state.

The second requirement for reaching the state overlap is that someone else is
speaking. Hence we add a transition from nonOverlap to overlap labeled with the
condition [in othersSpeaking], meaning that the transition will only be carried
out if the condition that the orthogonal statechart is in state othersSpeaking
evaluates to true. We simply use the Outside chart to keep track of whether the
other DPs are speaking or silent. We add another transition and label it with
the condition [in othersSilent]. Finally we need the statechart to emit the
events that we are interested in – overlap and overlapResolved. Since entering overlap means that there is an overlap and leaving it (in what way it may be)
means that the overlap is resolved, we add the emission of the events as
onEntry/onExit actions. The Inside Chart can be seen in Figure 4.

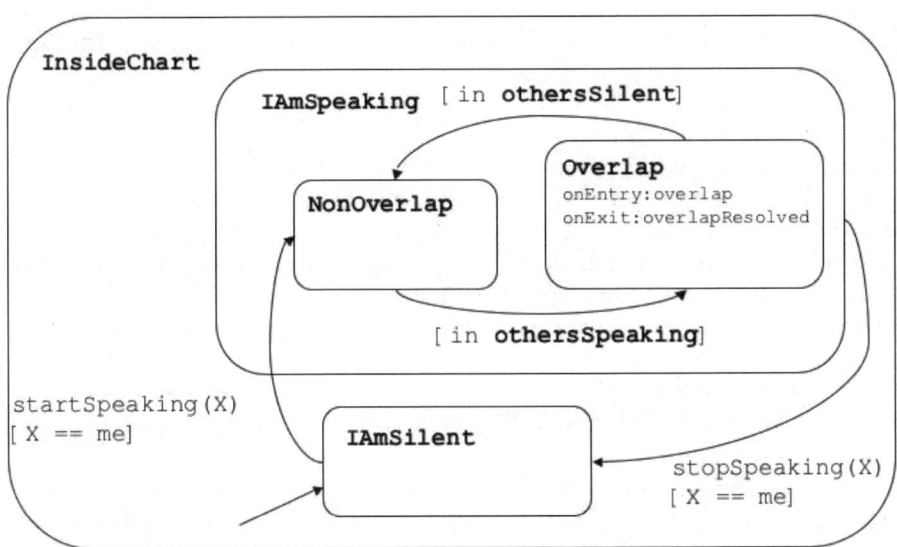

Fig. 4. The Inside Statechart

5.3   The TRP Chart

Let us now turn to the TRPs. We assume that the machine starts out in a state
called freeTrp, meaning that we assume that in the start of a dialogue, anyone
has the right to self-select to make contribution. In the freeTrp state we add the
onEntry action to emit the event freeTRP.

When someone starts speaking we will leave the freeTrp state, emitting the
event noTRP. To achieve this, we add an onExit action – to emit the event noTRP.
Unless the current speaker selects the other speaker as the next speaker, the up-
coming TRP will be a free TRP. We introduce the state freeTrpComingUp for this
purpose. It will not have any onEntry or onExit actions.

As soon as the current speaker(s) stops speaking, we will make a transition to the `freeTrp` state. How should we keep track of who is still speaking? We do not have to, since our Outside chart already does this for us. We simply add a transition from `freeTrpComingUp` to `freeTrp` with the label `[in othersSilent]`.

There is now only one event left to take care of – the `myTRP` event, signaling that I am the only DP with the right and obligation to speak. As the SSJ model states, this occurs when I am selected as next speaker by some other speaker. Selection is signaled to us with the event `addressing(X)`, so we add two states corresponding to the two we already have – `myTrpComingUp` and `myTrp` and also a transition from the first to the second with the label `[in silence]`. We also add a transition from `freeTrpComingUp` to `myTrpComingUp`, labeled with the event `addressing(me)`, meaning that the addressee must evaluate to my name (or identifier). To emit the correct events, we add the actions `onEntry:myTRP` and `onExit:noTRP`.

Let us take a look at the case when another DP is selected as next speaker. If we deploy the TM as it looks right now, the TRP occurring when the other DP is the only one with the right and obligation to speak will show up as a `freeTRP`, which is not what we desire. We need to add another state and two transitions.

We add a state `otherSelected` with a transition from `freeTrpComingUp`, labeled `addressing(X) [X!=me]`, which will ensure that when another party (not me) is addressed, we will end up in the `otherSelected` state.

Our TM is almost ready, but there is an important transition missing. Right now the statechart have three *cul-de-sacs* from which no transition is possible, and since we are not interested in having final states, we need to add transitions from these three states to the `freeTrpComingUp` state. In the statechart formalism used, we accomplish this by wrapping all the TRP states into one superstate and then by adding a transition going from that superstate to `freeTrpComingUp`. We label the transition `startSpeaking(_)`. This means that every time someone starts speaking, we will end up in the `freeTrpComingUp`. The chart can be seen in figure 5.

Two Problems and Their Solutions. There are two problems with the TRP chart as it looks right now. First, one agent can hold the turn forever as the TRP chart can get stuck in the `otherSelected` state. Second, mispredictions of TRPs can in certain cases cause the TRP chart not to retract a TRP even though the misprediction is known in other parts of the state chart. We present the problems and their respective solutions in this section.

One Agent Can Hold the Turn Forever. Say that agent A, equipped with our turn manager, and some other agent B, are engaged in dialogue. A asks "What time is it?" and B does not reply. Transcribed to a list of input events it will look like `startSpeaking(A)`, `addressing(C)`, `stopSpeaking(A)`. At this point in dialogue, A's TM is in state `otherSelected`. The only way to move the machine out of the state is to read an event `startSpeaking(X)`.

Say that B did not understand the question, or did not hear it, or maybe did not even perceive that somebody were trying to tell it something, or even heard the question, but deliberately did not answer it. In this case, we will not read a `startSpeaking(X)` event simply because no-one will start speaking.

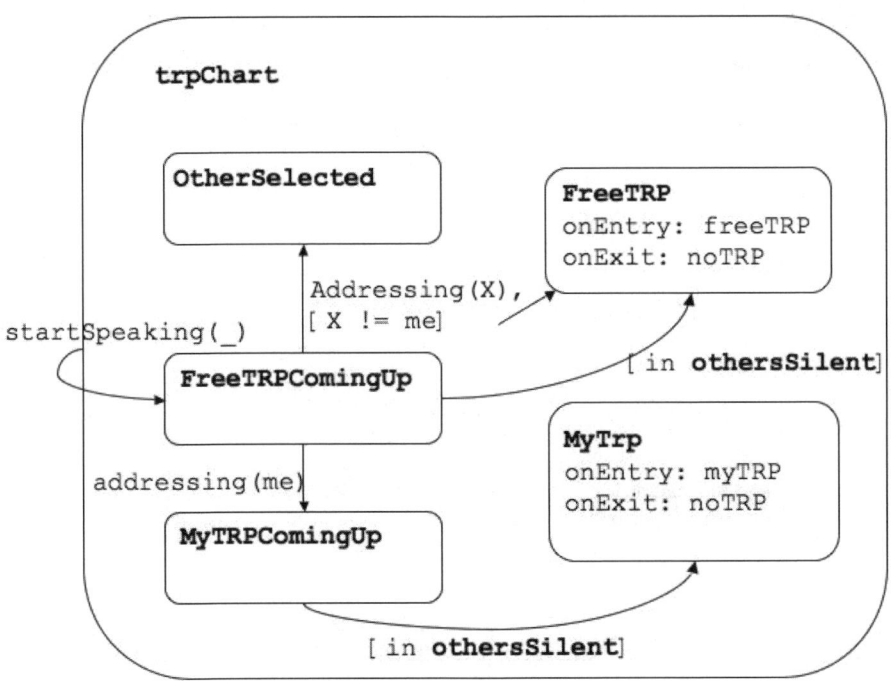

Fig. 5. The TRP Statechart

This may be solved either internally in the `TRP Chart` by adding a `othersTrp` state and timers that will trigger transitions from `myTrp` to `othersTrp` respectively to the `freeTrp` state, or external to the TM, for instance elsewhere in the Dialogue Manager. We will select the first solution, and the `TRP Chart` with the necessary changes is shown in Figure 6.

TRP Timeouts. At the end of section 5.1 we mentioned that the Outside chart signals, by a `trpTimeOut` event, to the TRP chart when a speaker which we thought was about to stop speaking actually did not. We need to take appropriate action when this event occurs. What does this event mean to us? The event is important only when the TRP states are active, when we have indicated a TRP when there were actually none. We will add transitions from the TRP states back to the respective "comingUp" states, labeling them with `trpTimeOut/noTRP`, indicating that the TRP was canceled. This addition is also shown in Figure 6. This makes our turn manager complete.

6 Summary and Conclusions

In this paper, we have described the motivations for and the construction of a turn manager for conversational agents. We have shown that an implementation

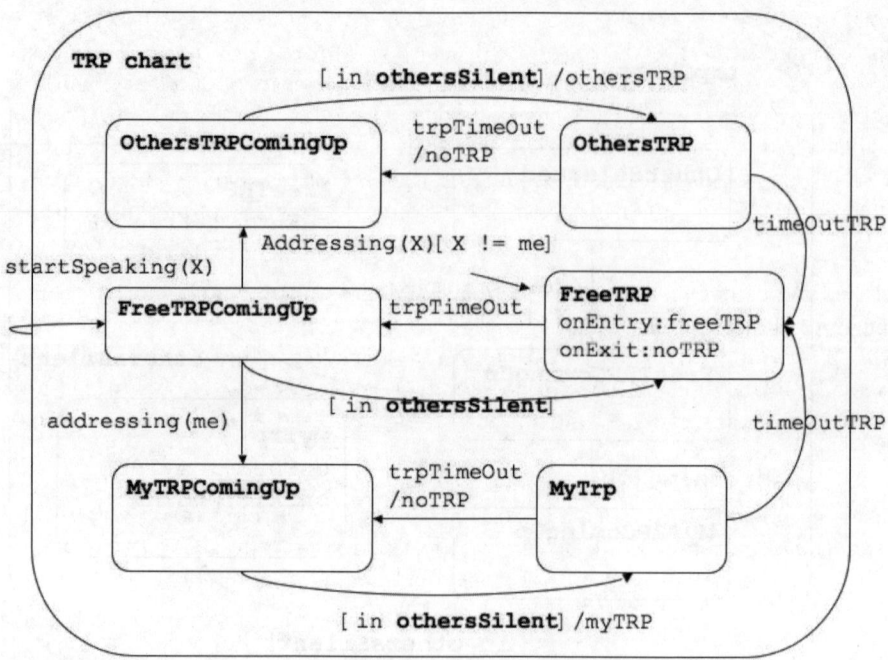

Fig. 6. The improved TRP Chart

using Harel statecharts is possible, and that a transition from the theory described by [9] to an state-based implementation is straightforward. The result is a highly modular statechart with three simple substates or modules, each of them dealing with one well-defined part of the turn taking problem.

The turn manager will be used in [6], which covers dialogue management, using Harel statecharts, for artificial conversational agents capable of engaging in multi-party dialogue.

By solving the turn-taking issue, we enable multi-party dialogue with artificial conversational agents for use in games, information services and chats. By designing (and implementing) the turn and dialogue management components of artificial conversational agents in Harel statecharts, proposed to become an integral part of VoiceXML, we hope that our work will become available for VoiceXML applications.

Acknowledgments

I would like to thank my supervisors Torbjörn Lager and Staffan Larsson for valuable comments, input and ideas. I also wish to thank two anonymous reviewers for valuable input.

References

[1] Barnett, J., Auburn, R., Bodell, M., Helbing, M., Hosn, R., K.R., (eds): State chart xml (scxml): State machine notation for control abstraction. Web document, http://www.w3.org/TR/2006/WD-scxml-20060124/ (2006)

[2] Cassell, J., Bickmore, T. W., Vilhjalmsson, H. H., Yan, H.: More than just a pretty face: affordances of embodiment *Intelligent User Interfaces* (2000) 52-59

[3] Edlund, J., Heldner, M., Gustafson, J.: Utterance segmentation and turn-taking in spoken dialogue systems. *Computer Studies in Language and Speec* **8** (2005) 576–587

[4] Harel, D.: Statecharts: A visual formalism for complex systems. *Science of Computer Programmin* **8** (1987) 231–274

[5] Hulstijn, J., Vreeswijk, G.A.W.: Turntaking: a case for agent-based programming. Technical report, Institute of Information and Computing Sciences, Utrecht University (2003)

[6] Kronlid, F.: Turn and Dialogue Management in Multi Party Dialogue Systems PhD. thesis, Göteborg University. (in prep)

[7] McGlashan, S., Burnett, D. C., Carter, J., Danielsen, P., Ferrans, J., Hunt, A., Lucas, B., Porter, B., Rehor, K., Tryphonas, S. (eds):   Voice Extensible Markup Language (VoiceXML) Version 2.0   Web document, http://www.w3.org/TR/2004/REC-voicexml20-20040316/ (2004)

[8] Ricordel, P., Pesty, S., Demazeau, Y.: About Conversations between Multiple Agents. 1st International Workshop of Central and Eastern Europe on Multi-Agent Systems, CEEMAS'99, SPIIRAS, pp. 203-210, Saint Petersburg, (1999).

[9] Sacks, H., Schegloff, E.A., Jefferson, G.: A simplest systematics for the organization of turn-taking for conversation. *Language* **50** (1974) 696–735

[10] Schegloff, E.A.: Overlapping talk and the organization of turn-taking for conversation. *Language in Society* **29**(1) (2000) 1–63

Inducing Perspective Sharing Between a User and an Embodied Agent by a Thought Balloon as an Input Form

Satoshi V. Suzuki[1,2] and Hideaki Takeda[2,3]

[1] DCISS, IGSSE, Tokyo Institute of Technology
[2] National Institute of Informatics
[3] University of Tokyo

Abstract. Accepting the perspectives of others often provides people with novel cues for discovering and solving problems. However, human cognitive limitations and differences in attitude between people make this difficult. In this study, a psychological experiment was conducted to examine how blank thought balloons emitted from an embodied agent encourages perspective sharing between a user and an embodied agent. In the experiment, participants ($N = 39$) were asked to do one of these tasks: reading a thought balloon emitted from an embodied agent, or filling in a speech balloon, or a thought balloon with predicting its content. It is suggested that filling in a blank thought balloon promoted the user to accept the perspective of the embodied agent from the experimental results. Embodied agent technologies for perspective sharing between a user and others are discussed through comparison between the experimental environment and practical problems, and degree of participants' understanding of experimental environment.

1 Introduction

Perspective sharing with others in often needed in ordinary human social activity. For example, you may discover another perspective when conversing with a child by bending down to share physical perspective with the child. Developing the "personal view" of a prospective user can lead to proper interface design [1]. In fact, taking the perspective of minority can often reveal flaws in majority's opinion in group discussion [2]. Furthermore, taking perspective of a teacher in mathematical problem solving can help learners find out the reasons for their own mistakes [3]. All of this evidence implies that perspective sharing with others can have an important role in problem discovering and solving.

We tried to discover a way to let a user accept perceived perspective of an embodied agent by a blank thought balloon emitted from the agent. Embodied agents are social actors that have potential to change the user's attitude [4]. Moreover, despite the ability of an embodied agent to interact with a user via body expression, achieving corresponding modality between the user and the agent should be difficult in most cases because of device constraints. For example, Takeuchi et al. [5] claimed that the user often unconsciously responds to

M. Klusch, M. Rovatsos, and T. Payne (Eds.): CIA 2006, LNAI 4149, pp. 96–108, 2006.

the agent's body (e.g., eyes, ears, and mouth) as if the agent's body was a real human body in a display, in spite of the existence of devices and sensors to sense the user's body (e.g., a Web camera, a microphone, and a speaker). However, from the viewpoint of interface design, this user's response to the embodied agent is inappropriate, since the agent's body cannot sense the user's body without using special devices and sensors. One of the solutions for this modality mismatch should be perspective sharing between the user and the embodied agent. In this study, we suggest the strategy of prompting perspective sharing with blank thought balloons emitted from an embodied agent. We also point out the problems in this strategy.

In this paper, first, the definition of two levels of perspectives, phenomenal level and representational level, is described. Then we explain that acceptance of perceived embodied agents' perspectives at the representational level by the user should be driven by perspective sharing either at the phenomenal level or at the representational level, and that the perspective sharing via blank thought balloons emitted from the embodied agent occurs at the representational level. After the argument of roles of balloon interface in user interface design, we depict a psychological experiment to examine the influence of blank thought balloons to perspective sharing between a user and an embodied agent at the representational level. Discussion on the acceptance of perceived perspective of the embodied agent by the user via the blank thought balloons follows.

2   Perspective Sharing with an Embodied Agent

We introduce the terms on perspective defined by Vogeley and Fink [6]. There are two levels of description in perspective. One is *phenomenal level (P-level)* which mentions perspective in virtual space; the other is *representational level (R-level)* which refers to perspective on a cognitive level conceptualized by the observer. Moreover, *first-person-perspective* and *third-person-perspective* respectively refers to the perspective of the user and that of the embodied agent in the P-level, and *egocentric perspective* and *allocentric perspective* respectively mentions the perspective of the user and that of the embodied agent in the R-level. Then, *perspective sharing* means the acceptance of allocentric perspective by the user.

Furthermore, triggers of perspective sharing exist at both the P-level and the R-level as shown in Fig. 1. *P-level trigger* occurs when the user perceives and accepts the third-person-perspective in virtual space, while *R-level trigger* occurs when the user perceives and accepts the allocentric perspective directly. One of approaches to accomplishing the perspective sharing with the P-level trigger is the body orientation correspondence between the user and the embodied agent [7, 8]. Arranging the agent's body orientation to correspond with the user's in virtual space, the user can easily know how the agent sees the virtual space, so the user can easily inspect the allocentric perspective of the agent. However, perspective sharing with P-level trigger may depend on the user's degree of perceived immersiveness in the virtual space. That is, it may be hard

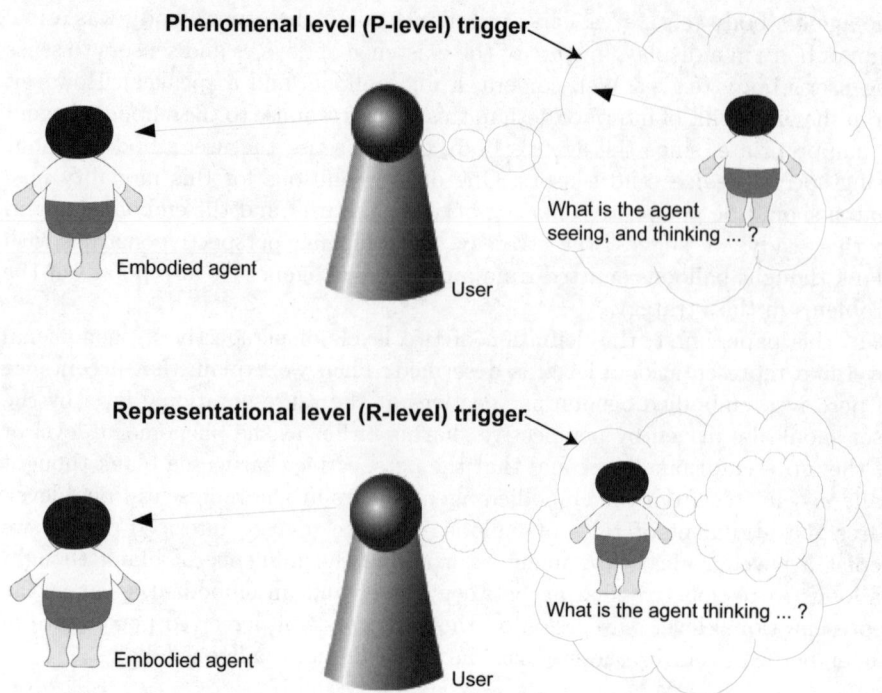

Fig. 1. Difference of triggers in perspective sharing

for the user to perceive his/her body as if it existed in the virtual space only by the body orientation correspondence between the user and the agent. The perspective sharing with R-level trigger can solve this problem, and one of the R-level trigger candidates is filling in the blank thought balloon emitted from the embodied agent.

3   Related Works

In this section, the related works on balloons in comics and comic-like interface, balloon media and acoustic media in embodied agent interface, and automatic attitude change of a user by a social actor are discussed.

3.1   Balloons in Comics and Comic-Like Interface

Balloons has been used to express character's utterance and reflection beyond time and space [9]. The balloons that express the character's utterance are called *speech balloons*, and those that express the character's reflection are called *thought balloons*. Some comic-like interface (e.g., Comic Chat [10], ComicDiary [11]) adopted balloon interface to express the character's utterance and reflection, and some helps and tips for using software have been displayed with pop-up balloons in user interface design [12], but no studies referred to the influence of blank thought balloons as a means of perspective sharing. Thus, we attempt to argue this problem.

3.2 Balloon Media Versus Acoustic Media

Some embodied agent interfaces adopt acoustic media to express the utterances of embodied agents [13]. In addition, another interfaces adopt both acoustic media and balloon media (e.g., Microsoft Agent). Expressing agent's reflection only using acoustic media may be difficult without using special devices. The influence of thought balloon media is thus worth inspecting.

3.3 Automatic Attitude Change of a User by a Social Actor

Some studies have reported that automatic attitude change of a user when interacting with a social actor (including an embodied agent and a computer) could be observed in some situations. Moon [14] discovered that the answer of a user who responded to perceived private information of a computer with keyboard input contained user's private information, that is, the user unconsciously reciprocated private information to the computer. Additionally, Moon also claimed that the user's reciprocation of personal information was promoted after some exchanges of self-introduction between the user and the computer, comparing with the situation without such exchanges. Sundar [15] found that the quality of interaction between a user and a computer decreased when the user must consider who created or operated the computer. Although the quality of interaction could be kept if the user could have enough interaction with the computer, that the user knows the structure of the computer at their first contact should be harm to the relationships between the user and the computer. These phenomena should also be observed in human-agent interaction, and they suggest that the deep human-agent interaction at their first contact requires cognitive burden to a user.

4   Psychological Experiment

We conducted a psychological experiment to examine the perspective sharing between a user and an embodied agent when the user filled in a blank thought balloon emitted from the embodied agent. Comparing this condition with two others, one in which a blank *speech* balloon to be filled in was emitted from the agent, and another in which no blank balloons appeared, the influence of the blank *thought* balloon on relationships between the user and the agent was investigated.

4.1 Predictions

Based on the argument in Section 3, the hypothesis that *a user can improve understanding the allocentric perspective via filling in a blank thought balloon* was suggested. Then, we predicted the following for the experiment:

P1 The length of content of thought balloons filled in by the user is longer than that of speech balloon.

P2 The frequency of perceived real intention of the embodied agent in thought balloons filled in by the user is higher than that in speech balloons.

P3 The impression of work of the embodied agent by the user is evaluated better when the user fills in the blank thought balloons emitted from the agent.

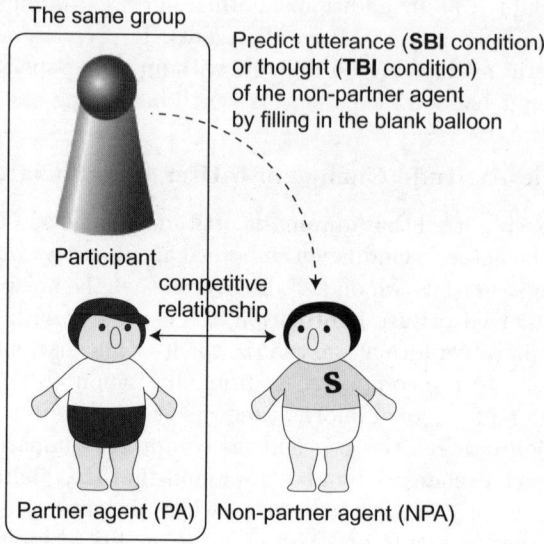

Fig. 2. Relationship among a participant, a partner agent, and a non-partner agent

4.2   Experimental Design

The two embodied agents shown in Fig. 2, partner agent (PA) and non-partner agent (NPA), appeared in the experiment. Each agent gave the participant pieces of advice for the task of the participant. Participants were told to interact with the PA about preference of pictures before the task. After the participant finished the task, he/she evaluated the quality of advice from the two agents. Before the evaluation, each agent had the opportunity to appeal to the participant that it had made an effort to let the participant finish the work as quickly as possible. PA expressed this appeal to the participant via a speech balloon. The reaction to the PA by the NPA was changed dependent on three experimental conditions. In "no balloon input" (**NBI**) condition, the NPA just answered the PA via a speech balloon. In "speech balloon input" (**SBI**) condition, the participant was told to fill in a speech balloon input emitted from the NPA, predicting how the NPA would answer the PA. In "thought balloon input" (**TBI**) condition, the participant was told to fill in a thought balloon input emitted from the NPA, predicting what the NPA would think about PA's appeal. Then, there existed one independent variable for these three experimental conditions (between-participant).

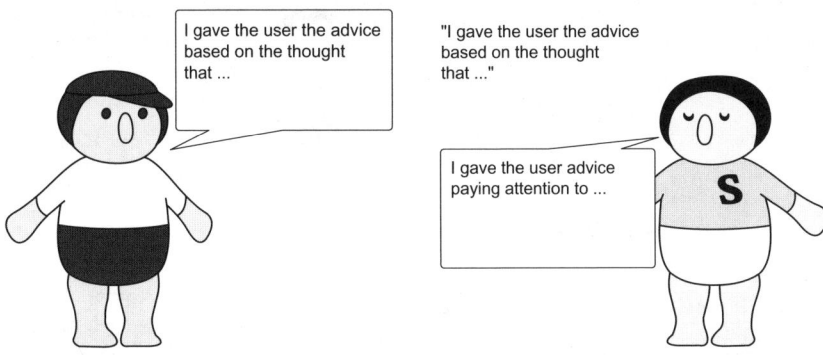

Fig. 3. Speech of a partner agent

Fig. 4. Speech of a non-partner agent in **NBI** condition

Fig. 5. A speech balloon input emitted from a non-partner agent in **SBI** condition

Fig. 6. A thought balloon input emitted from a non-partner agent in **TBI** condition

4.3 Participants

We collected valid experimental data from thirty-nine participants (20 males and 19 females, mean age: 22.9 (SD: 3.56) years old). The groups of participants consisted of Japanese undergraduate and graduate students and post-doctoral researchers. They were randomly assigned to one of the three experimental conditions, and there were 13 participants for each condition.

4.4 Procedure

Each participant was told that this experiment was to evaluate the quality of advice in an object-searching task. The experiment consisted of two parts. In the first part, the PA was introduced to the participant as a partner in the object-searching task and he/she interacted with PA. Three pairs of pictures (cat, toy, and beach) were exhibited to the participant, and he/she chose either

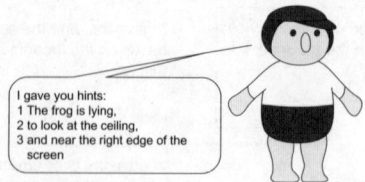

Fig. 7. Example of advice from an embodied agent

Points for the **PA**	14	13	12	11	10	9	8	7	6	5	4	3	2	1
Points for the **NPA**	1	2	3	4	5	6	7	8	9	10	11	12	13	14

Fig. 8. Reward distribution matrix (upper: for the partner agent, lower: for the non-partner agent)

of the picture for each pair based on his/her preference. Then, the PA told the participant that the PA liked the same picture that he/she had chosen. In the second part, the NPA appeared first, and the participant was told that the PA and the NPA were competing with each other. The participant was told to find an object instructed on the screen from the picture. While the participant was searching the object, either the PA or the NPA gave advice for finding the object. Each piece of advice from the PA or the NPA consisted of three parts. The first part was shown at the outset, and the second and the third part were shown 20 and 40 seconds, respectively, after the participant started to search for the object This timing was prepared to let the participant depend on the agent's advice. If the participant took beyond 120 seconds to find the object, the location of the object was displayed to him/her. The PA and the NPA took turns to give the participant a piece of advice. Each picture contained four objects to be searched for, and the participant worked on the object-searching task for four pictures. The pictures were excerpted from Wick [16].

After the participant finished the task for each picture, he/she evaluated the quality of the advice from the PA and the NPA as the procedure explained in Section 4.2. The size of the input form and font was the same in the **SBI** and the **TBI** condition. Based on the previous study [17], the participant was told to distribute 15 points between the two agents as a reward in accordance with the matrix in Fig. 8, and was told that the quality of the advice would be adjusted based on his/her evaluation.

Finally, the participant answered a paper-and-pencil questionnaire about the experiment. Then the participant was debriefed, thanked, and dismissed. Finishing the experiment took about 30–40 minutes for each participant.

The experimental environment was developed with Macromedia Flash, and run as a projector application on a laptop PC (OS: Windows XP). This application was displayed in full-screen mode in 1024 × 768 display resolution. Experimental data was collected via the WWW using a CGI program.

4.5   Measures

These measures were adopted:

Length of balloon content. We counted the number of words in the balloon content. Since this measure could not be used for the **NBI** condition, we compared this between the **SBI** and **TBI** conditions.

Depth of balloon content. Two judges who did not know the intent of the experiment evaluated the depth of the balloon content using a 5-point scale. The definition of the depth of the balloon was adopted from the depth of self-disclosure [18], because the content of the thought balloon would contain self-disclosure of the agent. The depth of the balloon was defined as how much these conditions satisfied comprehensively:

– Containing comprehensive tendency of behavior rather than specific behavior in a certain situation
– Containing original contents
– Containing invisible contents such as motivation, emotion, and imagination rather than actual actions and events
– Containing weak points of the NPA
– Containing response unfavorable for the PA
– Containing content with strong emotion

Then, averaged value between the two judges was adopted for the variable of the depth of the balloon content.

The correspondence rate between two judges was 59.6%. The value of correspondence rate was relatively low, but including the data evaluated differently by the two judges by only one point, the correspondence rate increased to 86.5%. This measure could not be used for the **NBI** condition, then the values in the **SBI** and **TBI** conditions were compared.

Reward distribution for NPA. This is the number of points that the participant distributed to the NPA. We compared the values in all of the three conditions.

5   Result

This section describes the results of the experiment.

5.1   Content of Balloons

Table 1 shows the median value of length and depth of balloon content for each condition. The results of Wilcoxon rank sum test showed that the value of the depth of balloon content in the **TBI** condition was consistently larger than in the **SBI** condition throughout the experiment. However, while the balloon content in the **TBI** condition on object-searching task in the first picture was significantly longer than that in the **SBI** condition, the difference between them vanished as the task went on.

Table 1. Median value (quartile deviation in parenthesis) of length and depth of balloon content

	SBI cond. ($n = 13$)		TBI cond. ($n = 13$)		Statistics values of Wilcoxon rank sum test	
	length	depth	length	depth	length	depth
1st picture	5.0 (1.50)	2.0 (0.25)	9.0 (2,00)	2.5 (0.50)	30.0**	36.0**
2nd	5.0 (1.00)	2.0 (0.50)	5.0 (1.50)	3.5 (1.00)	80.5	38.5**
3rd	6.0 (0.50)	2.0 (0.25)	6.0 (1.50)	3.0 (1.00)	78.5	37.0*
4th	6.0 (1.00)	2.0 (0.25)	6.0 (1.50)	3.0 (1.00)	89.0	41.0*

**: $p < .01$, *: $p < .05$

Table 2. Mean value (SD in parenthesis) of reward distribution for NPA

	NBI cond. ($n = 13$)	SBI cond. ($n = 13$)	TBI cond. ($n = 13$)	Statistics values of $F(2, 36)$
1st picture	8.38 (3.07)	7.00 (3.08)	8.08 (2.47)	0.825
2nd	7.38 (2.06)	7.85 (2.23)	7.15 (3.26)	0.244
3rd	7.77 (2.20)	8.54 (2.30)	6.92 (2.90)	1.37
4th	7.23 (1.36)	8.23[a] (1.42)	6.77[a] (1.59)	3.40 *

*: $p < .05$

[a]: Difference between them was significant according to multiple comparison using Holm's method ($p < .05$)

5.2   Evaluation of Advice from Two Embodied Agents

Table 2 represents the mean value of reward distribution for the NPA for each condition. The reward distribution of the PA can be found by subtracting this value from 15, therefore there were little differences of reward distribution between the PA and the NPA. As the task went on, while the value in the **SBI** condition showed a tendency to increase, the value in the other condition showed a tendency to decrease. Although there were no significant differences of the values among these conditions until the task for third picture, significant difference in the value in the **SBI** condition and in the **TBI** condition was observed at the task for fourth picture.

6   Discussion

Considering the experimental data obtained, the influence of filling in the blank thought balloon on perspective sharing with R-level trigger is discussed. Possible applications and future work are also suggested.

6.1   Perspective Sharing with Representational-Level Trigger

First, the length of the balloon content in the **TBI** condition was shorten after the object-searching task in the second picture. This may be because of fatigue of the participant derived from the object-searching task. Nevertheless, the depth of the balloon content in the **TBI** condition was not influenced by such fatigue, and the participants in the **TBI** condition kept on trying to write down the allocentric perspective of the NPA in the blank thought balloons.

The results of analysis of balloon content in Section 5.1 implies that blank thought balloons emitted from an embodied agent induce a user to inspect the allocentric perspective of the agent. Although the influence of fatigue derived from the tasks might exist, the participants in the **TBI** condition showed the attitude to inspect allocentric perspective of the NPA. Next, we investigated the content of the balloons filled in by the participants in detail. When the object-searching task for the first picture was finished, the PA said "I gave you pieces of advice while paying attention to the explanation of the shapes of the objects." In the **SBI** condition, the participants filled in the blank speech balloon with "I gave you pieces of advice while paying attention to the location and things around the target objects" or "I gave you pieces of information on the location behind which the target object was hidden." Additionally, the participants responded to the question "What did you think when you fill in the balloon?" with answers like "I filled in the balloon considering the correspondence of the PA's utterance." On the other hand, in the **TBI** condition, although some participants filled in the blank thought balloon in a similar way that of the participants in **SBI** condition, a different tendency in filling in the blank speech balloon appeared. For example, when the object-searching task for first picture finished, the participants in the **TBI** condition filled in the blank thought balloon with "It did not make sense to give the advice until it regards to how the target object had posed or what kind of features the target object had" or "It should be clear that the first piece of advice regards to the location of target object." Such competing message by NPA hardly appeared in **SBI** condition, notwithstanding the participants have been repeatedly told that the PA and the NPA were competing with each other. The participants' consideration of this competitive situation between PA and NPA in **TBI** condition might have influenced the salient decline of the reward distribution for the NPA.

6.2   User's Understanding of Situation Around Two Embodied Agents

Participants seem to have had difficulty to understand both the situation around the PA and the NPA and relation between human-agent interaction and the object-finding tasks shown in Fig. 2. Taking into account the previous study [17], the reward distribution for NPA should be relatively low among the three conditions since the user tends to have prejudice in favor of user's "teammate" [4]. Therefore, two problems exist in the discussion of the experimental results:

- The influence of interactivity between a user and an embodied agent did not explicitly appear in this experiment.
- The understanding of social relationships among the user, the PA, and the NPA was inadequate except for in some participants in the **TBI** condition.

The absence of the influence of interactivity is a problem since one of the advantages of computer-supported environment is interactivity [4]. Without the interactivity, this experimental results can be easily replicated even without interactivity (e.g. paper media). Thus, investigation of the influence of interactivity with different approaches from this study should be investigated.

Moreover, the social relationships among the participant, the PA, and the NPA were not understood by the participants until they filled in the blank thought balloon considering the situation among them. Consequently, understanding social relationships among the participant, the PA, and the NPA only with cover stories explained in the experiment and the initial interaction between the participant and PA seem to be hard for him/her. One of the solutions for these problems is to increase the opportunity for "rapport building" between a user and embodied agents [19]. Also considering the Moon's study [14] discussed in Section 3.3, it should be important to build rapport between a user and embodied agents whose perceived allocentric perspectives were different from the user's before the situation to enable a user to accept the agents' perceived allocentric perspective. Another solution should be addressing the procedural issues in the experiment, since the object-searching tasks were too hard for the participants to solve considering the situation among them, the PA, and the NPA. More understandable scenarios should be explored for the experiment.

6.3   Possible Application and Future Work

In this experiment, we predicted that the user could consider the situation of his/her "enemy" through filling in a blank thought balloon emitted from the NPA and that changes would occur in the user's allocentric perspective, similar to changes that occur in the opinion of a debate participant after considering the thought of a "devil's advocate" [2]. As mentioned in Section 1, there are many situations in which people need to accept perspective from others in ordinary life. For example, in the situation that the user needs to try to take the minority's allocentric perspective to solve problems, an interface to let the user accept the minority's allocentric perspective should contribute to the user's solving of the problems. It is worth attempting to induce perspective sharing with the blank thought balloon emitted from an embodied agent in other real problem solving situations.

7   Conclusion

In this study, through a psychological experiment that attempted to induce a user to accept perceived allocentric perspective of an embodied agent by filling in blank thought balloons, the possibility was explored of embodied agent technologies that let the user understand the perspective of others. The experimental results suggested that filling in a blank thought balloon emitted from the embodied agent may induce the user's acceptance of perceived allocentric perspective, but without establishment of social relationships between the user and the agent, the user has difficulty inspecting the perceived allocentric perspective. Finally, through introducing embodied agent technologies into practical situations, we intend to extract design principles of embodied agents that can let a user understand others' allocentric perspective that are different from his/hers.

References

[1] Norman, D.A.: Cognitive artifacts. In Carroll, J.M., ed.: Designing interaction: Psychology at the human-computer interface. Cambridge University Press, Cambridge (1991) 17–38

[2] Janis, I.L.: Groupthink: Psychological Studies of Policy Decisions and Fiascoes. 2nd edn. Houghton Mifflin Company, Boston, MA (1982)

[3] Morita, J., Miwa, K.: Changes of inferences caused by obtaining different perspectives: Analysis based on analogical reasoning. In: Proceedings of the 4th International Conference on Cognitive Science. (2003) 463–468

[4] Fogg, B.J.: Persuasive Technology: Using Computers to Change What We Think and Do. Morgan Kaufmann Publishers, San Francisco, CA (2003)

[5] Takeuchi, Y., Watanabe, K., Katagiri, Y.: Social identification of embodied interactive agent. In: Proceedings of the 13th International Workshop on Robot and Human Interactive Communication (RO-MAN 2004), Kurashiki, Japan (2004) 449–454

[6] Vogeley, K., Fink, G.R.: Neural correlates of the first-person-perspective. Trends in Cognitive Sciences **7**(1) (2003) 38–42

[7] Suzuki, S.V., Takeda, H.: Inducing change in user's perspective with the arrangement of body orientation of embodied agents. In: Proceedings of the 15th IEEE International Symposium on Robot and Human Interactive Communication (RO-MAN 2006). (in press)

[8] Okamoto, M., Okamoto, K., Nakano, Y.I., Nishida, T.: Supporting the creation of immersive CG contents with enhanced user involvement. In: Proceedings of the Symposium on Conversational Informatics for Supporting Social Intelligence and Interaction — Situational and Environmental Information Enforcing Involvement in Conversation, AISB'05: Social Intelligence and Interaction in Animals, Robots and Agents, Hatfield, UK (2005) 87–96

[9] Harrison, R.P.: The cartoon: Communication to the quick. Sage, Beverly Hills, CA (1981)

[10] Kurlander, D., Skelly, T., Salesin, D.: Comic Chat. In: Proceedings of the 23rd Annual Conference on Computer Graphics and Interactive Techniques (SIGGRAPH96), ACM Press (1996) 225–236

[11] Sakamoto, R., Nakao, K., Sumi, Y., Mase, K.: ComicDiary: Representing individual experiences in comics style. In: Proceedings of the 25th International Conference on Computer Graphics and Interactive Techniques (SIGGRAPH 2001). (2001) 158

[12] Cooper, A., Reimann, R.M.: About Face 2.0: The Essentials of Interaction Design. Wiley, Indianapolis, IN (2003)

[13] Cassell, J., Sullivan, J., Prevost, S., Churchill, E., eds.: Embodied Conversational Agents. MIT Press, Cambridge, MA (2000)
[14] Moon, Y.: Intimate exchanges: Using computers to elicit self-disclosure from consumers. Journal of Consumer Research **26** (2000) 323–339
[15] Sundar, S.S., Nass, C.: Source orientation in human-computer interaction. Communication Research **27**(6) (2000) 683–703
[16] Wick, W.: Can You See What I See?: Picture Puzzles to Search and Solve. Cartwheel Books, New York (2003)
[17] Tajfel, H., Billig, M.G., Bundy, R.P., Flament, C.: Social categorization and intergroup behavior. European Journal of Social Psychology **1** (1971) 149–177
[18] Altman, I., Taylor, D.A.: Social penetration: the development of interpersonal relationships. Holt, Rinehart, and Winston, New York (1973)
[19] Bickmore, T., Cassell, J.: Small talk and conversational storytelling in embodied conversational interface agents. In: Proceedings of the AAAI Fall Symposium on Narrative Intelligence, Cape Cod, MA (1999) 87–92

Agent-Based Analysis and Support
for Incident Management

Mark Hoogendoorn[1], Catholijn M. Jonker[2], Jan Treur[1], and Marian Verhaegh[3]

[1] Vrije Universiteit Amsterdam, Department of Artificial Intelligence
De Boelelaan 1081a, 1081 HV Amsterdam, The Netherlands
{mhoogen, treur}@cs.vu.nl
[2] Radboud University Nijmegen, Nijmegen Institute of Cognition and Information
Montessorilaan 3, 6525 HR Nijmegen, The Netherlands
C.Jonker@nici.ru.nl
[3] Quartet Consult, Jaap Edenlaan 16, 2807 BR Gouda, The Netherlands
info@quartetconsult.nl

Abstract. This paper presents an agent-based approach for error detection in incident management organizations. The approach consists of several parts. First, a formal approach for the specification and hierarchical verification of both traces and properties. Incomplete traces are enriched by enrichment rules. Furthermore, a classification mechanism is presented for the different properties in incident management that is based on psychological literature. Classification of errors provides insight in the functioning of the agents involved with respect to their roles. This insight enables the provision of dedicated training sessions and allows software support to give appropriate warning messages during incident management.

1   Introduction

The domain of incident management is characterized by sudden events which demand immediate, effective and efficient response. Due to the nature of incident management, those involved in such processes need to be able to cope with stress situations and high work pressure. In addition to that, cooperation between these people is crucial and is not trivial due to the involvement of multiple organizations with different characteristics (e.g. police, health care, fire department). As a result of these difficulties, often errors occur in an incident management process. If such errors are not handled properly, this may have great impact on the successfulness of incident management.

Research within the domain of computer science and artificial intelligence is being performed to see whether automated systems can improve the current state of affairs in incident management (see e.g. [12]). One of the problems is that the information available is incomplete and possibly contradictory and unreliable. As a result, more advanced techniques are needed to enable automated systems to contribute an improvement of the incident management process.

This paper presents an agent-based approach to monitor, analyze and support incident management processes by detecting occurring errors and providing support to avoid such errors or to limit their consequences. The approach is tailored towards the characteristics of incident management. First of all, the approach includes a method which deals with incomplete information. In addition, a diagnostic method based on

M. Klusch, M. Rovatsos, and T. Payne (Eds.): CIA 2006, LNAI 4149, pp. 109–123, 2006.
© Springer-Verlag Berlin Heidelberg 2006

refinement within the approach can signal whether certain required properties of the incident management organization are not satisfied, and pinpoint the cause within the organization of this dissatisfaction. The approach is based on the organizational paradigm nowadays in use in agent systems [1,4] which allows the abstraction from individual agents to the level of roles. Such an abstraction is useful as typically specification of the requirements in this domain is done on the level of roles (e.g. the police chief should communicate a strategy for crowd control). In case errors are observed in role behavior, they are classified to have more insight in what kind of errors are often made by a particular agent participating in the organization, in order to propose a tailored training program for this agent. In the future the approach as a whole can be incorporated in cooperating software agents for monitoring and providing feedback in training sessions, and software agents which can even monitor incident management organizations on the fly, giving a signal as soon as errors are detected, and providing support to avoid their occurrence or to limit their consequences.

Section 2 introduces the domain of incident management and, more specifically, the situation in the Netherlands. Thereafter, Section 3 introduces the formal language used to specify traces and behavior. Section 4 presents an approach for handling incomplete information by means of enrichment rules whereas Section 5 presents properties in the form of hierarchies for incident management organizations. Furthermore, Section 6 presents the classification scheme for errors, including specific incident management decision rules. Results of a case study are presented in Section 7 and finally, Section 8 is a discussion.

2   The Domain of Incident Management

In this Section, a brief introduction to the domain of incident management in the Netherlands is given. In the Netherlands four core organizations are present within incident management: (1) the fire department; (2) the police department; (3) health care, and (4) the municipalities involved. The first three parties mentioned each have their own alarm center in which operators are present to handle tasks associated with the specific organization.

A trigger for starting up an incident management organization is typically a call to the national emergency number, which is redirected to the nearest regional alarm center in which all three parties have their own alarm center. The call will be redirected to the most appropriate alarm center of the three parties. In case the operator of that alarm center considers the incident to be severe enough to start up the full incident management organization, he informs the alarm centers of the other organizations as well. Initially, the three alarm centers will send the manpower they think is appropriate for the incident reported. After the manpower has arrived on the scene, each part of the organization in principle acts on its own, each having a different coordinator of actions. In the case of the fire department this is the commander of the first truck to arrive, for health care it is the paramedic of the first ambulance and for the police there is no such coordinator as they have a supporting role. Each of the coordinators are in charge until the dedicated operational leaders of the organization arrive at the scene. The responsibilities of the organizations are briefly described as follows: the fire department takes care of the so called "cause and effect prevention", the health care organization is in charge of providing medical care, and the police takes care of routing of the various vehicles and crowd control. After the initial phase without structural coordination, an organization is formed in order to coordinate all actions of the individual organizations in case this is still necessary. The fire department is in charge of the operational side of this organization and the mayor of the municipality is in charge of the policy part. The mayor is responsible for the formation of the disaster staff for coordinating policy decisions, and is therefore informed of the situation. The operational coordination structures are formed after deliberation between the various parties on the scene has resulted in a mutual demand for such a coordination structure. In case it is decided to form the operational and/or disaster staff, the operators of the alarm centers start warning the relevant people. For more details on the full coordination structure, see [8].

3   Modeling Method Used

This section describes the language TTL (for Temporal Trace Language) [6] used for expressing dynamic properties as well as the expression of traces. Furthermore, the language meta-TTL is introduced for second-order dynamic properties.

3.1   The Language TTL for Dynamic Properties

In TTL [6], ontologies for states are formalized as sets of symbols in sorted predicate logic. For any ontology Ont, the ground atoms form the set of *basic state properties* BSTATPROP(Ont). Basic state properties can be defined by nullary predicates (or proposition symbols) such as hungry, or by using n-ary predicates (with n>0) like has_temperature(environment, 7). The *state properties* based on a certain ontology Ont are formalized by the propositions (using conjunction, negation, disjunction, implication) made from the basic state properties and constitute the set STATPROP(Ont).

In order to express dynamics in TTL, important concepts are *states*, *time points*, and *traces*. A *state* S is an indication of which basic state properties are true and which are false, i.e., a mapping S: BSTATPROP(Ont) → {true, false}. The set of all possible states for ontology Ont is denoted by STATES(Ont). Moreover, a fixed *time frame* T is assumed which is linearly ordered. Then, a *trace* γ over a state ontology Ont and time frame T is a mapping γ : T → STATES(Ont), i.e., a sequence of states $γ_t$ (t ∈ T) in STATES(Ont). The set of all traces over ontology Ont is denoted by TRACES(Ont).

The set of *dynamic properties* DYNPROP(Ont) is the set of temporal statements that can be formulated with respect to traces based on the state ontology Ont in the following manner. Given a trace γ over state ontology Ont, a certain state at time point t is denoted by state(γ, t). These states can be related to state properties via the formally defined satisfaction relation, indicated by the infix predicate |=, comparable to the Holds-predicate in the Situation Calculus. Thus, state(γ, t) |= p denotes that state property p holds in trace γ at time t. Likewise, state(γ, t) |≠ p denotes that state property p does not hold in trace γ at time t. Based on these statements, dynamic properties can be formulated in a formal manner in a sorted predicate logic, using the usual logical connectives such as ¬, ∧, ∨, ⇒, and the quantifiers ∀, ∃ (e.g., over traces, time and state properties). For example, consider the following dynamic property for a pattern concerning belief creation based on observation:

if	at any point in time t1 the agent observes that the situation is a disaster,
then	there exists a time point t2 after t1 such that
	at t2 in the trace the agent believes that the situation is a disaster

This property can be expressed as a dynamic property in TTL form with free variable γ as follows:

$$\forall t{:}T \; [\; state(\gamma, t) \models observes(itsadisaster) \Rightarrow \exists t' \geq t \; state(\gamma, t') \models belief(itsadisaster) \;]$$

The set DYNPROP(Ont, γ) is the subset of DYNPROP(Ont) consisting of formulae with γ occurring in which is either a constant or a variable without being bound by a quantifier. For a more elaborate explanation of TTL, see [6].

3.2 The Language Meta-TTL for Second-Order Dynamic Properties

The formalizations of the properties sometimes take the form of second-order dynamic properties, i.e., properties that refer to dynamic properties expressed within TTL. Such second-order dynamic properties are expressed in meta-TTL: the meta-language of TTL. The language meta-TTL includes sorts for DYNPROP(Ont) and its subsets as indicated above, which contain TTL-statements (for dynamic properties) as term expressions. Moreover, a predicate holds on these sorts can be used to express that such a TTL formula is true. When no confusion is expected, this predicate can be left out. To express second-order dynamic properties, in a meta-TTL statement, quantifiers over TTL statements can be used.

4 Handling Incompleteness of Information by Enrichment Rules

The trace of occurrences as logged during or reported from an incident management process usually is incomplete and therefore difficult to analyze. To overcome this incompleteness problem, additional assumptions have to be made on events that have occurred but are not explicitly mentioned in the logged trace. Such assumptions are addressed in this section. These extra assumptions enrich the trace with elements that are derived from the information in the trace itself, for example at later time points in case an analysis is performed afterwards. An example is the assumption that if at some time point an estimation of the situation is communicated, then at previous time points the necessary information to make that assessment was received or observed by the communicating role.

Addition of such elements to enrich a trace are based on rules which express that given certain trace elements, an additional element can be assumed. These rules in principle can be of two forms: Strict rules which can always be applied and provide conclusions that are certain, and defeasible rules which are used in case strict rules are insufficient to obtain a trace with a reasonable amount of information. However, it is not always possible to claim that a rule is a strict rule. Therefore, such rules are considered premises for the whole analysis.

Examples of such rules are presented below. Rule EP1 states that everybody present on the scene is assumed to have an internal judgment about the seriousness of the disaster:

EP1: **Internal judgment at scene**

if	at time t role R is present at the scene
and	situation S is the case
and	S is classified as being a disaster
then	there exists a later point in time t2 < t+d at which R has an internal judgment that this situation is a disaster

Formal:

∀ R:ROLE, t:TIME, S:SITUATION
[state(γ, t) |= physical_position(R, scene) &
state(γ, t) |= current_situation(S) &
state(γ, t) |= disaster(S)]
⇒ ∃t2>t & t2 < t+d [state(γ, t2) |= internal_judgment(R, disaster(S))]

Furthermore, in case a role receives a communication that the situation is a disaster and this role does not communicate that he does not believe it being a disaster, then it is assumed that he has the internal judgment that it concerns a disaster:

EP2: **Internal judgment based on communication**

if	at time t R1 communicates to R2 that the current situation S is a disaster
and	there exists no time point at which R2 communicates to R1 he thinks the situation is not a disaster
then	at every time point t2 > t R2 interprets the current state of affairs as being a disaster

∀R1,R2:ROLE, P:POSITION, t:TIME, S:SITUATION
[state(γ, t) |= communication_from_to(R1, R2, disaster(S)) &
¬∃t'>t [state(γ, t') |= communication_from_to(R2, R1, not(disaster(S)))]]
⇒ ∀t2 > t [state(γ, t2) |= internal_judgment(R2, disaster(S))]

5 Property Hierarchies for Incident Management Organizations

This section presents generic properties for incident management organizations in the Netherlands. The properties are presented in property hierarchies, which has as an advantage that diagnosis of properties can be done in a top down fashion. Such a diagnostic process starts by checking highest level property, and in case such a property is not satisfied pinpoints the error by gradually going down the tree to the unsatisfied properties.

5.1 Warning of Relevant Parties

The warning of relevant parties by the operator is a high level property stating that: "the operator should alarm all necessary parties in case it is informed of an incident":

P1(d): **Warn relevant parties**

if	at time t the operator is informed about an incident type I by a role R1,
and	for incident type I role R2 should be informed according to the disaster plan
then	there exists a time t2 later than t and before t + d at which R2 is informed about the incident type I

∀I:INCIDENT_TYPE, t:TIME, R1, R2:ROLE
[state(γ, t) |= communication_from_to(R1, operator, I) &
 state(γ, t) |= according_to_plan_should_be_involved_in(R2, I)]
 ⇒ ∃t2 > t & t2 < t + d [state(γ, t2) |= communication_from_to(operator, R2, I)]]

This property can be refined into a number of similar properties restricted to specific categories of roles that should be informed. For diagnosis, at the highest level property P1(d) can be checked, for example with the result that P1(d) is not satisfied which means that not all relevant parties were informed (but without information on which specific categories were not informed). At one level lower, the diagnosis can be refined by checking the refined properties, resulting in an indication of which of the categories of relevant roles were not informed.

5.2 First Arriving Ambulance

Second, the behavior of the first arriving ambulance is addressed. First, a formal definition of the first arriving ambulance is given:

first_arriving_ambulance(γ:TRACE, t:TIME, A:AMBULANCE)
An ambulance is the first arriving ambulance if:
the ambulance arrives at the scene of an incident at time t
and there does not exist a time t' < t at which another ambulance arrived at the scene of the incident

[state(γ, t) |=physical_position(A, scene) & ¬∃t'< t, [∃B:AMBULANCE [state(γ, t') |=physical_position(B, scene)]]]

On the highest level, the first arriving ambulance behavior is described by three important aspects: (1) signaling the green alarm light; (2) communicating a situation report, and (3) presence of at least one person belonging to the ambulance until the officer on duty arrives at the scene:

P2: First arriving ambulance global behavior
if	at a time t ambulance A is the first to arrive at the scene
and	at time t3 > t the officer on duty arrives at the scene
then	for all t2 ≥ t and t2 < t3 at least one person belonging to the ambulance should be present at the ambulance
and	for all t4 ≥ t the ambulance is signaling the green alarm light
and	there exists a time t5 later than t at which the driver of that ambulance communicates a correct interpretation of the situation to the operator.

∀A:AMBULANCE, t, t2:TIME
[first_arriving_ambulance(γ, t, A) &
state(γ, t2) |= physical_position(officer_on_duty, scene) &
¬∃t'''< t2 [state(γ, t''') |= physical_position(officer_on_duty, scene)]]
⇒
∀t3 < t2
   [t3 ≥ t ⇒ [∃R:ROLE [state(γ, t3) |= physical_position(R, A)]]]
& ∀t4 > t [state(γ, t4) |= alarm_lights(A, green)]
& ∃t5 > t, X:SITUATION[state(γ, t5) |= communication_from_to(driver, operator, situation_description(X)) &
                        situation(X)]]

This property can be related to lower level properties as shown in Figure 1. When trying to diagnose why the highest level property is not satisfied, the properties on the lower level can be checked. In case such a property is not satisfied, and it concerns a leaf property, at least one cause for the non-fulfillment of the high-level property has been found. Otherwise, go further down the tree to find the cause. In the tree a number of

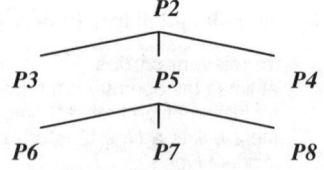

Fig. 1. Property hierarchy for the first arriving ambulance

properties are present to enable satisfaction of P2. First of all, the signaling of the green light, as expressed below.

P3: First ambulance green light behavior
if at a time t ambulance A is the first to arrive at the scene
then for all later points in time t2 the ambulance is signaling the green light.

∀A:AMBULANCE, t:TIME
[first_arriving_ambulance(γ, t, A) ⇒ ∀t2:TIME > t [state(γ, t2) |= alarm_lights(A, green)]]

Second, the presence of a person belonging to the ambulance for the time until the officer on duty is present:

P4: First arriving ambulance personnel presence
if at a time t ambulance A is the first to arrive at the scene
and at time t3 > t the officer on duty arrives at the scene
then for all t2 ≥ t and t2 < t3 at least one person belonging to the ambulance should be present at the ambulance

∀A:AMBULANCE, t, t2:TIME
[first_arriving_ambulance(γ, t, A) &
state(γ, t2) |= physical_position(officer_on_duty, scene) &
¬∃t'''< t2 [state(γ, t''') |= physical_position(officer_on_duty, scene)]]
⇒ ∀t3 < t2 [t3 ≥ t ⇒ [∃R:ROLE [state(γ, t3) |= physical_position(R, A)]]]

Finally, a property expressing the communication of the correct situation to the operator:

P5(d): First arriving ambulance interpretation
if at a time t ambulance A is the first to arrive at the scene
then at a later point in time t2 < t + d the driver of that ambulance communicates a correct interpretation of the situation

∀A:AMBULANCE, t:TIME
first_arriving_ambulance(γ, t, A)
⇒ ∃X:SITUATION, t2:TIME < t + d & t2>t
  state(γ, t2) |= physical_position(driver, A) &
  state(γ, t2) |= communication_from_to(driver, operator, situation_description(X)) &
  state(γ, t2) |= situtation(X)]

Note that parameter d includes the time to interpret the situation plus the time to start communicating that particular interpretation. Testing whether the interpretation was correct can be performed afterwards (e.g., the amount of casualties). The property P5 can be refined again into three lower level properties. First of all, when arriving at the scene, the paramedic should investigate the current state of affairs:

P6(d): Paramedic investigation
if at a time t ambulance A is the first to arrive at the scene
and at time t a paramedic is in the ambulance
then at a later point in time t2 < t + d the paramedic of that ambulance will start an investigation and not be at the ambulance any more

∀A:AMBULANCE, t:TIME
[first_arriving_ambulance(γ, t, A) &
state(γ, t) |= physical_position(paramedic, A)]]
⇒ ∃t2:TIME < t + d & t2 > t
  [state(γ, t2) |= not physical_position(paramedic, A) & state(γ, t2) |= investigating(paramedic)]

Second, the paramedic will return, communicating the current situation:

P7(d): Paramedic communication
if at a time t ambulance A is the first to arrive at the scene
and at time t the paramedic is in the ambulance

and   at time t2 the physical position of the paramedic is not inside the ambulance
then   at a later point in time t3 < t2 + d the paramedic of that ambulance will communicate a
           correct interpretation of the situation to the driver

∀A:AMBULANCE, t,t2:TIME
[first_arriving_ambulance(γ, t, A) &
 state(γ, t) |= physical_position(paramedic, A) & t2 > t &
 state(γ, t2) |= not physical_position(paramedic, A) &
 state(γ, t2) |= investigating(paramedic)]
⇒ ∃t3:TIME < t2 + d & t3 > t2, X:SITUATION
   [state(γ, t3) |= physical_position(paramedic, A) &
    state(γ, t3) |= communication_from_to(paramedic, driver, situation_description(X)) &
    state(γ, t3) |= situtation(X)]

Finally, once the driver has received the communication, he will communicate this to
the operator:

P8(d): Driver communication
if   at a time t the driver of the first ambulance at the scene receives a situation description
           from the paramedic
then   at a later point in time t2 < t + d the driver of that ambulance communicates a correct
           interpretation of the situation to the operator

∀A:AMBULANCE, t,t2:TIME, X :SITUATION
[first_arriving_ambulance(γ, t, A) &
 state(γ, t2) |= communication_from_to(paramedic, driver, situation_description(X))
⇒ ∃t3:TIME < t2 + d & t2 > t [state(γ, t3) |= communication_from_to(driver, operator, situation_description(X))]

5.3 Disaster Staff Activation

Furthermore, properties have been specified for the formation of the disaster staff and
activities following from the disaster staff. On the highest level the correctness of these
processes in the disaster staff can be described as follows: In case the operator has the
internal judgment that the current situation is a disaster, the operational leader will
eventually output actions belonging to a strategy communicated by the disaster staff.

P9: Successful disaster staff
if   at time t the operator judges the current situation as a disaster
then   there exists a later point in time t2 at which the disaster staff communicated a strategy
and   there exists an even later time at which the operational leader communicates an action
           appropriate for the strategy according to the disaster plan.

∀t:TIME
[state(γ, t) |= internal_judgement(operator, disaster)
⇒ ∃t2:TIME > t, S:STRATEGY
   [state(γ, t2) |= communication_from_to(disaster_staff, operational_leader, S) &
    ∃t3:TIME > t2, A:ACTION, R:ROLE
    [state(γ, t3) |= appropriate_action_according_to_plan(S, A) &
     state(γ, t3) |= accompanying_role(A, R)] &
     state(γ, t3) |= communication_from_to(operational_leader, R, perform(A))]

Such properties can be related to lower-level properties as shown in Figure 2. On the
intermediate level, three properties are present. First, the correct initiation of a disaster
staff is expressed:

P10: Correctly activated disaster staff
if   at time t the operator interprets the current situation being a disaster
then   at a later point in time t2 the disaster staff will be informed (and assumed to be present
           as a result)

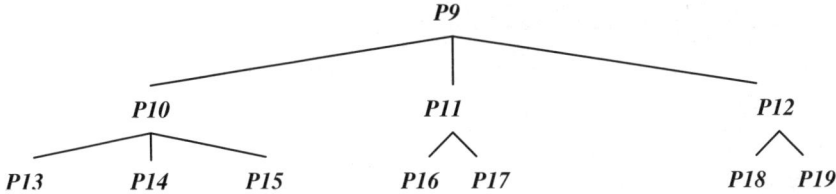

Fig. 2. Property hierarchy for the disaster staff activation and functioning

∀t:TIME, R:ROLE
[state(γ, t) |= internal_judgement(operator, disaster) &
state(γ, t) |= part_of(R, disaster_staff)
⇒ ∃t2:TIME > t + d [state(γ, t2) |= communication_from_to(operator, R, form_disaster_staff)]]

Thereafter, in case the disaster staff is formed, it should be active, which is characterized by an output in the form of a strategy:

P11: Active disaster staff
if   at time t the organizational unit called disaster staff is informed
then   at a later point in time t2 > t the organizational unit outputs a strategy S

∀t:TIME
[state(γ, t2) |= part_of(R, disaster_staff) &
state(γ, t2) |= communication_from_to(operator, R, form_disaster_staff)
⇒ ∃S:STRATEGY, t2 > t [state(γ, t2) |= communication_from_to(disaster_staff, operational_leader, S)]]

Finally, such a strategy should lead to actions be taken by the operational leader:

P12: Active operational leader
if   at time t the operational leader is informed of a strategy S to be applied
then   at a later point in time t2 > t the operational leader will command the appropriate actions according to the disaster plan to the roles.

∀t:TIME, S:STRATEGY, A:ACTION, R:ROLE
[state(γ, t2) |= communication_from_to(disaster_staff, operational_leader, S) &
state(γ, t) |= appropriate_action_according_to_plan (S, A) &
state(γ, t) |= accompanying_role(A, R)
⇒ ∃t2:TIME > t state(γ, t2) |= communication_from_to(operational_leader, R, perform(A))]

Each of these intermediate properties can again be split up to properties for individual roles within the organization. In order to obtain property P10 a number of properties need to hold. First of all, the mayor should be warned by the operator:

P13(d): Warn mayor
if   at time t the operator interprets the current situation being a disaster
then   at a later point in time t2 > t and t2 < t +d the operator communicates the occurrence of a disaster to the mayor.

∀t:TIME
[state(γ, t) |= internal_judgement(operator, disaster) &
⇒ ∃t2:TIME > t & t2 < t + d [state(γ, t2) |= communication_from_to(operator, mayor, disaster)]

Thereafter, the mayor should decide to form the disaster staff:

P14: Form disaster staff
if   at time point t the mayor interprets the current state of affairs as being a disaster
then   at a later point in time t2 > t the mayor forms the organizational unit called disaster staff

∀t:TIME
[state(γ, t) |= internal_judgement(mayor, disaster) &
¬∃t'< t [state(γ, t') |= internal_judgement(mayor, disaster)] &
⇒ ∃t2 > t [state(γ, t2) |= communication_from_to(mayor, operator, form_disaster_staff)]

Finally, in case the mayor communicates the decision to form the disaster staff, the operator should warn the appropriate parties:

P15(d): Warn rest disaster staff
if   at time t the operator receives the request of the mayor to form the disaster staff
and   role R is part of the disaster staff
then   at a later point in time t2 > t and t2 < t +d the operator communicates to role R that the disaster staff is being formed.

∀t:TIME, R:ROLE
state(γ, t) |= communication_from_to(mayor, operator, form_disaster_staff) &
state(γ, t) |= part_of(R, disaster_staff)
⇒ ∃t2:TIME > t + d [state(γ, t2) |= communication_from_to(operator, R, form_disaster_staff)]]

Regarding the intermediate property P11 the following properties need to hold for satisfaction of the intermediate property. First, after the mayor has decided to form the disaster staff he will eventually request advice from his disaster staff.

P16: Start deliberation
if   at time t the mayor decides to form the disaster staff
then   at a later point in time t2 > t the mayor starts a deliberation within the disaster staff by requesting advice

∀t:TIME
[state(γ, t) |= communication_from_to(mayor, operator, form_disaster)
⇒ ∃t2:TIME > t [state(γ, t2) |= communication_from_to(mayor, disaster_staff, request_advice)]]

After such advice is received, he should choose the appropriate strategy:

P17: Choose strategy
if   at time t starts a deliberation within the disaster staff by requesting advice
then   at a later point in time t2 the mayor communicates a strategy to the operational leader

∀t:TIME
[state(γ, t) |= communication_from_to(mayor, disaster_staff, request_advice)
⇒ ∃S:STRATEGY, t2:TIME > t state(γ, t2) |= communication_from_to(mayor, operational_leader, S)]

Finally, the intermediate property P12 is refined to two other properties. First, the operational leader should discuss the strategy with his operational team:

P18: Choose action
if   at time t the mayor communicates a strategy S to the operational leader
then   at a later point in time t2 > t the operational leader requests his operational team for advice how to implement S

∀t:TIME, S:STRATEGY
[state(γ, t) |= communication_from_to(mayor, operational_leader, S)
⇒
∃ t2:TIME > t state(γ, t2) |= communication_from_to(operational_leader, operational_team, request_advice(S))]

Finally, the operational leader communicates actions to be performed, based on the advices obtained in the discussion.

P19: Communicate action
if   at time t the operational leader request his operational team for advice how to implement S
then   at a later point in time t2 the operational leader will communicate actions appropriate for strategy S according to the disaster plan

∀t:TIME, S:STRATEGY, A:ACTION, R:ROLE
[state(γ, t) |= communication_from_to(operational_leader, operational_team, request_advice(S)) &
state(γ, t) |= appropriate_action_according_to_plan (S, A) &
state(γ, t) |= accompanying_role(A, R)
⇒ ∃ t2:TIME > t state(γ, t2) |= communication_from_to(operational_leader, R, perform(A))]

5.4 Ambulance Routing

Finally, properties are specified regarding ambulance routing. The police should act as follows:

P20: Route plan includes all wounded nests
if   at time t there are n wounded nests
and   at a later time point t2 > t the police communicates details concerning the route to be taken by the ambulances to cpa (the central ambulance post)
then   this communication should contain such a route description that ambulances will be sent to all wounded nests.

∀W:WOUNDED_NEST, R:ROUTE_PLAN, t:TIME
[state(γ, t) |= physical_position(W, scene) &
state(γ, t) |= communication_from_to(police, cpa, R)]
⇒ state(γ, t) |= route_passes_wounded_nest(R, W)

An alternative property not following standard procedure expresses that the routing is done based explicitly on victim locations:

P21: Send ambulance to all wounded on the scene
if   at time t there is a wounded person at a position P
then   at a later time point t2 an ambulance will be sent to position P
and   at an even later time point t3 that ambulance will be at position P

∀W:WOUNDED, P:POSITION, A:AMBULANCE, t:TIME
[state(γ, t) |= physical_position(W, P) &
⇒ ∃t2 > t [state(γ, t2) |= communication_from_to(operator, A, goto(P))] &
∃t3 > t2 [state(γ, t3) |= physical_position(A, P)]

This high-level property can be decomposed into three other properties. First of all, a wounded person will result in a communication to the operator of the physical position of this wounded person:

P22: Communicate wounded location
if   at time t there is a wounded person at a position P
then   at a later time point t2 this position will be communicated to the operator

∀W:WOUNDED, P:POSITION, t:TIME
[state(γ, t) |= physical_position(W, P) &
⇒ ∃R:ROLE, t2 > t [state(γ, t2) |= communication_from_to(R, operator, physical_position(W, P))]]

For every communication received by the operator, he eventually communicates the location to an ambulance:

P23: Send ambulance to wounded
if   at time t a wounded person is communicated to be at a position P
then   at a later time point t2 an ambulance will be sent to position P

∀W:WOUNDED, P:POSITION, R:ROLE, t:TIME
[state(γ, t) |= communication_from_to(R, operator, physical_position(W, P))
⇒ ∃t2 > t, A:AMBULANCE [state(γ, t2) |= communication_from_to(operator, A, goto(P))]]

Finally, once the ambulance gets this communication it will arrive at the location at a later point in time:

P24: Ambulance arrives at wounded

if   at time point t an ambulance is sent to position P

then   at a later time point t2 that ambulance will be at position P

∀P:POSITION, A:AMBULANCE, t:TIME

[state(γ, t2) |= communication_from_to(operator, A, goto(P))

⇒ ∃t2 > t [state(γ, t3) |= physical_position(A, P)

6 Human Error Types

This Section presents a classification scheme for the properties in incident management. Such a classification can help to determine the dedicated training needed. The human error classification presented by James Reason [9] is therefore adopted, who introduces a General Error Modeling approach which identifies three basic error types: (1) skill based slips; (2) rule based mistakes, and (3) knowledge based mistakes. This classification scheme is also used in [2] in which incident management is investigated. Rule based, and knowledge based errors come into play after the individual has become conscious of a problem, which is not the case for skill based slips. In that sense, skill based errors generally precede detection of the problem whereas rule based and skill based mistakes arise during subsequent attempts to find a solution to the problem. Skill based and rule based level error occur when humans use stored knowledge structures whereas knowledge based errors occur when such knowledge structures have been exhausted. Errors are much more likely to occur at the knowledge based level.

For the properties specified for incident management the following classification scheme is used. Skill based properties are those properties that are part of the very basic training of incident management workers. For example, how to start the water pump on a fire truck. A property is classified as a rule based property in case an incident management plan literally includes the property. Finally, a property is called a knowledge based property in case an incident management plan states that a decision needs to be taken, but does not specify how to come to this solution. Using this classification scheme, none of the properties from Section 5 are routine based, whereas properties P1, P3, P5, P6, P8, P13, P14, P15, P16, P19, P22, and P24 are rule based properties. Finally, properties P7, P17, P18, P20, and P23 are knowledge base properties. Note that only the leaf properties are categorized as these are the properties that define the individual role behavior within the organization.

In order to identify which types of error the different participants in the incident management organization are making, the following formula expressed in meta-TTL is used:

Type Error ≡

∀γ:TRACE, t_1, t_2:TIME, A:AGENT, R:ROLE, P:DYNPROP, Q:DYNPROPEXPR, S:SITUATION, X:PROPERTY_TYPE

[holds_in_period(has_role(A, R), γ, t_1, t_2) &

holds_in_period(S, γ, t_1, t_2) &

holds_in_period(relevant_for(P, R, S), γ, t_1, t_2) &

holds_in_period(type_for(P, R, X), γ, t_1, t_2) &

holds_in_period(has_specification(P, Q(R, γ, c_1, c_2)), γ, t_1, t_2) &

¬holds(Q(R, γ, t_1, t_2))]

⇒ makes_error_of_type(A, R, P, X, γ, t_1, t_2)

This expresses that if an agent A is allocated to a particular role R in a particular period between t_1 and t_2 in trace γ, and a situation S occurs in that same period in which property P is relevant for role R whereby the type of property P for role R is of type X (where X is either skill based, rule based or knowledge based), and the property has a specification which does not hold in the fragment of this trace, then an error of type X is made concerning property P by role R played by agent A.

7 Case Study

As a means to validate the approach presented above, a disaster which has been thoroughly investigated in the Netherlands is taken as a case study. The disaster concerns a bar fire which occurred in Volendam, the Netherlands, at New Years Night of the year 2001. The logs of the disaster have been thoroughly described in [7] and have been formalized using the approach presented in Section 3. Thereafter, the trace enrichment rules from Section 4 have been applied. A part of the resulting trace is shown in Figure 3, which uses the same ontology as used for the formalization of the properties in Section 5. On the left side of the Figure, the atoms are shown that occur during the incident management whereas the right side shows a timeline where a dark box indicates an atom being true at that time point and a gray box indicates the atom being false. The trace is used to verify whether the properties as specified in Section 5 indeed hold for the Volendam disaster. The following properties were shown not to hold: P2, P4, P5, P7, P8, P9, P10, P14, and P20. In other words, in the Volendam case study the first ambulance did not comply to the global desired behavior because the information was not communicated properly, and because there exist time points at which nobody was present at the ambulance. Furthermore, the disaster staff was not activated properly because the mayor did not communicate that the disaster staff should be formed, and finally the ambulance routing of the police was incorrect, but luckily the direct routing of the health care services was satisfied. These results exactly comply to the conclusions in the disaster report [7] which resulted from a thorough investigation of a committee specialized in incident management.

8 Discussion

This paper presents an agent-based approach which can be used for error detection in incident management organizations. The approach consists of several parts. First, a formal approach for the specification of both traces and properties that can be verified against these traces is presented. In domains like incident management, traces might be incomplete. Therefore, enrichment rules for these traces are identified to cope with this incompleteness. Furthermore, the properties that ought to be verified against these traces can be specified in a hierarchical fashion: in case the highest level property is not satisfied, the cause of this dissatisfaction can be determined by looking at the properties one level deeper in the tree, which continues until a leaf property is found which is not satisfied. Finally, a classification mechanism is presented for the different properties based on psychological literature. In case an error is observed such a classification immediately gives insight in the functioning of a particular agent playing a role, which enables performing dedicated training sessions or giving appropriate warning messages.

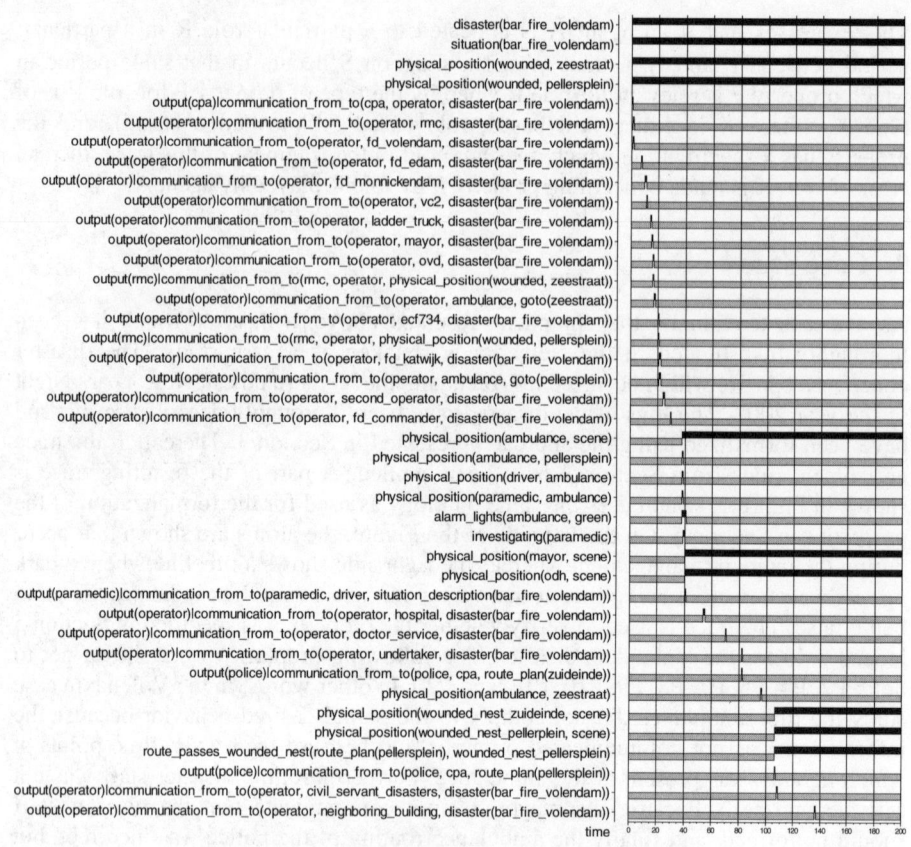

Fig.3. Partial trace of the Volendam case study

In the future, the approach presented can be incorporated in personal agents of people involved in incident management. Such agents automatically log all incoming and outgoing information in the form of traces and have knowledge on the property the particular role the agent is playing is required to fulfill. In case properties are observed not to be satisfied, a reminder or warning can for instance be given to the person. Such agents can be useful for training sessions, as it can be observed what kind of mistakes a person typically makes, but could possibly even be used during actual incident management.

In the field of information agents, support systems have also been developed for incident management (see e.g. [11]). In such systems however, the agents do not check whether errors are made, but simply provide people with information to make sure they are aware of their tasks. This does however not offer a mechanism to detect errors and avoid a chain of unwanted events. Approaches for e.g. detection of protocols (see e.g. [10]), also called overhearing, have been introduced. These approaches are however more focused on recognizing patterns, not on detection of errors.

Error detection itself is another related research field. In [3] behavioral properties for a parallel computing system can be specified, and can be checked on the fly. The properties are however specified as simple sequences of states, whereas the TTL language as used in this paper has the ability to express timing parameters between these states, often a necessity in incident management. In [5] properties for error detection are specified by means of a finite state machine which again does not allow for time parameter specification.

Acknowledgements

The authors wish to thank the anonymous reviewers for their useful comments and the Dutch Ministry of Economic Affairs for funding this research. Finally, the authors would like to thank the Netherlands Institute for Fire Service and Disaster Management for sharing their expertise in the domain of incident management.

References

1. Boissier, O., Dignum, V., Matson, E., Sichman, J. (eds.), Proc. of the 1st Workshop From Organizations to Organization Oriented Programming in MAS (OOOP), 2005.
2. Duin, M.J. van, Learning from Disasters (in Dutch), PhD Thesis, Leiden, 1992.
3. Fromentin, E., Raynal, M., Garg, V.K., and Tomlinson, A., On the Fly Testing of Regular Patterns in Distributed Computations, Information Processing Letters 54:267-274, 1995.
4. Giorgini, P., Müller, J., Odell, J. (eds.), Agent-Oriented Software Engineering IV, LNCS, vol. 2935, Springer-Verlag, Berlin, 2004.
5. Jard, C., Jeron, T., Jourdan, G.V., and Rampon J.X. "A general approach to trace-checking in distributed computing systems", In *Proc. IEEE International Conference on Distributed Ccomputing Systems*, pp. 386-404, Poznan, Poland, June, 1994.
6. Jonker, C.M., Treur, J. Compositional verification of multi-agent systems: a formal analysis of pro-activeness and reactiveness. International. Journal of Cooperative Information Systems, vol. 11, 2002, pp. 51-92.
7. Ministry of the Interior, Investigation Bar Fire New Years Night 2001 (in Dutch), SDU Publishers, The Hague, 2001.
8. Municipality of Amsterdam, Disaster Plan (in Dutch), 2003.
9. Reason, J., Human Error, Cambridge University Press, 1990.
10. Rossi, S., Busetta, P, Towards Monitoring of Group Interactions and Social Roles via Overhearing, In: Klusch, M., Ossowski, S., Kashyap, V., and Unland, R. (eds), Cooperative Information Agents VIII, LNAI 3191, Spinger-Verlag, pp. 47-61, 2004.
11. Storms, P.A.A., Combined Systems: A System of Systems Architecture, In: Proceedings of ISCRAM 2004, pp. 139-144, May 2004, Brussels.
12. Walle, B. van, and Carle, B. (eds.), Proceedings of ISCRAM 2005, 2005.

A Distributed Agent Implementation of Multiple Species Flocking Model for Document Partitioning Clustering

Xiaohui Cui and Thomas E. Potok

Oak Ridge National Laboratory
Oak Ridge, TN 37831-6085
{Cuix, potokte}@ornl.gov

Abstract. The Flocking model, first proposed by Craig Reynolds, is one of the first bio-inspired computational collective behavior models that has many popular applications, such as animation. Our early research has resulted in a flock clustering algorithm that can achieve better performance than the K-means or the Ant clustering algorithms for data clustering. This algorithm generates a clustering of a given set of data through the embedding of the high-dimensional data items on a two-dimensional grid for efficient clustering result retrieval and visualization. In this paper, we propose a bio-inspired clustering model, the Multiple Species Flocking clustering model (MSF), and present a distributed multi-agent MSF approach for document clustering.

Keywords: Swarm, Bio-inspired, Clustering, Agent, Flocking, VSM.

1 Introduction

Currently, more and more digital document data is being generated as part of the ubiquitous and pervasive use of computing systems, information systems, and sensor systems. It is a challenge to efficiently and effectively analyze this data. Clustering analysis is a descriptive data mining task, which involves dividing a set of objects into a number of clusters. The motivation behind clustering a set of data is to find inherent structure inside the data and expose this structure as a set of groups [1]. The data objects within each group should exhibit a large degree of similarity while the similarity among different clusters needs be minimal [9]. Document clustering is a fundamental operation used in unsupervised document organization, automatic topic extraction and information retrieval. It provides a structure for organizing a large body of text for efficient browsing and searching. There are two major clustering techniques: partitioning and hierarchical [9]. Many document clustering algorithms can be classified into these two groups. In recent years, it has been recognized that the partitioning techniques are well suited for clustering a large document dataset due to their relatively low computational requirements [18]. The best-known partitioning algorithm is the K-means algorithm and its variants [17]. This algorithm is simple, straightforward and based on the firm foundation of analysis of variances. One drawback of the K-means algorithm is that the clustering result is sensitive to the selection of the initial cluster centroids and may converge to the local optima, instead of the global one. The other limitation of the K-means algorithm is that it generally requires a prior knowledge of the probable number

M. Klusch, M. Rovatsos, and T. Payne (Eds.): CIA 2006, LNAI 4149, pp. 124–137, 2006.
© Springer-Verlag Berlin Heidelberg 2006

of clusters for a document collection. Therefore, there is a demand for more efficient algorithms for document clustering.

New algorithms based on biological models, such as ant colonies, bird flocks, and swarm of bees etc., have been invented to solve problems in the field of computer science. These algorithms are characterized by the interaction of a large number of agents that follow the same rules and exhibit complex, emergent behavior that is robust with respect to the failure of individual agents. The Flocking model is one of the first collective behavior models that have been applied in popular applications, such as animation. In addition to being used to simulate group motion, which has been used in a number of movies and games, The Flocking model has already inspired researches in time varying data visualization [12, 20] and spatial cluster retrieval [6, 7]. In this paper, we propose a bio-inspired clustering model, the Multiple Species Flocking clustering model (MSF), and present a distributed multiple agent MSF approach for dynamic updated text clustering.

The remainder of this paper is organized as follows: Section 2 provides a general overview of the basic Flocking model. A new multiple species flocking (MSF) model is proposed and a MSF model clustering algorithm is described in section 3. In section 4, a Multi-Agent Scheme for Distributed Dynamic Document Clustering is presented. Section 5 provides detailed experimental design, setup and results in comparing the performance of the multi-agent implementation for clustering the dynamic updated document collection on the cluster computer and a single processor computer. Section 6 describes the related works in the traditional and bio-inspired document clustering area. The conclusion is in Section 7

2   Modeling of Flocking Behavior

Social animals or insects in nature often exhibit a form of emergent collective behavior known as *'flocking'*. The Flocking model is a bio-inspired computational model for simulating the animation of a flock of entities. It represents group movement as seen in the bird flocks and the fish schools in nature. In this model, each individual makes its movement decisions on its own according to a small number of simple rules that it reacts to its neighboring members in the flock and the environment it senses. These simple local rules of each individual generate a complex global behavior of the entire flock. The basic Flocking model was first proposed by Craig Reynolds [14], in which he called each individual as "boid". This model consists of three simple steering rules that each boid need to execute at each instance over time: (1) Separation: Steering to avoid collision with other boids nearby; (2) Alignment: Steering toward the average heading and match the velocity of the neighbor flock mates (3) Cohesion: Steering to the average position of the neighbor flock mates.

As shown in Figure 1, in the circled area of Figure 1(a), 1(b) and 1(c), the boid's (located in the center of the small circle with grey background) behavior shows how a boid reacts to other boids' movement in its local neighborhood. The degree of locality is determined by the range of the boid's sensor (The semi-diameter of the big circle). The boid does not react to the flock mates outside its sensor range because a boid steers its movement based only on local information. These rules of Reynolds's boid flocking behavior are sufficient to reproduce natural group behaviors on the computer.

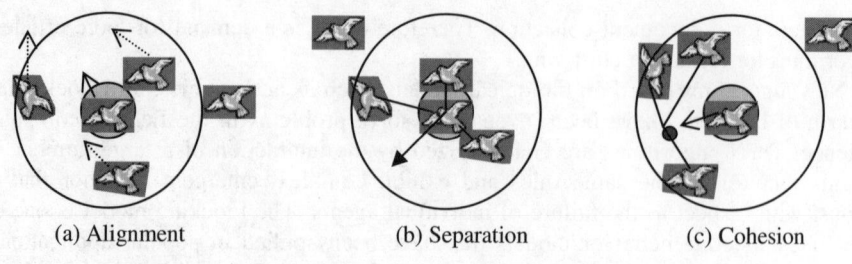

(a) Alignment   (b) Separation   (c) Cohesion

Fig. 1. The three basic rules in the boid

3 The Multiple Species Flocking (MSF) Model

Our early experiments [3] indicate these three rules in Reynolds's flocking model will eventually result in all boids in the simulation forming a single flock. It can not reproduce the real phenomena in the nature: the birds or other herd animals not only keep themselves within a flock that is composed of the same species or the same colony creatures, but also keep two or multiple different species or colony flocks separated. To simulate this nature phenomenon, we propose a new Multiple Species Flocking (MSF) model to model the multiple species bird flock behaviors. In the MSF model, in addition to these three basic action rules in the Flocking model, a fourth rule, the feature similarity rule, is added into the basic action rules of each boids to influence the motion of the boids. Based on this rule, the flock boid tries to stay close to these boids that have similar features and stay away from other boids that have dissimilar features. The strength of the attracting force for similar boids and the repulsion force for dissimilar boids is inversely proportional to the distance between the boids and the similarity value between the boids' features.

In the MSF model, we use the following mathematical equations to illustrate these four action rules for each boid:

Alignment Rule:

$$d(P_x, P_b) \leq d_1 \cap (P_x, P_b) \geq d_2 \Rightarrow \vec{v}_{ar} = \frac{1}{n} \sum_x^n \vec{v}_x . \tag{1}$$

Separation Rule:

$$d(P_x, P_b) \leq d_2 \Rightarrow \vec{v}_{sr} = \sum_x^n \frac{\overline{\vec{v}_x + \vec{v}_b}}{d(P_x, P_b)} . \tag{2}$$

Cohesion Rule:

$$d(P_x, P_b) \leq d_1 \cap (P_x, P_b) \geq d_2 \Rightarrow \vec{v}_{cr} = \sum_x^n (\overrightarrow{P_x - P_b}) . \tag{3}$$

Feature Similarity Rule:

$$v_{ds} = \sum_x^n \frac{(S(B, X) - T) * (\overrightarrow{P_x - P_b})}{d(P_x, P_b)} . \tag{4}$$

where v_{ar}, v_{sr}, v_{cr} and v_{ds} are velocities driven by the four action rules, $d(P_x, P_b)$ is the distance between boid B and its neighbor X, n is the total number of the boid B's local neighbors, v_b and v_x is the velocity of boid B and X, d_1 and d_2 are pre-defined distance values and $d_1 \succ d_2$, $\overrightarrow{P_x - P_b}$ calculates a directional vector point. $S(B,X)$ is the similarity value between the features of boid B and X. T is the threshold for separating similarity and dissimilarity boids.

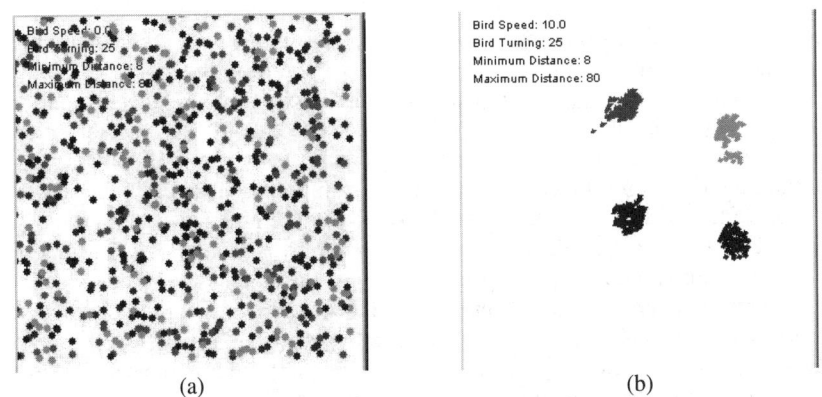

(a)   (b)

Fig. 2. Multiple species bird flocking simulation

To achieve comprehensive flocking behavior, the actions of all four rules are weighted and summed to give a net velocity vector demanded for the active flock boid.

$$v = w_{sr}.v_{sr} + w_{ar}.v_{ar} + w_{cr}.v_{cr} + w_{ds}.v_{ds} \; . \tag{5}$$

where v is the boid's velocity in the virtual space and $w_{sr}, w_{ar}, w_{cr}, w_{ds}, w_{dd}$ are pre-defined weight values.

Figure 2 shows the result of our multiple species bird flock simulation by using multiple agents system in which the MSF model is implemented in each simulation agent. In this simulation, there are four different boid species and each species have 200 boids. We use four different colors, green, red, blue and black, to represent different species. All together, 800 boids are simulated in the environment. At the initial stage, each boid is randomly deployed in the environment as shown in Figure 2(a). Each color dot represents one boid agent. There is no central controller in the simulation. Each boid agent can only sense other boids within a limited range and move in the simulation environment by following these four action rules of the MSF model. Although there is no intention for each boid to form a same species group and to separate different species from each other, after several iterations, as shown in Figure 2(b), the boids in the same species (shown as in same color) are grouped together and different species are separated. This phenomenon represents an emergent clustering behavior.

4   The MSF Clustering Algorithm

The MSF model could offer a new way to cluster datasets. We applied the MSF model to developing a document collection clustering algorithm called MSF Clustering algorithm. The MSF clustering algorithm uses a simple and heuristic way to cluster input data, and at the same time, maps the data to a two-dimensional (2D) surface for easy retrieval and visualization of the clustering result, processing both tasks simultaneously. In the MSF clustering algorithm, we assume each document vector is projected as a boid in a 2D virtual space. Each document vector is represented as a feature of the boid. Following the simple rules in MSF model, each boid determines its movement by itself in the virtual space. Similar to the bird in the real world, the boids that share similar document vector features (same as the bird's species and colony in nature) will automatically group together and became a boid flock. Other boids that have different document vector features will stay away from this flock. In this algorithm, the behavior (velocity) of each boid is only influenced by the nearby boids. The boid's four MSF action rules react to this influence and generate the boid's new moving velocity. Although this influence on each bird is locally, the impacts on the entire boid group is global. After several iterations, the simple local rules followed by each boid results in generating a complex global behavior of the entire document flock, and eventually a document clustering result is emerged.

We evaluated the efficiency of the MSF algorithm and the K-means algorithm on document collection that includes 112 recent news articles collected from the Google news. This news article collection has been categorized by human and manually clustered into 11 categories. For the purpose of comparing, the Ant document clustering [8] and the K-means clustering algorithms were implemented by Java language and applied to the same real document collection dataset, respectively. The K-means algorithm implementation was given the exact clustering result number as the prior knowledge. Our early research [3] shows that the Ant clustering algorithm can not come out any useful result if the algorithm only given a limited number of iteration (300 iterations) for refining the result. In this experiment, each algorithm was given 100 fixed iterations to refine the clustering result and only the MSF clustering algorithm and K-means algorithm can generate reasonable results. As shown in Figure 2(b), the clustering results generated by the MSF clustering algorithm can be easily recognized by human eyes because of their visual characteristic. In our experiments, the clustering result of the MSF clustering algorithm is retrieved by human looking at the visual flock picture that generated by the virtual boids on the screen. We compared the average results of these two algorithms from ten separate experiments. The results of the clustering algorithm were evaluated by comparing it with the prior knowledge of the classification of the document collection. The F-measure was used as the quality measure. The results are listed in Table 1. The results indicate that the flocking algorithm achieves better result compared to the K-means for document clustering although the K-means algorithm has prior knowledge of the exact cluster number.

Table 1. Performance results of the K-means and MSF clustering algorithms

Algorithms	Average cluster result number	Average F-measure value
MSF	9.105	0.7913
K-means	(11)	0.5632

5 Distributed Agent Implementation of MSF Clustering Algorithm

The MSF clustering algorithm can achieve better performance in document clustering than the K-means and the Ant clustering algorithm. This algorithm can continually refine the clustering result and quickly react to the change of individual data. This character enables the algorithm suitable for clustering dynamic changed document information, such as the text information stream. However, the computational requirement for real-time clustering a large amount of text collection is high. In the information society of today, tremendous amounts of text information are continuously accumulated. Inevitably, the MSF clustering algorithm approach of using single processor machine to cluster the dynamic text stream requires a large amount of memory and a faster execution CPU. Since the decentralized character of this algorithm, a distributed approach is a very natural way to improve the clustering speed of this algorithm. In this paper, we present a distributed multi-agent based flocking approach for clustering analysis of dynamic documents and balance the computation load on cluster nodes.

5.1 Distributed Agent Scheme for Document Clustering

In the MSF clustering algorithm, the document parse, similarity measurement and boid moving velocity calculation are the most computational consumption parts. The distributed implementation can divide these computational tasks into smaller pieces that may be scheduled to concurrently run on multiple processors. In order to achieve better performance using distributed computing, several issues must be examined carefully when designing a distributed solution. First is the load balance. It is important to keep load balancing among processing nodes to make sure each node have approximately the same workload. The environment state synchronization is the second issue need to be considered. It is very important for a distributed implementation to develop a synchronization algorithm, which is capable of maintaining causality. Third is reducing the communication between nodes, including communication overhead of the environment state synchronization and control of message exchange between nodes. Based on these requirements, we developed a distributed agent based implementation of the MSF clustering algorithm for clustering analysis of the text datasets. In this distributed agent based implementation, boids are modeled and implemented in terms of agents, which makes boids pro-active, adaptive and communicable. The distributed agent based implementation supports distributed load balance in a very natural way. Since each boid agent is implemented to perform document retrieval, parse, similarity comparison and moving velocity calculation independently, it is straight-forward to have different agents run on different machines to achieve a load balance. Since agent can be added, removed or moved to other machine without interrupting other agent's running, the system can be scalability and pro-activity to the change of work load.

One major concern in designing this distributed agent based MSF implementation is how to ensure agents be synchronized at any time when they must interact or exchange data. In a distributed system, environment information is spread out among the processors involved in the system. An agent doesn't know other agent's information if it is not informed, it has to commute with other agents to collect enough information, does an exhaustive search to find out which agents are located within its range, and calculates the force that it is pushed to travel based on it's neighbor agents' information. All these require that each agent in the system have a global view of other agents' status information. As such, it is necessary to develop a communication schemes to update the agent's information on different processors. One easy communication scheme is broadcast. As shown in Figure 3(a), each agent in the system broadcast its status information to all other agents wherever they are located in the same node or different nodes. Each agent will also use the information it received from other agents' broadcast to find out its neighbor boid mates and calculate the next moving velocity. In this scheme, each agent has a global view of the entire system status. However, the broadcast will use so much bandwidth that makes the network bandwidth in a computer cluster become a bottleneck of the system when the agent number increased. In this report, we proposed an environment status sharing scheme by using location proxy agent. As shown in Figure 3(b), there is a location proxy agent on each node. Each agent will only inform its status to the location proxy agent in the same node. The agent also inquires the location proxy agent to find out its neighbor mates. At every time step, after collecting the status of all agents that located in the same host, location proxy agents will broadcast this information to other proxy agents that located on different nodes, which enable the location proxy agent on each node to have global view of the whole system.

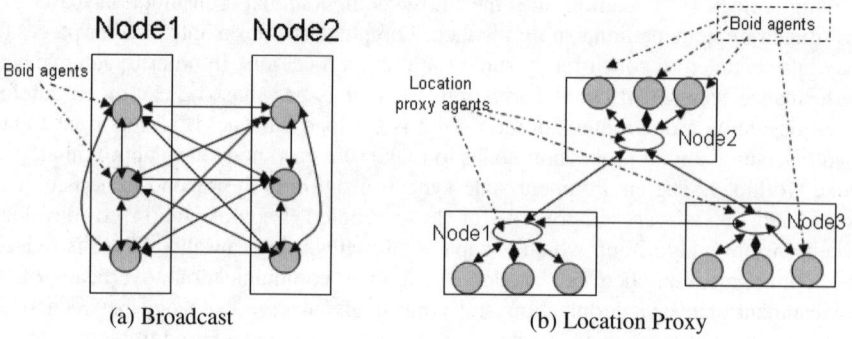

(a) Broadcast   (b) Location Proxy

Fig. 3. The architectures of different communication schemes

5.2 Datasets

The document dataset used in this study is derived from the TREC-5, TREC-6, and TREC-7 collections [10] and represented as a set of vectors $X=\{x_1, x_2, ..., x_n\}$, where the vector x_i corresponds to a single object and is called *"feature vector"* that contains proper features to represent the object. The feature value is represented using the Vector Space Model (VSM) [16]. In this model, the content of a document is formalized as a point in a multi-dimensional space and represented by a vector x, such as $x=\{w_1, w_2, ...w_n\}$, where $w_i(i = 1,2,...,n)$ is the term weight of the term t_i in one document. The term weight value w_i represents the significance of this term in a document. To calculate the term weight, the occurrence frequency of the term within a document and in the entire set of documents needs to be considered. The most widely used weighting scheme combines the Term Frequency with Inverse Document Frequency (TF-IDF) [15]. The TF-IDF weight w_{ij} of term i in document j is given in following equation:

$$w_{ji} = tf_{ji} * idf_{ji} = \log_2(1 + tf_{ji}) * \log_2(\frac{n}{df_{ji}}) .$$

(6)

Where tf_{ji} is the number of occurrences of term i in the document j; df_{ji} indicates the term frequency in the document collections; and n is the total number of documents in the collection.

Calculation of the TF-IDF weight value needs the knowledge of word frequency in the entire document collection and the total number of documents in the collection. If a single document is added or removed from the document collection, the TF-IDF scheme will need recalculate the TF-IDF value of all documents processed. It is difficult to use the TF-IDF scheme to convert streaming textual information into vectors. To address these issues, a modified TF-IDF scheme, Term Frequency / Inverse Corpus Frequency (TF-ICF) [13], is adopted to calculate the term weight value of each term in the document vector. In TF-ICF scheme, the TF portion is same as the TF portion in TF-IDF. The IDF calculation that uses document collection in TF-IDF is replaced with information gathered from a large, static corpus of documents in TF-ICF. The corpus includes more than 250,000 documents that contain almost all of the typically used English words. The weight w_{ij} of term i in the document j can be calculated by the following TF-ICF equation:

$$w_{ji} = \log_2(1 + tf_{ji}) * \log_2(\frac{n+1}{C_i+1}) .$$

(7)

where C_i is the number of documents in the corpus C where term i occurs.

Before translating the document collection into TF-ICF VSM, the very common words (e.g. function words: "a", "the", "in", "to"; pronouns: "I", "he", "she", "it") are stripped out completely and different forms of a word are reduced to one canonical form by using Porter's algorithm [11].

As we indicated in the previous session, the nature of the MSF clustering algorithm enable the algorithm continually refine the clustering results and quickly react to the change of the document contents. This character makes the algorithm suitable for cluster analyzing dynamic changed document information. In this report, the performance of these algorithms on clustering dynamic updated document collections is studied. To simulate the dynamic updated document collection, the document vector of each agent is periodically updated with a new document vector and the old document vector is considered as expired. To easily compare the performance of different scenario, in this study, each agent's document feature will be updated for ten times during the entire life of the system execution. In each experiment, the system will run 1000 cycles and the average document update gap is 100 time-steps.

5.3 Multi-agent Platform

The distributed MSF clustering algorithm is implemented on a (Java Agent DEvelopment Framework (JADE) agent platform. JADE is a software framework fully implemented in the Java language and is a FIPA compliant agent platform. As a distributed agent plate form, the JADE agent can be split on several hosts. The OS on each host is not necessary same. The only required environment is a Java virtual machine (JVM). Each JVM is a basic container of agents that provide a complete run time environment for agents and allow several agents to concurrently execute on the same container, JVM.

5.4 Experimental Design and Results

The simulation experiment in this study is to illustrate the performance enhancement by comparing the run time of executing the MSF clustering distributed agent implementation on a three-node cluster machine and a single processor machine.

In the MSF clustering distributed agent implementation, each boid is implemented as a Jade agent. Each agent has the ability to calculate its moving velocity based on the four actions rules as we discussed in the previous session. Each agent carries a feature vector representing a document vector. The environment used in the experiment consists of a continuous 2D plane, in which boid are placed randomly on a grid within a 4000×4000 squire unit area. All experiments were carried out on an experiment Linux computer cluster machine. The cluster machine consists of one head node, ASER and three cluster nodes, ASER1, ASER2, and ASER3, which are connected with a Gigabit Ethernet switch. Each node contains a single 2.4G Intel Pentium IV processor and 512M memory. To compare the performance, we utilize a *starter* agent that initiates the boid agent process and measures time. The running times for different number of agents is recorded using java's System.currentTimeMillis() method and the unit is milliseconds.

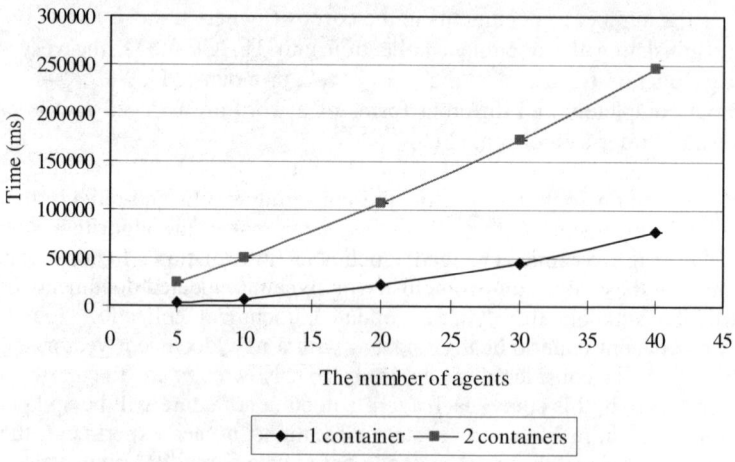

Fig. 4. The running time for boid agents deployed in one JADE container and two JADE containers

JADE allows multiple JADE containers (JVM) running on the same host while agents can be deployed in different containers. Our preliminary experiment is to test the performance impact when the boid agents running in multiple JADE containers. The running time of a different number of boid agents executed in one container or two containers are measured and recorded, separately. The experiment result is shown in Figure 4. As shown in this figure, the running time for the same amount of agents in a single container is much less than that in two containers. The main reason is that the communication between agents located in different JADE containers is much slower than the communication between agents located in the same JADE container. To reduce the communication delay, in the following experiments, all agents located in same host are assigned in the same container. At the same time, to reduce the impact of the JADE system computational requirement, in all simulation experiments, the main JADE system container runs on the head node of the cluster, which is not counted in the simulation nodes. Every simulation experiment will be executed for ten times. Reported results are the average time over 10 simulation runs of 1000 cycle each. The running time does not include the time for starting and finishing agents. It only counts the time consumed during boid agents start moving in the 2D space and stop moving after 1000 cycles.

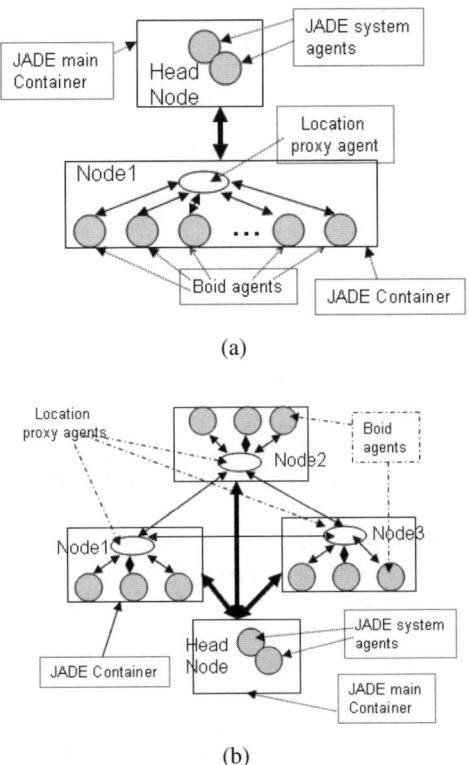

(a)

(b)

Fig. 5. The architecture of the single processor model and the distributed model

In the single processor model, all boid agents are executed on one cluster node. In the distributed model, the boid agents are equally distributed on three nodes, each node has one location proxy agent to collect the agent position and the location proxy agent on each node will exchange agent position information at every step. The architecture of the single processor model and the distributed model are represented in Figure 5(a) and 5(b), respectively. Different numbers of boid agents are tested on both simulation and the boid agent's execution time to finish 1000 circle is recorded. Because the distributed model requires three processes to simulate the document clustering, the time is the average time consumption for all agents running on different node after 1000 cycles. The experiment results are shown in Figure 6. The "Three nodes" curve line in Figure 6 indicates the time consumption of the document clustering simulation executed on the three nodes cluster machine. The "One node" curve line indicates the time consumption of the document clustering simulation executed on the single node machine.

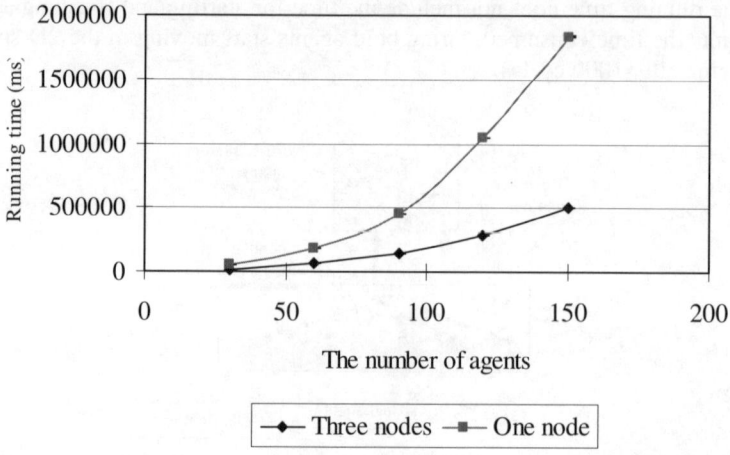

Fig. 6. The running time for 3 node cluster machine and one single processor machine

As shown in Figure 6, when the number of agents is 30, there is no significant difference on consumption time between the three node cluster machine and the single processor machine. When the number of agents is more than 60, it takes the three node cluster machine much less time than the single node machine. Before the total boid agent number reach 120, the three nodes simulation didn't cut the total running time into one third of the total time of the single node machine because of the communication overhead when location proxy agent updating status with other location proxy agents located on the other nodes. However, the running time consumption on the single node machine increases faster than that on the three node machine. Once the total boid agent number researches 120, the time required for running on the single node machine is more than three times of that on the three node machine. One possible reason is each node having limited memory (512M). In single node model, when more than 120 agents running on single node, depending on the documents that these agents represent, the memory requirement for the simulation may be larger than the actual memory of the computer node, which cause the computer system use the virtual memory (hard disk space) and the time requirement for finishing the simulation is largely increased. In the distributed model, the boid agents are evenly deployed on three different cluster nodes. Each node only have one third of the total boid agents and the memory requirement is related smaller than single node model. This will avoid the agent system exceed the node's physical memory limitation.

6 Related Works

To deal with the limitations existed in the traditional partition clustering methods, in recent years, a number of computer scientists have proposed several approaches inspired from biological collective behaviors to solve the clustering problem, such as Genetic Algorithm (GA) [2], Particle Swarm Optimization (PSO) [4, 19], Ant clustering [8, 22] and Self-Organizing Maps (SOM) [21]. Within these clustering algorithms, the Ant clustering algorithm is a partitioning algorithm that does not require a prior knowledge of the probable number to clusters or the initial partition. The Ant clustering algorithm was inspired by clustering of corpses and eggs observed in the real ant colony. Deneubourg et al [5] proposed a "Basic Model" to explain the ants' behavior of piling corpses and eggs. In their study, a population of ant-like agents randomly moved in a 2D grid. Each agent only follows one simple rule: randomly moving in the grid and establishing a probability of picking up the data object it meets if it is free of load or establishing a probability of dropping down the data object if it is loading the data object. After several iterations, a clustering result emerges from the collective activities of these agents. Wu [22] and Handl [8] proposed the use of the Ant clustering algorithms for document clustering and declared that the clustering results from their experiments are much better than those from the K-means algorithm. However, in the Ant clustering algorithm, clustered data objects do not have mobility by themselves. The movements of data objects have to be implemented through the movements of a small number of ant agents, which will slow down the clustering speed. Since each ant agent, carrying an isolated data object, does not communicate with other ant agents, it does not know the best location to drop the data object. The ant agent has to move or jump randomly in the grid space until it finds a place that satisfies its object dropping criteria, which usually consumes a large amount of computation time. In this paper, we present a novel MSF clustering approach for document clustering analysis. Similar as the Ant clustering algorithm, the MSF clustering algorithm is a partitioning algorithm and does not require a prior knowledge of the cluster number in the datasets. It generates a clustering of a given set of data through projecting of the high-dimensional data items on a two-dimensional grid for easy retrieval and visualization of the clustering result. However, the MSF clustering algorithm is more efficient than the Ant clustering algorithm because each document object in the collection is projected as an agent moving in a virtual space, and each agent's moving activity is heuristic as opposed to the random activity in the Ant clustering algorithm.

7 Conclusion

In this study, we proposed a new multiple species flocking (MSF) model and presented a distributed multi-agent approach for the MSF clustering algorithm. In this algorithm, each document in the dataset is represented by a boid agent. Each agent follows four simple local rules to move in the virtual space. Agents following these simple local rules emerge complex global behaviors of the whole flock and eventually the agents that carrying document belong to the same class will gradually merge together to form a flock. All agents are evenly deployed on different nodes in a distributed computing environment for load balancing purposes. On each node, a location proxy agent is introduced for maintaining the agents' location and synchronizing the status between nodes in the cluster machine.

The advantage of the MSF clustering algorithm is the heuristic principle of the flock's searching mechanism. This heuristic searching mechanism helps bird agents quickly form a flock and reactive to the change of any individual document. Since the bird agent in the algorithm continues fly in the virtual space and join the flock it belongs to, new results can be quickly re-generated when the information stream is continually feed into the system.

Acknowledgments. Prepared by Oak Ridge National Laboratory, P.O. Box 2008, Oak Ridge, Tennessee 37831-6285, managed by UT-Battelle, LLC, for the U.S. Department of Energy under contract DE-AC05-00OR22725.

References

1. Anderberg, M.R.: Cluster Analysis for Applications. Academic Press, Inc., New York (1973)
2. Casillas, A., De Gonzalez Lena, M.T., Martinez, R.: Document clustering into an unknown number of clusters using a genetic algorithm. 6th International Conference, TSD 2003, Sep 8-12 2003, Vol. 2807. Springer Verlag, Heidelberg, D-69121, Germany, Ceske Budejovice, Czech Republic 43-49
3. Cui, X., Gao, J., Potok, T.E.: A Flocking Based Algorithm for Document Clustering Analysis. Journal of System Architecture (2006)
4. Cui, X., Potok, T.E.: Document Clustering Analysis Based on Hybrid PSO+K-means Algorithm. Journal of Computer Sciences Special Issue (2005) 27-33
5. Deneubourg, J.L., Goss, S., SendovaFranks, N., Detrain, C., Chretien, L.: The dynamics of collective sorting robot-like ants and ant-like robots. Proceedings of the first international conference on simulation of adaptive behavior on From animals to animats. MIT Press, Cambridge, MA, USA 356-363
6. Folino, G., Forestiero, A., Spezzano, G.: Discovering clusters in spatial data using swarm intelligence. 7th European Conference, ECAL 2003, Sep 14-17 2003, Vol. 2801. Springer Verlag, Heidelberg, Germany, Dortmund, Germany 598-605
7. Folino, G., Spezzano, G.: Sparrow: A Spatial Clustering Algorithm using Swarm Intelligence. 21st IASTED International Multi-Conference on Applied Informatics, Feb 10-13 2003, Vol. 21. Int. Assoc. of Science and Technology for Development, Calgery - Alberta, T3B OM6, Canada, Innsbruck, Austria 50-55

8. Handl, J., Knowles, J., Dorigo, M.: Ant-based clustering and topographic mapping. Artificial Life **12** (2006) 35-61
9. Jain, A.K., Murty, M.N., Flynn, P.J.: Data clustering: a review. ACM Computing Surveys 31 (1999) 264-323
10. NIST: TREC (Text Retrieval Conference). http://trec.nist.gov (1999)
11. Porter, M.F.: An algorithm for suffix stripping. Program 14 (1980) 130-137
12. Proctor, G., Winter, C.: Information flocking: data visualisation in virtual worlds using emergent behaviours. Virtual Worlds First International Conference, VW'98 Proceedings, 1-3 July 1998. Springer-Verlag, Paris, France 168-176
13. Reed, J.: TF-ICF: A New Term Weighting Scheme for Clustering Dynamic Data Streams. Technical Report. Oak Ridge National Laboratory (2006)
14. Reynolds, C.W.: Flocks, Herds, and Schools: A Distributed Behavioral Model. Computer Graphics (ACM) 21 (1987) 25-34
15. Salton, G., Buckley, C.: Term-weighting approaches in automatic text retrieval. Information Processing & Management 24 (1988) 513-523
16. Salton, G., Wong, A., Yang, C.S.: A vector space model for automatic indexing. Cornell Univ., Ithaca, NY, USA (1974) 34
17. Selim, S.Z., Ismail, M.A.: K-Means-Type Algorithms: A Generalized Convergence Theorem and Characterization of Local Optimality. IEEE Transactions on Pattern Analysis and Machine Intelligence PAMI-6 (1984) 81-87
18. Steinbach, M., Karypis, G., Kumar, V.: A comparison of document clustering techniques. KDD Workshop on Text Mining
19. Van D. M., D.W., Engelbrecht, A.P.: Data clustering using particle swarm optimization. 2003 Congress on Evolutionary Computation, 8-12 Dec. 2003, Vol. Vol.1. IEEE, Canberra, ACT, Australia 215-220
20. Vande Moere, A.: Information flocking: time-varying data visualization using boid behaviors. Proceedings. Eighth International Conference on Information Visualization, 14-16 July 2004. IEEE Comput. Soc, London, UK 409-414
21. Vesanto, J., Alhoniemi, E.: Clustering of the self-organizing map. IEEE Transactions on Neural Networks 11 (2000) 586-600
22. Wu, b., Shi, Z.: A clustering algorithm based on swarm intelligence. 2001 International Conferences on Info-tech and Info-net. Proceedings, 29 Oct.-1 Nov. 2001, Vol. vol.3. IEEE, Beijing, China 58-66

Coverage Density as a Dominant Property of Large-Scale Sensor Networks

Osher Yadgar[1] and Sarit Kraus[2]

[1] SRI International, 333 Ravenswood Avenue Menlo Park, CA 94025-3493, USA
yadgar@ai.sri.com
[2] Bar Ilan University, Ramat Gan, Israel
sarit@cs.biu.ac.il

Abstract. Large-scale sensor networks are becoming more present in our life then ever. Such an environment could be a cellular network, an array of fire detection sensors, an array of solar receptors, and so on. As technology advances, opportunities arise to form large-scale cooperative systems in order to solve larger problems in an efficient way. As more large-scale systems are developed, there is a growing need to (i) measure the hardness of a given large-scale sensor network problem, (ii) compare a given system to other large-scale sensor networks in order to extract a suitable solution, (iii) predict the performance of the solution, and (iv) derive the value of each system property from the desired performance of the solution, the problem constraints, and the user's preferences.

The following research proposes a novel system term, the *coverage density*, to define the hardness of a large-scale sensor network. This term can be used to compare two instances of large-scale sensor networks in order to find the suitable solutions for a given problem. Given a *coverage density* of a system, one may predict the solution performance and use it jointly with the preference and the constraints to derive the value of the system's properties.

1 Introduction

On December 2, 2004, tsunami waves hitting the shores of Sri Lanka, India, Indonesia, and Thailand caused a loss of 300,000 lives and a tremendous tragedy for millions. Using current technology, sensors in the ocean could have sensed the creation and advancement of tsunami waves. A well-organized and well-managed network of such sensors using wireless communication could have produced an alarm that would have alerted control centers spread along the shores of the four countries. This alarm could have saved the lives of many of the victims. Studying the role of the different properties of such large-scale agent systems and tuning them according to the system constraints is in the core of this work. We will refer to large-scale agent systems capable of sensing objects as *large-scale sensor networks*.

Large-scale agent systems focus on the behavior of multiagent systems with many agents. As this is a relatively new research area, the number of agents

M. Klusch, M. Rovatsos, and T. Payne (Eds.): CIA 2006, LNAI 4149, pp. 138–152, 2006.

needed to consider a multiagent system as a large-scale agent system has not yet been defined [28]. It became clear to us that researchers do not tend to refer to scale of large scale agent system by means other than the number of agents. Researchers may discuses system properties, but never include them as part of their large scale agent system definition. We claim that this system property is misleading. In this paper we prove that claim and suggest a better system property. We will introduce the *coverage density* and will show how this large-scale sensor network property can be used to predict the performance of a given instance of a large-scale agent system capable of sensing objects.

In the next section we survey related work. We will then introduce the *coverage density* term as a tool for classifying large-scale sensor network. Next we will demonstrate how to use the *coverage density* to predict the performance of a large-scale sensor network and to choose the values of the system properties. A simulator based on our previous work on large-scale sensor networks' architecture and challenges will be introduced. We will then report simulation results of a total of 50 years of CPU time examining hundreds of thousands of different agents and goals. We will conclude by showing how these results establish our claim that *coverage density* is a dominant property of large-scale sensor networks.

2   Related Work

Focusing on the number of agents forming large-scale agent system, the research community holds different opinions about how many agents may form a large-scale agent system. In some cases, thousands of agents are considered to be a large-scale agent system [7], [22], while in other cases hundreds compose such a system [3], [4], [23], [24] and there are even cases where only dozens of agents are considered to be a large-scale system [13].

We suggest that certain large-scale agent systems, i.e. large-scale sensor networks, should be measured relative to their context, such as the size of their problem space, and not simply by the number of participating agents.

Recent technology has made small low-cost devices available to build sensor networks [5], [8], [9], [10], [11], [27]. Wireless sensor networks benefit from technology advances in micro-electro-mechanical systems (MEMS) [25]. These advances have facilitated the development of low-cost simple wireless sensors. Combining the information gathered from thousands of such sensors is a very difficult problem [12]. However, solving this problem may lead to an efficient way of producing global information. As we have witnessed, such information could save lives. We will use the *coverage density* property to support this technological development. *Coverage density* may be used to (i) measure the hardness of a given large-scale sensor network problem, (ii) compare a given system to other large-scale sensor networks in order to extract a suitable solution, (iii) predict the performance of the solution, and (iv) derive the value of each system property from the desired performance of the solution, the problem constraints, and the user's preferences.

The term *sensor coverage* is traditionally used to denote the effectiveness of a sensor network [1], [15], [16], [17], [18], [14], [26]. Previous studies have shown that increasing the The *sensor coverage* increases the number of tracked objects. Gage [6] defines the coverage as a "spatial relationship that adapts to specific local conditions to optimize the performance of some function". Gage distinguishes between three basic types of coverage behavior: blanket coverage, where the objective is to achieve a static arrangement of sensors that maximizes the detection rate of targets appearing within the coverage area; barrier coverage, where the objective is to achieve a static arrangement of sensors that minimizes the probability of undetected targets passing through a barrier; and sweep coverage, where the objective is to move a group of elements across a coverage area to balance between maximizing the detection rate and minimizing the number of missed detections. Gage specifies that a sweep is equivalent to a moving barrier. The *coverage density* is different from the *sensor coverage*. The *coverage density* considers the many properties of a given system and is related to the problem space and time as well as to single-agent characteristics, while *sensor coverage* is related only to the geometrical alignment of the sensors.

3   The Coverage Density

Many properties influence the-scale and the hardness of a given problem. When designing a solution for a large-scale sensor network problem the different aspects of the system's properties should be considered. Properties such as the number of agents and the quality of the sensors, may be related to each other. For instance, given a limited budget, the system designer should consider whether to use many cheap sensors or a small number of expensive sensors. A classifying tool, the *coverage density*, is proposed to classify large-scale sensor networks and to predict the performance of different property configurations. This predicting tool can be used to design the system in order to meet imposed constraints such as budget limitations, battery supply, or technological constraints. The *coverage density* defines the time it takes to cover an area equal to the size of the controlled zone. The following definition formalizes this notation:

Definition 1. *i. let A be a set of n agents such that $A = \bigcup_{i \in N} a_i$ whereas $N = \{0, 1, ..., n-1\}$.*

ii. let $w_{a_i}(t)$ be the area covered by the sensor of agent a_i at a given time t. The agent may detect objects in this area at time t.

The measurement units of the area are square meters.

iii. Let agent coverage, $\overline{w_{a_i}}$, be the average area covered by the sensor of agent a_i such that $\overline{w_{a_i}} = \frac{\int w_{a_i}(t) \cdot dt}{\int dt}$.

The measurement units of the agent coverage are $\frac{square\ meters}{second}$.

iv. Let total coverage, $\overline{W_A}$, be the average area covered by the sensors of all the agents such that $\overline{W_A} = \sum_0^{n-1} \overline{w_{a_i}}$.

The measurement units of the total coverage are $\frac{square\ meters}{second}$.

v. *Let Z be the size of the controlled area.*

vi. *Coverage density ρ is the total coverage divided by the size of the controlled area such that $\rho = \frac{W_A}{Z}$.*

The measurement units of the coverage density, ρ, are $\frac{1}{second}$.

The *coverage density* denotes the amount of the controlled area that can be covered rather than the area that is actually covered. There may be an overlap of agent coverage such that, for example, a value of 100% *coverage density* does not reflect coverage of all the controlled area. A *coverage density* of 100% will result in full coverage only when the sensors have no overlapping coverage. We do not require such a constraint in sensor alignment.

4   Using the Coverage Density

To examine the role of the *coverage density* on large-scale sensor networks we used our hierarchical large-scale agent system architecture, the Distributed Dispatcher Manager (DDM) [19], [20], [21], and applied it to the Autonomous Negotiating Teams (ANTs) [2] problem.

4.1   The DDM Hierarchy

The DDM is designed for efficient coordinated resource management in large-scale agent systems; the model makes use of a hierarchical group formation to restrict the degree of communication between agents and to guide processes in order to very quickly combine partial information to form a global assessment. Each level narrows the uncertainty based on the data obtained from lower levels. DDM organizes the sensing agents in teams, each with a distinguished team leader agent. A team is assigned to a specific sector of interest. Each such agent can act autonomously within its assigned sector of interest while processing local data. Teams are themselves grouped into larger teams. Communication is restricted to flow only between an agent (or team) and its team leader agent. Each team leader is provided with an algorithm to integrate information obtained from its team members. Each individual information-collecting agent can extend its local information through the application of causal knowledge. The causal knowledge may be inaccurate and noisy, and therefore it only constrains the set of possible solutions that could be associated with a collection of data measurements.

In some cases naive distribution of thousands of agents will not be efficient, thus a load balancing mechanism may be required. Therefore, a load balancing mechanism is applied to the hierarchical architecture of the DDM. This mechanism dynamically balances the ratio between agents and goals throughout the controlled area. While applying the load balancing mechanism, the DDM strives to balance the ratio between agents and goals in each hierarchy level from the top down. Each level directs only its immediate subordinate level. The directed level, then, directs its own immediate subordinate level and so on. We will refer to DDM activating the load balancing algorithm as LB and to DDM not activating the load balancing algorithm as NLB.

4.2   The ANTs Challenge

We developed a simulator to study large-scale problems associated with the application of DDM. The ANTs challenge [2] was chosen as the test case of DDM, and simulated Doppler radars were selected as sensors. The key task of the ANTs challenge is to detect and track moving objects while using low-cost hardware. The simulation consists of an area of a fixed size in which Doppler sensors attempt to extract the object state functions of moving targets. Doppler sensors are attached to mobile agents named samplers. The ANTS program uses Doppler sensors that may activate its beam in three different directions. According to the ANTS specific Doppler radar, only one direction may be activated at a time. The orientations of the beams are 0, 120 and 240 degrees. Each of these sensors may move and spin around its center. Given a measurement of a Doppler radar the target is located based on the following equation:

$$R_i^2 = \frac{k \cdot e^{\frac{-(\theta_i - \beta)^2}{\sigma}}}{\eta_i} \tag{1}$$

Where, for each sensed target, i, R_i is the distance between the sensor and i; θ_i is the angle between the sensor and i; η_i is the measured amplitude of i; β is the sensor beam angle; and k and σ are characteristics of the sensors and influence the shape of the sensor detecting area.

A sampler agent may sense targets only when it is not moving. While sensing, a sampler agent may detect targets located within a short distance from it. We refer to this distance as the *range of interaction*. The number of sampler agents, the time spent on detection versus the time spent on movement, and the range of interaction characterize the system. As we will see, these characteristics determine the quality of the solution. Balancing these characteristics results in a desired system quality under given limitations, such as budget.

5   Experiments

One hundred and fifty different personal computers running Windows XP, Windows 2000, and Linux operating systems were used to simulate hundreds of scenarios for four consecutive months. Each scenario simulated 7 days of target tracking. A total of 50 years of CPU time were logged, examining hundreds of thousands of different agents and goals.

While using the basic settings (Table 1) we simulate a 400,000,000 square meter area. In this area, agents track moving targets. At a given time 1,000 targets are moving in the area. In total, during 7 days, 13,635 targets enter and exit the controlled area at any given time. Each target has an initial random location along the border and an initial random velocity as high as 50 kilometers per hour in a direction that leads inward. Targets leave the area when reaching the boundaries of the area. Each target that leaves the area causes a new target to appear at a random location along the border and with a random velocity in

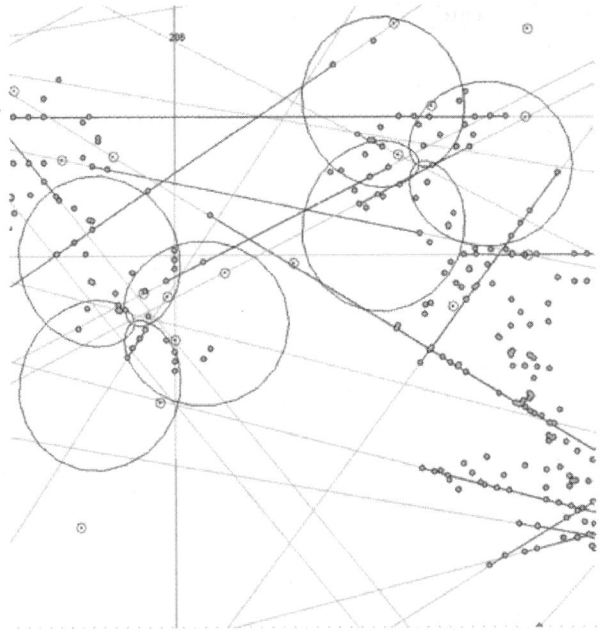

Fig. 1. Simulation of two sensors

a direction that leads inward. Therefore, each target may remain in the area for a random time period.

There are 5,000 Doppler agents and each of them contains a Doppler with a beam range of 50 meters. Since the Doppler beam is essentially a circle while the range of interaction is its diameter (Figure 1), the area covered by the beam is 1,963 square meters. Every Doppler senses targets for 10 seconds and then moves for 5 seconds. That is, on the average, the *agent coverage* , $\overline{w_{a_i}}$, is 1,309 $(\frac{m^2}{s})$. Using 5,000 similar Dopplers leads to a *total coverage*, $\overline{W_A}$, of 6,544,985 $(\frac{m^2}{s})$. Dividing the *total coverage* by the size of the controlled zone results in a *coverage density* of 1.64%. In each experiment, we vary one of the parameters of the environment, keeping the other values of the environment parameters as in the basic settings.

As stated earlier, the *coverage density* ρ characterizes the size of a given large-scale sensor network problem. As ρ decreases, the size of the problem increases. In the following sections we present a study on the properties that affect ρ. We will show how different sets of properties, having similar *coverage density* values, achieve similar results. We will establish a strong correlation between the *coverage density* and system performance as opposed to the other properties, such as the number of agents.

We will begin studying the *coverage density* by changing the number of sensing agents. As the number of sensing agents increases, the *coverage density* grows (Table 2 - left). The number of sensing agents not only influences the *coverage*

Table 1. Experiment basic settings

$Z\ (m^2)$	400,000,000
Agent properties	
Range of interaction (m)	50
Sensing time (sec)	10
Moving Time (sec)	5
$w_{a_i}(t)$ when sensing (m^2)	1,963
$w_{a_i}(t)$ when moving (m^2)	0
$\overline{w_{a_i}}\ \left(\frac{m^2}{sec}\right)$	1,309
Number of agents	5,000
$\overline{W_A}\ \left(\frac{m^2}{sec}\right)$	6,544,985
$\rho\ \left(\frac{1}{sec}\right)$	**1.64%**

density but also holds an important role in distributing the solution and reducing the computation load. We will show that up to a certain point, decreasing the *coverage density* by reducing the number of agents slightly affects the amount of tracked targets. In our load balancing algorithm case, having only 3,000 agents, which is a *coverage density* of 0.98%, yields results almost equivalent to the results of situations with a much larger number of agents. Having only 3,000 agents moderately reduces the tracked target percentage in comparison to not using the load balancing algorithm. Using fewer agents will reduce the tracked target percentage more dramatically. After focusing on the impact that changing the quantity of agents has on the system, we proceeded to study the impact of changing the quality of the sensor agents.

The range of interaction in the basic settings was 50 meters. In the following section we compare the behavior of DDM while using sensors with different ranges of interaction. This range reflects the complexity and the cost of the sensors. As the range of interaction increases, the sensor is likely to be more complex and expensive. Therefore, there may be an interest in using sensors with smaller ranges of interaction. However, decreasing the range of interaction increases the *coverage density* and therefore increases the scale of the problem. We will show how decreasing the *coverage density* by reducing the range of

Table 2. How changing one property while keeping the other as in the basic settings influences the *coverage density*

Agent population		Range of interaction		Moving vs. sensing time	
value	ρ	value	ρ	value	ρ
1000	0.33%	13	0.11%	2:1	0.82%
2000	0.65%	25	0.41%	* **1:2**	**1.64%**
3000	0.98%	* **50**	**1.64%**		
4000	1.31%	100	6.54%		
* **5000**	**1.64%**	200	26.18%		
7000	2.30%				
8000	2.63%				
9000	2.95%				

* **belongs to the basic settings**

interaction influences DDM performance with and without the load balance algorithm (Table 2 - middle).

The next property affecting the *coverage density* is the ratio between the sensing time and the moving time (Table 2 - right). As in the range of interaction, the ratio affects the cost of using DDM. Activating the sensor for longer periods of time is likely to cost more if the energy of producing the electromagnetic beam is expensive. On the other hand, a more mobile sensor may cost more if the fuel needed to drive a sensor around the controlled zone is expensive. Activating the sensor for longer periods of time at the expense of movement time decreases the *coverage density* and therefore reduces the scale of the problem. We will show that this period of time influences the performance of DDM with and without the load balancing mechanism. We will also show how to compensate for using simple and less expensive sensors by increasing the period of the sensing time.

6   Results

In the following sections we will show that system performance is strongly correlated to the *coverage density* rather than to the number of agents, the range of interaction, and the sensing/moving time. In Figures 2 ,3 ,4 the *coverage density* value is included below the X axis in parentheses. Results of DDM applying load balancing are in black, while DDM without load balancing is in gray. The results of the basic setting are denoted in bold symbols.

6.1 Agent Population

We investigated the influence of the *coverage density* through changing the number of sensor agents. During this investigation we ran different scenarios. Each scenario had the same properties (see Table 1) with a different number of sensor agents. In the first scenario, there were 1,000 agents; in the second, 2,000 agents; in the third, 3,000 agents; in the fourth, 4,000 agents; in the fifth, 5,000 agents; in the sixth, 7,000 agents; in the seventh, 8,000 agents; and in the eighth, 9,000 agents. The *coverage densities* of the scenarios were 0.33%, 0.65%, 0.98%, 1.31%, 1.64%, 2.30%, 2.63%, and 2.95%, respectively, whereas the basic setting trial had a *coverage density* of 1.64%.

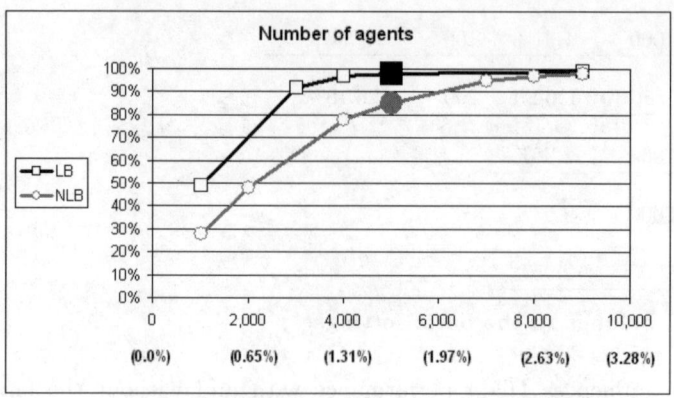

Fig. 2. Tracking percentage as a function of the number of agents

Following Figure 2, one can see an improvement in performance as the number of agents increases. Note that an increment of the number of agents reflects a corresponding increment of the *coverage density* (Table 2). The improvement is achieved regardless of whether the a load balancing mechanism is used. The results show that the system can efficiently utilize additional resources. However, the improvement is significant only up to a certain number of agents. For NLB it is 7,000 agents and for LB it is 4,000. In the next paragraphs we will show that the major influence on the system performance is the *coverage density* and not just the number of agents.

6.2 Range of Interaction

Another property influencing the *coverage density* is the sensor maximum range of interaction. In this part of the study we varied the range of interaction and compared the performance with and without load balance. In different settings, the maximum detection range of each sensor was 13, 25, 50,100, and 200 meters. This translates to coverage densities of 0.11%, 0.41%, 1.64%, 6.54%, and 26.18%, respectively.

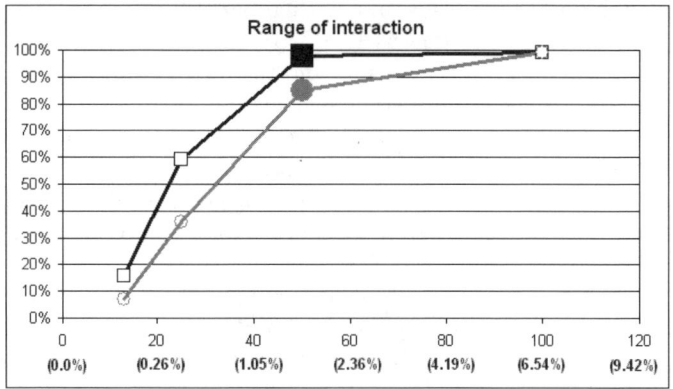

Fig. 3. Tracking percentage as a function of the range of interaction

In Figure 3 one can see that the system performs better as the range of interaction increases. That may be explained by the fact that each sensor may detect
more targets as its range increases. Once again, the improvement is presented
for both NLB and LB cases and is significant up to a certain point. We can
see that keeping the number of agents constant does not imply that the performance of the system will stay constant. However, as in the case of the number
of agents, increasing the range of interaction reflects a corresponding increment
of the *coverage density* (Table 2). We can see that in both cases increasing the
coverage density leads to better performance.

6.3 Sensing and Moving Time

In the basic settings each agent repeats the following activities: (i) it senses
targets for 5 seconds and then (ii) it moves for 10 seconds. The ratio between

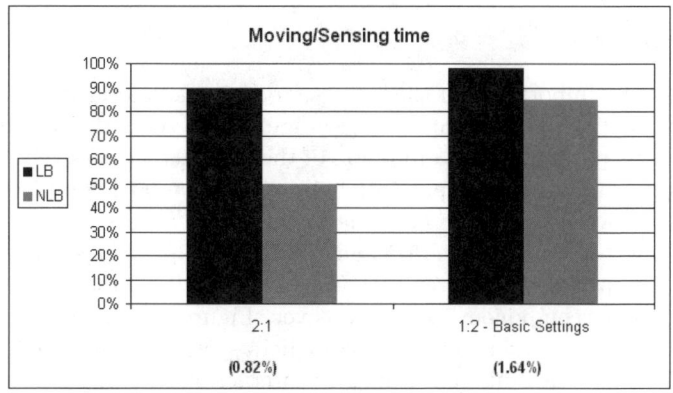

Fig. 4. Tracking percentage as a function of the sensing-moving ratio

the moving time and the sensing time is therefore 1:2 in the basic setting case. In this case the *coverage density* was 1.64%. To check the impact of the *coverage density* on the ratio between the sensing and the moving times we compared the basic settings to settings with different sensing and moving times. We increased the sensing period to 20 seconds while the moving period remained at 10 seconds. The ratio between the sensing time and the moving time in this case was 2:1 and the *coverage density* was 0.82%. The fact that the *coverage density* in this setting was lower than for the basic settings suggests that the problem of accurately identifying the targets' trajectories is harder.

Looking at Figure 4 we can see that once again keeping the number of agents constant does not ensure achieving the same performance. Moreover, it supports our findings that decreasing the *coverage density* decreases performance. In this case we decreased the *coverage density* from 1.64% to 0.82%, and the performance dropped from 98% to 90% while we applied a load balancing and from 85% to 50% while we did not.

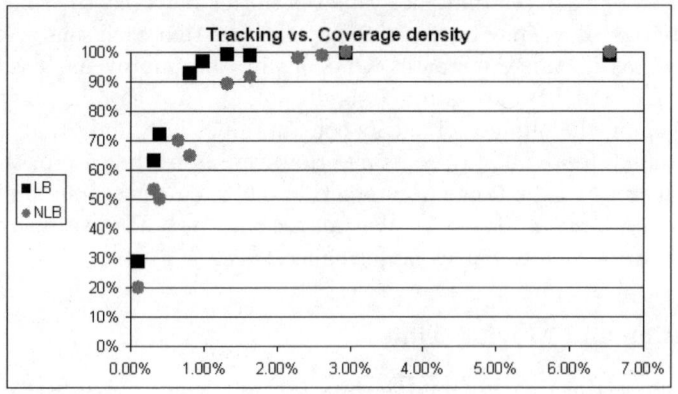

Fig. 5. Integrated results: performance vs. the *coverage density*

6.4   Integration

To establish the importance of the *coverage density* definition we compared the tracking percentage of different settings. Figure 5 presents the results reported in the previous paragraphs as a function of the *coverage density*. The results are the aggregation of the results presented above. Looking at Figure 5, one cannot distinguish between the different scenario sets. The results of all the sets are situated along the curve of the LB and the NLB graphs. This proves that the important characteristic of large-scale sensor networks is the *coverage density* and not a single component of it. Moreover, Figure 6 demonstrates that the number of agents does not necessarily predicts system performance. When we used 5,000 agents with different ranges of interaction or sensing/moving times, the system performed differently. The same results presented in Figure 6 were measured for the sensing/moving time and the range of interaction properties.

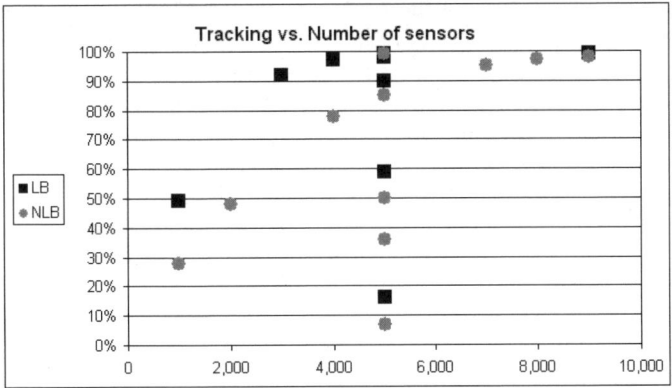

Fig. 6. Integrated results: number of agents

To compare the correlation between system performance and its properties, we calculated the correlation coefficient of each property. We used only the measurements that described a contribution to system performance. For example, we considered all the results up to 5,000 agents for the *Agent population* property with load balancing (see Figure 2). We did that because there is no sense in looking for correlation after the system reaches its full utilization. The correlation coefficient for the *Agent population* property with load balancing was 0.2 and without load balancing was 0.32. For the *Range of interaction* property with load balancing the coefficient was 0.79, while without the load balancing it was 0.68. The *Sensing/moving time* property had the worst correlation of 0.08 with load balancing and -0.16 without load balancing. The best correlation was achieved by the *coverage density* and had the value of 0.86 with load balancing and 0.89 without load balancing. These results prove that the *coverage density* has a strong correlation to system performance.

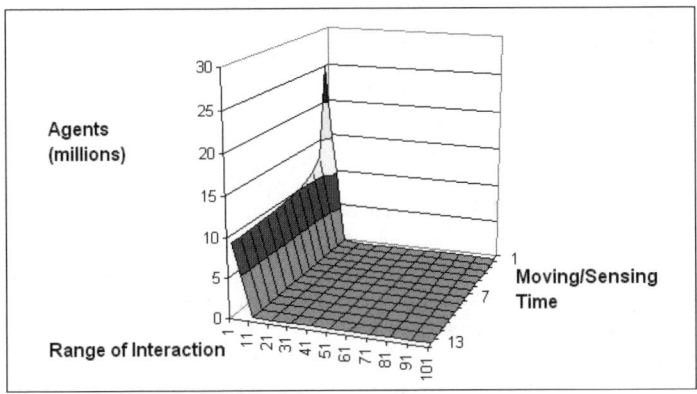

Fig. 7. Different settings that have the coverage density of the basic settings (1.64%)

To further depict the uses of the *coverage density*, Figure 7 presents the different alternatives for the basic settings. The figure illustrates an isogram surface of a continuous variation of the three property dimensions. Recalling that the *coverage density* is correlated to the multiplication of these three properties, each point on the surface represents a certain number of agents, an interaction range, and a moving-sensing ratio that result in the same *coverage density* of 1.64%, which is the same *coverage density* of the basic settings.

7 Conclusions

Coverage density defines the time needed to cover an area equal to the size of the controlled zone. We have shown that there is a strong correlation between the *coverage density* of a system and its behavior. In comparing large-scale sensor networks having different *coverage densities*, we have proven that system properties such as the number of agents, the range of detection of each agent, and the agent's activation time have the same influence on the number of detected objects. For instance, by analyzing only the number of objects a large-scale sensor network successfully detects, one may not know whether there is a large number of cheap sensors or a small number of expensive ones. Given this fact, we introduced a way to achieve the same system results with different preferences. As a result, a system designer may find it easier to achieve a certain level of system performance under given specific constraints, such as budget limits.

References

1. A. Howard, M. J Matarić and G. S. Sukhatme, 'Mobile Sensor Network Deployment using Potential Fields: A Distributed, Scalable Solution to the Area Coverage Problem', *Proceedings of the 6th International Symposium on Distributed Autonomous Robotics Systems (DARS02)*, pages 299-308, Fukuoka, Japan, 2002.
2. Autonomous Negotiating Teams (ANTs) website, *Darpa*, http://www.rl.af.mil/tech/programs/ants/
3. C. Intanagonwiwat, R. Govindan, D. Estrin, J. Heidemann and F. Silva, 'Directed Diffusion for Wireless Sensor Networking', *IEEE/ACM Transactions on Networking*, **11(1)**: 2-16, February 2003.
4. C. Ortiz, K. Konolige, R. Vincent, B. Morisset, A. Agno, Mi. Eriksen, D. Fox, B. Limketkai, J. Ko, B. Steward and D. Schulz, 'Centibots: Very Large Scale Distributed Robotic Teams', *AAAI*, 1022-1023, 2004.
5. D. Ganesan, A. Cerpa, Y. Yu, W. Ye, J. Zhao and D. Estrin, 'Networking Issues in Sensor Networks', *Journal of Parallel and Distributed Computing (JPDC)*, Special Issues on Frontiers in Distributed Sensor Networks, **64(7)**, 799–814, 2004.
6. D.W. Gage, 'Command Control for Many-Robot Systems', *Proceedings of AUVS92, 19th Annual Technical Symposium and Exhibition of the Association for Unmanned Vehicle Systems*, Huntsville AL, pages 22-24, June 1992.
7. E. Ogston, B. Overeinder, M. van Steen and F. Brazier, 'A Method for Decentralized Clustering in Large Multi-agent Systems', *AAMAS*, pages 789-796, 2003.

8. G. Asada, M. Dong, T. S. Lin, F. Newberg, G. Pottie, H. O. Marcy and W. J. Kaiser, 'Wireless Integrated Network Sensors: Low Power Systems on a Chip', *IEEE ESSCIRC '98*, pages 9-16, September 1998

9. G.J. Pottie and W.J. Kaiser, 'Wireless Integrated Network Sensors', *Communications of the ACM*, **43(5)**: 551-558, 2000.

10. I. F. Akyildiz, W. Su, Y. Sankarasubramaniam and E. Cayirci, 'Wireless Sensor Networks: A Survey', *Computer Networks* **38(4)**: 393-422, 2002.

11. J. Liu, L. F. Perrone, D. M. Nicol, M. Liljenstam, C. Elliott and D. Pearson, 'Simulation Modeling of Large-scale Ad-Hoc Sensor Networks', *Proceedings of Euro-SIW01, European Simulation Interoperability Workshop*, 2001.

12. K. Bult, A. Burstein, D. Chang, M. Dong, M. Fielding, E. Kruglick, J. Ho, F. Lin, T. H. Lin, W. J. Kaiser, H. Marcy, R. Mukai, P. Nelson, F. Newberg, K. S. J. Pister, G. Pottie, H. Sanchez, O. M. Stafsudd, K. B. Tan, C. M. Ward, S. Xue and J. Yao, 'Low Power Systems for Wireless Microsensors', *Proceedings of International Symposium on Low Power Electronics and Design*, pages 17-21, 1996.

13. K. H. Low, W. K. Leow and M. H. Ang Jr., 'Task Allocation via Self-Organizing Swarm Coalitions in Distributed Mobile Sensor Network', *AAAI*, pages 28-33, 2004.

14. K. Kar and S. Banerjee, 'Node Placement for Connected Coverage in Sensor Networks', *Proceedings of WiOpt 2003: Modeling and Optimization in Mobile, Ad Hoc and Wireless Networks*, March 2003.

15. M. A. Batalin and G. S. Sukhatme, 'Multi-robot Dynamic Coverage of a Planar Bounded Environment', *IEEE/RSJ International Conference on Intelligent Robots and Systems*, 2002.

16. M. A. Batalin and G. S. Sukhatme, 'Spreading Out: A Local Approach to Multi-Robot Coverage', *Proceedings of 6th International Symposium on Distributed Autonomous Robotic Systems*, 373-382, 2002.

17. M. A. Batalina and G. S. Sukhatmea, 'Sensor Coverage using Mobile Robots and Stationary Nodes', *Proceedings of the SPIE*, volume 4868: 269-276, Boston, MA, August 2002.

18. M. Cardei and J. Wu, 'Coverage in Wireless Sensor Networks', *Handbook of Sensor Net*, M. Ilyas and I. Mahgoub (eds), CRC Press, 2004.

19. O. Yadgar, 'Efficient Algorithms in Large-scale Agent Systems', PhD Thesis, Bar-Ilan University, 2005.

20. O. Yadgar, S. Kraus and C. Ortiz, 'Scaling Up Distributed Sensor Networks: Cooperative Large-scale Mobile-Agent Organizations', in *Distributed Sensor Networks: A Multiagent Perspective*, pp. 185-218, Kluwer publishing, 2003.

21. O. Yadgar, S. Kraus and C. Ortiz, 'Hierarchical Information Combination Process for Large-scale Task and Team Environments', in *Communications in Multiagent Systems*, Springer-Verlag, 2003.

22. P. J. Turner and N. R. Jennings, 'Improving the Scalability of Multi-agent Systems', *Proceedings of the First International Workshop on Infrastructure for Scalable Multiagent Systems*, Springer-Verlag, pages 246-262, Barcelona, Spain, June 2000.

23. P. Scerri, R. Vincent and R. Mailler, 'Comparing Three Approaches to Large Scale Coordination', *Proceedings of the First Workshop on the Challenges in the Coordination of Large Scale Multi-agent Systems*, July 2004.

24. P. Scerri, Y. Xu, E. Liao, J. Lai and K. Sycara-Cyranski, 'Scaling Teamwork to Very Large Teams', *AAMAS*, pages 888-895, 2004.

25. R. Niu, P. Varshney, M.H. Moore and D. Klamer, 'Decision Fusion in a Wireless Sensor Network with a Large Number of Sensors', *Proceedings of the Seventh International Conference on Information Fusion*, Stockholm, Sweden, June 2004.

26. S. Shakkottai, R. Srikant and N. Shroff, 'Unreliable Sensor Grids: Coverage, Connectivity and Diameter', *Proceedings of the IEEE INFOCOM*, pages 1073-1083, 2003.

27. T. H. Lin, H. Sanchez, R. Rofougaran and W. J. Kaiser, 'CMOS Front End Components for Micropower RF Wireless Systems', *Proceedings of the 1998 International Symposium on Low Power Electronics and Design*, pages 11-15, 1998.

28. V. Lesser, C. Ortiz and M. Tambe (ed), 'Distributed Sensor Networks: A Multiagent Perspective', Kluwer Publishing, 2003.

Selecting Web Services Statistically

David Lambert and David Robertson

School of Informatics, University of Edinburgh
d.j.lambert@sms.ed.ac.uk,
dr@inf.ed.ac.uk

Abstract. Service oriented computing offers a new approach to programming. To be useful for large and diverse sets of problems, effective
service selection and composition is crucial. While current frameworks offer tools and methods for selecting services based on various user-defined
criteria, little attention has been paid to how such services act and interact. Similarly, the patterns of interaction might be important at a level
other than that of the user-programmer. Semantic agreement between
services, and the patterns of interaction between them, will be an important factor in the usability and success of service composition. We
argue that this cannot be guaranteed by logic-based description of individual services. We have developed a simple but apparently effective
technique for selecting agents and interactions based on evidence of their
prior performance.

1 Introduction

Service oriented computing is already a key part of e-Science, business, and government computing. Web services in particular offer a compelling vehicle for
distributing software functionality, offering a common platform for traditional
remote procedure call, developing Grid services, and nascent agent technologies.
They enable access to distributed resources such as databases, compute servers,
and physical objects like telescopes; obviate the difficulties of distributing, installing, and ensuring currency of software that must otherwise be deployed on
users' machines; and allow contracts and virtual organisations to be constructed
between organisationally distinct domains.

Tools like Taverna [1] make it straightforward for users to construct workflows
and select services to perform them. However, the available services are generally either hard-coded into the tools, or manually acquired from web pages or
UDDI registries. The problem of discovering suitable services for a task is known
as the connection problem, and one that the multi-agent community long ago
automated by introducing middle-agents [2], which provide a meeting point for
service providers and clients. Doing this for systems as open as web services, however, is a challenge that is somewhat greater than that faced by those working
with typically closed, laboratory-bound multi-agent systems.

Web, Grid, and agent services are currently treated as fungible black boxes,
when there is justification to believe they are not. In this paper, we present a

M. Klusch, M. Rovatsos, and T. Payne (Eds.): CIA 2006, LNAI 4149, pp. 153–167, 2006.

technique which allows matchmakers to construct an effective interaction pattern and populate it with an optimal set of services, in a manner that makes minimal demands on the user.

2   The Madness of Crowds

Middle-agents [2] connect clients, as service requesters, with service providers, by providing some mechanism for matching providers' capability advertisements with clients' requests for service. One of the most common types of such middle-agents is the matchmaker, on which we focus. A matchmaker is privy to both advertisements and requests, as opposed to say a yellow-pages like directory where clients can inspect adverts in privacy. Almost all matchmaking research to date has focused on the mechanisms for describing services and requirements, such as capability description languages [3]. This is also the favoured approach for the semantic web, which uses OWL-S [4] descriptions of the service. Using taxonomies of services, descriptions of inputs and outputs, and planning-like descriptions of pre-conditions and effects, the idea is that a matchmaker can reason about the relative merits of advertising services and select those that best suit the client.

Despite the obvious utility of logic based approaches, it is far from clear that they can in practice capture all the pertinent system features in a complex world. Where many individuals, companies, and organisations offer ostensibly similar services, it is unlikely that many services will fully match their specification, or perform their task equally well [5]. In open systems, one cannot rely on the intelligence and familiarity of the expert, the insight of the designers and implementers, nor goodwill between investigators. Some particular reasons for the insufficiency of logic-based descriptions are:

- *The capability description language lacks expressiveness.* This does not imply a criticism of the language: it is unreasonable to expect any general purpose capability description language to allow the communication of arbitrarily complex capabilities and restrictions in every imaginable domain. However, it would frequently be possible for matchmakers, especially domain-specific ones, to discover such constraints.
- *User ignorance of ability of the language to express a characteristic, or of the effect of declaring it.* As expressible features or limitations become more complex, and services more common, it becomes increasingly likely that a user would be unaware of her ability to aid the matchmaker.
- *User expectation that the information will not be used by clients or matchmakers.* In an negative example of 'early-adopter syndrome', it is not unreasonable to expect service providers will refrain from supplying this kind of data until they observe a significant portion of the agent ecosystem using it.
- *Not wanting to express particular information.* In some instances, there is an incentive for service providers to keep the description of their services as general as possible, though not to the extent of attracting clients they has

no possibility of pleasing. Alternatively, the provider may not wish to be terribly honest or open about her service's foibles.

— *Comprehensive descriptions too expensive to generate or use.* Even if none of the above hold, it would often simply not be worthwhile for the service provider to analyse and encode the information. Further, in the case of web, semantic web and Grid services, it is reasonable to expect that users are discouraged by standards flux from investing much time in this endeavour.

We claim that even with the best will, it will often simply be too expensive in time, money, computation, or human brainpower, to fully describe services. Even then, as is shown in [6], it is not unreasonable to expect the reasoners (and hence any matchmakers using them) to differ in their interpretation in some cases.

Compounding this difficulty of correctly describing individual services is the one of finding agents that work well together. Our aim is to enable interactions between two or more agents, where one or more services must be found to satisfy the interaction's initiator. Why might this happen, and what can we do to overcome this obstacle to widespread use of multiple-service interactions in real-world operation?

— *'Social' reasons.* For instance, different social communities, or communities of practice, may each cluster around particular service providers for no particular reason, yet this would result in improved performance on some tasks if agents were selected from the same social pool.
— *Strategic (or otherwise) inter-business partnerships.* For example, an airline may have a special deal with other airlines or car-hire companies that would lead to a more satisfied customer.
— *Components designed by same group.* Organisations that seem to have nothing in common may well be using software created by a single group. Such software would be more likely to inter-operate well than software from others.
— *Different groups of engineers held differing views of a problem, even though the specification is the same.* Thus, the implementations are subtly incompatible, or at least do not function together seamlessly.
— *Particular resources or constraints shared between providers.* For example, in a Grid environment, a computation server and a file store might share a very high bandwidth connection, leading to improved service.
— *The inter-relationship is not known to the service provider.* Some of the dependencies may be extremely subtle, or simply not obvious.
— *Ontology mapping*
   Sometimes ontology mapping will work perfectly, in other cases, it would be better to select those services that share a native ontology.
— *Gatewaying issues* It is quite likely that many services will be provided via gateways, and that these will make semantic interaction possible and affordable, but more error prone than systems designed explicitly to interact.
— *Malice* It is hardly unknown for software vendors to ensure lock in by making their software deliberately fail to interact correctly with that of other vendors.

And, of course, we have the ever-present problem of bugs, which will often manifest themselves in such a way that some collaborating services will exercise them, and others will not.

The interaction is normally seen as secondary. If, instead, we treat it as a first-class object, neither emergent from agent behaviour, nor fixed by the client or server's interaction model, we can begin to examine some of its properties. Some such techniques include model checking [7], and ontology matching [8].

If, however, we made the interaction pattern known, and used a matchmaker to select our services, as well as, we could share empirical data about performance. This is our approach. It is made possible by our choice of interaction language, LCC. While conventional agent matchmaking is done by reference to the client's service request and the advertised capabilities of the providers, we make the protocol that drives the interaction the centrepiece. This implies:

- The purpose of the interaction is captured.
- Multi-agent dialogues, far from being impossible, are the norm.
- All agents can reason about the dialogue they are in, not just the initiator or broker.

What if, instead of simply choosing an agent and using its interaction model, we chose the interaction model, too? We can then apply our agent selection technique [9] to the question of how to construct the interaction.

In addressing all these problems we can use the evidence provided by clients on the effectiveness of services, discovering the actual performance of agents in the roles they claim to perform. Gathering enough data on any given service or interaction is hard work, and likely to be beyond the ability of any single agent. It is, however, a task for which a middle agent is ideally suited.

3   Framework

3.1   Lightweight Coördination Calculus

To describe the interactions, we use a language called the Lightweight Coördination Calculus (LCC) [10]. LCC is based on the Calculus of Communicating Systems (CCS) [11], and provides a simple language featuring message passing (denoted ⇒ for sending, and ⇐ for receiving) with the operators *then* (sequence), *or* (choice), and ← (if). An LCC protocol is interpreted in a logic-programming style, using unification of variables which are gradually instantiated as the conversation progresses. The rules governing execution of a protocol are in figure 2.

An LCC protocol consists of dialogue framework, expanded clauses, and common knowledge. The framework defines the roles necessary to conduct an interaction, along with the allowable messages and the conditions under which they can be sent. For our astronomy workflow (figure 3), the roles include *astronomer*, *astronomy-database*, and *black-hole-finder*. The expanded clauses note where each service has reached in the dialogue. The common knowledge records conversation-specific state agreed between the services.

$$
\begin{aligned}
Framework &::= Clause^* \\
Clause &::= Agent :: Def \\
Agent &::= a(Role, Id) \\
Def &::= Agent|Message|Def\ then\ Def|Def\ or\ Def|Def\ par\ Def \\
Message &::= M \Rightarrow Agent|M \Rightarrow Agent \leftarrow C|M \Leftarrow Agent|C \leftarrow M \Leftarrow Agent \\
C &::= Term|C \wedge C|C \vee C \\
Id, M, Type &::= Term \\
Term &::= Variable|Atom|Number|Atom(Term^+) \\
Atom &::= lowercase\text{-}char\ alphanumeric^* \\
Variable &::= uppercase\text{-}char\ alphanumeric^*
\end{aligned}
$$

Fig. 1. Grammar for the LCC dialogue framework

These rewrite rules constitute an extension to those described in [10]. A rewrite rule

$$
\alpha \xrightarrow{M_i, M_o, \mathcal{P}, O, \mathcal{C}, \mathcal{C}'} \beta
$$

holds if α can be rewritten to β where: M_i are the available messages before rewriting; M_o are the messages available after the rewrite; $\mathcal{P}$ is the protocol; O is the message produced by the rewrite (if any); $\mathcal{C}$ is set of collaborators before the rewrite; and $\mathcal{C}'$ (if present) is the—possibly extended—set of collaborators after the rewrite. $\mathcal{C}$ is a set of pairs of role and service name, e.g. $col(black\text{-}hole\text{-}finder, ucsd\text{-}sdsc)\}$. The same rewrite rules hold regardless of the implementation of the matchmaking function $recruit$. This enables us to apply other LCC tools, such as model-checkers and the interpreter itself, without alteration while allowing us to change $recruit$, and means clients can use their own choice of matchmaker and matchmaking scheme.

$$
\begin{array}{ll}
A :: B \xrightarrow{M_i, M_o, \mathcal{P}, \mathcal{C}, O} A :: E & if\ B \xrightarrow{M_i, M_o, \mathcal{P}, \mathcal{C}, O} E \\[2mm]
A_1\ or\ A_2 \xrightarrow{M_i, M_o, \mathcal{P}, \mathcal{C}, O} E & if\ \neg closed(A_2) \wedge A_1 \xrightarrow{M_i, M_o, \mathcal{P}, \mathcal{C}, O} E \\[2mm]
A_1\ or\ A_2 \xrightarrow{M_i, M_o, \mathcal{P}, \mathcal{C}, O} E & if\ \neg closed(A_1) \wedge A_2 \xrightarrow{M_i, M_o, \mathcal{P}, \mathcal{C}, O} E \\[2mm]
A_1\ then\ A_2 \xrightarrow{M_i, M_o, \mathcal{P}, \mathcal{C}, O} E\ then\ A_2 & if\ A_1 \xrightarrow{M_i, M_o, \mathcal{P}, \mathcal{C}, O} E \\[2mm]
A_1\ then\ A_2 \xrightarrow{M_i, M_o, \mathcal{P}, \mathcal{C}, O} A_1\ then\ E & if\ closed(A_1) \wedge A_2 \xrightarrow{M_i, M_o, \mathcal{P}, \mathcal{C}', O} E \\
& \quad \wedge collaborators(A_1) = \mathcal{C}' \\[2mm]
C \leftarrow M \Leftarrow A \xrightarrow{M_i, M_i \backslash \{M \Leftarrow A\}, \mathcal{P}, \mathcal{C}, \emptyset} c(M \Leftarrow A, \mathcal{C}) & if\ (M \Leftarrow A) \in M_i \wedge satisfied(C) \\[2mm]
M \Rightarrow A \leftarrow C \xrightarrow{M_i, M_i, \mathcal{P}, \mathcal{C}, \mathcal{C}', \{M \Rightarrow A\}} c(M \Rightarrow A, \mathcal{C}') & if\ satisfied(C) \wedge \\
& \quad \mathcal{C}' = recruit(\mathcal{P}, \mathcal{C}, role(A)) \\[2mm]
null \leftarrow C \xrightarrow{M_i, M_i, \mathcal{P}, \emptyset} c(null, \mathcal{C}) & if\ satisfied(C) \\[2mm]
a(R, I) \leftarrow C \xrightarrow{M_i, M_o, \mathcal{P}, \mathcal{C}, \emptyset} a(R, I) :: B & if\ clause(\mathcal{P}, C, a(R, I) :: B) \\
& \quad \wedge satisfied(C)
\end{array}
$$

$$
\begin{aligned}
collaborators(c(Term, \mathcal{C})) &= \mathcal{C} \\
collaborators(A_1\ then\ A_2) &= collaborators(A_1) \cup collaborators(A_2) \\
collaborators(A :: B) &= collaborators(A) \cup collaborators(B)
\end{aligned}
$$

Fig. 2. Rewrite rules governing matchmaking for an LCC protocol

While we use LCC as our framework, this paper's contribution regarding service selection does not require it. For our purpose, LCC's key provisions are support for multi-party dialogues, and for enabling the matchmaker and client to identify an ongoing interaction and determine the agents engaged in it. These requirements could be met by many other coördination approaches or simple extensions thereof, whether in Grid or web services domains.

3.2   Incidence Calculus

We use the incidence calculus [12] for our probabilistic calculations, It is a truth-functional probabilistic calculus in which the probabilities of composite formulae are computed from intersections and unions of the sets of worlds for which the atomic formulae hold true, rather than from the numerical values of the probabilities of their components. The probabilities are then derived from these incidences. Crucially, in general $P(\phi \wedge \psi) \neq P(\phi) \cdot P(\psi)$. This fidelity is not possible in normal probabilistic logics, where probabilities of composite formulae are derived only from the probabilities of their component formulae. In the incidence calculus, we return to the underlying sets of incidences, giving us more accurate values for compound probabilities.

$$
\begin{aligned}
i(\top) &= worlds & i(\bot) &= \{\} \\
i(\alpha \wedge \beta) &= i(\alpha) \cap i(\beta) & i(\alpha \vee \beta) &= i(\alpha) \cup i(\beta) \\
i(\neg \alpha) &= i(\top) \backslash i(\alpha) & i(\alpha \to \beta) &= i(\neg \alpha \vee \beta) = (worlds \backslash i(\alpha)) \cup i(\beta) \\
P(\phi) &= \frac{|i(\phi)|}{|i(\top)|} & P(\phi|\psi) &= \frac{|i(\phi \wedge \psi)|}{|i(\psi)|}
\end{aligned}
$$

The incidence calculus is not frequently applied, since one requires exact incident records to use it. Fortunately, that's exactly what the matchmaker has on hand.

4   The Matchmaker

First, we will explain the overall process of executing an LCC protocol, and the matchmaker's place in it. A client has a task or goal it wishes to achieve: using either a pre-agreed look-up mechanism, or by reasoning about the protocols available, the client will select a protocol, with possibly more than one being suitable. This done, it can begin interpreting the protocol, dispatching messages to other agents as the protocol directs. When the protocol requires a message to be sent to an agent that is not yet identified, the sender queries a matchmaker to discover services capable of filling the role. These new agents we term 'collaborators'. The matchmaker selects the service that maximises the probability of a successful outcome given the current protocol type and role instantiations. The protocol is then updated to reflect the agent's selection, and the term $col(Role, Agent)$, instantiated to the requested role and newly chosen agent, is stored in the protocol's common knowledge where it is visible to the participants and the matchmaker.

The success of a protocol and the particular team of collaborators is decided by the client: on completion or failure of a protocol, the client informs the matchmaker whether the outcome was satisfactory to the client. Each completed brokering session is recorded as an incident, represented by an integer. Our propositions are ground predicate calculus expressions. Each proposition has an associated list of worlds (incidents) for which it is true. Initially, the incident database is empty, and the broker selects services at random. As more data is collected, a threshold is reached, at which point the matchmaker begins to use the probabilities.

4.1   Selecting Agents

The traditional issue is selecting agents, so we will address this first. In our scenario, an astronomer is using the Grid to examine a black hole. Having obtained the LCC protocol in figure 3, she instantiates the *File* variable to the file she wants to work with, and runs the protocol. The protocol is sent first to a *black-hole-finder* service. This service, in turn, requires an *astronomy-database* to provide the file. If a black hole is found the *black-hole-finder* service will pass the data to a visualisation service. Finally, the client will receive a visualisation or notification of failure. Where is the inter-service variation? Consider that the astronomical data file is very large, and thus network bandwidth between sites will be a crucial factor in determining user satisfaction. Thus, some pairs of database and computation centre will outperform other pairs, even though the individuals in each pairing might be equally capable. Indeed, the 'best' database and compute centre may have a dreadful combined score because their network interconnection is weak.

If we imagine how the matchmaker's incidence database would look after several executions of this workflow (most likely by different clients), we might see something like this:

$i(protocol(\text{BLACK-HOLE-SEARCH}), [1, 2, \ldots, 25])$
$i(outcome(good), [1, 2, 3, 4, 6, 10, 11, 12, 16, 22, 23, 24])$
$i(col(astronomy\text{-}database, greenwich), [18, 19, 20, 21, 22, 23, 24, 25])$
$i(col(astronomy\text{-}database, herschel), [10, 11, 12, 13, 14, 15, 16, 17])$
$i(col(astronomy\text{-}database, keck), [1, 2, 3, 4, 5, 6, 7, 8, 9])$
$i(col(black\text{-}hole\text{-}finder, barcelona\text{-}sc), [8, 9, 16, 17, 24, 25])$
$i(col(black\text{-}hole\text{-}finder, ucsd\text{-}sdsc), [1, 2, 3, 4, 10, 11, 12, 13, 18, 19, 20])$
$i(col(black\text{-}hole\text{-}finder, uk\text{-}hpcx), [5, 6, 7, 14, 15, 21, 22, 23])$
$i(col(visualiser, ncsa), [1, 2, \ldots, 25])$

Each $i(proposition, incidents)$ records the incidents (that is, protocol interactions or executions) in which the proposition is true. We can see that the BLACK-HOLE-SEARCH protocol has been invoked 25 times, and that it has been successful in those incidents where *outcome(good)* is true. Further, by intersecting various incidences, we can compute the success of different teams of agents, and obtain predictions for future behaviour. Let us examine the performance of the Barcelona supercomputer:

$$i(col(black\text{-}hole\text{-}finder, barcelona\text{-}sc) \wedge outcome(good)) = \{16\}$$
$$P(outcome(good)|col(black\text{-}hole\text{-}finder, barcelona\text{-}sc)) = \frac{|\{16\}|}{|\{8,9,16,17,24,25\}|}$$

This performance is substantially worse than that of the other supercomputers on this task not because *barcelona-sc* is a worse supercomputer than *ucsd-sdsc* or *uk-hpcx*, but because its network connections to the databases required for this task present a bottleneck, reducing client satisfaction.

From this database, the matchmaker can then determine, for a requester, which services are most likely to lead to a successful outcome, given the current protocol and services already selected. That is, the matchmaker tries to optimise

$$argmax_s P(outcome(good)|\mathcal{P}, col(r, s) \cup \mathcal{C})$$

Where $\mathcal{P}$ is the protocol, $\mathcal{C}$ is the current set of collaborators, r is the role requiring a new service selection, and s is the service we are to select.

$a(astronomer(File), Astronomer) ::$
    $search(File) \Rightarrow a(black\text{-}hole\text{-}finder, BHF)$ then
    $\left(\begin{array}{l} success \Leftarrow a(black\text{-}hole\text{-}finder, BHF) \text{ then} \\ receive\text{-}visualisation(Thing, V) \leftarrow visualising(Thing) \Leftarrow a(visualiser, V) \end{array} \right)$ *or*
    $failed \Leftarrow a(black\text{-}hole\text{-}finder, BHF)$

$a(black\text{-}hole\text{-}finder, BHF) ::$
    $search(File) \Leftarrow a(astronomer(File), Astronomer)$ then
    $grid\text{-}ftp\text{-}get(File) \Rightarrow a(astronomy\text{-}database, AD)$ then
    $\left(\begin{array}{l} grid\text{-}ftp\text{-}sent(File) \Leftarrow a(astronomy\text{-}database, AD) \text{ then} \\ success \Rightarrow a(astronomer, Astronomer) \\ \quad\quad \leftarrow black\text{-}hole\text{-}present(File, Black\text{-}hole) \text{ then} \\ visualise(Black\text{-}hole, Astronomer) \Rightarrow a(visualiser, V) \end{array} \right)$ *or*
    $failed \Rightarrow a(astronomer(File), Astronomer)$

$a(astronomy\text{-}database, AD) ::$
    $grid\text{-}ftp\text{-}get(File) \Leftarrow a(black\text{-}hole\text{-}finder, BHF)$
    $grid\text{-}ftp\text{-}sent(File) \Rightarrow a(black\text{-}hole\text{-}finder, BHF) \leftarrow grid\text{-}ftp\text{-}completed(File, AD)$

$a(visualiser, V) ::$
    $visualise(Thing, Client) \Leftarrow a(\_, Requester)$ then
    $visualising(Thing) \Rightarrow a(\_, Client) \leftarrow serve\text{-}visualisation(Thing, Client)$

Note that LCC is being used only to coördinate the interaction: where appropriate, individual agents may use domain-specific protocols, such as Grid FTP, to perform the heavy lifting or invoke specific services outside of the LCC formalism and communication channel.

Fig. 3. LCC dialogue framework for astronomy workflow scenario

We have developed two algorithms for choosing services, although others are possible. The first, called RECRUIT-JOINT, fills all the vacancies in a protocol at the outset. It works by computing the joint distribution for all possible permutations of services in their respective roles, selecting the grouping with the largest probability of a good outcome.

The second approach, RECRUIT-INCREMENTAL, is to select only one service at a time, as required by the executing protocol. The various services already engaged in the protocol, on needing to send a message to an as-yet-unidentified service, will ask the matchmaker to find an service to fulfil the role at hand. RECRUIT-INCREMENTAL computes the probability of a successful outcome for each service available for role R given C (C being the collaborators chosen so far), and selects the most successful service. To illustrate RECRUIT-INCREMENTAL, imagine the workflow scenario. At first, the astronomer must ask the matchmaker to fill the *black-hole-finder* role. The *BHF* service's first action is to request the data file from an astronomy database. It therefore returns the protocol to the matchmaker, which selects the *astronomy-database* most likely to produce success, given that the *black-hole-finder* is already instantiated to *BHF*.

Both algorithms support the pre-selection of services for particular roles. An example of this might be a client booking a holiday: if it were accumulating frequent flier miles with a particular airline, it could specify that airline be used, and the matchmaker would work around this choice, selecting the best agents given that the airline is fixed. This mechanism also allows us to direct the matchmaker's search: selecting a particular service can suggest that the client wants similar services, from the same social pool, for the other roles, e.g. in a peer-to-peer search, by selecting an service you suspect will be helpful in a particular enquiry, the broker can find further services that are closely 'socially' related to that first one.

We can see from figure 5(a) that using this technique can substantially improve performance over random selection of agents which can individual meet the requirements. Which algorithm should one choose? In protocols where most roles are eventually filled, RECRUIT-JOINT will outperform RECRUIT-INCREMENTAL, since it is not limited by the possibly suboptimal decisions made earlier. RECRUIT-JOINT is also preferable when one wishes to avoid multiple calls to the matchmaker, either because of privacy concerns, or for reasons of communication efficiency. However, in protocols which rarely have all their roles instantiated, RECRUIT-JOINT can end up unfairly penalising those services which have not actually participated in the protocols they are allocated to. RECRUIT-INCREMENTAL is therefore more suitable in protocols where many roles go unfilled: total work on the broker would be reduced, and the results would probably be at least as good as for brokering all services.

4.2   Selecting Roles

So far, we have considered the case where the protocol is defined, and we simply need to select agents to fill the roles. What if the roles themselves are undefined, if the protocol is incompletely specified? What if we allowed agents to begin executing incomplete protocols? If the matchmaker could elaborate protocols at run time, selecting the elaboration based on prior experience? We will show one way to do this using the incidence calculus, in a very similar fashion to how we selected agents.

RECRUIT-JOINT(*protocol, database*)

1   *roles* ← ROLES-REQUIRED(*protocol*)
2   *collaborations* ← ALL-COLLABORATIONS(*protocol, database, roles*)
3   **for** *c* ∈ *collaborations*
4   **do** *quality*[*c*] ← PROBABILITY-GOOD-OUTCOME(*protocol, database, c*)
5   **return** ARGMAX(*collaborations, quality*)

RECRUIT-INCREMENTAL(*protocol, database, role*)

1   **for** *r* ∈ ACTIVE-ROLES(*protocol*)
2   **do** *collaborators*[*r*] ← COLLABORATOR-FOR-ROLE(*protocol, r*)
3   *candidates* ← CAPABLE-AGENTS(*database, role*)
4   **for** *c* ∈ *candidates*
5   **do** *collaborators*[*role*] ← *c*
6   *quality*[*a*] ← PROBABILITY-GOOD-OUTCOME(*database, collaborators*)
7   **return** ARGMAX(*candidates, quality*)

EMBELLISH-INCREMENTAL(*protocol, database, role*)

1   **for** *r* ∈ ROLE-DEFINITIONS(*protocol*)
2   **do** *role-definition*[*r*] ← DEFINITION-FOR-ROLE(*protocol, r*)
3   *candidates* ← AVAILABLE-ROLE-DEFINITIONS(*protocol,database,role*) *role*)
4   **for** *c* ∈ *candidates*
5   **do** *role-definition*[*role*] ← *c*
6   *quality*[*c*] ← PROBABILITY-GOOD-OUTCOME(*database, role-definitions*)
7   **return** ARGMAX(*role-definitions, quality*)

ARGMAX as used here does not always select the highest value. To improve the exploration of options, those entries that have low numbers of data points (i.e. have not often been selected previously) are preferentially chosen, and in other cases a random selection is sometimes made.

Fig. 4. Algorithms

Roles consist of an ordering of messages, together with constraints, and moves to other roles. It might be the case that just changing the ordering might make a large difference. For instance, if one is arranging to travel to a concert, it is preferable to obtain event tickets first, then organise transport. In our example, we take to problem of booking a trip involving a flight and hotel room. The LCC protocol is shown in figure 6. If we suppose that it is a preferable course of action to book the flight then the hotel room, since hotel room costs are more flexible that flight ones, we can expect a better outcome using *flight-then-hotel* rather than *hotel-then-flight*. Figure 5(c) shows the improvement in a simulation. The algorithm used is EMBELLISH-INCREMENTAL, shown in figure 4. EMBELLISH-INCREMENTAL works similarly to RECRUIT-INCREMENTAL, adding role definitions to the protocol as those roles are required at run-time. We have not provided equivalent to RECRUIT-JOINT, since this can inflate protocols with many roles that will remain unused.

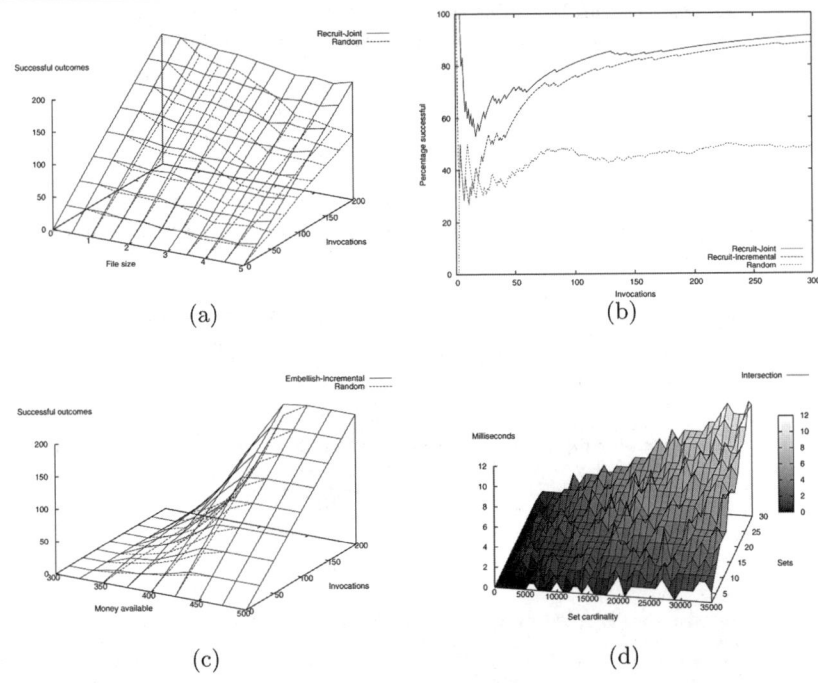

(a)   (b)

(c)   (d)

In (a), we see the improvement in task achievement using agent selection obtained using RECRUIT-JOINT versus random selection. Using the same scenario, but fixing the file size at 5 Gigabytes, (b) shows the relative performance of RECRUIT-JOINT, RECRUIT-INCREMENTAL, and random selection. We can see similar gains for selection of roles in (c), using the travel agent scenario. Performance of the underlying set calculus intersection operation is shown in (d).

Fig. 5. Simulation results

5   Discussion

Performance seems quite reasonable for very large sets. The core operation of this technique is set intersection, since for every collaboration or set of role definitions, the intersection of their incidences must be computed. By using a heap-sort like intersection algorithm, this can be done in order $O(n \log n)$. Figure 5(d) shows that we can quickly calculate intersections over large sets for reasonable numbers of sizable sets.

We note here two significant problems that seem to be inescapable issues intrinsic to the problem: trusting clients to evaluate protocol performance honestly and in a conventional manner; and the problems of locating mutually coöperative services in a large agent ecology. Since individual client services are responsible for the assigning of success metrics to matchmakings, there is scope for services

$$a(traveller, Traveller) ::$$
$$book\text{-}holiday(Src, Dst, Start, End, Money) \Rightarrow a(travel\text{-}agent, Agent)$$
$$\leftarrow travel\text{-}details(Src, Dst, Start, End, Money) \text{ then}$$
$$\left(\begin{array}{l} booking(Start, End, Cost) \Leftarrow a(travel\text{-}agent, Agent) \text{ then} \\ matchmaking(good) \Rightarrow a(matchmaker, matchmaker) \end{array} \right) \; or$$
$$\left(\begin{array}{l} failure \Leftarrow a(travel\text{-}agent, Agent) \text{ then} \\ matchmaking(bad) \Rightarrow a(matchmaker, matchmaker) \end{array} \right)$$

Note that the *travel-agent* role is not specified in the client's protocol! We leave it to the matchmaker to find one. The matchmaker, let us say, has the following role definitions available to it:

$$role(flight\text{-}then\text{-}hotel) \equiv a(travel\text{-}agent, Agent) ::$$
$$book\text{-}holiday(Src, Dst, Start, End, Money) \Leftarrow a(client, Client) \text{ then}$$
$$book\text{-}flight(Src, Dst, Start, End, Money) \Rightarrow a(airline, Airline) \text{ then}$$
$$\left(\begin{array}{l} no\text{-}flights \Leftarrow a(airline, Airline) \text{ then} \\ failure \Rightarrow a(client, Client) \end{array} \right) \; or$$
$$\left(\begin{array}{l} flight\text{-}booking(Flight\text{-}Cost) \Leftarrow a(airline, Airline) \text{ then} \\ flight\text{-}available(Src, Dst, Start, End, Money) \Leftarrow a(airline, Airline) \text{ then} \\ book\text{-}hotel(Location, Start, End, Money) \Rightarrow a(hotel, Hotel) \\ \quad \leftarrow is(Money\text{-}Left, Money - Flight\text{-}Cost) \text{ then} \\ \left(\begin{array}{l} hotel\text{-}booking(Hotel\text{-}Cost) \Leftarrow a(hotel, Hotel) \text{ then} \\ booking(Total\text{-}Cost) \Rightarrow a(client, Client) \\ \quad \leftarrow is(Total\text{-}Cost, Flight\text{-}Cost + Hotel\text{-}Cost) \end{array} \right) \; or \\ \left(\begin{array}{l} no\text{-}vacancy \Leftarrow a(hotel, Hotel) \text{ then} \\ failure \Rightarrow a(client, Client) \end{array} \right) \end{array} \right)$$

$$role(flight\text{-}then\text{-}hotel) \equiv a(travel\text{-}agent, Agent) ::$$
$$book\text{-}holiday(Src, Dst, Start, End, Money) \Leftarrow a(client, Client) \text{ then}$$
$$book\text{-}flight(Src, Dst, Start, End, Money) \Rightarrow a(airline, Airline) \text{ then}$$
$$\left(\begin{array}{l} no\text{-}flights \Leftarrow a(airline, Airline) \text{ then} \\ failure \Rightarrow a(client, Client) \end{array} \right) \; or$$
$$\left(\begin{array}{l} flight\text{-}booking(Flight\text{-}Cost) \Leftarrow a(airline, Airline) \text{ then} \\ flight\text{-}available(Src, Dst, Start, End, Money) \Leftarrow a(airline, Airline) \text{ then} \\ book\text{-}hotel(Location, Start, End, Money) \Rightarrow a(hotel, Hotel) \\ \quad \leftarrow is(Money\text{-}Left, Money - Flight\text{-}Cost) \text{ then} \\ \left(\begin{array}{l} hotel\text{-}booking(Hotel\text{-}Cost) \Leftarrow a(hotel, Hotel) \text{ then} \\ booking(Total\text{-}Cost) \Rightarrow a(client, Client) \\ \quad \leftarrow is(Total\text{-}Cost, Flight\text{-}Cost + Hotel\text{-}Cost) \end{array} \right) \; or \\ \left(\begin{array}{l} no\text{-}vacancy \Leftarrow a(hotel, Hotel) \text{ then} \\ failure \Rightarrow a(client, Client) \end{array} \right) \end{array} \right)$$

$$a(hotel, Hotel) ::$$
$$book\text{-}hotel(Location, Start, End, Money) \Leftarrow a(Role, Agent) \text{ then}$$
$$room\text{-}available(Location, Start, End, Money, Cost) \Rightarrow a(Role, Agent)$$
$$\quad \leftarrow room\text{-}available(Location, Start, End, Money, Cost) \text{ or}$$
$$no\text{-}vacancy \Rightarrow a(Role, Agent)$$

$$a(airline, Airline) ::$$
$$book\text{-}flight(Src, Dst, Start, End, Money) \Leftarrow a(Role, Agent) \text{ then}$$
$$flight\text{-}available(Src, Dst, Start, End, Money) \Rightarrow a(Role, Agent)$$
$$\quad \leftarrow flight\text{-}available(Src, Dst, Start, End, Money) \text{ or}$$
$$no\text{-}flights \Rightarrow a(Role, Agent)$$

$$a(matchmaker, matchmaker) ::$$
$$record\text{-}matchmaking\text{-}outcome(Outcome)$$
$$\quad \leftarrow matchmaking(Outcome) \Leftarrow a(Role, Agent)$$

Fig. 6. Booking a holiday with LCC

with unusual criteria or malicious intent to corrupt the database. The second question, largely unasked, is about the likely demographics of service provision. For some types of service, like search, we have already seen that a very small number of providers. For other tasks, a few hundred exist: think of airlines. For some, though, we may millions of service providers. Further, we must ask how many service types will be provided. Again, in each domain, we might have a simple, monolithic interface, or an interface with such fine granularity that few engineers ever fully understand or exploit it. The answers to these will impact the nature of our matchmaking infrastructure.

While our technique handles large numbers of incidences, it does not scale for very large numbers of services or roles. For any protocol with a set of roles R, and with each role having $|providers(r_i)|$ providers, the number of ways of choosing a team is $\prod_{r_i \in R} |providers(r_i)|$, or $O(m^n)$. No matchmaking system could possibly hope to discover all the various permutations of services in a rich environment, although machine learning techniques might be helpful in directing the search for groupings of services. How much of an issue this actually becomes in any particular domain will be heavily influenced by the outcomes to the issues discussed above.

6   Related Work

The connection problem arises in agent systems, semantic web, and grid environments. It is discussed in [2, 13, 14]. We consciously ignored methods like those found in [15], though they would be crucial in any real-world deployment: we believe our technique would usefully augment such systems. Similarly, several groups have attacked the workflow synthesis issue using automated planning [16]: we again suggest our method as an adjunct to other techniques, not a replacement.

Two studies have investigated the issue of using previous performance records. In [5] we first see the use of records to improve selection. In [17] this technique is combined with description logic concepts to improve matching of OWL-S requests.

Most work has been restricted to the case of selecting a single agent for a single role. Although current interactions are primarily client-server, we can imagine a future where match-made agent interactions are more distributed, involve many agents, and operate in a more peer-to-peer manner. It can be expected that these newer forms of dialogue will make even greater use of, and demands upon, matchmaking services than do current modes of employment. Our problem conception—matchmaking multiple roles for the same dialogue—is anticipated by the SELF-SERV system [18], though we believe our approach is novel in detecting emergent properties that are not known to the operator, and is more transparent, requiring less intervention (that is, specification of service parameters) from the client.

7   Conclusion

Distributed computing is becoming commonplace, and automated discovery of these systems will become crucial, too. The current, dominant model of service provision can be characterised by noting that: workflow execution happens on one machine dedicated to the purpose, whether the client's, a workflow server, or a middle agent, and other services are used as remote procedure calls; that the workflow is never exported beyond the machine; that services are selected based only on their capability as advertised through logical descriptions; and that information recorded about success or otherwise is, at best, held only by the machine which discovered it.

In this paper we made four claims: that services may not be totally described by their service advertisements; that services may interact in odd ways; that interaction patterns may be as important as the interacting objects; and that a simple, statistical matchmaker can be of help in solving all three problems.

We have shown that the successful completion of a task may depend not only on the advertised abilities of services but on their collective suitability and inter-operability. We also showed that the structure of the interaction can be important. We presented a simple, but effective, technique for detecting successful groupings of services, and choosing those interaction patterns that suit them best. We highlighted the intractability of the problem in environments with large numbers of available provider services and/or roles. We can sum up the traditional model of matchmaking as *static and action-oriented*. Our approach is *dynamic and interaction-oriented*, allowing us to respond to actual performance, and better support agent selection and protocol synthesis.

Further work remains. Practical issues of managing a large database of incidences must be resolved: can the task be distributed, either across clusters, like current Internet search engines, or in a peer-to-peer way? What scope is there for applying machine learning? Is our current description of services sufficient, and if not, how do we integrate more sophisticated notions of service description?

References

1. Oinn, T.M., Addis, M., Ferris, J., Marvin, D., Greenwood, R.M., Carver, T., Pocock, M.R., Wipat, A., Li, P.: Taverna: a tool for the composition and enactment of bioinformatics workflows. Bioinformatics **20** (2004) 3045–3054
2. Decker, K., Sycara, K., Williamson, M.: Middle-Agents for the Internet. In: Proceedings of the 15th International Joint Conference on Artificial Intelligence, Nagoya, Japan (1997)
3. Wickler, G., Tate, A.: Capability Representations for Brokering: A Survey (1999)
4. Martin, D., Burstein, M., Hobbs, J., Lassila, O., McDermott, D., McIlraith, S., Narayanan, S., Paolucci, M., Parsia, B., Payne, T., Sirin, E., Srinivasan, N., Sycara, K.: Owl-s: Semantic markup for web services (2004)
5. Zhang, Z., Zhang, C.: An improvement to matchmaking algorithms for middle agents. In: Proceedings of the first international joint conference on Autonomous agents and multiagent systems, ACM Press (2002) 1340–1347
6. Pan, Z.: Benchmarking DL Reasoners Using Realistic Ontologies. In: OWL: Directions and Experiences, Galway, Ireland (2005)
7. Osman, N., Robertson, D., Walton, C.: Run-time model checking of interaction and deontic models for multi-agent systems. In: Proceedings of the European Multi-Agent Systems Workshop, 2005. (2005)

 8. Besana, P., Robertson, D., Rovatsos, M.: Exploiting Interaction Contexts in P2P ontologoy mapping. In: Proceedings of the second international workshop on peer-to-peer knowledge management. (2005)
 9. Lambert, D., Robertson, D.: Matchmaking multi-party interactions using historical performance data. In: Proceedings of the Fourth International Joint Conference on Autonomous Agents and Multi-Agent Systems (AAMAS-05). (2005) 611–617
10. Robertson, D.: A lightweight method for coordination of agent oriented web services. In: Proceedings of the 2004 AAAI Spring Symposium on Semantic Web Services, California, USA (2004)
11. Milner, R.: Communication and concurrency. Prentice-Hall, Inc., Upper Saddle River, NJ, USA (1989)
12. Bundy, A.: Incidence calculus: A mechanism for probabilistic reasoning. Journal of Automated Reasoning **1** (1985) 263–284
13. Wong, H., Sycara, K.: A Taxonomy of Middle-agents for the Internet. In: 4th International Conference on Multi-Agent Systems (ICMAS 2000). (2000)
14. Klusch, M., Sycara, K.: Brokering and matchmaking for coordination of agent societies: a survey. In: Coordination of Internet agents: models, technologies, and applications. Springer-Verlag (2001) 197–224
15. Paulucci, M., Kawamura, T., Payne, T.R., Sycara, K.: Semantic Matching of Web Services Capabilities. In: The Semantic Web — ISWC 2002: Proceedings. (2002)
16. Blythe, J., Deelman, E., Gil, Y.: Planning for workflow construction and maintenance on the grid (2003)
17. Xiaocheng Luan: Adaptive Middle Agent for Service Matching in the Semantic Web: A Quantitative Approach. PhD thesis, University of Maryland, Baltimore County (2004)
18. Zeng, L., Benatallah, B., Dumas, M., Kalagnanam, J., Sheng, Q.Z.: Quality driven web services composition. In: WWW '03: Proceedings of the twelfth international conference on World Wide Web, New York, NY, USA, ACM Press (2003) 411–421

Conversation-Based Specification and Composition of Agent Services

Quoc Bao Vo and Lin Padgham

School of Computer Science and Information Technology
RMIT University - Australia
{vqbao, linpa}@cs.rmit.edu.au

Abstract. There is great promise in the idea of having agent or web services available on the internet, that can be flexibly composed to achieve more complex services, which can themselves then also be used as components in other contexts. However it is challenging to realise this idea, without essentially programming the composition using some process language such as BPEL4WS or OWL-S process descriptions. This paper presents a mechanism for specifying the external interface to composite and component services, and then deriving an appropriate internal model to realise a functioning composition. We present a conversation specification language for defining interaction protocols and investigate the issue of synchronous and asynchronous communication between the composite service and the component services. The algorithm presented computes a valid orchestration of components, given the interface specification of the desired composite service, interface specifications of available components, and some mapping rules between parameters to deal with ontological issues.

1 Introduction

Web services have been growing enormously in popularity over the last few years, as people see the potential of the world wide web to provide a repository of program components, in much the same way as it currently provides a repository of information pages. Agent technology for open systems has also had significant activity, with a number of standards developed by FIPA [16] to support interoperability. As web services start to incorporate more semantics, and greater focus is put on aspects such as automated discovery and composition, the gap between agents and web services narrows. Many of the issues are identical.

A vision of intelligent agents in an open Internet environment is that they would be able to locate services to assist them in achieving their goals and autonomously combine them in an appropriate manner forming composite services. In this paper we describe an approach to provide greater automated support for composition of services, whether they are seen as web or agent services.

There have been a number of languages for modelling and describing web services developed as well as frameworks for web service composition. Process modelling languages such as BPEL4WS [5], BPML [6] or WSCI [19] provide concrete ways for composite services to be manually described. There has been significant work on using workflows to support automated composition (e.g. [18,9] and references therein). One

M. Klusch, M. Rovatsos, and T. Payne (Eds.): CIA 2006, LNAI 4149, pp. 168–182, 2006.

common approach is to map workflows to Petri-nets as a formal model to allow reasoning. Using a similar idea, Narayanan and McIlraith [11] propose a framework for web service composition in which web service descriptions in OWL-S [12] are mapped to Petri-nets to allow formal verification and simulation and to Situation Calculus [13] to allow automatic composition. This approach requires that the services to be composed be atomic. As the process model description of the composite service must be given, such a mechanism should be more precisely described as service orchestration. On the other hand, the problem of synthesising the process model of a targeted composite service has been largely neglected with the notable exception of the work by Berardi et al [2,1]. As such, two major goals of the work presented in the present paper are to introduce an expressive language for describing conversational services and to achieve a mechanism to synthesise the process models of the composite services.

Several composition frameworks employ finite state machines or transition systems to formally describe either input/output messages or behaviours with environmental preconditions and effects. These include: the message-based approach (a.k.a. the Mealy model), (e.g. [4]) the activity-based approach (a.k.a. the Roman model) (e.g. [2]), and Traverso and Pistore's [17] approach which performs composition using an AI planner (based on a symbolic model checking approach). For a more thorough discussion of the various approaches, the reader is referred to [1]. Most of these approaches aim to describe web services using formal models such as process algebras, Petri-nets and finite state machines, to allow formal properties of the services to be verified. Our aim is rather to provide a simple language to allow the exported behaviours as well as the interface of a web service to be described in a way that will enable us to automatically produce an executable process model that realises a composite service. The description language proposed in our paper takes a major inspiration from a rich literature on component-based software engineering and communication protocols [20,14].

The main contribution of this paper is a mechanism that allows for automated synthesis of the internal process of a composite service, given the interface description of both component services and the desired composite service. In order to achieve this we also (i) specify a conversation specification language that allows specification of interactions with other entities; (ii) provide a synchronous semantics for the conversations between services; and (iii) provide a framework of mediation to allow communications between services to be monitored by a mediator. The mediator synchronises the possibly asynchronous message flow between services to ensure they adhere to a given synchronous semantics of the entire system.

2   Modelling and Describing Services

Agent or web services are software artefacts whose functionalities are made available over the Internet by the providing organisation. In order for them to be discovered and deployed by users or other applications, they must be described in a language interpretable by the users or client applications. Our model of services is an extension of the model of e-services introduced by Mecella and Pernici [10] as well as description of software components developed within the component-based software engineering community (see e.g. [20]). The key aspect of these representations of a software component is that they specify not only the static interfaces of the component but also its behaviour and evolution over time.

In our model a service is an event-driven component whose events are sending and receiving of messages. As such, the description of a service comprises an *external interface*, i.e. the input/output messages that can be exchanged between a service and its clients, and a *system dynamics* specification of the service. The system dynamics comprises an interaction protocol, i.e. the sequences of actions to be invoked, to allow the service to converse with its client applications or users. The *interaction protocol* describes a set of *sequencing constraints*, i.e. legal orderings of messages, by means of a finite-state grammar. The finite-state grammar consists of a set of named states and a set of transitions, one transition for each message that can be received or sent from a particular state. Formally, a transition is of the form:

```
<S> : <dir><msg>-> <S>
```

where <S> is the symbolic name of a state; <dir> is the direction of the message which can be either "!" (*send*) or "?" (*receive*); <msg> is the name of a message described in the external interface.

The above description of a service comprises the *external schema* which is made available on the Internet to allow a user or a client application to discover the service and to correctly interact with it.

Example 1. The following gives a *Banking Service* specification, describing how a client (of the bank) who has an account with the bank can interact with the service to carry out certain transactions.

```
Service Banking {
 Interface {
  RECEIVE enterPIN(Account acc, EncryptedPIN PIN);
  RECEIVE requestTransfer(Account toAcc, float amount);
  RECEIVE requestBalance();
  SEND invalidPIN();
  SEND authorised();
  SEND overdrawn();
  SEND transactionApproved();
  SEND currentBalance(float balance);
 };
 Protocol {
  States { 0(init,final), 1, 2, 3,
           4, 5(final), 6(final) };
  Transitions {
   0 : ?enterPIN          -> 1;
   1 : !invalidPIN        -> 0;
   1 : !authorised        -> 2;
   2 : ?requestTransfer   -> 4;
   2 : ?requestBalance    -> 3;
   3 : !currentBalance    -> 0;
   4 : !transferApproved  -> 5;
   4 : !overdrawn         -> 6;
  };
 };
};
```

Note that many transitions of a service also require some preconditions as well as have certain effects. For instance, the transition !authorised requires the precondition that the PIN entered is valid for the account. Or, the transition !transferApproved results in changes in the database including the balance of the current being deducted

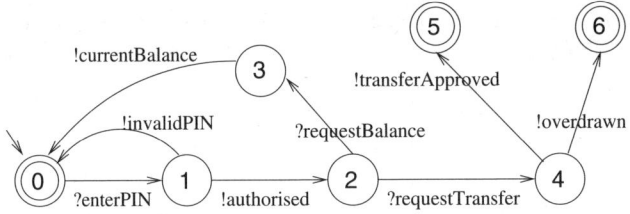

Fig. 1. The interaction protocol of a banking service

the amount entered and the balance of the account to which the money is transferred being increased by a corresponding amount. Besides the fact that not all transitions require a precondition or produce some effects, incorporating such conditions to the protocol description significantly increases the complexity of the framework and makes reasoning about the protocols and the composite service more difficult.

Let S be the external schema of a service. We denote by $States(S)$ the set of states of the interaction protocol of S, $Transitions(S)$ the set of transitions of the interaction protocol of S, and $init_S$ the initial state of the interaction protocol of S. As illustrated in Figure 1, the interaction protocol of a service defines a finite-sate machine (FSM), with edges between states being labelled by !<message> or ?<message>. A protocol also has a (possibly empty) set of *final states* in which it is valid for no further transitions to be carried out with this service (instance). A *mixed state* is a state from which at least one outgoing transition is labelled by a receive message and at least one outgoing transition is labelled by a send message.

2.1 A Model for Composite Services

There are situations in which a client request can not be satisfied by any single available service, but a *composite service* obtained by combining some available services might fulfill such a request. The services used to form a composite service are referred to as *component services*. When an organisation wishes to introduce a composite service based on a collection of existing services, at least two basic tasks need to be accomplished. In the first task, the organisation must produce a specification of how to coordinate the component service to allow the client request to be fulfilled. It is normally required that the specification be executable, i.e. there is an execution engine to execute the specification. Secondly the composite service must be made available as a normal service, i.e. its external schema must be exported and made available on the Internet to allow potential clients to discover and deploy it. It is the former task which is the focus of our current work, though we will also briefly discuss how an external schema is extracted from a composite service at the end of the paper.

Example 2. We now discuss a simple example of service composition involving the banking service discussed in Example 1 and the following *Airline Service*:

```
Service Airline {
 Interface {
  RECEIVE flightRequest(Flight flightID);
  RECEIVE cancelBooking(Flight flightID);
```

```
RECEIVE bookFlight(Flight flightID );
SEND flightUnavailable();
SEND pricingInfo(Price price);
SEND confirmTicket(details);
};
Protocol {
States { A(init,final), B, C, D(final), E, F(final) };
Transitions {
  A : ?flightRequest      -> B;
  B : !flightUnavailable -> A;
  B : !pricingInfo        -> C;
  C : ?cancelBooking      -> D;
  C : ?bookFlight         -> E;
  E : ?confirmTicket      -> F;
 };
};
};
```

A client request to purchase a ticket to fly on one of the flights provided by the above airline involves both the *Airline Service* and the *Banking Service* to allow the following functionalities: request for availability on a specified flight, information about the ticket price (in case a seat on the specified flight is available), and purchasing the ticket by transferring an appropriate amount from the client bank account to the airline (or the service provider) bank account. The message flow behaviour of this composite service and its interaction protocol are depicted in Figure 2.

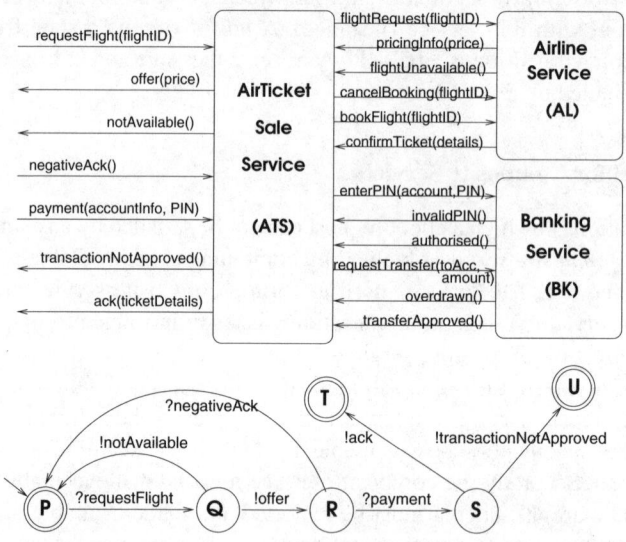

Fig. 2. A simple composite service for online Air Ticketing

To realise the composite service *AirTicket Sale Service*, on the one hand an external schema consisting of an interface and an interaction protocol with messages such as offer(), payment(), transactionNotApproved(), etc. must be exported and made available to the clients. On the other hand, a mechanism to coordinate the component services *Airline Service* and *Banking Service* must be introduced to allow the functionalities of the composite service to be correctly achieved. This is known as the problem of *composition synthesis* which is concerned with producing a specification of how to coordinate the existing services to realise the functionality of a desired composite service.

2.2 Problem Formalisation

Gerede et al [7] formalise the activity-based composition synthesis problem which was originally proposed by Berardi [1] based on finite state automata whose transitions between states are labelled by activities. The problem of message-based service composition has been discussed in the work of Hull et al [4,8]. Given a set of available services whose external schemata are made available, we would like to construct a composite service that meets certain criteria. While there could be several way in which such criteria could be expressed, we will require that the external schema of the composite service be provided. This leads us to a similar starting point to that of Gerede et al's [7] formalisation of the activity-based composition synthesis problem, *viz.* the composition system.

Definition 1. A *composition system* $\mathcal{C}$ is a pair $(S^T, \mathcal{S})$ where S^T is the external schema of the *target* (or, *desired*) service to be composed and $\mathcal{S} = \{S^1, \ldots, S^n\}$ is a set of external schemata specifying the available component services to be used in the composition of the desired service.

Essentially, in a composition system $\mathcal{C}$, the set of component services is fixed with their external schemata required to be fully specified. We require that the target service to be composed also be clearly specified in terms of its input/output messages and its interaction protocol. It is the task of a composer to construct a mechanism to coordinate the component services so that the specification of the target services is satisfied. We henceforth refer to this mechanism as the internal model of the target composite service. For convenience, we introduce the following notations: Given the external schema S of a service, $Messages(S)$ denotes the set of messages declared in the interface of S, and let $\tau \in Transitions(S)$, the function $Dir(S, \tau)$ will be ? if τ is a receiving message in S and will be ! otherwise. We will also write a transition as $s : m \to s'$ where $s, s' \in States(S)$ and $m \in Messages(S)$.

The internal model M of a composite service will have both message based transitions, with which it communicates with component services and the user, and also internal transitions to allow control of internal processing to capture the required business logic of the service.

Definition 2. A *realisation* of the composite service S^T, within a composition system $\mathcal{C} = (S^T, \mathcal{S})$, is a finite state machine (FSM) $M = (Q, \Sigma, \delta, q_0, F)$ where Q is a finite set of *states*, Σ denotes the set of transitions, $\delta : Q \times \Sigma \to 2^Q$ is the transition function, $q_0 \in Q$ is the *initial state*, and $F \subseteq Q$ is the set of *final states*. The realisation M of a composite service S^T is required to satisfy the following conditions:

1. $\Sigma = comm^M \cup trans^M$ where $comm^M = \{<?|\,!>m : m \in msg^M\}$ is the set of communicative acts such that $msg^M \subseteq Messages(S^T) \cup \bigcup_{S \in \mathcal{S}} Messages(S)$, and $trans^M$ consists of the set of transitions denoting the internal computations of the composite service.

2. There is an isomorphism $\imath : Q \rightarrow States(S^T)$ such that: (i) $\imath(q_0) = init_{S^T}$, and (ii) for each transition $(u : m \rightarrow v) \in Transitions(S^T)$, there exist two states $q, r \in Q$ such that $\imath(q) = u$ and $\imath(r) = v$, and $q \xrightarrow{\chi^*} r$, where χ^* is a sequence of transitions from $\Sigma \setminus Messages(S^T)$ such that m occurs in χ^*.

Moreover, in order for the composite service to behave correctly, certain properties need to be guaranteed. A *composition state* for a composition system $\mathcal{C} = (S^T, \{S^1, \ldots, S^n\})$ with a realisation $M = (Q, \Sigma, \delta, q_0, F)$ is a tuple $\langle s^1, \ldots, s^n, q \rangle$ where $s^i \in States(S^i)$ $(i = 1, \ldots, n)$ and $q \in Q$. An *execution trace* over $(\mathcal{C}, M)$ is a (possibly infinite) sequence $\sigma_0 \rightarrow_{m_1} \sigma_1 \rightarrow_{m_2} \sigma_2 \rightarrow \ldots$, where

- each σ_i is a composition state for $(\mathcal{C}, M)$;
- $\sigma_0 = \langle init_{S^1}, \ldots, init_{S^n}, q_0 \rangle$, and
- $\sigma_{i+1} = \langle s^1_{i+1}, \ldots, s^n_{i+1}, q_{i+1} \rangle$ iff $\sigma_i = \langle s^1_i, \ldots, s^n_i, q_i \rangle$, and there exists $\kappa \in \{1, \ldots, n\}$ such that (i) $\tau = (s^\kappa_i : m_i \rightarrow s^\kappa_{i+1}) \in Transitions(S^\kappa)$; (ii) $q_{i+1} \in \delta(q_i, !m_i)$ if $Dir(S^\kappa, \tau) = ?$ and $q_{i+1} \in \delta(q_i, ?m_i)$ otherwise; and (iii) for each $\ell \in \{1, \ldots, n\}$ such that $\ell \neq \kappa$, $s^\ell_{i+1} = s^\ell_i$.

By definition, $Exec\_Tree(\mathcal{C}, M) = \{\sigma : \sigma$ is an execution trace over $(\mathcal{C}, M)\}$. $Exec\_Tree(\mathcal{C}, M)$ is a tree whose root is the initial composition state σ_0. Two desirable properties of a realisation of a composition system $\mathcal{C}$ are *freedom of deadlock* and *freedom of unspecified receptions*.[1]

Definition 3. A realisation $M = (Q, \Sigma, \delta, q_0, F)$ of a composition system $\mathcal{C}$ is said to be *free of unspecified receptions* iff for all $\sigma \in Exec\_Tree(\mathcal{C}, M)$ such that $\sigma = \sigma_0 \rightarrow_{m_1} \ldots \sigma_k$, where $\sigma_k = \langle s^1_k, \ldots, s^n_k, q_k \rangle$, the following hold:

- for all $\ell \in \{1, \ldots, n\}$, if (i) $s = s^\ell_k$ is not a mixed state in the protocol of S^ℓ, (ii) $(s : m \rightarrow s') \in Transitions(S^\ell)$, and (iii) $Dir(S^\ell, m) = !$, then there exists $\sigma' = \sigma_0 \rightarrow_{m_1} \ldots \sigma_k \rightarrow_m \sigma_{k+1}$ such that $\sigma' \in Exec\_Tree(\mathcal{C}, M)$ and σ_{k+1} is the same as σ_k at every position except from the ℓth position where s^ℓ_k is replaced by s' and the last position where q_k is replaced by q' for some $q' \in Q$.
- let $u = q_k$, for all $m \in msg^M$, if $q' \in \delta(q, !m)$ then there exists $\sigma' = \sigma_0 \rightarrow_{m_1} \ldots \sigma_k \rightarrow_m \sigma_{k+1}$ such that $\sigma' \in Exec\_Tree(\mathcal{C}, M)$ and there exists $\mu \in \{1, \ldots, n\}$ and σ_{k+1} is the same as σ_k at every position except from the μth position where s^μ_k is replaced by s' for some $s' \in States(S^\mu)$ and the last position where q_k is replaced by q'.

Essentially, a composition system $\mathcal{C}$ with a realisation M has no unspecified receptions if and only if (i) whenever an execution trace σ can reach a point where the realisation M is in a state where it can send a message m then some service from the composition system $\mathcal{C}$, be it a component service or the constructed composite service, will be in a state where it can receive that message, and (ii) whenever an execution trace σ can reach a point where a service from the composition system $\mathcal{C}$ is in a state where (ii.a) it can send a message m and (ii.b) it can not receive any message, then the realisation M will be in a state where it can receive that message.

---

[1] The notions of freedom of deadlock and freedom of unspecified receptions was first introduced by Brand and Zafiropulo [3]. Definition 3 is adapted from [20].

Definition 4. A realisation $M = (Q, \Sigma, \delta, q_0, F)$ of a composition system $\mathcal{C}$ is said to be *free of deadlocks* iff for all finite execution trace $\sigma \in Exec\_Tree(\mathcal{C}, M)$ such that $\sigma = \sigma_0 \rightarrow_{m_1} \ldots \sigma_k$, where $\sigma_k = \langle s_k^1, \ldots, s_k^n, q_k \rangle$, then either

- $s_k^1, \ldots, s_k^n$ are final states of $S^1, \ldots, S^n$, respectively, or
- there exists $\sigma' \in Exec\_Tree(\mathcal{C}, M)$ such that σ is a strict prefix of σ'.

Definition 5. A realisation $M = (Q, \Sigma, \delta, q_0, F)$ of a composition system $\mathcal{C}$ is an *internal model* of $\mathcal{C}$ if M is free of unspecified receptions and free of deadlocks.

Example 3. The following is an internal model of the composition system involving the **Banking Service**, the **Airline Service** and the **AirTicket Sale Service** in our running example:[2]

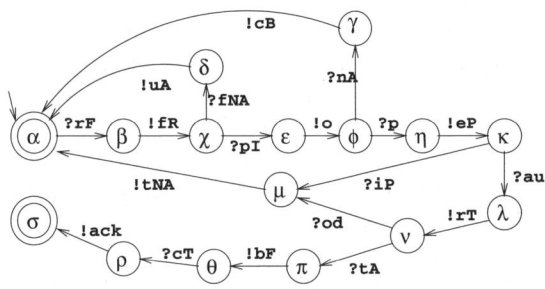

Fig. 3. An internal model for online Air Ticketing composite service

Theorem 1. *There exists an algorithm to check whether a realisation M is an internal model of a given composition system $\mathcal{C}$.*

3   Asynchronous Communication

Under our formulation of the synchronous semantics, the finite-state machines describing the protocols of the component services and the composite service on the one side and the internal model of the composite service on the other side are required to advance atomically. That is, when a message m is sent, one side must be in a state that enables it to send m and the other side is in a state that enables it to receive m. Hence, the finite-state machines describing one of the components and the internal model advance synchronously, so that the sending and receipt of a message are considered an atomic action under this abstraction. However, as discussed by Yellin and Strom [20], the synchronous semantics can be implemented without requiring the components to send and

---

[2] The following abbreviations for message names are used: rF (requestFlight), fR (flightRequest), fNA (flightUnavailable), uA (notAvailable), pI (priceInformation), o (offer), nA (negativeAck), cB (cancelBooking), p (payment), eP (enterPIN), iP (invalidPIN), au (authorised), rT (requestTransfer), od (overdrawn), tA (transferApproved), tNA (transactionNotApproved), bF (bookFlight), cT (confirmTicket).

receive messages atomically. The only requirement is that the communicating components always agree on the execution trace, i.e. the order of messages sent and received.

While the synchronous semantics significantly simplifies the reasoning about communicating systems, in particular, composite services and their internal models, this restriction may severely hamper the applicability of our model to most application domains in which services are required to be dynamically discovered and plugged in to obtain the composite services. The standard way to achieve asynchronism is to use unbounded memory to store the parameters sent from one component to another without requiring the sending component to halt its process to wait for its mate to receive the messages it sends. Although the asynchronous semantics are easier to implement in comparison to the synchronous semantics, it is hard to reason about systems of communicating components under these semantics. In general, properties of the system such as deadlock or existence of unspecified receptions are undecidable [3].

Given a composition system $C = (S^T, \{S^1, \ldots, S^n\})$ and a realisation $M = (Q, \Sigma, \delta, q_0, F)$ for C, properties of the composite service embodied by M and C such as deadlock, unspecified receptions, etc. can be investigated by considering the product automaton constructed from $S^1, \ldots, S^n$, and S^T and M. This is the approach taken by, e.g. Gerede et al. [7]. In our representation, we will have to take into account not only the interaction states the FSMs are in, but also the state of the FIFO channels containing the (asynchronous) messages exchanged between different components of the system.[3] A *configuration* is a pair $\langle \mathcal{I}, \mathcal{M} \rangle$ where

- $\mathcal{I}$ denotes the (global) interaction state, called *i-state*, of the production machine constructed from $S^1, \ldots, S^n$, and S^T and M;
- $\mathcal{M}$ denotes the (communication) medium state, call *m-state*, of the composite service.

There will be n duplex FIFO channels to allow messages between the components $S^1, \ldots, S^n$ and the realisation M to be stored. We denote the content of the queue storing the messages from M to S^i (resp. from S^i to M) by ω^i (resp. $\overline{\omega^i}$). The symbol ϵ denotes the empty sequence. Finally, an i-state is a tuple $(s^1, \ldots, s^n, q)$ where $s^i \in S^i$ $(i = 1, \ldots, n)$ and $q \in Q$.

Without loss of generality we will assume that the sets of messages of $S^1, \ldots, S^n$ and S^T are disjoint. A transition from one configuration $c = \langle (s^1, \ldots, s^n, q), (\omega^i, \overline{\omega^i})_{i=1}^n \rangle$ to another configuration c' is labelled by α which is either an activity from the set of activities Σ of the realisation M or a message from $\bigcup_{i=1}^n Messages(S^i)$ satisfying the following conditions:

1. If $\alpha = !m$ and $m \in Messages(S^k)$ for some $k \in \{1, \ldots, n\}$, then

   (a) If $(s^k : \alpha \to w^k) \in Transitions(S^k)$, then (i) the i-state of c' is the same as that of c except for s^k being replaced by w^k; and (ii) the content of the FIFO queue from S^k to M is updated by $m.\overline{\omega^k}$ (was $\overline{\omega^k}$ before the update).

---

[3] Another attribute of a configuration is the state of the world, e.g. the content of databases, ticketing and reservation systems, etc. This will be part of the future work to extend the framework introduced in this paper.

(b) If $q' \in \delta(q, \alpha)$, then (i) the i-state of c' is the same as that of c except from q being replaced by q'; and (ii) the content of the FIFO queue from M to S^k is updated by $m.\omega^k$.

2. If (i) $\alpha = ?m$ and $m \in Messages(S^k)$ for some $k \in \{1, \ldots, n\}$, (ii) $(s^k : \alpha \rightarrow w^k) \in Transitions(S^k)$, and (iii) the content of the FIFO queue from M to S^k is $m.\omega$ for some sequence of messages ω, then (a) the i-state of c' is the same as that of c except from s^k being replaced by w^k; and (b) the updated content of the FIFO queue from M to S^k becomes ω.

3. If (i) $\alpha = ?m$ and $m \in Messages(S^k)$ for some $k \in \{1, \ldots, n\}$, (ii) $q' \in \delta(q, \alpha)$, and (iii) the content of the FIFO queue from S^k to M is $m.\omega$ for some sequence of messages ω, then (a) the i-state of c' is the same as that of c except from q being replaced by q'; and (b) the updated content of the FIFO queue from S^k to M becomes ω.

4. Otherwise, the system reaches the special configuration error.

The above definition of configurations constitutes the states of the production FSM of a composition system $\mathcal{C}$ and its realisation. Based on this FSM and its reachability graph, standard notions such as deadlocks and unspecified receptions can be defined.

Definition 6. (Reachable configurations.) Let $\mathcal{C} = (S^T, \{S^1, \ldots, S^n\})$ be a composition system and $M = (Q, \Sigma, q_0, \delta, F)$ a realisation of $\mathcal{C}$, a configuration c is *reachable* if either $c_0 = \langle (init_{S^1}, \ldots, init_{S^n}, q_0), (\epsilon^2)_{i=1}^n \rangle$, called the *initial configuration* of $\mathcal{C}$ and M, or for some $r \geq 1$, $\exists c_1, \ldots, c_r, \exists \tau_1, \ldots, \tau_r$ such that $c = c_r$ and τ_i is the transition from c_{i-1} to c_i as defined above, for $i = 1, \ldots, r$.

A *deadlock* is a reachable configuration where all channels are empty and no component is in a state to send a message or move to another state under a non-communicative act.

Definition 7. (Deadlock.) Let $\mathcal{C} = (S^T, \{S^1, \ldots, S^n\})$ be a composition system and $M = (Q, \Sigma, q_0, \delta, F)$ a realisation of $\mathcal{C}$, a configuration $c = \langle (s^1, \ldots, s^n, q), (\epsilon)_{i=1}^n \rangle$ is called *deadlock* if it is reachable and

1. $\not\exists i \in \{1, \ldots, n\}$ s.t. $\exists m \in Messages(S^i)$ and $s^i : !m \rightarrow w$, for some $w \in States(S^i)$, and
2. $\not\exists \sigma \in \Sigma$ s.t. $\exists q' \in Q$ and $q' \in \delta(q, \sigma)$ unless $\sigma = ?m$ for some message m.

An *unspecified reception* is a reachable configuration c where the head of an incoming channel cannot be consumed by the related component at c or any reachable configuration from c.

Definition 8. (Unspecified reception.) Let $\mathcal{C} = (S^T, \{S^1, \ldots, S^n\})$ be a composition system and $M = (Q, \Sigma, q_0, \delta, F)$ a realisation of $\mathcal{C}$, a configuration $c = \langle (s^1, \ldots, s^n, q), (\omega^i, \overline{\omega^i})_{i=1}^n \rangle$ is an *unspecified reception* if it is reachable and $\exists k \in \{1, \ldots, n\}$ s.t. either

1. $\omega^k = m.\omega$ for some sequence of messages ω and $s^k : ?m \rightarrow s \notin Transitions(S^k)$ for any $s \in States(S^k)$; or

2. $\overline{\omega^k} = m.\omega$ for some sequence of messages ω and there does not exist any reachable configuration from c that puts the realisation M into a state q' where $\delta(q', ?m)$ is defined.

From the above definitions of deadlock configurations and unspecified receptions as well as the construction of the transition relation between configurations, the following theorem can be established:

Theorem 2. *Let* $C = (S^T, \{S^1, \ldots, S^n\})$ *be a composition system and* $M = (Q, \Sigma, q_0, \delta, F)$ *a realisation of* C, *a configuration* c *is* **error** *if and only if* c *is either deadlock or an unspecified reception.*

4 Synthesis Approach to Service Composition

We now wish to use the results of the semantic definition of asynchronous communication to define an algorithm which will build an internal model for a specified composite service, using a provided set of components.

Most existing approaches to service composition are based on a programmer provided description of the process model for the composite service in a language such as OWL-S. This is typified, e.g., by Narayanan and McIlraith [11], Sirin et al [15], and Traverso and Pistore [17]. These approaches aim at producing a sequence of service instances that meet the provided description for the composite service. Our interest is in synthesising the process model itself, along similar lines to the work of Berardi et al [2,1].

To aid in developing the internal model that interacts with component services as well as exporting the desired behaviour (i.e. the message interface and protocol of the target service), we introduce rules to allow interface mapping.[4] An *interface mapping* consists of a set of parameter mapping rules $\mathcal{P}$ which essentially express the relationships between the parameters of component services and the parameters of the target service, given by the following syntax:

```
<par_mapping> ::=
    [when <msg0>] forward <msg1> as <msg2>  |
    [<Function>] <par_or_const>+ -> <par>;
<msg> ::= <service_name>::<msg_name>;
<par_or_const> ::= <constant>  |  <par>;
<par> ::= <service_name>::<msg_name>.<par_name>;
```

Example 4. *The parameter mapping rules for our running example include:*[5]

$$\text{ATS} :: \text{requestFlight}.\textit{flightID} \rightarrow \text{AL} :: \text{flightRequest}.\textit{flightID} \tag{1}$$

$$\text{AL} :: \text{pricingInfo}.\textit{price} \rightarrow \text{ATS} :: \text{offer}.\textit{price} \tag{2}$$

$$\text{forward } \text{AL} :: \text{flightUnavailable as } \text{ATS} :: \text{notAvailable} \tag{3}$$

$$\text{forward } \text{ATS} :: \text{ack as } \text{AL} :: \text{bookFlight} \tag{4}$$

$$\text{ATS} :: \text{requestFlight}.\textit{flightID} \rightarrow \text{AL} :: \text{bookFlight}.\textit{flightID} \tag{5}$$

---

[4] Such rules could potentially be derived using an ontology service, however that is outside the scope of the current work.

[5] In this example and the following, we use the following abbreviation for the sake of presentation: ATS for **AirTicket Sale Service**, AL for **Airline Service**, and BK for **Banking Service**.

The idea behind our algorithm is fairly simple. By constructing the (asynchronous)[6] execution tree of the product FSM of a composition system we will be able to explore all possible execution traces as well as the *error* configurations. After deleting the branches of the execution trees that lead to error configurations, the remaining tree (if not empty) provides us with the possible process models for the target service.

The algorithm of constructing the internal model $M = (Q, \Sigma, q_0, \delta, F)$ for a given composition system $(S^T, \{S^1, \ldots, S^n\})$ proceeds as follows. First, as M must realise S^T, let $\mathcal{A}$ be a set such that there is an isomorphism $\imath : Q \to States(S^T)$. Our algorithm begins with creating a unique name q_0 to denote the initial state of M and thus, $\imath(q_0) = init_{S^T}$. To construct the execution tree for a composition system $\mathcal{C}$ and its internal model M, the common approach is to consider the set of all possible configurations (see Section 3) and construct all possible transitions between the configurations based on the messages that can be sent between components and the internal model. This is the approach taken, e.g. by Gerede et al [7]. The problem with this approach is the space explosion issue. As the execution of the whole system will either happen within the internal model or have an effect on the FIFO channels connecting the internal model with the component services, our approach will actually revolve around the internal model and the FIFO channels. Thus we will introduce the following set of (incomplete) configurations: Let $\{\theta_1, \ldots, \theta_k\} \subseteq \{1, \ldots, n\}$, then $c = \langle (s^{\theta_1}, \ldots, s^{\theta_k}), q, (\omega^i, \overline{\omega^i})_{i=1}^n \rangle$ is an *i-configuration*. Then initially the execution tree $\mathcal{T}$ contains only one single node labelled by the i-configuration $c_0 = \langle (), q_0, (\epsilon^2)_{i=1}^n \rangle$, i.e. no component service has been taken into account and all FIFO channels are empty.

Definition 9. *Let a composition system $\mathcal{C} = (S^T, \{S^1, \ldots, S^n\})$ be given. If the FSM $M = (Q, \Sigma, q_0, \delta, F)$ is an internal model of $\mathcal{C}$, then the isomorphism $\imath$ can be constructed as follows:*

- *$\imath(q_0) = init_{ST}$;*
- *let $m \in Messages(S^T)$ and $u^T, v^T \in States(S^T)$ such that $u^T \,! m \to v^T$ (resp. $u^T ?m \to v^T$). If $\exists q, r \in Q$ such that $r \in \delta(q, !m)$ (resp. $r \in \delta(q, ?m)$) then $\imath(q) = u^T$ and $\imath(r) = v^T$.*

It is straightforward to show that if M is an internal model of $\mathcal{C}$ then $f \in F$ if and only if $\imath(f)$ is a final state of S^T. An i-configuration $c = \langle (s^{\theta_1}, \ldots, s^{\theta_k}), q, (\omega^i, \overline{\omega^i})_{i=1}^n \rangle$ is *final* if for each $i \in \{1 \ldots k\}$, s^{θ_i} is a final state of S^{θ_i} and $q \in F$.

Let B be an branch on an execution tree $\mathcal{T}$ whose leaf is labelled by the configuration $c = \langle (s^{\theta_1}, \ldots, s^{\theta_k}), q, (\omega^i, \overline{\omega^i})_{i=1}^n \rangle$ such that c is non-final, the following rules allow one to construct an execution tree:

Extension rule on component services: Let $S^\kappa \in \{S^{\theta_1}, \ldots, S^{\theta_k}\}$, for each $m \in Messages(S^\kappa)$: (i) if $s^\kappa : !m \to s'$ for some $s' \in States(S^\kappa)$ then any transition

---

[6] We note that we do not provide duplex FIFO channels for the communication between M and its client. Rather we simply assume that whenever M is in a state that enables it to receive a message from its client it will repeatedly come back to the same state until the expected message arrives. Whenever M is in a state that enables it to send a message to its client, it simply does so, assuming that its client is ready to accept it or that there is a queue where the message will be stored.

from c to another valid configuration c' may contain an update by replacing s^κ with s' and enqueueing the message m to ω^κ; (ii) if $s^\kappa : ?m \to s'$ for some $s' \in States(S^\kappa)$ and the first element of the queue $\overline{\omega^\kappa}$ contains m then any transition from c to another valid configuration c' may contain an update by replacing s^κ with s' and removing the message m from $\overline{\omega^\kappa}$.

Extension rule on the composite service: (i) if $\imath$ maps q to some state $s \in States(S^T)$ then for each $m \in Messages(S^T)$, if $s : ?m \to s'$ for some $s' \in States(S^T)$ then any transition from c to another valid configuration c' may contain an update by replacing q with a new state q' and storing the message m to an array containing user's inputs for future uses; (ii) if the configuration c is such that the constructed model is required to send a message m then, based on the parameter mapping rules, a set of minimal requirements for m will be calculated. Each minimal requirement consists of a set of service parameters that are used to derive m (according to the parameter mapping rules). For each minimal requirement $\mathcal{MR}$, we introduce a new branch on the execution tree indicating the set of services required for this branch of execution. For each service $S^\kappa \in \mathcal{MR}$, we add its initial state $init_{S^\kappa}$ to the resulting configuration. Note that this mechanism allows several instances of a single service to be deployed on one execution trace.

Closure rule: When the configuration c is an error configuration as described in the preceding section, the transaction leading from the parent node N (on the execution tree $\mathcal{T}$) to c is deleted and marked as inapplicable. Then, unless there is another transaction from N which is not marked inapplicable, the node N also becomes invalid and the transaction leading to N must also be marked as inapplicable. This process is recursively carried out further to the predecessors of N.

Observe that the internal model M of the composite service can be straightforwardly derived from an execution tree as the set of states of M is made explicit in the configurations on the execution tree. In addition to the set of messages sent or received by M, the internal computation transitions such as $require(S^{\theta_1}, \ldots, S^{\theta_k})$ can also be easily extracted from the execution tree. Furthermore, in the extended version of the paper in which we take into account the preconditions and effects of transitions, each minimal requirement (leading to a new branch on the execution tree) is associated with a condition under which the requirement is applicable. Several minimal requirements may be applicable under one single condition.

5   Related Work

Our approach is similar to the one taken by Yellin and Strom [20] in which a language for protocol specification is introduced for software components. Yellin and Strom, however, only deal with synchronous communication between two processes whose communication protocols are given, and building an adaptor for collaborating components whose protocols may not be directly compatible. We on the other hand deal also with asynchronous communication between services as well as building an internal model to interact with the component services in a way that satisfies the specification of the composite service.

Bultan et al. [4] also introduce a formal model for Web services (based on Mealy finite state machines) to allow conversations between services to be specified and reasoned about. Their framework employs a peer-to-peer orchestration mechanism rather than a mediated approach as pursued in our work. Furthermore, they require a composition architecture of the composite service to be given so that the execution of the composite service can be carried out on a peer-to-peer basis.

Gerede et al's [7] framework is probably closest to the spirit of our approach. The delegator of a composition system plays the role of the execution tree presented in our paper. However, they assume that the messages sent and received by services are identical and, more importantly, that the communication between services is synchronous.

There has been a vast literature on AI planning-based approaches to Web service composition (e.g. see [11,15,17]). One major requirement for these approaches to work is that the description of the process model of the composite service must be given (usually in OWL-S). These approaches then produce an instantiation for the given process model to meet the user's goal by looking for a sequence of applicable instances of available component services. It is this process model (or, more precisely, its unfolded execution tree) that we wish to synthesise in the work presented in the present paper.

Berardi and her group [1,2] appear to tackle a similar problem to the one we are trying to tackle in this paper. Their composition model, however, is based on a Roman model. It is not clear how the communication problem, especially in the presence of asynchronous communication, will be addressed in their framework.

6   Conclusion and Future Work

The approach to the problem of Web service composition introduced in this paper is based on a rich literature in component-based software engineering. Our composition algorithm requires service specifications of the component services and the target composite service. We further require that a set of parameter mapping rules be provided to allow messages to be sent by the internal models of the composite service to be synthesised. We examine the conditions under which a configuration (i.e. the state of the production FSM) is an error configuration. The algorithm has then been constructed in such a way that error configurations and execution traces leading to error configurations are eliminated.

There are several directions we could pursue to extend the framework presented in this paper: (i) so far we have not taken into account the preconditions and effects of a service. This requires our model to be augmented to be able to represent the state of the world and to reason about changes made by services; (ii) the problem of failure handling is a more challenging problem which requires careful investigation into different mechanisms to fix errors that occur during the execution or instantiation of the composite process model.

References

1. D. Berardi. *Automatic Service Composition: Models, Techniques and Tools*. PhD thesis, Università di Roma, "La Sapienza", 2005.
2. D. Berardi, D. Calvanese, G. D. Giacomo, M. Lenzerini, and M. Mecella. Automatic Composition of E-services That Export Their Behavior. In *Service-Oriented Computing - ICSOC 2003, First International Conference, Trento, Italy, December 15-18, 2003, Proceedings*, pages 43–58. Springer-Verlag, 2003.
3. D. Brand and P. Zafiropulo. On communicating finite-state machines. *Journal of the ACM*, 30(2):323–342, 1983.
4. T. Bultan, X. Fu, R. Hull, and J. Su. Conversation specification: a new approach to design and analysis of e-service composition. In *WWW '03: Proceedings of the 12th international conference on World Wide Web*, pages 403–410, New York, NY, USA, 2003. ACM Press.
5. Business Process Execution Language for Web Services. http://www-128.ibm.com/developerworks/library/specification/ws-bpel/, Feb, 2005.
6. Business Process Modeling Language. http://www.bpmi.org/bpml-spec.htm, March, 2001.
7. C. E. Gerede, R. Hull, O. H. Ibarra, and J. Su. Automated composition of e-services: lookaheads. In *ICSOC '04: Proceedings of the 2nd international conference on Service oriented computing*, pages 252–262, New York, NY, USA, 2004. ACM Press.
8. R. Hull, M. Benedikt, V. Christophides, and J. Su. E-services: a look behind the curtain. In *PODS '03: Proceedings of the twenty-second ACM SIGMOD-SIGACT-SIGART symposium on Principles of database systems*, pages 1–14, New York, NY, USA, 2003. ACM Press.
9. S. Lu. *The Semantic Correctness of Transactions and Workflows*. PhD thesis, Computer Science Dept., State University of New York at Stony Brook, USA, 2002.
10. M. Mecella and B. Pernici. Building flexible and cooperative applications based on e-services, 2002.
11. S. Narayanan and S. A. McIlraith. Simulation, verification and automated composition of web services. In *WWW '02: Proceedings of the 11th international conference on World Wide Web*, pages 77–88. ACM Press, 2002.
12. OWL-S 1.1 Release. http://www.daml.org/services/owl-s/1.1/, November, 2004.
13. R. Reiter. *Knowledge in Action: Logical Foundations for Specifying and Implementing Dynamical Systems*. MIT Press, Cambridge, Massachussets, 2001.
14. K. Saleh. Synthesis of communications protocols: an annotated bibliography. *SIGCOMM Comput. Commun. Rev.*, 26(5):40–59, 1996.
15. E. Sirin, B. Parsia, D. Wu, J. Hendler, and D. Nau. HTN planning for web service composition using SHOP2. *Journal of Web Semantics*, 1(4):377–396, 2004.
16. The Foundation for Intelligent Physical Agents. http://www.fipa.org/.
17. P. Traverso and M. Pistore. Automated composition of semantic web services into executable processes. In *Proceedings of International Semantic Web Conference 2004*, pages 380–394. Springer-Verlag, 2004.
18. W. M. P. van der Aalst, T. Basten, H. M. W. Verbeek, P. A. C. Verkoulen, and M. Voorhoeve. Adaptive workflow-on the interplay between flexibility and support. In *International Conference on Enterprise Information Systems*, pages 353–360, 1999.
19. Web Service Choreography Interface. http://www.w3.org/TR/wsci/, August, 2002.
20. D. M. Yellin and R. E. Strom. Protocol specifications and component adaptors. *ACM Trans. Program. Lang. Syst.*, 19(2):292–333, 1997.

Evaluating Dynamic Services in Bioinformatics

Maíra R. Rodrigues[1,*] and Michael Luck[1]

School of Electronics and Computer Science, University of Southampton
Southampton SO17 1BJ, UK

Abstract. In dynamic applications characterised by a variety of alternative services with the same functionality but heterogeneous results, agents requesting services must find an efficient way to select a service provider from alternatives. In this context, this paper proposes an evaluation method to analyse the outcome of dynamic service, in order to provide a guide for agents in future decision-making over alternative interaction partners. We consider the application of the evaluation method to the bioinformatics domain and present empirical results that support the need for dynamic evaluation of services in that domain.

1 Introduction

Bioinformatics is a new field of research characterised by the application of computer technology to the management and analysis of biological data (i.e., to gather, store, analyse and merge genome and protein related information) [1]. Because of the vast quantities of data being generated by several genome and protein sequencing efforts, a large variety of services have been developed to analyse such data. These services are not only heterogeneous in terms of functionalities and results, they are also distributed over the Internet, and in continuous update. Such a dynamic, distributed and heterogeneous environment imposes restrictions on the task of managing and analysing biological data and services, and points to the suitability of an agent-based approach. When an agent is engaged in this kind of environment and needs to delegate to, or request a bioinformatics service from, another agent, it is likely that it will find many alternative agents providing similar services.

In essence, there are three ways of selecting a service provider from alternatives: by random selection; by identifying the best provider based on the service or provider description given by the providers themselves; or by identifying the provider with the best outcomes over previous interactions. Random selection may allow providers offering poor services to be selected over those offering better services. Selection based on descriptions given by providers does not guarantee that providers are giving correct information or that the described properties are valid when services are performed in different contexts. The more efficient way to select is the third option, by identifying partners with good outcomes

---

* The first author is supported by Coordenação de Aperfeiçoamento de Pessoal de Nível Superior (CAPES) of the Brazilian Ministry of Education.

M. Klusch, M. Rovatsos, and T. Payne (Eds.): CIA 2006, LNAI 4149, pp. 183–197, 2006.

over previous interactions. This method is based on the assumption that, when services manifest a certain regularity of behaviour, a provider that performed well in the past is likely to perform well again in a similar situation. If the aim of evaluation is to provide some *criterion for future decision-making* over alternative interaction partners, then this offers a reasonable way to proceed.

In order to determine the best outcome in this way, however, agents requesting services must perform an *evaluation* of services after they are executed and the results are received. This evaluation should reflect the satisfaction of the user with the service outcome, which can be in relation to the quality of the interface, the provider's availability to perform the service when requested, the time taken to execute, the quality of the content returned, and so on. For example, the evaluation allows a requester to identify, among the possible providers, the one with the best attributes in a similar situation, like highest quality of results and lowest time to complete the request.

Although the application of multi-agent systems to the management and analysis of bioinformatics data has already been proposed [2,3], previous work is concerned with high-level management and integration of bioinformatics tools and data, and does not address the evaluation of individual bioinformatics services.

In response, this paper proposes an evaluation method to analyse service outcomes, in order to provide a guide for agents in future decision-making over alternative interaction partners. This evaluation is needed to determine how *satisfied* an agent is with a service it has requested and received.

The paper starts with an analysis of the issues concerning evaluation of dynamic services, followed by a description of the proposed evaluation method to be embedded in the agents' internal architecture. We introduce a scenario in the bioinformatics domain in which we evaluate services for protein identification, and end by presenting empirical results that support the need for dynamic evaluation of those services.

2   Evaluation of Dynamic Services

When evaluating a service, independent of the context or domain in which the evaluation is taking place, we must consider which characteristics may be important to analyse during evaluation, since evaluators are usually interested in several aspects of the service. For example, when evaluating the food in a restaurant, customers might take into account the quality of the ingredients, the way the food was presented, and the price. Similarly, to evaluate computing services like search engines, users must consider, for example, the time taken to complete the query, the relevance of the content returned to the user in relation to the query, and the way results were presented. The number of characteristics to be evaluated in a service varies according to the evaluator and the type of the service; that is, the more complex the service, the more aspects might be relevant to observe.

Dynamic services are considered here both as the services changing constantly through new versions and updates, and the services that, despite manifesting regular behaviour when working under similar conditions, can vary their performance depending on the parameter configurations used. An example of such dynamic services are those in the bioinformatics domain, in which the dynamism is a consequence of the great amount of information resulting from continuing genomic and proteomics research. Also, some bioinformatics services, like those related to comparison and search against gene or protein databases, vary their performance according to *both* the quality of the input data used for comparison and search, and the configuration parameters used for execution.

However, because the performance of dynamic services can change from one execution to another, evaluations have to be undertaken every time a service is executed. In addition, the evaluation should be associated with context information, to allow future analysis of service results under different contexts. More specifically, we identify four distinct issues to be addressed by an evaluation method in this context, as follows.

1. *Consistency*: the evaluation method must deliver an evaluation measure that allows comparison between evaluations, even if they were generated at different points in time. This is important when interactions between agents are repeated over time under different conditions, and when new services appear.

2. *Generality*: the evaluation method must be general enough to be applied to different types of service. Having one general method that can be applied in all situations is more advantageous than having to define specific methods for different types of services. A consequence of this generality is the need to support evaluation according to multiple attributes, since agents with different goals may be interested in evaluating different attributes of the service.

3. *Continuity*: the evaluation process must occur every time agents interact, instead of only once, since the performance of services may change from one interaction to another if different input configurations are used, if services are updated, or if new data has been published.

4. *Discriminated information*: the evaluations provided by the evaluation method must alow flexible decision-making in the future service selection process, so services can be selected either by comparing evaluations of particular attributes, or by comparing a single evaluation that combines the measures of all attributes.

2.1 Alternative Approaches

Traditional evaluation approaches calculate the evaluation of a service using scoring or utility functions, which return a quantitative evaluation for the service [4,5,6]. Utility functions can be calculated based on observed values only, or on the comparison of observed and expected values. In the first case, which we refer to as the *absolute evaluation* approach, the utility is derived from values that are observed directly from service outcomes, and the evaluation of a service depends only on its performance and is not influenced by expected performance

[4,6]. In the second case, which we refer to as *relative evaluation* approach, the utility of a service or attribute is derived from the comparison of values from the outcome of the service at hand with those of a similar service, or with expected values [7].

The main difference between these two approaches is that absolute evaluation yields independent measures, while relative evaluation renders comparative measures which require either information about a similar service, or the identification of ideal or expected performance.

As an alternatively to quantitative measures, service evaluation can also use qualitative measures by using classification functions (or rules), which appear in several approaches in web services literature [8,9,10]. These classify services or service attributes according to pre-defined quality categories, such as *terrible*, *poor*, *acceptable*, *good*, or *excellent* for services, and *low*, *medium*, or *high* for attributes response time and cost. The classification function applies pre-defined thresholds to determine the evaluation of a service or attribute so that, for example, the attribute response time is evaluated as *high* when it is less than 10 seconds, as *low* when it is more than 100 seconds, and so on. In addition to evaluation categories, similar approachers consider probabilistic values to represent the degree of pertinence to a specific category, as in evaluating service s_1 to be *good* with a probability of 0.8 [8,10].

If we consider the periodicity of the evaluation process, we can observe that relative evaluation methods, which are based on the comparison of evaluations of similar services, are more suitable for low frequency and bootstrapping evaluations. Since more than one service must be evaluated during the evaluation process so that comparison is possible, when evaluations occur more frequently, it is more costly for agents to evaluate two or more services at once than to evaluate only one through an absolute evaluation method.

Regarding the characteristics of the evaluated service, it has to be considered that for services which have several possible variations in parameter configuration and each of these can yield a distinct result, it is difficult to identify expected measures of performance. Thus, in this case, absolute evaluation methods are more suitable than relative evaluation methods which are based on expected values.

Finally, to guarantee consistent comparisons between evaluations generated at different points in time, it is more appropriate to use absolute measures than relative ones, because in relative evaluation methods measures are dependent on another service's performance or to an expected value. If the services used as a comparative basis, or the expected values, change from one evaluation to the other, the comparison of evaluations can lose consistency. For absolute evaluation methods, however, the evaluation process is independent of other services and expected performance, so evaluation measures are not biased.

3   General Evaluation Scheme

Considering the issues concerning the evaluation of dynamic services identified previously and the analysis of alternative evaluation approaches, we propose a general evaluation method based on absolute evaluation measures. This approach is more suitable for generating evaluations that can be consistently compared, is less costly over repeated interactions, and does not require the identification of expected performance values (which is not trivial for services influenced by different input configurations like bioinformatics services). The approaches to address the dynamic services' evaluation issues are described in the following.

First, to provide generality, the evaluation must take place over multiple attributes of a service. Thus, agents requesting services with different functionalities may have individual sets of evaluation attributes, but follow the same evaluation scheme.

Second, to ensure continuity and consistency, all attributes must be evaluated according to an independent utility function, which receives as input values that are directly observed from the service outcome. The definition of utility functions based on measures directly observed from results, instead of based on similarity or expected measures, allows the evaluation to be performed after each interaction, since it is independent of other services or specific input configurations.

The choice for *observable* measures as input for utility functions instead of expected or ideal values, also avoids relative evaluations that are not desirable for two main reasons. If expectation values change, evaluations based on old expectations will not be correctly compared with those based on a different, new expectation value. Also, if the service being evaluated is very dynamic and sensitive to different input conditions, it becomes difficult to determine what value to expect.

Finally, to have discriminated information, the evaluation method must generate individual evaluations for each attribute instead of a single evaluation measure. If necessary, a single evaluation measure should be calculated during the selection process. This is because, to combine all attributes in one evaluation, the evaluator would have to consider the relevance of each attribute by assigning different weights according to its preference. However, if the evaluator's preferences change over time and, as a consequence, the weights assigned to each attribute, consistent comparison between evaluations is not possible. The components and processes that implement the solutions described above are presented in the next sections.

3.1 Evaluation Attributes

All services need to be evaluated in relation to certain attributes. For example, to evaluate a database, an evaluator agent usually distinguishes between the aspects it wants to assess, which could be the quality of the data entries, and data access performance. We call these aspects *evaluation attributes*, which indicate what is relevant to evaluate in a service or resource.

Bioinformatics services deal mainly with the analysis of biological data related to DNA and protein sequences aiming at identifying their function in living organisms as well as their structure. From a user's perspective, these services must be capable of identifying all information that is related to the biological data being analysed, so they can have hints about its function and structure. Also, it is important that any similarities that are identified by bioinformatics services are correct by a high degree of confidence. Such data-related aspects are also found in traditional web search engine evaluation metrics [12], with the difference that in traditional web search the query data is usually known. In addition, services in bioinformatics usually handle great amounts of data, and thus service results can take hours or even days to complete. In this case, performance-related aspects also have to be evaluated. Although evaluation criteria regarding performance are generally applied in the evaluation of web services [13], they are not considered in many benchmarks for bioinformatics services [18,11], which are mainly concerned with data-driven aspects. Based on this analysis, we have identified four evaluation attributes for bioinformatics services which consider both data and performance-related aspects of these services, as described below.

- *Sensitivity* refers to the ability to identify all significant information that is related to the input data independent of its quality.
- *Accuracy* indicates whether result errors were generated from service execution. An algorithm for comparing the similarity of a protein sequences with a sequence database, for example, must be accurate enough to return only matches that are related to the input and to avoid random matches.
- *Reliability* relates to the capacity of the service to deliver results as expected, and to recover results when there is a failure during execution. A reliable service must have a very low frequency of failure.
- *Performance* indicates the time needed to complete a task.

Depending on the service being evaluated, other attributes, in addition to those described above, can be considered for evaluation and added to the list of attributes (see [12] and [13] for an extensive list of possible attributes). We consider similar services as types, and the only constraint on the choice of evaluation attributes is that services of the same type must be evaluated using the same set of evaluation attributes, to guarantee a consistent comparison between them. The choice of a set of evaluation attributes for an agent is related to the objective of the evaluation. For an agent receiving a service, the evaluation is intended to measure its satisfaction with the service results.

3.2   Result Measures

Evaluation attributes are measured in terms of elements that can be directly observed from the service results. For example, the sensitivity of a search engine may be measured in relation to the number of matched hits that are related to the input query, and its performance may be measured in terms of the time taken to complete the search. We call these computable elements *result measures*.

Using a more specific view, we define result measures as pieces of information derived from service results that can be used to determine the service's utility. Result measures are service-dependent, since they relate to the function and purpose of a service.

We distinguish between two types of measures: *static measures* and *dynamic measures*. Static measures are those whose values do not change, or rarely change, from one execution to another, and dynamic measures are those whose values tend to change when the inputs or external conditions vary from one execution to the other. The distinction between these two types of measures is important when considering the continuity of the evaluation process and the characteristics of the services being evaluated.

The accuracy attribute, for example, can be defined in terms of both static and dynamic measures. In case of database search engines, a static measure for the search engine's accuracy would be, for example, whether new entries submitted to the database are verified by human-experts (a curated database is generally considered more accurate than a non-curated one). This measure does not change over time and, thus, can be evaluated only once instead of every time the service is used. A dynamic measure for the search engine's accuracy would be the number of matched items returned by the search algorithm that are not relevant to the input query (the fewer the number of irrelevant matches, the more accurate the search engine). Different from the static measure, the dynamic measure can vary from one execution to another when different input data or parameter configurations are used. Thus, the evaluation of dynamic measures must be performed every time the service is used.

3.3   Evaluation Functions

An agent that is involved in an interaction and wants to evaluate a service of type t, uses a set of evaluation attributes represented by $A_t = \{a_i, .., a_n\}$. Each evaluation attribute a_i in a set A_t has its own evaluation function, which is expressed in terms of utility. To measure an attribute's utility, we take into account the result measures associated with that attribute.

When more than one attribute is evaluated, all utility measures must be on the same scale to allow their future combination in a single measure by the selection mechanism. To guarantee that utility measures (U_i) for attributes a_i and $i = \{1, .., n\}$ are on the same scale, we define a basic, normalized function which is:

- $U_i = b^c$, for decreasing utility attributes; and
- $U_i = b^{\frac{1}{c}}$, for increasing utility attributes.

Where $b \in (0, 1)$ defines how strict the range of acceptable values is (it alters the shape of the curve in Figure 1) and c represents the result measure associated with attribute a_i. The range of acceptable values is higher for $b > 0.5$ and smaller for $b < 0.5$. According to the function, for decreasing utility attributes the utility will be higher for smaller values of their results measures (c), as shown in Figure 1. For increasing utility attributes the utility is higher for higher values of their result measures (c).

3.4   Storing Evaluations

After the evaluation for an attribute is calculated, it is stored by the evaluator agent as an *evaluation tuple*:

$$(r, p, s, C_j, a_i, U_i)$$

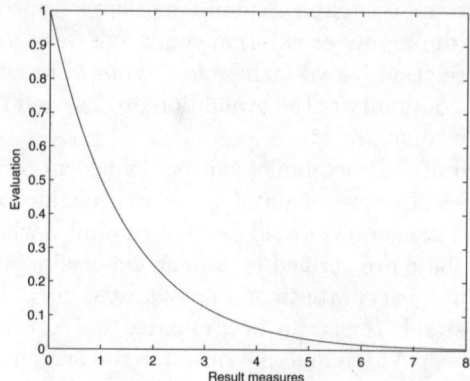

Fig. 1. General utility function for evaluation attributes with $b = 0.5$

where r is the agent requesting the service, p is the agent providing the service, s is the service being evaluated, C_j is the input configuration for service s in the current interaction, a_i is the attribute being evaluated, and U_i is the evaluation of this attribute.

3.5   Evaluation Process

For each type of needed service, the evaluator must identify a set of attributes which it considers relevant to evaluate. Also, for each identified evaluation attribute, the result measures that best define that attribute need to be determined and applied to the utility function for that attribute. For dynamic measures, repeated evaluations are more relevant since they allow the analysis of service behaviour under different input configurations.

Every time an agent receives a service, it initiates an evaluation process for that service, which is carried out by the evaluation method. The input for the evaluation method is the service result itself, or information about the service execution process. The output is a set of evaluations, one for each evaluation attribute of the service. The evaluation process for an agent r when interacting with a partner p, and evaluating a service s which was performed using an initial configuration C_j, follows the steps below.

1. For each evaluation attribute a_i in A_t do
   (a) Compute the *result measure* associated with evaluation attribute a_i based on service result information.
   (b) Calculate the *evaluation* U_i for a_i using its associated evaluation function, which takes as input the result measures.
   (c) Store the evaluation for the individual attribute evaluations together with related information in the *evaluation tuple* (r, p, s, C_j, a_i, U_i).

4   Applying the Evaluation Method

In this section we consider the application of the proposed evaluation method to the bioinformatics domain. In particular, we evaluate services that are used in *proteomics* research [1].

Identification of the proteins which are present in particular cells or tissues of living organisms is one of the main goals of proteomics research. This task is carried out with the help of what is known as a *MS/MS search engine*[1], which receives as input a data file containing a list of peptides from an unknown protein called the *spectra*, and uses *matching algorithms* to search the unknown peptides against a database of known protein sequences. The output is the list of peptides which matched the database, and the protein sequences to which they are associated. The premise behind MS/MS search engines is that if two proteins have similar peptide sequences, they probably have similar function and structure, even if they come from different organisms or different cells.

Alternative MS/MS search engines are publicly available, and differ from each other mainly in the implementation of the matching algorithm. Examples of such search engines are Mascot[14], Tandem[15], and OMSSA[16], some of which run on remote servers, while others run as local services.

Although there are alternative MS/MS search engines with the same functionality, they can yield heterogeneous results for the same input data. Thus, from a user perspective, the evaluation of these search engines can provide a criterion for future selection. In addition, MS/MS search engines are very sensitive to initial configurations and to the quality of the input data, as shown in empirical studies described in [17,18,11]. As a consequence, some services may be more suitable for data with a certain quality or for particular configuration setting than others. This means that, even if one search engine performs better when using a particular configuration setting, it may vary its performance when working with a different configuration setting. Thus, MS/MS search engines need a repeated evaluation process, and in terms of their dynamic attributes.

In this context, in the following sections we apply the proposed evaluation method to evaluate MS/MS search engines and show empirical results that support the need for a repeated evaluation in case of dynamic services.

4.1   Identifying Evaluation Attributes

Experiments for protein identification usually have two focuses: identification of a single protein from unknown input data, or identification of more than one protein from multiple, unknown inputs. In both cases, relevant attributes to be evaluated by the requester are the service *sensitivity*, *accuracy*, and *performance*. The first attribute evaluates the capacity of the search engine to match relevant proteins, which are those associated with a higher number of peptides. The

---

[1] MS/MS is a specific type of input received by the search engines, which comes from mass spectrometry machines.

second attribute, accuracy, evaluates the capacity of the search engine to identify true matches and to avoid false positives. Finally, service performance measures the time taken from the input submission until the results are received.

4.2 Identifying Result Measures

Each evaluation attribute is measured according to concrete values that can be observed from parsed service results or from the execution process. For MS/MS search engines, the result measures used to evaluate each attribute are as follows.

Sensitivity. The sensitivity of a MS/MS search engine is related to its ability to identify all matches that are related to the input spectra. All search engines have a *significance value* associated to each protein match, which represents the chance of that match being a random match. If this value is above a certain threshold, the protein match is considered a *true positive*. Thus, for this scenario, we measure the sensitivity of a MS/MS search engine in terms of the *number of proteins* identified above the significance threshold, and the *number of peptides* matching the proteins (the *peptide ratio*). The higher the number of significant protein matches and the number of peptides per identified protein, the higher the sensitivity of the search engine.

Both result measures can be directly identified by parsing the search result. The number of proteins is calculated by counting all protein matches returned that are above a significance threshold. A simple way of calculating the number of peptides per protein might be by the simple average of peptide concentrations per matching protein as follows:

$$peptide\_ratio = \frac{1}{n} \times \sum_{i=1}^{n} pp(i)$$

where n is the total number of proteins, and $pp(i)$ is the number of peptides matching protein i.

Accuracy. For general Internet search engines like Google or Altavista, a common approach to measure accuracy is to observe the number of occurrences of the query in the matching web site [12]. However, the main difference between MS/MS search engines and general web search engines is that users of the latter engines submit keywords or expressions with the goal of finding related information, while MS/MS search engine users usually submit data with an unknown identity with the goal of finding similar data that could give a hint about the identity or origin of the submitted data.

The submission of unidentified data to search engines makes it difficult for the evaluator to determine the accuracy of the matched results. Unless users submit data which is already known, they cannot determine whether the match is a false positive without further investigation or relying on a detailed human expert analysis.

Although determining whether a result is accurate without further investigation is a very difficult task, some approaches have been proposed in [18] and [11] that can provide some kind of result validation, as described below.

- *Search with multiple input files*: this sends multiple input files from the same protein and analyses each result individually to identify those matches that were common for all input files and those that were not. The idea is that searching with multiple input files from the same original protein sample reduces the chance of *false positives* from being repeated in all individual results, so that they can be identified as 'odd' (false positive) matches.
- *Corroborate results of different services*: this repeats the request sent to one service in a different service and compares the matches given by both. The premise is that services give top hits similar enough to validate each other's results and, thus, the comparison of different results can identify both *true positives* and *false positives* that are between the best hits.
- *Compare matched protein masses with expected mass*: usually, before starting a MS/MS search, requesters have some idea of the mass of the protein that is present in the input file. Thus, the result can be validated by comparing the mass of top match proteins with the expected mass. True matches must have similar mass to the expected one.

Apart from the fact that the corroboration approach depends on another service, any of these approaches could be adopted to determine the service accuracy, since all provide concrete, observable result measures to be used by the proposed evaluation method. For example, if we take the *number of false positives* as a result measure for service accuracy, all three validation approaches provide different ways of getting the information, and the choice of which to adopt is left to specialist users. For the scope if this paper, we do not implement the evaluation of this attribute in the empirical study.

Performance. The performance of a MS/MS search engine can be measured by the *response time*, which represents the amount of time a requester has to wait for the service result. The response time differs from processing time because the former considers the influence of network traffic. From the point of view of a requester, it is more relevant to consider the performance of the MS/MS service in terms of response time.

As with the other result measures, the response time can be determined during the execution process. In the current approach, contextual information that might be useful in determining external factors like network traffic or provider overhead are not considered. However, if services are repeatedly evaluated, it may be possible to identify such variations in performance.

4.3   Evaluation Functions

Since search engines match each individual entry in an input file with the database, the size of the input file (the number of entries) will influence some evaluation attributes like performance and sensitivity. In other words, the larger the input file, the bigger the expected response time for the service, and the higher the expected number of matching proteins and peptide ratio.

In this context, the evaluation of each attribute of the MS/MS search engine considers the size of the input data in addition to the respective result measures.

Sensitivity. The utility function that evaluates the sensitivity attribute is given in terms of result measures associated with that attribute, in this case the number of proteins and peptide ratio. A desirable service is one given a result with a higher number of significant protein matches and a higher concentration of peptides per protein, indicating that there was a big coverage of the protein sequence. The utility function that reflects the desirable result is in the form:

$$U_s = 0.5^{sm}$$

where sm (sensitivity measure) is the relation between the number of proteins returned by the service, peptide ratio, and the input size (in Kbytes).

$$sm = \frac{input\_size}{protein\_number \times peptide\_ratio}$$

Here, the service sensitivity increases as the number of identified proteins and associated peptides increase. Thus, the value of sm is calculated in an inverted form (with a decreasing value for higher result measures) to reflect this behaviour in the utility function. Since the number of proteins is usually much smaller than the peptide ratio, the latter has a bigger contribution to the utility.

Performance. A desirable result in terms of performance will have small values for response time. Thus, the evaluation of service performance is given by the normalized utility function:

$$U_p = 0.5^{rt}$$

where rt is the relation between the service response time and the size of the input file, and is given by the following:

$$rt = \frac{response\_time}{input\_size}$$

The response time is given in seconds, and the input size is given in Kbytes. According to the function, service performance will be higher for smaller values of rt and, consequently, for smaller response times.

4.4   Results

We apply the proposed evaluation method to evaluate four different search engines, two locally and two remotely accessed. These search engines are Mascot remote [14], Tandem local and remote [15], and OMSSA local [16].

For this empirical study, the requests were submitted to all services using the same input spectra (580.8Kb), and two different input configurations, as shown in Table 1. Configurations C_1 and C_2 have different settings for parameters *Taxonomy* and *Fixed Modifications*, while the others are kept the same. We repeated the evaluation process for each input configuration using the same spectra to observe the changes in evaluation results.

Results for the evaluation of the four different MS/MS search services according to the *sensitivity* attribute are shown in Table 2, and the services with best

Table 1. Initial configurations for MS/MS search services

Parameter	C_1	C_2
Database	NCBInr	NCBInr
Enzyme	Trypsin	Trypsin
Taxonomy	*Mammals*	*All entries*
Fixed Modifications	*Carbamidomethyl* (C)	*None*
Potential Modifications	None	None
Peptide Tolerance	2.0Da	2.0Da
Fragment Tolerance	0.8Da	0.8Da
Missed Cleavages	1	1

evaluation for this attribute using each configuration are highlighted in bold. Here we observe that, for configuration C_1 *Mascot* has a better sensitivity, but for configuration C_2, *Tandem local* is better. Evaluation results for the performance attribute are shown in Table 3. Here, we observe that *Tandem local* has better performance when using configuration C_1, but *Tandem remote* is better when configuration C_2 is used. From this results we observe that, if the evaluation process had not been repeated after the first interaction with Tandem local, a requester interested in finding the best service in terms of sensitivity would have the wrong information that Mascot would perform better when using configuration C_2 as well.

Similarly, if the evaluation process had not been repeated after an interaction with Tandem remote, a requester interested in finding the best service in terms of performance would have the incorrect information that Tandem local would present better performance also for configuration C_2.

Moreover, the results show that dynamic services, like those presented on this empirical study, despite having similar functionally, can yield heterogeneous

Table 2. Evaluating MS/MS search services according to the sensitivity attribute

Service	protein_number		peptide_ratio		Sensitivity	
	C_1	C_2	C_1	C_2	C_1	C_2
Mascot	**13**	40	**10**	9	**0.045**	0.327
Tandem Local	8	**36**	11	**51**	0.010	**0.803**
Tandem Remote	2	3	9	6	1.9E-10	1.9E-10
OMSSA Local	31	31	4	4	0.039	0.039

Table 3. Evaluating MS/MS search services according to the performance attribute

Service	response_time (sec)		Performance	
	C_1	C_2	C_1	C_2
Mascot	172	200	0.814	0.787
Tandem Local	**11**	41	**0.986**	0.952
Tandem Remote	26	**37**	0.969	**0.956**
OMSSA Local	2581	2489	0.045	0.051

results under different configurations. Thus, there is a need to dynamically evaluate services to improve the efficiency of future selection of alternative services.

5 Conclusion and Future Work

We have presented a general evaluation method for dynamic services to be used by agents in bioinformatics applications. We discuss the issues for efficient evaluation of dynamic services, which include the adoption of a repeated evaluation process, the use of absolute evaluations, and the generation of comparable evaluations, and describe the components of the evaluation method.

We apply the evaluation method to evaluate services for protein identification, and show the importance of a dynamic evaluation process for those services through empirical results. Results show that there is a need to dynamically evaluate services to have more accurate information about their results, so that agents requesting services in dynamic environments can improve the selection of alternative services in the future. Future work aims to develop selection strategies for agents using service evaluation, considering both individual attribute evaluations and a combined evaluation of different attributes.

Although the evaluation method targets services in the proteomics domain, it can also be applied to services in other domains that share the same characteristics of dynamism (where different evaluation criteria may be required, but using the same method).

References

1. Campbell, A.M., Heyer, L.J.: Discovering Genomics Proteomics and Bioinformatics. Benjamin Cummings, San Francisco CA (2002)
2. Bryson, K., Luck, M., Joy, M., Jones, D.T.: Applying agents to bioinformatics in geneweaver. In: Cooperative Information Agents IV. Volume 1860 of Lecture Notes in Artificial Intelligence. Springer-Verlag (2000) 60–71
3. Decker, K., Zheng, X., Schmidt, C.: A multi-agent system for automated genetic annotation. In: Fifth International Conference on Autonomous Agents, Montreal (2001) 433–440
4. Edwards, W., Newman, J.R.: Multiattribute evaluation. In Sullivan, J.L., Niemi, R.G., eds. Volume 26 of Quantitative Applications in the Social Sciences. Sage, CA (1982) 7–94
5. Russel, S., Norvig, P.: Intelligent Agents. In: Artificial Intelligence: A Modern Approach. Prentice Hall, New Jersey (1995) 31–50
6. Yoon, K.P., Hwang, C.: Multiple attribute decision making: An introduction. In Lewis-Beck, M.S., ed. Volume 104 of Quantitative Applications in the Social Sciences. Sage, CA (1995) 1–75
7. Caverlee, J., Liu, L., Rocco, D.: Discovering and ranking web services with BASIL: a personalized approach with biased focus. In: International Conference on Service-oriented Computing, New York, ACM Press (2004) 153–162
8. Casati, F., Castellanos, M., Dayal, U., Shan, M.: Probabilistic context-sensitive and goal-oriented service selection. In: Second International Conference On Service Oriented Computing, New York USA (2004) 316 – 321

9. Chakraborty, D., Jaiswal, S.K., Misra, A., Nanavati, A.A.: Middleware architecture for evaluation and selection of 3rd party web services for service providers. In: IEEE International Conference on Web Services, IEEE Press (2005)

10. Day, J., Deters, R.: Selecting the best web service. In: Conference of the Centre for Advanced Studies on Collaborative research, Ontario Canada, IBM Press (2004) 293–307

11. Kapp, E.A., Schtz, F., Connolly, L.M., *et al*: An evaluation, comparison, and accurate benchmarking of several publicly available ms/ms search algorithms: Sensitivity and specificity analysis. Proteomics **5**(13) (2005) 3475–3490

12. Dhyani, D., Wee, K., Showmick, S.S.: A survey of web metrics. ACM Computing Surveys **34**(4) (2002) 469–503

13. Lee, K., Jeon, J., Lee, W., Jeong, S., Park, S.: Qos for web services: Requirements and possible approaches. Working group note, W3C (2003)

14. Perkins, D.N., Pappin, D.J.C., Creasy, D.M., Cottrell, J.S.: Probability-based protein identification by searching sequence databases using mass spectrometry data. Electrophoresis **20**(18) (1999) 3551–3567

15. Craig, R., Beavis, R.C.: A method for reducing the time required to match protein sequences with tandem mass spectra. Rapid communications in mass spectrometry **17** (2003) 2310–2316

16. Geer, L.Y., Markey, S.P., Kowalak, J.A., *et al*: Open mass spectrometry search algorithm. Proteomics Research **3** (2004) 958–964

17. Boutilier, K., Ross, M., Podtelejnikov, A.V., Orsi, C., Taylor, R., Taylor, P., Figeys, D.: Comparison of different search engines using validated ms/ms test datasets. Analytica Chimica Acta **534** (2005) 11–20

18. Chamrad, D.C., Korting, G., Stuhler, K., Meyer, H.E., Klose, J., Bluggel, M.: Evaluation of algorithms for protein identification from sequence databases using mass spectrometry data. Proteomics **4**(3) (2004) 619–628

A Classification Framework of Adaptation in Multi-Agent Systems

César A. Marín and Nikolay Mehandjiev

School of Informatics, University of Manchester
PO Box 88, Sackville St. Manchester M60 1QD, UK
Cesar.Marin@postgrad.manchester.ac.uk,
Nikolay.Mehandjiev@manchester.ac.uk

Abstract. This paper proposes a classification framework to help with the understanding and integration of contributions in the field of adaptive multi-agent systems. This framework is used to highlight gaps in the field and derive directions for further research. The need for this framework has arisen from the proliferation of fragmented streams of research, aiming to enable adaptation of agent systems to rapidly changing circumstances and requirements. Multi-agent systems are purported to provide flexible support for users and organisations in dynamic and complex open environments because of their capabilities of autonomous problem-solving. However, exploring the boundaries of flexibility quickly uncovers limitations when agents have to adapt to situations which have not been considered during design time. This issue has been addressed by different research groups using approaches such as flexible systems, evolutionary computation, control systems, and complex adaptive systems. Nevertheless, exchange of ideas between different groups is rare, and systematic analysis of achievements is overdue. The classification framework proposed here is used for such analysis and covers both the analysis and the results in terms of directions for future work.

Keywords: adaptive multi-agent systems, classification framework, ecosystem.

1 Importance of Adaptive Multi-Agent Systems

Business and organisation environments are characterised with distributed, decentralised, and highly dynamic business processes where unpredictable situations occur frequently [1]. In addition, the increase of unstructured information and knowledge augments the complexity to these environments, and this has led to the development of complex systems for organisations' support. Software agents are increasingly seen as an appropriate technology to build supporting systems for such environments because of their ability to build distributed multi-agent systems (MASs), and their capabilities of autonomous problem-solving [2]. But MAS cannot easily cope with the increase of complexity and frequent changes occurring in its environment. For this reason, "agents must possess a pervasive property of human behaviour: adaptation"[3], which in turn "is not an emergent property but should be a fundamental characteristic" [4] in MAS.

M. Klusch, M. Rovatsos, and T. Payne (Eds.): CIA 2006, LNAI 4149, pp. 198–212, 2006.

Building a MAS for complex and dynamic environment is not a straightforward goal to achieve. It is difficult to anticipate all potential situations an agent may be involved in, and specify the agents' optimal behaviour whilst designing them. This is why in recent years research interest has been attracted to the field of adaptive MAS (AMAS) [5,6]. A number of researchers work in the area, following diverse and fragmented approaches, such as flexible systems, evolutionary computation, control systems, and complex adaptive systems. However, exchange of ideas between different groups is rare, and thus systematic analysis of achievements is overdue.

To facilitate this systematic analysis of achievements, we propose a classification framework of contributions in the field of AMAS. The framework is based on three key elements of the adaptation nature itself. Other approaches, e.g. system and user dimensions, are considered out of the scope of this paper. The elements of the adaptation nature which we consider are: (1) Environment: focusing on the environmental changes as one of the reasons for adaptation; (2) System: the interactions within AMAS; and (3) Boundary/Relation: the strength of the relation between the AMAS and its environment. Combining these three dimensions leads to five adaptation classes. Using these classes it is possible to analyse past achievements and set future research goals.

In order to present our classification framework we have organised this paper as follows: in the next section, a brief definition of AMAS is provided. In Section 3, the classification framework is presented along with some representative examples to illustrate each section of the framework. Section 4 gives a comparison of our framework with another classification approach. Section 5 uses the framework to derive directions of further research effort in adaptation in MASs. Finally a brief summary and conclusions are given in Section 6.

2   Definition of Adaptive Multi-Agent System

From the biological point of view, *adaptation* "is the process whereby an organism fits itself to its environment. Roughly, experience [and learning] guide changes in the organism's structure so that as time passes the organism makes better use of its environment for its own ends" [7]. The vision of adaptive agent was defined by Maes [8] as an agent that becomes better at reaching its objectives. In terms of the two main approaches for agent modelling and environment interaction, Guessoum suggests that an adaptive agent would be that who combines the *cognitive* and the *reactive* approaches where the cognitive approach relates to the traditional artificial intelligence (AI) way to represent the world by symbolic models and planning; and the reactive approach refers to the simpleminded agent that reacts rapidly to events without the need to use complex reasoning [4]. Jacques Pitrat goes further (as cited by [4]) and states that an adaptive agent is that who has knowledge about its own structure and evolutionary capacities (i.e. meta-knowledge), so that it can dynamically modify its behaviour by changing its own structure.

Now, considering Pitrat's definition of adaptive agent and Guessoum's considerations for AMASs [4], let us define an AMAS as *a MAS situated in an open environment and capable to self-modify its structure and internal organisation by varying its elements' interactions according to environmental changes*. This definition helps us to identify several key elements in both the AMAS and its environment upon which we base our framework: environmental changes, AMAS internal interactions and the strength of the relation between the AMAS and its environment. The rationale for using these elements will be described in the next section in order to establish our classification framework. Then we use it to analyse existing contributions in the field of AMAS, and to derive directions for future work.

3   Our Contribution: Classification Framework of Adaptation in Multi-Agent Systems

There have been several attempts to develop AMASs and they have provided good results for their particular domain. But looking at all of them together it is not possible to foresee where the research efforts are aiming at. This is where the importance of this framework surfaces, since it provides a useful tool to analyse the proliferation of fragmented streams of research aiming to enable adaptation of agent systems to rapidly changing circumstances and requirements. The framework is also used to highlight gaps in the field and to derive suggestions for further research.

The definition of AMAS given in Section 2 helps us to identify key elements in both the AMAS and its environment upon which we base our framework: (1) the environmental changes which are clearly the main reason for AMAS to adapt itself; (2) the AMAS internal interactions which are one of the "guiding"[8] and "engineering"[9] principles to enable adaptation; and (3) the relation between the AMAS and its environment because of the obvious need to consider the degree at which AMAS adaptations affect the environment. Using these key elements it is now possible to draw the classification framework as follows:

Nature of environmental change: the assumed nature of change can be used to characterise the environment either as discrete or continuous. A *discrete environment* is that whose events are discrete, i.e., changes does not occur smoothly. As a consequence, the environment has states assigned to it and possible event types are known in advance, but occurrence time may be unknown. A *continuous environment* is that whose events occur gradually, i.e. there are no discrete changes. Therefore the environment can be modelled as a function agents try to either manipulate, anticipate or optimise. Additionally, event types might be unknown as well as occurrence time. We consider other agents as separate from the environment and a part of the AMAS.

Nature of AMAS internal interactions: the nature of interactions can be used to characterise the AMAS either as static or dynamic. A *static AMAS* is that whose internal interactions are predefined. In other words, agent types are developed to interact specifically with agents of certain types. Additionally, the number of agent types is fixed and small, and the agent diversity is low. On

Table 1. Classification framework of adaptation in MASs. Combining environment types, AMAS internal interaction types, and the strength type of the relation between AMAS and its environment is possible to group adaptation achievements into five different classes.

		Relation w/ Env	Environment	
			Discrete	Continuous
A	Static	Strong	Automaton	Control System
M		Weak	Semi – Isolated Evolution	
A	Dynamic	Weak	Complex Interactions	
S		Strong	Ecosystem	

the other hand, a *dynamic AMAS* is that whose internal interactions are not predefined. That is, agents are not restricted to interact with agents of specific types. They interact freely creating complex structures and organisations. Moreover, there is usually a high diversity of agent types which is neither fixed nor predefined. As a consequence, complex behaviours can emerge [4,7,9].

Nature of the strength of the relation between AMAS and its environment: the nature of the strength of this relation can be either weak or strong. A *strong relation* is that in which a single change in the AMAS behaviour affects the environment almost immediately. A *weak relation* is that in which a single change in the AMAS behaviour does not affect the environment. It gets influenced after a collection of consecutive changes takes place though. The collection size is determined by the AMAS itself and depends on the particular implementation.

As a result of combining types of environment, AMAS and relation, five different adaptation classes can be obtained as shown in Table 1: Automaton, Control System, Semi-Isolated Evolution, Complex Interactions, and Ecosystem. Each adaptation class is explained in the following subsections along with representative examples from literature. It is important to highlight that we are not evaluating the results presented in literature, but we are (a) using the examples to illustrate the classes of the framework, and also (b) analysing and classifying the different attempts to enable adaptation in MASs.

3.1 Adaptation as an Automaton

The strong relation of a static AMAS with a discrete environment leads to have adaptation as an Automaton. In this class, agents have a fixed action set and the environment has a fixed state set. Agent actions and events bring the environment to different states in a similar way as an automaton works. So, all possible states in the environment are known in advance, and thus AMAS actions are predefined and event types are known in advance. Therefore, AMAS adapts its behaviour according to the current environment state and to the state it wants to bring the environment to. Examples of approaches embraced by researchers working in this category are the following:

A social reasoning for adaptation [10] endows each agent with a knowledge base in which the environment is modelled in a discrete way. Agents have different goals and different sets of actions they use to make plans. Agents may not reach their goals by their own, so they infer they need to cooperate in order to reach them. Agents re-plan and consider other agents' goals, i.e. one agent may infer that it can help other agents to achieve their goals first in order to achieve its own goal later. So, adaptation is enabled when a logical conclusion dictates a modification to original plans.

Interaction experience organisation [11] allows agents to acquire proficiency for further adaptations. It generates agent classes whilst interacting with other agents. Classes are created explicitly in terms of a deterministic finite automaton. Adaptation is enabled by analysing other agents' possible actions according to the current state. An argument-based negotiation example using an implementation of this framework is explained in [12], where agent conversations are used to construct discrete models of other agents.

A generic architecture for adaptive agents development [13] manages reusable software components for adaptation. It selects the proper reusable software components, available in advance, according to the current environment situation. Thus, adaptation is limited to the amount of available components and to the environment states those components were originally developed for. In [14], a similar approach is presented for mobile agents.

A memory-based adaptation [15] allows agents to store environment local observations in a rolling memory window in a discrete manner. Actions are predefined and explicitly represented as states in an automaton. Local observations trigger transitions and bring the automaton to new states, i.e. agents react to local observations.

A feature in common to all approaches belonging to the Automaton class of this framework is the assumption that the environment can be in a number of discrete states, and that the AMAS can control these states, or at least that it has correct responses for each of such states. *In conclusion, the perception of adaptation as an Automaton relies on the assumption that only foreseen events will happen in the environment.* This assumption is questionable when MASs are purported to provide support in open environments.

3.2   Adaptation as a Control System

The strong relation of a static AMAS with a continuous environment lets us have adaptation as a Control System. In this class, the environment is perceived by the agents as an input function (or a set of them) instead of states. Environment alterations are sensed throughout the input function. Agents have a fixed action set and can tune the degree at which these actions affect the environment. Thus, agents have to either manipulate, anticipate or optimise the input function according to their tasks or goals, resembling in this way a control system. In this class, events might not be unexpected because it could be possible to anticipate a situation due to input function tendency. Nevertheless, event types might be unknown because agents cannot see (or do not care) what is causing a specific function outcome. Examples of approaches followed by researchers working in this class are the following:

A load balancing framework for distributed environments [16] allows agents to adapt their structure to optimise load balancing. Agents perform operations such as composition and decomposition where two agents can merge into a single one, and one agent can split into two agents, respectively. By performing these two operations, agents adapt their structure in order to optimise load balancing of different sites they are performing in whilst task deadlines are met.

An economic model [17] enables agents to make investment decisions in a stock market environment. Each agent is represented by a learning classifier system (LCS). And the environment consists of a set of variables about prices, splits and dividends, etc. The input function is the profit obtained by previous decisions. Adaptation is reached by tuning internal LCS parameters in order to optimise the benefits, i.e. get better profits.

An adaptive organisational policy [18] permits agents to allocate tasks and resources in several organisations. A task allocation protocol (TAP) is used within an organisation to form agent teams and distribute workload among them. This distribution is made according to current task throughput which is the function organisations try to optimise. When one organisation needs more resources (agents) to perform its assigned tasks, it uses a resource allocation protocol (RAP) to hire agents from other organisations. This quickens an adaptation process in each organisation where TAP rearranges agent coalitions whilst maximising task throughput.

Adaptive economic firms [19] are studied to deal with the exploration-exploitation dilemma. The environment consists of other firms (i.e. agents) in a market where each of them tries to optimise its own resources. Firms are modelled as LCSs with meta-rules attached to them. The latter consider current performance and elapsed time to decide either to explore for new strategies or to exploit strategies already learnt whilst optimising resources.

A dynamic opponent modelling [20] for football (soccer) simulation environments allows agents to use statistical information to predict opponents' behaviours. Agents create opponent classes using statistical information about opponents' movements, such as speed and displacement in several time intervals according to their relative position with the modelling agent. Classes are used to adjust agents' behaviours to those of the opponents' whilst playing a match. Adaptation is enabled by selecting the best action from a fixed set, according to the predicted opponents' behaviour, i.e. their movements.

A characteristic commonly found in all approaches from the Control System class of our framework is the assumption that environmental events are reflected on the input function agents acquire. And therefore, the AMAS assumes it has all the means to control its environment because it can either manipulate, anticipate or optimise this function. *In conclusion, perceiving adaptation as a Control System depends on the assumption that only events reflected on the input function will happen in the environment.* This dependence may be problematic when MASs have to provide support in open environments.

3.3   Adaptation as a Semi-isolated Evolution

A weak relation of a static AMAS with its environment would, using the proposed framework, classify adaptation as Semi-Isolated Evolution. Examples from literature of this class show that there is no significant difference for an AMAS inhabiting in either a discrete or continuous environment. In this class, adaptation is usually accomplished by modifying agents' internal structure using evolutionary computation. These modifications are made in a separated stage from operation, and AMAS internal interactions are utilised for adaptation evaluation. Therefore, AMAS adapts itself semi-isolated from the environment. Examples of approaches pursued by researchers working in this category are the following:

The evolution of MAS structure [21] concede the creation of new agents using the idea of a genetic algorithm (GA). The three main GA operators (selection, crossover and mutation) were changed in order to be applied on agent behaviours and actions. Agents are selected according to current performance, then their behaviours are "crossed over" to produce new agents. Finally, a random mutation process is applied to the new generation. In this way, the original MAS behaviour is adapted to create a better one throughout generations.

The evolution of behaviours [22] permits micro air vehicles (MAVs) —agents— to cooperate in surveillance tasks. Each agent's behaviour is depicted by a population of stimulus-response rule sets. Each individual in the population (i.e. an entire rule set) is represented by a chromosome as in a classical GA. Stimuli are acquired by sensors and responses are actions such as speed and turn angle. Rule sets in each MAV are evolved (adapted) by a modified GA after each simulation in order to maximise coverage area in following runs.

Strategy evolution [23] for playing the Iterated Prisoner's Dilemma (IPD) game in noisy environments allows agents to adapt their strategies throughout generations. Each agent has a set of strategies which are evolved offline using a GA, i.e. after playing IPD using the same set of strategies the GA is utilised to improve the set for following runs. Nothing in the environment is affected whilst strategies are evolving.

An advice-exchange mechanism [24] in the pursuit domain allows learning agents to improve their performance by sharing information. Predators (agents) are considered either as GAs combined with neural networks or as Q-learning agents. The environment consists of a grid with several predators and a prey they have to catch. Predators request for and give episodic advice to peers in order to learn from others' experience. After each trial, own and others' experience are used to produce better performance for following trials.

A common feature in all approaches from the Semi-Isolated Evolution class is that adaptation is separated in a different stage from operation. *In conclusion, adaptation as Semi-Isolated Evolution assumes that AMAS remains suited to its environment in-between adaptation stages.* This assumption is incompatible with our view of continuous adaptation.

3.4   Adaptation as Complex Interactions

A weak relation of a dynamic AMAS with its environment leads to have adaptation as Complex Interactions. Examples from literature of this class show that there is no significant difference for an AMAS inhabiting in either a discrete or continuous environment. The flexibility AMASs can exhibit depends mainly upon agent interactions because of the complex behaviours they allow to emerge [4,7,9]. Thus, dynamic AMAS interactions along with a weak relation with the environment permits a higher degree of adaptation than the previous class (see Sect. 3.3), but the impact on the environment is still poor. Examples of approaches are not very common:

Emergent design system [25] is the combination of Complex Adaptive Systems (CASs) [7] and soft computing for adaptive construction of structures (e.g. buildings). Adaptive agents represent different types of basic building blocks (e.g. beams, columns) and their interactions allow the emergence of higher order building blocks (e.g. walls, rooms) from the bottom to the upper levels of the structure. The interactions represent both information and connection mechanisms between every basic building block, so that when a new one is added to the structure it propagates its impact through all interactions (i.e. connections) already established in the structure. This impact is analysed locally and it can trigger a re-organisation process at different levels. There is no mention of resource limitations, e.g. the space required for the final structure nor the availability of basic building blocks.

In summary, AMAS dynamic interactions allow the emergence of complex behaviours which could be regarded to provide enough flexibility for adaptation to unexpected, unknown situations. But there is a poor consideration of AMAS adaptation's impact on the environment. *In conclusion, AMA assumes the environment will provide unlimited resources for AMAS to consume.* This assumptions may be far from realistic when MASs are purported to give support in open environments with limited resources.

3.5   Adaptation as an Ecosystem

A strong relation of a dynamic AMAS with its environment leads to have adaptation as an Ecosystem. An ecosystem has been previously characterised as a CAS by Holland in [7]. This term is used to refer to a system in which a large number of individuals or agents exist. These agents interact together and the whole system exhibits behaviours beyond those of the agents'. In this class AMAS has a strong relation with its environment resembling a natural ecosystem. Examples of approaches from literature of this class show that there is no significant difference for an AMAS inhabiting in either a discrete or continuous environment. In a similar way as in previous class (Sect. 3.3), dynamic AMAS interactions allow complex behaviours to emerge [4,9,7], so that they could be regarded to provide enough flexibility for adaptation. The strong relation with the environment removes the assumption of an AMAS having unlimited resources from the environment. Examples of approaches in this class are the following:

An ecosystem model called ECHO [7] consists of agents living in an environment of spatially distributed sites. Each site contains a different fountain of diverse resources which allow the proliferation of agent diversity. Agents consist of a chromosome of eleven sub-strings grouped into two sets, one for agent interactions (external tags) and the other one for resource processing control (internal conditions). According to the resources agents process from the environment, agents can either combat, trade or mate. During these interactions agents consume resources from the agents they interact with as well. The interaction type depends upon the internal conditions and the resources agents consume due to the current interaction. Because of these interactions, the whole population adapts itself until an equilibrium is reached. As a consequence, complex relationships arise such as symbiosis, food chain, and aggregated individuals. In the latter, complex structures emerge by having agents forming coalitions which in turn may form larger organisms. The emergence of complex structures along with the site distribution grant emergence of different species. If a change occurs in the environment, the population adapts itself again in order to find a new equilibrium. Nevertheless, no empirical proof of these claims was presented.

A toolkit for agent application development DIET [26] (Decentralised Information Ecosystem Technologies) is based upon the idea of ecosystem dynamics in order to overcome common MAS issues such as adaptability. It consists of a three-layered architecture from which the lower one is of our interest: the core layer. It contains different types of agents (or infohabitants) that are only capable to communicate locally with peers and migrate from one environment to another. The environment contains resources (memory and CPU) agents have to share. One computer may hosts more than one environment and several networked computers create a distributed world. When an environment (or a computer) becomes unavailable agents re-allocate themselves according to available resources in the remaining environments. Local interactions and agent migrations allow the whole population to adapt itself to resource variations and the availability of environments. Nevertheless, a representative example of an application using the DIET architecture was not presented.

In summary, the dynamic interactions along with the major role the environment plays in this class allows an AMAS to adapt itself to environmental events (at least in theory). Adaptation is accomplished by the whole set of agents, not by single ones, which allows the emergence of complex structures and behaviours. *In conclusion, the soundness of these examples along with the the lack of supporting experiments reported by their authors make a gap where further research efforts is suggested to be allocated.*

4   Related Classification and Analysis Approach

The alternative classification framework of Hayes-Roth [3] uses for classification the aspects of the adaptive intelligent system (AIS) that are to be adapted: (1) perception strategy; (2) control mode; (3) reasoning tasks; (4) reasoning methods; and (5) meta-control strategy. Although on first glance these dimensions are orthogonal to those used in our classification, a deeper analysis of the assumptions and mode of thinking underlying the descriptions of these dimensions allows us to draw mappings between the two classification frameworks. Indeed, most of the systems which focus on adapting their perception strategy could be classified as belonging to the Automaton class of our framework because agents have to switch its perceptual strategy (from a fixed set of available strategies) according to information needs and resource limitations. Systems which focus onto the adaptation of their control mode can be seen as belonging to the Control System class because the focus is on the degree agents guide its behaviours according to own-action constraints and environment uncertainty, i.e. the degree granted by environment uncertainty at which plan actions can be interleaved. Like the first dimension of perception strategy, the third dimension where the focus is on adapting reasoning tasks can be mapped onto the Automaton category because it relates to the adaptation of potential reasoning tasks to dynamic objectives, i.e. either to interrupt or resume tasks according current events. The fourth dimension can, like the second one, be classified as a Control System due to the adaptation of reasoning methods according to internal model construction of the world and the demand for model usage. Finally, the meta-control strategy adaptation can also be mapped onto the Control System class because it relates to the allocation of computing resources among different internal configurations of competing and complementary tasks in order to maximise behaviour utility.

These adaptation dimensions for an AIS are sound and give a good first insight on what agents (and their developers as well) should consider to enable adaptation. Each dimension is well explained with appropriate examples and references to the classical (non-adaptive) AI approaches. However, Hayes-Roth only considers adaptation in individual agents, i.e. the notion of a MAS is not even taken into account, and MAS can render trivial the adaptation problems considered, such as computing resource allocation, diverse task accomplishment because of the MAS distributed nature and different autonomous problem-solving capabilities. And thus, complex behaviour emergence is not allowed because of the lack of agent interactions [4,7,9]. *In summary, the classification framework proposed here is a broader view of adaptation because it includes Hayes-Roth's dimensions of adaptation and adds additional views and considerations about complex interactions found in MAS.*

5   Further Work on Adaptation in MASs: Ecosystem

The analysis in Sect. 3.1–3.5, demonstrates that current research efforts on adaptation in AMAS are centred in the five adaptation classes proposed in this paper. And we have presented the main characteristics and flaws of each class along with representative examples. However there are still gaps in research when tackling adaptation as ecosystems. So, we argue that the Ecosystem class is where research efforts on AMAS should be concentrated in the future. Holland [7] originally presented a set of ideas of how adaptation in complex environment can be accomplished by agents as an ecosystem (or CAS). He presented a set of properties for this purpose which other authors have agreed with [9,25,27,28]. The properties are aggregation, non-linearity, flow and diversity. In Sect. 3.5 examples of approaches from the Ecosystem class were presented (ECHO [7] and DIET [26]), but not enough experimental support was given by their authors. Here, we present a few experiments carried out by other authors to support the original approaches.

In [29] the first experiments carried out with ECHO [7] were presented. They statistically measured evolutionary activity and diversity throughout several runs of ECHO simulations whilst expecting complex ecologies to emerge. They showed that as population increases and stabilises, diversity drops and stabilises. They concluded that the use of evolutionary activity statistics help to analyse the emergence in ecological complexity. In addition, they suggest to address research efforts in this direction.

Smith and Bedau in [28] presented a deeper study on ECHO [7] emergence. They ran a set of experiments incorporating characteristics explained by Holland such as agent interaction rules (for trading, mating and combating). They analysed the evolution of population size and variety of different genotypes. These analyses were made across different mutation rates to variate population convergence. As a result, they demonstrated complex relationships surface such as simple trading. However, complex structures did not emerge, as claimed by Holland. And thus, they argue that Holland's ideas are correct, the problem is that we still have to figure out how to address them.

In [30,31], experiments of emergent group formation using the DIET toolkit [26] are presented. They set a scenario where users have an interest category and they look for other users who share the same interest, and therefore the same information. Each user creates a DIET environment with several mobile agents which in turn know their user's interests. Agents navigate through other available environments whilst assessing each of them in order to determine the best one with more available resources. Then each agent moves to the preferred environment and spend a specific time there sharing user information with other agents and acquiring information from other users. Agents store all these data (preferred environment and agents inhabiting within it) in an internal chromosome. Next, agents return to their original environment for an evolutionary process, i.e., a GA is applied to all agents, so that a new population of agents is generated with biased information about preferred environments and agents living within. Then, the process starts again and continues until the agent population converges to set of most preferred environments. As a result, agent groups are formed whilst optimising resources across all environments. The problem with these experiments is that the original idea was addressed using a classical evolutionary computation approach, i.e. a GA, and because of it these experiments can be classified as Semi-Isolated Evolution and not in the Ecosystem class. As with the previous example, the problem is that we still have to figure out how to address Holland's ideas.

The Ecosystem approach seems more suitable where complexity and unpredictability govern environments in which MAS must provide enough flexibility.

Experiments on ECHO and DIET show some feasibility of the Ecosystem approach, although there is still a lack of ways for addressing Holland's ideas and more realistic experiments and applications. *Based on the principles underlying these experiments and ideas, we argue that the Ecosystem class of adaptation is the most promising foundation for future work on AMAS.*

5.1   So, How Could We Address Adaptation as an Ecosystem?

We believe that in order to accomplish adaptation within the Ecosystem class, it is necessary to draw features from nature and combine ideas and principles from AMAS and biology communities, rather than take the limited approach of simulating artificial ecosystems as suggested by [32]. From the AMAS community, we can embrace the properties for adaptation introduced by Holland [7]. These properties are aggregation, non-linearity, flow and diversity. Parunak [9] envisaged a set of engineering principles for MAS development. Some of these principles dictate that agents should: (1) not be abstract functions; (2) be decentralised; (3) be diverse; (4) dissipate flows in order to orient themselves; (5) have catching and sharing information mechanisms; and (6) execute concurrently.

The biology community, following a separate research line from the AMAS community and with different objectives, have been deriving descriptive formulae for analysing Holland's properties for adaptation. Kolasa [33] presents an approach for hierarchical structure emergence from sub-components' aggregation. Maurer [34] describes how aggregated communities emerge from species diversity according to environment resources. Otsuka [35] introduces a descriptive model for substance flow among producers, consumers and decomposers within an ecosystem, and tries to answer the question of how different organisms with different strategies form an ecological system. Green [36] presents a review on complexity theory in order to explain non-linearity and emergence in ecological systems.

The AMAS community has been figuring out properties and principles to develop AMAS. Biology community has been proposing descriptive model of how ecological systems work in reality whilst giving support to properties and principles for AMAS. *In conclusion, we suggest to build AMAS as ecosystems by using biology findings about ecological system mechanics which support Holland's ideas for adaptation.*

6   Conclusions

We analysed different approaches for adaptation in MASs taken by researchers. We characterise the environment nature as discrete or continuous. And AMAS is characterised by its internal interactions as static or dynamic. The relation between the AMAS and its environment was then characterised according to its strength as weak or strong. Our classification framework contains five adaptation classes derived by combining environment, AMAS and their relation characterisations: Automaton, Control System, Semi-Isolated Evolution, Complex Interactions, and Ecosystem. The main advantage of our classification framework over other analysis approach found in literature is that we actually encompass that approach within our framework.

Adaptation in MASs is clearly desirable for open environments, such as organisations, where unexpected situations frequently occur, and complexity and unpredictability are in constant growing. Seeing adaptation in MASs using the presented analysis framework helps one to visualise previous attempts and address future research according to the required adaptation scope. Our suggestion is to address research efforts on adaptation as Ecosystems. In order to do this, we suggest to look at biology findings about ecological system mechanics [33,34,35,36] which support Holland's [7] ideas for adaptation. We are not claiming to build virtual living organisms (cf. [32]) but to construct systems that really help users and support organisations under the Ecosystem approach.

There are some open questions in AMAS research field that still need to be studied: (1) Can an AMAS be always adaptable? Or is there a limit where adaptation cannot longer continue? (2) How can we predict emergent behaviours from a collection of adaptive agents? (3) What is the degree at which users would allow a set of adaptive entities to manipulate sensitive information and processes?

Acknowledgements

César A. Marín thanks the support provided by the Consejo Nacional de Ciencia y Tecnología (CONACyT) through contract No. 197297.

References

1. Jennings, N.R., Norman, T.J., Faratin, P.: ADEPT: an agent-based approach to business process management. SIGMOD Record 27(4) (1998) 32–39
2. Jennings, N., Faratin, P., Johnson, M., Brien, P., Wiegand, M.: Using intelligent agents to manage business processes. In: First International Conference on The Practical Application of Intelligent Agents and Multi-Agent Technology (PAAM96), London, UK (1996) 345–360
3. Hayes-Roth, B.: An architecture for adaptive intelligent systems. Artificial Intelligence 72(1–2) (1995) 329–365
4. Guessoum, Z.: Adaptive agents and multiagent systems. IEEE Distributed Systems Online 5(7) (2004) http://dsonline.computer.org/.
5. Kudenko, D., Kazakov, D., Alonso, E., eds.: Adaptive Agents and Multi-Agent Systems II. Lecture Notes in Artificial Intelligence. Springer Berlin / Heidelberg, Heidelberg, Germany (2005)
6. Alonso, E., Kudenko, D., Kazakov, D., eds.: Adaptive Agents and Multi-Agent Systems: Adaptation and Multi-Agent Learning. Lecture Notes in Artificial Intelligence. Springer Berlin / Heidelberg, Heidelberg, Germany (2003)
7. Holland, J.: Hidden Order: How Adaptation Builds Complexity. Helix books. Addison-Wesley (1995)
8. Maes, P.: Modeling adaptive autonomous agents. Artificial Life 1(1–2) (1994) 135–162
9. Parunak, H.V.D.: Go to the ant: Engineering principles from natural mutli-agent systems. Annals of Operation Research 75 (1997) 69–101

10. Sichman, J.S., Demazeau, Y.: Exploiting social reasoning to enhance adaptation in open multi-agent systems. In Wainer, J., Carvalho, A., eds.: 12th Brazilian Symposium on Artificial Intelligence (SBIA 95), Campinas, Brazil, Springer-Verlag (1995) 253–263

11. Rovatsos, M., Weiß, G., Wolf, M.: An approach to the analisys and design of multiagent systems based on interaction frames. In: First International Conference on Autonomous Agents and Multiagent Systems (AAMAS 2002), Bologna, Italy, ACM Press (2002) 682–689

12. Rovatsos, M., Rahwan, I., Fischer, F., Weiss, G.: Adaptive strategies for practical argument-based negotiation. In: Proceedings of the 2nd International Workshop on Argumentation in Multi-Agent Systems (ArgMAS), Utrecht, The Netherlands (2005)

13. Splunter, S.V., Wijngaards, N.J., Brazier, F.M.: Structuring agents for adaptation. In Alonso, E., Kudenko, D., Kazakov, D., eds.: Adaptive Agents and Multi-Agent Systems: Adaptation and Multi-Agent Learning. Lecture Notes in Artificial Intelligence. Springer Berlin / Heidelberg, Heidelberg, Germany (2003)

14. Amara-Hachmi, N., Fallah-Seghrouchni, A.E.: Towards a generic architecture for self-adaptive mobile agents. In Alonso, E., Guessoum, Z., eds.: Proceedings of the Fifth Symposium on Adaptive Agents and Multi-Agent Systems (AAMAS-05), Paris, France (2005)

15. Lerman, K.: A model of adaptation in collaborative multi-agent systems. Adaptive Behavior 12(3-4) (2004) 187–197

16. Fatima, S.S., Uma, G.: An adaptive organizational policy for multi agent systems — AASMAN. In: 3rd International Conference on Multi-Agent Systems (ICMAS 1998), Paris, France, IEEE Computer Society (1998) 120–127

17. Schulenburg, S., Ross, P.: An adaptive agent based economic model. In: Learning Classifier Systems, From Foundations to Applications, London, UK, Springer Berlin / Heidelberg (2000) 263–282

18. Fatima, S.S., Wooldridge, M.: Adaptive task resources allocation in multi-agent systems. In: AGENTS '01: Proceedings of the Fifth International Conference on Autonomous Agents, Montreal, Canada, ACM Press (2001) 537–544

19. Rejeb, L., Guessoum, Z.: The exploration-exploitation dilemma for adaptive agents. In Alonso, E., Guessoum, Z., eds.: Proceedings of the Fifth European Workshop on Adaptive Agents and Multi-Agent Systems, Paris, France (2005)

20. Marín, C.A., Peña Castillo, L., Garrido, L.: Dynamic adaptive opponent modeling: Predicting opponent motion while playing soccer. In Alonso, E., Guessoum, Z., eds.: Fifth European Workshop on Adaptive Agents and Multiagent Systems, Paris, France (2005)

21. Vacher, J.P., Galinho, T., Lesage, F., Cardon, A.: Genetic algorithms in a multi-agent system. In: INTSYS '98: Proceedings of the IEEE International Joint Symposia on Intelligence and Systems, Washington, USA, IEEE Computer Society (1998)

22. Bassett, J.K., De Jong, K.A.: Evolving behaviors for cooperating agents. In: ISMIS '00: Proceedings of the 12th International Symposium on Foundations of Intelligent Systems, London, UK, Springer-Verlag (2000) 157–165

23. O'Riordan, C.: Evolving strategies for agents in the iterated prisoner's dilemma in noisy environments. In Kudenko, D., Kazakov, D., Alonso, E., eds.: Adaptive Agents and Multi-Agent Systems II. Volume 3394 of Lecture Notes in Artificial Intelligence. Springer Berlin / Heidelberg, Heidelberg, Germany (2005) 205–215

24. Nunes, L., Oliveira, E.: Advice-exchange between evolutionary algorithms and reinforcement learning agents: Experiments in the pursuit domain. In Kudenko, D., Kazakov, D., Alonso, E., eds.: Adaptive Agents and MultiAgent Systems II. Volume 3394 of Lecture Notes on Artificial Intelligence. Springer Berlin / Heidelberg, Heidelberg, Germany (2005) 185–204

25. Voss, M.S.: Complex adaptive systems + soft computing = emergent design systems (EDS). In Hamza, M.K., ed.: Artificial Intelligence and Soft Computing, IASTED/ACTA Press (2000) 29–35

26. Marrow, P., Koubarakis, M., van Lengen, R., Valverde-Albacete, F., Bonsma, E., Cid-Suerio, J., Figueiras-Vidal, A., Gallardo-Antolin, A., Hoile, C., Koutris, T., Molina-Bulla, H., Navia-Vazquez, A., Raftopoulou, P., Skarmeas, N., Tryfonopou-los, C., Wang, F., Xiruhaki, C.: Agents in decentralised information ecosystems: The DIET approach. In: Proceedings of the AISB'01 Symposium on Information Agents for Electronic Commerce, York, UK, SSAISB (2001) 109–117

27. Levin, S.A.: Ecosystems and the biosphere as complex adaptive systems. Ecosystems 1(5) (1998) 431–436

28. Smith, R., Bedau, M.A.: Is ECHO a complex adaptive system? Evolutionary Computation 8(4) (2000) 419–442

29. Smith, R., Bedau, M.: Emergence of complex ecologies in ECHO. In: Proceedings from the international conference on complex systems on Unifying themes in complex systems, Perseus Books (2000) 473–486

30. Hoile, C., Wang, F., Bonsma, E., Marrow, P.: Core specification and experiments in DIET: a decentralised ecosystem-inspired mobile agent system. In: First International Conference on Autonomous Agents and Multiagent Systems (AAMAS 2002), Bologna, Italy, ACM Press (2002) 623–630

31. Marrow, P., Hoile, C., Wang, F., Bonsma, E.: Evolving preferences among emergent groups of agents. In Alonso, E., Kudenko, D., Kazakov, D., eds.: Adaptive Agents and Multi-Agent Systems: Adaptation and Multi-Agent Learning. Lecture Notes in Artificial Intelligence. Springer Berlin / Heidelberg, Heidelberg, Germany (2003) 159–173

32. Olson, R.L., Sequeira, R.A.: Emergent computation and the modeling and management of ecological systems. Computers and Electronics in Agriculture 12(3) (1995) 183–209

33. Kolasa, J.: Complexity, system integration, and susceptibility to change: Biodiversity connection. Ecological Complexity 2(4) (2005) 431–442

34. Maurer, B.A.: Statistical mechanics of complex ecological aggregates. Ecological Complexity 2(1) (2005) 71–85

35. Otsuka, J.: A theoretical characterization of ecological systems by circular flow of materials. Ecological Complexity 1(3) (2004) 237–252

36. Green, D.G., Sadedin, S.: Interactions matter–complexity in landscapes and ecosystems. Ecological Complexity 2(2) (2005) 117–130

Market-Inspired Approach to Collaborative Learning

Jan Tožička, Michal Jakob, and Michal Pěchouček

Gerstner Laboratory
Department of Cybernetics, Czech Technical University
Technická 2, Prague, 166 27, Czech Republic
{tozicka, jakob, pechouc}@labe.felk.cvut.cz

Abstract. The paper describes a decentralized peer-to-peer multi-agent learning method based on inductive logic programming and knowledge trading. The method uses first-order logic for model representation. This enables flexible sharing of learned knowledge at different levels of abstraction as well as seamless integration of models created by other agents. A market-inspired mechanism involving knowledge trading is used for inter-agent coordination. This allows for decentralized coordination of learning activity without the need for a central control element. In addition, agents can participate in collaborative learning while pursuing their individual goals and maintaining full control over the disclosure of their private information. Several different types of agents differing in the level and form of knowledge exchange are considered. The mechanism is evaluated using a set of performance criteria on several scenarios in a realistic logistic domain extended with adversary behavior. The results show that using the proposed method agents can collaboratively learn properties of their environment, and consequently significantly improve their operation.

1 Introduction

There are two different perspectives from which learning in multi-agent systems can be viewed. The first, perhaps the more pragmatic one views multi-agent systems as a possible tool for solving complex learning problems. The second perspective is driven by the understanding that adaptivity is one of the fundamental properties of any intelligent system. This perspective then considers machine learning as a set of techniques using which intelligent agents and multi-agent systems can adapt in changing environments. Although quite different at the first sight, each emphasizing different priorities and seemingly different goals, both perspectives should ultimately lead to similar core principles and techniques, and should be therefore viewed as dual rather than conflicting.

This is exactly the case with the collaborative learning mechanism described in this article. Although primarily designed to equip multi-agent systems with adaptation abilities, it could be also used as a distributed machine learning algorithm. The algorithm combines first-order logic as a basis for knowledge representation

M. Klusch, M. Rovatsos, and T. Payne (Eds.): CIA 2006, LNAI 4149, pp. 213–227, 2006.

and learning with market principles for decentralized inter-agent coordination. Altogether, the method addresses some of the difficult challenges posed by learning in the multi-agent environment, including the distribution of learning sub-tasks, inter-agent communication, and the coordination of the learning activity.

The proposed method has been implemented within the cognitive-reflective agent framework [1]. In this framework, learned models are represented as encapsulated components that can be integrated with agent's reasoning layer in a plug-and-play manner. This offers several important advantages. The learned theory can be immediately operationalized in guiding agent's behavior. Second, the theory or its parts can be easily exchanged between agents. Finally, agents can rapidly reconfigure their reasoning to match the characteristics of the changing environment.

1.1   Structure of the Paper

In Section 2, we review some of the existing work relevant to our multi-agent learning method. Section 3 then introduces inductive logic programming, which forms the basis of our approach. The proposed collaborative multi-agent learning method based on knowledge trading is described in Section 4. Section 5 evaluates the method on a set of scenarios and discusses the obtained experimental results. Finally, we summarize our work in Section 6.

2   Survey of Existing Work

In this section, we give a brief overview of existing work on multi-agent machine learning and its application to distributed data mining. As our method builds strongly on logic- and market-based approaches, we examine both of them in greater detail.

2.1   Machine Learning in Multi-Agents Systems

The majority of research on learning in multi-agent systems focuses on reactive reward-based approaches and their application to inter-agent coordination [2]. Considerably less work exists on higher-level concept learning and the role of explicit inter-agent communication in multi-agent learning. Panait and Luke [3] present an exhaustive review of cooperative methods for multi-agent learning. They discuss the role of communication in learning, distinguishing between direct and indirect communication.

Weiss [4] proposes a classification scheme distinguishing between three classes of multi-agent learning mechanisms, depending on the amount of cooperation among agents: *multiplication*, *division* and *interaction*. In Weiss'es classification, the collaborative method presented in this papers uses the interaction mechanism. In contrast to the division mechanism which only allows the exchange of raw training examples (see also coactive learning [5]), interaction mechanisms involve higher-level exchange of models created during learning. Apart from potentially speeding up the learning process, this has an additional significant benefit of protecting the privacy of individual agents, and is therefore crucial in domains where agents have private data sources.

2.2   Logic-Based Learning in Multi-Agent Systems

Kazakov [6] discusses the application of ILP for single-agent learning in the multi-agent setting. Agents individually learn the properties of the environment using a Progol ILP system. In contrast to our approach, no communication between agents takes place.

Hernandez [7] discusses the application of the first-order decision tree induction system ACE to learn about the applicability of plans in the BDI architecture. There is no inter-agent communication beyond plain observation exchange and the learning system is not integrated into agent's reasoning architecture.

Alonso [8] advocates the application of ILP and other logic-based techniques for learning in complex multi-agent domains such as conflict simulations.

2.3   Market-Based Approaches to Learning

Market-based techniques have become a popular approach to coordination in multi-agent and multi-robot systems. However, there is currently only a very limited work on the application of such techniques to multi-agent learning. A notable exception is the work by Wei et al. [9] presenting a market mechanism for the aggregation of the output of multiple learning agents.

2.4   Distributed Data Mining

Distributed data mining is an important application area for the proposed method and multi-agent learning techniques in general. *Data mining* [10] is concerned with the analysis of possibly massive amounts of data. Various distributed data mining methods [11,12,13] have been proposed to address the scalability issues limiting the applicability of centralized data mining techniques. Klusch et al. [14] analyze the benefits of the multi-agent approach to distributed data mining, especially in open, heterogeneous environments with plurality of different data sources and data mining methods.

3   Inductive Logic Programming

In this section, we introduce inductive logic programming which forms the basis of our multi-agent learning method. Inductive Logic Programming (ILP) [15] systems fall into the category of machine learning algorithms. They use domain-specific background information, encoded by means of a predicate logic theory, and pre-classified sample data in the form of first-order ground facts, to construct a predicate logic theory for deriving data classification. In most cases, the first-order logic language for expressing both the background theory and the learned theories is constrained to a list of Horn clauses, i.e., to the grammar of Prolog programs. In our implementation, the quality of created theories is evaluated using F_1 measure [16].

ILP is a suitable learning method for the use in multi-agent systems (e.g. [6]) because it represents both the input to the learing process, i.e., the examples and the background knowledge, as well the output learned theory in first-order logic (or in its Horn fragment). Due to the expressivity and the well-defined semantics of first-order representations, learned models can be easily exchanged among agents and reused in agent's further learning or reasoning processes. This feature of ILP is particularly important for collaborative multi-agent learning.

In our case, the sets of positive and negative examples are agents' observations classifying situations occurring in agent's environment. The objective of learning is to create a model which can predict these classifications. Background theory B contains agent's common knowledge including the knowledge describing the context (i.e., relational and temporal properties) of training examples. In addition, individual Horn rules in the created theory are assigned weights specifying how many positive and negative observations they cover. These weights are then used during situation classification to get finer than just binary classification.

4   Collaborative Learning with Knowledge Trading

In this section, we describe our collaborative learning method based on knowledge trading. On the single-agent level, the mechanism uses ILP as an inductive method for generating predictive models from examples (observations) an agent receives. On the inter-agent level, the ILP is complemented with a trading mechanism through which agents can trade observations and (sub-)theories. Agents in the system differ with respect to whether they create models and whether and how they trade them with others.

4.1   Knowledge Trading Protocol

Interaction between agents in the system is governed by a variant of the Contract-Net-Protocol (Figure 1). The seller, i.e., the agent offering its theory, sends Call-for-Proposal messages containing the meta-description of its theory to other agents. The meta-description contains the information used to calculate the F_1 measure, i.e., the number of covered positive and negative examples, and the number of all positive examples in the training set.

Each recipient, i.e., a potential buyer evaluates the offered theory and, if it finds the theory useful, replies with a meta-description of the knowledge it wants to offer in exchange. The knowledge offered can be either a set of recipient's observations (i.e., a training set and a background knowledge) or its own generalized theory. Note that agents are not allowed to resell knowledge acquired from other agents.

Next, the seller evaluates received proposals and selects the sellers that have proposed attractive knowledge. It then sends them the *accept* message with its theory and receives the proposed knowledge as a reply.

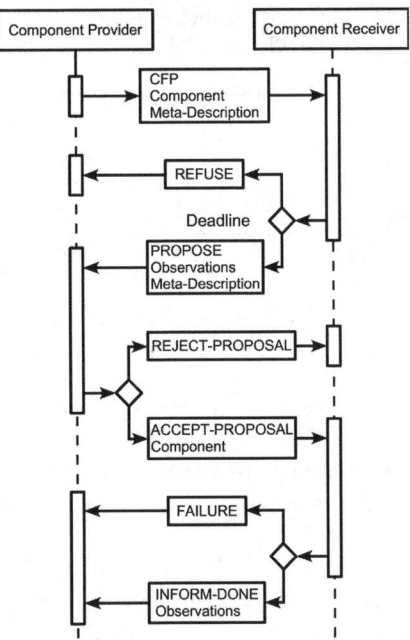

Fig. 1. The knowledge trading protocol used in the collective learning

4.2   Agent Classification

A range of collaborative learning agents can be implemented using the above trading protocol. In order to categorize them, we introduce several agent classification properties:

learning: an agent is called *learning* if it creates its own theory; otherwise it is called *non-learning*

offering: learning agents can be further classified as *offering* or *non-offering* depending on whether or not they actively offer the learned model (i.e., whether they can play the role of the provider in the trading protocol)

trading: an agent is called *trading* if it participates in knowledge barter when asked by an offering agent; otherwise it is called *non-trading*; furthermore, an agent can either trade *rules* or raw *observations*

Table 1 summarizes possible types of agents under the proposed classification schema.

4.3   Types of Agents

Not all possible types of agents are used in our collaborative learning mechanism. A^D, for example, is a totally non-adaptive agent, and is therefore not an interesting member of a collaboratively learning agent society. Similarly, agent

Table 1. Types of agents that can be implemented based on the three introduced classification properties: *learning, offering* and *trading*

Types of Agents		Non-Trading	Trading	
			Observations	Rules
Non-Learning		A^D	A^L	N/A
Learning and	Non-Offering	A^S	A^{O-}	A^{R-}
	Offering	A^P	A^O	A^R

A^P never participates as a recipient in a knowledge barter. Although its behavior might be interesting in some heterogeneous societies, it is currently not used in our system. Finally, as preliminary tests with the agents of type A^{O-} and A^{R-} have not yield good results, the agents have been excluded from experiments discussed in this paper.

The remaining agent types (A^S, A^O, A^R, and A^L) have been experimentally evaluated and are described in greater detail below. Experimental results involving these agents are then provided in Section 5.

A^S – **Simple Agent.** does not communicate with other agents and therefore does not participate in the collaborative learning process. The agent learns in isolation, creating its own theory based solely on its own observations. It is therefore expected to converge more slowly to a target theory than collaborative agents. It has been implemented for comparison purposes only.

A^O – **Observation-Based Agent.** offers its created theory for trading and buys theories offered by other agents in exchange for its observations. It buys theories of all sizes (i.e., even theories covering only a small number of positive examples), however, in exchange it offers only a subset of its observations covering the same number of positive examples as the theory bought does. The agent thus uses the number of covered positive examples as the measure of theory quality. This is an appropriate choice in the domain considered (see Section 5.2) as observations representing positive examples contain the most valuable knowledge. In other domains, a different theory quality measure can be more suitable.

A^R – **Rule-Based Agent.** trades theories for theories, both as the offering agent or as the recipient in a knowledge barter. In both cases, it accepts all theories that are better than its own. Theories worse than its own theory are accepted only with the probability equal to the ratio between the quality of the offered theory and the quality of agent's own theory (which is always lower than 1).

Bought theories are appended to agent's own theory, and the positive examples covered by the newly acquired theory are removed from agent's observation set. The ILP learning algorithm is subsequently invoked to derive a theory covering only the remaining, uncovered observations. This significantly speeds up the learning process because the time complexity of ILP grows exponentially with the size of the training set.

Communication bandwidth required by rule-based agents is significantly lower than the bandwidth needed by observation-based agents. This is due to *compression* performed by the inductive learning algorithm: in most cases, the size of the generalized model is significantly smaller than the size of the training set from which it was generated.

A^L – **Lazy Agent.** does not create a theory on its own. Instead, similarly to A^O agents, it buys other agents' theories in exchange for its observations. The lazy agent is very lightweight regarding its computational requirements. However, it needs higher communication bandwidth to communicate its observations.

5   Experiments

This section describes the empirical tests we have conducted to evaluate the performance of the proposed collaborative learning mechanism. First, we briefly outline the implementation of the method and introduce the domain in which learning takes place. Next, we describe experiments performed involving different types of agents and collaborative communities. Finally, we present and discuss the experimental results obtained.

5.1   Reflective-Cognitive Agent Architecture

The proposed learning method has been implemented within the reflective-cognitive agent architecture, a modular Java-based architecture for the design and implementation of autonomous intelligent agents [1]. The reflective-cognitive agent is composed of two parts (Figure 2):

- **the reasoning layer** implements agent decision-making. The layer is implemented using a modular approach based on the component architecture. Agent's reasoning can be reconfigured by adding/removing new reasoning components in run-time. ILP model is an example of the reasoning module that can be integrated with the agent reasoning cycle.
- **the reflective-cognitive (RC) layer** manages the reasoning layer. It implements closed-loop adaptation by monitoring agent's performance and modifying the reasoning layer, in order to optimize agent's operation in the changing environment. The modification is of agent's behavior is achieved through adding, removing and possibly fine-tuning components of the reasoning layer. The RC layer can also communicate with other agents' RC layers in order to exchange and integrate components created by other RC agents in the system.

5.2   Domain Description

The domain ACROSS [17] used in the empirical evaluation is a logistic scenario extended with adversarial behavior. In the domain, truck transporter agents carry

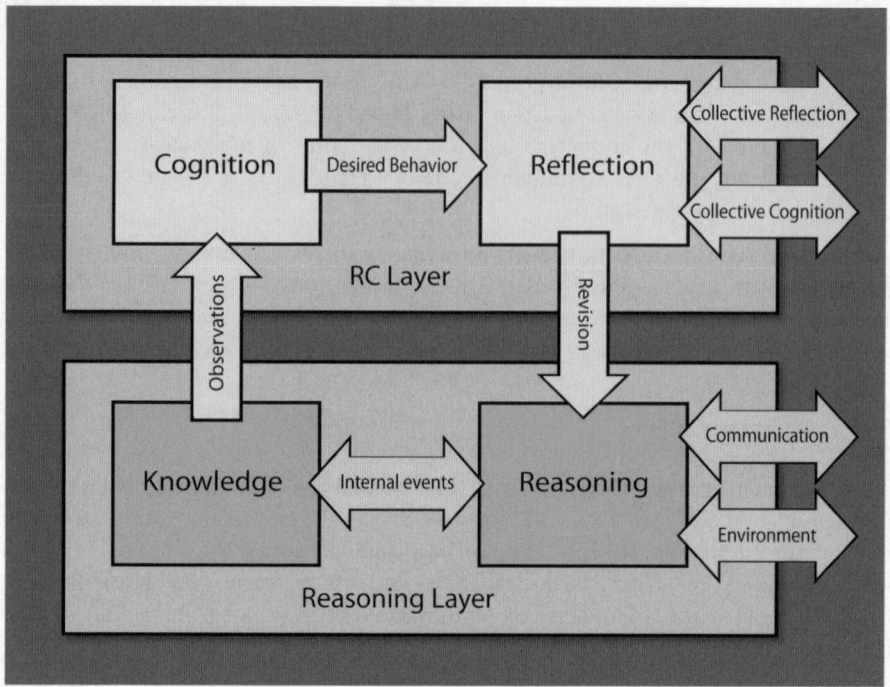

Fig. 2. The scheme of Reflective-Cognitive agent's architecture

goods between producers and consumers. The transporter agents are able to form coalitions in order to improve their chances when competing for transport tasks.

In addition to the transporter agents, adversarial *bandit agents* that can attack and rob transporter agents are present in the domain. The activity of bandit agents is not the same everywhere. Instead, each bandit agent has a set of preferences specifying in which areas and under which conditions it attacks. These preferences are described by a relational theory taking into account the properties of the road network in the scenario. Bandit agents also have some restrictions on the transporter agents and the situations in which they attack (e.g., *transporters of tribe Northlanders carrying cargo to a location not producing this cargo*). The situation description is the part of the agent's observations that do not belong to the training set used for ILP learning. A training example is generated whenever an agent is robbed (a positive example represented by predicate *holdup*), or when it safely passes a road (a negative example represented by predicate *noholdup*).

In experiments, transporter agents try to learn bandits' restrictions in order to operate more safely. Each transporter agent is provided with an ILP system, using which it generates a theory predicting bandits' behavior. It does not attempt to create a theory covering all possible circumstances but only those relevant to its properties and regions in which it operates (e.g., transporter's tribe or its home city's region).

5.3   Example

Let us illustrate learning in ACROSS with an example. In this case, a bandit agent uses the following rule do decide whether or not to attack:

```
attack(Transporter):-
    endCity(Transporter, C1),
    cityRegion(C1, 'Central'),
    startCity(Transporter, C2),
    cityRegion(C2, 'Central'),
    notEqual(C1, C2).
```

This bandit agent attacks only transporter agents carrying goods between two different cities in the Central region.

Operating in this domain, a transporter agent could learn the following rule[1] representing its view of bandit agent's behavior:

```
attack(Transporter):-
    endCity(Transporter, C1),
    cityTribe(C1, 'Midlanders'),
    startCity(Transporter, C2),
    cityPopulation(C2, 'village').
```

On the first sight, the rule learned by the transporter agent looks quite different to the actual rule guiding the bandit agent's behavior. However, because of the fact that most locations in the Central region belong to the Midlanders tribe (and vice versa), and some locations next to the border of the Central region are villages, this rule in fact closely approximates the actual behavior of the bandit agent.

Note that the rule learned by the agent uses variables and a conjunction of different predicates to concisely express a condition that covers a large number of specific situations. The same condition would have to be represented as a long enumeration of specific cases if relational, logic-based learning was not used.

5.4   Experiment Scenario Setup

We have used simple A^S , observation-based A^O , rule-based A^R and lazy A^L agents in our experiments (see Section 4.3 for the detailed description of agent types). Using these agents, we have designed two sets of scenarios with (i) homogeneous, and (ii) heterogeneous societies of agents.

Homogeneous society consists of N agents of the identical type. Only learning agents are considered for homogenous societies as societies consisting of non-learning agents only would have no adaptation ability, and are thus not interesting for our study. Altogether, we thus have the following three agent societies:

---

[1] This is just an example, the learned model usually consists of several rules of this kind.

- **SC-1** consists of N simple agents
- **SC-2** consists of N observation-based agents
- **SC-3** consists of N rule-based agents

Note that while observation-based agents solely share their observations, rule-based agents share created models, and use them to filter out covered positive examples from their training sets. As a result, each rule-based agent tries to cover a different area of the whole learning space. This leads to the emergence of specialization in the agents, and to a spontaneous decomposition of the learning task based solely on the decentralized knowledge trading mechanism. In all these scenarios, we have evaluated average properties over all N participating agents.

Heterogeneous societies have been used in the second set of experiments. Out of a number of possible combination, we have decided to evaluate societies consisting of a mixture of observation-based and lazy agents. This decision was motivated by the need to evaluate the performance trade-offs of lazy agents. Specifically, we have considered the following two societies:

- **SC-4** consists of a single lazy agent and observation-based agents as the rest, i.e., $(N - 1) \times A^O + 1 \times A^L$
- **SC-5** consists of a balanced mixture of lazy and observation-based agents, i.e., $(N/2) \times A^O + (N/2) \times A^L$

In the both experimental scenarios we have focused on the behavior of lazy agents.

5.5   Evaluation Criteria

We have measured the following properties:

prediction quality is defined as the number of robberies. This measure shows the number of agent's false negative predictions, i.e., how many times a road classified as *safe* was not successfully passed.

communication load is measured as the amount of data transferred during knowledge exchange.

computational load is measured as the amount of CPU time consumed by the ILP system. This property generally depends on two factors: (i) the number of ILP invocations, and (ii) the length of each ILP run.

5.6   Results

Let us now present experimental results obtained on the described scenarios using the above defined evaluation criteria. All results are summed over tens of simulation cycles and averaged over five simulation runs.

Results for the Scenarios with Homogeneous Society of Agents. In the case of scenarios involving homogenous societies, we have measured the average per-agent value of each evaluation criteria. Each society consisted of five

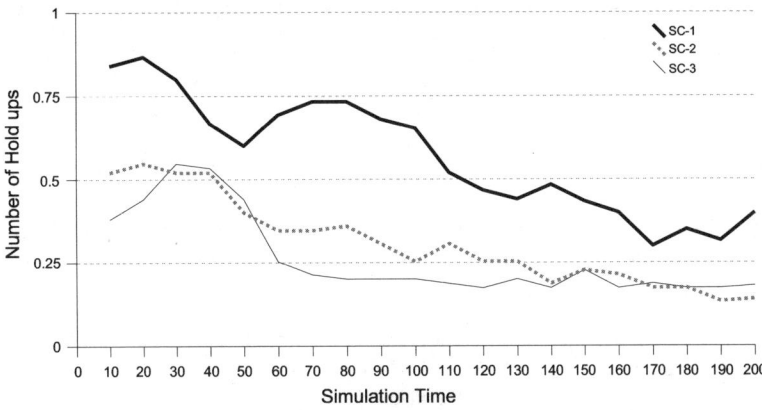

Fig. 3. Number of robberies during the simulation. This illustrates how well the learned theory covers positive examples, i.e., dangerous roads in our scenario. The average number of robberies for A^D agent without learning capability is approximately 0.8.

learning transporter agents and three bandit agents randomly passing the map and robbing transporters they met whenever their restrictions allowed it.

Graph 3 shows how fast the agents adapt to the domain in the sense of minimizing the number of robberies. We can see that all agents improve their behavior (agents without learning capability have an expected robbery probability of 0.8 approximately), but the agents sharing their knowledge learn much faster, particularly at the beginning of the simulation – in as little as ten cycles the number of robberies was decreased to nearly one half. Both these observations were expected, unlike the rather surprising one that A^O agents only slightly outperformed A^R agent during the first half of the experiment. At the end of the experiment agents perform similarly well.

Graph 4 shows how many bytes were sent on average by each agent communicating its knowledge. A^S agents (in SC-1 scenario) do not communicate at all. A^O agents (in SC-2 scenario) communicate approximately 20-times more on average then A^R agents (in SC-3 scenario). While during the initial 50 cycles this ratio is less then 10:1 (A^O:A^R), it rises up to approximately 40:1 in the middle of the experiment, and finally converges to 20:1.

Finally, Graph 5 shows the computational demand of ILP learning. A theory induction operation is started after each holdup event to ensure that the agent would not repeat its misjudgment. A^S agents (in SC-1 scenario) consume a lot of resources because they run time-consuming ILP even if their knowledge is only slightly improved – this can be improved using batch learning where a new theory would be created only if the agent has acquired at least some minimal number of new observations, on the expense of a possible increase in the number of robberies. A^O (in SC-2 scenario) and A^R (in SC-3 scenario) agents have similar computational requirements on average, though in the first half of experiments A^R agents are less time-consuming. This is caused by two factors: first, the

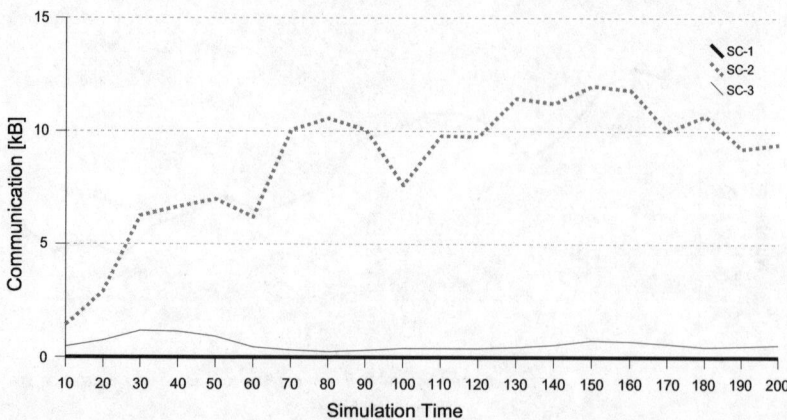

Fig. 4. Communication traffic during collective reasoning. It is the number of kilobytes of contents of messages during knowledge exchange. Note that there is no communication in SC-1 scenario.

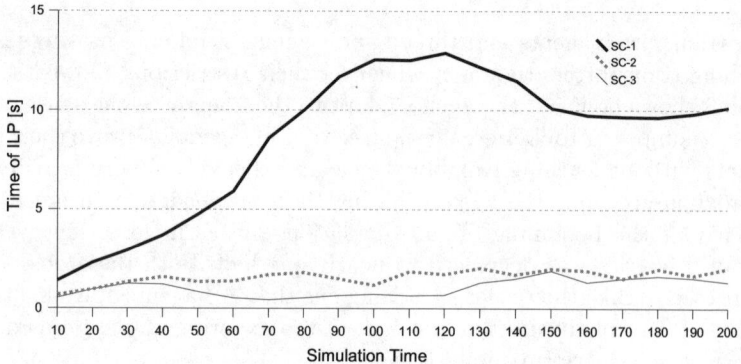

Fig. 5. Time needed to create theories using ILP system on state-of-the-art machine

training set of an A^O agent grows much faster as it receives other observations[2]; second, the filtration of positive examples used by A^R agents very often filters the positive examples out of the trainig set. A society of A^R agents can be therefore recommended to run on slower machines: even if the ILP ran more often (when aggregated over all the agents), the time-consumption of individual runs was smaller than in the case of A^O agents.

Results of Scenarios with the Heterogeneous Agent Society. A^L agents in SC-4 scenario always buy new rules offered by other agents in the community (A^O in our case). The better the rules are, the higher number of positive examples they cover, and therefore the more expensive they are. As a result, A^L agents

---

[2] Note that this can lead to flooding in some cases, e.g., when these observations are irrelevant for the receiving agent.

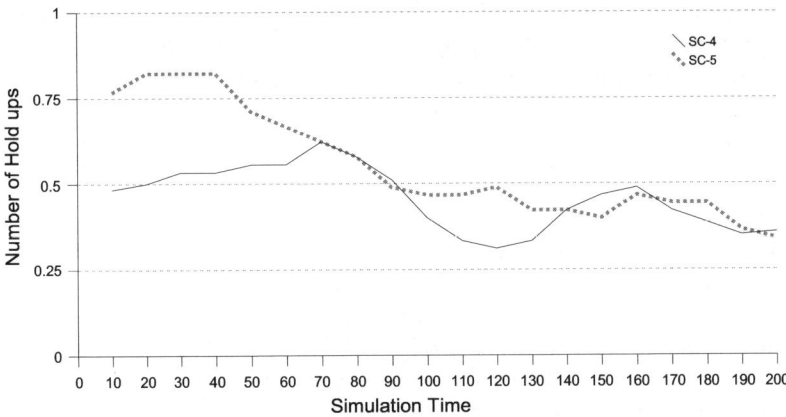

Fig. 6. Number of hold-ups during the simulation in SC-4 and SC-5 scenarios. It illustrates how well the created theory covers positive examples, or dangerous roads in our scenario.

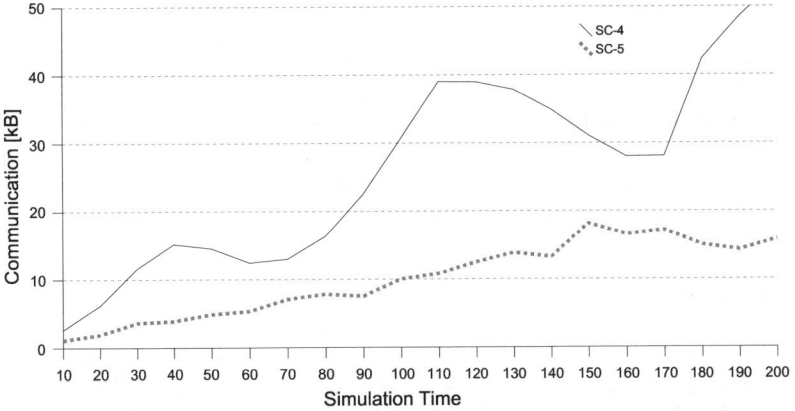

Fig. 7. Communication traffic during collective reasoning in SC-4 and SC-5 scenarios. It is the number of kilobytes of contents of messages during knowledge exchange.

have to send more observations in exchange. This leads to an unlimited growth in communication traffic until all supplying agents have perfect theories and do not improve them any more.

The last graph (Figure 6) demonstrates that if there is only a small number of A^L agents in the community (SC-4 scenario), they are fairly successful from the beginning of the simulation but later they improve very slowly. A higher proportion of A^L agents in the community (SC-5 scenario) causes slower learning in the beginning, though later it reaches the performance of SC-4 scenario. This is partially caused by the difficulty of the learning task because $N/2$ agents were able to cover dangerous roads with good accuracy.

Graph 7 illustrates the growth of communication traffic during the simulation. Higher communication load in SC-4 scenario corresponds to a higher number of A^O agents offering their knowledge to A^L agents. Note that the time needed to run ILP in SC-4 and SC-5 scenarios is zero as we measured A^L (lazy) agents only.

6   Conclusions

In this paper, we have presented collaborative learning agents that can share their knowledge using a simple trading protocol. Depending on their roles in the trading protocol, we have identified several types of knowledge trading agents. We have evaluated the performance of both homogenous and heterogeneous communities of such agents with respect to several criteria, including the quality of learned models and the communication and computational resources required. The experiments have shown that agents trading generalized models outperform agents exchanging raw observations only. Even the latter, however, outperform non-collaborative agents in terms of model quality and computational resources required. Altogether, the proposed mechanism allows effective distributing learning without the need for a central coordinator or other centralized resources. In consequence, it enables the creation of robust and scalable peer-to-peer learning systems.

Acknowledgement

We gratefully acknowledge the support of the presented research by Army Research Laboratory project N62558-03-0819.

References

1. Foltýn, L., Tožička, J., Rollo, M., Pěchouček, M., Jisl, P.: Reflective-cognitive architecture: From abstract concept to self-adapting agent. In: DIS '06: Proceedings of the Workshop on Distributed Intelligent Systems, IEEE Comp. Soc. (2006)
2. Kudenko, D., Kazakov, D., Alonso, E., eds.: Adaptive Agents and Multi-Agent Systems II: Adaptation and Multi-Agent Learning. In Kudenko, D., Kazakov, D., Alonso, E., eds.: Adaptive Agents and Multi-Agent Systems II: Adaptation and Multi-Agent Learning. Volume 3394 of LNCS., Springer (2005)
3. Panait, L., Luke, S.: Cooperative multi-agent learning: The state of the art. Autonomous Agents and Multi-Agent Systems 11(3) (2005) 387–434
4. Weiss, G., Dillenbourg, P.: What is 'multi' in multi-agent learning? In: P. Dillenbourg (Ed) Collaborative-learning: Cognitive and Computational Approaches. Elsevier, Oxford (1999) 64–80
5. Grecu, D.L., Becker, L.A.: Coactive Learning for Distributed Data Mining. In: Proceedings of the Fourth International Conference on Knowledge Discovery and Data Mining (KDD-98), New York, NY (1998) 209–213
6. Kazakov, D., Kudenko, D.: Machine learning and inductive logic programming for multi-agent systems. In: Multi-Agent Systems and Applications. Volume 2086 of LNAI., Prague, Czech Republic, Springer Verlag (2001) 246–270

7. Guerra-Hernandez, A., Fallah-Seghrouchni, A., Soldano, H.: Learning in BDI multi-agent systems. In: in Proceedings of CLIMA 2003. (2004) 185–200
8. Alonso, E., d'Inverno, M., Kudenko, D., Luck, M., Noble, J.: Learning in multi-agent systems. Knowledge Engineering Review **16**(3) (2001) 277–284
9. Wei, Y.Z., Moreau, L., Jennings, N.R.: Recommender systems: a market-based design. In: AAMAS '03: Proceedings of the second international joint conference on Autonomous agents and multiagent systems, New York, NY, USA, ACM Press (2003) 600–607
10. Hand, D., Mannila, H., Smyth, P.: Principles of Data Mining. A Bradford Book The MIT Press Cambridge (2001)
11. Kargupta, H., Chan, P., eds.: Advances in Distributed and Parallel Knowledge Discovery. In Kargupta, H., Chan, P., eds.: Advances in Distributed and Parallel Knowledge Discovery, MIT/AAAI Press (2000)
12. Park, B., Kargupta, H.: Distributed Data Mining: Algorithms, Systems, and Applications. In Ye, N., ed.: Data Mining Handbook. IEA (2002) 341–358
13. Giannella, C., Bhargava, R., Kargupta, H.: Multi-agent systems and distributed data mining. In Klusch, M., Ossowski, S., Kashyap, V., Unland, R., Laamanen, H., eds.: Cooperative Information Agent VIII. LNAI 3191, Springer-Verlag, Heidelberg (2004) 1–15
14. Klusch, M., Lodi, S., Moro, G.: Agent-based distributed data mining: The kdec scheme. In: AgentLink. Number 2586 in LNCS, Springer (2003)
15. Muggleton, S., Raedt, L.D.: Inductive logic programming: Theory and methods. Journal of Logic Programming **19/20** (1994) 629–679
16. van Rijsbergen, C.J.: Information Retrieval. Butterworths, London (1979)
17. Šišlák, D., Rehák, M., Pěchouček, M., Rollo, M., Pavlíček, D.: $\mathcal{A}$-**globe**: Agent development platform with inaccessibility and mobility support. In Unland, R., Klusch, M., Calisti, M., eds.: Software Agent-Based Applications, Platforms and Development Kits, Berlin, Birkhauser Verlag (2005) 21–46

Improving Example Selection for Agents Teaching Ontology Concepts

Mohsen Afsharchi and Behrouz H. Far

Department of Electrical and Computer Engineering,
University of Calgary, Calgary, Canada
{mafsharc, far}@ucalgary.ca

Abstract. We present a method to improve the positive examples selection by teaching agents in a multi-agent system in which a team of agent peers teach concepts to a learning agent. The basic idea in this method is to let a teacher agent expand the features it uses to describe a concept in its ontology by additional features. This resembles the typical behavior of human teachers who describe concepts from different viewpoints in the hope that one of these viewpoints comes close to the viewpoint of a learner. The extended feature set is then used to select positive examples that together with negative examples are communicated to the learner agent. The learner uses concept learning techniques to integrate the new concept into its own ontology. An experimental evaluation shows a significant learning improvement compared to the previous approach.

1 Introduction

Knowledge sharing is an integral property of multi-agent systems (MAS). In the past, knowledge sharing among agents was usually assumed to be instantaneous and fail safe and therefore, if one agent learns something all the others have learned it. Recently many researchers have argued that if two agents have different internal knowledge representations (e.g. distinctive ontologies) the knowledge sharing is hard to be accomplished. Therefore the idea of having agents *learn* concepts from the other agents has been suggested [1,7,9,11]. In our recent work, we have presented a general method for having an agent learn concepts and their features from several other agents [1].

In this method an agent (learner agent) that wants to learn a concept will query the other agents (teacher agents) about this concept by providing features (and their values) or examples that it thinks are associated with the concept. Then the teacher agents provide the learner with a set of positive and negative examples from their understanding of the concepts (i.e. concepts known by them) that seem to fit the query. These sets are further analyzed by the learner using several concept learning techniques to get a better understanding of the concept. Better understanding is equivalent to (a) identifying concepts' relevant features and (b) identifying the proper location of the concept in the concept hierarchy.

Note that the effectiveness of the learning strongly depends on the precision of the positive and negative examples that the peer agents send to the learner.

M. Klusch, M. Rovatsos, and T. Payne (Eds.): CIA 2006, LNAI 4149, pp. 228–242, 2006.

These examples should be selected in a way that covers the broad area of the concept being learned from different viewpoints. Of special importance are the positive examples that they should provide the learner with all features that discriminate the particular concept from other concepts.

When human tutors teach concepts to human learners, they usually explore and explain the concept from various viewpoints, so that the learner can select the viewpoint that fits best into his/her own view of the world. This essentially means that the teacher should investigate alternative ways to characterize a concept.

In this paper, we improve our general concept teaching/learning scenario by devising mechanisms to help teacher agents create alternative viewpoints of a concept in order to improve the selection of positive examples. More precisely, we use ideas from the area of feature selection in text classification (see [4,12]) to have a teacher agent find all the characteristic features of a concept using the examples this teacher associates with the concept. Then the teacher ranks theses examples associated with the concept based on the characteristic features and sends the highest ranking example to the learner.

The structure of this paper is as follows. After a brief introduction of the concepts in Section 2 the learning process is described in Section 3 and a method for positive example selection using added features and example ranking is introduced in Section 4. An intuitive example using real data set is given in Section 5 followed by related works and conclusions in Section 6 and 7.

2   Basic Definitions

In this section, we provide a brief definition of each of the two basic concepts involved in our system which are ontologies and agents. Also we provide the instantiations of these concepts that we require for our methods.

2.1   Ontologies and Concepts

The usage of the term "ontology" in (computer science) literature faces problems very similar to the usage of the term "agent": there is no agreed-upon formal definition for the term, but nevertheless it is used very intensively and there are many systems that come with a (somehow) built-in definition of the term. Common to most usages of the term ontology is that it is considered to be a way for representing concepts (or objects) in a hierarchy with additional ways of defining relationships among the concepts (or objects).

This is reflected by Stume's formal definition (see [9]) who defines a *core ontology* as a structure $\mathcal{O} := (C, \leq_C, R, \sigma, \leq_R)$. Where C and R are two disjoint sets and the elements of C are called *concept identifiers* and the elements of R are so-called *relation identifiers*. $\leq_C$ is a partial order on C called *concept hierarchy* or *taxonomy* and $\leq_R$ ia a partial order on R, named *relation hierarchy*. $\sigma : R \rightarrow C^+$ is a function providing a signature for a relation such that $|\sigma(r_1)| = |\sigma(r_2)|$ for every $r_1, r_2 \in R$ with $r_1 \leq_R r_2$ and for every projection π_i $(1 \leq i \leq |\sigma(r_1)|)$

of the vectors $\sigma(r_1)$ and $\sigma(r_2)$ we have $\pi_i(\sigma(r_1)) \leq_C \pi_i(\sigma(r_2))$. If $c_1 \leq_C c_2$ for c_1, $c_2 \in C$, then c_1 is called a *subconcept* of c_2 and c_2 is a *superconcept* of c_1. Obviously, the relation $\leq_C$ is supposed to be connected with how concepts are defined. In the literature, taxonomies are often built using the subset relation, i.e. we have

$$C_i \leq_C C_j \text{ iff for all } o \in C_i \text{ we have } o \in C_j.$$

This definition of $\leq_C$ produces a partial order on C as defined above and we will use this definition in the following for the ontologies that our agents use.

The Stume's definition of ontology $\mathcal{O}$ lacks the precise treatment of the conecpts, C. Many works in databases and machine learning define concepts as collections of objects that share certain *feature* instantiations. In the following we assume that we have a set of features $\mathcal{F} = \{f_1, ..., f_n\}$ and for each feature f_i we have its domain $D_i = \{v_{i1}, ..., v_{im_i}\}$ that defines the possible values the feature can have. Then an object $o = ([f_1 = v_1], ..., [f_n = v_n])$ is characterized by its values for each of the features (often one feature is the identifying name of an object and then each object has a unique feature combination). By $\mathcal{U}$ we denote the set of all (possible) objects. In machine learning, often every subset of $\mathcal{U}$ is considered as a concept. In databases and in this work we want to be able to characterize a concept by using feature values. Therefore, a *symbolic concept C_k* is denoted by $C_k([f_1 = V_1], ..., [f_n = V_n])$ where $V_i = \{v'_{i1}, ..., v'_{ij_i}\} \subseteq D_i$ (if $V_i = D_i$ then we often omit the entry for f_i). An object $o = ([f_1 = v_1], ..., [f_n = v_n])$ is *covered* by a concept C_k, if for all i we have $v_i \in V_i$. In an ontology according to the definition above, we assign a concept identifier to each symbolic concept that we want to represent in our ontology.

Note that the objects must possess all the features of the concept C_k in order to be covered by it. But it does not necessarily mean the objects should not possess other features that not exhibited in the C_k. As we stated previously the $V_i \subseteq D_i$ and that means the V_i is not necessarily equals with D_i. This naturally allows the objects to have an extended set of features resulting in a potential ability to teach the concept from a different viewpoint.

From the point of view of knowledge representation the really interesting part of ontologies are the relations R that a particular ontology allows. This is also the part where we see a lot of discrepencies among different authors. In general, all possible relations between tuples of concepts can be used in ontologies, but usually researchers assume a small set of built-in relations and tool developers sometimes throw in the possibility to have (limited) user-defined relations. But unfortunately, different ontologies can use the same relation identifiers for different built-in relations, so that there is quite some confusion in this area. Therefore, if we have two systems build by different people using ontologies over the same set $\mathcal{U}$ it is very important to either identify those relations that occur in both ontologies or to find ways the knowledge contained in the (usage of) relations in one ontology can be used in communications between the systems. In this work, we will show such a usage for one relation that we have called `is-similar-to` with $\sigma(\text{is-similar-to}) \in C^2$.

2.2   Agents

A general definition that can be instantiated to most of the views of agents in literature sees an agent $\mathcal{A}g$ as a quadruple $\mathcal{A}g$ $\{Sit, Act, Dat, f_{Ag}\}$. Sit is a set of situations the agent can be in, the representation of a situation naturally depending on the agent's sensory capabilities, Act is the set of actions that $\mathcal{A}g$ can perform and Dat is the set of possible values that $\mathcal{A}g$'s internal data areas can have. In order to determine its next action, $\mathcal{A}g$ uses $f_{Ag} : Sit \times Dat \rightarrow Act$ applied to the current situation and the current values of its internal data areas.

As we want to focus on the knowledge representation used by agents, so we look more closely at Dat. We assume that every element of Dat of an agent $\mathcal{A}g$ contains an ontology area $\mathcal{O}_{Ag}$ as defined in the previous subsection that represents the agent's view and knowledge of concepts. For the concepts in the taxonomy of $\mathcal{O}_{Ag}$ there might be additional data, beyond features, that the agent requires from time to time. Naturally, there will be additional data areas representing information about the agent itself, knowledge about other agents and the world that the designer of the agent may want to be represented differently than in $\mathcal{O}_{Ag}$. In the rest of this paper, we will concentrate on how the agent uses and manipulates its ontology.

3   Learning Process

In this section we provide a brief discussion about the multi-agent concept learning we presented in [1]. We will see how we changed this general scheme to improve positive example selection in Section 4.

We have developed a method that demonstrates how an agent can learn new concepts for its ontology with the help of other agents. This naturally assumes that not all agents have the same ontology (otherwise learning would not be necessary). In fact, we additionally assume that there are only some base features $\mathcal{F}_{base} \subseteq \mathcal{F}$ that are known and can be recognized by all agents and that there are only some base symbolic concepts C_{base} that are known to all agents by name, their feature values for the base features and the objects that are covered by them. Outside of this base common knowledge, individual agents may come with additional features they can recognize and additional concepts they know. Given this setting, agents will develop problems in working together, since the common grounds for communication are not there. To solve this problem, agents need to acquire the concepts outside of C_{base} that other agents have, at least those concepts that are needed to establish the necessary communication to work together on a given task. The basic idea is to have an agent *learn* a required concept (or at least a good approximation) of it with the *help* of the other agents.

3.1   Interaction Scheme

Although we want all agents to be able to learn new concepts, for explaining our interaction scheme we designate one agent, $\mathcal{A}g_L$, as the one that wants to learn a new concept and the other agents, $Ag_1,...,Ag_m$, will be its teachers. Ag_L has an ontology $\mathcal{O}_L = (C_L, \leq_C, R_L, \sigma_L, \leq_{R_L})$ and knows a set of features $\mathcal{F}_L$. Analogously, Ag_i has as ontology $\mathcal{O}_i = (C_i, \leq_C, R_i, \sigma_i, \leq_{R_i})$ and knows a set of features $\mathcal{F}_i$. For a concept c known to the agent Ag_i, this agent has in its data areas a set $pex_i^c \subseteq \mathcal{U}$ of positive examples for c that it can use to teach c to Ag_L. Part of Act_L are actions QueryConcept, AskClassify, Learn, and Integrate, while part of the Act_is are the actions FindConcept, CreateNegEx, ReplyQuery, ClassifyEx and ReplyClass; all with appropriate arguments. These actions form our interaction scheme in the following manner:

1. Ag_L determines it needs to know about a particular concept c_{goal} and performs QueryConcept("c_{goal}") to inform the other agents about this need.
2. Each agent Ag_i reacts to Ag_L's query by:
   (a) performing FindConcept("c_{goal}"), which leads to a set of candidate concepts C_i^{cand},
   (b) selecting the "best" candidate c_i out of C_i^{cand},
   (c) selecting a given number of elements out of $pex_i^{c_i}$, thus creating p_i,
   (d) performing CreateNegEx(c_i) to produce a given number of (good) negative examples for c_i, which we call the set n_i,
   (e) performing ReplyQuery($path(c_i),p_i,n_i$).
3. Ag_L collects the answers $(path(c_i),p_i,n_i)$ from all agents and uses a learner to learn c_{goal} from these combined examples (action Learn($(p_1,n_1),...,(p_m,n_m)$)). If there are conflicts, then it resolves them with the help of the other agents using AskClassify (resp. ClassifyEx and ReplyClass by the other agents.
4. Ag_L uses the learned c_{goal} and the collected $path(c_i)$s from the other agents to construct an ontology path C_{path} leading to c_{goal} within its ontology $\mathcal{O}_L$ (action Integrate($path(c_1),...,path(c_m)$)).

The result of this learning/teaching scheme is the description of c_{goal} in terms of Ag_L's feature set $\mathcal{F}_L$ and an updated ontology $\mathcal{O}_L^{new} = (C_L^{new}, \leq_C, R_L, \sigma_L, \leq_{R_L})$. Ag_L will also create a set $pex_L^{c_{goal}}$ in case another agent wants Ag_L to teach it c_{goal}.

3.2   Selecting Positive and Negative Examples

While supplying the learner with more examples normally are the better, in our case we have to take into account that the more objects from the positive and negative examples are selected, the more expensive the communication becomes and the more effort Ag_L will have to spent on learning. On the other hand, less examples usually means less precise learning result. Therefore the number of examples communicated to Ag_L by each agent should be selected as a parameter of the whole system.

For negative examples, since every concept other than queried concept c_j can be categorized as its counter concept, the number of associated objects (which naturally are negative examples) could be potentially very high. This big volume of the negative examples makes the selection of a subset of them a crucial task. As we elaborated negative example selection and improvement and reported the result [1], in Section 3.3 we briefly explain this problem.

For positive examples, Since each agent Ag_i stores for each concept c_j a set $pex_i^{c_j}$ of positive examples , i.e. a set of objects covered by c_j, coming up with positive example objects for a concept known to Ag_i does not seem to be a big problem, because selecting the appropriate number of elements for p_i could be realized by randomly sampling $pex_i^{c_i}$. But as we will show in Section 4, applying the *viewpoint* of the teacher agents to select better positive examples can make a significant improvement in the learner's effectiveness. In Section 4 we present two algorithms to extract discriminative features and ranking positive examples respectively.

3.3   Selecting Negative Examples by Ontology Guidance

Selecting negative examples for a concept is not easy. Obviously, the set of negative examples nex^c for a concept c is defined as
$$nex^c = \mathcal{U} - \{o|o \text{ covered by } c\}.$$
This can be a very large set and usually different elements of this set provide learners with a different quality of advice. Good negative examples are examples that "nearly" are in the set covered by the concept, a kind of "near-misses" that allow to highlight the borders of a concept. The fact that our agents have ontologies allows us to do a better job in selecting negative examples than randomly selecting out of nex^{c_i} (by Ag_i). The key for this better selection is to make use of the taxonomy information Ag_i has and the relations in R_i. The later naturally depends on what relations are available.

Let us first look at the possibilities that the *taxonomy* offers. Each superconcept of the concept c_i –that Ag_i sees as the best concept to answer Ag_L's query– can be used to limit the set of negative examples $nex_i^{c_i}$ that Ag_i should consider for its answer. As a superconcept of c_i, these concepts share a lot of feature values with c_i, so that the elements in their set of positive examples that are not covered by c_i are good candidates for "near-misses". In fact, sibling concepts of c_i or its superconcepts are even better source for negative examples since all their positive examples are not covered by c_i.

Since all agents use the same relation $\leq_C$, all agents can use the taxonomy information to limit the pool of negative examples to choose from. But also information provided by some other relations can be used. As an example, let us look at the usage of the relation `is-similar-to` that we mentioned earlier. The motivation for `is-similar-to` is to allow to express the similarity between two concepts that are far away from each other in the taxonomy tree, but that share a lot of feature values. This makes `is-similar-to` a perfect candidate for helping with the selection of negative examples. After collecting all candidates in $nex_i^{c_i}$, we again select the given number of examples for n_i as a random sample.

Note that an `is-similar-to`-relation can be automatically computed for a given C_i and $\mathcal{F}_i$ by introducing a similarity measure sim_i^f on feature values for each feature $f \in \mathcal{F}_i$ with domain D: $sim_i^f : D \times D \rightarrow [0..1]$. We can create out of this a similarity measure $sim_i^{\mathcal{U}}$ for objects by, for example, summing up the similarities for each feature. More formally, let $o = ([f_1 = v_1], ..., [f_n = v_n])$ and $o' = ([f_1 = v_1'], ..., [f_n = v_n'])$, then

$$sim_i^{\mathcal{U}} = \sum_{j=1}^{n} sim_i^{f_j}(v_j, v_j')$$

where $sim_i^{f_j}(x, y) = 0$, if $f_j \notin \mathcal{F}_i$.

Out of this, we can create is-similar-to$_i$ between two concepts c and c', if $sim_i^{\mathcal{U}}(o, o') \geq simthreshold$ for all $o \in pex_i^c$ and $o' \in pex_i^{o'}$, with $simthreshold$ as a given parameter. While it would be better to use all objects covered by c and c', this can be impossible or at least very expensive, so that we suggest to use the examples that are already there.

4   Positive Example Selection by Discriminative Feature Selection and Example Ranking

Technically, there is a set of objects associated with each concept c_j for the teacher agent Ag_i as positive examples, and if c_j is selected as an answer to a query, this set is simply available for the teacher to select positive examples and send it to the learner. Randomly selection of the positive examples is the most straightforward way which while keeps the selection process easy, does not guarantee the comprehensiveness of the positive examples. That is because the set of positive examples should cover the border of the concept as well as the body of the concept. Therefore good subset of positive examples are examples that cover the whole space of positive examples.

One very important issue here is that, the selection of positive examples is the point that the teacher can exert its unique view in the teaching of a specific concept, therefore, the teacher agent should utilize some methods to reflect its viewpoint. Similar to the teaching process in human beings we used the feature describing a concept as a point that the teacher can express its viewpoint. Apart from the features in the concept definition in the ontology, there might be some other very characterizing features in the positive examples which the teacher agent can rely on in the teaching of the concept by selecting the positive examples using them. We believe that these characterizing features are the features that are more discriminatory than other features in the examples. Fortunately, there is a very close relation between the technical problem we mentioned in the previous paragraph and the teaching from different viewpoints. By selecting the subset of positive examples using more discriminative features, the teacher agent not only exerts its unique point of view, but it has a criterion to arrange the selected subset in a very comprehensive way.

To identify discriminative features and select examples based on them, we introduced a new action SelectPosEx(c_i) and replaced the section (c) of step 2 of our general interaction scheme as follows: performing SelectPosEx(c_i) to select a given number of good elements out of $pex_i^{c_i}$, thus creating p_i. In SelectPosEx we use the differences of features between the given positive examples ($pex_i^{c_k}$)

and negative examples $(nex_i^{C_k})$ to calculate the *feature strength* in discrimination between the positive and negative examples. We also use feature strength to identify more discriminative features which we call them *core features*, and denote them by $\mathcal{CF}$. Then we use $\mathcal{CF}$, to extract good positive examples from $pex_i^{C_k}$ and we call them *distinctive positive examples* (p_i).

4.1   Identifying Discriminative Features

We identify the discriminative features based on the notion called *Relief* which we borrowed the idea from [5] Using *ReliefF* which is a more robust algorithm from Relief family we developed an algorithm to identify the discriminative features. This algorithm constructs the set of core features of pex, $\mathcal{CF}$, by ranking the feature strengths among the features that are exhibited in pex and nex.

The key idea of our method , given in Algorithm 1, is to estimate the strength of features according to how well their values distinguish between examples that are near to each other. For that purpose, given a randomly selected example e_i (line 3), algorithm searches for its k nearest neighbors from the pex, called nearest hit P, and k others from the nex, called nearest miss N (line 4). It updates the strength estimation $W[F]$ for the set of all features F depending on their values for e_i, P, and N (lines 6 and 7). If e_i and majority of k examples in P are different in their values for the feature f then the the feature f separates examples in the same concept which is not desirable so we decrease the strength estimation $W[f]$. On the other hand if e_i and majority of k examples in N are different in their values for the feature f then the feature f separates a positive example from negative examples which is desirable so we increase the strength estimation $W[f]$. The k is a user definable parameter which increase the robustness of the algorithm against the noisy data. The whole process is repeated for m times, where m is also a user defined parameter.

Function $diff(f, e_i, e_j)$ calculates the difference between the values of the feature f for two instances e_i and e_j. For nominal features it is define as:

$$diff(f, e_i, e_j) = \begin{cases} 0; value(f, e_i) = value(f, e_j) \\ 1; otherwise \end{cases}$$

and for numerical features as:

$$diff(f, e_i, e_j) = \frac{|value(f, e_i) - value(f, e_j)|}{\max(f) - \min(f)}$$

The algorithm then determine ϕ as the average of $W(F)$. Obviously because the teacher is interested in the feature in pex it filters the set of features and add to the $\mathcal{CF}$ all features which are seen at least in one e in pex and $W(f) > \theta$.

4.2   Extracting Distinctive Positive Examples

We have shown how to compute feature strengths and determine ϕ so as to select a set of discriminative features for formulating the core features $(\mathcal{CF})$ of

---

Algorithm 1. Calculate the vector of W of estimations of the features strenght

---

1. set all weights $W[F] := 0.0$
2. **for** $i = 0$ to m **do**
3.   Randomly select an example e_i
4.   find k nearest hit examples in pex, P
5.   find k nearest miss examples in nex, N
6.   **for all** f in F **do**

7. $$W[f] = W[f] - \sum_{j=1}^{k} diff(f, e_i, P_j)/(m \cdot k) + \sum_{j=1}^{k} diff(f, e_i, N_j)/(m \cdot k)$$

8.   **end for**
9. **end for**
10. $\phi \frac{1}{|F|} \sum_{i=1}^{|F|} W[f_i]$
11. **for all** f in F **do**
12.   **if** $f > \phi$ and $f \in pex$ **then**
13.   append f to $\mathcal{CF}$
14.   **end if**
15. **end for**

---

the positive examples . Another important issue is, given an example, what is the criterion, in order to consider it a potential distinctive positive example?

Algorithm 2 shows the mechanism that we utilized to select the set of distinctive positive examples. The key idea of our procedure , given in Algorithm 2, is to estimate the distance of every positive examples from their peers in the negative side and use this estimation to assess the distribution of the examples in the whole space of positive examples. For that purpose, for every example e_i (line 3), algorithm searches for its k nearest neighbors from the nex, called nearest miss N (line 4). To find theses nearest misses we used the similarity function that we presented in the previous section. the algorithms then updates the distance estimation $\mathcal{D}[e_i]$ for the set of all features $\mathcal{CF}$ depending on their values for e_i and each example in N using the $diff$ function(lines 5, 6 and 7). Obviously the examples with minimum value of $\mathcal{D}[e_i]$ are in the border and as the value goes higher the examples go farther from the border. In order to select more comprehensive set of positive examples, the teacher agent selects the examples that are not very close to each other assuming that the close examples do not add so much to the learner knowledge and its accuracy. The $dist$ function calculates the distance of the selected example e_j with candidate example e_i. If the value of distance is greater than θ for all selected examples, then teacher adds it to the set of selected positive example p (line 12 and 13). The value for θ is selected based on the number of examples the teacher can send to the learner and the average distance between examples.

Function $diff(f, e_i, e_j)$ is defined similar to the previous section and function $dist$ is defined based on the $diff$ function as follows:

$$dist(e_i, e_j) = \sum_{k=1}^{|\mathcal{CF}|} diff(f_k, e_i, e_j)$$

Algorithm 2. Select the set of p of comprehensive positive examples

---

1. set all distances $\mathcal{D}[pex] := 0.0$
2. **for** $i = 0$ to $|pex|$ **do**
3.   select an example e_i
4.   find k nearest miss examples in nex, N
5.   **for all** f in $\mathcal{CF}$ **do**
6. $\mathcal{D}[e_i] = \mathcal{D}[e_i] + \sum_{j=1}^{k} diff(f, e_i, N_j)/k$
7.   **end for**
8. **end for**
9. $p = \emptyset$
10. **while** there is e_i in pex **do**
11.   take out of pex an example e_i such that $\mathcal{D}[e_i]$ is minimum
12.   **if** $dist(e_i, e_j) > \theta$ for all $e_j \in p$ **then**
13.   append e_i to p
14.   **end if**
15. **end while**
16. return p

---

5   Experimental Results

We have conducted several experiments using the general setup of our multi-agent system from [1], in which the teacher agents have some differences in their "world view", simply because there are different ways how to organize the objects in the world, but where there is nevertheless a large agreement on many things. We changed the process of positive example selection to enable the teacher agents to reflect their specific "viewpoint" by selecting some examples that they *think* are more distinctive positive examples.

5.1   The University Units and Courses Domain

The Course catalog ontology domain has been chosen as the basic set up for our multi-agent system. (see [3]). The set of objects $\mathcal{U}$ consists of files describing the courses offered by Cornell University, the University of Washington and the University of Michigan. The domain is additionally structured according to the university units of these universities, which creates different ontologies for each of them. In fact, our teacher agents will be agents that each represents one of these 3 universities ($\mathcal{A}g_C$, $\mathcal{A}g_W$, $\mathcal{A}g_M$). The course files (and unit structure) for Cornell and Washington were taken from [3], the ones for Michigan from their web site at [10]. A course file contains course identifier, course description and the prerequisites of a course. The three universities together offer 19061 courses(which naturally is the total number of examples in the system) and each university's ontology has at least 166 concepts on top of their courses. For each of the following examples, our agents used their full ontologies even if we report only on parts of them.

Borrowing some ideas from the field of information retrieval, to represent the courses in terms of features, we had a little bit of preparation to do. The course description, that is the main feature in our method of learning, usually determines by which organizational units a course should be taught and the descriptions are text-based. Defining concepts based on objects that consist of natural language texts is not easy, but an area of quite a lot of interest and practical applications. One way of defining features for such texts to group them is to look for particular words in the texts or word combinations (see [4]). Unfortunately, there is a lot of substitutivity in these word combinations, so that we need features that allow us to express this substitutivity. For example, feature $f_{\texttt{picture,photo,figure}}$: text $\rightarrow$ Boolean is true for a text t, if either $\texttt{picture}$ or $\texttt{photo}$ or $\texttt{figure}$ occurs in t. For our application domain, it is not clear what substitutivities should be considered (just synonyms are not what we are looking for here), so that we base our features for the course descriptions on what we call a set $\mathcal{K}$ of key words. Then we have a feature for each possible subset of $\mathcal{K}$ (excluding the empty set) as described above. Different key sets create different feature sets.

To instantiate Algorithm 1 and 2 for our context we first used the similarity function of section 3.3 to find k nearest hit for each document example e_i. The same process is done to find k nearest miss document. To calculate feature weights, W, we needed to realize a $diff$ function which was compatible with our context. In the information retrieval domain one common scheme, to weight a keyword is known as "term frequency inverse document frequency" and originally for a keyword(i.e term) i in document j is defined as:

$$\omega_{i,j} = tf_{i,j} * \ln \frac{N}{n}$$

where $tf_{i,j}$ is the frequency of the keyword i in document j, N is the total number of documents which naturally in our context is the number of documents both in pex and nex, and n is the number of documents where keyword i occurs at least once. To make this weighting scheme works with our features, we substitute keywords by the set of keywords that we use for our system. Therefore for example in addition to "differential" and "equation" we also count the occurrences of "differential equation" in documents as a single feature. Based on this definition we instantiate the $diff$ function as follows:

$$diff(f, e_i, e_j) = |\omega_{f,e_i} - \omega_{f,e_j}|$$

5.2 Different Positive Example Selection Comparison

To show the efficiency of the learner when a concept thought from different viewpoints, we conduct some interesting experiments. For first experiment, similar to our experiment in [1], we assumed that the learning agent is supposed to provide someone at a university with suggestions for how a unit concerned with $\texttt{Greek}$ should be characterized. This learning agent would pose a query based on providing a key set out of its own key set of words, in our example this query key set would be $\{\texttt{greek,program,attic,literature}\}$. We also further

Table 1. Classification result for concept **greek** and **mathematics**

n%	greek				mathematics			
	DPE	RS1	RS2	RS3	DPE	RS1	RS2	RS3
10	0.006	0.000	0.000	0.000	0.002	0.000	0.000	0.000
20	0.017	0.000	0.000	0.001	0.011	0.000	0.000	0.000
30	0.031	0.001	0.008	0.011	0.078	0.000	0.001	0.000
40	0.093	0.031	0.011	0.021	0.181	0.021	0.012	0.009
50	0.188	0.069	0.083	0.052	0.289	0.105	0.145	0.098
60	0.390	0.128	0.116	0.102	0.366	0.254	0.227	0.191
70	0.510	0.219	0.223	0.190	0.432	0.321	0.309	0.268
80	0.612	0.381	0.350	0.324	0.511	0.390	0.384	0.329
90	0.691	0.439	0.402	0.491	0.580	0.481	0.472	0.448
100	0.780	0.582	0.562	0.577	0.641	0.571	0.521	0.514

assumed that the relevant concepts in C_{base} are $C_{base}=$ {university} and the relevant concepts in $\mathcal{F}_{base}$ are created using the key set $\mathcal{K}_{base} =$ {class, course, program, literature,modern, attic,classic, culture, prose, graduate,seminar,grammar,drama,greek}.

Based on the above mentioned assumptions, we enabled our agents to apply Algorithm 1 to come up with the core features representing the unique viewpoint of each agent. A subset of the core feature key set which is not common with $\mathcal{K}_{base}$, for each agents were as follows:

$CF_C =$ {democritus,religion,english,herodotus,medieval}
$CF_W =$ {tragedy,orator,antique,myths,archeology}
$CF_M =$ {modern,epic,classic,odyssey, ancient,aristotelian,aeneid}.

Then we let the agents to extract positive examples using CF and Algorithm 2 and send them to the learner. In the learner side and in order to evaluate the efficiency of our method in selecting distinctive positive examples, we first trained the learner with the set of distinctive positive examples (DPE) and test it against the set of all 1016 positive examples associated with concept **greek** in the world of three agents. Column DPE of Table 1 shows the percentage of the true classification that the learner did. To see how our method improves the efficiency of whole process of learning we also trained the learner with three different random set(e.g. RS1, RS2 and RS3) of positive examples(which obviously associated with concept which is being learned). Column **greek** in the Table 1 shows the major improvement in the classification where the accuracy of DPE (78 %) is 19.8 more than the best random set(58.2%) . The experiment is repeated n times, where n is the percentage of the positive examples used in training.

We repeated the experiment for the concept **mathematics** with query key set: {mathematics,program,science,calculus} and the key set $\mathcal{K}_{base} =$ {class, course, program, science, calculus, mathematics, school, graduate,

Table 2. Average classification accuracy for nine concepts

n%	DPE	RS1	RS2	RS3
10	0.003	0.000	0.000	0.000
20	0.012	0.000	0.000	0.000
30	0.043	0.001	0.003	0.001
40	0.114	0.028	0.016	0.023
50	0.206	0.109	0.091	0.078
60	0.327	0.202	0.190	0.161
70	0.438	0.267	0.274	0.211
80	0.551	0.377	0.361	0.356
90	0.649	0.448	0.421	0.463
100	0.733	0.560	0.549	0.554

seminar,systems,number, solution}. A subset of core features for each agents were as follows:

$\mathcal{CF}_C=$ {vector,elementary,statistics,geometry,function,proof}
$\mathcal{CF}_W -$ {equation,logic,linear,fourier,integral }
$\mathcal{CF}_M =$ {algebra,matrices,graph,theorem,dynamics,logarithm }.

Column mathematics in the Table 1 shows the major improvement(64.1%-57.1% =7%) in the classification when we test the learner over 2117 positive examples associated with concept mathematics in the world of three agents. In addition to mathematics and greek we repeated our experiment for seven other concepts: computer science, linguistics, german, japanese, chemistry, physics and chinese. Table 2 shows the average result for nine concepts. Again we see a significant improvement in classification accuracy(17.3%)

6   Related Works

Most works in the multi-agent concept learning did not focus on the quality of the positive and negative examples. The Williams's work [11] introduced the idea of using learning to improve the mutual understanding about a concept between two agents. In contrast to our method, Williams uses only a flat repository of concepts, not a real ontology. The learning is used to have only two agents develop a common feature description about a particular concept assuming that the agents share the same perception of objects. Also there is no concentration on the quality of examples. [7] presents a method how one agent can train another agent to recognize a concept by providing selected positive training examples. while the multi-agent dimension is not addressed and no usage of ontologies is made, the quality of examples also not addressed.

Researchers have studied various aspects of feature selection. Different feature selection methods can be broadly categorized into the wrapper model [4] and the filter model [8,6]. The wrapper model uses the predictive accuracy of a predetermined learning algorithm to determine the goodness of the selected subsets. The filter model separates feature selection from classifier learning and selects feature subsets that are independent of any learning algorithm. It relies on various measures of the general characteristics of the training data such as distance, information, dependency, and consistency. According to the availability of class labels, there are feature selection methods for supervised learning [5].

7   Conclusion

We presented a method to improve the process of positive example selection by teaching agent in multi-agent systems that a group of agents try to teach a concept to a learning agent. We established our method base on the reflection of the viewpoints of the teacher agents. Similar to the behavior of human beings, the teacher agents express their viewpoints with the features that they think are more discriminatory. Then they use these features to extract more distinctive positive examples which naturally characterize the queried concept better. We found this method very useful in monotonous distribution over whole positive example space. Our experimental results revealed the improvement of the learner effectiveness using this new method of positive example selection. As a future work we will expand the method for better selection of negative examples and we will analyze the behavior of the selected subset of the negative examples over the whole space of negative examples.

References

1. M. Afsharchi, B.H. Far, J. Denzinger: Ontology-Guided Learning to Improve Communication between Groups of Agents, Proc. AAMAS-06 (in press), 2006. http://www.enel.ucalgary.ca/ afsharch/aamas06.pdf
2. R. Kohavi and G.H. John. Wrappers for feature subset selection. Artificial Intelligence, 97(1-2): 273324, 1997.
3. Illinois Semantic Integration Archive. http:// anhai.cs.uiuc.edu/archive/, as seen on Jan 30, 2005.
4. D. Koller, M. Sahami: Hierarchically Classifying Documents Using Very Few Words, Proc. ICML-97, 1997, pp. 170–178.
5. M. Robnik-Sikonja, I. Kononenko: Theoretical and Empirical Analysis of ReliefF and RReliefF. Machine Learning Journal, Volume 53, 2003, pp. 23–69.
6. M.A. Hall. Correlation-based feature selection for discrete and numeric class machine learning. In Proceedings of the Seventeenth International Conference on Machine Learning, pages 359366, 2000.
7. S. Sen, P.P. Kar: Sharing a concept, AAAI Tech Report SS-02-02, Stanford, 2002.
8. H. Liu, H. Motoda, and L. Yu. Feature selection with selective sampling. In Proceedings of the Nineteenth International Conference on Machine Learning, pages 395402, 2002.
9. G. Stumme: Using Ontologies and Formal Concept Analysis for Organizing Business Knowledge, in J. Becker, R. Knackstedt (Eds.): Wissensmanagement mit Referenzmodellen – Konzepte für die Anwendungssystem- und Organisationsgestaltung, Physica, 2002, pp. 163–174.

10. University of Michigan academic units. http:// www.umich.edu/units.html, as seen on Jan 30, 2005.
11. A.B. Williams: Learning to Share Meaning in a Multi Agent System, Autonomous Agents and Multi Agent Systems 8(2), 2004, pp. 165–193.
12. Y. Yang, Y., J.P. Pedersen: A Comparative Study on Feature Selection in Text Categorization. Proceedings of the Fourteenth International Conference on Machine Learning (ICML'97), 1997, pp412-420.

Egalitarian Allocations of Indivisible Resources: Theory and Computation

P.-A. Matt and F. Toni

Department of Computing, Imperial College London,
South Kensington Campus, London SW7 2AZ, UK
{pmatt, f.toni}@imperial.ac.uk

Abstract. We present a mechanism for collaboration and coordination amongst agents in multi-agent societies seeking social equity. This mechanism allows to compute egalitarian allocations of indivisible resources to agents, reached via progressive revisions of social consensus. Egalitarian allocations are allocations with maximal egalitarian social welfare, where the egalitarian social welfare is given by the minimum worth (utility) assigned by agents to the resources they are given by the allocation. Egalitarian allocations are useful in a number of applications of multi-agent systems, e.g. service agents, satellite earth observation and agent oriented/holonic manufacturing systems. The mechanism we propose is distributed amongst the agents, and relies upon an incremental construction whereby agents join progressively in, forcing a revision of the current set of agreements amongst the prior agents. The mechanism uses search trees and a reduction operator simplifying the search for egalitarian allocations. We finally show how to reduce the negotiation time using social order-based coordination mechanisms and make agents find consensus efficiently using well-suited resource-preference orders.

1 Introduction

The emergence of societies of artificial agents, such as software agents, domestic or industrial robots, is a development with huge potential significance in the near future. For this significance to materialise, it is important that agent-designers render agents as autonomous as possible, by specifying decision-making strategies and rules of interaction. It is also important, from a global perspective, to clarify the properties a society of agents should exhibit in order to benefit applications.

To tackle this issue, we follow a worth-oriented paradigm adapted from the area of social choice theories [1,2,3] and welfare economics [4,5,6]. In this paradigm, agents assign a measure of worth to each of the possible states of affairs they may encounter, to represent, intuitively, the notion of goal satisfaction. In particular, we focus on states of affairs resulting from the allocation of indivisible resources to agents. Resources serve as an abstraction for objects, commodities, tasks, services, computational power etc.

Research in multi-agent systems so far focused mostly on utilitarianism, i.e. selfish agents trying to maximise their own good without concern for the global

M. Klusch, M. Rovatsos, and T. Payne (Eds.): CIA 2006, LNAI 4149, pp. 243–257, 2006.

good of the society. Although appropriate for applications such as combinatorial auctions [7], utilitarian principles dangerously threaten cooperation between agents working in teams, because they are highly elitist by often generating situations where only a small percentage of agents detain the totality of the resources, preventing the others to achieve their goals. Moreover, purely artificial 'servants' may have no particular need of behaving selfishly and agent-designers do have the power to enforce specific interaction protocols and chosen reasoning strategies, in particular cooperative ones.

In our opinion, self-interest, natural within human societies, may be counterproductive in artificial societies. By shifting from natural to artificial societies, it is possible, and beneficial in some applications of resource allocation for cooperative agents, to abandon the utilitarian model. Egalitarian allocations allow to maximise the welfare of the agent that is less 'well-off' in the society, in terms of the worth it assigns to resources it is allocated. When agents are endowed with egalitarian strategies, they combine their actions for the global good of the society. This can be a fruitful approach in the resource allocation case: agents' cooperation allows better repartition of the resources, resulting in simultaneous quality improvements in the wide panel of services offered or set of tasks performed by the agents [8].

A recent overview of socially optimal allocations of resources achieved by means of negotiation can be found in [9]. Interestingly, the paper proves that any sequence of strongly equitable deals (see [9] for a definition) will eventually result in an egalitarian allocation. This purely theoretical result provides however no indication to designers of multi-agent systems on how agents can compute these deals. In this paper, we provide a new negotiation mechanism for solving in a distributed manner, and without any approximation, indivisible resource allocation problems so that the egalitarian social welfare of the multi-agent system is maximised, in the case where the worth of resources to agents is represented in terms of semi-linear utility functions. It is assumed that agents are willing to fully cooperate when working in teams. One may think of agents serving or acting for the interest of a common symbolic 'master' that in practice could correspond to an individual, company or institution of any kind.

Egalitarian allocations correspond to natural solutions in a number of application areas, and in particular for service-oriented multi-agent systems, where for example control of or access to services needs to be negotiated amongst agents. In this application, worth and utilities may respectively correspond to agents' competence in managing services and using the services. Then, the egalitarian approach would allow maximising the minimum competence in managing/using services in the system. Another application is earth observation via satellites [18,16], where an egalitarian approach is advisable as observation satellites are a scarce and highly expensive resource, usually co-exploited by several entities all expecting fairness in the exploitation process. A third field for application and perhaps the most obvious one, is agent-oriented [19,20] or holonic manufacturing systems [21]: agents can play the role of flexible self-organizing production units in a factory, where production platforms, raw materials and semi-finished products are utilised in function of the market's conditions. Factories are typically environments where no agent should be under-exploited and it is thought egalitarian principles can bring better productivity. A very interesting list of other practical applications has been given in [13].

The remainder of this paper is structured as follows. In section 2, we give a formal introduction to the resource allocation problem we tackle. In section 3, we introduce a general method to solve the problem efficiently and distributedly. Section 4 is dedicated to experiments on the time complexity required for solving allocation problems and the comparison of several social order-based coordination techniques for conducting negotiations and decision-making heuristics based on resource-preference orders. Section 5 draws some conclusions, compares our approach with related work and identifies some directions for future research.

2   Preliminaries

When several agents within a multi-agent system compete for the same resources, they need to overcome a complex conflict of interest, especially when agents need (or lack) many resources and have similar preferences. Autonomous agents need to solve the resulting resource allocation problem on their own, but cooperative agents also aim at finding a solution which is socially acceptable.

In this paper, we will refer to the agents and resources involved in a resource allocation problem as $a_1, a_2, \ldots, a_n$ and $r_1, r_2, \ldots r_m$, respectively, where the number of agents (n) and resources (m) are assumed to be strictly positive integers. We will assume that the resources are indivisible, so that a resource may be allocated only entirely and to one agent at most. We will use the following definition of allocation of resources to agents.

Definition 1. *Let $G = \{a_{i_1}, \ldots, a_{i_g}\}$ be a non-empty subset of $\{a_1, \ldots, a_n\}$ of cardinality $g \leq n$. G represents a* group *of g agents. An* allocation *for G is a Boolean table $A = ((A_{i,j}))_{g \times m}$ of g lines and m columns*

$$A^{\{i_1,\ldots,i_g\}} = \begin{pmatrix} i_1 : A_{i_1,1} \; A_{i_1,2} \; \cdots \; A_{i_1,m} \\ \cdots \; \cdots \; \cdots \; \cdots \; \cdots \\ i_g : A_{i_g,1} \; A_{i_g,2} \; \cdots \; A_{i_g,m} \end{pmatrix} \; s.t. \; \forall j \in \{1,\ldots,m\} : \sum_{i,a_i \in G} A_{i,j} \leq 1.$$

We say that a_i gets r_j if and only if $A_{i,j} = 1$.

The inequalities in definition 1 sanction that each resource is allocated to one agent at most and indivisibility is expressed by the Boolean quantities. When clear from the context, we omit the agents indexes in the allocations, as done here-after. As an example, given the group $G = \{a_1, a_2, a_3\}$ and resources r_1, r_2, r_3, r_4, a possible allocation is

$$A = \begin{pmatrix} 1 \; 0 \; 0 \; 0 \\ 0 \; 0 \; 1 \; 1 \\ 0 \; 0 \; 0 \; 0 \end{pmatrix}$$

According to it, a_1 gets r_1, a_2 gets r_3 and r_4 and a_3 gets no resource.

In our framework, agents in a multi-agent systems are abstractly characterised by their own preferences concerning the resources to be distributed. These preferences are given via a global utility table:

Definition 2. *A* utility table *is a matrix* $U = ((u_{i,j}))_{n \times m}$ *with n lines and m columns of coefficients $u_{i,j} \in \mathbb{R}^+$. For each $1 \leq i \leq n$ and $1 \leq j \leq m$, $u_{i,j}$ is referred to as the* utility *of resource r_j for agent a_i.*

The utility of a resource for an agent provides a measure of its contribution to the agent's welfare.

A reasonable and convenient assumption is to consider that the welfare of an agent resulting from an allocation of resources is semi-linearly distributed over the resources, as given by the following definition:

Definition 3. *For any $1 \leq i \leq n$, the welfare of agent a_i resulting from allocation A is given by the equation $w_i(A) = c_i + \sum_{j=1}^{m} u_{i,j} A_{i,j}$ where $c_i \in \mathbb{R}^+$.*

The coefficient c_i intuitively represents the welfare of a_i prior to any allocation of resources. By our definition of welfare, basically all the resources that are given to a_i increase its welfare: the individual utilities of resources sum up. This simple model captures the idea that: the more resources agents get the higher their welfare, and agents prefer resources that contribute most to their welfare. However, this model does not capture the synergies resources may have when put together. This simplification enables us to avoid having to treat the allocation problem as a complex combinatorial one, as is for instance the case in combinatorial auctions.

Let us now introduce an optimality criterion on allocations, borrowed from the areas of social choice theories and welfare economics and having an *egalitarian* flavour. Informally, we are after allocations that maximise the egalitarian social welfare of the multi-agent system, defined metaphorically as the welfare of the 'unhappiest' agent in the system. Formally:

Definition 4. *The* egalitarian social welfare *of an allocation A for $\{a_1, \ldots, a_n\}$ is $sw_e(A) = Min\{w_i(A) | i = 1, \ldots, n\}$. An* egalitarian allocation *is an allocation A^* with maximal egalitarian social welfare.*

As an example, given agents a_1, a_2, a_3, resources r_1, r_2, r_3, r_4, and tables

$$U = \begin{pmatrix} 0.9 \, 0.3 \, 0.0 \, 1.2 \\ 0.2 \, 0.5 \, 0.7 \, 0.3 \\ 0.4 \, 0.4 \, 0.9 \, 0.8 \end{pmatrix}, \quad \begin{pmatrix} c_1 \\ c_2 \\ c_3 \end{pmatrix} = \begin{pmatrix} 0.6 \\ 0.2 \\ 0.5 \end{pmatrix}$$

then, $A^* = \begin{pmatrix} 1 \, 0 \, 0 \, 0 \\ 0 \, 1 \, 1 \, 0 \\ 0 \, 0 \, 0 \, 1 \end{pmatrix}$ with $sw_e(A^*) = 1.3$, since $\begin{pmatrix} w_1(A^*) \\ w_2(A^*) \\ w_3(A^*) \end{pmatrix} = \begin{pmatrix} 1.5 \\ 1.4 \\ 1.3 \end{pmatrix}$.

We will use this example as a running example throughout the paper.

Note that there may be multiple egalitarian allocations within a society, but they all have the same egalitarian social welfare that we will denote sw_e^*.

Intuitively, by maximising the egalitarian social welfare in a society, we increase the chances that all agents are given enough resources to achieve their objectives. The notion of egalitarian social welfare contrasts with the more popular notion of utilitarian social welfare, amounting to the sum (or average) of all agents' welfare values. When utilitarian social welfare is maximised, resources are given to the agents that best use them, in terms of their individual welfare. But this may cause that other agents become inactive and incapable of achieving their objectives, which can be very ineffective, especially when the artificial society is supposed to provide a wide panel of services at the same time, as is the case e.g. in grid computing.

In the next section we give a method for constructing egalitarian allocations. Note that finding an egalitarian allocation of resources is a very hard search problem since there are exactly $(n+1)^m$ possible allocations to explore (that is the number of Boolean matrices of size $n \times m$ with at most one 1 per column). This means, for example, that even for a small multi-agent system with 9 agents and 10 resources to share, there are ten billions possible allocations to consider! Thus, the complexity of the decision-making problem the agents are confronted with when trying to compute an egalitarian allocation is huge.

3   Computation of Egalitarian Allocations

In this section we present an algorithm allowing agents to compute egalitarian allocations by working together, while taking autonomous decisions. When building an egalitarian allocation, two problems need to be solved at once: 1) finding the value sw_e^* of the optimal egalitarian social welfare and 2) actually finding an egalitarian allocation for the whole set of agents, with welfare sw_e^*.

3.1   Computing the Optimal Egalitarian Social Welfare

To solve the first problem, we will perform a dichotomous search. Dichotomy is a simple and elegant mechanism guaranteeing arbitrary precision and enabling fast estimation of the optimal social welfare. In this dichotomous search, an upper bound (ub) and lower bound (lb) for this optimal value are updated iteratively. These bounds are initialised as follows:

$$ub_0 = Min\{c_i + \sum_{j=1}^{n} u_{i,j} | i = 1 \ldots n\} \; ; \; lb_0 = Min\{c_i | i = 1 \ldots n\}$$

Roughly, the upper bound corresponds to an allocation where the eventually unhappiest agent is given all the resources and the lower bound corresponds to an allocation where it is given no resource. Clearly, the value of the optimal egalitarian social welfare lies somewhere between those bounds. The imprecision of our estimation is equal to their difference.

Definition 5. *Let $k \in \mathbb{N}$. Let ub_k and lb_k denote estimated upper and lower bounds of sw_e^* at iteration k: $lb_k \leq sw_e^* \leq ub_k$. Let m_k be the mean of ub_k and*

lb_k, defined as $m_k = (ub_k + lb_k)/2$. A is a satisfying allocation at iteration k iff its egalitarian social welfare is greater than m_k:

$$sw_e(A) \geq m_k.$$

Assume now that the agents are endowed with reasoning capabilities that enable them to detect whether the set of satisfying allocations is empty or not. If this set is empty, i.e. the optimal egalitarian social welfare cannot be greater than the mean, then the upper bound can be updated with the value of the mean:

$$ub_{k+1} = m_k \; ; \; lb_{k+1} = lb_k \; ; \; m_{k+1} = (ub_{k+1} + lb_{k+1})/2$$

Otherwise, the optimal social welfare is at least equal to the mean and the lower bound can be assigned to the value of the mean:

$$ub_{k+1} = ub_k \; ; \; lb_{k+1} = m_k \; ; \; m_{k+1} = (ub_{k+1} + lb_{k+1})/2$$

In both cases, one of the bounds is updated and the estimation imprecision is divided by two. After k iterations, the imprecision on sw_e^* is divided by 2^k. The constructed sequences all converge to the same limit:

Theorem 6 (Convergence). $\lim_{k \to \infty} lb_k = \lim_{k \to \infty} ub_k = \lim_{k \to \infty} m_k = sw_e^*$

Proof. The sequences $(lb_k)_{k \in \mathbb{N}}$ and $(ub_k)_{k \in \mathbb{N}}$ are adjacent sequences, respectively monotonic increasing and monotonic decreasing. This proves they converge to the same limit, so $(m_k)_{k \in \mathbb{N}}$ also converges and its limit is the same. The common value of these three sequences is obviously sw_e^*.

We therefore dispose of an efficient estimation procedure in which the imprecision converges towards zero at exponential speed. Note that theorem 6 can actually be strengthened. Indeed, in practice the agents would represent the utilities $u_{i,j}$ and the parameters denoted c_i by means of a finite number of digits d, i.e. with a precision of 10^{-d}. Then:

Theorem 7 (Fast termination). *The optimal egalitarian social welfare is computed after a number of dichotomous search steps equal to $floor(log_2 \frac{ub_0 - lb_0}{10^{-d}}) + 1$.*

Proof. Since sw_e^* is a sum of parameters represented with d digits it also has the same number of digits. The interval $I_k = [lb_k, ub_k]$ can contain a maximum of N_{max} such numbers, where $N_{max} = floor((lb - ub)/10^{-d})) + 1$. When N_{max} equals 1, the target sw_e^* can be precisely identified as the unique real number with d digits in this interval. As long as the length of I_k, i.e. $L(I_k) = ub_k - lb_k = 2^{-k}(ub_0 - lb_0)$, is strictly smaller than 10^{-d}, N_{max} is equal to 1. Basic calculus shows that this happens for the smallest integer k such that $k > log_2(\frac{ub_0 - lb_0}{10^{-d}})$.

3.2   Computing an Allocation with Optimal Egalitarian Social Welfare

Having shown how to compute the value of the optimal egalitarian social welfare in a society, we now turn to how to best construct satisfying allocations for this value. These correspond to egalitarian allocations. We present a method whereby, at each iteration k of the dichotomous search, the agents will go through a multiple-phase process (up to n phases), by constructing groups of increasing size: the first group contains one agent, the second contains two agents, etc.

In the dichotomous search process, the set of satisfying allocations for the society, at any iteration, need not be explicitly constructed, as only the (non-)emptiness of the set of all satisfying allocations matters. Thus, trivially, the agents are allowed to restrict the search to any subset of the set of satisfying allocations obtained by applying an *invariance operator*, namely an operator on sets preserving the properties of emptiness and non-emptiness.

Then, basically, our idea is to use an invariance operator that reduces as much as possible the search space. We will use an invariance operator defined in terms of the following binary relation on allocations for groups:

Definition 8. *Let A and B be two allocations for a group G. Then $B \preceq A$ if and only if for all resources j, $1 \leq j \leq m$:*

$$\sum_{i, a_i \in G} B_{i,j} \leq \sum_{i, a_i \in G} A_{i,j}$$

The inequality means that if a resource j is allocated according to B then it is also allocated according to A. The relation $\preceq$ is reflexive and transitive. Also, not all allocations can be compared with this relation (i.e. $\preceq$ is not a total relation). Moreover, $\preceq$ is not anti-symmetrical, so $\preceq$ is not an order relation.

Definition 9. *Let A and B be two allocations for a group G. Then B minors A if and only if $B \preceq A$ and A is* equivalent *to B if and only if $B \preceq A$ and $A \preceq B$.*

When considering the satisfying allocations, we eliminate every allocation that is either minored by or equivalent to another one. We repeat these simplifications until a fix point is reached. This process enables to construct/implement a reduction operator with the property of being an invariance operator:

Definition 10. *Let S be a set of allocations. A frugal reduction $F(S)$ of S is a subset of S such that (i) any allocation in S is minored by a allocation in $F(S)$, and (ii) no allocation in $F(S)$ is minored by another one in $F(S)$.*

Note that frugal reductions are not guaranteed to be unique, but the frugal reduction operator has the merit of being an invariance operator.

Theorem 11 (Invariance of F). *The frugal reduction operator F is an invariance operator.*

Proof. Since $F(S) \subseteq S$ trivially holds for all S, the frugal reduction of the empty set is the empty set. If S is not empty, it contains an element that is minored by an element in $F(S)$, so $F(S)$ is not empty either.

The problem of determining an egalitarian allocation then amounts to determining whether the frugal reduction of the satisfying set for the final iteration of the dichotomous search, giving the optimal egalitarian social welfare, is empty or not and, if not, to find one of its elements. In fact, we compute all of them.

Note also that, by using frugal reductions, resources are not wasted since only minimal allocations are kept (see example in figure 1). This is particularly useful when resources are scarce or expensive because leftovers can be re-used for other allocations. Note that utilitarianism does not have this property: any available resource is systematically consumed. In a nutshell, strict egalitarianism implicitly captures resource management policies.

$$F(\{ \begin{pmatrix} 1\,0\,1\,0 \\ 0\,1\,0\,0 \\ 0\,0\,0\,1 \end{pmatrix}, \begin{pmatrix} 0\,1\,0\,0 \\ 0\,0\,1\,0 \\ 0\,0\,0\,1 \end{pmatrix}, \begin{pmatrix} 0\,1\,0\,0 \\ 0\,0\,1\,0 \\ 1\,0\,0\,0 \end{pmatrix}, \begin{pmatrix} 0\,0\,1\,0 \\ 0\,1\,0\,0 \\ 1\,0\,0\,0 \end{pmatrix} \}) = \{ \begin{pmatrix} 0\,1\,0\,0 \\ 0\,0\,1\,0 \\ 0\,0\,0\,1 \end{pmatrix}, \begin{pmatrix} 0\,1\,0\,0 \\ 0\,0\,1\,0 \\ 1\,0\,0\,0 \end{pmatrix} \}$$

Fig. 1. The frugal reduction operator filters both redundancies (superfluous agreements) and allocations that over-consume resources (inefficient solutions). The agents save memory and time and the society manages its resources better (here either r_1 or r_4 is preserved).

Below, the term *(minimal collection of) agreements* for a group G, denoted $Ag(G)$, will stand for a frugal reduction of the set of satisfying allocations for G. Now we present an efficient decision-making procedure to build minimal collections of agreements for the full set of agents at each iteration of the dichotomous search, via a multi-phase process whereby agents progressively join in, starting from an initial group consisting of a single agent. At each phase, a minimal collection of agreements is built for the current group, if possible, and, when a new agent joins the group, the prior set of agreements is revised to provide a minimal collection for the newly formed group. If no agreements can be found the search is abandoned. In order to collect the minimal collection of agreements for a group to which a new agent has been added, we will use sets of trees, or in other words forests.

Suppose an agent $a_{i'}$ wants to start a new group $G' = \{a_{i'}\}$ or join an existing group $G = \{a_{i_1}, a_{i_2}, ..., a_{i_g}\}$ to form the new group or $G' = G \cup \{a_{i'}\}$. In order to build the minimal collection of agreements for G', $a_{i'}$ constructs a forest of trees whose nodes are pairs of the form $(Z, w(Z))$, where Z is a *fuzzy allocation* for G' and $w(Z)$ is its welfare, defined below.

Definition 12. *A fuzzy allocation is a table* $Z = ((z_{i,j}))_{(g+1) \times m}$ *with* $g+1$ *lines and* m *columns and whose coefficients* $z_{i,j}$ *belong to* $\{1, 0, -1\}$:

$$F = \begin{pmatrix} i_1 : z_{i_1,1} & z_{i_1,2} & \cdots & z_{i_1,m} \\ \cdots & \cdots & \cdots & \cdots & \cdots \\ i_g : z_{i_k,1} & z_{i_k,2} & \cdots & z_{i_g,m} \\ i' : z_{i',1} & z_{i',2} & \cdots & z_{i',m} \end{pmatrix}$$

The set of allocations encoded by a fuzzy allocation Z is the set of allocations for G' according to which each agent a_i in the group G' gets r_j if $z_{i,j} = 1$ and does not get r_j if $z_{i,j} = -1$.

The coefficients equal to 0 in a fuzzy allocation leave the information as to which agents gets the corresponding resource unspecified.

Definition 13. *The signature of a fuzzy allocation Z is obtained by replacing in Z all the coefficients equal to -1 by 0.*

Intuitively, the signature of a fuzzy allocation is the allocation in the set encoded by Z that allocates fewest resources.

Definition 14. *The welfare of a fuzzy allocation Z, denoted $w(Z)$, is the egalitarian social welfare of the signature of Z. If $w(Z)$ is greater than m_k, at some iteration k, then Z is said to be* satisfying.

Definition 15. *A node $(Z, w(Z))$ in a tree is called*

- positive *iff $w(Z) \geq m_k$ (i.e. Z is satisfying)*
- open *iff it is not positive but the allocation in the set encoded by Z in which all the resources not used by the agents in G are used by the new agent $a_{i'}$ is satisfying (if $G' = \{a_{i'}\}$ any resource can be used)*
- negative *iff it is neither positive nor open.*

The trees are constructed as follows. The roots of the trees constituting the forest of a phase are constructed from the positive leaves of the trees in the previous phase. More precisely, $Ag(G')$, the minimal collection of agreements for G', is computed from the positive leaves of the trees in the forest for G' (as we will see below). The roots of the trees in the forest for G' are pairs $(Z, w(Z))$ where the first g lines of Z take their values in (one of) the agreements in $Ag(G)$ and all the coefficients in the last line (corresponding to the newly added agent $a_{i'}$) are equal to zero. Negative and positive nodes have no children, only open nodes do. Consider an open node $N = (Z, w(Z))$. Let j_0 be the index of a resource r_j that $a_{i'}$ could use, i.e. $z_{i',j_0} = 0$ and that does not have a null utility. Such an index exists since the node is open. Then the left and right children of N, denoted $(Z_L, w(Z_L))$ and $(Z_R, w(Z_R))$, respectively, are defined as follows:

$$Z_{L;i',j_0} = 1, \ Z_{R;i',j_0} = -1 \text{ and } \forall j \neq j_0 : \ Z_{L;i',j} = Z_{R;i',j} = Z_{i',j}$$

The agents build the tree by constructing the descendants of all open nodes. Thus, the trees all have a strictly binary structure. The process terminates finitely because there is a finite number of resources. In fact, the depth of a tree is bounded by the number of resources $a_{i'}$ can use.

Figures 2 and 3 illustrate the construction of trees in a forest, for our running example at step $k = 1$, where the allocations must have a welfare greater than $m_1 = 1.225$. Here and in the rest of the paper, we ignore the index of agents in fuzzy allocations if clear from the context.

We will refer to fully constructed trees (namely trees whose only leaves are positive or negative nodes) as *frugal trees*. Frugal trees have an interesting property: their leaves 'hide' a frugal reduction of their root:

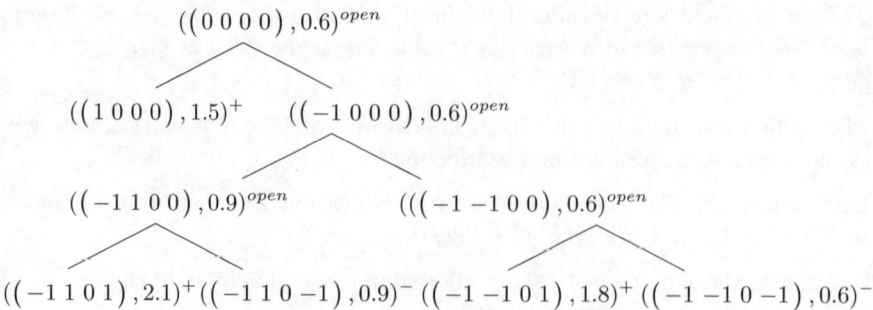

Fig. 2. a_1 finds first three satisfying allocations (1 0 0 0), (0 1 0 1) and (0 0 0 1). The second one, which is minored by the third one, will be eliminated by frugal reduction.

$$\left(\begin{pmatrix} 1\ 0\ 0\ 0 \\ 0\ 0\ 0\ 0 \end{pmatrix}, 0.2\right)^{open}$$

$$\left(\begin{pmatrix} 1\ 0\ 0\ 0 \\ 0\ 1\ 0\ 0 \end{pmatrix}, 0.7\right)^{open} \qquad \left(\begin{pmatrix} 1\ 0\ 0\ 0 \\ 0\ -1\ 0\ 0 \end{pmatrix}, 0.2\right)^{-}$$

$$\left(\begin{pmatrix} 1\ 0\ 0\ 0 \\ 0\ 1\ 1\ 0 \end{pmatrix}, 1.4\right)^{+} \qquad \left(\begin{pmatrix} 1\ 0\ 0\ 0 \\ 0\ 1\ -1\ 0 \end{pmatrix}, 0.7\right)^{-}$$

Fig. 3. a_2 examines the first allocation found by a_1 and this search leads to one agreement between the two agents: a_1 takes r_1 and a_2 takes r_2 and r_3

Theorem 16 (Frugal tree). *Given a fuzzy allocation Z, let L be the set of positive leaves of a frugal tree with root $(Z, w(Z))$, and let S be the set of signatures for all elements of L. Then, there exists a frugal reduction $F(\Sigma)$ of the set Σ of satisfying allocations encoded by Z such that $F(\Sigma) \subseteq S$.*

Proof. By construction of the tree, the union of the sets encoded by its leaves is equal to the set encoded by the root. A property of negative nodes is that they encode sets that do not contain satisfying allocations. So, all the satisfying allocations are in the union of the positive nodes (recall that open nodes are not leaves). By $\preceq$-minimality of the elements in the frugal reduction, they can only be the allocation in the positive node consuming least resources, i.e. be signatures of positive nodes. Hence the inclusion.

Applying the frugal reduction operator after having collected the signatures for the leaves enables the agents to ignore superfluous agreements. The reason why we do not lose any useful agreement by working only on the positive nodes is justified by the following lemma, where the role of the set of signatures is played by S and the set of satisfying allocations for the root is played by Σ:

Lemma 17 (Elimination). *If $F(\Sigma) \subseteq S \subseteq \Sigma$ then $F(S) = F(\Sigma)$ (namely, a frugal reduction of S is also one of Σ).*

Proof. Any allocation in Σ is minored by an allocation in $F(\Sigma)$ which in turn is minored by an allocation in $F(A)$. No allocation in $F(A)$ is minored by another in $F(A)$.

This lemma justifies the idea that the agents should apply the reduction operator on the positive leaves of the frugal trees so as to minimise the computational effort in the next phase, by minimising the number of trees to explore/construct and therefore save both time and memory.

By virtue of the following theorem, harvesting the positive leaves of a frugal tree and filtering through the frugal reduction operator, one ends up with a minimal collection of agreements for the new group.

Theorem 18 (Agreements coverage). *There exists a frugal reduction of the minimal collection of agreements for G' that is included in $F(X)$, where X is the union of all positive nodes in all trees in the forest constructed for G'.*

Proof. We will prove that indeed, the frugal reduction of the union is also a frugal reduction of the satisfying agreements for G'. We simply check that the two points defining a frugal reduction hold. The second point is trivial since the frugal reduction of the union is a frugal reduction. The first point holds because we started from a complete set of minimal agreements for G and have taken a complete set of their minimal extensions.

As an illustration of the overall mechanism, consider our running example with three agents, four resources and the tables in section 2. Then

– at iteration $k = 0$: $lb_0 = 0.2$ $ub_0 = 1.9$ $m_0 = 0.55$

$$Ag(\{1\}) = \{(0\,0\,0\,0)\}\,;\; Ag(\{1,2\}) = \{\begin{pmatrix}0\,0\,0\,0\\0\,1\,0\,0\end{pmatrix}, \begin{pmatrix}0\,0\,0\,0\\0\,0\,1\,0\end{pmatrix}, \begin{pmatrix}0\,0\,0\,0\\1\,0\,0\,1\end{pmatrix}\}\,;$$

$$Ag(\{1,2,3\}) = \{\begin{pmatrix}0\,0\,0\,0\\0\,1\,0\,0\\1\,0\,0\,0\end{pmatrix}, \begin{pmatrix}0\,0\,0\,0\\0\,1\,0\,0\\0\,0\,1\,0\end{pmatrix}, \begin{pmatrix}0\,0\,0\,0\\0\,1\,0\,0\\0\,0\,0\,1\end{pmatrix}, \begin{pmatrix}0\,0\,0\,0\\0\,0\,1\,0\\1\,0\,0\,0\end{pmatrix}, \begin{pmatrix}0\,0\,0\,0\\0\,0\,1\,0\\0\,0\,0\,1\end{pmatrix}\}$$

– at iteration $k = 1$: $lb_1 = 0.55$ $ub_1 = 1.9$ $m_1 = 1.225$

$$Ag(\{1\}) = \{(1\,0\,0\,0), (0\,0\,0\,1)\}\,;\; Ag(\{1,2\}) = \{\begin{pmatrix}1\,0\,0\,0\\0\,1\,1\,0\end{pmatrix}, \begin{pmatrix}0\,0\,0\,1\\0\,1\,1\,0\end{pmatrix}\}\,;$$

$$Ag(\{1,2,3\}) = \{\begin{pmatrix}1\,0\,0\,0\\0\,1\,1\,0\\0\,0\,0\,1\end{pmatrix}\}$$

– at iteration $k = 2$: $lb_2 = 1.225$ $ub_2 = 1.9$ $m_2 = 1.5625$

$$Ag(\{1\}) = \{(0\,0\,0\,1)\}\,;\; Ag(\{1,2\}) = \{\begin{pmatrix}0\,0\,0\,1\\1\,1\,1\,0\end{pmatrix}\}\,;\; Ag(\{1,2,3\}) = \{\}$$

– at iteration $k = 3$: $lb_3 = 1.225$ $ub_3 = 1.5625$ $m_3 = 1.39225$

$$Ag(\{1\}) = \{(1\,0\,0\,0), (0\,0\,0\,1)\}\,;\; Ag(\{1,2\}) = \{\begin{pmatrix}1\,0\,0\,0\\0\,1\,1\,0\end{pmatrix}, \begin{pmatrix}0\,0\,0\,1\\0\,1\,1\,0\end{pmatrix}\}\,;$$
$$Ag(\{1,2,3\}) = \{\}$$

– at iteration $k = 4$: $lb_4 = 1.225$ $ub_4 = 1.39225$ $m_4 = 1.308625$

$$Ag(\{1\}) = \{(1\,0\,0\,0),(0\,0\,0\,1)\} \; ; \; Ag(\{1,2\}) = \{\begin{pmatrix} 1\,0\,0\,0 \\ 0\,1\,1\,0 \end{pmatrix}, \begin{pmatrix} 0\,0\,0\,1 \\ 0\,1\,1\,0 \end{pmatrix}\}$$
$$Ag(\{1,2,3\}) = \{\}$$

– at iteration $k = 5$: $lb_5 = 1.225$ $ub_5 = 1.308625$ $m_5 = 1.2668125$

$$Ag(\{1\}) = \{(1\,0\,0\,0),(0\,0\,0\,1)\} \; ; \; Ag(\{1,2\}) = \{\begin{pmatrix} 1\,0\,0\,0 \\ 0\,1\,1\,0 \end{pmatrix}, \begin{pmatrix} 0\,0\,0\,1 \\ 0\,1\,1\,0 \end{pmatrix}\}$$
$$Ag(\{1,2,3\}) = \{\begin{pmatrix} 1\,0\,0\,0 \\ 0\,1\,1\,0 \\ 0\,0\,0\,1 \end{pmatrix}\}$$

At this point the algorithm terminates (as $ub_5 - lb_5 < 10^{-1}$) correctly computing A^* given in section 2.

4   Consensus Search and Coordination Heuristics

Two issues have been left open regarding the computation of egalitarian allocations: (i) the choice of resource indexes for splitting open nodes (in the *search for consensus*) and (ii) the election criterion for an agent to join the current group (referred to as *coordination* criterion). In this section we provide solutions to these issues in an experimental setting, as they play no role at the theory level. The solutions will be stated in the form of heuristics.

The way an agent performs consensus search is determined by a node-splitting strategy, i.e. a rule for choosing the resource index on which to split an open node in the search tree. In our experiments, the reference strategy consists in following the order of appearance of the (yet un-allocated) resources in their natural order r_1, r_2, r_3, etc. We call this the *random node strategy (RN)*. This strategy is compared to two other strategies based on resource preferences. These strategies are called *least-useful strategy (LU)* and *most-useful strategy (MU)*. The splitting index chosen when following LU (resp. MU) is the one of the unused resource having the lowest (resp. greatest) utility for the new agent.

Coordination is determined by the election criterion/order applied for selecting the next agent to join the group and enter in negotiation with it. The simplest order, that we call *random order (RO)*, is the natural order of the agents $a_1, a_2, ..., a_n$. This criterion serves as a reference for performance comparisons. We define two other orders, based on the welfare of the agents, which enables to order them socially. The *lowest welfare strategy (LW)* gives priority to the remaining agent with lowest welfare, whereas the *highest welfare strategy (HW)* gives priority to the remaining agent with highest welfare.

Figure 4 summarises some experiments comparing, in the first three columns, the consensus search strategies (RN, LU and MU) while keeping the coordination heuristic fixed to RO, and, in the last two columns, the social orders LW and HW for coordination, while keeping MU for the consensus search. We evaluate in seconds the average computational time needed to solve randomly generated problems whose sizes are indicated in the (n, m) column. The number of agents

(n, m)	$RO - RN$	$RO - LU$	$RO - MU$	$HW - MU$	$LW - MU$
$(1, 1)$	0.0945	0.1065	0.1010	0.0110	0.0060
$(2, 2)$	0.3635	0.4075	0.3145	0.0245	0.0180
$(3, 3)$	0.9600	1.1345	0.8640	0.0320	0.0365
$(4, 4)$	2.4090	2.8825	2.0175	0.1000	0.1110
$(5, 5)$	7.4655	9.6015	6.0310	0.2450	0.1405
$(6, 6)$	20.7670	27.6690	15.6435	0.8785	0.7125
$(7, 7)$	74.6614	105.4960	51.6125	4.4810	2.2935

Fig. 4. Influence of the nodes-splitting strategy for social consensus (RN, LU, MU) and the agents selection order for coordination (RO, HW, LW) on the total decision-making time. The combined LW-MU heuristic divides the negotiation time by nearly 30.

is taken equal to the number of resources and this number varies from 1 to 7. The table U and coefficients c_i are generated according to a uniform distribution between 0 and 1. We use 2 digits of precision for the utilities ($d = 2$). The computational time is averaged over 20 problems for each dimension and the different strategies are systematically assessed with respect to the same cases for fair comparisons. The experiments have been carried with Maple 10 on a 1.07 GHz G4 processor. The first three columns show that for a fixed random order of negotiation, following the MU strategy gives the best results. When splitting open nodes with respect to most useful resources first, the depth of the search tree's branches is minimised. Then keeping the MU strategy (last two columns), we discover that using monotonic social orders to coordinate negotiations leads to solutions very fast, with a slight superiority of the increasing order over the decreasing one. The agents that must join the group first are those with lowest welfare (LW). When these two best strategies are combined (LW-MU), the improvement is considerable: the total time required for the negotiations is divided by nearly 30.

5   Conclusion

We presented a sound method that guarantees agents to find an allocation of resources that exactly maximises the egalitarian social welfare of the society they constitute. The method relies upon a dichotomous search terminating after a 'small' number of steps. In the search process, agents examine and update the value of the optimal egalitarian social welfare that can be collectively achieved given their personal preferences, expressed in terms of utilities they assign to sets of resources. Our method uses binary search trees and forests of Boolean fuzzy allocations as well as a frugal reduction operator that simplifies the reasoning process of the agents by eliminating appropriately any superfluous agreements they might come up with. The solutions are efficient as far as they never overconsume resources.

The proposed mechanism allows consensus to be found with 'minimal' disclosure of information about the agents' preferences. Also, the mechanism can be nicely be distributed over the agents, with important computational advantages: the agents themselves carry the computational burden and the agents' master is relieved of all supervising work.

We proved empirically that the agents reason collectively much faster when giving priority to the most useful resources and can efficiently coordinate the sequence of their negotiations by using monotonic increasing social orders.

Dall'Aglio and Maccheroni [10] recently proved the existence of fair divisions between agents in the case of strongly subadditive and strongly continuous utility functions. In this paper, we have assumed additivity (semi-linearity) of the utility functions but have considered a finite set of indivisible resources. As Golovin [12] puts it: 'little is known about the computational aspects of finding [...] fair allocations [...] with indivisible goods' and 'early work in operations research focused on special cases that are tractable, or on exponential time algorithms for general models [13]'. In this family of models [13,14], resources are allocated to activities, not agents. Under such formalism, the problem comes down to determining the appropriate levels of activity (represented as simple scalar variables). But when resources are allocated to agents, this notion collapses and one is led to handle vectorial variables with components for each resource, as in our case. Hence, although those models and our own all aim at solving the same ultimate application, they are not formalised as equivalent mathematical problems. Our intuition is that agents should first be assigned to tasks considering their capabilities (e.g. via coalition formation [8]) and then be allocated the resources.

The computational aspects of fair allocations of indivisible goods have been studied by [11]. This work however differs from ours in that in [11] fairness is achieved by minimising envy. According to Brams and King [15], 'while envy may be ineradicable if one desires to help the worst off, it is not clear that abandoning the maximin criteria to avoid it is a better alternative'.

[12] and [16] investigated the complexity of finding fair allocations of indivisible goods. [17] considered the problem of finding approximate max-min fair allocations for agents with additive utilities. In this paper, we have given a new negotiation mechanism for solving in a distributed manner, and without any approximation, indivisible resource allocation problems in the extended case of semi-linear utility functions.

Future work will be dedicated to the design of protocols and policies for implementing the allocation mechanism in distributed settings, to the study of complexity and scalability issues and to an experimental comparison to other methods.

Acknowledgements

This work was partially funded by the Sixth Framework IST programme of the EC, under the 035200 ARGUGRID project. The second author has also been supported by a UK Royal Academy of Engineering/Leverhulme Trust senior fellowship.

References

1. K. J. Arrow: Social Choice and Individual Values. John Wiley and Sons (1963)
2. A. K. Sen: Collective Choice and Social Welfare. Holden Day (1970)
3. H. Moulin: Axioms of Cooperative Decision Making. Cambridge University Press (1988)
4. J. Rawls: A Theory of Justice. Harvard University Press (1971)
5. J. C. Harsanyi: Can the Maximin Principle Serve as a Basis for Morality? American Political Science Review **86:2** (1996) 269–357
6. U. Endriss, N. Maudet, F. Sadri and F. Toni: Resource Allocation in Egalitarian Agent Societies. MFI (2003) 101–110
7. T. Sandholm: Algorithms for Optimal Winner Determination in Combinatorial Auctions. Artificial Intelligence **135** (2002)
8. O. Shehory and S. Kraus: Methods for task allocation via agent coalition formation. Artificial Intelligence **101:1–2** (1998) 165–200
9. U. Endriss, N. Maudet, F. Sadri and F. Toni: Negotiating Socially Optimal Allocations of Resources. Journal of Artificial Intelligence Research **25** (2006) 315–348
10. M. Dall'Aglio and F. Maccheroni: Fair division without additivity. The American Mathematical Monthly **112** (2005)
11. R. Lipton, E. Markakis, E. Mossel and A. Saberi: On approximately fair allocations of indivisible goods. Proceedings of EC'04 (2004)
12. D. Golovin: Max-Min Fair Allocations of Indivisible Goods. CMU-CS-05-144 (2005)
13. H. Luss: On equitable resource allocation problems: A lexicographic minimax approach. Operations Research **47:3** (1999) 361–378
14. G. Yu: On the max-min 0-1 knapsack problem with robust optimization applications. Operations Research **44** (1996) 407–415
15. S.J. Brams and D.L. King: Efficient Fair Division: Help the Worst Off or Avoid Envy? Rationality and Society **17:4** (2005) 387-421
16. S. Bouveret, M. Lemaître, H. Fargier and J. Lang: Allocation of indivisible goods: a general model and some complexity results. AAMAS (2005) 1309–1310
17. I. Bezakova and V. Dani: Allocating indivisible goods. ACM SIGecom Exchanges **5:3** (2005) 11–18
18. M. Lemaître, G. Verfaillie and N. Bataille: Exploiting a Common Property Resource under a Fairness Constraint: a Case Study. IJCAI (1999) 206–211
19. S. Bussmann: Agent-Oriented Programming of Manufacturing Control Tasks. ICMAS (1998) 57–63
20. S. Bussmann and K. Schild: Self-Organizing Manufacturing Control: An Industrial Application of Agent Technology. ICMAS (2000) 87–94
21. R. Babiceanu and F. Chen: Development and Applications of Holonic Manufacturing Systems: A Survey. Journal of Intelligent Manufacturing **1:17** (2006) 111–131

Iterative Query-Based Approach to Efficient Task Decomposition and Resource Allocation

Michal Pěchouček[1], Ondřej Lerch[2], and Jiří Bíba[1]

[1] Department of Cybernetics, Faculty of Electrical Engineering
Czech Technical University in Prague
Technická 2, Prague, 166 27, The Czech Republic
{pechouc, biba}@labe.felk.cvut.cz
[2] Department of Software Engineering, Faculty of Nuclear Engineering
Czech Technical University in Prague
Břehová 7, Prague, 115 19, The Czech Republic
ondrej.lerch@gmail.com

Abstract. Intelligent coordination in complex multi-agent environments requires sophisticated mechanisms for suboptimal *task decomposition* and efficient *resource allocation* provided by the the agents. Besides the quality of coordination (i.e. efficiency of decomposition and resource allocation) we need to handle also computational efficiency restriction such as fast response time and limited communication traffic among the agents as well as optimization of the amount of private knowledge disclosure, during collaboration patterns negotiation among the semi-collaborative agents. We present a novel contracting mechanism based on the use of the approximated acquaintance model, a structure where the agents store the information about the states, capabilities and resources of possible collaborators. We suggest an approach of iterative construction of the partially-linear acquaintance models that is beneficial mainly in complex agent communities.

1 Introduction

This paper presents a novel contracting mechanism based on the use of the *acquaintance model*, a knowledge structure representing agents' mutual awareness. An appropriate use of the acquaintance models reduces the communication traffic requirements and reduces the computational requirements on agent's decision making. This approach provides the most significant benefits in system with larger amount of agents (tens to hundred of agents) and with very high number of operational alternatives (i.e. ways how a single request can be handled). Besides operational efficiency improvements, the use of acquaintance models also provides an elegant mechanism for avoiding private knowledge disclosure.

The presented approach has got its applicability potential in the logistics and supply chain management domains, where complex business interaction needs to be optimized. Especially the knowledge disclosure aspect is very important in this domain. The acquaintance model based contracting has been deployed in the OOTW (operations other then war) humanitarian relief provision scenarios [1]. Besides, this efficient coordination mechanism can be used in manufacturing domains (illustrated in [2]), resource

M. Klusch, M. Rovatsos, and T. Payne (Eds.): CIA 2006, LNAI 4149, pp. 258–272, 2006.

leverage in larger (possibly ad-hoc) networking environment [3], telecommunication, and others.

We will be working with a community of agents where each agent can act as a **service provider** (agent that provide some service or product) or a **service requester** (agent that request services or products). The algorithm will be illustrated on a single contract case, where there is only one requester and n providers. However, the algorithm is designed so that each agent can be a provider and a requester at the same time and the agents can also contract each other (similar to [4]). The problem is to find best decomposition of a specific task into granular services and the most optimal contracting among the community of possible service providers.

As mentioned earlier, the presented problem integrates two deliberation activities (i) *decomposition* and (ii) *contracting* (delegation). The main difficulty is that efficiency of decomposition depends on how well the subtasks can be contracted, while contracting depends on how the task is decomposed. Both deliberation processes are deeply interlinked.

1.1 Existing Contracting Mechanisms

Contracting is one of the most important problems that has been studied in the field of multi-agent system. The most widely used approaches to contracting are based on the *contract-net-protocol* [5]. Here the requester broadcasts the call for proposals within a community of potential providers. The providers reply with a collaboration bids. The requester selects the most optimal bid and sets a contract. The contract-net-protocol can be also multi-staged, that is understood as an auction. There are several auctioning mechanisms available in the community: *English auction, Dutch auction, seal-bid auction, Vickery auction* [4].

The problem with the classical contract-net-protocol is that it may get stuck in local optimum. This happens primarily if we are trying to balance a load in a nontrivial network of n requester and n providers. That is why several variants of the original O-contract-net-protocol have been suggested. C-contract-net-protocol works similarly to the classical protocol while the subject of negotiation is not a single task but a collection of tasks. The S-contract-net-protocol works with agents who are not selling and buying tasks but they swap the tasks between two agents instead. Similarly, the M-contract-net-protocol arrange swapping among several (more than 2) agents. It has been proved that with a finite number of agents and tasks, the $OSCM$-contract-net-protocol protocol that combines all these variants can always find a globally optimal solution in a finite number of steps [6].

While the concept of delegation, task decomposition and commitments have been also widely studied in the multi-agent community [7], [8] [9] our focus will be mainly centered around linking the contracting and decomposition activities within the community of collaborating agents.

1.2 Acquaintance Models

As mentioned previously, use of the acquaintance models is going to be a central concept of the presented contracting mechanism. The *acquaintance model* is computational model of agents' mutual awareness, built by each of the agents. The acquaintance model is a collection of agent's social knowledge [10] available from previous interaction or provided by independent monitoring mechanisms. The acquaintance model may contain both the inevitable information for setting any kind of collaboration (such as the *white-page* information – IP addresses, ACL, port-number) and an optional information that can improve the quality of collaboration (such as information about the services available, free capacities, overall load of the agents and others). The acquaintance model can also contain non-public information such as trust models or models of the other agent's internal mental states (e.g. commitments, intentions).

There have been several specific architectures of the acquaintance model designed in the past – *tri-base* (3bA) acquaintance model [11], *twin-based model* [12], acquaintance model in ARCHON [13]. In the remaining parts of the article the specific architecture of the acquaintance model is unimportant, as we will be discussing how the knowledge is maintained and exploited on an abstract level. However, there is one clear distinction between the existing acquaintance models and the abstract acquaintance model we will be using in our experiments. Unlike the listed models, we will be using the concept of acquaintance models for representing an *approximate social knowledge*. Such knowledge is an estimated information about the other agents and may be constructed by various approximation mechanisms and limited interaction among the agents.

1.3   Task Decomposition and Resource Allocation Approaches

A task decomposition and a resource allocation is one of the most crucial points of inter-agent cooperation. There have been proposed various approaches based on concepts like market mechanisms, task/resource clustering, load balancing, etc. Both the problems of the task decomposition and the resource allocation are often substantially mutually dependent and generally belong to class of NP-complete or even NP-hard tasks. This is caused by complex dependences between subtasks that particular tasks consist of (e.g. precedence constraints) as well as by a need for sharing different special resources among more tasks.

Interesting results are obtained by means of combining the agent approach with non-deterministic optimization approaches like genetic algorithms in order to obtain solutions of complex problems in a reasonable time and quality. An approach combining the agent paradigm with genetic algorithms (GA) was presented in [14]. Resource allocation in a computational grid is done in three steps: (i) rough task clustering negotiated by the agents "possessing" (representing) particular resources – the tasks are clustered so that tasks with a more intensive messaging are assigned to nodes inter-connected by means of better communication lines , (ii) optimal mapping of task clusters to resource clusters by means of GA and (iii) recursive distribution of the task clusters to appropriate resource clusters. The tasks could require specific resources and were assumed to be inter-connected.

Another approach exploiting hierarchical grid topology and execution time prediction was presented in [15]. In a task farming problem (i.e. several independent tasks are to be executed in parallel so that the execution time is minimized) an execution time prediction is used to choose resources/nodes for their execution and the job scheduling is done by means of GA. The tasks may be generally of different kinds (i.e. require different types of resources/services). When considering only one-service tasks, the scheduling is done by means of a Roulette Wheel Selection according to predicted execution times of the jobs at particular nodes.

An agent-oriented solution exploiting market mechanisms was introduced in [16]. The system TRACE consists of multi-agent organizations that are allowed to allocate dynamically task and resources in order to efficiently process incoming stream of tasks. Each agent may be assigned only a task that is capable to handle (i.e. the agent is equipped with resources/abilities required for the particular task). There are distinguished permanent and marketable agents and each organisation has own resource manager agent. The tasks arrive arbitrarily to permanent agents who become responsible for the tasks. If an agent determines that the task cannot be proceeded within a given deadline, the task is decommitted within the organization. The resource manager collects an information about decommitted tasks and handles renting or offering marketable agents from or to other organizations. The decommitted tasks are then sent to permanent agents again. The determination of need for marketable agents is carried out by means of a market mechanism. Together with the decommitted task the resource manager is paid a decommitment penalty by the permanent agent. The higher is the contribution, the higher priority has the decommitted task. The resource manager calculates an equilibrium task allocation and participates in a market competition for available marketable agents. As soon as the market approaches an equilibrium (number of all offered marketable agents at given price is equal to number of required ones), it hires the agents and provides them with a necessary amount of domain information concerning the tasks they are hired for.

Another market mechanism was presented in [17]. There was provided an explicit formal description of an agent utility which differs in the subject of minimization when allocating the tasks on the resources, i.e. either (i) the total-duration or (ii) the total-price. While the one objective function is minimized the other is considered as a constraint. The *grid task agents* compete for resources handled by *grid resource agents*. The grid resource agents aim to maximize their utility as well as the grid task agents do – thus the grid resource agents update the prices with respect to a demand and the grid task agents offer prices with respect to demanded amount of resources and available budget. The bargaining process is finished when an equilibrium between demanded and offered resources is achieved. The negotiation between grid task agents and grid resource agents is held indirectly by means of a grid market that gathers information of all the actual negotiations (a global market view) and provides it to negotiating parties while multiple independent negotiations are facilitated.

In special cases the task decomposition and resource allocation problems may be solved polynomially or pseudo-polynomially provided the properties and requirements of the tasks are restricted. A simplification consists e.g. in reducing the number of available resources (e.g. scheduling only for two dedicated processors) or in relaxation of task inter-dependences (e.g. there are missing precedence constraints among the subtasks). An interesting simplification consists in reducing the number of resource types required to an only type while multiple resources are available for processing. In this paper we focus on an "as-soon-as-possible" task decomposition and resource allocation of tasks requiring only one type of resource/service while minimizing the total duration.

2   Problem Definition

In this section we will formally define the coupled problem of decomposition and contracting. We will denote R as a requester agent, S as a type of service that requester R request in order to complete its task, a_t as a total amount of service S that requester R requests, n as a number of providers offering the service type S, P_j as a provider agent offering service S, where $j = \{1, ..., n\}$ and $d_j(a)$ as a duration for the agent P_j to deliver the amount a of service S.

The **decomposition** of the service S in amount a_t to agents $P_1, \ldots, P_n$ is an arbitrary vector of non-negative integers $(a_1, \ldots, a_n)$, where

$$a_j \in \mathbb{Z}^+, \quad \sum_{j=1}^{n} a_j = a_t. \tag{1}$$

If a_j equals 0, then the provider P_j is not contracted at all.

The **overall duration** of decomposition $(a_1, \ldots, a_n)$ is defined as

$$d(a_1, \ldots, a_n) = \max_j d_j(a_j) \quad j \in \{1, \ldots, n\}, a_j > 0. \tag{2}$$

The explanation of (2) is as follows: if the requester agent contracts the service S in total amount a_t using the decomposition $(a_1, \ldots, a_n)$, then it means that each agent $P_j \in \{P_1, \ldots, P_n\}$ has to perform S in amount a_j. The whole task is therefore performed when the last agent performs its sub-task. Those agents for which $a_j = 0$ are not contracted at all, and therefore duration $d_j(0)$ is not taken into account.

Our primary effort is to find **optimal decomposition** that minimizes (2), that is to find the vector $(a_1^{min}, \ldots, a_n^{min})$ such that

$$(a_1^{min}, \ldots, a_n^{min}) = \arg \min_{a_1, \ldots, a_n} d(a_1, \ldots, a_n), \tag{3}$$

where $(a_1, \ldots, a_n)$ fulfill (1).

In this work, we focus on the task decomposition to minimize the overall **duration** (2). Another important task is to decompose the task to minimize the overall **price**. Let us assume that the price of service S in amount a equals $p_j(a)$ if the task is performed by the provider P_j. The overall price of decomposition $(a_1, \ldots, a_n)$ is defined as

$$p(a_1, \ldots, a_n) = \sum_j p_j(a_j) \quad j \in \{1, \ldots, n\}, a_j > 0. \tag{4}$$

The difference between the overall duration (2) and overall price (4) is that the overall duration is the maximum of durations $d_1(a_1), \ldots, d_n(a_n)$ while the overall price is the sum of prices $p_1(a_1), \ldots, p_n(a_n)$. In our work, we focused on overall duration minimization since in the real-world scenario, the lowest price decompositions are $(0, \ldots, 0, a_j = a_t, 0, \ldots, 0)$ where P_j is the cheapest provider. This is caused by the fact that providers offer better price per 1 amount if contracted for more amounts.

In this work we consider an only *type* of service to be decomposed (in contrast to decomposing a bunch of different services). While the choice of the overall price as the only objective function makes the decomposition rather trivial, the choice of the overall duration remains still reasonable in a case of need for meeting a deadline (it is necessary to get the service as soon as possible and the price is less important).

Though, in the real-world scenarios the price is hardly completely ignored – more likely it is set as an optimization constraint and a **constrained decomposition problem** is solved: we minimize the duration $d(a_1, \ldots, a_n)$ under the condition that the price $p(a_1, \ldots, a_n)$ is smaller or equal than predefined constant p_{max}. An even more probable constrained decomposition problem is introduced by the vice versa setting: a deadline is set as the constraint and the subject of optimization is the price: we minimize the price $p(a_1, \ldots, a_n)$ under the condition that the duration $d(a_1, \ldots, a_n)$ is smaller or equal than the predefined constant d_{max}. Finally, an interesting problem is also **combined decomposition problem** that takes into account both decomposition duration and price and uses a joint minimization criterion

$$f_\alpha(a_1, \ldots, a_n) = \alpha \cdot d(a_1, \ldots, a_n) + (1 - \alpha) \cdot p(a_1, \ldots, a_n),$$

$0 \leq \alpha \leq 1$, which includes both the duration and the price. The coefficient α determines if we prefer the minimization of duration or price.

However, in our work, we actually do not cover neither the combined decomposition problem nor the constrained decomposition problem and minimize the overall duration only (i.e. we cover cases when it is necessary to obtain the service as soon as possible).

3   Solution

We have designed a straightforward decomposition mechanism that finds the most optimal decomposition given the right objective function and available data [18]. The decomposition algorithm is polynomial and easy to construct. Its behavior, however, depends strongly on the data stored in the acquaintance models of the agents. In the following we will discuss the decomposition algorithms and two approaches how the acquaintance model can be constructed and maintained – *Batch-Query AM Construction* and *Iterative-Query AM Construction*. The decomposition algorithm and acquaintance model construction are demonstrated on a simple scenario of decomposition a service between two providers (see section 4).

3.1   Decomposition Algorithm

For purposes of this paper, we introduce a decomposition algorithm derived from the algorithm presented in [18], however, with significantly smaller complexity. We assume that durations $d_j(a)$ can only take discrete values, that is $d_j(a) \in \mathbb{Z}^+$, and that the functions $d_j(a)$ are extended to the point $a = 0$ by $d_j(0) = 0$. We can now construct pseudo-inverse function $a_j(d)$ as

$$a_j(d) = \max \{a \in \{0, \ldots, a_t\} \mid d_j(a) \leq d\}, \, a \in \mathbb{Z}^+. \tag{5}$$

The meaning of (5) is as follows: if $a_j(d) = \tilde{a}$ then the provider P_j is able to produce $\tilde{a}$ pieces of S in the duration $\tilde{d} \leq d$, but he is not able to produce more pieces than $\tilde{a}$. Function a_j is queried pseudo-inverse to d_j since if d_j is injective, then $a_j(d_j(a)) = a$. Let us point out that we do not assume so far that functions d_j are increasing.

Now in the time d, provider P_j produces service S in the amount of $a_j(d)$, therefore all providers can produce amount of

$$a(d) = \sum_{j=1}^{n} a_j(d). \tag{6}$$

If we want to produce service S in the amount $a \geq a_t$ in the shortest possible duration $d = d_{min}$, we simply search for a decomposition $(a_1(d), \ldots, a_n(d))$ which provides the smallest d such that $a(d) \geq a_t$, that is

$$d_{min} = \min \{d \in \{0, 1, 2, \ldots\} \mid a(d) \geq a_t\}. \tag{7}$$

For simplicity, let the amount provided by the provider j is denoted as

$$a_j^{min} = a_j(d_{min}) \qquad j = \{1, \ldots, n\}, \tag{8}$$

i.e. $(a_1^{min}, \ldots, a_n^{min}) = (a_1(d_{min}), \ldots, a_n(d_{min}))$ and the overall provided amount is denoted

$$a_{min} = a(d_{min}). \tag{9}$$

Then the found n-tuple $(a_1^{min}, \ldots, a_n^{min})$ is the optimal decomposition of service S in amount $a_{min} \geq a_t$. Let us prove this simple assertion. First of all, $\sum_{j=1}^{n} a_j^{min}$ has to be equal to a_{min} which holds according to (6), (8) and (9). Second of all, $(a_1^{min}, \ldots, a_n^{min})$ is really optimal for amount $a_{min} \geq a_t$. In any duration $\tilde{d} < d_{min}$ all providers cannot altogether produce $\tilde{a} \geq a_{min}$ amounts as d_{min} is chosen according to (7). Therefore a_t pieces of service S cannot be produced in duration smaller than d_{min}[1].

The problem is that a_{min} may be generally greater than the desired amount a_t. Let us make further assumption that functions $d_j(a)$ are increasing, that is

$$d_j(a) \leq d_j(\tilde{a}) \qquad a < \tilde{a}.$$

According to previous algorithm, for a given a_t we can construct a decomposition $(a_1^{min}, \ldots, a_n^{min})$, which is optimal decomposition of amount $a_{min} \geq a_t$. If $a_{min} > a_t$, we may decrease amounts $a_1^{min}, \ldots, a_n^{min}$ arbitrarily till the decreased amounts $\hat{a}_1, \ldots \hat{a}_n$ fulfill $\sum_{j=1}^{n} \hat{a}_j = a_t$. Of course, $(\hat{a}_1, \ldots \hat{a}_n)$ is the decomposition for a_t, but assuming that functions $d_j(a)$ are increasing, it is also optimal. Explanation is as follows: according to the construction of $(a_1^{min}, \ldots, a_n^{min})$, we cannot produce $\tilde{a} \geq a_t$ pieces of S in the duration $\tilde{d} < d_{min}$. As $\hat{a}_j \leq a_j^{min}$, then also $d(\hat{a}_j) \leq d(a_j^{min})$ and therefore $d(\hat{a}_1, \ldots, \hat{a}_n) \leq d(a_1^{min}, \ldots, a_n^{min})$, which proves that $(\hat{a}_1, \ldots, \hat{a}_n)$ is the optimal decomposition for amount a_t. Duration $d(\hat{a}_1, \ldots, \hat{a}_n)$ cannot in fact be smaller than duration $d(a_1^{min}, \ldots, a_n^{min})$, as it would be in contradiction to the construction of $(a_1^{min}, \ldots, a_n^{min})$, therefore $d(\hat{a}_1, \ldots, \hat{a}_n) = d(a_1^{min}, \ldots, a_n^{min})$.

Let us summarize the algorithm that finds optimal decomposition $(\hat{a}_1, \ldots, \hat{a}_n)$ of service S in amount a_t. We assume that there are n agents $P_1, \ldots, P_n$ that perform S

---

[1] Note that both the amounts and durations are considered to be non-negative integers.

and that the requester knows durations $d_j(a)$ for all amounts $a \in \{1, \ldots, a_t\}$ and all agents $P_1, \ldots, P_n$. We also assume that the functions $d_j(a)$ are increasing. The algorithm works as follows:

1. We gradually take $d = \{0, 1, 2, \ldots\}$ and calculate $a(d)$ according to (6) till we find $d = d_{min}$ such that $a(d) \geq a_t$. Such smallest d we denote d_{min} and corresponding amount $a(d_{min})$ we denote a_{min}.
2. We put $a_j^{min} = a_j(d_{min})$, if $a_{min} = \sum_{j=1}^{n} a_j^{min}$ is already equal to a_t, then $(a_1^{min}, \ldots, a_n^{min})$ is the optimal decomposition for a_t. Otherwise, we decrease amounts $(a_1^{min}, \ldots, a_n^{min})$ arbitrarily till the decreased amounts $(\hat{a}_1, \ldots, \hat{a}_n)$ fulfill $\sum_{j=1}^{n} \hat{a}_j = a_t$.
3. Amounts $(\hat{a}_1, \ldots, \hat{a}_n)$ create optimal decomposition of S in amount a_t for providers $P_1, \ldots, P_n$.

The operation of the decomposition algorithm is based on an assumption that the objective function (i.e. delivery times) $d(a_j)$ are known for all the possible amounts of services a_j. The main argument of this article is that these data are not available in the complex or semi-trusted domains. Instead of working with a data-structure representing all possible $d(a_j)$, we will work with approximated knowledge stored in the acquaintance models.

In the following we present two ways how to construct, maintain and use an approximated acquaintance model.

3.2   Batch-Query AM Construction

The simplest approach to building a well informed acquaintance model representing the agent's services is to send several query messages asking 'what if I wanted this amount of that service':

```
(query
        :requester R
        :provider P
        :content (deadline S a^(k) d(a^(k)) ))
```

where $a^{(k)}$ are amounts corresponding to an uniform division of space of the total required amount a_t into N different amounts $a^{(1)}, \ldots, a^{(N)}$ while $N \in \mathbb{N}$ and to find out about the corresponding delivery times for these amounts. The remaining part of the acquaintance model would be approximated by partially linear function. It is easy to see that the quality of such model would strongly depend on N, the number of query messages sent between the provider and requester.

The batch-query acquaintance model construction algorithm where the requester wants to find an optimal decomposition of service S in the amount a_t works in the following steps:

1. Requester agent finds all agents that provide service S, let us suppose that those agents are $P_1, \ldots, P_n$.
2. Requester agent queries all providers $P_1, \ldots, P_n$ for amounts $a^{(1)}, \ldots, a^{(N)}$, where $a^{(k)}$ is defined by

$$[!t]a^{(1)} = 1, \quad a^{(k)} = \lfloor \frac{(k-1) \cdot a_t}{N-1} \rfloor, \tag{10}$$

where $k \in \{2, \ldots, N\}$ and $N \in \mathbb{N}$ is a predefined constant equal for all providers

3. Requester agent collects all responses from the providers. This allows us to define approximate durations $\tilde{d}_j(a)$, approximate amounts $\tilde{a}_j(d)$ and the approximate total amount $\tilde{a}(d)$. In our case, we approximate the function $d_j(a)$ by partially linear function $\tilde{d}_j(a)$ according to

$$\tilde{d}_j(a) = l(a|a^{(1)}, \ldots, a^{(N)}, d_j(a^{(1)}), \ldots, d_j(a^{(N)})). \tag{11}$$

$$\tilde{a}_j(d) = \max \{a \in \{0, \ldots, a_t\} \mid \tilde{d}_j(a) \le d\}. \tag{12}$$

$$\tilde{a}(d) = \sum_{j=1}^{n} \tilde{a}_j(d), \tag{13}$$

provided that function $l(x)$ produces partially liberalization function with parameters $x_1, \ldots, x_k, y_1, \ldots, y_k$ and is defined as

$$l(x|x_1, \ldots, x_k, y_1, \ldots, y_k) = \frac{y_{j+1} - y_j}{x_{j+1} - x_j} \cdot (x - x_j) + y_j. \tag{14}$$

for $x_j \le x \le x_{j+1}$ and $l_0(x) = l(x)$ for $x \ne 0$ and $l_0(x) = 0$ for $x = 0$.

4. We gradually take $d = \{0, 1, 2, \ldots\}$ and calculate $\tilde{a}(d)$ according to (13) till we find $d = \tilde{d}_{min}$ such that $\tilde{a}(d) \ge a_t$.

$$\tilde{d}_{min} = \min \{d \in \{0, 1, 2, \ldots\} \mid \tilde{a}(d) \ge a_t\}.$$

Such smallest d we denote $\tilde{d}_{min}$ and corresponding amount $\tilde{a}(\tilde{d}_{min})$ we denote $\tilde{a}_{min}$.

5. We put $\tilde{a}_j^{min} = \tilde{a}_j(\tilde{d}_{min})$. We decrease amounts $(\tilde{a}_1^{min}, \ldots, \tilde{a}_n^{min})$ arbitrarily till the decreased amounts $(\hat{a}_1, \ldots, \hat{a}_n)$ fulfill $\sum_{j=1}^{n} \hat{a}_j = a_t$.

6. Amounts $(\hat{a}_1, \ldots, \hat{a}_n)$ create decomposition found by the algorithm that approximates optimal decomposition of service S in amount a_t for requesters $P_1, \ldots, P_n$.

3.3 Iterative-Query AM Construction

The above presented algorithm has proved to be efficient and pragmatic solution for our contracting/decomposition problem. The key difficulty is that its behavior is parameterized by the constant N determining the amount of messages sent in the acquaintance model construction phase. As there is no a priori knowledge about the distribution of the providers' services[2] $d_j(a)$, the appropriate granularity (and hence the parameter N) is unknown before the requests are broad-casted. This property makes the algorithm rather inflexible.

If N is reasonably high the model is very precise, while it also represents substantial amount of unneeded information. If the implementation does not allow parallel querying, this algorithm may also increase the communication traffic substantially. Not only

---

[2] By when which amount of service is available.

communication traffic matters. We may also assume that every piece of information that provider discloses has to be payed for by the requester (this assumption reflects the fact that a high amount of information disclosure is likely to be just unwanted by the provider).

This is why we suggest a novel approach to building the acquaintance model based on flexible approximation of the available information. Only one specific amount of the requested service is queried before contracting is initiated. This value is used for very imprecise approximation that is encoded in the acquaintance model. Based on this imprecise model decomposition is computed and appropriate providers are queried for availability their resources. If the bids provided by the providers are close enough to the values approximated by the acquaintance model, the providers are contracted accordingly. If the bids are different then expected, the information provided in the bid is used for refinement of the acquaintance model. New decomposition is computed again and all the process is repeated until the bids are close to the values in the acquaintance model. See below for more detailed specification of the iterative-query acquaintance model construction algorithm:

1. Let us set N equal to 2 and query all providers $P_1, \ldots, P_n$ for $a = \{1, a_t\}$, where a_t is desired total amount. We therefore estimate the real distributions $d_j(a)$ by linear distributions $\tilde{d}_j(a) = \alpha_j a + \beta_j$ which match with $d_j(a)$ for $a = 1, a_t$.
2. For those approximations we find optimal decomposition $a_1^{min}, \ldots, a_n^{min}$ and set $a_1^{(s)}, \ldots, a_n^{(s)}$ equal to $a_1^{min}, \ldots, a_n^{min}$.
3. For the amounts $a_j^{(s)}$ the requester broadcasts appropriate queries to the providers and collects the replies with the values $d_j(a_j^{(s)})$.
4. Provided that $|d_j(a_j^{(s)}) - d_j^{(e)}(a_j^{(s)})| \leq \Delta$, the acquaintance model is regarded as precise enough for the specific contract and the decomposed amounts $(a_1^{(s)}, \ldots, a_n^{(s)})$ can be contracted[3]. The algorithm terminates here.
5. If the algorithm did not terminate in the step 4, the requester inserts new $d_j(a_j^{(s)})$ value into its acquaintance model and carries out new linear approximation and return to step 2.

4   Experiments

Properties and efficiency of the listed contracting mechanisms have been empirically tested on a high number of experimental settings. In the following we will show how precise gets the requester's acquaintance model with an increasing number of query messages sent to providers. In other words, how much of providers social knowledge needs to be disclosed for a specific quality of this acquaintance model. We will compare the batch-query AM construction with iterative-query AM construction in a simple scenario where a service requester is building the acquaintance models of two different service providers. We will show how difficult is for the requester to construct the acquaintance model with:

---

[3] Δ is an a priori defined error of the admissible acquaintance model precision.

- **piecewise linear objective function:** a real provider's resource availability is represented by a piecewise linear function – such a function may represent duration of processing a certain amount of data in dependence on the tasks already scheduled at a specific node of a computational grid – let say that the tangent of the objective function is given by the computational load of the node in time – thus during the time when the node is less loaded the same amount of data is processed quicker than during a time when the node is more loaded (see Figure 1a) and
- **piecewise constant objective function:** a real provider's resource availability is represented by a piecewise constant function – such a function can represent e.g. total delivery time of a specific order that may be transportees in a number of batches (trucks) and delivery time is identical for several different volumes of the cargo (see Figure 1b).

Let the decomposition and acquaintance model construction be demonstrated on the following simple scenario: let a requester requires 1000 items to be jointly delivered from two providers – `seller1` and `seller2`, whose objective functions are given in Figure 1a. The requester thus needs to approximate in its acquaintance model the

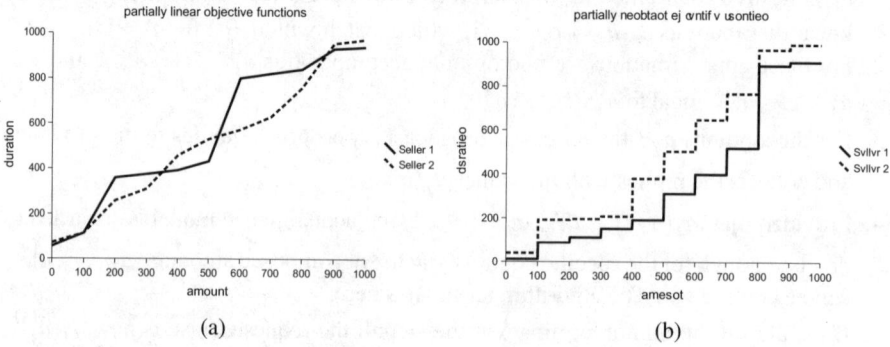

Fig. 1. (a) Piecewise *linear* objective function — (b) Piecewise *constant* objective function

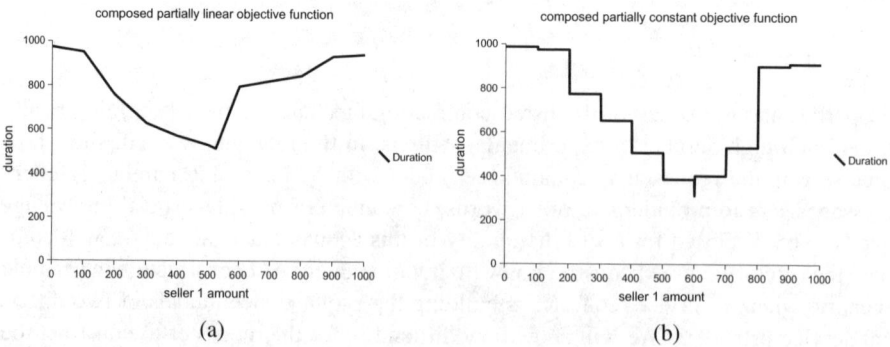

Fig. 2. (a) Composed piecewise *linear* objective function — (b) Composed piecewise *constant* objective function

functions `seller1`(*amount*) and `seller2`(*amount*). According to (2) the function to be minimized (i.e. total duration) is given by max(`seller1`(*amount*), `seller2`(1000 − *amount*)) − see Figure 2a.

If this function is supposed to be minimized the optimal solution would be to contract `seller1` for 520 units and `seller2` for 480 units. This contract can be delivered within 512 time units. In Figure 3a the straight solid line shows the optimum decomposition. The thick dashed line gives the solution suggested by the batch-query AM construction mechanism. In the horizontal axis there is N – the number of queries sent to the providers. It is seen that the batch-query AM construction mechanism provides results close to optimum with N around the value 40. The thick solid line gives the solution suggested by the iterative-query AM construction mechanism. The iterative-query AM construction mechanism provides optimal solution after 8 iteration of the algorithm. Similar argument is demonstrated on the graph in Figure 3b. Here the acquaintance model provides an estimation of the delivery due time of the optimal contract as defined above.

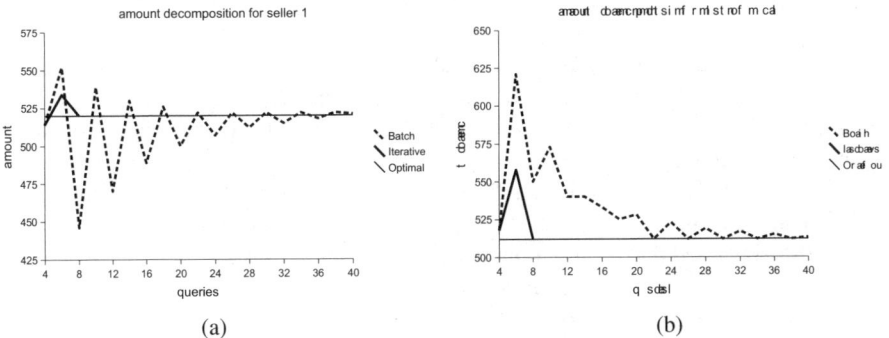

Fig. 3. Approximation of piecewise *linear* objective function in acquaintance model: (a) decomposition — (b) delivery time

The optimal delivery time 512 unites is estimated by the batch-query AM constructed model after sending 40 queries (i.e. 20 iterations – in each iteration queries are sent to both the providers) while iterative-query AM construction mechanism requires only 8 queries.

An interesting result has been obtained when working with the piecewise constant functions. Here the optimal decomposition - `seller1` providing 600 items and `seller2` 400 items – is hard to detect by the batch-query algorithms. The graph in Figure 2b (that is again a composition of the partially constant objective functions of the two sellers) shows that this optimal solution lies on the specific pike.

The graphs on Figures 4a and 4b show that batch-query algorithms have not find an optimal decomposition even after 40 queries and delivery due date has been estimated 380, while the optimal delivery is 312 units. The iterative-query algorithm managed to find the optimal solution by means of 14 queries.

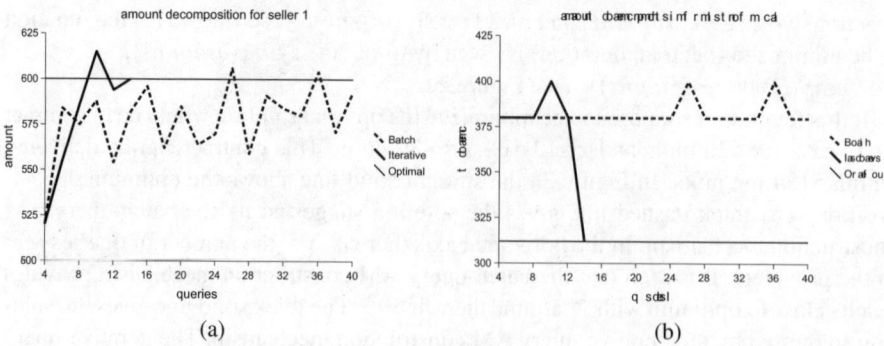

Fig. 4. Approximation of piecewise *constant* objective function in acquaintance model: (a) decomposition — (b) delivery time

5   Conclusions and Future Work

This partially theoretical and in parts experimental paper introduces a novel mechanism for efficient task decomposition and subcontracting in non-trivial communities of agents. The key novel idea is centered around an assumption that the quality of the acquaintance model can be iteratively improved by learning from obtaining unsatisfactory bids. Efficiency of the presented mechanism have been illustrated on two different examples – partially linear and partially constant distribution of services. The whole formal model and substantially richer set of experiments is available in [18].

It needs to be noted that besides obvious advantages, there also several disadvantages of the iterative-query algorithm. Mainly, the iterative-query algorithm is for the same quantity of message exchange generally slower. It is caused by the fact that in the case of batch-query algorithm, messages are sent to every provider in parallel (or perhaps in a single message). In the case of iterative-query algorithm, new queries are generated on the ground of previously received proposals. Therefore, we think that the iterative-query algorithm is particularly suitable in the domains, where:

- (i) the service amount granularity is very fine and it is technically impossible to enumerate all the amounts and (ii) the N parameter is not known a priori
- where the providers are motivated to minimize the amount of disclosed information (or the requester needs to pay for every information it receives when building the acquaintance model)
- getting the right $d_j(a_j)$ values takes the providers specific amount of time (e.g. given by measurement or non-trivial computation)

In real-life the $d_j(a_j)$ values in competitive environments also often depend on various other aspects such as past contracting track record, other providers providing to the same requester, providers not providing the respective requester, trust, etc.

A major disadvantage of the presented decomposition method is the fact that its results substantially depend on the chosen accuracy of the acquaintance model (i.e. the choice Δ for the iterative-query AM construction mechanism). Both the underestimation and overestimation of the objective functions may cause a deviation of the achieved decomposition from the optimum that possibly result in an increase of the real delivery time with respect to the expected $d_j(a_j)$.

The goal of the introduced contracting mechanism was a minimization of the overall duration of the service delivery. While a complementary problem may be a minimization of the overall price, in real-world environments both the duration and price are rather mutually inter-dependent and balance each other. In our future work we would like to explore such settings in which the price and duration are mutually dependent – this results in solving either a *constraint decomposition problem*, i.e. (i) minimization of duration under a maximum price constraint or (ii) minimization of price under maximum duration constraint or a *combined decomposition problem* when (iii) both the price and duration are minimized. In our future work we would like to carry out also experiments on scalability and to run the system populated with a substantially greater number (tens to hundreds) of negotiating agents.

Acknowledgement

This work was supported by the Ministry of Education, Youth and Sports of the Czech Republic under the grant no. MSM6840770013.

References

1. Pěchouček, M., Mařík, V., Bárta, J.: A knowledge-based approach to coalition formation. IEEE Intelligent Systems **17**(3) (2002) 17–25
2. Pěchouček, M., Tožička, J., Mařík, V.: Meta-reasoning methods for agent's intention modelling. In: Autonomous Intelligent Systems: Agents and Data Mining. Berlin: Springer (2005) 134–148
3. Rehák, M., Pěchouček, M., Tožička, J., Šišlák, D.: Using stand-in agents in partially accessible multi-agent environment. In: Proceedings of Engineering Societies in the Agents World V, Toulouse, October 2004. Number 3451 in LNAI, Springer-Verlag, Heidelberg (2005) 277–291
4. Sandholm, T.: Distributed Rational Decision Making. In: Multiagent Systems: A Modern Approach to Distributed Artificial Intelligence. MIT Press, Cambridge, MA. (1999) 201–258
5. Smith, R.G.: The contract net protocol: High level communication and control in a distributed problem solver. In IEEE Transactions on Computers **C-29**(12) (1980) 1104–1113
6. Sandholm, T., Lesser, V.: Coalitions among computationally bounded agents. Artificial Intelligence **94**(1-2) (1997) 99–137
7. Tambe, M.: Towards flexible teamwork. Journal of Artificial Intelligence Research **7** (1997) 83–124
8. Sycara, K., Decker, K., Pannu, A., Williamson, M., Zeng, D.: Distributed intelligent agents. IEEE Expert **11**(6) (1996) 36–46
9. Grosz, B., Kraus, S.: Collaborative plans for complex group action. Artificial Intelligence **86**(2) (1996) 269–357
10. Mařík, V., Pěchouček, M., Štěpánková, O.: Social knowledge in multi-agent systems. In Luck, M., Mařík, V., Štěpánková, O., eds.: Multi-Agent Systems and Applications. LNAI, Springer-Verlag, Heidelberg (2001)
11. Pěchouček, M., Mařík, V., Štěpánková, O.: Role of acquaintance models in agent-based production planning systems. In Klusch, M., Kerschberg, L., eds.: Cooperative Infromation Agents IV - LNAI No. 1860, Heidelberg, Springer Verlag (2000) 179–190

12. Cao, W., Bian, C.G., Hartvigsen, G.: Achieving efficient cooperation in a multi-agent system: The twin-base modeling. In Kandzia, P., Klusch, M., eds.: Cooperative Information Agents. Number 1202 in LNAI, Springer-Verlag, Heidelberg (1997) 210–221

13. T., W.: ARCHON: An Architecture for Multi-agent System. Ellis Horwood, Chichester (1992)

14. Sanyal, S., Jain, A., Das, S., Biswas, R.: A hierarchical and distributed approach for mapping large applications to heterogeneous grids using genetic algorithms. In: Proceedings. IEEE International Conference on Cluster Computing, Los Alamitos, CA, USA, IEEE Comput. Society (2003) 496–9

15. Gao, Y., Rong, H., Huang, J.Z.: Adaptive grid job scheduling with genetic algorithms. Future Generation Computer Systems **21**(1) (2005) 151–61

16. Fatima, S.S., Wooldridge, M.: Adaptive task and resource allocation in multi-agent systems. In: Proceedings of the Fifth International Conference on Autonomous Agents, New York, NY, USA, ACM (2001) 537–44

17. Li, C., Li, L.: Competitive proportional resource allocation policy for computational grid. Future Generation Computer Systems **20**(6) (2004) 1041–54

18. Lerch, O.: Effcient contraction mechanisms for virtual enterprises operation. Master's thesis, Czech Technical University (2005)

Multilevel Approach to Agent-Based Task Allocation in Transportation

Martin Rehák, Přemysl Volf, and Michal Pěchouček

Department of Cybernetics and Center for Applied Cybernetics
Czech Technical University, Technická 2, Prague, 166 27, Czech Republic
{mrehak, volf, pechouc}@labe.felk.cvut.cz

Abstract. We present a hybrid algorithm for distributed task allocation problem in a cooperative logistics domain. Our approach aims to
achieve superior computational performance by combining the classic
negotiation techniques and acquaintance models from agent technology
field with methods from the operation research and AI planning. The
algorithm is multi-stage and makes a clear separation between discreet
planning that defines the tasks and allocation of resources to available
tasks. Task allocation starts with centralized planning based on acquaintance model information that prepares a framework for efficient distributed negotiation. The subsequent distributed part of the task allocation
process is parallel for all tasks and allows the agents to optimally allocate
their resources to proposed tasks and to further optimize the allocation
by negotiation with other agents. Parallel execution of the task allocation mechanism allows the algorithm to answer the planning request in
predictable time, albeit at expense of possible non-optimality. In the experiments, we evaluate the relative importance of OR and negotiation
parts of the task allocation process.

1 Introduction

In this contribution, we present a hybrid approach to distributed planning and
task allocation problem in the domain of cooperative logistics. The key use case
of the suggested planning algorithm is to organize the transport of large quantities of humanitarian aid sent to the disaster area, using the available *resources* –
vehicles. The vehicles are operated by several self-interested *transporter agents*
who are reluctant to provide *complete* information about their capabilities, services and current status. On the other hand, the transporters are ready to share
the necessary amount of information (referred to as *semiprivate knowledge*) and
negotiate with others about available delivery services and contracts' acquisition. The effort is planned and organized by *requestors* (humanitarian agents)
who decompose the aid distribution into appropriate tasks and allocate these
tasks among the transporters in an efficient manner. This planning and task allocation problem (formally specified in Section 2) is obviously computationally
very complex and there is no easy way how to identify an optimal solution, even
with complete and centralized knowledge.

M. Klusch, M. Rovatsos, and T. Payne (Eds.): CIA 2006, LNAI 4149, pp. 273–287, 2006.
© Springer-Verlag Berlin Heidelberg 2006

Existing multi-agent approaches tackle the problem using the negotiation and auction based approaches [1,2], where each agent retains its own private information and task definition and allocation is negotiation-based. Even though the *Contract-Net-Protocol* [3] (CNP) based solutions are widely used in industrial environment and provide rather efficient mechanisms for distributed task allocation they suffer from important limitations in our application domain:

- undesirable need to implicitly communicate substantial amount of private knowledge (when initiating a contract-nct-protocol and when replying with a proposal),
- they found locally optimal solution for a single specific contract while being inefficient for a batches of contracts and
- the need to backtrack and re-negotiate if the problem features a set of interdependent actions

The problems with undesirable knowledge disclosure can be partially addressed by forming *alliances* and other organizational structures that structure the information dispersion in the community. Semiprivate information (see 2.1) shared within the alliance in its effect reduces future requirements for sharing private information outside the alliance [4]. The problems related to optimization of higher number of requests were addressed in parts by extension of the original CNP to *OSCM*-CNP that can always find a globally optimal solution in a finite number of steps [5]. In our work we have combined the concept of semi-private knowledge sharing (as defined in [4]) and Extended Contract-Net-Protocol (ECNP) as described in [1] and further extended towards practical application by [2]. This protocol achieves the result by using the negotiation between the requestor and perspective providers.

When the perspective requestor wishes to solve the task by ECNP, it asks other agents to cover the task completely or at least partially. Agents submit their bids, the best ones are selected and provisionally granted the task. The rest of the task is auctioned again and new auctions are organized until the whole task is covered. If the remaining task can not be covered, the algorithm must achieve consistency by backtracking – revocations of provisionally granted tasks and auctioning new ones, as the tasks may be mutually dependent. For example, in case of transport from A to C via B, we have to allocate either the complete trajectory, or BOTH $A \rightarrow B$ and $B \rightarrow C$. If we provisionally grant the $A \rightarrow B$ and later fail to allocate $B \rightarrow C$, $A \rightarrow B$ must be revoked. Problem gets more complex when we consider the consistency of quantities between dependent actions, parallelism of actions and limitations regarding the use of single resource contributing to several subtasks. Even with a unique central requestor, the planning problem is completely decentralized and requires intensive communication. Consequently, this approach introduces computational performance problems when it plans in large state spaces. Such planners outperform manual planning [6], but mathematical programming techniques will typically offer better performance. On the other hand, mathematical programming-based solutions require centralized knowledge and precise problem formulation. The agent-based approach brings more flexibility than classical approaches as the agents may combine many sources and types of knowledge to prepare the plan, each agent contributing its knowledge, reasoning and resources. Agents don't need to be aware of each other's resource availability, provided that they are syntactically and semantically interoperable. This allows the agents to avoid explicit disclosure of their private information, while not completely solving the implicit disclosure problem stated above.

The main contribution of this paper is the integration of classical AI and operational research 'heavy duty' solvers with multi-agent techniques to efficiently address the existing limitations of multi-agent approach, while not compromising the solution flexibility. We argue that the abstract models of collaboration in agent systems as they are now used within the multi-agent system community have severe drawbacks – they are well suited for simple reasoning and limited amount of knowledge, while little scalable. Their performance tends to degrade with increasing problem complexity and shift of the focus from qualitative to quantitative reasoning. Therefore, we suppose that the AI/OR techniques are a very good fit for agent reasoning due to their high performance and little or no scalability problems. The traditional problems related to their application – restrictive applicability conditions (e.g. linearity and certainty) are solved by modern methods [7] and on the other side, acquaintance models [8] provide the necessary knowledge inputs for the model, as well as an efficient mechanisms for its maintenance.

Specifically, the main difference when comparing our approach with ECNP is the separation of planning and task allocation. In the planning phase, we elaborate and merge alternative plans how to accomplish the task (e.g roads to take and intermediary storage locations), so that we obtain a directed bipartite graph with all the alternatives included and merged – an abstract plan as formally defined in section 2. AI planners perform very well in this task. Then, in the task allocation phase, we alternate the use of OR techniques and negotiation to perform the task allocation, as described in Section 3. In Section 4 we empirically evaluate the algorithm by measuring the influence of negotiation step on the quality of the solution.

2   Problem Statement

In the logistics planning problem we consider (see Fig 1), we address the transport of goods from single start location to terminal location[1] using the resources belonging to self-interested agents. Therefore, we must (i) prepare a sequence/graph of actions to perform and (ii) allocate resources to these actions in order to maximize the expected amount of delivered goods. In the formal problem presentation below, we present the problem from the perspective of the requestor – the agent denoted A_0 that leads the collaborative planning and task allocation process.

---

[1] This formal simplification doesn't reduce the generality of our approach - in case of need, we may define formal zero-cost actions between the initial/terminal objective and the real terminal objective for each part of the cargo, provided that we impose appropriate restrictions on these actions.

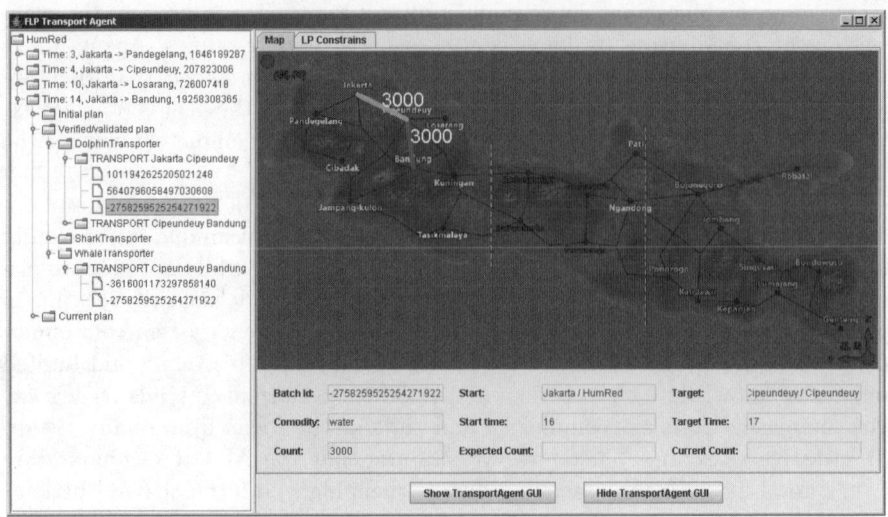

Fig. 1. Domain Map With Plan Example

To describe the plan we follow the approach proposed by [9] and instead of decomposing the plan into the action-state graph, we will describe it using actions and objectives (called objects in [9]). In this representation, the global state is defined as a combination of local state of all objectives.

An ***abstract plan*** (e.g. route plan), typically prepared by AI techniques in the first phase of the planning, is a directed bipartite graph, where one side is composed of ***objectives*** (corresponding to locations in our case), defined by the set $O = \{o_0(start), o_1, o_n(terminal)\}$, with each member defined as $o_i = (prer_{o_i}, allows_{o_i})$. Both the $prer_{o_i}$ and $allows_{o_i}$ are subsets of the action set $Ac = \{a_1, a_2, ... a_m\}$ that forms the other side of the bipartite graph. Ac contains ***actions*** a_i (transports) linking the objectives, where each action is defined as $a_i = (prer_{a_i}, allows_{a_i})$. The sets $prer_{a_i}$ and $allows_{a_i}$ are subsets of O. By definition, we always start from a single *start objective* o_0 (with no prerequisites: $prer_{o_0} = \emptyset$) and terminate in a *terminal objective* that corresponds to the achieved goal state: $allows_{o_n} = \emptyset$. [2]

Batches constitute the cargo that is transported. Each batch p_i from the set P is defined by its size $size(p_i)$ and *type* (liquid, bulk, etc...) that defines the resources (e.g. type of the vehicle) that may carry it. We assume that all batches can be split during transport; we denote $p_i^{a_j}$ the part of the batch allocated to action a_j.

The transport problem is being solved by ***agents*** from the set $Ag = \{A_0...A_k\}$, including the requestor A_0. Each agent is modelled by other agents as a tuple

---

[2] Therefore, in our graph, the nodes are defined as $Ac \cup O$, while the directed edges describe the relations expressed in *allows* and *prer* sets of each action or objective. We may also note that the global state of the system is defined by the state of all objectives.

of its resources $A_i = (res_{A_0}(A_i))$ – in our case, aggregate information about its vehicles. All **resources**, regardless of their owner agent form a set $R_{A_0} = \{r_1^{A_i}, r_2^{A_j}, r_l^{A_j}\}$, where the super index of each resource denotes the agent to which this specific resource belongs. Each resource is described by a tuple $r_i^{A_j} = (A_j, allowed_{r_i}, cap_{r_i})$, where the A_j denotes the owner agent of the resource, $allowed_{r_i}$ is a set of actions (transports) to which the resource can be assigned, and cap_{r_i} defines its capacity.

Tasks are a result of the planning process. They form a set $T = \{t_{a_1}...t_{a_m}\}$, and each task corresponds to a single action a_i of the abstract plan. It is defined as $t_{a_i} = (batch_{t_{a_i}}, com_{t_{a_i}})$, where $batch_{t_{a_i}}$ is a set of batches (or their fractions) transported in the scope of the task and $com_{t_{a_i}}$ is a set of **commitments** – each commitment[3] $c = (a_i, A_j, r_k^{A_j}, p_l^{a_i}, cap)$ is an assignment of a specific resource r_k (and consecutively its owner A_j) to one partial batch $p_l^{a_i}$ from the set $batch_{t_{a_i}}$ and cap determines the assigned capacity. If the resource capacity allows it, one resource r_k can be committed to more than one batch/action and a single partial batch $p_l^{a_i}$ can be covered by several commitments – in such case, we denote $cap(r_k^{a_i})$ the aggregate size of all commitments from the task t_{a_i} to which the resource r_k is committed. Commitments of agents' resources relative to a single task define a **team** working on the task as a set $E = \{e_{a_1}, e_{a_2}, ..., e_{a_m}\}$. Each such team $e_{a_i} \subset Ag$ contains all the agents contributing their resources to the task t_{a_i}. A union of all teams from the set E contains all agents participating at project solution. According to [4], it is equivalent to the coalition.

2.1   Public, Semi-private and Private Information

In order to plan efficiently, the agents must share appropriate information. The amount of shared knowledge must be carefully sized with respect to self-interestedness of the agents. They are not ready to provide their competitors with more information than necessary. This principle leads us towards definition of several knowledge sharing levels defined in [4]:

- *Public knowledge* is accessible to any agent in the system.
- *Semi-private knowledge* is mutually shared within groups of trusted agents.
- *Private knowledge* is accessible only to the owner agent and never shared with anyone else

While public knowledge includes information about agent identity, existence, location and basic annotation of provided services–*type* of the resources $res_{A_0}(A_i)$ it offers, but without any information concerning their capacity, number or restrictions, private knowledge contains the detailed information about its resources, including their individual capacity, restrictions, locations and other information. Semi-private knowledge collects information that facilitates the planning process and enables collaborators to prepare the plans easier than by

---

[3] Formally, until being evaluated and updated by bidding agents, commitments must be regarded to as mere *commitment opportunities*.

negotiating all possible options. For each agent A_i, it includes the information about its resources *aggregated* by type and including the restrictions regarding their use on the set Ac – typically, we include a set of roads that this specific vehicle/group can cover. Such compromise provides enough knowledge for the first stage of the planning process, and detailed task allocation is then finalized in the course of negotiation without exposing more data than necessary[4].

3   Algorithm Presentation

This section provides an overview of the planning algorithm we suggest, combining the social model and linear programming planner with bounded and well-focused negotiations in the later stages of the process. The planning process proceeds as follows (see also Fig 2):

1. **Initial Planning**: Requestor uses its social knowledge and planning capabilities in order to prepare the initial plan. This happens in two phases:

(i) abstract plan construction and
(ii) task allocation to the agents.

2. **Local Plan Evaluation**: Initial plan is evaluated by the respective agents:

(i) the members evaluate the plan and match the proposed commitments with their available resources and
(ii) make an attempt to trade the proposed commitments within teams working on the same tasks to optimize the allocation of their resources.

3. **Coherence & Verification**: The requestor incorporates the proposals, including the traded tasks information, into the task allocation problem from the initial planning phase and solves the problem again.

4. **Plan Execution**: Final commitments are received by members, may be swapped and the plan is executed.

3.1   Initial Planning

In the first phase of the plan, we assume that the requestor (denoted A_0 and materialized as a humanitarian agent in our scenario) has a goal to accomplish and is obliged to cooperate with other agents. It uses its social knowledge to draft a preliminary plan in the following steps.

Constructing the Abstract Plan. The first step is a preparation of the abstract plan – an action-objective bipartite graph capturing the relationship between initial and terminal objectives (states). This graph typically describes

---

[4] Note that the sets R as perceived by various agents are not identical due to the fact that they don't have the access to the same information.

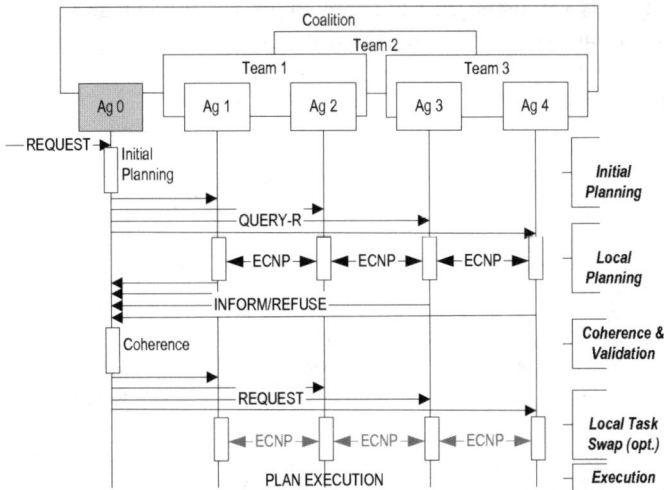

Fig. 2. Overview of the protocol phases: Agent A_0 is a requestor and has decomposed the global task into three tasks

and integrates several alternative solutions of the abstract planning problem. Shared objectives of these solutions allow flexible task assignments to actions from different original sub-plans and their seamless combination. Abstract plan must contain at least one path connecting the initial and terminal objective – if no such path can be identified, agent A_0 is unable to solve the planning problem.

Constructing the abstract plan is a computationally exponential problem in complex domains. Recent advancements in the field of AI planning provided very efficient techniques for constructing the plans in reasonable amount of time such as GraphPlan [10], SAT-Plan or their variants. These techniques implement a sophisticated breadth-first search based on expansion of the bipartite graph or iterative propositionalization of the planning problem. In the experiments presented in Section 4, we have used a pre-prepared static plans in order to achieve repeatability between various configurations tested. In the general case, the choice of the appropriate algorithm for this stage of planning depends on the complexity of the domain and specific requirements regarding computational efficiency and desired solution quality.

Task Allocation. Once an acceptable abstract plan is established, requestor proceeds with the allocation of batches and resources to individual actions in the plan, while respecting the constraints defined in the objectives. Note that for sake of computational efficiency, some actions and objectives from the abstract plan can be removed during this phase if there are no resources or batches to allocate to them. Then, we use a linear programming (or its variants [7]) that either provides an acceptable initial task allocation T, or identifies the constraints that prevent the agent from finding the solution.

The constraints we define for the problem are the following. The first equation expresses the node equilibria - conservation of goods in each node.

$$\forall o_i \in O \setminus \{o_0, o_n\}, \forall p_j \in P : \sum_{a_k \in prer(o_i)} size(p_j^{a_k}) = \sum_{a_l \in allows(o_i)} size(p_j^{a_l}) \quad (1)$$

The initial node has a simpler relation, declaring that we can't take away more cargo than available:

$$\forall p_j \in P : size(p_j) \geq \sum_{a_l \in allows(o_0)} size(p_j^{a_l}) \quad (2)$$

while the terminal node doesn't introduce any constraint.

Furthermore, for each action a_i (elementary transport) and each batch p_j, we must ensure that the commitments cover the whole partial batch $p_j^{a_i}$ ($size(p_j^{a_i} \leq p_j$) due to the possible parallelism):

$$\forall a_i \in Ac, \forall p_j \in P : p_l^{a_i} = \sum_{c \in com_{t_{a_i}} : batch(c) = p_l^{a_i}} cap(c) \quad (3)$$

then, we must also make sure that no resource is used beyond its capacity. To do so, we must determine the sets of actions that may share a resource in the scope of the plan. Therefore, we introduce an ordering on the set of actions Ac in the abstract plan. This partial ordering relationship is defined by causality in the plan: we say that $a_i < a_j$ iff a_j belongs to the transitive closure of the set $allows_{a_i}$, meaning that a_i shall be completed before a_j starts. Partiality of the ordering relation defines the relation of resource allocation *compatibility* between two actions. Actions a_i and a_j are compatible, iff $a_i < a_j$ or $a_j < a_i$. Otherwise, they are incompatible and can't share single resource. The set *incompatible*(a_j) used below includes all actions from Ac incompatible with the action a_j.

$$\forall r_i \in R \forall a_j \in Ac : cap(r_i) \geq \sum_{a_k \in a_j \cup incompatible(a_j)} cap(r_i^{a_k}) \quad (4)$$

In practice, the above relationships generated for different actions is often identical and duplicate restrictions are removed from the problem specification for sake of performance. Alternatively, we may decide that the resources can be used only for single action within the plan, and then the set $a_k \in a_j \cup incompatible(a_j)$ encompasses the whole Ac. This restriction can reflect maintenance and required downtime requirements.

Besides the restrictions, we need to set-up the **utility function** for which we optimize:

$$U_m = \sum_{p_i \in P} size(p_i^{o_n}) \quad (5)$$

where $p_i^{o_n}$ denotes the part of the batch p_i delivered to the terminal objective o_n and $ag(c)$ the agent committing to c. This simple function maximizes the amount of the cargo delivered to the objective. Extension of this function to more specific forms that may include transport prices and/or trustfulness of individual agents is straightforward, even if the formulation must be kept strictly linear. Linearity limitations can be partially addressed by iterative application of the solver and the use of FLP methods [7] that allow us to handle the uncertainty in social knowledge. These methods are especially relevant when we also consider the trustfulness of individual agents.

Once the solution of the above problem is identified, requestor determines all perspective participants (owners of resources assigned to various tasks) and queries each perspective member whether it is capable and willing to participate. Therefore, each perspective participant A_i is sent a structure: $cma_{A_i} = (coalmem, assign)$, where the set $coalmem$ lists all coalition members and the set $assign$ lists the relevant information about tasks the agent's resources are assigned to, defined as $(e_{a_j}, com_{t_{a_j}}(A_i))$, where j is an action (task) index and $com_{t_{a_j}}(A_i)$ are commitments suggested to agent A_i on task t_{a_j}.

3.2 Local Plan Evaluation

When the agents A_i (selected by the requestor in the previous step) receive the proposals from the requestor, they must use their private knowledge to create the bid reflecting their preferences and local situation. At this level, we handle several issues that are ignored by the requestor's first-level planning – resource granularity (unknown to the planning agent due to the privacy issues) and relations between the resources assigned to different tasks. In the first round, each agent assigns its resources to the commitments that are the best fit for available resources, trying to cover all commitments. Then, it will offer the excess capacity of the resources assigned to the task t_{a_j} to all members of the team e_{a_j} using the multi-phase auction mechanism described in [1]. This step is designed to eliminate the resource allocation inefficiencies that are due to the possible requestor's lack of knowledge about actual resources or a side effect of selected planning method. More formally (see also Fig. 3), to start the the negotiations, each agent A_i working on task t_{a_j} broadcasts a CFP message containing its free capacity to all team $e_{t_{a_j}}$. If the other team members are interested in using this capacity for the task they were allocated, they submit their bid. Agent A_i selects one or more bids and answers them with a temporary grant, making them binding *for the bidders*; other are refused. When the agent A_i participates in several teams, it can now reshuffle its resources between the tasks to use them in an optimal manner. Once the resource reallocation is terminated, all compatible temporary grants are confirmed, while the others may be refused (In case the agent has replaced the original resource with a lower-capacity one.). If appropriate, agent can now offer the new free capacity for trading using the same protocol.

Note that the auctioning and negotiation takes place only within the single task team, therefore minimizing the knowledge dispersion and communication load. On the other hand, agents may therefore miss a better task allocation. Once the negotiation is finished, all team members send their answers to the requestor. The answer is a list of commitments that are actually *binding* for each agent, but may differ from those originally assigned to the agent as: **(i)** the agent is not always able to cover the whole assigned commitment and commits

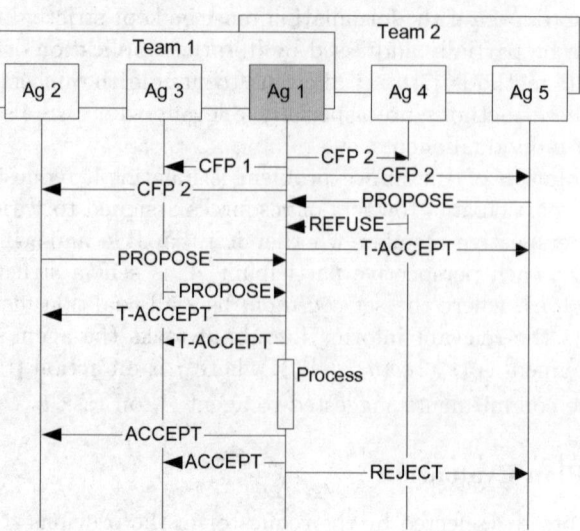

Fig. 3. Use of the ECNP to allocate agent's resources across two different teams. Agent A_1 first temporarily accepts the offer from A_5, but later on finds a better resource allocation and prefers to commit larger resource to *team 1*. Therefore, it rejects the bid from A_5.

only to a part of the original commitment or **(ii)** it notifies the requestor about the transfer of the whole commitment or its part to other team member (this member lists this commitment in its turn as covered). When the agents submit their binding commitments to the requestor, they have an alternative to offer the free capacity of the resources they've allocated to the task to the requestor - the requestor may include use it to cover other batches from the same task, as specified by relation 6. While this remains an attractive optimization feature, this approach has two major drawbacks – the requestor can easily guess the capacity of agent's resources and the free resources can not be used on another task. Positive influence of the negotiation in this step is clearly visible while analyzing the experimental results presented in Section 4.

3.3   Coherence and Verification Phase

In this phase, requestor receives the answers from the participants and must re-combine them into a globally coherent plan. As the initial planning has produced a coherent plan, the plan is coherent when all proposed commitments were covered by members. If not, the requestor must add all updated commitments/refusals from the agents to the initial plan and perform the new calculation to make sure that the condition 1 is valid for the final plan.

Updated commitments are included as follows (refusals or previously unassigned commitments are considered as commitments with 0 capacity):

$$\forall a_i \in Ac, \forall r_j \in R : cap(r_j^{a_i})^{prop} \geq cap(r_j^{a_i})^{final} \tag{6}$$

It is at this stage of planning process when we also detect the failure to execute the plan altogether – the proposals (or actually refusals) from the members may be mutually incompatible. If the requestor manages to find an acceptable planning outcome, it prepares the final commitments (with the quantities assigned that are less or equal to the binding ones proposed by members) and re-submits them to the participants.

3.4   Plan Execution

As the proposals by the agents were binding, participating agents shall be all able to start performing the assigned tasks immediately. Alternatively, when the final commitments are lower than the ones they have proposed, they may change their resource allocation or trade the assignments with their peers in the team in the same way as in the Local Plan Evaluation phase, provided that they manage to honor their commitments.

4   Experiments

In order to evaluate the significance of team-wide negotiation phase (e.g during Local Plan Evaluation), we have compared the performance of the algorithm with and without this feature. The experiment provides a comparison of our distributed hybrid approach with centralized planner working with the same information, while the role of the participating agents is reduced to the allocation of tasks to their specific resources (vehicles).

To perform the experiment, we have used the ACROSS scenario [11] based on 𝒜-globe multi-agent platform. In this scenario, we simulate a population dispersed in communities on an island. These communities need to trade their production to satisfy their needs, creating the demand for transport. This demand is covered by **Transporter agents**, representing transport companies owning one or more vehicles, each company with its own private preferences regarding the cooperation rules, transport actions it can perform and vehicles of various type and capacity. Into this setting, we introduce a humanitarian catastrophe that partially disables a local production in a predetermined area. **Humanitarian Agent** then tries to address the emergency using its own stock of goods, that must be transported to the affected area. Transport is organized by the Humanitarian Agent as a requestor (with centralized planning capability) and Transporters, who provide their resources.

The scenarios we compare differ by the abilities of the plain transporter agents - in one case, they only use their own resources to cover the assigned transport requests. In the second case, they perform the peer-to-peer ECNP-based negotiation as described in Section 3.2. In the result of our experiments, we will see to which extent this extension increases the performance, while keeping the explicit (shared social knowledge) or implicit (disclosed as a negotiation side effect) private information disclosure low.

As a reasonably domain-independent measure of planning quality, we use the resource utilization efficiency: the ratio of the actual cargo loaded on the

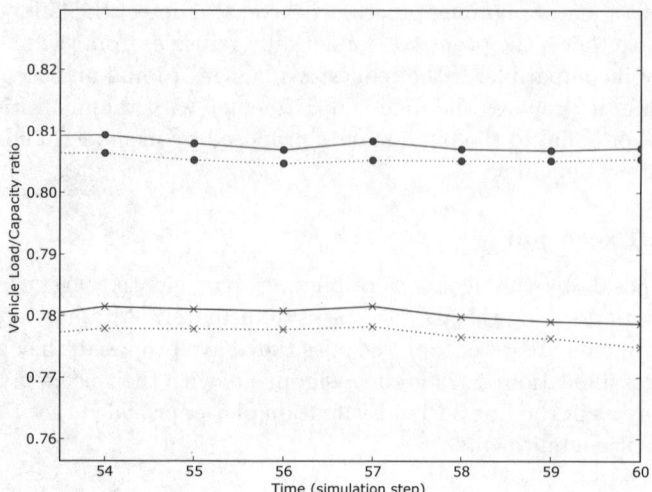

Fig. 4. Performance of the various variants of the algorithm evaluated by resource usage. Full lines represent the solution with Formula 4 in its nominal form, while the dotted lines present the planner performance when all actions are considered incompatible for resource sharing aspects. Values with circular points were obtained with ECNP, crossed points without.

individual vehicles compared to their capacity. Such metrics evaluates the whole task allocation part of the planning process, from the initial planning down to the assignment of batches to individual vehicles within transporter fleet. On the other hand, it doesn't reflect the abstract planning phase quality. We consider this as a correct decision, because we concentrate on task allocation and the abstract planning is (i) highly domain dependent and (ii) easy to validate independently of the rest of the planning process. The experiments were performed in the situations differing by the requested quantity of the cargo to transport and the results were aggregated. However, in all cases, the demand exceeds the supply of available resources given their limitations.

As we can see in Fig 4, the overall behavior of the system is stable (except for a brief startup period not represented in figure) and the differences between the quality of the solution are relatively minor, with the use of the ECNP negotiation phase as a biggest differentiator. Even if the difference due to the ECNP use is only about 3 percentage points, this modest improvement is caused by the fact that in most cases, there is only a limited potential for improvement. Most contracts require simply the use of the full available capacity, and the ratio of plans where the negotiation can improve the results is relatively small. In the similar manner, we can see that the difference due to the introduction of more or less restrictive approach to resource planning is negligible, less than a fraction of percentage point. However, we feel that even these improvements are crucial. Besides their clear economic interest, they improve the planning process by pushing the solution closer to Pareto-optimality and while the heavy duty methods still do most of the planning work (as we can clearly see from the results), the negotiation process reaches the locally optimum solution that can not be further easily improved. This feature is important for industrial applications, as the clients are often not satisfied by solutions that are not locally optimal, even if the overall result approximates the global optimum close enough.

Please note that with respect to the framework described in this paper, we have omitted the last phase of the ECNP negotiation and used a fixed base of abstract plans to achieve repeatability between experimental runs.

5   Conclusions and Future Work

In this paper, we have presented an algorithm for cooperative task allocation in an environment with self-interested agents. While our algorithm remains a distributed solution, it uses the concept of social knowledge to delegate important part of the planning to single agent in the community. In the same time, the individual agents still retain control of their resources and protect their private information.

The algorithm presented in this paper has several properties that make it interesting for industrial applications:

Reduced communication is a result of the use of the social knowledge in the *initial planning* step of the algorithm. Instead of several rounds of auctions, action decomposition and backtracking, requestor uses its social knowledge to compose balanced task teams and pre-assign commitments to each potential member.

Increased parallelism is also a consequence of the initial planning introduction and separate abstract planning step. Pre-assigned teams of agents negotiate in parallel on the problem that was already decomposed and tentatively allocated, instead of sequential negotiation in the ECNP, where the tasks are allocated successively, one after another, and frequent backtracking is required.

Iterative reduction of the solution space is another key feature – each step of the planning, centralized or distributed, reduces the solution space. Initial planning performs the greatest reduction, as the actions/tasks are selected, resources pre-allocated and agent teams created. Local planning phase then further clarifies resource allocation and team composition and the results of this phase are incorporated as additional restrictions for the planning problem solved in the coherence and validation phase – we ensure that any overall solution will respect the commitments received from participating agents and can be executed. The final solution is restricted by the boundaries of the initial planning with additional restrictions. If the plan can not be implemented due to the member refusal or resource incompatibility, the situation is detected in the coherence planning step. In the algorithm as suggested, we don't allow any backtracking (except the team-scale negotiation), increasing the outcome predictability. On the other hand, the algorithm as presented doesn't guarantee that the result it returns will be the optimal plan. We don't consider this as a serious drawback, because none of the comparably efficient algorithms currently in use can guarantee such result.

Thanks to the above features, our solution offers **fast response times**. We assume that the centralized planning steps (e.g. initial planning and coherence phase) can be performed rapidly in most practical setups, as the separate tasks of route finding (abstract planning) and linearized task allocation can be solved in polynomial time. During the negotiation and local plan evaluation phase, the size of the problem is already significantly reduced, and the agents only allocate the assigned (or traded) tasks to available resources. While this problem is NP complete in general case of indivisible batches, its relatively small size and batch divisibility make this problem easily solvable by application of appropriate heuristics (as in our implementation) or standard search algorithms[5]. In practice, as we always restrict the time to answer in the each stage of interaction protocol (as a protection against communication failures), the time to return the solution is determined by twice the negotiation timeout plus the time required to solve the centralized planning.

In our future work, we plan to benchmark the results against an implementation of the ECNP-based planning and task allocation mechanism. However, such benchmark presents several important challenges to tackle – we must make sure that the implementation of the ECNP is good enough for a fair comparison and that the underlying planning problem (or a set of problems) will not disadvantage any of the evaluated solutions.

Acknowledgment

Effort sponsored by the Air Force Office of Scientific Research, Air Force Material Command, USAF, under grant number FA8655-04-1-3044. The U.S. Government is authorized to reproduce and distribute reprints for Government purpose notwithstanding any copyright notation thereon. The views and conclusions contained herein are those of the author and should not be interpreted as necessarily representing the official policies or endorsements, either expressed or implied, of the Air Force Office of Scientific Research or the U.S. Government.

References

1. Fischer, K., Muller, J.P., Pischel, M., Schier, D.: A model for cooperative transportation scheduling. In: Proceedings of the First International Conference on Multiagent Systems., Menlo park, California, AAAI Press / MIT Press (1995) 109–116
2. Perugini, D., Lambert, D., Sterling, L., Pearce, A.: A distributed agent approach to global transportation scheduling. In: The 2003 IEEE/WIC International Conference on Intelligent Agent Technology (IAT 2003), Halifax, Canada (2003) 18–24
3. Smith, R.G.: The contract net protocol: High level communication and control in a distributed problem solver. In IEEE Transactions on Computers **C-29**(12) (1980) 1104–1113

---

[5] Required quality of this algorithm depends on the number of available resources and assigned batches (for each cargo type), but even relatively large problems can be solved using mixed-integer programming approaches like branch-and-bound algorithm [12].

4. Pěchouček, M., Mařík, V., Bárta, J.: A knowledge-based approach to coalition formation. IEEE Intelligent Systems **17**(3) (2002) 17–25
5. Sandholm, T.: Contract types for satisficing task allocation: I theoretical results. In: Proceedings of the AAAI Spring Symposium. (1998)
6. Perugini, D., Lambert, D., Sterling, L., Pearce, A.: Agent-based global transportation scheduling in military logistics. In: AAMAS '04: Proceedings of the Third International Joint Conference on Autonomous Agents and Multiagent Systems, Washington, DC, USA, IEEE Computer Society (2004) 1278–1279
7. Carlsson, C., Fullér, R.: Fuzzy Reasoning in Decision Making and Optimization. Physica Verlag, Springer, Heidelberg (2002)
8. Pěchouček, M., Mařík, V., Štěpánková, O.: Role of acquaintance models in agent-based production planning systems. In Klusch, M., Kerschberg, L., eds.: Cooperative Infromation Agents IV - LNAI No. 1860, Heidelberg, Springer-Verlag, Heidelberg (2000) 179–190
9. Witteveen, C., Roos, N., van der Krogt, R., de Weerdt, M.: Diagnosis of single and multi-agent plans. In: AAMAS '05: Proceedings of the fourth international joint conference on Autonomous agents and multiagent systems, New York, NY, USA, ACM Press (2005) 805–812
10. Miguel, I., Jarvis, P., Shen, Q.: Flexible graphplan. In Horn, W., ed.: Proceedings of the Fourteenth European Conference on Artificial Intelligence. (2000) 506–510
11. Šišlák, D., Rehák, M., Pěchouček, M., Rollo, M., Pavlíček, D.: *A*-**globe**: Agent development platform with inaccessibility and mobility support. In Unland, R., Klusch, M., Calisti, M., eds.: Software Agent-Based Applications, Platforms and Development Kits, Berlin, Birkhauser Verlag (2005) 21–46
12. Lawler, E.L., Wood, D.E.: Branch-and-bound methods: A survey. Operations Research **14**(4) (1966) 699–719

Learning to Negotiate Optimally in Non-stationary Environments

Vidya Narayanan and Nicholas R. Jennings

Intelligence, Agents, Multimedia
School of Electronics and Computer Science
University of Southampton SO17 1BJ, UK
{vn03r, nrj}@ecs.soton.ac.uk

Abstract. We adopt the Markov chain framework to model bilateral negotiations among agents in dynamic environments and use Bayesian learning to enable them to learn an optimal strategy in incomplete information settings. Specifically, an agent learns the optimal strategy to play against an opponent whose strategy varies with time, assuming no prior information about its negotiation parameters. In so doing, we present a new framework for adaptive negotiation in such non-stationary environments and develop a novel learning algorithm, which is guaranteed to converge, that an agent can use to negotiate optimally over time. We have implemented our algorithm and shown that it converges quickly in a wide range of cases.

1   Introduction

Automated negotiation plays a key role in resolving conflicts in multiagent systems in which individual agents have different stakes in a joint operation. Now, in many such cases, agents have little information about one another, and, in addition, the environment changes as a result of interactions between them [4]. Thus, learning about the other agents in the system and about their common environment becomes essential for effective performance. In particular, while an agent is engaged in negotiations, it has to learn about the *negotiation parameters* and *strategies* [10] of its opponents if it is to bargain optimally in such non-stationary environments.

Generally speaking, reinforcement learning, in particular Q-learning, is often used in multiagent systems since it does not need a model for learning and can be used online [4], [11]. In this vein, several researchers have adopted the stochastic game framework for multiagent reinforcement learning and have developed solution techniques like *Nash Equilibrium* [4], [9] and best response strategies [12]. Others, like [2], have used *fictitious play* techniques to analyse learning in games. However our problem is different. We are not trying to model learning in multiagent systems using game theory, but rather, we are trying to develop negotiation techniques for multiagent systems for which learning is necessary. Therefore, we believe that reinforcement learning, in which agents learn to maximize a reward signal, is not best suited for our purposes. Moreover, reinforcement learning algorithms rely on the assumption that the underlying environment is stationary (i.e., the parameters and strategies of the opponent do not change over time,

M. Klusch, M. Rovatsos, and T. Payne (Eds.): CIA 2006, LNAI 4149, pp. 288–300, 2006.

they are simply unknown). Now, this is clearly not the case in many realistic negotiation encounters, so we need to look at other learning methods.

Some of the first models to discuss the need for learning in negotiations among agents were [5] and [7]. However, while these papers discuss the concept of reasoning based on experience among negotiating agents, they do not explicitly develop a learning model. In [13] this notion is formally modelled, as a sequential learning mechanism based on a Bayesian belief update process. Specifically, a very general framework is adopted for the negotiation in which multiple agents bargain for multiple items. The *a priori* model that the agents have of their opponents is constantly updated using current information which is received as a signal from the environment. In particular, given the prior knowledge of an agent and the newly incoming information, the posterior distribution of the knowledge of the agents is computed using Bayesian rules. However, this model does not capture the non-stationarity in the environment. By this, we mean that, although the agents are assumed not to know the distribution of players' strategies and their negotiation parameters, it is assumed that this distribution does not change over time. Now, this is a serious shortcoming in the types of open environment in which multiagent systems are often deployed and is something that we wish to rectify in this work. Thus, in our case, the agent has to learn how its opponents change their strategies and then respond optimally to them. We have used Bayesian learning in our model because we believe it is more suitable than other forms of learning, like reinforcement or supervised learning, to represent uncertainties in the negotiation process as a probability function and then update this based on signals received from the environment.

In particular, we consider negotiation between a pair of agents over a single issue (price). We use the non-stationary Markov chain framework to model the negotiation process and prove, for the first time, an important estimation property for these processes (namely that the future distribution of the states can be obtained given their initial distribution and the probabilities of state change during the process). Within this framework, at each stage in the negotiation process, the agent uses Bayesian updating to learn the strategy that its opponent is most likely to use and, based on this, determines what it should adopt to maximise its payoff at that stage of the negotiation process. In so doing, we analytically prove that in repeated negotiations our algorithm converges to the actual optimal strategy at every stage of the negotiation process. We verify this by means of an example problem, and have shown that our algorithm is at least 200% more effective than random estimation. Our empirical results also show that, on average, the algorithm converges within 24 iterations and that each iteration takes 18.92 seconds.

The rest of the paper is organized as follows: Section 2 presents the basics of our negotiation model, Section 3 the learning model, Section 4 our empirical results. Finally, Section 5 concludes.

2   The Negotiation Model

In this section, we detail the basic concepts that we will use in our model. First, we define the notion of a *stochastic process* and the corresponding notion of a *Markov Chain* in order to use it to capture the uncertainty in our domain. Then, to provide a grounding for our learning algorithm, we give the *Bayesian probability rule* and explain how it is used in Bayesian learning techniques. Finally, we present the concept of mixed strategy profiles in the context of classical game theory which we will use as a framework to describe the strategies that our negotiating agents will use.

Turning first to stochastic processes and Markov Chains, let the real random variable $(r.r.v)$, X, be defined as a function that maps a space of events to a real number. Formally, if Ω represents the space of events and $\Re$ represents the set of all real numbers, then $X : \Omega \rightarrow \Re$. The probability that $X = a$ where $a \in \Re$ is represented as $Pr(X = a)$. A sequence of $r.r.vs$ that is indexed by some parameter, n, where $n \in T$ and T is a suitable index set, is represented as X_n and is called a *Stochastic Process*. A *realization* of a stochastic process $X_n, n \in T$, is an assignment to each $n \in T$, of a possible value of X_n. Now, there are two important sets associated with stochastic processes:

- *State Space S*: This is the space in which possible values of X_n lie. If $S = 0, 1, 2, 3, ..$ then the associated process is called a discrete state process. In our model the state space is discrete.
- *Index Parameter T*: If $T = 0, 1, 2, 3, ...$ (i.e., if T takes only discrete values) then X_n is called a discrete time stochastic process. Again, in our model, we assume that T is discrete.

We also need to define the concept of the *conditional probability* of random variables. Thus, if A and B represent two events, then the *conditional probability* of event A given that event B occurred is defined by:

$$Pr\{A|B\} = \frac{Pr\{A \text{ and } B\}}{Pr\{B\}} \tag{1}$$

We now move onto Markov processes.

Definition 1. A *first order* Markov process is a stochastic process that satisfies the following condition:

$$Pr\{X_{n+1} = x | X_n = x_n, X_{n-1} = x_{n-1}, ...\} = Pr\{X_{n+1} = x | X_n = x_n\} \tag{2}$$

Intuitively, this means that the probability of any future behaviour of the process, when its present state is known exactly, is not changed by any additional information about its past states. That is, the Markov Process is *memoryless*. This property of the stochastic process enables elegant mathematical analysis. Now, it is not unreasonable to suppose that the negotiation strategy at a particular stage is dependent only on the immediately preceding stage, since a single offer captures the entire decision making that preceded it. Therefore we model the negotiation process as a Markov process. Here, the probability $P = Pr\{X_{n+1} = x | X_n = x_n\}$ is called the *one-step transition probability function* and it is fundamental to the study of Markov processes and, as such, to our model. This function **P** is usually represented as a matrix where each entry (i, j) is given by $P_{ij} = Pr\{X_{n+1} = j | X_n = i\}$. A Markov process, for which S and T are discrete, is called a *Markov chain* and, so therefore, can our model.

Having introduced Markov chains, we now define the notions on which the learning component of our model is based. Specifically, our agent updates its beliefs using a

Bayesian update rule. Such Bayesian analysis is often used to estimate the most probable underlying model for a random process, based on some observed data or inference [13], and we choose it here because it enables us to represent the uncertainty in the environment as probability functions and it gives us a formal procedure to update these functions based on our observations. Now, let $A_1, A_2, ..., A_n$, represent n random events. Then, we let $X_n, t = 0, 1, ...$ be the stochastic process we are trying to estimate. Each of these n events can be thought to represent the hypothesis that the parameters of $\{X_n, t = 0, 1, ...\}$ belong to sets $T_1, T_2, ..., T_n$. Finally, we let the event B represent the set of observed data. Now, *Bayes rule* can be stated as:

$$Pr\{A_i|B\} = \frac{Pr\{B|A_i\} \times Pr\{A_i\}}{\sum Pr\{B|A_i\} \times Pr\{A_i\}} \tag{3}$$

where $Pr\{A_i\}$ is the prior probability of model A_i in the absence of any information, $Pr\{B|A_i\}$ is the likelihood that observation B was produced given that the model was A_i, and $Pr\{A_i|B\}$ is the posterior probability of the model being A_i given the observation is B. Our learning agent will use these inference rules to estimate the underlying randomness of the negotiation process.

Our final discussion in this section refers to the strategies that the agents will use in the negotiation process. In classical game theory, a *Strategic-Form* game has three elements:

1. the set of players $i \in I$, where $I = 1, 2, ..., n$
2. the *pure-strategy space* S_i, for each player i, and
3. *payoff functions* u_i that give player $i's$ utility $u_i(s)$ for each *profile*, $s = (s_1, s_2, ..., s_n)$, of strategies

Therefore in game theory a *strategy* is perceived as an action choice of a player that has a *utility* associated with it. Often the objective in games is to determine a strategy s_i that will maximise player $i's$ payoff given the strategy set, s_{-i}, that the other players use. Also, notice that the u_i that player i receives depends on the strategies of all the players in the game and is not related to an isolated strategy that i may use. In the definition of a strategic game we called the strategy space a *pure-strategy*, this is because game theorists often refer to an alternate strategy space called the *mixed-strategy space*. The mixed-strategy space is a probability distribution over the space of pure-strategies and for mathematical ease of analysis it is often more convenient to deal with the mixed-strategy space [3]. Thus in our problem the agent will learn the mixed-strategy profile of its opponent and evolve a strategy in response to that strategy that earns it maximum payoff. In this sense, our negotiation problem can be considered as a two-player strategic game.

Having introduced the main concepts that we use in our model, we are now ready to describe the learning component and outline the solution procedure we have developed.

3 The Learning Model

The main objective of our agent is to learn the mixed-strategy profile of its opponent and determine a strategy in response to this profile that maximises its pay-off at each stage of the negotiation process. This learning problem is complicated by the fact that the agent has no information about its opponent and that the strategy that the opponent uses may well change during the course of the negotiation. Now, to model this process of change in the strategies of the opponent, we use a *non-stationary Markov chain*. Formally, a *non-stationary Markov chain* is a Markov chain (see Section 2) whose one-step transition probability function, $\mathbf{P(t)} = Pr\{X_{n+1} = x | X_n = x_n\}$, varies with time [8]. If we define the state space, S, associated with this non-stationary Markov chain to be the space of all possible strategies that the opponent can employ, and the corresponding time dependent transition probability function, $\mathbf{P^n(t)}$, to represent the probability that the strategy of the opponent changes at each step n of the game and that this probability function itself is a function of time, then this framework gives us a powerful tool to describe and analyse the non-stationary negotiation process that we are trying to model. Therefore, we adopt this mathematical formulation in this work.

Now, if $\mathbf{P^n(t)}$ were specified as a function of time, then we could obtain the strategy profile of the opponent at each stage of the negotiation process using standard stochastic process analysis [6] and then obtain a strategy that maximises our own payoff using maximization algorithms [1]. But since this function is unknown in our problem, the agent has to learn it from interactions with the opponent and the environment. In Bayesian learning, as explained in Section 2, the probability of a hypothesis being true is continuously updated by signals that are received from the environment and, as such, is well suited to modelling uncertainty in the environment. In our problem, in order to learn the function, $\mathbf{P^n(t)}$, we propose that the learning agent initially has a finite number of hypotheses [1] of the possible distributions of $\mathbf{P^n(t)}$ which it updates using Bayesian inference rules. This means that in successive negotiations, by updating the different hypotheses, the agent comes closer to estimating the true value of $\mathbf{P^n(t)}$ and, therefore, to estimating the true optimal strategy in response to its opponent's play.

Formally, we consider two agents say buyer X and seller Y, negotiating over price. We assume that the buyer is learning to respond to the strategy of the seller. Now, we assume that there is a payoff function, $u_{s_x}^n(t)$, associated with X, which depends on the strategy s that X uses in response to Y at each step, n, of the negotiation. $X's$ objective in the negotiation is to find a strategy profile that maximises $u_{s_x}^n(t)$ which we assume is known to X. Therefore, X must learn the strategy profile of Y in order to determine an optimal response strategy. To describe how X learns this strategy within the Markov chain, we need to first define some of its properties. In stationary Markov chains, the probability of moving from state i to state j in n time steps is represented as P_{ij}^n and is given by [6]:

$$P_{ij}^n = \sum_{k=0}^{m} P_{ik}^r \times P_{kj}^s \qquad (4)$$

where m is the total number of states, k is some intermediate state and $r + s = n$. Intuitively, this means that the probability of moving from one state to another in a certain number of steps, n, is equivalent to the probability of moving from the first state to an intermediate state, k, in r steps together with the probability of moving from

---

[1] This assumption reduces the search space while allowing us to represent the uncertainty in the problem.

k to the final state in the remaining number of steps. Now, from matrix algebra, we recognise equation 4 as the formula for matrix multiplication, so the n-step transition matrix, represented by P^n, is equal to $P^{(n)}$ or that the entries P_{ij}^n in P^n are equal to the entries in the matrix $P^{(n)}$, which is the nth power of the one-step transition matrix P. It follows that if the probability of the process initially being in state j is p_j, (i.e., $Pr\{X_0 = j\}$), then the probability of the process being in state k, at time n is:

$$p_k^n = \sum_{j=0}^{m} p_j P_{jk}^n \qquad (5)$$

where m is the total number of states. Thus in our problem if we know the initial distribution of the opponent's strategies we can calculate the probability that the opponent uses a certain strategy after n time steps. This is the main reason for using the Markov chain framework to model the negotiation process. In our model, however, the Markov chain is non-stationary and, therefore, we need to prove, an equivalent result for the non-stationary case (this has not previously been done). Here, since $\mathbf{P^n(t)}$ is a function of time, at each step of the process we have a different transition probability matrix. Here, we propose that to obtain p_k^n as a function of time, we need to multiply n different transition matrices. We now formally state and prove this result.

Theorem 1. *In non-stationary Markov chains, the probability of moving from state i to state j in n time steps, during time instant t, is represented as $P_{ij}^n(t)$ [2] and is given by:*

$$P_{ij}^n(t) = \sum_{k=0}^{m} P_{ik}^r(u) \times P_{kj}^s(v)$$

where m is the total number of states, k is some intermediate state, $r + s = n$ and u, v are time instants at which the transitions occur.

Proof. We prove the result when $n = 2$. The event of moving from state i to state j can happen in mutually exclusive ways, of going to some intermediate state $k \in \{0, 1, 2..., m\}$ in the first transition and then moving from state k to state j in the next transition. Now, because of the Markovian assumption that the transition probability is independent of the history of the process, the probability of the second transition is simply $P_{kj}(v)$ and, by definition, the probability of the first transition is $P_{ik}(u)$. Therefore, by the law of total probability: $P_{ij}^2(t) = \sum_{k=0}^{m} P_{ik}^1(u) \times P_{kj}^1(v)$. In the general case, by breaking up the first r steps and then the next s steps into a series of single step transitions and again by using, the law of total probability for each transition, the proof is obtained. □

Thus, in the non-stationary case also, given the probability that initially the process was in, say state j (i.e., $p_j^0(0) = Pr\{X_0(0) = j\}$), then the probability that it is in state k after n time steps and at time t is represented as $p_k^n(t) = Pr\{X_n(t) = k\}$ and is given by:

---

[2] Here n represents the number of time steps and t represents the fact that the transition probability $P_{ij}^n(t)$ is a function of time.

$$p_k^n(t) = \sum_{j=0}^{m} [p_j^0(0)] \times [Q_{jk}^n(t)] \qquad (6)$$

where $Q_{jk}^n(t) = [P^0(0)] \times [P^1(1)]... \times [P^{n-1}(t-1)]$.

Therefore, we now have a means of obtaining the probability distribution of the process and, thereby, the probability distribution of strategies at any stage in the negotiation process given an initial distribution of strategies and the transition probability matrices.

Now, we come to the main issue of learning the transition probability matrices. As already stated, we propose to do this using Bayesian inference rules. However, to do this we must assume that the learning agent, in our case the buyer X, has some knowledge about the negotiation process. Specifically, in order to update its hypothesis about the strategy distribution of Y from the offers that it receives, it has to know how the offer generation process depends on the strategy selection process. To this end, let us assume that S, the set of all possible strategies that Y can use, and as such constitutes the state space of our Markov chain, is given by $S = \{s_0^o, s_1^o, ..., s_m^o\}$. Therefore, Y switches between the strategies in S according to the transition probability matrix $\mathbf{P^n}(t)$, which varies with time. We let $O_n(t)$ represent a sequence of offers made by Y and $O_n^p(t)$ represent the event that the offer at the nth step of the process at time t is p. We also let $H_n(t)$ represent a sequence of finite sets of hypotheses about $\mathbf{P^n}(t)$ during the negotiation process. Therefore $H_n(t) = \{H_n^1(t), ..., H_n^k(t)\}$, where k is some finite positive integer. We assume that the hypothesis representing the true value of the transition probability function also belongs to $H_n(t)$. Then the objective of our learning algorithm is to update each of these hypotheses $\{H_n^i(t) \in H_n(t)\}$ at every step n of the negotiation. The steps of the algorithm are detailed in Algorithm 1. In more detail, using Bayes rule we have for each hypothesis, at step n of the process that:

$$Pr\{H_n^i(t)|O_n^p(t)\} = \frac{Pr\{H_n^i(t)\} \times Pr\{O_n^p(t)|H_n^i(t)\}}{\sum_k^{i=0} [Pr\{H_n^i(t)\}] \times [Pr\{O_n^p(t)|H_n^i(t)\}]} \qquad (7)$$

We call $Pr\{H_n^i(t)|O_n^p(t)\}$ the likelihood function, L. Thus each $H_n^i(t)$ is updated in the light of the incoming offer $O_n^p(t)$. Now, B uses the hypothesis $H_n^{new}(t) = \sum_k^{i=0} \{Pr\{H_n^i(t)|O_n^p(t)\} \times H_n^i(t)\}$ to find the strategy used by the opponent. Therefore the learning agent weights the different hypotheses by the probabilities of their occurring in order to form a new hypothesis about $\mathbf{P^n}(t)$. Because of this construction of the new hypothesis we can show that, as $t \to T$ where T is sufficiently large, $H_n^{new}(t)$ approaches the true value of $\mathbf{P^n}(t)$ (see theorem 2 for details). Then, according to $u_{s_x}^n(t)$, the agent determines the strategy $s_{max}^n(t)$ that maximises $u_{s_x}^n(t)$ at each step of the negotiation process. We denote this maximum value of the payoff function by $u_{s_{max}}^n(t)$. This completes the solution procedure for determining the best response strategy to the opponent's play and consequently the maximum payoff at each step of the negotiation process.

Here, it is important to note that according to this algorithm, the agent learns across successive negotiations and not within a single negotiation process. Therefore, we claim that in repeated negotiations using our algorithm, the agent learns to use the optimal

Algorithm 1. The Adaptive Negotiation Algorithm

1. **for** $(t = 0, 1, 2, ..., T)$

2.   **for** $(n = 0, 1, 2, ..., t_{terminal})$

3.   **initialize** $H_n^i(t) \in H_n(t)$ as an arbitrary distribution.

4.   **input** opponent offer $p \in Domain\{O_n(t)\}$

5. $Pr\{H_n^i(t+1)\} \leftarrow Pr\{H_n^i(t)|O_n^p(t)\}$ using equation 7

6.   **assign** $H_n^{new}(t) = \sum_{i=0}^k \{Pr\{H_n^i(t)|O_n^p(t)\} \times H_n^i(t)\}$

7.   **assign** $[P^n(t)] = H_n^{new}(t)$

8.   **compute** $[(s_1^o, s_2^o, ..., s_m^o)]^n(t)$ using equation 6

9.   **compute** $s_{max}^n(t) = \max [(s_1, s_2, ..., s_m)]^n(t) \times u_x^n(t) \times [(s_1^o, s_2^o, ..., s_m^o)]^n(t)]^T$ s.t $\sum_{i=0}^m s_i = 1$ and $s_i \geq 0 \,\forall i$

10.   **compute** $u_{s_{max}}^n(t)$

11.   **next** n

12. **next** t

strategy and earn maximum payoff at each stage of the negotiation process. In order to prove this claim we need the following lemma.

Lemma 1. After a sufficiently large time T, the real probability distribution over the future rational play of a game is ϵ-close to what player i *believes* the distribution is [5].

Here, ϵ-close implies that we can approach arbitrarily close to the actual distribution and rational play means that at each stage of the negotiation the players take the action that maximises their pay-offs. Having stated Lemma 1, we are now ready to prove our main result.

Theorem 2. *In the non-stationary negotiation process, the sequence of nth step strategies $\{s_{max}^n(0), ..., s_{max}^n(t), s_{max}^n(t+1), ..., \}$ and the corresponding sequence of nth step payoff functions, $\{u_{max}^n(0), ..., u_{max}^n(t), u_{max}^n(t+1), ..., \}$, after a sufficiently large time T, are ϵ-close to the true optimal strategy and the corresponding maximum payoff function at the nth step of the negotiation process.*

Proof. According to Lemma 1, in a systematic belief update process, the learner eventually comes arbitrarily close to the true distribution after a sufficiently large time T. Since the process by which our learning agent estimates the strategy of the opponent is constructed as a Bayesian belief process, the sequence of updated probabilities,

$\{Pr\{H_n^0(t)|O_n^p(t)\}, ..., Pr\{H_n^i(t)|O_n^p(t)\}, ..., Pr\{H_n^k(t)|O_n^p(t)\}\}$ *comes arbitrarily close to* $\{0, ..., 1, ..., 0\}$ *for some* $i \in \{0, 1, 2, ..., k\}$ *as* $t \to T$. *This implies that* $H_n^i(t)$ *is the true hypothesis. Therefore,* $H_n^{new}(t) = \sum_k^{i=0}\{Pr\{H_n^i(t)|O_n^p(t)\} \times H_n^i(t)\}$, *by construction, and, therefore,* $H_n^{new}(t) \to H_n^i(t)$ *as* $t \to T$. *Since the opponent determines its strategy at each step using* $H_n^{new}(t)$ *and since our agent determines its optimal strategy and the maximum payoff at each step in response to this updated opponent strategy, the result is proved.*   □

Thus we have analytically shown that our algorithm converges. We now present an example to illustrate this operation (and in section 4 we explore the actual speed of convergence). Specifically, in this problem, we make the following assumptions:

1. The strategy space S of the opponent consists of two strategies, $S = \{s_1, s_2\}$.
2. At each time step n of the negotiation, the learning agent has a set of three hypotheses about the possible value of $\mathbf{P^n(t)}$.

We now describe the solution procedure in our problem.

- Here as specified in Step 3 of algorithm 1, we initialize, $H_0^i(0) \in H_0(0)$.

$$H_0^1(0) = \begin{bmatrix} 0.5 & 0.5 \\ 0.5 & 0.5 \end{bmatrix}$$

$$H_0^2(0) = \begin{bmatrix} 1 & 0 \\ 0 & 1 \end{bmatrix}$$

$$H_0^3(0) = \begin{bmatrix} 0 & 1 \\ 1 & 0 \end{bmatrix}$$

Now the agent is unaware of the true value of $\mathbf{P^n(t)}$, but has arbitrary probabilities assigned to each of these hypotheses about $\mathbf{P^n(t)}$.
- Let $\{Pr(H_0^1(0)) = 0.5\}, \{Pr(H_0^2(0)) = 0.25\}, \{Pr(H_0^3(0)) = 0.25\}$ and offer of opponent, $O_0(0) = 100$.
- Then according to Step 4 in algorithm 1, we observe the offer of the opponent and assume that $Pr\{O_0(0)|H_0^1(0)\} = 0.6$, $Pr\{O_0(0)|H_0^2(0)\} = 0.2$ and $Pr\{O_0(0)|H_0^3(0)\} = 0.2$ (here we assume arbitrary values for $Pr\{O|H\}$, but we are in the process of studying the offer patterns of traders in different domains in order to get an accurate representation for these values).
- Using Step 5, we update probabilities as $Pr\{H_0^1(0)|O_0(0)\} = 0.75$, $Pr\{H_0^2(0)|O_0(0)\} = 0.125$ and $Pr\{H_0^3(0)|O_0(0)\} = 0.125$.
- From Step 6, we determine $H_0^{new}(0) = (0.75) \times H_0^1(0) + (0.125) \times H_0^2(0) + (0.125) \times H_0^3(0)$.
- Step 7 specifies the strategy profile of the opponent. The initial profile is assumed to be given as $[0.2, 0.8]$ (i.e., $Pr\{S = s_1^o\} = 0.2, Pr\{S = s_2^o\} = 0.8$) and the payoff function of the agent is:

$$u_x^o(0) = \begin{bmatrix} 1 & 0 \\ -2 & 3 \end{bmatrix}$$

- From Step 8, to determine its strategy profile, $[s_1, s_2]$ and the corresponding payoff function, the agent solves the linear program:
  $max [s_1, s_2] \times u_x^0(0) \times [0.2, 0.8]^T$ s.t $s_1 + s_2 = 1$ and $s_1, s_2 \geq 0$.
  The strategy profile thus obtained is denoted as $s_{max}^0(0)$ and the payoff function is $u_{max}^n(0)$.
- We do this for every time step n of the negotiation process and obtain $\{s_{max}^0(0), s_{max}^1(0), ...\}$ and $\{u_{max}^0(0), u_{max}^1(0), u_{max}^2(0), ...\}$
- We then repeat this for every negotiation during time instants $t = 0, 1, 2, 3, ...$ and obtain the sequences $\{s_{max}^0(0), s_{max}^0(1), s_{max}^0(2), ...\}$, $\{s_{max}^1(0), s_{max}^1(1), s_{max}^1(2), ...\}$, $\{s_{max}^3(0), s_{max}^3(1), ...\}$ and the corresponding payoff sequences.

In this case the two sequences converge within 4 iterations to the optimal values at each step of the negotiation process. Having proved that our algorithm converges, we need to determine the rate of this convergence and the factors that influence this. This can only be done empirically and our results are presented in the next section.

4   Empirical Results

We have run experiments by varying the number of hypotheses for $\mathbf{P^n(t)}$. Specifically, we have experimented with both 2×2 and 3×3 matrices representing the strategy profiles. We have found that using our algorithm, the agent on an average (computed by varying the number of hypotheses ie., the number of 2×2 and 3×3 matrices) learns the maximum payoff within 13.6 iterations for 2×2 matrices and on an average within 23.6 iterations for 3×3 matrices. On an average, each iteration takes 7.44 seconds to complete for 2×2 matrices and 18.92 seconds for 3×3 matrices. We have also experimented by changing the elements of the transition matrices. Our results indicate that the rate of convergence is independent of variations in the patterns of the opponent's offers. But it depends on the number of hypotheses for $\mathbf{P^n(t)}$ at each step of the negotiation. However, since the computation of updated probabilities is a simple arithmetic operation and since this computation alone is affected by the number of matrices, the time for convergence does not drastically increase with the number of matrices. This is shown in tables 1 and 2 and figure 1 shows the actual convergence of the algorithm during successive iterations at a *single step* of the negotiation process. In figure 1 the optimal value line for the payoffs is computed by assuming that the opponent's strategy profile is known to the agent. The other line corresponds to the agent learning the opponent's strategy profile and therefore the optimal payoff value, using our algorithm, as illustrated in the example problem. In figure 1 we used 2×2 matrices to represent the opponent's strategy profiles and assumed 2 hypotheses for $\mathbf{P^n(t)}$ at each step of the negotiation.

Now, in general, if we assume that there are k hypotheses for $\mathbf{P^n(t)}$, then in the random case the probability of finding the true hypothesis is always $1/k$ (i.e., this probability does not improve with time). However, the convergence of our algorithm is guaranteed by theorem 2 and therefore our estimation of the true $\mathbf{P^n(t)}$ improves with each iteration and eventually converges. With this and the fact that the algorithm converges on an average within 1315 seconds even with 10 hypotheses and 3 strategies, we claim that our algorithm is k times more effective than random estimation. Therefore even in

Table 1. Dependence of rate of convergence on number of hypotheses for 2×2 matrices

No of Hypotheses	Offer Distribution	Average Iterations	Average Time for Iteration in secs
2	Arbitrary	2	2.7
4	Arbitrary	4	4.6
6	Arbitrary	11	7
8	Arbitrary	21	10.1
10	Arbitrary	30	12.8

Table 2. Dependence of rate of convergence on number of hypotheses for 3×3 matrices

No of Hypotheses	Offer Distribution	Average Iterations	Average Time for Iteration in secs
2	Arbitrary	7	6.2
4	Arbitrary	15	12
6	Arbitrary	25	18.4
8	Arbitrary	29	26.7
10	Arbitrary	42	31.3

the case when there are only 2 hypotheses at each step n for $\mathbf{P^n(t)}$ our algorithm is 200% more effective than random estimation. Obviously, as we increase the number of hypotheses, which allows for a more general representation of $\mathbf{P^n(t)}$ and therefore of the uncertainty in the problem, the effectiveness of our algorithm over random estimation increases proportionally.

5 Conclusions and Future Work

In this work we have developed a new framework, using Markov chains, for studying negotiation in non-stationary environments. This is a general framework which can be used to study decision making in many stochastic systems like market places and auctions. Within this framework, we have derived, for the first time, an important result for non-stationary Markov chains that computes the distribution of the random variable, which defines it, at any future step of the process given its initial probability distribution and the transition probability matrices at each step of the process. Then, using this framework we have developed an algorithm to learn a strategy in response to a non-stationary opponent's play and proved that it converges to the optimal strategy in repeated negotiations. Unlike previous work in this area, our algorithm does not assume knowledge of the opponent's strategy profile and, as such, is a powerful tool to analyse negotiations in real world environments where such uncertainty is common. Our algorithm is also explicitly designed to deal with cases in which the strategy profile is not only unknown, but changes with time during the course of the negotiation process itself. This significantly extends the state of the art in the field of automated negotiations in non-stationary, real world environments. For such cases, we have proved, analytically, that our algorithm converges. Our empirical results indicate that the algorithm converges within reasonable timeframes to the true hypothesis even when the number of hypotheses is large. Also, in our algorithm, the states of the Markov chain represent

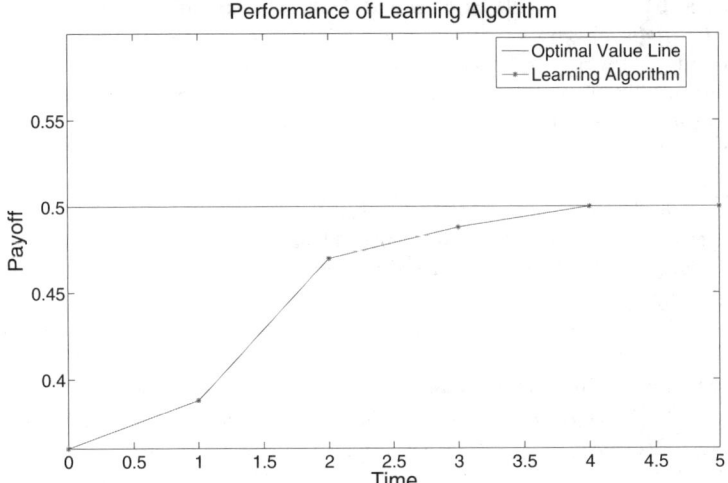

Fig. 1. Convergence to Optimal Strategy

the strategies that are available to the opponent and the actual uncertainty in the problem is represented by the number of hypotheses. Therefore we need not increase the number of states to represent greater uncertainty in the domain. The algorithm is also vastly more accurate than random estimation.

In our future work, we intend to use the structure of the Markov chain to develop a more formal model for the likelihood function in the Bayesian belief update process which would help us to reduce the computation effort involved in updating the agent's knowledge even in complicated real world scenarios. We are also in the process of doing statistical analysis to estimate the number of hypotheses that are required to get an accurate representation of the dynamism in exemplar real world domains like mobile communications and we also intend to extend the algorithm to learn the opponent's negotiation parameters along with its strategy profile and to study negotiation when the opponent is also changing its strategies in response to our agent's adaptivity. Finally, we intend to do a detailed comparative study between other machine learning techniques, like Reinforcement learning and Bayesian methods in automated negotiations, for non-stationary environments. This study would also provide a more effective benchmark than random estimation for our algorithm.

References

1. J. Filar and K. Vrieze. *Competitive Markov Decision Processes*. Springer, 1996.
2. D. Fudenberg and D.K Levine. *The Theory of Learning in Games*. The MIT Press, 1998.
3. D. Fudenberg and J. Tirole. *Game Theory*. MIT Press, 1991.
4. J. Hu and M.P. Wellman. Multiagent reinforcement learning: Theoretical framework and an algorithm. *Proceedings of the 11th International Conference on Machine Learning: 242-250*, 1998.

5. E. Kalai and E. Lehrer. Rational learning leads to nash equilibrium. *Econometrica, 61(5):1019–1045*, 1993.
6. S. Karlin and H. Taylor. *First Course in Stochastic Processes*. Academic Press, 1974.
7. S. Kraus and V.S. Subrahmanian. Multiagent reasoning with probability, time, and beliefs. *International Journal of Intelligent Systems 10(5): 459-499*, 1995.
8. V. Kulkarni. *Modelling and Analysis of Stochastic Systems*. Chapman Hall/CRC, 1996.
9. M.L. Littman. Markov games as a framework for multi-agent reinforcement learning. *Proceedings of the 11th International Conference on Machine Learning: 157-163*, 1994.
10. V. Narayanan and N. R. Jennings. An adaptive bilateral negotiation model for e-commerce settings. *Proc. 7th Int. IEEE Conf on E-Commerce Technology, Munich, Germany: 34-39*, 2005.
11. R.S. Sutton and A.G. Barto. *Reinforcement Learning: An Introduction*. The MIT Press, 1998.
12. M. Weinberg and J. Rosenschein. Best-response multiagent learning in non-stationary environments. *The Third International Joint Conference on Autonomous Agents and Mutli-Agent Systems:506-513*, 2004.
13. D. Zeng and K. Sycara. Bayesian learning in negotiation. *Int. J Human-Computer Studies(1998), 48:125-141*, 1998.

Eliminating Interdependencies Between Issues for Multi-issue Negotiation

Koen Hindriks, Catholijn M. Jonker, and Dmytro Tykhonov

Nijmegen Institute for Cognition and Information, Radboud University, Montessorilaan 3,
6525 HR Nijmegen , The Netherlands
{C.Jonker, K.Hindriks, D.Tykhonov}@nici.ru.nl}

Abstract. In multi-issue negotiations, issues may be negotiated independently or not. In the latter case, the utility associated with one issue depends on the value of another. These issue dependencies give rise to more complex, non-linear utility spaces. As a consequence, the computational cost and complexity of negotiating interdependent issues is increased significantly compared to the case of independent issues. Several techniques have been proposed to deal with this increased complexity, including, for example, introducing a mediator in the negotiation setting. In this paper, we propose an alternative approach based on a weighted approximation technique to simplify the utility space. We show that given certain natural assumptions about the outcome of negotiation the application of this technique results in an outcome that closely matches with the outcome based on the original, interdependent utility structure. Moreover, using the approximated utility structure, each of the issues can be negotiated independently which ensures that the negotiation is computationally tractable. The approach is illustrated by applying and testing it in a case study.

1 Introduction

Negotiation is a process by which a joint decision is made by two or more parties [7]. The parties first express contradictory demands and then move towards agreement by a process of concession making. Negotiation is an important method for agents to achieve their own goals and to form cooperation agreements, see e.g. [2,10,11]. Raiffa [8] explains how to set up a preference profile for each negotiator that can be used during negotiation to determine the utility of exchanged bids. For more information on utility and other game theoretic notions the reader is referred to e.g. [3]. Representing agent's preferences in terms of mathematical formulae expressing relationships between values of issues and the utility of bids allows the development of software support for negotiations. The complexity of these relationships determines the computational complexity of the negotiation process. One way to avoid such computational complexity is, as proposed in e.g. [4], to build up profiles as combinations of independent and simple evaluation functions per issue. This approach corresponds to the way the average human tackles negotiation. Humans tend to simplify the structure of their preferences ([12]) and prefer to negotiate one

M. Klusch, M. Rovatsos, and T. Payne (Eds.): CIA 2006, LNAI 4149, pp. 301–316, 2006.

issue at a time, which means that issues influence the utility of a bid independently from each other. Absence of issue dependencies allows for the use of efficient nego-tiation strategies. Until now this approach is only applicable if the values of the dif-ferent attributes in the domain are independent from each other. However, in some domains the issues are interdependent.

In some domains, however, issue dependencies influence the overall utility of a bid. In such cases it is no longer possible to negotiate one issue at a time and Klein at al in [5] argue that there is no efficient method that an agent can use to negotiate mul-tiple issues, even if the agent tries to guess the opponent's profile. The authors pro-pose to use a mediator who uses a computationally expensive evolutionary algorithm that can solve non-linear optimization tasks of high dimensionality. Bar-Yam [1] shows that in a multi-issue negotiation with issue dependencies the utility can only be described by non-linear functions of multiple issue variables.

In this paper, we present a new approach to tackle the complexity problem of a utility space with interdependent issues that is based on the following observations. First, not all bids are equally important for negotiation: there are some bids which are not acceptable for the agent or are too optimistic to be an outcome of the negotiation. In effect, it is possible to indicate an expected region of utility of the outcome. Sec-ond, in real life cases a profile can be modeled by utility functions that are far from "wild"; they have a structure that is far from random. This paper proposes weighted averaging as a method to approximate complex utility functions with simpler func-tions that is based on these observations. Furthermore, the method provides a way to check the adequacy of the approximation by a measure of the introduced error.

The paper is organized as follows. The next section provides a formal definition of utility spaces containing interdependencies between issues. Section 3 describes the approximation method for eliminating such dependencies. A leading case study is used throughout the paper to illustrate the method. The theme of Section 4 is the analysis of the approximation with respect to the original utility space in the same negotiation setup. Section 5 summarizes the paper with conclusions about the pro-posed approximation method.

2   Utility of Interdependent Issues

The overall utility of a set of independent issues can be computed as a weighted sum of the values associated with each of the separate issues. As is common (see e.g. [4,8]), an evaluation function is associated with each issue variable and the utility of a bid then is computed by the following weighted sum of the issue evaluation functions:

$$u(x_1, x_2) = w_1 ev_1(x_1) + w_2 ev_2(x_2) \tag{1}$$

In equation (1), the (weighted) contribution of each issue to the overall utility only depends on the value associated with that issue and the contribution of a single issue can be modeled independently from any other issues. Evaluation functions for inde-pendent issues thus have the same properties as the utility function associated with the bids that consist of multiple issues: it maps issue values on a closed interval [0; 1].

This setup can be used for issue values that are numeric (e.g., price, time) as well as for issue values taken from ordered, discrete sets (e.g., colors, brands).

Bid utility functions that are weighted sums of the contribution of single issue values to the overall utility cannot be used, however, for modeling dependencies between issues. The value of one issue may depend on that of another, thus influencing the utility of a bid that includes both issues. For two issues, dependencies between these issues give rise to a generalization of equation (1) to:

$$u(x_1, x_2) = w_1 ev_1(x_1, x_2) + w_2 ev_2(x_1, x_2) \tag{2}$$

It is easy to generalize (2) to more than two issues. In that case, dependencies between selected subsets of issues instead of all issues may have to be considered.

As an illustrative example of dependent issues, in this paper, we consider the negotiation of an employment contract where two important issues are at stake: the number of days that have to be worked and the number of days that childcare will be provided by an employer. In the example, the candidate employee additionally has to take into account a dependency between these two issues: working time (issue variable x_1) needs to be balanced with the time s/he needs to spend with his/her child (issue variable x_2). Assuming that the partner of the candidate is working too and can take responsibility for only part of the childcare, the candidate has promised that s/he will take care of the child for at least 2 days, either by taking care in person, or by finding professional childcare. Thus the child care issue is really important and in case the employer proposes a contract for 5 days our candidate will try to negotiate a result which includes at least 2 days of childcare. In terms of utility, bids with 5 working days and less than 2 days of childcare have a low utility (e.g. $u(5,0)\approx0.1$, $u(5,1)\approx0.5$). In case the employer proposes a contract for only 4 days, the candidate will need to negotiate a result including only one day of childcare and a bid of 4 working days and one day of childcare has an acceptable utility value associated with it (e.g. $u(4,0)\approx0.25$, $u(4,1)\approx0.55$) though the candidate would prefer to work more. With respect to bids of the employer that require the candidate to work 3 days or less, there is no problem regarding the caretaking of the child. In that case, the childcare issue has much less influence on the value of the bid (e.g. $u(3,0)\approx0.35$, $u(3,1)\approx0.55$. Even in this relatively simple example, the values associated with each of the issues cannot be modelled independently and overall utility cannot be calculated using equation (1). The contribution of the childcare issue to overall utility depends on the number of working days associated with the other issue and vice versa in a way that introduces non-linear dependencies between the issues. Such non-linear dependencies can only be modelled by equation (2). To make the example concrete, the candidate's preferences are modelled using the following evaluation functions:

$$ev_1(x_1, x_2) = 0.01x_1^2 + 0.03x_1x_2 + 0.028x_2^2 \tag{3}$$

$$ev_2(x_1, x_2) = -0.04x_1^2 + 0.13x_1x_2 - 0.11x_2^2 + 1 \tag{4}$$

Figure 1 shows the utility space of the candidate employee defined by the evaluation functions (3) and (4) and weights $w_1 = w_2 = 0.5$.

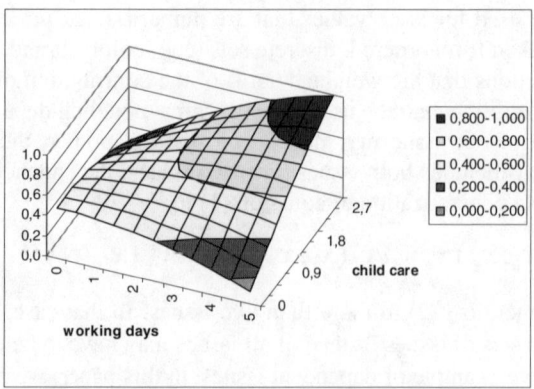

Fig. 1. Utility space of the candidate employee with issue dependencies

The representation of a complex, interdependent utility space by evaluation functions as in equation (2) is similar to the model proposed in [5]. In contrast with Klein et all., who discuss binary issues only, however, we allow multi-valued, discrete, as well as continuous issues. Even so, they show that the computational complexity of searching through a utility space based on issue dependencies grows exponentially and cannot be handled efficiently by either agent when the opponent's utility function is unknown. Such complex negotiations are most efficiently handled by revealing the utility functions of the negotiating agents to a mediator that is trusted by both parties (cf. [5]). Computationally simple and efficient approaches covered in [6] mostly rely on the independence of issues to determine their next bid and are not applicable.[1]

3   A Method for Approximating Complex Utility Spaces

Due to the inherent computational complexity and the limited number of negotiation strategies that can be used to handle issue dependencies in negotiations, it would be beneficial to have methods that simplify the negotiation process of dependent issues without using a mediator. One particularly interesting option is to investigate the complexity of the utility space itself and try to eliminate the dependencies between issues. In case issue dependencies can be eliminated, various alternatives for efficient negotiation become available: Searching through the utility space of multi-issue bids becomes feasible and negotiation strategies for independent issues can be applied.

In this section, a method based on weighted approximation is proposed to eliminate issue dependencies. It uses an averaging technique in which some general observations about negotiation have been integrated and which can take available knowledge about a negotiation domain into account. In particular, knowledge about the relative importance of bids and about outcomes which reasonably can be expected are part of the weighted averaging method.

---

[1] As we discuss below, however, the approach can be adapted by using exhaustive search through the utility space, but becomes intractable and in practice works only for small utility spaces.

Although elimination of issue dependencies implies a loss of information and accuracy with regard to utility, it is shown in this paper that if the influence of one issue on the associated value of another issue is "reasonable" (i.e., the utility space is not too wild) a good approximation of the complex utility space can be obtained.

The averaging technique proposed in this paper for eliminating dependencies is valid for utility spaces that have a certain "smooth" structure. The technique averages the values of bids close to each other. Therefore, utilities should not fluctuate too much from one bid to another within the proximity range set by the technique. In real life, common negotiations, this limitation on the applicability of the method is not seen as a problem considering that it is cognitively hard to make sense of wildly fluctuating utility spaces. As an indication, we think that the techniques are applicable to utility functions that can be modeled by polynomial functions of modest power. If the nature of the utility space is not clear, the applicability of the proposed techniques has to be tested for that case. A case study illustrates that the elimination of dependencies does not result in significant changes of the negotiation outcome. Additionally, a method for analyzing and assessing the difference between the original and approximated utility space is provided. This method analyze and assess the results can always be applied to arbitrary utility spaces.

Our main objective thus is to find and present a method for transforming a utility space $u(x_1, x_2)$ based on dependent issues that can be represented by equation (2) to a utility space $u'(x_1, x_2)$ without such dependencies that can be represented by equation (1). There exist various techniques to transform complex (utility) spaces with non-linear functional dependencies between variables to spaces which are linear combinations of functions in a single variable [13]. For our purposes, we are particularly interested in the linear separability of non-linear evaluation functions of dependent issues. The main idea is to transform a utility space $u(x_1, x_2)$ into an approximation $u'(x_1, x_2)$ of that space by approximating each of the evaluation functions $ev_i(x_1, x_2)$ by a function $ev'_i(x_i)$ in which the influence of the values of other issues x_j, $j \neq i$, on the associated value $ev_i(x_1, x_2)$ have been eliminated. Mathematically, the idea is to "average out" in a specific way the influence of other issues on a particular issue.

The weighted averaging method takes as input a utility space based on non-linear issue dependencies (i.e. issues cannot be linearly separated[2] and transforms it into a utility space that can be defined as a weighted sum of evaluation functions of single issues (i.e. issues are independent). The weighted averaging method consists of the following steps:

1. As a first step, estimate the utility of an expected outcome that is reasonable (given available knowledge). This estimate is called the "m-point" and is used to define a region of utility space where the actual outcome is expected to be.
2. Select a type of weighting function. The selection of a weighting function is based on the amount of uncertainty about the estimated m-point (expected outcome) in the previous step.

---

[2] In geometry, when two sets of points in a two-dimensional graph can be completely separated by a single line, they are said to be linearly separable. In general, two groups are linearly separable in n-dimensional space if they can be separated by an $n - 1$ dimensional hyperplane.

3. Calculate an approximation of the original utility space based on non-linear issue dependencies using the m-point and the weighting function determined in the previous step. The result of this step is a utility space that can be defined as a weighted sum of evaluations of independent issues (a function of the form of equation (1)).[3]

4. Perform an analysis of the difference of the original and approximated utility space by means of a δ-function to assess the range of the error for any given utility level. In this final step, based on the assessment, thresholds for breaking off the negotiation or accepting opponent's bids can be reconsidered.

Finally, the results of the approximation method can be used in combination with a particular negotiation strategy. In section 4, we study the results of using an approximated utility space for the child care example in a negotiation strategy and compare the results with an approach based on the original utility space. The sections below explain each of the steps in more detail and illustrate how these steps achieve the objective of eliminating issue dependencies.

3.1 Estimate an Expected Outcome

Any approach based on using uniform arithmetical averaging methods has the effect of discarding information uniformly. Such an approach does not take the final goal of negotiation into consideration: the negotiation outcome. A uniform averaging method is indifferent to the fact that even before negotiation starts it can be assumed that certain regions of the utility space are more relevant to the negotiation than others. Some general observations about the structure of utility spaces that can be associated with negotiations taken from actual practice provide additional insight that can be used to increase the effectiveness of an approximation technique.

Consider, to make clear what we mean, a worst case scenario in which two agents A and B associate completely opposite utilities with bids. In other words, what is valuable for agent A is of no value for agent B. Formally, we can express this opposition in terms of utility functions as follows:

$$u_A(x_1, x_2) = 1 - u_B(x_1, x_2)$$

(5)

Given these utility functions, it is easy to see that the Nash product is 0.25 with associated utility values $u_A(x_1,x_2)=u_B(x_1,x_2)=0.5$ and the same point within the utility space is an efficient negotiation outcome when using Kalai-Smorodinsky criteria, that is, a Pareto-optimal outcome with equal utilities for both parties. Assuming such opposite interests, none of the agents would accept a bid which has a utility below 0.5.

Typically, however, negotiations do not fit such worst case scenarios and there is something to gain for both parties. Formally, this means that there exist acceptable negotiation outcomes, i.e. bids, with associated utilities that are higher than 0.5. In such cases, the utility spaces of the negotiating opponents are not completely opposite as expressed by (11). This line of reasoning makes clear that in general we may as-

---

[3] In the more general case of more than two issues, an evaluation function may depend on more than two issues and one of those issues has to be selected to be separated from the other issues.

sume that the expected outcome of the negotiation is located somewhere in the open utility interval (0.5; 1) and this region in the utility space is generally of more importance in a negotiation.

It follows from the previous considerations that some regions within the utility space are more important for obtaining a good negotiation outcome than others and in the approximation method proposed should be approximated as good as is possible. As a first step to identify these regions, an agent can estimate an expected outcome which would identify with some probability one of the more relevant points in the utility space. We call this point the "m-point".

An agent will be able to estimate an expected outcome with reasonable exactness only if it has some knowledge about the opponent's profile. In that case, as we illustrate below, the m-point can be computed in two steps. But even if an agent lacks any information whatsoever about its opponent an m-point can be based on considerations of the agent's own utility space. In the latter case, we propose that the m-point can be identified with the average of the break-off point (an agent breaks off a negotiation in case any utility with a lower utility is proposed) and the maximum utility in the utility space. In the childcare example, the break-off point equals 0.37, which is equal to the minimum utility that still satisfies the candidate employee's childcare constraint.

A second, more informed method to determine an expected outcome can be used when the agent does have some information, e.g. based on previous experience, concerning the opponent's profile. In the childcare example, assuming that the employer will take the child care request seriously into consideration, but will try to minimize his contribution in this regard, bids with 1-2 child care days are reasonable to expect. Additionally, it may be more or less certain that the employer prefers the employee to work as much as possible and that these issues are independent from the other. Then, as an estimated model of the opponent's profile, the following evaluation functions can be used, which, using equal weights of .5, specified by:

$$ev_1(x_1) = x_1/5 \tag{6}$$

$$ev_2(x_2) = (3 - x_2)/3 \tag{7}$$

An estimate of the expected outcome can now be computed from the agent's own utility space and the educated guess of the opponent's utility space using Kalai-Smorodinsky criteria, which ensures that a Pareto-optimal outcome is selected and the expected outcome is not strongly biased in favour of either one of the parties (see figure 8). Calculating the utility in our example yields $m=0.74$. This estimate may still be quite uncertain, but we will discuss this issue more extensively below. The estimated outcome only defines one parameter of the approach.

3.2 Select Weighting Function

As discussed above, not all points within the utility space are equally important for obtaining a good negotiation outcome. To take into account the relative importance of certain regions within the utility space, we introduce a weighting function associating a weight with each point (its "importance") in the utility space. In general, there are two useful considerations that can be made which provide clues for constructing an appropriate weighting function.

The first consideration is that a certain range of utility values are of particular interest in the negotiation. Also, certain bids may be more "appropriate" than others in a negotiation. As an example, bids with utility values below a break-off point are less significant than other bids and do not have to be approximated as well as others. In the childcare example, provided with the relevant domain knowledge, it is moreover unreasonable for our candidate employee to propose to do no work and at the same time to request 5 childcare days.

The first consideration concerning the approximation of the utility space can be given a formal interpretation by associating the highest weight with the expected outcome (the "m-point" identified above, located within the (0.5;1) interval).

The second consideration is the fact that an agent may be more or less uncertain about its estimate of the utility of the negotiation outcome. To take this into account, we propose to use two different functions depending on the level of uncertainty that the agent has about the estimate of the m-parameter. In case the agent does not have information about the opponent, nor any past experience with the particular negotiation domain and is quite uncertain about the most probable outcome, a relatively broad range of utility values around the expected outcome should be assigned a high weight. As a consequence, bids in a rather wide neighborhood of the m-point are equally important for the negotiation and only extreme points (with utilities close to one or zero) do not have to be approximated very accurately. Given a relatively large uncertainty, we propose to use a polynomial function of the second order, which is rather flat near the m-point and declines closer to the extreme utilities (see figure 2a). The corresponding weighting function ψ then can be computed as follows:

$$\psi(x_1, x_2) = \frac{2}{m} u(x_1, x_2) - \frac{1}{m^2} u^2(x_1, x_2) \tag{8}$$

In the case the agent is reasonably certain about the estimate, for example, when the most probable region of the negotiation outcome is well defined on the basis of domain knowledge, knowledge about the opponent or experience gained in previous negotiations, a weighting function with a stronger differentiation of utilities values can be used. In that case, a Gaussian function that is defined in terms of a maximum point m and spread σ can be used that assigns high weights only to bids with a utility close to the expected outcome m (see figure 2b):

$$\psi(x_1, x_2) = e^{-\frac{(u(x_1, x_2) - m)^2}{\sigma^2}} \tag{9}$$

The spread parameter σ provides an indication of the agent's certainty about expected outcome. In both cases, the m-parameter represents the expected outcome and is a point in the interval (0.5; 1); ψ assigns the m-point the maximal weight of 1.0.

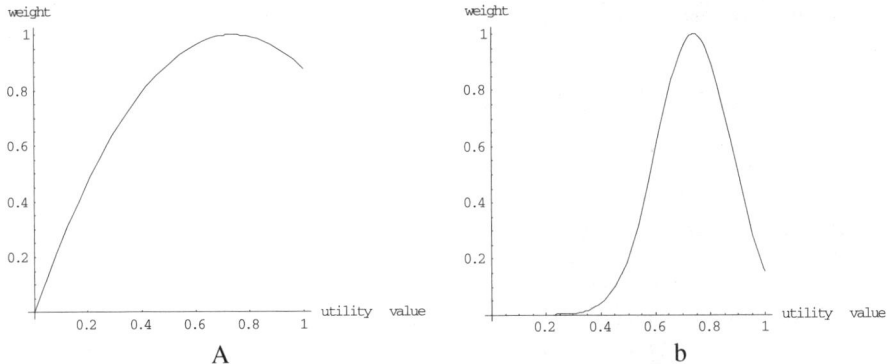

Fig. 2. Example of ψ function for $m=0.74$

In our example, an educated guess of the opponent's profile could be made and therefore a Gaussian weighting function is selected and a value for the "spread" σ needs to be determined. To this end, we use the 3σ rule (or "Empirical rule"), which says that (most likely) 99,7% of all outcomes will be in the interval $(m - 3\sigma, m + 3\sigma)$, which gives us $\sigma = (0.37+0,74)/(2*3) = 0,19$.

3.3   Compute Approximation of Utility Space

Using the weighting function ψ a weighted approximation technique can be defined. The weighted approximation technique proposed here first multiplies each evaluation value with its corresponding weight and then averages the resulting space by integration. In the equation below, a function ω is introduced instead of ψ since the weighting must be normalized over the interval of integration. The range of integration is identical to the range of the integrated issue.[4]

$$ev'_i(x_1) = \int_{\xi_1}^{\xi_2} \omega_2(x_1, x_2) ev_i(x_1, x_2) dx_2 \tag{10}$$

Formally, the weighting function ω is defined by:

$$\omega_2(x_1, x_2) = \frac{\psi(x_1, x_2)}{\int_{\xi_1}^{\xi_2} \psi(x_1, x_2) dx_2} \tag{11}$$

So far we have been assuming a negotiation with only two issues. It is not difficult, however, to generalize the approximation technique to arbitrary numbers of issues. In case a negotiation involves N issues with interdependencies between these issues, and

---

[4] If the issue has discrete values, integration simply means summation over all these values.

evaluation functions $ev_i(x_1,x_2,...,x_N)$ for the ith issue are given, equation 14 generalizes to the equation below:

$$ev'_i(x_i) = \int_V \omega_i(x_1,x_2,...,x_N) ev(x_1,x_2,...,x_N) dV \qquad (12)$$

Here V is a volume of $N-1$ dimensionality build on the dimensions $\{x_1,x_2,...,x_{i-1},x_{i+1},...,x_N\}$. Of course, not all issues have to depend on all others. The approximation technique can be applied sequentially for each evaluation function in the negotiation setup, which involves dependencies between issues.

As an illustration, we apply the weighted averaging technique to our employment contract negotiation. Figure 4 shows the ψ-functions for the original utility space using a polynomial function (8) for the left chart and a Gaussian function (9) for the right one. The flat section in the middle of the left chart represents a rather wide neighborhood of the m-point: this corresponds to the expected outcome and weights in its neighborhood are high. Outside this region the weighting function slowly declines to zero. For the Gaussian function (right chart) we obtain a different picture: the function has high values (close to 1) for the small band of bids with utility values close to the m-point and declines rapidly for the remainder of the utility space.

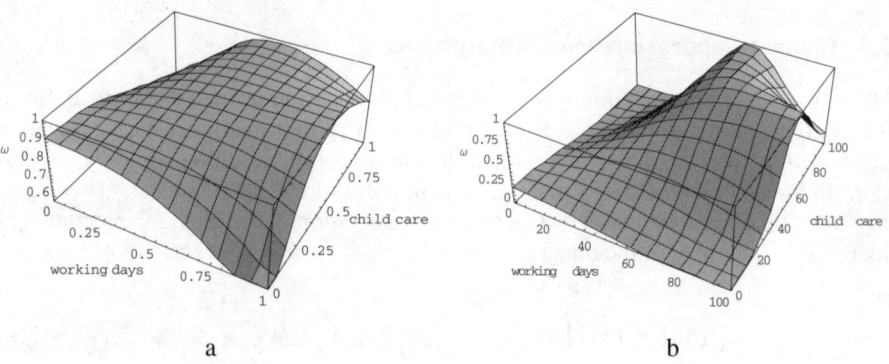

a   b

Fig. 3. Examples of ψ-functions for the employee's utility space: (a) polynomial function with m=0.74; (b) Gaussian function with m=0.74 and σ=0.19

We apply expressions (10) and (11) to the evaluation functions of our employment contract negotiation example to derive an approximated utility space without interdependencies from the original utility space. Figure 5 shows the utility spaces obtained by approximation with a polynomial weighting function (a) and a Gaussian weighting function (b).

The utility spaces obtained by approximation with the polynomial and Gaussian weighting functions have a similar structure. However, the Gaussian weighting function due to its stronger utility discrimination power makes it more precise in the vicinity of the m-point. This is explained in more detail in the next section.

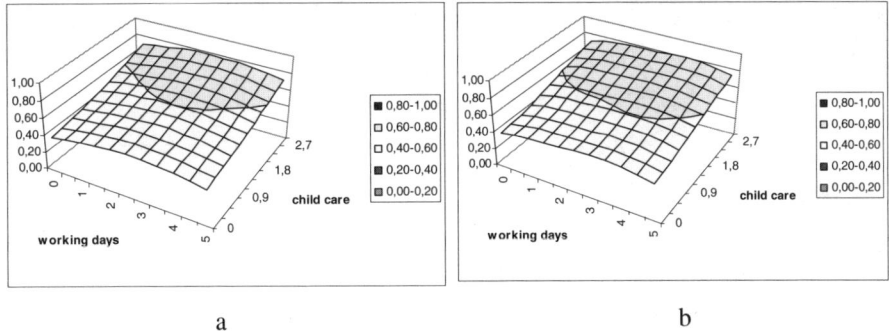

a   b

Fig. 4. The approximation by (a) the weighted averaging method using a polynomial weighting function with m=0.74 and (b) the Gaussian weighting function with m=0.74, sigma=0.19

3.4 Analyze Difference δ with Original Utility Space

The technique presented approximates the original utility space and consequently, introduces an error in the utility associated with bids. To obtain a measure for the distance of the values of bids in the original utility space compared to the bids in the approximated utility space, a difference function δ can be defined as follows:

$$\delta(x_1, x_2) = |u(x_1, x_2) - u'(x_1, x_2)| \qquad (13)$$

As is to be expected, the δ-values for the approximation using the Gaussian weighting function shift the utility considerably for some bids. For certain bids in the childcare example, the difference is almost 0.5. However, this only is the case for bids that are unreasonable and are not relevant for reaching a negotiation outcome. In particular, this shift in utility occurs for bids that involve more days of child care than working days. Approximations of the utility of bids that are close to the m-point are very good and close to zero.

To see the effect of the weighted averaging method near the m-point we take a section in the original utility space for the m-point (m=0.74 for our negotiation example). By fixing the utility to 0.74, an expression can be obtained for the value of one of the issues as a function of another one:

$$u(x_1, x_2) = 0.74 \quad \Rightarrow \quad x_1 = f(x_2) \qquad (14)$$

The function thus obtained can be substituted into the expression of the delta function (10). This provides us with the values of δ for a fixed utility as a function of only one of the issues, and can be obtained for other utility values in a similar way.

The δ-values obtained by weighted averaging with the polynomial weighting function and the Gaussian weighting function for utility equal to 0.74 are rather small for both (see Figure 6b), but weighted averaging with a Gaussian function produces smaller approximation errors: it is almost twice as good. For bids with utilities of 0.9 the δ-values (see Figure 6c) rise in comparison with that of 0.7, however, the Gaussian weighting function still gives a better result. For bids with a utility of 0.5 (see Figure 6a) the δ-values are quite similar.

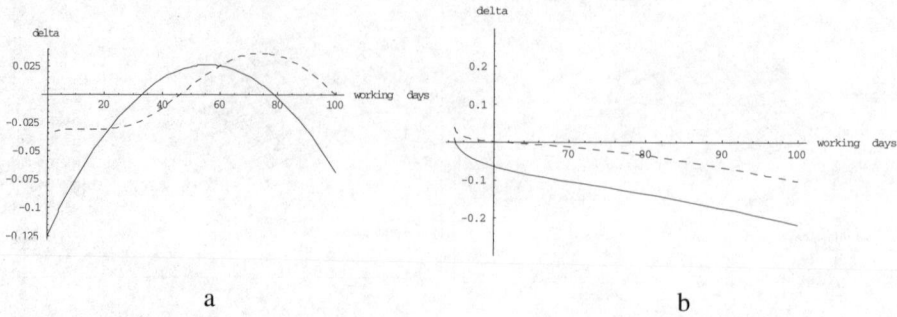

Fig. 5. Graphs depicting values of the δ functions for utility equal to (a) - 0.5, (b) – 0.7 in the original space based on a polynomial weighting function (solid line), and a Gaussian weighting function (dashed line).

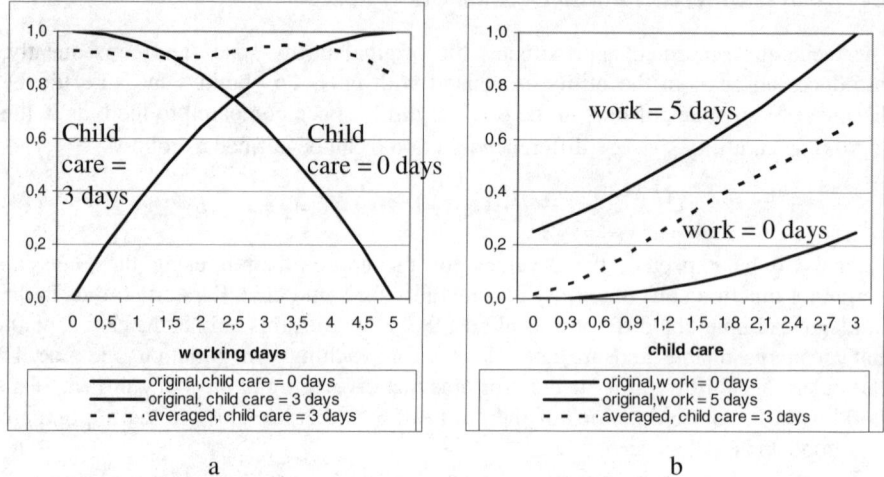

Fig. 6. Original and averaged utility values running through maximum δ-point

In figure 7, a worst case analysis is illustrated. It presents the utilities for extreme values of childcare (figure 7a) and for the number of working days (figure 7b) that run through the maximum δ-value, corresponding to the bid with 0 working days and 3 days of childcare. It shows that the evaluation function associated with 0 days of child care (0 working days) is almost mirrored with respect to the evaluation function associated with 3 days of child care (5 working days). In effect, this shows that our child care example presents a serious test for our approximation method that somehow has to average these differences.

4 Case Study

In this section, a particular negotiation strategy is used to study the bids that an agent will offer during a negotiation using the original as well as the approximated utility space. The negotiation strategy that an agent decides to use should not only fit the agent's personality profile and culture, its experience in general and the current domain and negotiation partner, but it also has to be applicable given the utility space.

A transformation of the utility space will have an effect on the negotiation process as well as on the negotiation outcome. To assess the impact of the weighted averaging approximation method, a negotiation strategy is applied to the employment contract example. Here, we use the ABMP-strategy proposed by Jonker and Treur [4].

The ABMP-strategy determines a bid in two steps: the strategy first (a) determines the target utility for the next bid, and then (b) determines a bid that has that target utility. The (b) part of the strategy is very efficient for independent utility spaces. For the purpose of comparison, however, we can use exhaustive search through the complete utility space to find a bid in the second step, provided that the space is discretized in a suitable manner (using small enough steps). In this way, the first step (a) in the ABMP-strategy followed by the second step (b) using exhaustive search can be applied to the original utility space whereas the original ABMP strategy can be applied to its approximation.

An additional check is incorporated into the strategy when the approximated utility space is used to avoid the risk of accepting bids with low utilities in the original space that have much higher utilities in the approximated space. The bids with high δ-values, that have shifted significantly due to application of the averaging method, can be filtered out in this additional step. The check applies both to a received bid as well as to the computation of a proposal for a new bid. When the agent receives a bid from its opponent, the agent has to calculate the associated original utility as well and compare it with the bid acceptance threshold. When a new bid is send to the opponent, the agent also has to check the associated utility in the original space to ensure that the bid is not worse than the current utility acceptance level. If the bid does not satisfy this condition, then agent has to find an alternative bid with the same utility value but with different issue values. These new values can be selected by systematically going through the bid space using (variants of) equation (12). This procedure guarantees that the agent will never propose or accept a bid which has a very low utility in the original utility space.

This additional check is computationally cheap, involving only a simple calculation using the original utility equations. Still, the computational costs may increase again since an agent may repeatedly need to find new bids that are acceptable. The probability of finding an appropriate bid, however, is high in regions close to the m-point. Adding a check thus still results in significant reduction of the computational costs compared with exhaustive search.

In our experiments, the same profile of the employer was used in the original as well as in the approximated case.

Figure 8a shows the outcome space build up out of the utilities of the employer and employee per bid. Each point on the chart represents one bid. The coordinates of the bid are the utilities of the opponents (x-coordinate is the employer's utility of the bid, y-coordinate is the employee's utility of the bid). The Nash product, see e.g., [8], representing a bid with the highest utilities simultaneously for both opponents of the original utility space equals 0.53 and corresponds to a bid of 5 working days with 2.5 days of childcare, which satisfies the employee's constraints. The Kalai-Smorodinsky solution is 1.5 days of child care and 5 working days. This bid is found by locating a bid on the Pareto-optimal frontier, which is closest to the line drawn from points with utilities of (0; 0) to points with utilities (1; 1), see e.g., [8]. This bid represents a negotiation outcome where both parties get the same utility. Using the ABMP strategy with exhaustive search for both parties, the negotiation lasts 4 rounds (4 bids from each side, the employer starts) and finishes when the employee accepts a bid of 2 days of childcare with 4.5 working days.

Figure 8b presents the result using the original ABMP strategy for both parties, where the profile of the employee has been approximated. The bids in the utility space are now concentrated around the employees original and approximated utility level of 0.7 (the m-point) with some spread towards lower utilities. The Nash product shifts to the bid of 5 working days and 1.5 days of childcare and the Kalai-Smorodinsky solution now is 4 working days and 1.5 days of childcare.

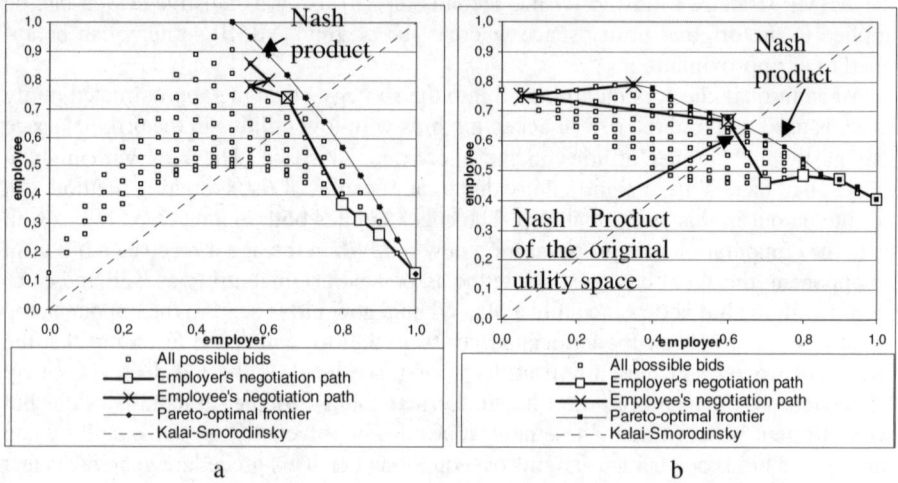

a   b

Fig. 7. Outcome space, optimality criteria, and negotiation paths (a) for the original utility space of the employee, and (b) for the approximated utility space of the employee

The original outcome space and the approximated one are significantly different. However, the difference is not critical for the negotiation itself due to the fact that most of the bids for which the difference is significant will not be used in a negotiation and we basically aim for the efficient solutions (Kalai-Somorindinsky point, and Nash Product). Also note that the bids are shifted only on the vertical axis (employee's utility), because the employer's profile remains the same.

The negotiation performed for the same setup but using the approximated employee's utility space is also finished in 4 rounds as in the previous experiment and also results in a deal of 4.5 working days and 2 days of childcare.

This example shows that the approximation procedure leads to some shifts in the efficient outcomes of the negotiation with respect to Nash and Kalai-Smorodinski. However, it also confirms that these bids and those around them preserve their meaning for the negotiator. Negotiation outcomes for both utility spaces are rather close even though the negotiation paths are different.

5 Conclusion

In this paper we introduced a new approach that allows agents to deal with complex utility functions in a negotiation environment with interdependent issues. Instead of representing the negotiation task as an optimization task for interdependent issues we propose an approximation method to simplify the agent's utility using the observation that in common negotiation settings the expected negotiation outcome is approximately known and the insight that the nature of utility spaces for such common negotiation settings has enough structure to make our approach applicable. The method provides a means to analyze the impact of the approximation on a particular utility space, thereby making it possible to determine up front, whether or not the approximation is useful in any particular domain.

The main advantage of the proposed method is that it enables applicability of a wider range of computational negotiation strategies without introducing a mediator into the negotiation. Available information about the domain and the most probable negotiation outcome can be used to increase the accuracy of the method in the utility area around the expected outcome, which is most important for the negotiation. The additional check that compares the utility of exchanged bids with the utility of the original utility space during a negotiation prevents an agent from accepting low-utility bids in the original space with a high δ (error) in the approximated space. This check in itself is computationally cheap and ensures reasonable negotiation performance.

Robu at al. in [9] propose a graph-based technique to learn complex opponent's profiles. The authors propose an algorithm of exponential computational complexity for searching through a learned utility space of the opponent. The main interest in [9], however, is the scalability of a model for representing an opponent's profile which is different from the approach proposed here to simplify an agent's profile.

In future research, we want to identify in more detail which classes of utility functions can be approximated by weighted averaging sufficiently accurate. Another interesting direction for research would be a modeling experiment with humans, to gain a better understanding of the nature of the complexity of human preferences and the ways in which humans simplify the negotiation task.

References

[1] Bar-Yam, Y., (1997). *Dynamics of complex systems.* Reading, Mass., Addison-Wesley.

[2] Barbuceanu, M., Lo, W.K., (2001), Multi-attribute Utility Theoretic Negotiation for Electronic Commerce. In: Dignum, F, and Cortés, U., (eds.), Agent-Mediated Electronic Commerce III, Lecture Notes in Computer Science, Vol. 2003, Springer – Verlag, pp.15-30.

[3] Binmore, K., (1992), Fun and Games: A Text on Game Theory, D.C. Heath and Company, Lexington.

[4] Jonker, C.M., Treur, J., An Agent Architecture for Multi-Attribute Negotiation. In: B. Nebel (ed.), *Proceedings of the 17th International Joint Conference on AI, IJCAI'01,* 2001, pp. 1195 – 1201.

[5] Klein, M., Faratin, P., Sayama, H., and Bar-Yam, Y., (2002), Negotiating Complex Contracts. In: Autonomous Agents and Multi-Agent Systems, Bologna, Italy: AAAI Press. Paper 125 of the Center for eBusines@MIT. http://ebusiness.mit.edu.

[6] Lai, G., Li, C., Sycara, K., and Giampapa, J., (2004). *Literature Review on Multi-attribute Negotiations.* Technical Report CMU-RI-TR-04-66, Cornegie Mellon University, Robotics Institute.

[7] Pruitt, D.G., (1981), Negotiation Behavior, Academic Press.

[8] Raiffa, H., Richardson, J., and Metcalfe, D., (2002). *Negotiation Analysis: The Science and Art of Collaborative Decision Making*, Cambridge, MA: Belknap Press of Harvard University Press.

[9] Robu, V., Somefun, D.J.A., La Poutre, J.A., (2005). Complex Multi-Issue Negotiations Using Utility Graphs, *Proceedings of the Fourth International Joint Conference on Autonomous Agents and Multi-Agent Systems (AAMAS'05),* Utrecht, The Netherlands, July 2005, pp. 280-287.

[10] Rosenschein, J.S., and Zlotkin, G., (1994). *Rules of Encounter: Designing Conventions for Automated Negotiation Among Computers.* MIT Press.

[11] Sierra, C., Faratin, P., and Jennings, N.R., (1997), A service-oriented negotiation model between autonomous agents. In: Boman, M., and Velde, W. van de (eds), Multi-Agent Rationality: Proceedings of the 8th European Workshop on Modelling Autonomous Agents in Multi-Agent World, MAAMAW'97, Lecture Notes in Artificial Intelligence, Vol.1237, Springer-Verlag, pp. 17 – 35.

[12] Thompson, Leigh, (2000), The Mind and Heart of the Negotiator, Prentice-Hall.

[13] Wang, I-J., Chong, E. K. P., Kulkarni, S. R., (1996), Weighted Averaging and Stochastic Approximation, *Proceeding of the 35th Conference on Decision and Control,* Kobe, Japan, December 1996, pp. 1071-1076.

The Distortion of Cardinal Preferences in Voting

Ariel D. Procaccia and Jeffrey S. Rosenschein

School of Engineering and Computer Science
Hebrew University, Jerusalem, Israel
{arielpro, jeff}@cs.huji.ac.il

Abstract. The theoretical guarantees provided by voting have distinguished it as a prominent method of preference aggregation among autonomous agents. However, unlike humans, agents usually assign each candidate an exact utility, whereas an election is resolved based solely on each voter's linear ordering of candidates. In essence, the agents' cardinal (utility-based) preferences are embedded into the space of ordinal preferences. This often gives rise to a *distortion* in the preferences, and hence in the social welfare of the outcome.

In this paper, we formally define and analyze the concept of distortion. We fully characterize the distortion under different restrictions imposed on agents' cardinal preferences; both possibility and strong impossibility results are established. We also tackle some computational aspects of calculating the distortion. Ultimately, we argue that, whenever voting is applied in a multiagent system, distortion must be a pivotal consideration.

1 Introduction

Social choice mechanisms have long been in the service of computer-scientists, a tool in the quest to reach consensus among agents. The problem is especially acute, as multiple heterogeneous, self-interested agents may (and often do) have conflicting preferences. Voting is a well-studied and well-understood method of preference aggregation, with numerous applications in multiagent systems. In practice, an election is held, and the winning candidate is declared to be the agreed choice; the candidates can be beliefs, joint plans [7], schedules [9], movies [8], or indeed entities of almost any conceivable sort.

A *social choice function*, also known as a *voting protocol*, is used to determine the winner of an election. The agents specify their preferences by reporting a linear order relation on the candidates. Such *ordinal* preferences are only natural when the voters are humans; a human might prefer, say, Ehud Olmert to Benjamin Netanyahu as the prime minister of Israel, but would probably find it impossible to evaluate each candidate precisely in terms of utility.

For computational agents, on the other hand, calculating utilities is a way of (artificial) life. In fact, even in settings where voting is used, it is usually assumed that agents compute the utility of each alternative. For instance, Ghosh et al. [8] describe a movie recommender system that relies on voting; with the guarantees provided by voting schemes, the system is able to generate convincing explanations for different recommendations, and is robust to small errors in the evaluation of the user's preferences. Aspects of these preferences are represented as dimensions, and every movie has

M. Klusch, M. Rovatsos, and T. Payne (Eds.): CIA 2006, LNAI 4149, pp. 317–331, 2006.

a value (or utility) with respect to each dimension. The exact utilities are not taken into account: one movie is preferred over another with respect to a dimension if the former's utility is greater than the latter's.

So in some settings, designers of multiagent systems do away with exact *cardinal* (utility-based) preferences in order to exploit different properties of voting. Essentially, the cardinal preferences of agents are embedded into the space of ordinal preferences over candidates, in a way somewhat reminiscent of embeddings of metric spaces [10]. This embedding of preferences entails a degree of *distortion*, which depends on the properties of the social choice function used in the election.

Informally, we define the distortion of a social choice function to be the maximal ratio between the total utility of the candidate that maximizes social welfare, and the total utility of the candidate that is elected. The maximum is taken over all possible cardinal preference profiles, subject to certain restrictions.

We first explore distortion when the only restriction imposed on cardinal preferences is that all voters have the same sum of utilities for candidates. We establish some strong impossibility results regarding the degree of distortion in this model. Further, we show that these results also hold in an alternative model, where utilities are not constrained, but weighted voting is used. Another impossibility result is computational in nature: we prove that a decision problem associated with the computation of distortion is $\mathcal{NP}$-hard.[1]

The impossibility results mentioned above suggest that distortion is an obstacle that should be taken into account when applying voting in multiagent systems. Nevertheless, they motivate us to examine a model where the preferences of users are more restricted; in this context, we reformulate distortion as *misrepresentation*. We examine the misrepresentation of different well-known social choice functions. In addition, we analyze complexity issues related to calculating misrepresentation.

The paper proceeds as follows. In Section 2 we review some relevant issues in social choice theory. In Section 3, we put forward results concerning the distortion of social choice functions in models where preferences are little constrained. In Section 4, we examine the more specific setting of misrepresentation, especially with respect to important social choice functions. Finally, we give our conclusions in Section 5.

2   Preliminaries

In this section we give a brief introduction to classic social choice theory. Readers are urged to consult [3] for more information.

Let N be the set of voters, $|N| = n$, and let C be the set of candidates, $|C| = m$; we assume that $n \geq 2$ and $m \geq 3$, unless explicitly stated otherwise. We usually use the index i to refer to voters, and the index j to refer to candidates. When we discuss attributes of voters or candidates, the index of a voter usually appears in superscript, whereas the index of a candidate appears in subscript.

Let $\mathcal{L}$ be the set of all linear orders[2] on C. Each voter has ordinal preferences $\succ^i \in \mathcal{L}$. We refer to $\succ = \langle \succ^1, \ldots, \succ^n \rangle \in \mathcal{L}^N$ as an *ordinal preference profile*.

---

[1] Many recent articles have explored other computational aspects of voting; see for example [5,6,12,2].

[2] Binary relations that satisfy antisymmetry, transitivity, and totality.

Given $\succ^i$, let $j_1, \ldots, j_m$ be indices of candidates such that $j_1 \succ^i j_2 \succ^i \cdots \succ^i j_m$; we denote by p_l^i the candidate that voter i ranks in the l'th place, i.e., $p_l^i = j_l$. We denote by l_j^i the position in which candidate j is ranked by voter i; it holds that $p_{l_j^i}^i = j$.

2.1   Social Choice Functions

A *social choice function*, also known as a *voting protocol*,[3] is a function $F : \mathcal{L}^N \to C$, i.e., a mapping from preferences of voters to candidates. We shall consider the following voting protocols:

- *Scoring protocols* are defined by a vector $\alpha = \langle \alpha_1, \ldots, \alpha_m \rangle$.[4] Given $\succ \in \mathcal{L}^N$, the score of candidate j is $s_j = \sum_i \alpha_{l_j^i}$. The candidate who wins the election is $F(\succ) = \text{argmax}_j s_j$. Some of the well-known scoring protocols are:
  - *Borda*: $\alpha = \langle m - 1, m - 2, \ldots, 0 \rangle$.
  - *Plurality*: $\alpha = \langle 1, 0, \ldots, 0 \rangle$.
  - *Veto*: $\alpha = \langle 1, \ldots, 1, 0 \rangle$.
  Some of our results (in particular regarding complexity) concentrate on scoring protocols, as these voting protocols can be concisely represented by the vector α.
- *Copeland*: we say that candidate j beats j' in a pairwise election if $|\{i \in N : l_j^i < l_{j'}^i\}| > n/2$. The score s_j of candidate j is the number of candidates that j beats in pairwise elections, and $\text{Copeland}(\succ) = \text{argmax}_j s_j$.
- *Maximin*: the maximin score of candidate j is the candidate's worst performance in a pairwise election: $s_j = \min_{j'} |\{i \in N : l_j^i < l_{j'}^i\}|$, and $\text{Maximin}(\succ) = \text{argmax}_j s_j$.
- *Single Transferable Vote* (STV): the election proceeds in rounds (a total of $m - 1$ rounds); in each round, the candidate with the fewest votes ranking him first among the remaining candidates is eliminated.
- *Plurality with Runoff*: similar to STV, but there are only two rounds. After the first round, only the two candidates that maximize $|\{i \in N : l_j^i = 1\}|$ survive. In the second round, a pairwise election is held between these two candidates.
- *Bucklin*: for any candidate j and $l \in \{1, \ldots, m\}$, let $B_{j,l} = \{i \in N : l_j^i \leq l\}$. It holds that $\text{Bucklin}(\succ) = \text{argmin}_j (\min\{l : |B_{j,l}| > n/2\})$.

It is also to possible to consider weighted voting. A voter i with weight K and preferences $\succ^i$ is taken into account as K voters, each with preferences $\succ^i$.

2.2   Properties of Social Choice Functions

In this subsection we formulate several criteria that are commonly used to compare social choice functions.

- Majority criterion: $[\exists j \in C \text{ s.t. } |\{i \in N : l_j^i = 1\}| > n/2] \Rightarrow F(\succ) = j$.
- Participation: if $F(\succ) = j$ and one adds a ballot that ranks j above j', then the winner is not j' (it is better to vote honestly than not to vote at all).

---

[3] We use the two terms interchangeably.

[4] More formally, a scoring protocol is defined by a sequence of such vectors, one for each value of m, but we abandon this formulation for clarity's sake.

- Monotonicity: If $F(\succ) = j$, and $\succ'$ is an ordinal preference profile where some of the voters rank j higher compared to $\succ$ (but none rank j lower), then $F(\succ') = j$.
- Consistency: if the electorate is partitioned in two and a candidate wins in both parts, then he wins overall.

3 Distortion of General Cardinal Preferences

Let $\mathcal{U} = (\mathbb{N} \cup \{0\})^C$ be the set of all possible cardinal preferences on C. Each voter is associated with preferences in $\mathcal{U}$, $\boldsymbol{u}^i = \langle u_1^i, \ldots, u_j^i \rangle$, where $u_j^i \in \mathbb{N} \cup \{0\}$ is voter i's utility for candidate j; denote $u_j = \sum_i u_j^i$, and denote the *cardinal preference profile* by $\boldsymbol{u} = \langle \boldsymbol{u}^1, \ldots, \boldsymbol{u}^n \rangle \in \mathcal{U}^N$.

When voting is used to aggregate preferences, agents' cardinal preferences are translated into ordinal preferences in the natural way.

Definition 1. *Let $\boldsymbol{u} \in \mathcal{U}^N$ and $\succ \in \mathcal{L}^N$. $\succ$ is derived from $\boldsymbol{u}$ iff both of the following conditions hold:*

1. $\forall i \in N, j_1, j_2 \in C: u_{j_1}^i > u_{j_2}^i \Rightarrow j_1 \succ^i j_2$.
2. $\forall i \in N, j_1, j_2 \in C: u_{j_1}^i = u_{j_2}^i \Rightarrow j_1 \succ^i j_2 \vee j_2 \succ^i j_1$, but not both.

Definition 2. *Let F be a social choice function. The* distortion *of F with n voters and m candidates, denoted $\Delta_m^n(F)$, is $\max \frac{\max_j u_j}{u_{F(\succ)}}$, where the first maximum is taken over all $\boldsymbol{u} \in \mathcal{U}^N$ and $\succ \in \mathcal{L}^N$, under the restrictions that there exists $K \in \mathbb{N}$ such that for all voters i, $\sum_j u_j^i = K \geq 1$, and $\succ$ is derived from $\boldsymbol{u}$. It is additionally assumed that in case several candidates are tied in the election, the one that minimizes social welfare is elected.[5] If the denominator is 0 but the numerator is not 0, we write $\Delta_m^n(F) = \infty$, where $\infty > k$ for all $k \in \mathbb{N}$.*

Less formally, the distortion of F with n voters and m candidates is the worst-case ratio between the utility of the candidate that maximizes social welfare and the winner according to F, when one considers all possible cardinal preference profiles $\boldsymbol{u}$ with fixed utility-sum for each voter, and derived ordinal preference profiles $\succ$.

Remark 1. Clearly, when one eschews the assumption that $\sum_j u_j^i = K$ for all i, it is not possible to bound the distortion even when a small number of voters and candidates is considered. For example, assume $n = 3$ and $m = 2$, and F is the plurality protocol. Let $u_1^1 = c$ for some $c > 2$, $u_2^1 = 0$, $u_1^2 = u_1^3 = 0$, $u_2^2 = u_2^3 = 1$. The derived ordinal preference profile is $1 \succ^1 2, 2 \succ^2 1, 2 \succ^3 1$, therefore candidate 2 is chosen by the plurality protocol. The distortion is $c/2$.

The following proposition is a strong impossibility result; it implies that no voting protocol is optimal in terms of distortion, even for very small values of n and m.

Proposition 1. *Let F be a social choice function. Then $\Delta_2^3(F) > 1$.*

---

[5] This assumption is justified as we engage here in a *worst-case* analysis.

Proof. Consider the cardinal utility profile $u_1^1 = 3$, $u_2^1 = 2$, $u_1^2 = 0$, $u_2^2 = 5$, $u_1^3 = 3$, $u_2^3 = 2$. The only derived ordinal preference profile is $1 \succ^1 2$, $2 \succ^2 1$, $1 \succ^3 2$. Since $u_1 < u_2$, if $F(\succ) = 1$ then we are done. Otherwise, suppose $F(\succ) = 2$, and consider the cardinal preference profile $u_1^1 = 5$, $u_2^1 = 0$, $u_1^2 = 0$, $u_2^2 = 5$, $u_1^3 = 5$, $u_2^3 = 0$. Again, the only derived preference profile is $\succ$, but now $u_1 > u_2$. $\square$

Definition 3. *Let F be a social choice function. We say that F has* unbounded distortion *if there exists $m \in \mathbb{N}$ such that for all $k \in \mathbb{N}$, $\Delta_m^n(F) > k$ for infinitely many values of n.*

Proposition 2. *Let F be a scoring protocol with*

$$\alpha_2 \geq \frac{1}{m-1} \sum_{l \neq 2} \alpha_l \tag{1}$$

for some m. Then F has unbounded distortion.

Proof. Let n such that $m - 1$ divides n. Consider the profile $u \in \mathcal{U}^N$ where for every candidate $j \neq 1$, exactly $n/(m-1)$ voters i have utility $u_j^i = 1$ and $u_{j'}^i = 0$ for every $j' \neq j$. Let $\succ$ be a derived ordinal preference profile; define for all

$$P_{j,l} = \{i \in N : p_l^i = j\}.$$

It must hold that for all $j \neq 1$, $|P_{j,1}| = n/(m-1)$. Moreover, it is possible to derive an ordinal preference profile such that for all $j \neq 1$ and $l \neq 2$, $|P_{j,l}| = n/(m-1)$, and with respect to candidate 1, $|P_{1,2}| = n$. Without loss of generality, let $\succ$ be such a profile. The score of candidate 1 in this election is $n\alpha_2$, and the score of every other candidate is $\frac{n}{m-1} \sum_{l \neq 2} \alpha_l$. Further, it holds that $u_1 = 0$, and $u_j = n/(m-1)$ for all $j \neq 1$. By Equation (1) and the assumption that in case of a tie the candidate that minimizes utility wins, it follows that candidate 1 wins the election, but for any other candidate, say candidate 2, $\frac{u_2}{u_1} = \frac{n/(m-1)}{0}$. Thus, the distortion of F is unbounded. $\square$

It follows from Proposition 1 that in many reasonable scoring protocols, the distortion is unbounded. In particular:

Corollary 1. *The Borda and Veto Protocols have unbounded distortion.*

3.1   An Alternative Model

So far, we have analyzed the distortion with respect to cardinal preference profiles that satisfy, for all voters, i: $\sum_j u_j^i = K$. If one allows for weighted voting, it is possible to obtain a generalization of this model. Indeed, let $K^i = \sum_j u_j^i$, possibly $K^i \neq K^{i'}$ for $i \neq i'$. However, when an election is held based on a derived ordinal preference profile $\succ$, voter i has weight K^i. The definition of distortion can be reformulated in the obvious way to apply to this model; we denote the worst-case ratio between the candidate that maximizes utility and the one that wins the weighted election governed by F, when different K^i are allowed, by $\widehat{\Delta}_m^n(F)$.

The next proposition shows that the two models are equivalent with respect to distortion.

Proposition 3. *For all social choice functions F, n_1 and m, $\Delta_m^{n_1}(F) \leq \widetilde{\Delta}_m^{n_1}(F)$, and there exists $n_2 \geq n_1$ such that $\widetilde{\Delta}_m^{n_1}(F) \leq \Delta_m^{n_2}(F)$.*

Proof. For the first inequality, let $n_1, m \in \mathbb{N}$. Let $u \in \mathcal{U}^N$ and $\succ \in \mathcal{L}^N$ that maximize, in the first model, the ratio $\frac{\max_j u_j}{u_{F(\succ)}}$, subject to: for all i, $\sum_j u_j^i = K$, and $\succ$ is derived from u. In the second model, $F(\succ)$ is as before, since all voters have identical weights in the election (K). Therefore $\frac{\max_j u_j}{u_{F(\succ)}}$ in the second model is at least as large as in the first.

Regarding the second inequality, let $n_1, m \in \mathbb{N}$, and let $\widetilde{u} \in \mathcal{U}^N$ and a derived $\widetilde{\succ} \in \mathcal{L}^N$ that maximize the ratio $\frac{\max_j \widetilde{u}_j}{u_{F(\widetilde{\succ})}}$ (with weighted voting). $\widetilde{u}$ may not be a valid cardinal preference profile in the first model, but we construct a profile that is. Let $n_2 = \sum_i K^i$; for each one of the original voters $\widetilde{i} = 1, \ldots, n_1$, consider $K^{\widetilde{i}}$ voters i whose utility is $u_j^i = u_j^{\widetilde{i}} \cdot \prod_{\widetilde{i}' \neq \widetilde{i}} K^{\widetilde{i}'}$. Let $K = \prod_{\widetilde{i}} K^{\widetilde{i}}$; it holds that for all i, $\sum_j u_j^i = K$, hence u is valid in the first model. Further, for every candidate j it holds that $u_j = K \cdot \widetilde{u}_j$. Notice that $\widetilde{\succ}^{\widetilde{i}}$ can be derived from u^i for every voter i that corresponds to $\widetilde{i}$; denote the ordinal preference profile that is obtained by replicating $\succ^{\widetilde{i}}$ $K^{\widetilde{i}}$ times, once for each voter that corresponds to $\widetilde{i}$, by $\succ$. In the new election, we have $K^{\widetilde{i}}$ voters casting identical ballots to the one cast by voter $\widetilde{i}$, and this voter had weight $K^{\widetilde{i}}$ in the original election. Therefore, $F(\succ)$ with weighted voting is identical to $F(\succ)$ without. To conclude, we have obtained that:

$$\frac{\max_j u_j}{u_{F(\succ)}} = \frac{K \max_j \widetilde{u}_j}{K \widetilde{u}_{F(\widetilde{\succ})}} = \frac{\max_j \widetilde{u}_j}{\widetilde{u}_{F(\widetilde{\succ})}}. \qquad \square$$

Corollary 2. *Let F be a social choice function. Then $\widetilde{\Delta}_2^3(F) > 1$.*

Corollary 3. *Let F be a social choice function. F has unbounded distortion in the first model iff F has unbounded distortion in the second model.*

3.2 Complexity Issues

The existence of an algorithm that efficiently computes (or approximates) the distortion of a given voting protocol is, clearly, a basic prerequisite for comparing voting protocols in terms of distortion. As we shall see in Subsection 4.1, one of the building blocks of such an algorithm is a procedure that efficiently decides the following problem:

Definition 4. *In the MIN-SCORE-MAX-UTIL (MSMU) problem, we are given the number of voters n, the number of candidates m, a scoring protocol F defined by parameters $\alpha_1, \ldots, \alpha_m$, for each voter i, a sequence of nonnegative integers $b^i = \langle b_1^i, \ldots, b_m^i \rangle$, and $y, z \in \mathbb{N}$. We are asked whether there are n permutations on C, $\pi^1, \ldots, \pi^n$, such that for the cardinal preference profile u defined by $u_j^i = b_{\pi^i(j)}^i$ and a derived ordinal preference profile $\succ$, it holds that $u_1 \geq y$ but $s_1 \leq z$.*

To put it less formally, we are given a scoring protocol, and for each voter, a sequence of m numbers. We know what the utilities of each voter are in general, but it is still left to determine how each voter assigns these utilities to candidates. Essentially, this is equivalent to choosing an ordinal preference relation for each voter, and then assigning the maximal element in b^i to p_1^i, the second largest element to p_2^i, etc. — and this is the approach that will later become relevant.

Remark 2. It is not assumed here that $\sum_l b_l^i = K$ for all i.

Proposition 4. *MSMU is $\mathcal{NP}$-complete.*

Proof. Reduction from KNAPSACK; omitted due to space constraints.

4 Misrepresentation

Impossibility results regarding the general model, manifested above as Propositions 1, 2, and (to a lesser degree) 4, motivate us to impose restrictions on agents' possible cardinal preference profiles. In this section, we examine a slight variation on the concept of distortion that allows for possibility results.

Monroe [11] defines a measure of *misrepresentation*; using our notations, voter i's misrepresentation with respect to candidate j is $\mu_j^i = l_j^i - 1$. To put it differently, if voter i ranks candidate j first, then i's misrepresentation w.r.t. to j is 0, the misrepresentation w.r.t. the second highest-ranked candidate is 1, and so forth. The misrepresentation of candidate j is $\mu_j = \sum_i \mu_j^i$.

Definition 5. *Let F be a social choice function. The* misrepresentation *of F with n voters and m candidates, denoted $\mu_m^n(F)$, is $\max \frac{\mu_{F(\succ)}}{\min_j \mu_j}$, where the maximum is taken over all ordinal preference profiles $\succ^i$ and their associated misrepresentation values. If several candidates are tied in an election, the one that maximizes misrepresentation is elected.*

Misrepresentation values can, of course, be interpreted as cardinal preferences (e.g., $u_j^i = m - \mu_j^i - 1$), albeit restricted ones: a voter's ordinal preference relation $\succ^i$ fixes a (perfect) matching between candidates and the utilities $0, 1, \ldots, m - 1$.[6] Consequently, the misrepresentation of a social choice function F can be easily reformulated as distortion. In fact, similar results can be obtained, but the latter formulation favors candidates that are ranked last by few voters, whereas the former formulation rewards candidates that are placed first by many voters.

When is misrepresentation an issue? The following scenario provides a compelling, albeit somewhat artificial, example. Consider the meeting scheduling problem discussed in [9]: scheduling agents schedule meetings on behalf of their associated users, based on given user preferences; a winning schedule is decided in an election. Say three possible schedules are being voted on. These schedules, being fair, conflict with at most two of the requirements specified by any user. In other words, a user's misrepresentation with respect to a certain schedule is 0 if there are no conflicts, 1 if there is a single

---

[6] Unlike the general model, in the current setting there is a unique derivation of misrepresentation values from ordinal preferences, and vice versa.

conflict, and 2 if there are two conflicts.[7] In this case, having no conflicts at all is vastly superior to having at least one conflict, as even one conflict may prevent a user from attending a meeting. As noted above, this issue is taken into account in the calculation of misrepresentation — emphasis is placed on candidates that were often ranked first.

Proposition 1 stated that there is no social choice function with distortion 1. Clearly this is not the case here:

Proposition 5. *Let* $m \in \mathbb{N}$, *and let* F *be a scoring protocol with parameters* $\alpha_1 \geq \alpha_2 \geq \ldots \geq \alpha_m$. *Then* $\mu_m^n(F) = 1$ *for all* n *iff there exist* a *and* b *such that* $\alpha_l = -a \cdot l + b$ *for all* $l = 1, \ldots, m$.

Proof. Assume first that there exist a and b such that $\alpha_l = -a \cdot l + b$ for all $l = 1, \ldots, m$, and let $n \in \mathbb{N}$, $\succ \in \mathcal{L}^N$. Candidate j's score is:

$$\sum_i \alpha_{l_j^i} = \sum_i [-a \cdot l_j^i + b] = \sum_i [-a(\mu_j^i + 1) + b] = n[b - a] - a \sum_i \mu_j^i,$$

so the candidate that maximizes the score is the one that minimizes misrepresentation.

In the other direction, assume there do not exist a and b such that $\alpha_l = -a \cdot l + b$ for all $l = 1, \ldots, m$. It follows that there exist l_0, a and a' such that $a \neq a'$, and $\alpha_1 - \alpha_2 = a$ but $\alpha_1 - \alpha_{l_0} = a'(l_0 - 1)$, and $a, a' > 0$.[8] Assume w.l.o.g. that $a > a'$. Consider the following ballot: n' voters vote $2 \succ^i 1 \succ^i \ldots$, $n' - x$ voters rank $1 \succ^i 2 \succ^i \ldots$, and y voters cast their ballots in a way that $p_1^i = 1$, $p_{l_0}^i = 2$, for some $x, y \in \mathbb{N}$ (we have that $n = 2n' - x + y$). When comparing the scores of candidates 2 and 1, we have:

$$s_2 - s_1 = xa - ya'(l_0 - 1). \tag{2}$$

Further, it holds that:

$$\mu_2 - \mu_1 = -x + y(l_0 - 1). \tag{3}$$

It is sufficient to show that it is possible to make candidate 2 win the election, and in particular guarantee that candidate 2's score be higher than 1's, but simultaneously ensure that candidate 2's misrepresentation be higher than 1's. Indeed, by Equations (2) and (3) both conditions are satisfied whenever

$$\frac{x}{l_0 - 1} < y < \frac{a}{a'} \cdot \frac{x}{l_0 - 1}. \tag{4}$$

Choosing $x > 3(l_0 - 1)\frac{a'}{a-a'}$, it is possible to choose y that satisfies Equation (4). Moreover, it is clearly now possible to choose n' large enough so as to guarantee that candidate 2 wins the election, since for all candidates $j \neq 1, 2$, there are at most y voters such that $p_2^i = j$, and $\alpha_1 > \alpha_l$ for all $l \neq 1$.   □

Corollary 4. *For all* n, m, $\mu_m^n(Borda) = 1$.

---

[7] We implicitly assume that for each user there is one schedule with no conflicts, one with a single conflict, and one with two conflicts.

[8] It is safe to assume that $a > 0$ (and therefore $a' > 0$), because if $\alpha_1 = \alpha_2$ then the result is obvious.

Corollary 4 establishes the optimality of the Borda protocol in terms of misrepresentation. Unfortunately, this protocol is notoriously easy to manipulate, and is plagued by other disadvantages. Therefore, it is worthwhile to explore the misrepresentation of other protocols.

The concept of unbounded misrepresentation can be defined analogously to Definition 3. In the framework of misrepresentation, we have the following proposition.

Proposition 6. *Let F be a scoring protocol with parameters $\alpha_1 \geq \alpha_2 \geq \ldots \geq \alpha_m$. Then F has unbounded misrepresentation iff $\alpha_1 > \alpha_2$.*

Proof. Suppose first that $\alpha_1 > \alpha_2$. Let $n, m \in \mathbb{N}$, $\succ \in \mathcal{L}^N$, and assume w.l.o.g. that $\text{argmin}_j \mu_j = 1$ and $F(\succ) = 2$. Let $k = |\{i \in N : l_1^i = 1\}|$ be the number of voters that ranked candidate 1 first. The number of points candidate 2 received is at most $s_2 \leq (n - k)\alpha_1 + k\alpha_2$, and the number of points candidate 1 received is at least $s_1 \geq k\alpha_1$. We have:

$$(n - k)\alpha_1 + k\alpha_2 \geq s_2 \geq s_1 \geq k\alpha_1.$$

Therefore, $k \leq n\frac{\alpha_1}{2\alpha_1 - \alpha_2}$; this implies that $\mu_1 \geq n\frac{\alpha_1 - \alpha_2}{2\alpha_1 - \alpha_2}$. As $\mu_2 \leq n(m - 1)$, we have that

$$\frac{\mu_2}{\mu_1} \leq \frac{n(m - 1)}{n\frac{\alpha_1 - \alpha_2}{2\alpha_1 - \alpha_2}} = \frac{(m - 1)(2\alpha_1 - \alpha_2)}{\alpha_1 - \alpha_2}.$$

For a fixed m, this expression is a constant, even as n grows.

In the other direction, suppose $\alpha_1 = \alpha_2$, and consider $\succ \in \mathcal{L}^N$ where for all voters i, $1 \succ^i 2 \succ^i \cdots$. It holds that $\mu_1 = 0$, $\mu_2 = n$. We can assume w.l.o.g. that $F(\succ) = 2$, since in case of a tie a candidate that maximizes misrepresentation is elected, hence the winner must have misrepresentation at least as high as μ_2. The proposition follows from the fact that $\frac{\mu_2}{\mu_1} = \infty$. □

Corollary 5. *The Veto protocol has unbounded misrepresentation.*

Remark 3. Corollary 5 implies that the Participation, Monotonicity, and Consistency properties (even together) do not guarantee that a voting protocol has bounded misrepresentation, as the Veto protocol satisfies all three properties.

Proposition 7. *For all n, m, $\mu_m^n(Plurality) = \mu_m^n(Plurality\ with\ Runoff) = m - 1$.*

Proof. Omitted due to space constraints.

Proposition 8. *For all n, m, $\mu_m^n(Copeland) \leq m - 1$.*

Proof. Let $\succ \in \mathcal{L}^N$; w.l.o.g. suppose $\text{argmin}_j u_j = 1$ and $\text{Copeland}(\succ) = 2$. Additionally, denote by C' the set of candidates that candidate 2 beats in a pairwise election, $|C'| = k$. For each candidate $j \in C'$, at least $\lceil n/2 \rceil$ voters have $l_2^i < l_j^i$. Let $C^i = \{j \in C : l_2^i < l_j^i\}$; for all i, $l_2^i = m - |C^i|$. It holds that $\sum_i |C^i| \geq k\lceil n/2 \rceil$, but this implies that:

$$\mu_2 = \sum_i \mu_2^i = \sum_i (l_2^i - 1) = \sum_i [(m - 1) - |C^i|] \leq n(m - 1) - k\lceil n/2 \rceil.$$

We distinguish two cases:

Case 1: $k = m$. In this case, candidate 1 has not won the pairwise election against 2, and thus there are at least $\lceil n/2 \rceil$ voters i such that $l_2^i < l_1^i$. This implies that $\mu_1 \geq \lceil n/2 \rceil$, and hence $\frac{\mu_2}{\mu_1} \leq \frac{n(m-1)-m\lceil n/2 \rceil}{\lceil n/2 \rceil} \leq m - 2$.

Case 2: $k \leq m - 1$. Candidate 1 won at most k pairwise elections. In each pairwise election that 1 did not win against candidate j, at least $\lceil n/2 \rceil$ voters voted $l_j^i < l_1^i$. By the same reasoning as before, $\mu_1 \geq (m - k)\lceil n/2 \rceil$. Therefore,

$$\frac{\mu_2}{\mu_1} \leq \frac{n(m-1) - k\lceil n/2 \rceil}{(m-k)\lceil n/2 \rceil} \leq \frac{2m - k - 2}{m - k}. \tag{5}$$

The ratio in Equation (5) on the right is monotonic increasing as a function of k when $1 \leq k \leq m - 1$, and thus is bounded by $m - 1$. □

Proposition 9. *For all n, m, $\mu_m^n(Bucklin) \leq m$.*

Proof. Let $\succ \in \mathcal{L}^N$; assume w.l.o.g. that $\mathrm{argmin}_j u_j = 1$, and $Bucklin(\succ) = 2$. Let $l_0 = \min\{l \in \{1, \ldots, m\} : \exists j \text{ s.t. } B_{j,l} > n/2\}$. At least $\lceil n/2 \rceil$ voters i have $p_l^i = 2$ for $l \leq l_0$. Therefore, $\mu_2 \leq \lceil n/2 \rceil(l_0 - 1) + \lfloor n/2 \rfloor(m - 1)$. We now examine two cases.

Case 1: $l_0 = 1$. It cannot be the case that $B_{2,1} > n/2$ and $B_{1,1} > n/2$ simultaneously. Therefore, it must be true that at least $\lceil n/2 \rceil$ voters i have $l_1^i \geq 2$, and hence $\mu_1 \geq \lceil n/2 \rceil$. We have that $\frac{\mu_2}{\mu_1} \leq m - 1$.

Case 2: $l_0 \geq 2$. At most $\lfloor n/2 \rfloor$ voters i have $l_1^i \leq l_0 - 1$, therefore $\mu_1 \geq \lceil n/2 \rceil(l_0 - 1)$. It holds that

$$\frac{\mu_2}{\mu_1} \leq \frac{\lceil n/2 \rceil(l_0 - 1) + \lfloor n/2 \rfloor(m - 1)}{\lceil n/2 \rceil(l_0 - 1)}.$$

The ratio is maximized when $l_0 = 2$; it follows that $\frac{\mu_2}{\mu_1} \leq m$. □

Proposition 10. *For all n, m, $\mu_m^n(Maximin) \leq \frac{2}{\sqrt{5}-1}(m - 1) \approx 1.62(m - 1)$.*

Proof. Let $\succ \in \mathcal{L}^N$. Assume w.l.o.g. that $\mathrm{argmin}_j u_j = 1$, and $Maximin(\succ) = 2$. Additionally, suppose that candidate 2's Maximin score is k. With foresight, we denote $c = \frac{3-\sqrt{5}}{2}$. We distinguish two cases:

Case 1: $k > cn$. At least cn voters i have $l_2^i < l_1^i$. In the worst case, $(1 - c)n$ voters i vote $l_1^i = 1, l_2^i = m$, and cn voters have $l_2^i = 1$ and $l_1^i = 2$. Therefore, in this case,

$$\frac{\mu_2}{\mu_1} \leq \frac{(1 - c)}{c}(m - 1) \approx 1.62(m - 1).$$

Case 2: $k \leq cn$. There exists a candidate, w.l.o.g. candidate 3, s.t. at most k voters i have $l_1^i < l_3^i$, i.e., at least $(1 - c)n$ voters do not rank 1 first. Since $\mu_2 \leq n(m - 1)$, it holds that

$$\frac{\mu_2}{\mu_1} \leq \frac{n(m - 1)}{(1 - c)n} = \frac{1}{1 - c}(m - 1) \approx 1.62(m - 1).$$

This concludes the proof.[9]   □

---

[9] c was chosen such that $\frac{1-c}{c} = \frac{1}{1-c}$.

Algorithm 1

```
 1: procedure MIN-MISREP(n, m, α, y)
 2:     for l ← 0, y do                                          ▷ Initialization
 3:         a_{0,l} ← 0
 4:     end for
 5:     for k ← 1, n do
 6:         for l ← 0, y do
 7:             q ← min{l, m − 1}
 8:             a_{k,l} ← min_{p=0,...,q}(a_{k−1,l−p} + α_{p+1})    ▷ Induces rankings for candidate 1
 9:         end for
10:     end for
11:     return a_{n,b}
12: end procedure
```

Proposition 11. *For all n, m, $\mu_m^n(STV) \leq \frac{3}{2}(m − 1)$.*

Proof. Omitted due to space constraints.

Remark 4. It is easy to show that if F is a voting protocol that satisfies the majority criterion, then $\mu_m^n(F) \leq 2(m − 1)$.

4.1   Complexity Issues

In this subsection we address complexity issues related to calculating misrepresentation. We begin by reformulating the MSMU problem, presented in Section 3, in the context of misrepresentation.

Definition 6. *In the* MIN-SCORE-MIN-MISREPRESENTATION *(MSMM) problem, we are given the number of voters n, the number of candidates m, a scoring protocol F defined by parameters $\alpha = \langle \alpha_1, \ldots, \alpha_m \rangle$, and $y, z \in \mathbb{N}$. We are asked whether there exists $\succ \in \mathcal{L}^N$ such that it holds that $\mu_1 \leq y$ but $s_1 \leq z$.*

Unlike the general formulation of the problem, here we have:

Lemma 1. *MSMM can be decided in time polynomial in n and m.*

Proof. We describe a dynamic programming algorithm MIN-MISREP, given as Algorithm 1. The algorithm keeps a matrix $A = (a_{kl})_{k \in \{0,\ldots,n\}, l \in \{0,\ldots,y\}}$; entry a_{kl} is the minimal score candidate 1 may have under the constraints that k voters have cast their vote, and $\mu_1 \leq l$.

The correctness of the algorithm can be easily proven by induction on k. As $y = O(nm)$, the running time of the algorithm is $O(n^2 m^2)$. Now, the given instance of MSMM is a "yes" instance iff the output of MIN-MISREP is at most z: $a_{n,y} \leq z$.   □

We now consider the following problem:

Definition 7. *In the* LOSER-WITH-MIN-MISREPRESENTATION *(LWMM) problem, we are given the number of voters n, the number of candidates m, a scoring protocol F defined by parameters $\alpha_1, \ldots, \alpha_m$, and $y \in \mathbb{N}$. We are asked whether there exists $\succ \in \mathcal{L}^N$ such that it holds that $\mu_1 \leq y$ but candidate 1 loses the election.*

Lemma 2. *LWMM can be decided in time polynomial in n and m.*

Proof. Algorithm 1 can easily be adapted to return candidate 1's minimal score, under the former constraint that $\mu_1 \leq y$, and the additional constraint that exactly n' voters, $0 \leq n' \leq n$, satisfy $l_1^i = 1$. This can be accomplished, for example, by running MIN-MISREP once for each value of n', and assuming that n' voters have already cast their vote (ranking candidate 1 first), whereas the remaining $n - n'$ cast their vote according to the algorithm.

For each value of n', it is possible to assume the remaining voters rank candidate 2 as high as possible, i.e., candidate 2 receives $s_2 = (n - n')\alpha_1 + n'\alpha_2$ points. Clearly, there exists a value of n' such that $s_2 \geq s_1$ iff the given instance of LWMM is a "yes" instance.[10]   □

Given n, m, and α, we have shown so far that it is possible to find rankings $l_1^{i\ ALG}$ for candidate 1, such that the associated misrepresentation of candidate 1 satisfies:

$$\mu_1^{ALG} = \min\{\mu :\ \exists \succ \in \mathcal{L}^N\ \text{s.t.}\ \mu_1 = \mu \wedge \text{candidate 1 loses the election}\}.$$

Ultimately, we would like to be able to compute $\mu(F) = \max \frac{\mu_F(\succ)}{\min_j \mu_j}$; let $\succ^* \in \mathcal{L}^N$ that maximizes this ratio, let μ_j^* be the associated total misrepresentation values of candidates, s_j^* be the associated scores, and $l_j^{i\ *}$ be the associated rankings; assume w.l.o.g. that $\arg\min_j u_j^* = 1$, and $F(\succ^*) = 2$.

Definition 8. *Let F be a scoring protocol. F has the* popular loser property *iff the rankings $l_1^{i\ ALG}$ are identical to the rankings $l_1^{i\ *}$, up to the order of the voters.*

Definition 9. *Let F be a scoring protocol. F has the* even match property *iff, given s_1^*, the rankings $l_2^{i\ *}$ are the ones that maximize μ_2^*, under the constraint $s_2^* \geq s_1^*$.*

In other words, a scoring protocol has the popular loser property if any ordinal preference profile such that candidate 1 has maximal misrepresentation, under the constraint that candidate 1 is not the winner, is optimal in the sense that candidate 1's ranking by voters is identical to candidate 1's ranking in the preference profile that maximizes misrepresentation. A scoring protocol has the even match property if, once the above rankings for candidate 1 are known, in order to find the misrepresentation of the protocol it is sufficient to find rankings for candidate 2 that maximize candidate 2's misrepresentation, while guaranteeing that 2 has a higher score than 1.

Certainly, if F has both properties, then Lemma 2 is a step forward towards calculating the misrepresentation of F. But are there protocols that possess both properties?

Example 1. The Plurality and Veto protocols have the popular loser property and the even match property.

If so, some important protocols possess the properties. Characterizing more fully the protocols that possess both properties remains an open question.

---

[10] It is enough to demand a weak inequality in $s_2 \geq s_1$, as candidate 1 is the candidate that minimizes the score while achieving misrepresentation μ_1; if $s_2 = s_1$ then it must hold that $\mu_2 \geq \mu_1$, hence candidate 2 still wins the election.

Theorem 1. *Let F be a scoring protocol with the popular loser property and the even match properties. Then the problem of calculating $\mu_m^n(F)$ has a Fully Polynomial Time Approximation Scheme (FPTAS).*

Proof (Sketch). Observe the rankings $l_1^i{}^{ALG}$ fixed by the algorithm from the proof of Lemma 2, on the given input. By the assumptions, it is sufficient to find rankings l_2^i for candidate 2 in a way that μ_2 is maximal, under the constraint $s_2 \geq s_1^{ALG}$.

The above problem reduces to the exact KNAPSACK problem with cardinality constraints (E-kKP). In this problem, we are given n items, each with a weight w_i and a value v_i, and a weight limit K; the goal is to find a subset S of items of size k, that maximizes $\sum_{i \in S} v_i$, subject to $\sum_{i \in S} w_i \leq K$.

In our setting, l_2^i can take any value in $\{1, \ldots, m\} \setminus \{l_1^i{}^{ALG}\}$; let there be an item associated with each possible value of l_2^i, $i = 1, \ldots, n$ (there are $n(m - 1)$ items). The value of the item associated with $l_2^i = l$ is $\mu_2^i = l - 1$, and its weight is $\alpha_1 - \alpha_l$. Exactly n items are to be chosen; the weight limit is $n\alpha_1 - s_1^{ALG}$.

This is a polynomial time reduction. Indeed, given rankings l_2^i, $i = 1, \ldots, n$ such that $s_2 \geq s_1^{ALG}$, choose n corresponding items in the knapsack instance. The items' total value is exactly μ_2. Moreover, the total weight associated with the items is at most $n\alpha_1$ minus the total score of the associated rankings, which is at least s_1^{ALG}. The other direction is similar.

Caprara et al. [4] present an FPTAS for E-kKP. Therefore, for any $\epsilon > 0$, it is possible to find (in polynomial time) μ_2 such that $\mu_2 \leq \mu_2^* \leq (1 + \epsilon)\mu_2$. In addition, recall that $\mu_1^{ALG} = \mu_1^*$. Therefore:

$$\frac{\left(\frac{\mu_2^*}{\mu_1^*}\right)}{\left(\frac{\mu_2}{\mu_1^{ALG}}\right)} = \frac{\mu_1^{ALG}\mu_2^*}{\mu_1^*\mu_2} = \frac{\mu_2^*}{\mu_2} \leq 1 + \epsilon.$$

$\square$

5 Conclusions

We have defined the distortion of a social choice function as the worst-case ratio between the total utility of the candidate that maximizes social welfare, and the elected candidate. At first, we have focused on a model where, for all voters, the sum of utilities is identical. We have shown that every social choice function is distorted, even when the number of voters and the number of candidates are small. Moreover, we have established a sufficient condition for unbounded distortion — a result which implies that several well-known scoring protocols have unbounded distortion in the general model. We have shown our model to be equivalent, in terms of distortion, to another model where the voters' cardinal preferences are unconstrained, but each voter's weight is the sum of its utilities. Finally, we have proven that a problem associated with calculating distortion is $\mathcal{NP}$-complete when utilities are unconstrained.

Motivated by the impossibility results mentioned above and the work of Monroe [11], we have reformulated the concept of distortion as misrepresentation. The main difference between the two settings is, essentially, that in the misrepresentation setting voters' cardinal preferences are quite restricted. We have established a necessary and

Table 1. The misrepresentation of common voting protocols

Voting Protocol	Misrepresentation
Borda	1
Veto	Unbounded
Plurality	$= m - 1$
Plurality with Runoff	$= m - 1$
Copeland	$\leq m - 1$
Bucklin	$\leq m$
Maximin	$\leq 1.62(m - 1)$
STV	$\leq 1.5(m - 1)$

sufficient condition for a social choice function to be optimal in terms of misrepresentation, and have also characterized the scoring protocols with unbounded misrepresentation. More importantly, we have given bounds — in some cases tight — for the misrepresentation of specific voting protocols; these bounds are summarized in Table 1.

Last, we have tackled the problem of calculating misrepresentation. Moving through several sub-problems, we have ultimately demonstrated that there is a fully polynomial time approximation scheme (FPTAS) for this problem, when the voting protocol is a scoring protocol that possesses the popular loser and even match properties. It remains an open issue to characterize the scoring protocols that have these properties.

The results presented in Section 3 suggest that distortion may be a major obstacle for designers of multiagent systems who wish to apply voting. This is true, however, only if the agents' cardinal preferences are almost unconstrained. On the other hand, we have seen in Section 4 that restricting the preferences overturns some of the impossibility results.

In the context of restricted preferences, the results imply that the distortion of a voting protocol should be a major criterion in the comparison of different protocols — alongside other classical criteria like manipulability. For instance, whenever misrepresentation is a concern (as in the meeting scheduling example discussed in Section 3), one might prefer to employ the Borda protocol, which is optimal in terms of misrepresentation but highly manipulable, rather than the STV protocol, which is difficult to manipulate [1] but has high misrepresentation. In a three candidate example, STV's misrepresentation might be 3 times higher than Borda's; in the scheduling domain, this might imply three times as many conflicts with user preferences — certainly a steep price to pay for preventing strategic behavior.

We briefly mention two directions for future research. Our computational complexity analysis of distortion is rather rough. It seems true that calculating distortion (or even misrepresentation) in scoring protocols is $\mathcal{NP}$-complete, but currently there is no proof. Second, our approximation scheme relies on the popular loser and even match properties; it remains an open issue to characterize the scoring protocols that have these properties. Further, can these assumptions be abandoned?

Acknowledgment

This work was partially supported by Israel Science Foundation grant #039-7582.

References

1. J. Bartholdi and J. Orlin. Single transferable vote resists strategic voting. *Social Choice and Welfare*, 8:341–354, 1991.

2. J. Bartholdi, C. A. Tovey, and M. A. Trick. How hard is it to control an election. *Mathematical and Computer Modelling*, 16:27–40, 1992.

3. S. J. Brams and P. C. Fishburn. Voting procedures. In K. J. Arrow, A. K. Sen, and K. Suzumura, editors, *Handbook of Social Choice and Welfare*, chapter 4. North-Holland, 2002.

4. A. Caprara, H. Kellerer, U. Pferschy, and D. Pisinger. Approximation algorithms for knapsack problems with cardinality constraints. *European Journal of Operational Research*, 123:333–345, 2000.

5. V. Conitzer and T. Sandholm. Complexity of manipulating elections with few candidates. In *Proceedings of the National Conference on Artificial Intelligence*, pages 314–319, 2002.

6. E. Elkind and H. Lipmaa. Small coalitions cannot manipulate voting. In *International Conference on Financial Cryptography*, Lecture Notes in Computer Science. Springer, 2005.

7. E. Ephrati and J. S. Rosenschein. A heuristic technique for multiagent planning. *Annals of Mathematics and Artificial Intelligence*, 20:13–67, 1997.

8. S. Ghosh, M. Mundhe, K. Hernandez, and S. Sen. Voting for movies: the anatomy of a recommender system. In *Proceedings of the Third Annual Conference on Autonomous Agents*, pages 434–435, 1999.

9. T. Haynes, S. Sen, N. Arora, and R. Nadella. An automated meeting scheduling system that utilizes user preferences. In *Proceedings of the First International Conference on Autonomous Agents*, pages 308–315, 1997.

10. J. Matousek. *Lectures on Discrete Geometry*, chapter 15. Springer, 2002.

11. B. L. Monroe. Fully proportional representation. *American Political Science Review*, 89(4):925–940, 1995.

12. A. D. Procaccia and J. S. Rosenschein. Junta distributions and the average-case complexity of manipulating elections. In *Proceedings of the Fifth International Joint Conference on Autonomous Agents and Multiagent Systems*, pages 497–504, 2006.

Risk-Bounded Formation of Fuzzy Coalitions Among Service Agents

Bastian Blankenburg[1], Minghua He[2], Matthias Klusch[1], and Nicholas R. Jennings[2]

[1] German Research Center for Artificial Intelligence, Stuhlsatzenhausweg 3,
66123 Saarbrücken, Germany
{blankenb, klusch}@dfki.de
[2] School of Electronics and Computer Science, University of Southampton,
Southampton, SO17 1BJ, UK
{mh, nrj}@ecs.soton.ac.uk

Abstract. Cooperative autonomous agents form coalitions in order to share and combine resources and services to efficiently respond to market demands. With the variety of resources and services provided online today, there is a need for stable and flexible techniques to support the automation of agent coalition formation in this context. This paper describes an approach to the problem based on fuzzy coalitions. Compared with a classic cooperative game with crisp coalitions (where each agent is a full member of exactly one coalition), an agent can participate in multiple coalitions with varying degrees of involvement. This gives the agents more freedom and flexibility, allowing them to make full use of their resources, thus maximising utility, even if only comparatively small coalitions are formed. An important aspect of our approach is that the agents can control and bound the risk caused by the possible failure or default of some partner agents by spreading their involvement in diverse coalitions.

1 Introduction

In today's increasingly networked and competitive world, the appropriate utilization of pay per use Web services are considered as one major key to the success of commercial service oriented business applications in domains such as e-logistics, tourism, and entertainment. In the near future, intelligent service agents are not only supposed to search for, interact with, and compose, but also negotiate access to, and execute such Web services on behalf of its user, or other agents. In fact, they may exhibit some form of economically rational cooperation by forming coalitions to share the created joint monetary value while at the same time maximizing their own individual payoff. According to classical microeconomics, means and concepts of cooperative game theory are inherently well suited to this purpose. In this paper, we propose a protocol for resource-bounded computational rational agents to automatically form risk-bounded fuzzy coalitions in order to fulfill service requests with deadlines.

As opposed to traditional cooperative games, games with fuzzy coalitions allow the agents to be members of multiple coalitions with varying degrees of involvement. The notion of fuzzy coalitions was first introduced by Aubin and Butnariu (see [2,5]) to overcome some problems of traditional cooperative games in real-world settings. For

M. Klusch, M. Rovatsos, and T. Payne (Eds.): CIA 2006, LNAI 4149, pp. 332–346, 2006.

example, suppose that agent a_1 can independently benefit from cooperations with agent a_2 as well as with agent a_3. To realise both opportunities, a coalition of all three agents has to be formed, requiring a_2 and a_3 to agree on a coalition contract although they do not cooperate otherwise. Another drawback of non-overlapping coalitions emerges in the case of failure. If, in the above example, a_2 fails its task, thus reducing the coalition value, all members of the coalition are affected, including a_3, although it is not actually working together with a_2. In contrast, with fuzzy coalitions makes it is possible to form a coalition for each service request, without preventing other requests from being satisfied. This approach has the advantage that there are no unnecessary negotiations and contracts between agents which actually do not work together.

Additionally, using fuzzy coalitions allows the agents to lower their individual risk of monetary losses by participating in a number of coalitions, if coherent risk measure are considered. Assuming that agents are able to assess other agent's risk of failure in a coalition, we show how such risk-bounded coalition formation can be done. In particular, we consider the membership of an agent in a coalition as an investment, since the costly service execution takes place first. Rewards are received later only for successful and timely execution. We thus allow the agents to specify individual risk bounds in terms of the coherent financial risk measure *tail conditional expectation* (TCE). The adherence to these bounds is guaranteed by the proposed coalition formation protocol RFCF.

But as it turns out, we cannot directly use the existing solution concepts for cooperative games with fuzzy coalitions. The approaches taken by Aubin, Butnariu as well as Nishizaki and Sakawa (see [9]) all assume that the coalition value is a proportional function of the agents' membership degrees. As this assumption does not hold in our setting, we introduce appropriate extensions of the excess and surplus. We then show that it is possible to compute the surplus in polynomial time under some additional assumptions, similar to the approach taken in [10]. Stearns transfer scheme can then be used to compute Kernel-stable solutions for the game (see [11]).

The remainder of this paper is organized as follows: in section 2 we introduce our service agent and coalition model. In section 3, we introduce our notion of fuzzy coalition games among service provider agents. We then show how to compute the risk of fuzzy coalitions and fuzzy coalition structures in section 4. Section 5 is concerned with the stability of risk-bounded fuzzy coalitions. We propose our coalition formation protocol RFCF in section 6. In section 7 we discuss related work and conclude in section 8.

2 Agent Model

In this section we specify more precisely the environment of service agents that we consider in this paper.

We consider two types of agents: service request agents and service provider agents.

Definition 1. *Service Request Agent*

A service request agent sra requests exactly one (possibly complex) service s and some deadline d. It will pay a certain monetary reward $r \in \mathbb{R}$ for a successful execution of s before d. Otherwise, no reward is paid.

SRA denotes the set of all service request agents in the system.

On the other hand, service provider agents offer the execution of exactly one type of service. They are assumed to be computationally bounded, i.e. to have only limited resources per time for the execution of their service. For simplicity, we assume that the execution time for a service instance is a linear function of the resources devoted to it. This is reasonable in the case where the bounded resources are computing power and/or memory, for example.

Definition 2. *Service Provider Agent*
   A service provider agent *spa offers the execution of exactly one service s_{spa} and has the following properties:*

1. *Service Composition*
    (a) *spa is able to send* service advertisements *for s_{spa}.*
    (b) *given a requested service s and a set of service advertisements, spa has the ability to compute* service composition plans; *each such plan is a list of advertised services whose execution implements the requested service s.*
    (c) *each element of a plan $\mathcal{P}$ is called a* service instance *of the respective service.*
2. *Service Execution*
    (a) *spa can spend only some max. amount of resources per time in service executions.*
    (b) *the minimum execution time of an instance i of s_{spa} is denoted t_i^{min} (i.e. this is the execution time if spa devotes all its resources to it).*
    (c) *spa can split its resources and execute multiple instances of s_{spa} at the same time. The fraction of resources per time (wrt. the maximum) devoted to the execution of service instance i is denoted r_i.*
    (d) *the execution time t_i of service instance i is*

$$t_i = \frac{1}{r_i} \times t_i^{min}.$$

    (e) *spa might not be able to detemine t_i^{min} exactly in advance, but is able to specify a probability density function (PDF) $pdf_{t_i^{min}}$ over the values it might take.*
    (f) *there is a monetary cost for resource consumption of spa. We assume this is constant, so that because of Definition 2.2(d) the cost $cost_i$ for executing service instance i is also constant and does not depend on r_i.*

SPA denotes the set of all service provider agents in the system.

Note that because of the linear relationship assumed in Definition 2.2(d), it is easy to obtain the PDF of the execution time of a service instance i with a given fraction of resources per time r_i:

$$pdf_{t_i}(x) = pdf_{t_i^{min}}(r_i * x) \tag{1}$$

Example 1. As an example, we consider a medical service provider agent scenario. We assume that there are a number of these agents in the system, each offering medical information in one or more specific medical domains. A specific set of symptoms of a patient might have possible diagnosis in several domains. Thus, a full diagnosis as response to a request from e.g. a medical doctor might require a set of provider agents to collaborate. We assume that the medical personnel will request this information with specific deadlines to ensure the timely treatment of patients. Suppose that agent spa_1 gets a request from a doctor and realizes that it also needs spa_2 to provide a feasible diagnosis. spa_1 then estimates the runtime for its own service on the request and sends coalition proposal to spa_2. spa_2 then likewise estimates its runtime and sees that this coalition might actually fail, producing high costs. However, spa_2 has a further request from agent spa_3. While forming just the coalition spa_1 is too risky for spa_2, it is acceptable if the coalition with spa_3 is also formed.

3   Fuzzy Coalition Games of SPA Agents

In our setting, the capability of service provider agents to split their resources among different service instance executions makes it possible for them to take part in several service composition plan executions. This suggests to allow the agents to be a (partial) member of several coalitions. For this purpose, a number of authors (most notably Aubin, Butnariu and Nishizaki and Sakawa [2,5,9]) extended concepts from cooperative game theory to allow for *fuzzy coalitions*, where each agent is a member only to a certain *membership degree*. In our model, each fuzzy coalition will execute exactly one service composition plan. The membership degree represents the relative amount of resources they spend for their respective service instance executions in the plan. If the same group of agents decides to execute an additional plan, it simply forms an additional fuzzy coalition. We also disallow any members that are not actually involved in the execution of P.

Definition 3. *Fuzzy Coalition of Service Provider Agents*
   Let there be a request for a service ws from a service request agent sra and a plan P whose execution satisfies ws.

1. *$SPA_P \subseteq SPA$ is the set of service provider agents involved in P.*
2. *The* fuzzy coalition of service provider agents *$\widetilde{C}$ for sra and P is written as*

$$\widetilde{C} = (spa_1/mem_1, \ldots, spa_k/mem_k, sra, P)$$

   with $k = |SPA_P|$, $spa_j \in SPA_P$, $1 \leq j \leq k$; $mem_j \in [0,1]$ is a guaranteed minimum *for the fraction of resources per time r_i devoted by spa_j to any i of its service instances in P.*
3. *$mem(spa, \widetilde{C})$ is agent spa's membership in $\widetilde{C}$.*
4. *We write $spa \in \widetilde{C}$ if spa is a member of $\widetilde{C}$ with some positive membership, i.e. $mem(spa, \widetilde{C}) > 0$.*
5. *$\widetilde{C} \widetilde{\subseteq} \widetilde{C}'$ if $\forall spa \in \widetilde{C} : mem(spa, \widetilde{C}) \leq mem(spa, \widetilde{C}')$, where $\widetilde{C}$ and $\widetilde{C}'$ are fuzzy coalitions for the same service request agent and plan.*
6. *$\widetilde{C}(sra, plan)$ denotes the set of all fuzzy coalitions $\widetilde{C} = (., sra, plan)$.*
7. *$|\widetilde{C}|$ is the number of agents in $\widetilde{C}$.*

We also denote "fuzzy coalition" or just "coalition" instead of "fuzzy coalition of service provider agents" where the context is clear.

Because of the deadlines for service requests, $\tilde{C}$ either earns the reward r for the successful and timely execution of $\mathcal{P}$ from the requesting agent, or nothing otherwise. To specify coalition values for fuzzy service provider agent coalitions, we thus need to consider its probabilities of failure and success. For simplicity, we assume that the execution times of service instances are independent of each other and that the services in a plan $\mathcal{P}$ are executed sequentially. Then, the total execution time of $\mathcal{P}$ is the sum of the execution times of the individual service instances:

$$t_{\mathcal{P}} = \sum_{i \in \mathcal{P}} t_i \tag{2}$$

The PDF of the sum of two independent random variables A and B is given by the *convolution integral* over their individual PDFs pdf_A and pdf_B (see, e.g., [8], p. 113). I.e., with $x \in \mathbb{R}$:

$$pdf_{A+B}(x) = (pdf_A * pdf_B)(x)$$
$$= \int_0^\infty pdf_A(y) pdf_B(x - y) dy \tag{3}$$

For a plan $\mathcal{P}$ with $m \in \mathbb{N}$ service instances, the PDF of its execution time is therefore an $m - 1$ fold convolution over the individual service instance execution time PDFs. With $x \in \mathbb{R}^+$ (it is sufficient to consider only positive values since execution times are always positive).

$$pdf_{t_{\mathcal{P}}}(x) = (\cdots (pdf_{t_{i_1}} * pdf_{t_{i_2}}) \cdots * pdf_{t_{i_m}})(x) \tag{4}$$

For specific cases, there exist simple analytical solutions of the convolution. E.g., the convolution of two normal PDFs is again normal, as is the convolution of a normal PDF with an exponential one. But this is not the case for arbitrary distribution types. Fortunately, there are alternative ways to obtain the convolution, such as the pointwise multiplication of the Fourier Transform F of the PDFs:

$$f * g = F^{-1}(F(f)F(g)) \tag{5}$$

The Fast Fourier Transform algorithm efficiently approximates the Fourier Transform with complexity $k \log k$, where k is the number of sample points taken from the functions.

Suppose the agents executing a plan $\mathcal{P}$ agree to start the execution at time t_s. With the PDF of the execution time of a plan $\mathcal{P}$ and the deadline given for the respective service request, it is then easy to determine the probability that the plan execution exceeds this deadline, which we call the probability of failure (PoF):

$$PoF(\mathcal{P}, t_s, d) = \int_{d - t_s}^\infty pdf_{t_{\mathcal{P}}}(x) dx \tag{6}$$

Note that for $d < t_s$, we always have $PoF(\mathcal{P}, t_s, d) = 0$, since the plan execution time must be positive. Similarly, the probability of success (PoS) is:

$$PoS(\mathcal{P}, t_s, d) = 1 - PoF(\mathcal{P}, t_s, d) \tag{7}$$

Given the membership degrees, the PDF over the upper bound $\hat{t}_i$ for the execution time of a service instance $i \in \mathcal{P}$ of agent spa_k is, analogous to 1,

$$pdf_{\hat{t}_i}(x) = pdf_{t_i^{min}}(mem_k * x) \tag{8}$$

According to 4, we can then obtain the PDF of the upper bound $\hat{t}_\mathcal{P}$ for the execution time of the complete plan, and thus the probabilities of failure and success of the fuzzy coalition, denoted $PoF(\widetilde{C})$ and $PoS(\widetilde{C})$, resp. This enables us to determine a lower bound for the expected reward for $\widetilde{C}$, denoted $\underline{r}_{\widetilde{C}}$:

$$\underline{r}_{\widetilde{C}} = PoS(\widetilde{C}) \times r \tag{9}$$

To specify a value for the fuzzy coalitions, we further have to consider the costs that are generated by the service executions. The agents should reasonably stop the execution once the deadline is reached, since no additional reward can be obtained by any further work. However, to simplify things, we consider only the worst case, i.e. the case where maximum costs have been produced even if the coalition fails.

Definition 4. *Value of a Fuzzy Service Provider Agent Coalition*
Let there be a fuzzy coalition $\widetilde{C}$ with plan $\mathcal{P}$. The value $v(\widetilde{C})$ *of $\widetilde{C}$, also called* coalition value, *is defined as*

$$v(\widetilde{C}) = \underline{r}_{\widetilde{C}} - \sum_{i \in \mathcal{P}} cost_i$$

Although fuzzy coalition structures allow the agents to be a member in several coalitions at the same time, we still have to require that each agent does not allocate more resources to coalitions than it can actually provide. Formally, we have

Definition 5. *Feasible Fuzzy Coalition Structure*
For a fuzzy coalition $\widetilde{C}$, let $mem_{spa}^{\widetilde{C}}$ denote the membership degree of spa in $\widetilde{C}$, with $mem_{spa}^{\widetilde{C}} = 0$ if spa is not member of $\widetilde{C}$. A feasible fuzzy coalition structure $\mathcal{S}$ *for the agents in SPA is defined as a set of fuzzy coalitions with*

$$\forall spa \in SPA : \sum_{\widetilde{C} \in \mathcal{S}} mem_{spa}^{\widetilde{C}} \leq 1 \tag{10}$$

4   Risk of Fuzzy Coalition Structures

Given a variety of combination of coalitions that the agent can possibly join, rational agents will prefer coalitions with a high reward and a low PoF, i.e. a high expected value. But assume there is a coalition with a high expected value, but which also involves very high costs. If an agent cannot afford to lose more than some amount without compromising liquidity, even a low PoF of the coalition might be still too risky. To control and avoid such situations, a number of financial risk measures have been introduced in the literature (for a recent overview, see [7] and references therein).

For the definitions in the remainder of this section, we follow Artzner et al.[1], omitting certain details which are not important in our setting. Also, where Artzner et al. speak of *positions* (meaning investment positions), we speak of *strategies*, meaning an agent's decision with whom to coalesce and service requests to work on. Lastly, note that the definitions of VaR and other measures in [1] include the reward of a reference investment (e.g. interest rates) as a scaling factor, which we omit here for simplicity.

Definition 6. *Risk and Measure of Risk*

Let Ω denote the set of states of nature, and assume it is finite. Considering Ω as the set of outcomes of an experiment, we compute the final net worth of a strategy for each element of Ω. Risk is the investor's future net worth, which is described by a random variable. Let G be the set of all risks, that is the set of all real valued functions on Ω. A measure of risk r is a mapping $r: G \mapsto \mathbb{R}$.

According to [7], a widely known and used one is the Value-at-Risk (VaR), which also has become part of financial regulations. VaR calculates how much one may lose during a specified period given a probability and the capital should be used to control the risk.

Definition 7. *Value-at-Risk (VaR)*

Given $\alpha \in [0,1]$, the Value-at-Risk VaR^α at level α of the final net worth $X \in G$ with distribution P is

$$VaR^\alpha(X) = -\inf\{x \in \mathbb{R}: P(X \le x) > \alpha\}$$

Artzner et al. also introduce the notion of *coherent* risk measures.

Definition 8. *Coherent risk measure*

With $X, Y \in G, z \in \mathbb{R}$, a risk measure r is called coherent if it satisfies

1. *subadditivity: for all $X, Y \in G$: $r(X + Y) \le r(X) + r(Y)$*
2. *translation invariance: $r(X + z) = r(X) - z$*
3. *positive homogeneity: $\forall z \ge 0, r(zX) = zr(X)$*
4. *monotonicity: if $X \le Y$ then $r(Y) \le r(X)$*

As has also been shown in [1], VaR is not coherent, since it does not fulfill subadditivity. As it turns out (see below), this lack of superadditivity constitutes a major drawback in the design of a risk-bound coalition formation algorithm. Fortunately, a number of coherent measures which are derived from VaR have been proposed. Here, we employ the tail conditional expectation (TCE) which is coherent for continous distributions.

Definition 9. *Tail Conditional Expectation: given a probability measure P on Ω and a level α, the tail conditional expectation is defined by:*

$$TCE^\alpha(X) = -E_P\{X|X \le -VaR^\alpha(X)\}$$

Using this measure, each agent spa_i may individually specify a parameter α_i and a TCE-threshold $tTCE_i$, expressing that it will only accept coalition structures which satisfy

$$TCE^{\alpha_i}(u_i) \le tTCE_i$$

where u_i is agent spa_i's final net worth, i.e. the total net result from all coalitions it is involved in.

Proposition 1. *Let service provider agent spa_i be a member in a fuzzy coalition $\widetilde{C}$, let $cost_i$ be the cost for spa_i if $\widetilde{C}$ fails, and let $u_i(\widetilde{C}) > -cost_i$ be the payoff obtained by spa_i if $\widetilde{C}$ is successful. The $TCE^{\alpha_i}(\widetilde{C})$, i.e. the TCE^α restricted to consider only spa_i and $\widetilde{C}$, can be computed as follows:*

$$TCE^{\alpha_i}(\widetilde{C}) = \begin{cases} PoF(\widetilde{C})cost_i(\widetilde{C}) + PoS(\widetilde{C})(-u_i(\widetilde{C})) & PoF(\widetilde{C}) \leq \alpha_i \\ cost_i(\widetilde{C}) & PoF(\widetilde{C}) > \alpha_i \end{cases}$$

Proof. Let X_i be spa_i's net result from $\widetilde{C}$, with $X_i = u_i$ in case of success of $\widetilde{C}$ and $X_i = -cost_i$ in case of failure. Consider the first case, i.e. assume that $PoF(\widetilde{C}) \leq \alpha i$. Then the Value-at-Risk, i.e. the TCE^α restricted to consider only spa_i and $\widetilde{C}$, is $VaR^{\alpha_i}(\widetilde{C}) = -u_i$ because $P(X_i \leq -cost_i) = PoF(\widetilde{C}) \not> \alpha i$, but $P(X_i \leq u_i) = 1$ (since $PoS(\widetilde{C}) = 1 - PoF(\widetilde{C})$). Thus, the set of relevant outcomes considered in TCE^α includes both $X_i = -cost_i$ and $X_i = u_i$. In the second case, with $PoF(\widetilde{C}) > \alpha i$, we have $VaR^{\alpha_i}(\widetilde{C}) = cost_i$ because $P(X_i \leq -cost_i) = PoF(\widetilde{C}) > \alpha i$. Thus, the set of relevant outcomes considered in TCE^α contains only $X_i = -cost_i$, and the case $X_i = u_i$ is disregarded.

To obtain the TCE^{α_i} for a fuzzy coalition structure, we have to consider the probability of failure for each subset of fuzzy coalitions that spa_i is involved in, as well as the payoffs and costs for spa_i in these cases. The following follows directly from the independency of the PoF of different coalitions and the definition of VaR.

Corollary 1. *Let there be a fuzzy coalition structure S and let $S_{spa_i} \subseteq S$ be the subset of all coalitions involving spa_i. For each $S^*_{spa_i} \in 2^{S_{spa_i}}$ (including the empty set) let $cost_i(S^*_{spa_i})$ be the cost for spa_i if all coalitions in $S^*_{spa_i}$ fail, and let $u_i(S^*_{spa_i})$ be the net payoff obtained by spa_i from the coalitions in $S_{spa_i} \cup S^*_{spa_i}$ (i.e. the reward minus costs for the successful coalitions).*

The probability $PoF(S^*_{spa_i})$ that the coalitions in $S^*_{spa_i}$ fail while those in $S_{spa_i} \cap S^*_{spa_i}$ succeed is

$$PoF(S^*_{spa_i}) = \prod_{\widetilde{C} \in S^*_{spa_i}} PoF(\widetilde{C}) \times \prod_{\widetilde{C} \in S_{spa_i} \cap S^*_{spa_i}} PoS(\widetilde{C})$$

The $VaR^{\alpha_i}(S)$, i.e. the VaR^α restricted to consider only spa_i and S, is then

$$VaR^{\alpha_i}(S) = -min_{S^*_{spa_i} \in 2^{S_{spa_i}}} \{u_i(S^*_{spa_i}) : \sum_{\substack{S'_{spa_i} \in 2^{S_{spa_i}} \\ u_i(S'_{spa_i}) \leq u_i(S^*_{spa_i})}} PoF(S^*_{spa_i}) > \alpha_i\}$$

Having $VaR^{\alpha_i}(S)$, the computation of the $TCE^{\alpha_i}(S)$ is straight-forward. Please note that $VaR^{\alpha_i}(S)$ and thus also TCE^{α_i} depend on the agent's payoff. But as becomes clear in section 5, computing a stable payoff depends on the risk. Also, we have to consider each element in the power-set of coalitions that spa_i is involved in, making the complexity of this computation exponential. However, by bounding the number of coalitions an agent might be involved in, we obtain polynomial complexity. This is also shown in section 5.

5 Stability of Fuzzy Coalitions Structures

In this section, we finally show how a coalition's payoff should be distributed among its members. Cooperative game theory traditionally deals with the question how this can be done in a *stable* way. Stable means that no agent has a reasonable incentive to break its coalition(s). For games with fuzzy coalitions, several such solution concepts, including the Core and the Shapley Value, have been introduced in the literature[2,5,9]. Unfortunately, these assume a linear or even proportional relationship of the membership and coalition values. This does not hold in our case, because the coalition either gets the payoff or not, while the membership values determine the involved risk. But even considering the expected values does not help, since (a) the execution time of a service instance is characterized by an $\frac{1}{x}$-relationship wrt. to the membership (see Definition 2.2(d)) and (b) the actual probability of failure also depends on the underlying distributions of the service instance runtimes which might be arbitrary. We thus introduce a new variant of the $excess$ which is compliant with out setting. Since the excess is the basis for a number of solution concepts including the Core, Kernel and Nucleolus, this allows us to use these concepts. In this paper, however, we consider only the Kernel.

In crisp games, the excess of a coalition C wrt. a given coalition structure S with $C \notin S$ quantifies the difference in payoff that the agents in C obtain by forming C and leaving their resp. coalitions in S. Because each agent can be a member of only one coalition in a crisp coalition game, they then do not obtain any payoff from their former coalitions. But this is not the case in fuzzy coalition games. Here, it is possible to withdraw just some membership and put it into a new coalition. However, not all coalitions might be feasible wrt. the involved agents' individual risk bounds. We consider such coalitions not to be a feasible threat. Also, we exclude the case that an agent threatens to withdraw any amount membership from an existing coalition such that its own risk bound would be exceeded. While this makes sure that the hard risk bounds are taken into account, we also have to consider that more membership means a better chance of success. Thus, we regard the expected coalition values.

Definition 10. *Excess of a fuzzy coalition*
Let there be fuzzy coalition $\widetilde{C}$ and fuzzy coalition structures S and S' with $\widetilde{C} \in S'$, $\widetilde{C} \notin S$, S' is feasible, and $\forall \widetilde{C}' \in S', \widetilde{C}' \neq \widetilde{C} : \exists \widetilde{C}'' \in S : \widetilde{C}' \widetilde{\subseteq} \widetilde{C}''$. Further, let there be a payoff distribution u. We define

$$\widetilde{e}(\widetilde{C}, S', \widetilde{u})_{|TCE} := \underline{v}_{|TCE}(\widetilde{C}, S') - \sum_{spa_i \in \widetilde{C}} d_i(S, S')$$

with

$$\underline{v}_{|TCE}(\widetilde{C}, S') = \begin{cases} \underline{v}(\widetilde{C}) & \text{if } \forall spa_i \in \widetilde{C} : TCE^{\alpha_i}(S' \cup \widetilde{C}) \leq tTCE_i \\ 0 & \text{otherwise} \end{cases}$$

and

$$d_i = \sum_{\widetilde{C}^* \in S, \widetilde{C}' \in S', \widetilde{C}' \widetilde{\subseteq} \widetilde{C}^*} \underline{v}(\widetilde{C}') - \underline{v}(\widetilde{C}^*)$$

In crisp games, for a given configuration (S, u), the surplus of an agent a_i over another agent a_k with $a_i, a_k \in C \in S$ is then defined as the maximum excess of all coalitions including agent a_i but without agent a_k. For games with fuzzy coalitions, however, it is possible to threaten with a number of alternative coalitions at the same time. Also, only a membership transfer from coalitions that include both a_i and a_k should be considered. Finally, we require that all membership of a_i from such coalitions is transferred.

Definition 11. *Fuzzy coalition surplus*
   Let there be a fuzzy coalition structure S and payoff distribution u and agents a_i and a_k.

1. *A feasible fuzzy coalition structure S' with $\forall \widetilde{C} \in S', \widetilde{C} \notin S : a_i \in \widetilde{C}, a_k \notin \widetilde{C}$, $\forall C \in S, a_k \notin C : C \in S'$ and $\nexists \widetilde{C} \in S' : a_i, a_k \in \widetilde{C}$ is called an ik-fuzzy surplus* structure.
2. *The set of all ik-fuzzy surplus structures wrt. S is denoted $SS_{ik}(S)$*
3. *The fuzzy coalition surplus of a_i over a_k is*

$$\widetilde{s}_{ik|TCE} := \max_{S' \in SS_{ik}(S)} \{ \sum_{a_i \in \widetilde{C} \in S'} \widetilde{e}(\widetilde{C}, \widetilde{u})_{|TCE} \}$$

To compute a fuzzy coalition surplus it is thus not only necessary to identify the best set of agents that should form alternative coalitions when excluding the other agent, but also to find the best membership values for them wrt. feasibility and the individual agent risk thresholds.

Definition 12. *Let Q_{ik} denote a set of pairs $(sra, \mathcal{P})$ with $\mathcal{P}$ satisfies the request from sra, $a_i \in SPA_{\mathcal{P}}$ and $a_k \notin SPA_{\mathcal{P}}$. For a feasible coalition structure S, let $SS_{ik}(Q_{ik})$ denote the set of all ik-fuzzy surplus structures S' wrt. S such that for all pairs $(sra, \mathcal{P}) \in Q_{ik}$ there exists $\widetilde{C} \in \widetilde{C}(sra, \mathcal{P})$ with $\widetilde{C} \in S'$. We define the function $MaxS(Q_{ik}, S, u)$ to return $S^* \in SS_{ik}(Q_{ik})$ such that $\sum_{a_i \in \widetilde{C} \in S^*} \widetilde{e}(\widetilde{C}, \widetilde{u})_{|TCE}$ is maximized wrt. all other elements in $SS_{ik}(Q_{ik})$.*

Because the service instance runtime depends on the spent resources and thus the membership values by a $\frac{1}{x}$-relationship (see Definition 2.2(d)), $MaxS$ has to solve a nonlinear optimization problem. The complexity to compute a fuzzy coalition surplus is thus even worse than in the crisp case, where we have exponential complexity wrt. the number of agents in the system because of the exponential number of possible coalitions and excesses. Shehory and Kraus proposed to reduce this to a polynomial complexity by limiting the maximum coalition size[10]. We achieve the same effect for the fuzzy coalition surplus by not only bounding the number of agents in a coalition, but also the number of coalitions that an agent threatens to transfer membership to as well as the number of plans per set of agents.

Proposition 2. *Let $aMax \in \mathbb{N}$ be an upper bound for the number agents in a coalition and $\widetilde{C}Max \in \mathbb{N}$ be an upper bound for all sets $|Q_{ik}|$, i.e. the number of new coalitions including agent a_i and excluding agent a_k in the computation of $\widetilde{s}_{ik|TCE}$. Let further $\mathcal{P}Max$ be an upper bound for the number of plans that involve the same set of agents and let $n \in \mathbb{N}$ be the number of agents. Then the number of sets Q_{ik}, constrained by $\widetilde{C}Max$ and $\forall (sra, \mathcal{P}) \in Q_{ik} : \mathcal{P} \in PLANS$, is less or equal than $n^{(aMax \times \mathcal{P}Max)^{\widetilde{C}Max}}$.*

Proof. It was shown in [10] that the number of crisp coalitions with maximum size $aMax$ among n agents is bounded by n^{aMax}. Because each set of agents might be involved in multiple plans, this has to be multiplied $\mathcal{P}Max$ to obtain the upper bound for the number of considered coalitions. By the same argument as in the proof in [10], the number of sets of these coalitions with maximum size $\widetilde{C}Max$ is then bounded by $n^{(aMax \times \mathcal{P}Max)^{\widetilde{C}Max}}$.

In crisp games, the *kernel* of a cooperative game $(\mathcal{A}, v)$ with respect to a given coalition structure $\mathcal{S}$ is a set of configurations $(\mathcal{S}, u)$ wherein each pair of agents a_i, a_k in each coalition $C \in \mathcal{S}$ is in equilibrium wrt. their surplusses. That is the case if the agents cannot outweigh each other in $(\mathcal{S}, u)$ by having the option to get a better payoff in coalition(s) *not* in $\mathcal{S}$ excluding the opponent agent (agent i outweighs k, if $s_{ik} > s_{ki}$ and $u_k > w_i(C)$). Fortunately, having defined the surplus also for fuzzy coalitions, we can substitute it in this definition to obtain a definition for the kernel for games with fuzzy coalitions.

Definition 13. *Let there be a fuzzy coalition structure S and payoff distribution u. (S, u) is in the* **kernel** *of the fuzzy coalition game iff each pair of agents a_i, a_k in each fuzzy coalition $C \in S$ is in equilibrium wrt. their fuzzy coalition surplusses.*

To make a payoff distribution kernel-stable for a given coalition structure, Stearns *transfer scheme* can be used in the case of crisp games. The same can be applied here, since a side-payment from one agent to another will increase the former agent's payoff while lowering the latter agent ones.

6 Coalition Formation Protocol RFCF

In this section, we propose a fuzzy coalition formation protocol that guarantees to form coalitions which are in compliance with the agents' individual risk bounds. The negotiation is to be finished in a fixed amount of time in order to ensure a timely start service executions. In order to achieve polynomial complexity in the negotiation, some compromises have to be made. In particular, upper bounds for the risk of a coalition structure can be obtained by either considering only the self-values of the agents instead the actual utilities or by computing the risk for subsets of the structure and utilizing the subadditivity of TCE. The main drawback of using upper bounds for the risk is that it might prevent the formation of some coalitions which are then considered too risky although they are acceptable. We thus propose to execute a parallel process to continually improve the bound as long as there is time.

Before we give the actual definition of RFCF, we here provide a short outline of the protocol to emphasize the main ideas of the individual steps. In RFCF, each agent performs multiple tasks in parallel:

- **Composition Planning** - Composition plans are generated. Since only agents that can execute a plan together will form coalitions, this step is necessary to identify possibly worthwhile coalitions.
- **Coalition Negotiation**
  1. *Proposal generation* - The agent computes fuzzy coalitions such that their formation certainly leads to a feasible coalition structure while minimising the membership values. This way, no more membership (i.e. resources) than necessary is used, allowing the involved agents to possibly form additional coalitions later. A proposal is then send to the agents of the fuzzy coalition which maximises the value per membership.
  2. *Proposal evaluation* - From the received proposals, form feasible coalitions with acceptable risk the and maximal value per membership
  3. *Payoff distribution and risk bound update* - Use the transfer scheme to compute the Kernel-stable payoff distribution. Compute the single-coalition TCE and add it to previous coalition structure TCE bound to obtain an updated bound on the coalition structure TCE.
- **Risk Measure Computation** - Compute TCE for a new random subset of coalitions to obtain a tighter bound for the coalition structure TCE.

In the following definition of the algorithm, we use the following functions and constants:

- $\mathcal{P}Max$: the maximum number of plans to be considered for a set of agents
- $aMax$: the maximum coalition size
- $\widetilde{C}Max$: the maximum number of coalitions that an agent threatens to transfer membership to in the surplus computation
- $sra(\mathcal{P})$ Returns the service request agent for whose request $\mathcal{P}$ was generated.
- $findFuzzyCoalition(S, \mathcal{P}, risk)$: Computes a fuzzy coalition $\widetilde{C}$ such that the membership degrees in $\widetilde{C}$ are minimized while $S \cup \widetilde{C}$ is acceptable for all agents wrt. risk. Use $\widetilde{C}(sra(\mathcal{P}), \mathcal{P})$ as a starting point. If $risk = nil$ then compute an upper bound for $TCE^{\alpha_a}(S \cup \widetilde{C}(sra(\mathcal{P}), \mathcal{P}))$, otherwise use $risk$ as this upper bound. It is possible to efficiently implement this function by exploiting the monotonicity of the TCE wrt. to the membership values. If this is not possible or $|\widetilde{C}| > MaxCSize$, return nil
- $makeStable(S)$: Computes a new stable payoff distribution u^* for the fuzzy coalition structure S using the transfer scheme (see 5) and the bounds $\mathcal{P}Max$, $aMax$ and $\widetilde{C}Max$.

Algorithm 1. *RFCF*
  Each agent a performs:

Initialization:

1. $setPLANS := \emptyset$
2. $setPPPLANS := \emptyset$

3. $set PPPLANSRISK := \emptyset$
4. $set PROPS := new\ priority\ queue$
5. $set risk_a := TCE(\{a\}/1)$

Parallel Execution:

- *Composition plan generation: repeat (until terminated)*
    1. *Generate a new composition plan $\mathcal{P}$ for a random service request and for a set of agents for which the number of previously generated plans is less than $\mathcal{P}Max$.*
    2. $PLANS := PLANS \cup \mathcal{P}$
- *Coalition negotiation: repeat (until terminated)*
    1. *Proposal generation*
        (a) *set* $BestCoalition := nil$, $BestPayoffperMembership := 0$
        (b) *for each $\mathcal{P}$ in $PLANS$ do:*
            i. $\widetilde{C} := findFuzzyCoalition(S, \mathcal{P}, nil)$
            ii. *if $\widetilde{C} = nil$ then* $PLANS := PLANS \setminus \mathcal{P}$;
            $POSTPONEDPLANS := \cup \mathcal{P}$ *;next 1b*
            iii. *if $v(\widetilde{C})/|\widetilde{C}| > BestPayoffperMembership$ then*
            $PLANS := PLANS \setminus \mathcal{P}$; $BestCoalition := \widetilde{C}$;
            $BestPayoffperMembership := |\widetilde{C}|$
        (c) *if $BestCoalition = nil$ then for each $\mathcal{P}$ in $POSTPONEDPLANS$ do:*
            i. *if $PPPLANSRISK$ contains $(\mathcal{P}, .)$ then*
            $\widetilde{C} := findFuzzyCoalition(S, \mathcal{P}, PPPLANSRISK(\mathcal{P}))$
            ii. *if $\widetilde{C} = nil$ then next 1b*
            iii. *if $v(\widetilde{C})/|\widetilde{C}| > BestPayoffperMembership$ then*
            $PPPLANSRISK := PPPLANSRISK \setminus \mathcal{P}$;
            $BestCoalition := \widetilde{C}$; $BestPayoffperMembership := |\widetilde{C}|$
    2. *send $(BestCoalition, BestPayoffperMembership)$ as a proposal to all other agents*
    3. *Proposal evaluation*
        (a) *receive coalition proposals from all other agents and self*
        (b) *for each non-nil proposal $(\widetilde{C}, ppm)$, put $\widetilde{C}$ in $PROPS$ with priority ppm.*
        (c) *set $S^* = \emptyset$*
        (d) *while $PROPS$ is not empty do*
            i. *get and remove the highest priority coalition $\widetilde{C}$ from $PROPS$*
            ii. *if $\widetilde{C}$ is feasible, set $S^* := S^* \cup \widetilde{C}$*
    4. *Payoff distribution and TCE update*
        (a) *set $u^* = makeStable(S \cup S^*)$*
        (b) *do atomically: set $S := S \cup S^*$ and $u := u^*$*
        (c) *set $risk_a := risk_a + \sum_{\widetilde{C} \in S_a^*}(TCE_a(\widetilde{C}))$*
- *Risk measure computation of current structure: repeat (until terminated)*
    1. *randomly choose a previously unconsidered subset S^* from S_a*
    2. $risk_a := risk_a - \sum_{\widetilde{C} \in S^*} TCE_a(\widetilde{C}) + TCE_a(S^*)$

- *Risk measure computation of potential structures for postponed plans: repeat (until terminated)*
  1. *Randomly choose $\mathcal{P}$ from $PPPLANS$ such that $(\mathcal{P}, .) \notin PPPLANSRISK$*
  2. *Compute exact $TCE^{\alpha_a}(S \cup \widetilde{C}(sra(\mathcal{P}), \mathcal{P}))$ and put $(\mathcal{P}, TCE^{\alpha_a}(S \cup \widetilde{C}(sra(\mathcal{P}), \mathcal{P})))$ into $PPPLANSRISK$*
- *Termination of negotiation*
  1. *Wait(ExecutionStartTime)*
  2. *terminate all other tasks*
  3. *start service instance execution in my coalitions; terminate*

Proposition 3. *The runtime of the coalition negotiation section of the RFCF is polynomial.*

Proof. In the proposal evaluation, each agent orders the coalition proposals in the same way in the priority queue since the priority is defined as payoff per membership which is a global measure. Because of the bounds used in the surplus computation, the payoff distribution is done in polynomial time (see 5). All other steps in the coalition negotiation section are of less complexity.

7 Related Work

In the research field of fuzzy coalition formation, Nishizaki and Sakawa in [9] proposed a number of algorithms to compute solutions according to their concepts. They did however not propose a protocol that enables a coalition negotiation among computational autonomous agents. Also, as we have pointed out in section 1, they assume that the coalition value is a proportional function of the agents' membership degrees, which does not hold in our case.

Shehory and Kraus considered the formation of overlapping but non-fuzzy coalitions. They however focus on maximising the joint payoff of all agents rather than individual payoffs or minimising potential individual losses. In contrast, our approach focuses especially on the latter points. Thus, the motivations and the properties of the obtained solutions are very different.

There also exist approaches for the formation of non-overlapping coalitions which take uncertainty in the coalition values into account. These are also suitable to tackle the problem of reduced coalition values due to (partial) coalition failure in some cases. Probabilistic approaches, such as [6], usually consider the expected values of coalitions. This might lead to the case that a number of risk-neutral agents decide to form a high-risk coalition, excluding risk-averse agents to cooperate with them because overlapping coalitions are not allowed. In contrast, our approach allows for such cooperations by forming additional coalitions. Approaches that employ fuzzy coalition values, such as [3], account for a range of possible coalition values. However, the fuzzy coalition values are assumed to actually be fuzzy numbers or intervals. But this assumption is not compatible with our setting where a coalition value either produces a specific profit or a specific loss.

8   Conclusions

We have studied a setting of cooperative service provider agents that form fuzzy coalitions in order to share and combine resources and services to efficiently respond to market demands while bounding individual risk. We showed how a coherent risk measure, the TCE, can be used to assess the risk for agents when taking part in coalitions to satisfy service requests with deadlines. By splitting resources among different coalitions, an agent might lower its overall risk. Despite previous work on fuzzy coalitions in the literature, we found it necessary to give our own definitions for the fuzzy coalition game, including the excess and surplus for fuzzy coalitions. This is because of unrealistic assumptions in the cited models that do not hold in our setting. In the surplus computation, sets of alternative fuzzy coalitions have to be considered. As a consequence, we had to bound not only the maximum coalition size, but also the number of coalitions in these sets as well as the number of plans for a set of agents to obtain a polynomial computation time for the fuzzy coalition surplus.

References

1. P. Artzner, F. Delbaen, S. Eber, and D. Heath. Coherent measures of risk. *Mathematical Finance*, pages 203–228, 1999.
2. J.-P. Aubin. *Mathematical Methods of Game and Economic Theory*. North-Holland, 1979.
3. B. Blankenburg, M. Klusch, and O. Shehory. Fuzzy kernel-stable coalitions between rational agents. In *Proc. 2nd Int. Conference on Autonomous Agents and Multiagent Systems, Melbourne, Australia*, 2003.
4. R. N. Bracewell. *The Fourier Transform and Its Applications*. McGraw-Hill Science/Engineering/Math, New York, 3rd edition, 1999.
5. D. Butnariu. Stability and shapley value for an n-persons fuzzy game. *Fuzzy Sets and Systems*, 4:63–72, 1980.
6. G. Chalkiadakis and C. Boutilier. Bayesian reinforcement learning for coalition formation under uncertainty. In *Proc. 3rd Int. Conference on Autonomous Agents and Multiagent Systems, New York, USA*, 2004.
7. S. Cheng, Y. Liu, and S. Wang. Progress in risk management. *Advanced Modelling and Optimization*, 6(1):1–20, 2004.
8. G. R. Grimmett and D. R. Stirzaker. *Probability and Random Processes*. Oxford University Press, 3rd edition, 2001.
9. I. Nishizaki and M. Sakawa. *Masatoshi Fuzzy and multiobjective games for conflict resolution*, volume 64 of *Studies in Fuzziness and Soft Computing*. Physica-Verlag, Heidelberg, 2001.
10. O. Shehory and S. Kraus. Feasible formation of coalitions among autonomous agents. *Computational Intelligence*, 15(3):218–251, 1999.
11. R. E. Stearns. Convergent transfer schemes for n-person games. *Transactions of the American Mathematical Society*, 134:449–459, 1968.

A Simple Argumentation Based Contract Enforcement Mechanism

Nir Oren, Alun Preece, and Timothy J. Norman

Department of Computing Science, University of Aberdeen, Aberdeen, AB24 3UE, Scotland
{noren, apreece, tnorman}@csd.abdn.ac.uk

Abstract. Agents may choose to ignore contract violations if the costs of enforcing the contract exceed the compensation they would receive. In this paper we provide an argumentation based framework for agents to both decide whether to enforce a contract, and to undertake contract enforcement actions. The framework centers around the agent reasoning about what arguments to put forth based on a comparison between the utility it would gain for proving its case and the utility it loses for probing environment state.

1 Introduction

Open environments may contain self–interested agents with different levels of trust-worthiness. While self–interested, these agents may both cooperate and compete so as to increase their own utility. Many mechanisms have been proposed to ensure correct agent behaviour in such environments, and most make use of some form of implicit or explicit contract between the agents[1,17,6]. The purpose of such a contract is to lay out what is expected from each contracting party. Given norm-autonomous agents, i.e. agents which are able to decide whether to fulfil their normative requirements, contracts also allow for the imposition of penalties and compensation to the wronged party if any deviations from the agreed upon behaviour occurs. Sanctioning of agents often takes place through the use of a trust or reputation framework[11], or some monetary mechanism.

In the real world, minor contract violations are often ignored, either due to the loss in trust that would arise between the contracting parties, or due to the small compensation the wronged party would receive when compared to the overhead of enforcing the contract. Even major violations might not result in the wronged party being (fully) compensated, or the guilty party being penalised as the cost of proving the violation might exceed the compensation which would have been obtained by the victim, resulting in them not attempting to enforce the contract. While the former behaviour might be useful to replicate within multi-agent systems (due to increased efficiency), at first glance the latter behaviour seems undesirable. Such behaviour is however rational (and thus desirable in many settings), as it maximises an agent's gain. It could be argued that loss making contract enforcement actions, which might increase the society's welfare as a whole, are the responsibility of some "pro-bono" third party agents, rather than contract participants.

Contract enforcement costs are not constant in many scenarios. Referring again to a typical real world example, if a contract case goes to court, extra costs are incurred due

M. Klusch, M. Rovatsos, and T. Payne (Eds.): CIA 2006, LNAI 4149, pp. 347–359, 2006.
© Springer-Verlag Berlin Heidelberg 2006

not only to lawyer's fees, but also due to the cost of gathering evidence. As the case progresses, additional evidence might be needed, leading to further escalating costs. Some legal systems avoid this by having the loser of a case pay its opponent's fees.

The increasing complexity of artificial agent environments means that many of these scenarios have analogies within the agent domain. Agents interacting with each other on the web, virtual marketplace or a Grid do not trust each other and sign contracts before providing and consuming services. If one agent believes another did not fulfil its obligations, it may need to verify its belief by gathering large amounts of evidence. This evidence gathering might cost it not only computational, but also monetary resources as it might have to purchase information from other agents. In a similar manner, it might cost the accused agent resources to defend itself. Allowing for such behaviour can increase both the efficiency and robustness of agent environments.

In this paper we examine multiple issues related to this type of contract enforcement. We provide an argumentation/dialogue game based framework which allows agents to both decide and undertake contract enforcement actions. We also look at how aspects of this framework can tie into contracting languages. Our work forms part of the CONOISE-G project [12]. CONOISE-G centers around the creation and implementation of technologies designed to improve the performance and robustness of virtual organisations. Agents operating within the environment have their behaviour regulated by contracts, and contract monitoring and enforcement thus form a major part of the project focus.

When an agent believes that a contract it is participating in has been violated, it calculates the amount of utility it would (lose) gain by (not) enforcing the contract. While a net utility gain exists, the agent maintains its enforcement action, bringing up evidence as required. The action of presenting evidence decreases the agent's utility. The accused agent follows a similar process, computing how much utility it would lose by not defending itself, and paying for evidence it uses in its defence. This process ends when one agent either capitulates or has no further evidence to present, after which a decision regarding the status of the contract can be reached. While simple, we believe that this approach can both be useful in a large number of scenarios as well as provide the basis for more complicated techniques.

In the next section we formalise our framework, after which an small example is presented. Section 4 looks at the features of our framework, and places it within the context of related work. Finally, possible extensions to this work are discussed.

2   The Formalism

In this section, we describe our approach in detail. We are primarily interested in only one section of the contract enforcement stage, namely the point at which an agent attempts to prove that another agent has (or has not) broken a contract. Informally, the agent begins by determining how much utility it would gain by proving that it has been wronged, as well as what the net utility gain would be for not being able to prove its claims. A dialogue then begins between the accuser and the accused. In the course of this dialogue, evidence is presented from outside sources. Presenting this evidence costs, imposing an ordering on the best way to present the evidence, as well as possibly causing an agent to give up on its claims. Once the agents have made all the utterances they desire, an adjudication process can take place, determining whether an agent has been able to prove its case. The work presented here is an extension of the work described in [9,8].

We begin by describing the logical layer in which interaction takes place, and the way arguments interact with each other. We decided against using an abstract argumentation framework (such as the one described by Dung [3]) or a legal based argumentation framework (such as Prakken and Sartor's [15]) as our arguments are grounded and do not make use of any default constructs. Making use of our own logical formalism also helps simplify the framework.

After describing the logical level, we specify the dialogue game agents can use to perform contract monitoring actions, examining strategies agents can use to play the game, as well as looking at how to determine the winners and losers of an instance of the game. It should be noted that we discuss very few of our design decisions in this section, instead simply presenting the framework. An in depth examination of the framework is left for Section 4. The section concludes by describing how to transform a contract into a form usable by the framework.

2.1 The Argumentation Framework

Argumentation takes place over the language Σ, which contains propositional literals and their negation.

Definition 1. *Argument. An argument is a pair (P, c), where $P \subseteq \Sigma \cup \{\top\}$ and $c \in \Sigma$ such that if $x \in P$ then $\neg x \notin P$. We define $Args(\Sigma)$ to be the set of all possible arguments derivable from our language.*

P represents the premises of an argument (also referred to as an argument's support), while c stands for an argument's conclusion. Informally, we can read an argument as stating "if the conjunction of its premises holds, the conclusion holds". An argument of the form $(\top, a)$ represents a conclusion requiring no premises (for reasons detailed below, such an argument is not necessarily a fact).

Arguments interact by supporting and attacking each other. Informally, when an argument attacks another, it renders the latter's conclusions invalid.

An argument cannot be introduced into a conversation unless it is grounded. In other words, the argument $(\{a, b\}, c)$ cannot be used unless a and b are either known or can be derived from arguments derivable from known literals. Care must be taken when formally defining the concept of a grounded argument, and before doing so, we must (informally) describe the proof theory used to determine which literals and arguments are justified at any time.

To determine what arguments and literals hold at any one time, let us assume that all arguments refer to beliefs. In this case, we begin by examining grounded beliefs and determining what can be derived from them by following chains of argument. Whenever a conflict occurs (i.e. we are able to derive literals of the form x and $\neg x$), we remove these literals from our derived set. Care must then be taken to eliminate any arguments derived from conflicting literals. To do this, we keep track of the conflicting literals in a separate set, and whenever a new conflict arises, we begin the derivation process afresh, never adding any arguments to the derived set if their conclusions are in the conflict set.

Differentiating between beliefs and facts makes this process slightly more complicated. A literal now has a chance of being removed from the conflict set if it is in the set of known facts.

More formally, an instance of the framework creates two sets $J \subseteq Args(\Sigma)$ and $C \subseteq \Sigma$, while making use of a set of facts $F \subset \Sigma$ such that if $l \in F$ then $\neg l \notin F$ and if $\neg l \in F$ then $l \notin F$ (i.e. F is a consistent set of literals). J and C represent justified arguments and conflicts respectively.

Definition 2. Derivation. *An argument* $A = (P_a, c_a)$ *is derivable from a set* S *given a conflict set* C *(written* $S, C \vdash A$*) iff* $c_a \notin C$ *and* $(\forall p \in P_a (\exists s \in S \text{ such that } s = (P_s, p)$ *and* $p \notin C)$ *or* $P_a = \{\top\})$.

Clearly, we need to know what elements are in C. Given the consistent set of facts F and a knowledge base of arguments $\kappa \subseteq Args(\Sigma)$[1] , this can be done with the following reasoning procedure:

$$J_0 = \{A | A \in \kappa \text{ such that } \{\}, \{\} \vdash A\}$$
$$C_0 = \{\}$$

Then, for $i > 0, j = 1 \ldots i$, we have:

$$C_i^* = C_{i-1} \cup \{c_A, \neg c_A | \exists A = (P_A, c_A), B = (P_B, \neg c_A) \in J_{i-1}\}$$
$$C_i = C_i^* \backslash (C_i^* \cap F)$$
$$X_{i0} = \{A | A \in \kappa \text{ and } \{\}, C_i \vdash A\}$$
$$X_{ij} = \{A | A \in \kappa \text{ and } X_{i(j-1)}, C_i \vdash A\}$$
$$J_i = X_{ii}$$

The set X allows us to recompute all derivable arguments from scratch after every increment of i[2]. Since i represents the length of a chain of arguments, when $i = j$ our set will be consistent to the depth of our reasoning, and we may assign all of these arguments to J. Eventually, $J_i = J_{i-1}$ (and $C_i = C_{i-1}$) which means there are no further arguments to find. We can thus define the conclusions reached by a knowledge base κ as $K = \{c | A = (P, c) \in J_i\}$, for the smallest i such that $J_i = J_{i+1}$. We will use the shorthand $K(\kappa)$ and $C(\kappa)$ to represent those literals which are respectively derivable from, or in conflict with a knowledge base κ. C_i^* represents the conflict set before facts are taken into account.

2.2   The Dialogue Game

Agents make use of the argumentation framework described above in an attempt to convince others of their point of view. An agent has an associated private knowledge

---

[1] We assume that κ contains all our facts, i.e. $\forall f \in F, f \in \kappa$.

[2] This allows us to get rid of long invalid chains of arguments, as well as detect and eliminate arbitrary loops.

base (KB) containing its beliefs, as well as a table listing the costs involved in probing the system for the value of literals (M). An instance of the argumentation dialogue is centred around agents trying to prove or disprove a set of goals G. Utility gains and losses are associated with succeeding or failing to prove these goals. The environment also contains a public knowledge base recording the utterances made by the agents. This knowledge base performs a role similar to a global commitment store, and is thus referred to as CS below.

Definition 3. *Environment.* *An environment is a tuple* $(Agents, CS, F, S)$ *where Agents is the set of agents participating in the dialogue,* $CS \subseteq Args(\Sigma)$ *is a public knowledge base and* $F \subset \Sigma$ *is a consistent set of literals known to be facts.* $S \subseteq \Sigma$ *contains literals representing the environment state.*

Definition 4. *Agent.* *An agent* $\alpha \in Agents$ *is composed of a tuple* $(Name, KB, M, G, U_{win}, U_{draw}, U_{lose}, T)$ *where* $KB \subseteq Args(\Sigma)$, $G \subseteq \Sigma$, M *is a function allowing us to compute the cost of probing the value of a literal.* $U_{win}, U_{draw}, U_{lose} \in \mathbb{R}$ *are the utilities gained for winning, drawing or losing an argument.* $T \in \mathbb{R}$ *keeps track of the total costs incurred by an agent during the course of the argument.*

The monitoring cost function M expresses the cost incurred by an agent when it must probe the environment for the value of a literal. It maps a set of literals to a real number:

Definition 5. *Monitoring costs.* *The monitoring cost function* M *is a domain dependant function* $M : 2^{\Sigma} \rightarrow \mathbb{R}$

Representing monitoring costs in this way allows us to discount multiple probing actions, for example, it might be cheaper for an agent to simultaneously determine the cost of two literals than to probe them individually in turn.

Agents take turns to put forward a line of argument and ascertain the value of a literal by probing the environment. For example $\{((\top, a), (a, b)), b)\}$ is a possible utterance an agent could make, containing the line of argument $\{(\top, a), (a, b)\}$ and probing the environment for whether b is indeed in the environment state. Alternatively, an agent may pass by making an empty utterance $\{,\}$. The dialogue ends when CS has remained unchanged for as many turns as there are players, i.e. after all players have had a chance to make an utterance, but didn't. Once this has happened, it is possible to compute the literals derivable from CS, determine the status of an agent's goal expression, and thus compute who won the dialogue.

Definition 6. *Utterances.* *The utterance function*

$$utterance : Environment \times Name \rightarrow 2^{Args(\Sigma)} \times \Sigma$$

accepts an environment and an agent name, returns the utterance made by the agent. The first part of this utterance lists the arguments advanced by the agents, while the second lists the probed environment states.

Given an agent with a monitoring cost function M, we may compute the cost to the agent of making the utterance (Ar, Pr), where Ar is the line of argument advanced by the agent and Pr is the set of literals the agents would like to probe, as $M(Pr)$.

Definition 7. *Turns. The function*

$$turn : Environment \times Name \rightarrow Environment$$

takes an environment and an agent label, and returns a new environment containing the effects of the agent's utterance.

Given an environment $Env = (Agents, CS, F, S)$ *and an agent*
$\alpha = (Name, KB, M, G, U_{win}, U_{draw}, U_{lose}, T) \in Agents$, *we define the turn function as follows*

$$turn(Env, Name) = (NewAgents, CS \cup Ar, F \cup (Pr \cap S), S) \text{ where } Ar, Pr$$

are computed from the function $utterance(Env, Name) = (Ar, Pr)$, *and*

$$NewAgents = Agents \backslash \alpha \cup (Name, KB, M, G, U_{win}, U_{draw}, U_{lose}, T + M(Pr))$$

We may assume that the agents are named $Agent_0, Agent_1, \ldots, Agent_{n-1}$ where n is the number of agents participating in the dialogue. It should be noted that the inner workings of the *utterance* function are dependant on agent strategy, and we will describe one possible game playing strategy below. Before doing so however, we must define the dialogue game itself. Each turn of the dialogue game results in a new environment, which is used during later turns.

Definition 8. *Dialogue game. The dialogue game can be defined in terms of the turn function as follows:*

$$turn_0 = turn((Agents, CS_0, F_0, S), Agent_0)$$
$$turn_{i+1} = turn(turn_i, Agent_{i \bmod n})$$

The game ends when $turn_i \ldots turn_{i-n+1} = turn_{i-n}$.

CS_0 and F_0 contain the initial arguments and facts, and are usually empty. Note that the agent may make a null utterance $\{,\}$ during its move to (eventually) bring the game to an end. If we assume that our agents private knowledge bases contain only a finite number of arguments, it can easily be seen that the dialogue game will eventually end.

To conclude the dialogue game definition, we need to determine how much utility an agent gains at the end of a dialogue instance. An agent wins the game if it is able to prove all its goals. A draw occurs when the status of an agent's goals are unknown (either due to being indeterminable or in the conflict set).

Definition 9. *Agent utility. Given an environment* $= (Agents, CS, F, S)$, *and abbreviating an agent definition* $(Name, KB, M, G, U_{win}, U_{draw}, U_{lose}, T)$ *as* α, *the winning set of agents is defined as*

$$Agent_{win} = \{\alpha | \alpha \in Agents \text{ such that } G \subseteq K(CS)\}$$

The set of drawing agents is then defined as

$$Agent_{draw} = \{\alpha | \alpha \in Agents \text{ such that}$$
$$\forall g \in G, (g \in C(CS) \text{ or } \{g, \neg g\} \cap K(CS) = \{\})\}$$

All other agents are in the losing set: $Agent_{lose} = Agents \backslash (Agent_{win} \cup Agent_{draw})$.
An agent α may calculate its utility in such an environment by computing

$$U(\alpha) = \begin{cases} U_{win} - T & \text{if } \alpha \in Agent_{win} \\ U_{draw} - T & \text{if } \alpha \in Agent_{draw} \\ U_{lose} - T & \text{if } \alpha \in Agent_{lose} \end{cases}$$

Note that drawing (or even losing) a dialogue game may provide an agent with more utility than winning the game. At the end of the game, $K(CS)$ contains all literals which are agreed to be in force by the agents, while $C(CS)$ contains all conflicting literals.

2.3   The Heuristic

We are now in a position to define one possible technique for taking part in the dialogue game. We assume that our agent is rational and will thus attempt to maximise its utility. By using the reasoning procedure described in Section 2.1 over the environment's knowledge base CS, its knowledge base KB and the set of known facts F, an agent can both determine what literals are currently in force and in conflict, as well as determine the effects of its arguments. Given all possible arguments to advance $PA \in 2^{KB}$, we can define the resultant commitment store by computing $RCS = PA \cup CS$. If we call PF the set of possible facts which the agent an probe, we can compute the set of possible utterances as $PU = RCS \times PF$. By then performing the move for each PU and computing the agent's utility as if the game had ended, an ordering based on utility of the elements of PU can be generated. The agent then returns the element of PU which maximises its utility.

Given a set of possible utterances with equal utility, we use a secondary heuristic (as described in [9]) to choose between them: the agent will make the utterance which reveals as little new information to the opponent as possible. More formally,

Definition 10. *Making utterances. For an environment Env and an agent*
$\alpha = (Name, KB, M, G, U_{win}, U_{draw}, U_{lose}, T)$, *let* $PA \in 2^{KB}$, $RCS = PA \cup CS$.
We compute a set of possible facts accessible by the agent (PF) as[3]

$$PF = \{f, \neg f | f \in (K(RCS) \cup C(RCS)) \backslash F\} \text{ and } \{f, \neg f\} \cap S \neq \{\}$$

The set of all possible utterances is thus $PU = RCS \times PF$. *Let* $Env_{new}(Utt) = turn(Env, Name)$ *where Utt is the utterance function used within the turn function. We can compute the utility of Utt as* $U_{utterance}(Utt) = U(\alpha, Env_{new})$.
Then the agent will make the utterance $Utt = (Ar, Pr) \in PU$ *such that*
$max_{Utt \in PU}(U_{utterance}(Utt))$. *If multiple such possible utterances exist, we will choose one such that* $K(Ar \cup CS) - K(CS) + C(Ar \cup CS) - C(CS)$ *is minimised.*

Assuming that every probing action has an associated utility cost, such an agent would begin by attempting to argue from its beliefs, probing the environment only as a last

---

[3] The second part of the condition allows us a way of limiting the probing to only those facts which are in fact accessible, without having to know their value.

resort. This behaviour is reminiscent of the idea put forward by Gordon's pleadings game [4], where agents argue until certain irreconcilable differences arise, after which they approach an arbitrator to settle the matter.

It should also be noted that our framework allows for different probing costs to be associated with probing for a value or its negation. This makes sense in a contracting environment, as different sensors might be used to perform these two types of probing actions.

2.4   Contracts

To utilise such a framework in the context of contracting requires a number of additional features:

1. S, the set of facts which can be probed, must be defined.
2. T the agent's cost for performing the probing must also be determined.
3. G the set of agent goals must be computed.
4. The agent's winning, drawing and losing utilities must be set appropriately.
5. The agent's knowledge bases KB must be created to reflect the content of the contract, as well as any initial beliefs held by the agents regarding the environment state.
6. F_0, the set of known facts must be generated.

While all of these are contract specific, some guidelines can be provided due to the features of the framework. Given a two party contract, we can assign our agents plaintiff and defendant roles. Usually, they will have opposite goals, initially determined by a combination of the contract clauses and the the plaintiff's beliefs regarding the environment state. The set S, as well as the cost of performing the probing is determined by the contract, and the contract clauses, together with an agent's beliefs about the state of the world are used to determine an agent's KB. F_0 (and thus CS_0) will not be empty if certain facts about the environment state are already known.

Item 4 is interesting. Most legal systems operate under the requirement that a plaintiff prove their case either on the balance of probabilities, or beyond reasonable doubt. Given the binary nature of our framework, both reduce to the same level. This means that the winning and drawing utilities for the defendant will be the same, while the drawing and losing utilities of the plaintiff will be identical. For many contracts, The winning utility of the plaintiff will be the same as the losing utility of the defendant (reflecting the fact that the defendant will have to pay the plaintiff in the case of a loss).

To simplify matters, we assume that a contract is enforced in its entirety, i.e. all issues must be settled in favour of the plaintiff for them to win. We thus define a contract as follows:

Definition 11. Contract. *A contract consists of the tuple*
$(Plaintiff, Defendant, Clauses, Monitors, Issues, Penalty)$ *where Plaintiff and Defendant are labels, Clauses* $\in Args(\Sigma)$, *Monitors* $: \{Plaintiff, Defendant\} \times 2^\sigma \to \mathbb{R}$, *Issues* $\subseteq \Sigma$, *and Penalty* $\in \mathbb{R}$.

Given such a contract, as well as a set of states S, we can instantiate our framework as follows:

$$Environment = ((Agents_0, Agents_1), , , S)$$

$$Agents_0 = (Plaintiff, Clauses, M_{Plaintiff}, Issues, Penalty, 0, 0, 0)$$

$$Agents_1 = (Defendant, Clauses, M_{Defendant}, Issues, 0, Penalty, Penalty, 0)$$

Where $M_{Plaintiff}$ and $M_{Defendant}$ are computed by partially parameterising the $Monitors$ function with the appropriate label. Note that the defendant's goals are the same as the plaintiff's goals, but that it gains utility for "losing" or drawing the game, as this would mean it had successfully defended it's stance.

At this stage, contract enforcement is possible using the framework. We will now provide a short example to illustrate the framework in operation.

3   Example

We will look at a very simple scenario (taken from the service provision scenario described in [12]) where a provider agent has agreed to provide a movie service to a consumer agent, subject to restrictions on the movie framerate.

Given the following contract clauses

$$fr25 \rightarrow payPerson$$
$$\neg fr25 \rightarrow giveWarning1$$
$$wrongMovie \rightarrow giveWarning2$$
$$giveWarning1 \wedge giveWarning2 \rightarrow penalty$$

We assume that monitors exist for $fr25, giveWarning1$ and $giveWarning2$ at a cost of 5,10 and 20 respectively. Finally, let the penalty for contract violation be 30 units of currency.

Now let us assume that the consumer believes that it has been given the incorrect movie, and when the movie finally arrived, its framerate was below 25 frames per second (i.e. the literal $\neg fr25$ evaluates to true). Furthermore, the provider disputes all of this, believing that it provided the right movie at an appropriate framerate. After creating the agents using the method described in Section 2.4, the following conversation might take place (omitting brackets for the sake of readability where necessary):

$(P1)$ $(\{(\neg fr25, giveWarning1), (wrongMovie, giveWarning2),$
$\quad (\{giveWarning1, giveWarning2\}, penalty)\}, \{\})$
$(D2)$ $((\top, fr25), \{\})$
$(P3)$ $(\{\}, \{\neg fr25, fr25\})$
$(D4)$ $((\top, \neg wrongMovie))$
$(P5)$ $(\{\}, \{\neg giveWarning2, giveWarning2\})$
$(D6)$ $()$
$(P7)$ $()$

The plaintiff first puts forward its case, based on its beliefs. Since the agent attempts to reveal as little as possible, the defendant utters just enough to counter the plaintiff's argument. The plaintiff responds by giving proof for its argument, as that is all it can do. Note that the state of $fr25$ rather than $giveWarning1$ was probed due to its lower utility cost. This process repeats itself for $wrongMovie$, but since this literal is not directly observable, the agent must probe its conclusion instead. Finally, no more arguments are put forward, and the case is decided in favour of the plaintiff, who earns a net utility of 5.

Had the defendant attempted to argue for its beliefs regarding the state of $fr25$ in an earlier contract enforcement episode, then this round of argument may have begun with $\neg fr25$ already being an established fact (i.e. part of F_0). As can be seen it is difficult to provide an all encompassing domain independent set of rules to convert a contract, agents, and environment into a form suitable for a contract enforcement action.

While simple, the example should serve to illustrate how contract enforcement can take place using our framework. In the next section we will discuss the framework's properties in more detail, as well as look at related work and possible directions for future research.

4   Discussion

While we have focused on using our framework for contract enforcement, it can also be used in other settings. For example, given a non-adversarial setting where probing sensors still has some associated cost (for example, of network resources or time), an agent can reason with the framework (by generating an argument leading to its goals) to minimise these sensing costs.

The contract enforcement stage is only part of the greater contracting life-cycle. With some adaptation, our framework can also be used in the contract monitoring stage: by constantly modifying its beliefs based on inputs from the environment, an agent could continuously attempt to prove that a contract has failed; once this occurs contract enforcement would begin.

Contract enforcement and monitoring has been examined by a number of other researchers. Given a fully observable environment in which state determination is not associated with a utility cost, the problem reduces to data mining. Research such as [19] operates in such an environment, but focus more on the problem of predicting imminent contract failure. Daskalopulu et al. [2] have suggested a subjective logic [5] based approach for contract enforcement in partially observable environments. Here, a contract is represented as a finite state machine, with an agent's actions leading to state transitions. A central monitor assigns different agents different levels of trust, and combines reports from them to determine the most likely state of the system. While some weaknesses exist with this approach, most techniques for contract enforcement are similar in nature, making use of some uncertainty framework to determine what the most likely system state is, then translating this state into a contract state, finally determining whether a violation occurred. An argumentation based approach potentially has both computational as well as representational advantages over existing methods. In earlier work[10], we described a contracting language for service level agreements based on semantic web standards (called SWCL). One interesting feature of that work is the appearance of an explicit monitoring clause describing where to gather information regarding specific environment states. Most other contracting languages lack such a feature, and the addition of a monitoring cost would allow SWCL to be used as part of our framework. A related feature of our framework which, in a contracting context would require a language with appropriate capabilities, is the ability to assign different monitoring costs for determining whether a literal or its negation holds. In an open world environment, such a feature is highly desirable.

Argumentation researchers have long known that a dialogue should remain relevant to the topic under discussion [7]. This trait allows dialogue based systems to rapidly reach a solution. The approach presented here enforces this requirement due to the nature of the heuristic; any extraneous utterances will lead to a reduction in an agent's final utility. One disadvantage of our approach is that, as presented, the computational complexity of deciding what utterance to make is exponential in nature. Simple optimisations can be implemented to reduce the average case complexity, but in the worst case, all possible arguments must still be considered. Mitigating this is the fact that the number of clauses involved in a contract enforcement action is normally relatively small, making its use practical in the contracting domain.

Many different argumentation frameworks have been proposed in the literature ([16] provides an excellent overview of the field). We decided to design our own framework rather than use an existing approach for a number of reasons. First, many frameworks are abstract in nature, requiring the embedding of a logic, and then making use of some form of attacking relation to compute which arguments are, or are not in force. Less abstract frameworks focus on the non–monotonic nature of argument, often requiring a default logic be used. The manner in which agents reason using our heuristic, as well as the grounded nature of the subject of arguments in our domain makes the argumentation framework presented here more suitable than others for this type of work. However, we intend to show the relationship between our framework and sceptical semantics in existing argumentation frameworks in future work.

Legal argumentation systems often grapple with the concept of burden of proof (e.g. [13,14,18]). We attempt to circumnavigate the problem of assigning responsibility for proving the state of a literal to a specific agent by having agents probe for the value themselves as needed. This approach will not work in more complicated scenarios with conflicting sensors, and extending the framework to operate in such environments should prove interesting.

One quirk of our framework is that we do not do belief revision when agents are presented with facts. While adapting the method in which $NewAgents$ are created in Definition 7 is possible by setting the new agent's KB to be $KB \cup (\top, f) \forall f \in F$, and even remove any "obviously conflicting" beliefs, we are still unable to remove beliefs that arise from the application of chains of arguments. We would thus claim that an agent's beliefs are actually a combination of its private knowledge base KB, the public knowledge base CS and the set of presented facts F, rather than being solely a product of KB. Overriding beliefs with facts means our framework assigns a higher priority to fact based argument than belief based argument. This is reminiscent of many existing priority based argumentation frameworks such as [15].

Another possible area of future work involves reasoning about contracts with multiple weakly related clauses. Currently, an agent wins or loses an argument based on whether it can prove all its goals. This (unrealistic) assumption simplifies the problem greatly.

By enriching the framework with a more complicated reward function, an agent would be able to gain (or lose) utility by proving only some of its goals. Such work would probably need other enhancements such as opponent modelling and the integration of a planner to allow the agents to plan arguments further than just its next utterance.

Finally, the procedure used to transform a contract into an environment and agents for argumentation is very simple. Enhancing this procedure to make use of the full power of the argumentation framework requires further examination. This enhancement will allow for both the representation of, and dialogue regarding, more complex contracts, further increasing the utility of the framework. Another area of future work involves n–party contracts. While our framework provides support for such dialogue, agents, we have not examined what such contracts would look like, and this might be an interesting research direction to pursue.

5   Conclusions

Explicit or implicit contracts are the dominant method for specifying desired agent behaviour within complex multi-agent systems. Contract enforcement is necessary when agents are able to renege on their obligations.

In this paper we have presented an argumentation based framework for contract enforcement within partially observable environments for which querying sensors has an associated cost. This work can prove useful in a variety of settings, including untrusted (and trusted) distributed computing environments such as the Grid. While many interesting research questions remain, we believe that our framework provides a good starting point to model, and reason about such environments.

Acknowledgements

This work is partly funded by the DTI/EPSRC E-Science Core Program and BT, via a grant for the CONOISE-G project (http://www.conoise.org), a multi-university collaboration between Aberdeen, Cardiff and Southampton universities, and BT.

References

1. R. K. Dash, N. R. Jennings, and D. C. Parkes. Computational–mechanism design: A call to arms. *IEEE Intelligent Systems*, 18(6):40–47, 2003.
2. A. Daskalopulu, T. Dimitrakos, and T. Maibaum. Evidence-based electronic contract performance monitoring. *Group Decision and Negotiation*, 11(6):469–485, 2002.
3. P. M. Dung. On the acceptability of arguments and its fundamental role in nonmonotonic reasoning, logic programming and n-person games. *Artificial Intelligence*, 77(2):321–357, 1995.
4. T. F. Gordon. The pleadings game: formalizing procedural justice. In *Proceedings of the fourth international conference on Artificial intelligence and law*, pages 10–19. ACM Press, 1993.
5. A. Josang. Subjective evidential reasoning. In *Proceedings of the 9th International Conference on Information Processing and Management of Uncertainty in Knowledge-Based Systems*, pages 1671–1678, July 2002.

6. M. J. Kollingbaum and T. J. Norman. Supervised interaction – creating a web of trust for contracting agents in electronic environments. In *Proceedings of the First International Joint Conference on Autonomous Agents and Multi–Agent Systems*, pages 272–279, 2002.

7. D. Moore. *Dialogue game theory for intelligent tutoring systems*. PhD thesis, Leeds Metropolitan University, 1993.

8. N. Oren, T. J. Norman, and A. Preece. Arguing with confidential information. In *Proceedings of the 18th European Conference on Artificial Intelligence*, Riva del Garda, Italy, August 2006. (To appear).

9. N. Oren, T. J. Norman, and A. Preece. Loose lips sink ships: a heuristic for argumentation. In *Proceedings of the Third International Workshop on Argumentation in Multi-Agent Systems (ArgMAS 2006)*, pages 121–134, Hakodate, Japan, May 2006.

10. N. Oren, A. Preece, and T. J. Norman. Service level agreements for semantic web agents. In *Proceedings of the AAAI Fall Symposium on Agents and the Semantic Web*, pages 47–54, 2005.

11. J. Patel, W. Teacy, N. Jennings, and M. Luck. A probabilistic trust model for handling inaccurate reputation sources. In *Proceedings of Third International Conference on Trust Management*, pages 193–209, 2005.

12. J. Patel, W. T. L. Teacy, N. R. Jennings, M. Luck, S. Chalmers, N. Oren, T. J. Norman, A. Preece, P. M. D. Gray, Shercliff, P. J. G., Stockreisser, J. Shao, W. A. Gray, N. J. Fiddian, and S. Thompson. Agent-based virtual organisations for the grid. *International Journal of Multi-Agent and Grid Systems*, 1(4):237–249, 2005.

13. H. Prakken. Modelling defeasibility in law: Logic or procedure? *Fundamenta Informaticae*, 48(2-3):253–271, 2001.

14. H. Prakken, C. A. Reed, and D. N. Walton. Argumentation schemes and burden of proof. In *Workshop Notes of the Fourth Workshop on Computational Models of Natural Argument*, 2004.

15. H. Prakken and G. Sartor. A dialectical model of assessing conflicting arguments in legal reasoning. *Artificial Intelligence and Law*, 4:331–368, 1996.

16. H. Prakken and G. Vreeswijk. Logics for defeasible argumentation. In D. Gabbay and F. Guenthner, editors, *Handbook of philosophical logic, 2nd Edition*, volume 4, pages 218–319. Kluwer Academic Publishers, 2002.

17. Y. Shoham and M. Tennenholtz. On social laws for artificial agent societies: Off-line design. *Artificial Intelligence*, 73(1–2):231–252, 1995.

18. D. N. Walton. Burden of proof. *Argumentation*, 2:233–254, 1988.

19. L. Xu and M. A. Jeusfeld. *Pro-active monitoring of electronic contracts*, volume 2681 of *Lecture notes in Computer Science*, pages 584–600. Springer-Verlag GmbH, 2003.

A Fuzzy Approach to Reasoning with Trust, Distrust and Insufficient Trust

Nathan Griffiths

Department of Computer Science, University of Warwick,
Coventry, CV4 7AL, UK
nathan@dcs.warwick.ac.uk

Abstract. Multi-agent systems are based upon cooperative interactions between agents, in which agents provide information, resources and services to others. Typically agents are autonomous and self-interested, meaning that they have control over their own actions, and that they seek to maximise their own goal achievement, rather than necessarily acting in a benevolent or socially-oriented manner. Consequently, interaction outcomes are uncertain since commitments can be broken and the actual services rendered may differ from expectations in terms of cost or quality. Cooperation is, therefore, an uncertain interaction, that has an inherent risk of failure or reduced performance. In this paper we show how agents can use trust to manage this risk. Our approach uses fuzzy logic to represent trust and allow agents to reason with uncertain and imprecise information regarding others' trustworthiness.

1 Introduction

Cooperation is the foundation of all multi-agent systems. Agents typically lack the knowledge, capabilities or resources needed to achieve their objectives alone, and it is through cooperation that they are able to function effectively. Individual agents provide information, resources and services to others in exchange for some form of payment. In order to achieve flexibility and robustness, agents are typically given the autonomy to control their own individual goals and actions. By definition, however, this autonomy implies that agents have control over how they cooperate. In particular, agents determine for themselves when to initiate cooperation or assist others, when to rescind cooperative commitments, and how to conduct cooperative tasks. Consequently, where agents cooperate any one of them may change the nature of their contribution, or even cease to cooperate, at any time. For example, an agent may choose to delay the provision of information, perform a processing task to a reduced quality, or simply fail to fulfil its commitments. Such failures are costly to the remaining cooperating agents since their goals may not be achieved, or not achieved as effectively (i.e. to a lower quality or with an increased cost).

On entering into cooperation an agent begins an uncertain interaction in which there is a risk of failure (or reduced performance) due to the decisions and actions of another. To function effectively, an agent needs to manage this risk.

M. Klusch, M. Rovatsos, and T. Payne (Eds.): CIA 2006, LNAI 4149, pp. 360–374, 2006.

In this paper we show how agents can use the notion of trust, based on their individual experiences, to manage this risk by selecting appropriate interaction partners. Our approach uses fuzzy logic to represent trust and to allow agents to reason with uncertain and imprecise information. In addition to positive trust, we introduce the notions of negative trust (distrust) and insufficient trust (untrust and undistrust), and show how agents can use these concepts to increase the effectiveness of their interactions. Our approach to using fuzzy logic to represent trust was initially described in [4]. In this paper, we describe a refinement of the reasoning process, discuss how negative and insufficient trust can be incorporated into an agent's reasoning, and present our initial experimental results.

2 Background

2.1 Trust and Reputation

Trust and reputation are related, but distinct, concepts. The former represents an agent's *individual* assessment of the reliability, honesty etc. of another, while the latter is a *social* notion corresponding to a group assessment of such issues. Reputation is generally built by combining trust assessments (or recommendations) given by a group of agents to obtain a single value representing an estimate of reputation. The process of combining individual assessments or recommendations into a group notion generally requires agents to make their private assessments of others publicly available. Agents do not necessarily need to reveal the full details of their private assessments but they do need to reveal whether a given agent is considered trustworthy or not[1]. In some situations this can be undesirable from an individual's perspective, since it involves revealing private information that may reduce future effectiveness. For example, suppose that an agent α frequently cooperates with β, who reliably provides high quality and timely information. If α were to make its assessment of β's reliability and quality (i.e. its trustworthiness) public, then β may become overloaded and unreliable for α's future interactions.

In providing trust information to establish reputation, an agent might reduce the effectiveness of its own future interactions. For an agent to provide such information, there must be some intrinsic motivation for information sharing. In the absence of such a motivation, there will be insufficient information to assess reputation. There are also general issues with reputation concerning the subjectivity and context-specific nature of feedback [5]. Although in many situations the benefits of reputation might outweigh the individual cost of trust information sharing, it is useful in general to consider trust and reputation as separate, enabling agents to use trust without considering reputation.

Many of the existing applications of trust combine the notions of trust and reputation by using a global aggregation of individual trust into a reputation

---

[1] Other potential approaches, such as a polling mechanism, remove the need to make such private information public, however most existing approaches require the sharing of individual "trust recommendations".

assessment [13, 14, 15, 16]. Such research tends not to address how trust itself can be used in an individual's decision making. In this paper we focus specifically on trust from an individual's perspective, and do not consider reputation further. Our approach is complimentary to reputation-based models, and we view trust and reputation as both playing an important role in a complete system. Moreover, existing approaches also do not account for the roles of distrust and insufficient trust in the decision making process.

Existing models of trust can be categorised according to how trust is used: for achieving security or for enhancing quality of service [3]. In this paper we focus on the quality of service perspective to enable agents to maximise the "quality" of their interactions according to their current preferences.

2.2 Fuzzy Logic for Trust

Trust represents an individual's assessment of the reliability, honesty etc. of another, and the level of trust ascribed to an agent is based on the individual's experiences with that agent: positive experiences lead to positive trust and negative ones to distrust. However, although based on the known outcomes of previous experiences there is inherent uncertainty regarding the level of trust ascribed to an agent. For example, there is no guarantee that a previously reliable agent will continue to be so. Fuzzy logic offers the ability to handle uncertainty and imprecision effectively [12], and is therefore ideally suited to reasoning about trust. Inference using fuzzy logic copes with imprecise inputs, such as assessments of quality, and allows inference rules to be specified using imprecise linguistic terms, such as "very high quality" or "slightly late". Existing approaches have successfully used fuzzy logic to represent trust in multi-agent systems [8, 11] and peer-to-peer systems [14]. However, these existing techniques use trust as a means of establishing reputation, rather than focusing on individual trust in its own right. In this paper we aim to show how agents can enhance their interactions by using trust based on their individual experiences. Moreover, the existing approaches do not adequately consider the notions of negative and insufficient trust. We describe, in this paper, a method that uses fuzzy logic to make assessments about various aspects of trust, and allows agents to make decisions based on trust, distrust and insufficient trust. Before presenting our approach, however, we introduce some basic fuzzy concepts.

2.3 Basic Fuzzy Concepts

In classical set theory the membership of an object in a set is clearly defined: it is either a member or it is not. For example, a person of age 10 might be a member of the set *young*, and not of the set *old*. Such sets are required to have well-defined boundaries. However, the *concept* of young does not have a clear boundary, and in some contexts age 30 might be considered to be young, and not in others. *Fuzzy sets* are based on the notion of a *membership function*, $\mu(x)$, which defines the degree to which a fuzzy variable x is a member of a set. Full membership is represented by 1, and no membership by 0. The membership function $\mu(x)$

maps x into the interval $[0, 1]$. For example, age 35 might have a membership of 0.8 in a fuzzy set $\widetilde{y}$, representing young ages, and a 0.1 membership in the set $\widetilde{o}$ representing old ages. We use a tilde accent, $\widetilde{x}$, to indicate that a set x is a fuzzy set. The *universe of discourse* of a fuzzy set corresponds to the range of values that are considered, such as $[0, 130]$ for age.

Fuzzy sets are used to define *terms* with respect to a *variable*. For example, the sets $\widetilde{y}$ and $\widetilde{o}$ define the terms $\widetilde{young}$ and $\widetilde{old}$ respectively, on the variable *age*. Terms can be subjected to *modifiers* (also called *linguistic hedges*), such as very or slightly, which serve to modify, or hedge, the membership function from its original definition. The former example *concentrates* the membership function, while the latter *dilates* it. A discussion of the mathematical definition of such modifiers is beyond the scope of this paper, but we adopt Zadeh's definitions which follow the intuitive linguistic meanings [17]. For example, if we define $\alpha = \int_Y \frac{\mu_\alpha(y)}{y}$ then very $\alpha = \int_Y \frac{[\mu_\alpha(y)]^2}{y}$ and slightly $\alpha = \int_Y \frac{[\mu_\alpha(y)]^{0.5}}{y}$ (for further details see [12, 17]).

Relations between variables can be defined using *fuzzy inference rules* of the form:

> **if** $input_1$ is [modifier$_1$] $\widetilde{term_1}$ **and** $input_2$ is [modifier$_2$] $\widetilde{term_2}$
> **then** *output* is modifier' $\widetilde{term'}$

which define the relationship between antecedents ($input_1$ and $input_2$) and consequent (*output*), described by terms $\widetilde{term}_1$, $\widetilde{term}_2$ and $\widetilde{term}'$ and optional modifiers modifier$_1$, modifier$_2$ and modifier'. For example, we might have rules such as the following.

> (R1) **if** *age* is $\widetilde{young}$ **and** *income* is very $\widetilde{high}$
>   **then** *customerPotential* is $\widetilde{high}$
> (R2) **if** *age* is $\widetilde{old}$ **and** *income* is $\widetilde{low}$
>   **then** *customerPotential* is $\widetilde{medium}$

Rules are applied in parallel, and the conclusion membership degrees are aggregated by superimposing the resultant membership curves (i.e. by taking the fuzzy union of the resulting fuzzy sets). We adopt a Mamdani min-max approach to inference, such that the membership degree of the rule conclusions is clipped at a level determined by the minimum of the maximum membership values of the intersections of the fuzzy value antecedent and input pairs [7]. This ensures that the degree of membership in the antecedents is reflected in the output. We give an example of how Mamdani min-max inference operates for fuzzy trust in Section 5.

A crisp value can be obtained from the result of inference by *defuzzifying* the aggregated consequents. There are many methods for defuzzification, but for simplicity we take the centre of the area bounded by the membership curve. (Further discussion of the concepts introduced in this section can be found in [12].)

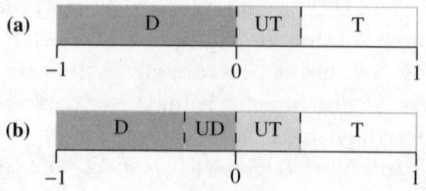

Fig. 1. (a) Marsh's notions of trust and, (b) our addition of undistrust, where D, UD, UT, and T correspond to distrust, undistrust, untrust, and trust respectively

3   Trust

Our proposed mechanism builds on existing work using service-oriented trust in agent-based systems. Trust is generally taken to be the belief that an agent will act in the best interests of another (i.e. that it will cooperate), even if given the opportunity to do otherwise (i.e. to defect) [1, 2]. When entering into cooperation an agent can use its trust of potential partners to evaluate the risk of failure. Most previous work on trust has concentrated the positive side of trust (analogous to assessing the extent to which an agent is reliable), and has largely ignored the notion of *distrust* (analogous to assessing the extent to which an agent is *un*reliable). Distrust is not simply the negation of trust [6], but rather it is an explicit belief that an agent will act against the best interests of another [9]. Alternatively, *untrust* corresponds to the space between distrust and trust, in which an agent is positively trusted, but not sufficiently to cooperate with. This view of trust, proposed by Marsh, is illustrated in Fig. 1(a). Marsh argues that distrust is an important concept, that can play an important role in an agent's reasoning, complimenting trust itself [9].

We concur with Marsh's view regarding the importance of distrust, and in this paper we provide a mechanism for agents to make use of distrust in their decision making. In addition to distrust, untrust and trust, however, we propose a new notion of *undistrust*. Untrust is defined as positive trust, but insufficient to support cooperation. For distrust to play a useful role in an agent's reasoning, we argue that a similar region of undistrust is needed, namely, a region of negative trust but insufficient to make definite conclusions in the reasoning process. Fig. 1(b) illustrates our definition of the notions of trust, distrust, untrust and undistrust. Although agents can not use untrust and undistrust to make definite conclusions regarding trust, they can still make use of the notions of untrust and undistrust in their reasoning regarding cooperation. For example, if there are no trusted agents with whom to interact then an agent may choose to interact with an untrusted, or even an undistrusted, agent provided that the cost of failure is relatively low (i.e. where it is better to have tried and failed that not to have tried at all).

4   Interaction Histories

Trust is based on an agent's individual experiences (since in this paper, as noted above, we do not consider reputation), and so each agent must keep track of its previous interactions. Some interactions may simply have a binary result of success or failure. However, typical cooperative interactions are more complex than simple succeed or fail tasks, and tasks may partially succeed, or be completed with different characteristics than expected. For example, an agent that has agreed to provide information may provide it late or with less detail than expected. This might not cause the goal of the receiving agent to completely fail, but it may cause the receiving agent's level of performance to reduce. Therefore, to enable agents to make effective use of trust we require them to represent more than a simple expectation about success or failure. We take a multi-dimensional view of trust as comprising the combination of the different dimensions of an interaction, such as the quality of a task or the cost imposed for executing it, in addition to whether an interaction was successful or not. Agents model such characteristics as *dimensions of trust*, which taken together give an assessment of an agent's trustworthiness. For illustrative purposes, in this paper we consider the dimensions of success, cost, and quality, although other dimensions are equally possible. The multi-dimensional approach provides a mechanism that allows agents to reason about the specific characteristics of an interaction where appropriate.

In order to assess trust an agent must evaluate its experiences in each of the trust dimensions. For each interaction, and in each dimension, an agent's expectations will have either been met or not met. Agents maintain a history of the interactions that they have had with each other agent, and track the number of successful and unsuccessful interactions for each dimension, in terms of whether their expectations were met. Thus, for each dimension, d, and agent that has been cooperated with, α, an agent maintains a value I_{α}^{d+} which corresponds to the number of interactions in which its expectations were met, and a value I_{α}^{d-} in which they were not met. From these values, the *experience*, e_{α}^{d}, in each dimension d, for each agent α, can be calculated as:

$$e_{\alpha}^{d} = \frac{I_{\alpha}^{d+} - I_{\alpha}^{d-}}{I_{\alpha}^{d+} + I_{\alpha}^{d-}}$$

Such experience values are the basic information from which an agent can assess the trustworthiness of others. They are crisp values in the interval $[-1, 1]$ and must be translated into fuzzy values in order to reason about trust. Experience values are based directly on an agent's interaction histories, and so they are not uncertain in themselves. Rather, the uncertainty for trust comes from a lack of information about other agents' future actions. Therefore, each experience value is fuzzified by translating it into a fuzzy value defined by the singleton fuzzy set whose membership function is 0 at all points except for e_{α}^{d} which has a membership of 1. Thus, the fuzzified experience is given by $E_{\alpha}^{d} = fuzzySingleton(e_{\alpha}^{d})$.

4.1   Purging Old Interactions

Agents keep track of the outcomes of their interactions by using a window of experiences that is maintained for each other agent. This window is bounded, such that there is an upper limit on the number of interactions that are recorded for any agent. The interaction window acts as a first-in first-out queue, and when full it is the earliest experiences that are removed to be replaced by new ones. Over time, however, the information stored may become outdated if the environment (particularly in terms of the character of the other agents) has changed and previous experiences are no longer relevant. Agents may change, and an agent that was reliable previously may no longer be so. To address this problem an agent purges outdated experiences from its interaction windows after a certain predefined period. Thus, even if an interaction window is not full, the record of experiences will be removed over time.

The delay between the occurrence of an interaction and the removal of its record from the interaction window is called the *purge lag*, and has a direct influence on how quickly an agent's trust assessments respond to changes in its environment. A small purge lag means that interaction records do not persist for long and so the effect of previous experiences decays quickly and trust assessments respond quickly to changes. However, a small purge lag also reduces the extent of the experiences that can be used to determine trust. If the purge lag is too small there will be insufficient experiences on which to base trust, and any small perturbations in others' reliability and honesty will have a significant effect on trust. Conversely, a large purge lag avoids magnifying the effects of small perturbations in others' reliability, but increases the number of interactions that are required to react to changes in the environment. Thus, trust assessments are slow to respond to change.

In determining trust it is important that an agent has sufficient experience on which to calculate trust. We define the confidence level in the experience for a particular dimension as the total number of interactions on which it is based.

$$confidence_\alpha^d = I_\alpha^{d+} + I_\alpha^{d-}$$

If this confidence level is below a predefined threshold then either a value of untrust or undistrust will be ascribed (for the success dimension), or a default value will be used (for other dimensions) as described in the following section. Note that there may be different levels of confidence for different dimensions. For example, there are likely to be fewer interactions relevant to quality than success, since only successful interactions will contribute to the quality dimension whereas all interactions will contribute to the success dimension.

5   Fuzzy Trust

We define fuzzy terms for experience in each of the dimensions in which agents record their interactions, in our case success, cost, and quality. Fuzzy terms are defined in reference to fuzzy variables, and for experience we define fuzzy

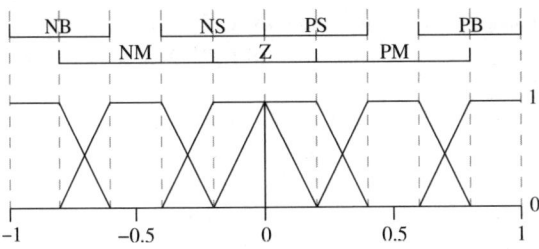

Fig. 2. Definition of fuzzy terms for experience, where NB, NM, NS, Z, PS, PM, and PB correspond to negative big, negative medium, negative small, zero, positive small, positive medium and positive big respectively

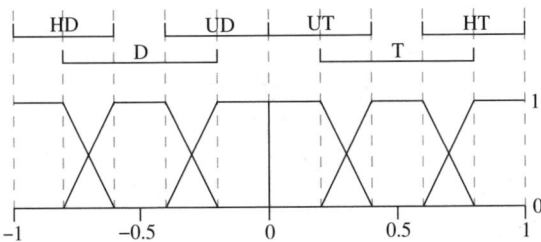

Fig. 3. Definition of fuzzy terms for trust, where HD, D, UD, UT, T, and HT correspond to high distrust, distrust, undistrust, untrust, trust, and high trust respectively

variables for each trust dimension. Thus, for our chosen dimensions we introduce E^s_α, E^c_α, and E^q_α corresponding to the experiences in the dimensions of success, cost, and quality for agent α respectively. The universe of discourse of these fuzzy variables is $[-1, 1]$, i.e. ranging from expectations never being met to expectations always being met. For each of these variables we define the terms: negative big, negative medium, negative small, zero, positive small, positive medium, and positive big. Other terms are possible, but these are sufficient for our purposes. The fuzzy sets that describe these terms are illustrated in Fig. 2.

In order to use fuzzy inference to determine trust, T_α, in an agent α we must also define trust as a fuzzy variable, with an associated set of fuzzy terms. The universe of discourse for trust is also $[-1, 1]$, i.e. complete distrust to complete trust, and we define the terms: high distrust, distrust, undistrust, untrust, trust, and high trust. These terms allow us to represent that there is insufficient trust for reasoning, in the form of untrust and undistrust, along with representing two degrees of trust and distrust. Again, other definitions are possible, but these are sufficient for our application. The fuzzy sets that describe these terms are illustrated in Fig. 3.

For each dimension we define a set of fuzzy inference rules that take the fuzzified experiences as antecedents and make conclusions regarding trust. The definition of these rules is the responsibility of the system developer, and we do not prescribe a particular rule set. In the experiments described in Section 6 we

$(R_{UT}1)$ **if** $confidence_\alpha^d < minConfidence$ **and** E_α^d is *positive* **then** T_α is $\widetilde{untrust}$

$(R_{UT}2)$ **if** $confidence_\alpha^d < minConfidence$ **and** E_α^d is *negative* **then** T_α is $\widetilde{undistrust}$

...

(R_T1) **if** E_α^d is $\widetilde{negativeBig}$ **then** T_α is $\widetilde{highDistrust}$

(R_T2) **if** E_α^d is $\widetilde{negativeMedium}$ **then** T_α is very $\widetilde{distrust}$ or $\widetilde{undistrust}$

(R_T3) **if** E_α^d is $\widetilde{negativeSmall}$ **then** T_α is $\widetilde{undistrust}$

(R_T4) **if** E_α^d is $\widetilde{zero}$ **then** T_α is $\widetilde{undistrust}$ or $\widetilde{untrust}$

(R_T5) **if** E_α^d is $\widetilde{positiveSmall}$ **then** T_α is $\widetilde{untrust}$

(R_T6) **if** E_α^d is $\widetilde{positiveMedium}$ **then** T_α is very $\widetilde{trust}$ or $\widetilde{untrust}$

(R_T7) **if** E_α^d is $\widetilde{positiveBig}$ **then** T_α is $\widetilde{highTrust}$

...

(R_Rn) **if** T_α is $\widetilde{highTrust}$ **and** F_α^c is $\widetilde{medium}$ **and** F_α^q is very $\widetilde{high}$ **then** R_α is $\widetilde{high}$

(R_Rm) **if** T_α is low $\widetilde{distrust}$ **and** F_α^c is $\widetilde{medium}$ **and** F_α^q is $\widetilde{high}$ **then** R_α is $\widetilde{low}$

Fig. 4. Example fuzzy inference rules

use the rules R_T1–R_T7 given in Fig. 4 along with additional rules of the form of R_Rn. Other rules are, of course, possible and can be easily incorporated into the system.

5.1 Determining Trust

Before determining the trustworthiness of an agent the assessor must check whether there have been sufficient previous interactions to calculate trust. All previous interactions will either have succeeded or failed (there is no notion of a 'partial' success), and so we use the success dimension to determine whether there is sufficient information to calculate trust. If there have not been sufficient interactions in the success dimension then the agent is ascribed a value of un-trust or undistrust according to whether the interactions that have taken place are positive or negative overall, i.e. whether e_α^d is positive or negative. Thus, the first step in determining the trust of an agent α is to check whether there is sufficient confidence, i.e. that $confidence_\alpha^s \geq minConfidence$. If there is not suffi-cient confidence then trust T_α is defined by the fuzzy terms $\widetilde{untrust}$ or $\widetilde{undistrust}$ with a membership degree determined by the level of confidence and value of experience, as defined in rules $R_{UT}1$ and $R_{UT}2$. (Note that before firing rules $R_{UT}1$ and $R_{UT}2$ in fuzzy inference confidence is fuzzified in a similar manner to that described above for experience.)

Provided that there have been sufficient previous experiences, then fuzzy infer-ence is used to calculate trust. To determine the trustworthiness of the potential interaction partners we must consider the inference rules for each of the trust dimensions. Each rule is considered in turn, and if there is a match between the input (i.e. E_α^d) and the fuzzy set defined by the antecedent of the rule, then the rule is fired. For example, if there is an overlap between the input E_α^d and the area defined by the term *negativeBig* then rule R_T1 is fired. If there is insufficient confidence in a particular dimension, the agent uses a default "experience" value

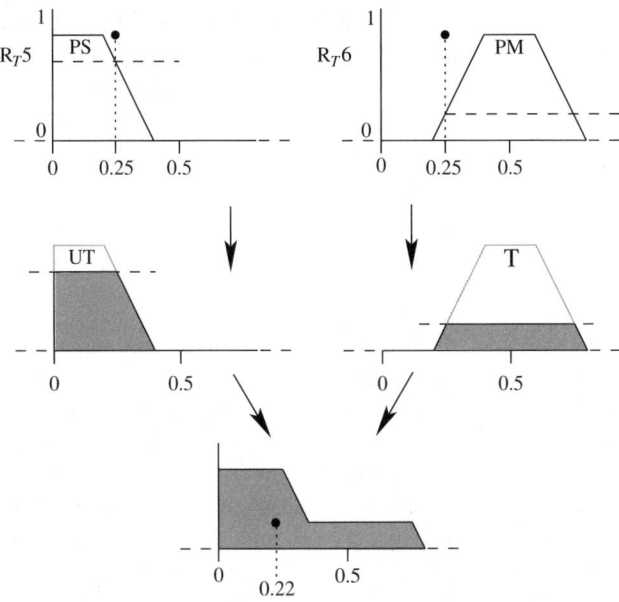

Fig. 5. A simple inference example showing the firing of rules R_T5 and R_T6

for that dimension, $default_d$. This value is determined by the the agent's trust disposition, with optimists using higher values than pessimists.

By way of example, suppose that for the success dimension we have determined that $E_\alpha^s = 0.25$ for agent α based on the experiences recorded in the interaction window. This crisp value is fuzzified as described above, and the fuzzy rules are then applied. In this case the input set matches with the antecedents of rules R_T5 and R_T6, i.e. $fuzzySingleton(0.25)$ overlaps with the sets defined by the terms *positiveSmall* and *positiveMedium*. Using Mamdani min-max inference the membership of the conclusion fuzzy set is clipped by the degree of membership of the antecedent. The outputs of the rules are then aggregated by taking the fuzzy union. This is shown graphically in Fig. 5. The process is then continued for the other dimensions, with the outputs from any matching rules being combined with the existing output by taking the fuzzy union. Once rules R_T1–R_T7 have be applied for all dimensions we have determined a fuzzy value for trust T_α. A crisp value can be determined by defuzzifying as shown in Fig. 5, in this case resulting in a trust of 0.22.

5.2 Distrust

Once the potential cooperative partners have been ascribed trust values, the selecting agent can filter out all those that are distrusted. Since trust is a fuzzy value, checking for distrust is not a crisp operation, but instead involves considering the extent that trust is a member of the fuzzy set *highDistrust*. A small membership in this set is (typically) insufficient to reject a partner whilst a high membership, indicating definite high distrust, should cause the agent to be rejected. Our approach is to check the *similarity*[2] of the fuzzy value T_α with the fuzzy value whose membership function is defined solely by the *highDistrust* fuzzy set. This can be thought of as checking the similarity of the T_α and *highDistrust* membership graphs. If the similarity is above a threshold, *maxDistrust*, then the agent concerned is rejected, and is no longer considered to be a potential cooperative partner.

5.3   Untrust and Undistrust

If the trust level ascribed to an agent is untrust or undistrust, then the trust level is considered insufficient to directly make a decision regarding the agent's suitability (i.e. to reject the agent or to cooperate). Intuitively, each agent who is ascribed untrust or undistrust should not be directly considered for selection (although it should not be completely rejected either). However, in hostile or highly dynamic environments this can lead to problems, since all agents may be either distrusted and so explicitly rejected, or untrusted and undistrusted and so not considered for cooperation. This gives rise to deadlock. To avoid this situation we provide the facility for untrusted and undistrusted agents to be considered for a proportion of interactions. If there are no trusted agents that have the required capabilities then with some probability, called the *rebootstrap* rate, the agent with the highest trust level from the set of untrusted and undistrusted agents will be selected.

5.4   Selecting an Cooperative Partner

Assuming that there is a set of trusted (i.e. with a trust level above untrust) agents, then one of them can be selected for cooperation. Agents might simply use trust alone to select which agent to cooperate with by selecting the most trusted. However, typically there is additional information with which to make a decision. For example, each of the alternative agents may advertise a cost and quality for the interaction. In this case, the selecting agent can incorporate such information into its decision making. Since these advertised values represent uncertain information (i.e. the actual cost and quality are unknown at the point of making a decision), they also lend themselves to fuzzy inference. Thus, we introduce fuzzy rules that combine trust with each of the other decision factors and determine a rating for each alternative potential interaction partner. Each

---

[2] The experiments described in Section 6 are obtained using the NRC FuzzyJ Toolkit [10]. We adopt the definition of similarity given in FuzzyJ, namely:

$$similarity(a, b) = \textbf{if } necessity(a, b) > 0.5$$
$$\textbf{then } possibility(a, b)$$
$$\textbf{else } (necessity(a, b) + 0.5) \times possibility(a, b), \text{ where}$$
$$necessity(a, b) = 1 - possibility(not\ a, b), \text{ and}$$
$$possibility(a, b) = max_x(min(\mu_a(x), \mu_b(x))).$$

of these factors F_i is a crisp value, which can be fuzzified as a singleton set. We define a set of inference rules that have fuzzy trust and the fuzzy decision factors as antecedents and the *rating* for an agent as conclusions. These factors are domain specific. In our example, we use the advertised cost and quality from an agent α, denoted F_α^c and F_α^q respectively. Suppose that we have defined the fuzzy terms *low*, *medium* and *high* for these factors, according to the universe of discourse defined by the range of potential advertised cost and quality values. Similarly, suppose that we have terms *low*, *medium*, *high* and *reject* defined for ratings, which has a universe of discourse of $[0, 1]$. We then define a set of rules of form illustrated by R_Rn and R_Rm in Fig. 4. Rule R_Rn states that if an agent is trusted, has a medium advertised cost and a high advertised quality, then it has a high rating. Similarly, rule R_Rm states that if an agent is ascribed low distrust (insufficient distrust to cause a rejection), has a medium advertised cost and high advertised quality, then it has a low rating. Similarly to calculating trust, each of these rules is applied in parallel using Mamdani min-max inference, and a crisp rating value for agent α is obtained by defuzzifying the fuzzy rating. To balance the importance of the various decision factors (including trust), agents can scale the inputs before performing inference. For example, if cost is not currently important then the input E_α^c would be multiplied by some reduction factor, r, where $0 < r < 1$.

In order to select an agent to cooperate with, the selecting agent calculates the rating value for each alternative, and selects the one with the highest rating. After the interaction, the interaction window is updated according to whether the interaction was successful, and whether the expected (as determined by advertised value) cost and quality were met.

5.5   Bootstrapping

Initially agents have insufficient experience for reasoning. Therefore, each agent goes through a bootstrapping phase in which partners are chosen randomly by way of exploration. During this bootstrapping phase agents that are distrusted, undistrusted, untrusted, and trusted have an equal chance of being selected.

6   Experimental Results

Our approach has been validated experimentally, using the NRC FuzzyJ Toolkit [10] to implement the fuzzy decision mechanism. We constructed a test stub to generate the complete set of possible interactions that an agent might have, i.e. the outcome that would result for each choice of potential cooperative partner. Using this set we can then evaluate the effectiveness of different configurations of the decision mechanism for each set of possible interactions. Thus, we can make direct comparisons about how effective a given configuration of the fuzzy decision mechanism is given exactly the same set of possible interactions. In this section we describe initial results obtained by simulating an agent using fuzzy trust to select its cooperative partners in an environment of 50 others from whom

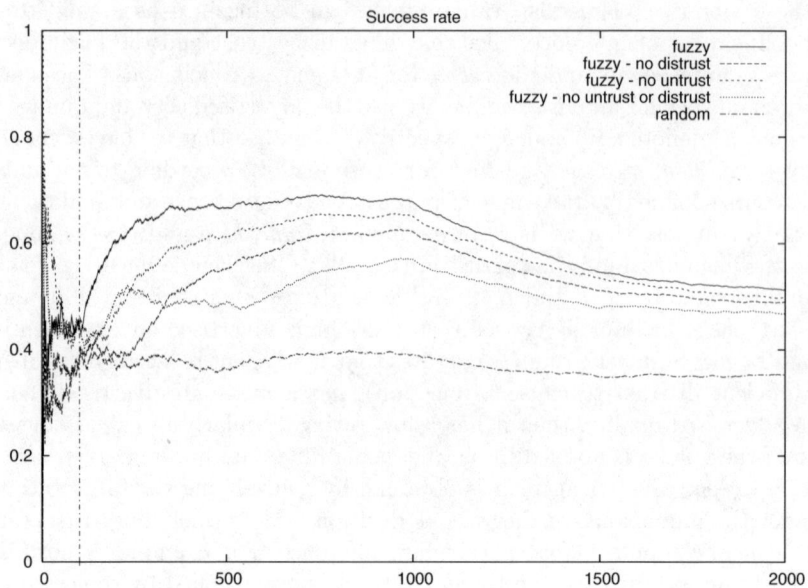

Fig. 6. The effect of reasoning with untrust and distrust on the success rate

a cooperative partner must be chosen each iteration (or cooperation avoided due to distrust or insufficient trust). The vertical line after 100 interactions signifies the end of the bootstrapping phase, and so to the left of this line agents are chosen randomly (from the set of agents that have the required capabilities). To the right of the bootstrapping line fuzzy trust is used to select a partner from the agents that have the required capabilities.

Fig. 6 shows the effectiveness of our decision mechanism on the success rate of cooperative interactions, and illustrates the usefulness of untrust and distrust. A random selection of cooperative partners is also shown for control purposes. The agents in the system were initially generated to be of average reliability, but were made less reliable after 1000 iterations. It can be seen that each of the fuzzy approaches give a significant increase in success rate. (Note that exactly the same generated "environment history" is used to obtain results for each approach.) Fig. 6 also shows that making explicit use of the notions of distrust, undistrust and untrust in decision making results in an increased success rate. The use of distrust alone (i.e. not using untrust and undistrust) gives a better result than using untrust and undistrust alone, and using positive trust alone (i.e. not using distrust, undistrust or untrust) gives the lowest success rate, although still significantly higher than a random selection.

The results shown in Fig. 6 are for a single generated "environment history". However, the actual success rate changes with the environment, since agents' reliability is different across environments. Fig. 7 shows the success rate and the rate that cost and quality expectations are met across a set of environments. The figures shown are averaged for 20 separate environments. It can be seen

Selection mechanism	Success rate	Cost rate	Quality rate
Fuzzy trust	0.64	0.73	0.84
Fuzzy trust (no distrust)	0.63	0.68	0.81
Fuzzy trust (no untrust or undistrust)	0.63	0.58	0.79
Fuzzy trust (no distrust, untrust or undistrust)	0.61	0.56	0.78
Random (control)	0.42	0.39	0.64

Fig. 7. Success rate and the rate that cost and quality expectations are met, averaged over a set of environments

that, as in Fig. 6, using trust gives a significant improvement in success rate over a random selection. Similarly, the use of distrust, undistrust and untrust also improves the success rate. When averaged over a set of environments the effect on the success rate of distrust, undistrust and untrust are similar. The use of fuzzy trust for decision making also has a significant effect on the rate at which cost expectations are met, with nearly a 35% improvement over a random selection. In the cost dimension, the use of untrust and undistrust has a greater effect than distrust, but the best results are again obtained by using distrust, untrust and undistrust together, giving a rise of 17% over using fuzzy trust that considers positive trust only (i.e. not using distrust, undistrust or untrust). We have obtained similar results in the quality dimension, as also shown in Fig. 7.

7   Conclusions

In this paper we have shown how fuzzy logic can be used to represent trust, and select appropriate agents for cooperation. We have proposed a new notion of *undistrust* and incorporated this, along with the notions of untrust and distrust proposed by Marsh [9], into the reasoning process. Our system is flexible; the fuzzy rules are specifiable by a system designer, and agents are able to scale inputs according to their current preferences regarding the relative importance of the trust dimensions. We have described initial experimental results that demonstrate the effectiveness of our approach in increasing the success rate, and the rate at which an agent's expectations are met in other trust dimensions. There are many areas of ongoing work, with our primary focus being additional experimentation to investigate different fuzzy rulesets and to consider the effect of different populations of reliable and unreliable agents. We also aim to integrate the model of individual fuzzy trust presented in this paper with existing models of reputation.

References

[1] C. Castelfranchi and R. Falcone. Principles of trust for MAS: Cognitive anatomy, social importance, and quantification. In *Proceedings of the Third International Conference on Multi-Agent Systems (ICMAS-98)*, pages 72–79, Paris, France, 1998.

[2] D. Gambetta. Can we trust trust? In D. Gambetta, editor, *Trust: Making and Breaking Cooperative Relations*, pages 213–237. Basil Blackwell, 1988.

[3] N. Griffiths. Trust: Challenges and opportunities. *AgentLink News*, 19:9–11, 2005.

[4] N. Griffiths. Fuzzy trust for peer-to-peer systems. In *Proceedings of the P2P Data and Knowledge Sharing Workshop (P2P/DAKS 2006)*, to appear.

[5] N. Griffiths and K.-M. Chao. Experience-based trust: Enabling effective resource selection in a grid environment. In P. Herrman, V. Issarny, and S. Shiu, editors, *Proceedings of the Third International Conference on Trust Management (iTrust 2005)*, pages 240–255. Springer-Verlag, 2005.

[6] N. Luhmann. Familiarity, confidence, trust: Problems and alternatives. In D. Gambetta, editor, *Trust: Making and Breaking Cooperative Relations*, pages 94–107. Basil Blackwell, 1988.

[7] E. H. Mamdani and S. Assilian. An experiment in linguistic synthesis with a fuzzy logic controller. *International Journal of Man-Machine Studies*, 7(1):1–13, 1975.

[8] D. W. Manchala. E-commerce trust metrics and models. *IEEE Internet Computing*, 4(2):36–44, 2000.

[9] S. Marsh and M. R. Dibben. Trust, untrust, distrust and mistrust — an exploration of the dark(er) side. In P. Herrman, V. Issarny, and S. Shiu, editors, *Proceedings of the Third International Conference on Trust Management (iTrust 2005)*, pages 17–33. Springer-Verlag, 2005.

[10] NRC Institute for Information Technology. The FuzzyJ toolkit. www.iit.nrc.ca/IR_public/fuzzy/fuzzyJToolkit2.html, 2006.

[11] S. D. Ramchurn, C. Sierra, L. Godo, and N. R. Jennings. Devising a trust model for multi-agent interactions using confidence and reputation. *Artificial Intelligence*, 18(9–10):833–852, 2004.

[12] T. J. Ross. *Fuzzy Logic With Engineering Applications*. John Wiley & Sons, 2nd edition, 2004.

[13] J. Sabater and C. Sierra. REGRET: A reputation model for gregarious societies. In *Proceedings of the First International Joint Conference on Autonomous Agents in Multi-Agent Systems (AAMAS-02)*, pages 475–482, 2002.

[14] S. Song, K. Hwang, R. Zhou, and Y.-K. Kwok. Trusted P2P transactions with fuzzy reputation aggregation. *IEEE Internet Computing*, 9(6):24–34, 2005.

[15] N. Stakhanova, S. Basu, J. Wong, and O. Stakhanov. Trust framework for P2P networks using peer-profile based anomaly technique. In *Proceedings of the Second International Workshop on Security in Distributed Computing Systems*, pages 203–209, 2005.

[16] L. Xiong and L. Liu. PeerTrust: Supporting reputation-based trust in peer-to-peer communities. *IEEE Transactions on Knowledge and Data Engineering*, 16(7):843–857, 2004.

[17] L. A. Zadeh. A fuzzy-set-theoretic interpretation of linguistic hedges. *Journal of Cybernetics*, 2(3):4–34, 1972.

Performative Patterns for Designing Verifiable ACLs

Nicola Dragoni and Mauro Gaspari

Dipartimento di Scienze dell'Informazione
via Mura Anteo Zamboni 7
40127 Bologna, Italy

Abstract. When people hear two actors reciting a conversation in a poem, they become attuned to the kinds of sounds that they are producing, which may not be apparent in the printed text of the poem. This result depends on certain habitual patterns of how people read or how things should be read in a performance. Performative patterns suggest certain kinds of rhythmic possibilities, time, timbre and intonation, which are not written on the page. Although their scope is quite different we claim that agents' conversations are subject to similar principles. In the same way agents' conversations are not completely specified by the logical description of the involved performatives and rules governing speech act interaction are needed to guarantee a reproducible and thus verifiable behaviour. In this paper we present a set of performative patterns for ACLs which specify how performatives should be executed in a concurrent and reactive way with respect to a given logical semantics. We provide a classification of the KQML and FIPA performatives in these patterns and we show how several properties of Multi-Agent Systems can be inferred and verified if an ACL adopt this approach.

1 Introduction

When people hear two actors reciting a conversation in a poem, they become attuned to the kinds of sounds that they are producing, which may not be apparent in the printed text of the poem. This result depends on certain habitual patterns of how people read or how things should be read in a performance. Performative patterns suggest certain kinds of rhythmic possibilities, time, timbre and intonation, which are not written on the page.

Similar patterns are also used by humans in conversation. Although a conversation might appear casual and confused, not related to a performance, it is normally ruled out by a given rhythm of turnover and accommodation. Basically people needs to coordinate their talk becoming speaker in interaction in a well-timed way [1].

Here we claim that agents' conversations are subject to similar principles. In the same way of a poem agents' conversation are not completely specified by the logical description of the involved performatives and rules governing speech act interaction are needed to guarantee a reproducible and thus verifiable behaviour.

In this paper we present a set of performative patterns for Agent Communication Languages (ACLs), which specify how performatives should be executed in a concurrent and reactive way with respect to an intended logical semantics. Our aim is to show that a mapping of ACLs performatives in these patterns is essential in order to design verifiable ACLs.

M. Klusch, M. Rovatsos, and T. Payne (Eds.): CIA 2006, LNAI 4149, pp. 375–387, 2006.
© Springer-Verlag Berlin Heidelberg 2006

The rationale behind the introduction of performative patterns can be illustrated by means of a simple example. Suppose that we want to prove a simple knowledge sharing property "two agents (A and B) know proposition p" (*KS(p)*) in an asynchronous Multi-Agent System *M* (*i.e.*, a Multi-Agent System where agents communicate using an asynchronous ACL). Suppose that M uses KQML as a communication language and that agent A already knows p.

If agent A executes the KQML performative *insert(B, A, p)* (which informally means: agent A asks agent B to insert a proposition p in its Knowledge Base (KB)) is it possible to demonstrate that *KS(p)* will hold in M? Intuitively the answer is yes, if certain conditions are verified. More precisely, if we assume that agent B is sincere, agent A does not unassert p, and both agent A and B do not terminate, we can prove that exists a time *t* after that *KS(p)* will hold in M. However, starting from the above informal specification, we have no way to calculate *t* exactly. We just know that this time exists.

The consequence of this is that it is not possible to use *KS(p)* to determine the future behaviour of agent A, when agent A needs to know the value of *KS(p)* to select its next action. Thus it is not possible to verify that A behaves correctly.

Several types of semantics for ACLs have been introduced to solve these problems. For example the KQML semantics defined in [2] introduces a set of conditions which specify when a given performative is enabled and define its effects on the mental states of agents. The most relevant information for our purpose is given by *postconditions* of the sender agent, that describe the state of the sender after the utterance of a performative. Informally, the postcondition of A is "A knows that B believes p", which means in other words that A knows that B has inserted p in its knowledge base.

Given this semantics agent A can infer *KS(p)* as soon as the insert performative is executed. Indeed agent A knows p and the insert postcondition states that: B knows that A knows p. However, since the ACL is asynchronous a mechanism to acknowledge agent A that agent B inserted p in its KB is needed. More precisely, when B receives an insert message it must execute an action (to assert p in its KB) and it must send back an acknowledgment to A. Agent A will be able infer *KS(p)* as soon as it receives this ack. This is an example of a *Do Action with Ack* pattern which is described in details in the next Section. If the performative is realized according to this pattern agent A will be able to select its next action using *KS(p)*, and the behaviour of A will be verifiable.

An additional problem arises if we consider possible failures of agents involved in this conversation. In similar way to actors that are able to improvise when unexpected events occur in a performance, agents should be able to react to failures of other agents. For example if agent A unexpectedly crashes, then *KS(p)* does not hold any more in M and agent B should be able to react properly to this event. Performative patterns deal with this issue introducing a failure continuation in each pattern which reacts to unexpected significant agent crashes[1]. If agent B crashes a failure continuation is activated and agent A will be informed that *KS(p)* does not hold any more. Thus, the behaviour of A will be still verifiable.

---

[1] Note that considering only crash failures is a common fault assumption in distributed systems, since several mechanisms can be used to detect more severe failures and to force a crash in case of detection [3].

In the next Section we give a detailed description of the performative patterns we propose and, successively, we provide a classification of KQML and FIPA conversation performatives in these patterns. Finally we show how properties of Multi-Agent Systems can be inferred and verified if an ACL adopts this approach.

2 Performative Patterns

A performative pattern has a *name* and is described by the following schema:

- A natural language **description** of the pattern's intuitive meaning.
- A **success condition** which describes a property that must hold when a pattern succeeds.
- A **success continuation** for a performative which specifies the behaviour (program) executed by an agent when a response or acknowledge is received from another agent or in general when a communication performative succeeds.
- A **failure continuation** for a performative which specifies the program executed by an agent when a critical crash failure occurs. In one-to-one performatives a critical failure occurs when the receiving agent has crashed. In one-to-many performatives a critical failure occurs when all the receiving agents have crashed.
- One or more **performative templates** that show an example of performatives involved in the pattern. For associating continuations to a performative we follow this form:

> performative(...)[**success_continuation + failure_continuation**]

Informally the semantics of the + operator is that only one of the two continuations can be called according to the concurrent behaviour of the performative pattern associated to the performative.

- One or more **predicates** which give a view at the agent level of significant concurrent events.
- A **concurrent behaviour** which describes the interactions among agents involved in the pattern. We use the following graphical notation:

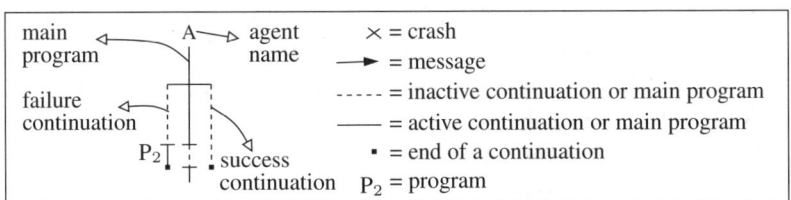

Following the above schema we describe each of the six performative patterns we propose for ACLs. Empty items are omitted.

- Pattern: **Assert**
    - **Description:** Agent A sends some content to agent B.
    - **Performative Templates:**
        - ∗ perf_name(B, A, content)
    - **Concurrent Behaviour:** Agent A sends an asynchronous message to B.

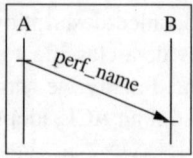

- Pattern: **Assert with Ack**

  - **Description:** Agent A sends some content to agent B. When B receives this message it sends a receipt notification to A.
  - **Success Condition:** Agent A knows that B has received the content.
  - **Success Continuation:** on_ack(P_1)
  - **Failure Continuation:** on_fail(P_2)
  - **Performative Templates:**
    * perf_name(B, A, content)[on_ack(P_1) + on_fail(P_2)]
  - **Concurrent Behaviour:** Agent A sends an asynchronous message to B. If B is alive (1), a receipt notification is sent to A. This acknowledge is handled by the success continuation of A and the program P_1 is executed. Otherwise, if B crashes before receiving A's message (2), then sooner or later the failure continuation of A will be executed (program P_2).

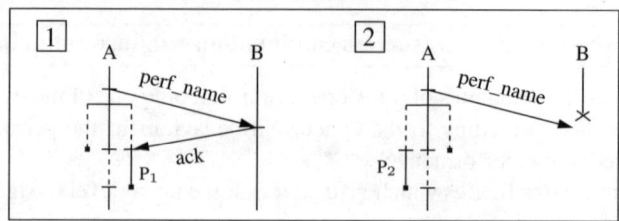

- Pattern: **Do Action with Ack**

  - **Description:** Agent A tells an agent B to perform some action. When B receives this message it sends a receipt notification to A.
  - **Success Condition:** Agent A knows that B has executed the actions.
  - **Success Continuation:** on_ack(P_1)
  - **Failure Continuation:** on_fail(P_2)
  - **Performative Templates:**
    * perf_name(B, A, actions)[on_ack(P_1) + on_fail(P_2)]
  - **Concurrent Behaviour:** Agent A sends an asynchronous message to B. If B is alive (1), a receipt notification is sent to A after B has executed the actions requested by A. This acknowledge is handled by the success continuation of A (program P_1). Otherwise, if A does not receive an ack because B has crashed (2), then sooner or later the failure continuation of A will be executed (program P_2).

- Pattern: **Request and Answer**
  - **Description:** Agent A asks an agent B for some knowledge K. Agent B answers to the request of A.
  - **Success Condition:** Agent A knows B's answer.
  - **Success Continuation:** on_answer(P_1)
  - **Failure Continuation:** on_fail(P_2)
  - **Performative Templates:**
    * request_name(B, A, K)[on_answer(P_1) + on_fail(P_2)]
    * answer_name(A, B, K)
  - **Concurrent Behaviour:** Agent A sends an asynchronous message to B. If B is alive (1), then it answers to the A's request. This reply is handled by the success continuation of A (program P_1). Otherwise, if A does not receive an answer because B has crashed (2), then sooner or later the failure continuation of A will be executed (program P_2).

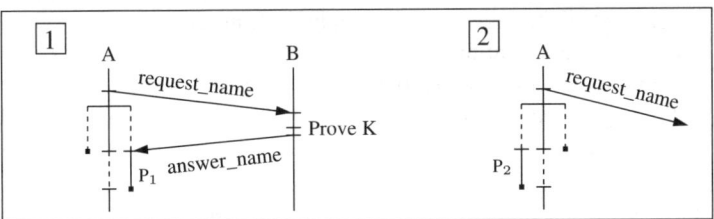

- Pattern: **Request and Answers**
  - **Description:** Agent A asks an agent B for some knowledge K. Agent B replies with one or more answers.
  - **Success Condition:** Agent A receives all the answers of B.
  - **Success Continuation:** on_answer(P_1)
  - **Failure Continuation:** on_fail(P_2)
  - **Performative Templates:**
    * request_name(B, A, K)[on_answer(P_1) + on_fail(P_2)]
    * answer_name(A, B, K)
    * end_name(A, B, K)
  - **Concurrent Behaviour:** Agent A sends an asynchronous request for knowledge to B which reply with one or more answers. Each reply is handled by the success continuation of A (program P_1) which remains active until A receives an end message (1). If A does not receive this message due to a crash of B (2), then the failure continuation is called (program P_2) and the success continuation is deactivated.

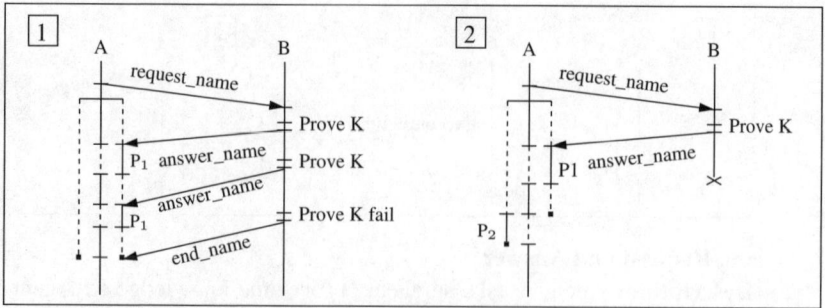

- Pattern: **Request to Everybody**
  - **Description:** Agent A asks all the available agents[2] which can provide some knowledge K for that knowledge. These agents answer to the request of A.
  - **Success Condition:** Agent A knows the answers of all the available agents.
  - **Success Continuation:** on_answer(P_1)
  - **Failure Continuation:** on_fail(P_2)
  - **Performative Templates:**
    * request_name(A, K)[on_answer(P_1) + on_fail(P_2)]
    * answer_name(A, B, K)
  - **Predicates:**
    * *all-answers(K)*: returns *true* if all the replies about K have been received.
  - **Concurrent Behaviour:** Agent A sends an asynchronous request for knowledge to available agents which reply with an answer. Each reply is handled by the success continuation of A (program P_1). Note that A does not wait for replies of crashed agents (1). If A does not receive any answer because all the agents have crashed (2), then the failure continuation of A is executed (program P_2).

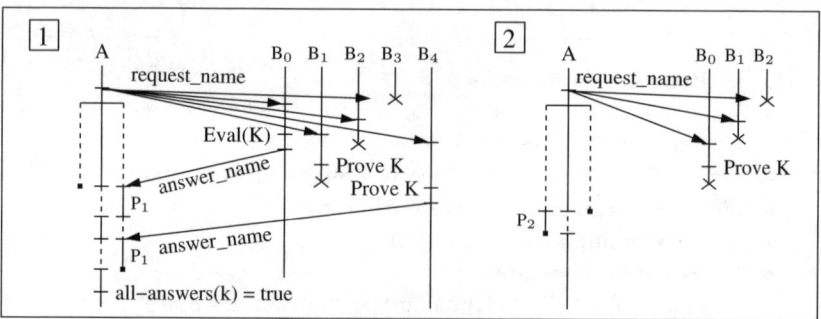

3   Classification of Standard Performatives

In Table 1 we provide a classification of KQML and FIPA performatives according to our performative patterns. For space constraints, we focus on standard *conversation*

---

[2] "Available agents" means agents which have not crashed when the multicast query is performed.

performatives only and therefore here we present a classification of a representative subset of their performatives[3]. However, all the omitted primitives could be mapped into our patterns.

Table 1. Classification of the KQML/FIPA ACL/FT-ACL communication performatives into performative patterns (possible answers to queries are enclosed in curly braces)

| | Communication Performatives | | |
Pattern	KQML	FIPA ACL	FT-ACL
Assert		inform, agree, failure, cancel, confirm, disconfirm, accept proposal, reject proposal	inform
Assert with Ack	advertise, tell, untell, error, sorry, deny		inform[... + ...]
Do Action with Ack	insert, uninsert, delete-one, delete-all, undelete, achieve, unachieve		insert
Request and Answer	ask-if, ask-all, ask-one {tell, untell, deny}	request, query if, query ref {inform, agree, cancel, failure} propose {accept proposal, reject proposal}	ask-one {tell}
Request and Answers	stream-all, subscribe {tell, untell, deny, eos}	subscribe {inform, cancel}	
Request to Everybody			ask-everybody {tell}

The criterion used to classify the performatives has been to consider the formal and informal semantics provided in the KQML/FIPA ACL specifications [2,4] trying to identify which pattern should be applied for verifying a performative. We have shown that the most relevant information for this purpose is given by *postconditions* and the

---

[3] More in detail, we omit some of the intervention and mechanics primitives and all the facilitation and networking primitives of KQML. We also omit some FIPA ACL macros (that is, primitives obtained as composition or extension of other communication primitives).

role of *preconditions* is not relevant, intuitively because performative patterns concern how communication acts should be executed and not if they should be executed or not.

In case of KQML, we have classified the *insert(B,A,p)* performative as a *Do Action with Ack* pattern. Note that the KQML primitive *tell(B,A,p)* (untell) belongs to a different pattern: *Assert with Ack*. The meaning of this performative is that "an agent A states to an agent B that A believes the content to be true". The postcondition of A is that "A knows that B knows that A believes p", which requires a receipt notification from B only (because A must only know that B has received the tell message about p). This is the reason because the performative is classified in the *Assert with Ack* pattern.

The classification of FIPA ACL performatives has been more problematic. FIPA ACL's semantic model is mainly based on the *rational effect* of each performative, which represents the purpose of a message (informally, what the sender agent hopes to obtain by sending the message). For instance, the rational effect of the *query-if* performative is that "the receiving agent has replied to the query of the sender agent". The problem with this semantic model is that, differently from KQML, the FIPA rational effect of a performative is not a postcondition of uttering the communicative act, but it represents just a constraint on the *intentions* of the sender. As a consequence, while the FIPA rational effect has been useful for understanding the intuitive meaning of a performative (what is the goal of the performative), on the contrary it has been useless from the point of view of verifying concurrent properties of the ACL. Therefore the classification of FIPA performatives has been mainly based on our "concurrent interpretation" of each performative.

3.1   Discussion

The classification of FIPA ACL performatives have been problematic for the main reason that some concurrent properties are not specified in the formal semantics of FIPA ACL primitives. As a consequence, often we had to understand the semantics of the primitives reasoning on their informal description. Moreover, the lack of specifications about *conversation policies* among FIPA agents made the classification task more difficult. A representative example could be the primitive *accept proposal*. The informal meaning of this primitive is "the action of accepting a previously submitted proposal to perform an action". The rational effect is: "the receiving agent (which previously made the proposal of performing an action) believes that the sender intends that the receiving agent will perform the action". But the information concerning the previous submission of a proposal is completely missing in the formal model. From a concurrent point of view this means that we have no way to constrain the execution of the accept proposal performative as a subsequent action to be performed for replying to a proposal. In other words, following the formal semantics of accept proposal we could use this performative independently from having received a proposal. Moreover, it is not clear (at least in the FIPA ACL's semantic model) which performatives enable the execution of an accept proposal.

Two main comments could be done observing the FIPA ACL column of Table 1. The first one concerns the absence of FIPA ACL performatives in the Do Action with Ack pattern. The reason of this lack is that, in FIPA ACL's semantic model, agents are not allowed to directly manipulate another agent's KB. This is also the reason because

KQML-like performatives such as insert, uninsert, delete-one, delete-all and undelete are absent in FIPA ACL.

The second comment is that, differently from KQML, none of the FIPA ACL performatives belongs to the Assert with Ack pattern. This is due to the meaning of the *rational effect* of the FIPA ACL's semantic model. As already remarked, the rational effect of a performative is not a postcondition on the sender (which must be true after the message has been sent/delivered) but it is just a *constraint on the "intentions of the sender agent"* [4]. In other words, a sender must intend the rational effect of the communicative acts it sends out. This is the key difference between KQML postconditions and FIPA ACL rational effect. For instance, the rational effect of the FIPA performative *inform* (which is used by a sender to inform the receiver that a given proposition is true) is that the receiver believes the content of the message. This represents the meaning of the performative *inform* in the intentions of the sender. Therefore we don't need a notification message from the receiver to the sender. Note that the analog KQML performative *tell* belongs instead to the Assert with Ack pattern because of its *postcondition* (the sender knows that the receiver knows that the sender believes some knowledge).

Finally, note that both the KQML and FIPA performatives do not deal with possible failures of agents. Thus despite they can be classified into our patterns their specification is not strictly conform to them. The consequence of this is that FIPA/KQML based Multi-Agent Systems are not verifiable in the presence of agent crashes.

4   Verifying Concurrent Properties in FT-ACL

In this Section we show how properties of Multi-Agent Systems can be inferred and verified if an ACL is fully conform to our patterns. To this purpose we use FT-ACL [5], an asynchronous ACL designed for specifying fault tolerant protocols in open Multi-Agent Systems, and we provide a fault tolerant specification of a *confident selection* protocol. The choice of FT-ACL instead of KQML or FIPA ACL is forced. Indeed FT-ACL has been designed and implemented taking into account the proposed performative patterns including failures.

FT-ACL Performatives. The FT-ACL conversation performatives (Table 2) are a small subset of those defined in KQML. Because of space constraints, we discuss only the FT-ACL performatives used in the subsequent protocol specification. Readers interested in a formal specification of FT-ACL can find it in [6], while an implementation is presented in[7].

The *ask-everybody* performative realizes a one-to-many anonymous interaction protocol which allows an agent A to ask all agents in the system which are able to deal with a knowledge p for an instantiation of p which is true in their KB. When A executes *ask-everybody*, an *ask-one* message is sent to all the agents interested in p. According to the Request to Everybody pattern the performative is associated with a success continuation $on\_answer(P_1)$ which is called each time A receives a reply to the multicast query and remains active until all the replies of not crashed agents have arrived. Instead, if no agents are able to reply because they have all crashed, then the failure continuation $on\_fail(P_2)$ is called. An agent replies to a query using the performative *tell*. Finally,

Table 2. FT-ACL conversation performatives

ask-one(B, A, p)[on_answer(P_1) + on_fail(P_2)]
inform(B, A, p)[on_ack(P_1) + on_fail(P_2)]
insert(B, A, p)[on_ack(P_1) + on_fail(P_2)]
ask-everybody(A, p)[on_answer(P_1) + on_fail(P_2)]
tell(B, A, p)

executing the performative *insert*, an agent A tells an agent B to insert p in its KB. This performative belongs to the Do Action with Ack pattern (Table 1). Therefore a success continuation *on_ack(P_1)* is called after B has inserted p in its KB and A has received an acknowledgment of this event. As a consequence, the program P_1 is executed by A. Instead, if p cannot be inserted in B's KB because B has crashed, then the failure continuation *on_fail(P_2)* is activated and A executes the program P_2.

Protocol Specification. The confident selection protocol is a contract net [8] based protocol for sharing knowledge with a selected agent only in a dynamic Multi-Agent System. A manager agent A selects an agent B from a set of agents to share with it some knowledge p. The selection is performed by means of negotiation.

If we assume that both the manager and the first selected agent do not crash[4], the following property can be considered at the end of this protocol:

Weak Confidentiality. *The manager agent knows that one agent (the confident) knows p*[5].

In Figure 1 we provide a FT-ACL based specification of the protocol using a prolog-like notation as in [9]. Agents react to messages received from other agents. Each agent has an associated *handler function* which maps the received message into the list of communication actions which must be executed when that message is received. H_A and H_{C_i} are the handler functions of the manager A and of the ith agent in the Multi-Agent System respectively. The manager A starts the protocol executing an ask-everybody performative (line 2). Each reply to this multicast query is handled by the continuation get_bids (lines 4-8) which stores the answer in A's KB (line 5) and checks if all the replies have arrived (line 6). If this is the case, then the best agent is selected (line 7) and an insert performative is executed to share the knowledge with it (line 8). An agent C_i replies to the multicast query of A with a bid for getting the knowledge (line 13). The winner agent receives an insert message from A (line 14) and consequently updates its KB (line 15).

Verification of the Weak Confidentiality Condition. To verify that the above protocol specification satisfies the weak confidentiality condition we have to show that:

---

[4] This assumption has been inserted for the sake of simplicity of the protocol specification (Figure 1). However, a similar property could be proved relaxing this constraint with the assumption that "at least one agent does not crash" (and not necessarily the "first selected agent").

[5] A stronger version of this property can be defined requiring that "only" the confident agent knows p. Due to space constraints we have chosen the weaker version.

1. The protocol terminates: it never goes in a deadlock situation despite crashes of agents.
2. At the end of the protocol, the manager agent (A) knows that one agent (B) knows p.

To show 1 we have to prove that agent A will never endlessly wait for answers from crashed agents. This deadlock situation could occurs when A is waiting for replies to its multicast query. But a deadlock in this situation is impossible because the multicast query is performed by means of the ask-everybody performative (line 2) which belongs to the Request to Everybody pattern. Therefore, we are sure that, if all the agents in the Multi-Agent System are crashed, then the failure continuation on_fail of A is executed. In this case a message of failure is sent to the starter of the protocol (line 11). Moreover, we are sure that each reply is handled by the success continuation of A which remains active until all the replies of not crashed agents have arrived (according to the Request to Everybody pattern). Thus if the manager and at least one agent do not crash the protocol terminates.

To show 2 we have to prove that, if at least one agent has not crashed, then sooner or later A will execute the success continuation (line 10) of the insert primitive (line 8). Since we have proved that the protocol cannot go in a deadlock situation, then we are sure that sooner or later the insert primitive will be executed by A. Therefore it remains to prove that A will receive the acknowledge message from the selected agent B, which for hypothesis it does not crash. This property holds because the insert performative belongs to the Do Action with Ack pattern. Therefore agent A will receives a notification

H_A:
1   handler(ask-one(A, Y, startCN(t))) ←
2   ask-everybody(A, bid(t, z))[on_answer(get_bids(m)) +
                                        on_fail(P_2)]

3
4   get_bids(tell(A, w, bid(t, z))) ←
5   update(bid(t, w, z)) ∧
6   all-answers(bid(t, _)) ∧
7   best_bid(t, B) ∧
8   insert(B, A, t)[on_ack(P_1) + on_fail(P_2)]

9
10   $P_1 \overset{def}{=}$ tell(Y, A, ProtocolOK)
11   $P_2 \overset{def}{=}$ tell(Y, A, ProtocolFailed)

H_{C_i}:
12   handler(ask-one(C_i, X, bid(t, z))) ←
13   bid(t, z) ∧ tell(X, C_i, bid(t, z))

14   handler(insert(C_i, x, t)) ←
15   updateKB(t)

Fig. 1. FT-ACL based specification of the Confident Selection protocol

message after B has inserted the content of A's message to its KB. In other words, at the end of the protocol the manager agent knows that a confident knows p. Thus the weak confidentiality property holds.

5   Related Work

One of the main challenges in agent communication is the design of verifiable semantics for ACLs. In [10] Wooldridge introduces this problem and presents a strong notion of verifiability: given a semantic framework for an ACL it must be possible to determine whether or not an agent is respecting this semantics for all the communication action it executes. In our approach we introduce a weaker notion of verifiability for an ACL which concerns the verifiability (with respect to a given semantics) of some properties of a Multi-Agent System specification in the presence of failures. Although the two approaches are complementary, we argue that a classification of performatives in concurrent patterns is necessary to extend the Wooldridge notion of verifiability to asynchronous Multi-Agent Systems where crash failures of agents may occur. The main advantages of FT-ACL with respect to current ACLs such as KQML [11] and the FIPA ACL [4] are that: it supports almost all the performative patterns (as shown in Table 1); it provides a set of fault-tolerant communication primitives; it is well integrated at the Knowledge Level [5]; it is the only ACL which supports an anonymous interaction protocol (*ask-everybody* performative) fully integrated with the dynamic nature of Multi-Agent Systems [5].

Some authors ([12,13,14]) propose conversation patterns to model the structure of dialogues in MAS. In these approaches the defined patterns constrain the set of admissible message sequences in agents' interaction. Although performative patterns may also have an influence on the sequence of admissible messages in a dialogue, they work at a different granularity. Performative pattern in general involve a single performative or two tigthly related performatives and state how these communication actions should be executed, with respect to a given ACL semantics. Additionally, performative patterns indicate when agent should react to unexpected significant agent crashes.

6   Conclusions

The main contribution of this work is to set up a criteria for defining verifiable ACL performatives for asynchronous Multi-Agent Systems where failures of agents may occur. We show that, if an ACL conforms to performative patterns, it is verifiable (*i.e.,* it is possible to verify some properties of Multi-Agent System specifications written in this language despite crashes of agents). Performative patterns can be effectively used by ACL designers and implementors to realize verifiable ACLs as soon as a mapping of ACLs performatives in these patterns is provided.

Acknowledgements

This work was partially funded by Ricerca Fondamentale Orientata - University of Bologna, Tecnologie e strumenti software per l'intrattenimento online (PI: Marco Roccetti) and by the Italian Ministry of University and Research, PRIN Project 2005015785_004: Linguaggi e verifica per Global Computing. The authors would like to thank the anonymous referees for their valuable comments on a draft of this paper. Also, the authors would like to thank Dr. Davide Guidi for his essential contribution to the design and implementation of the FT-ACL primitives.

References

1. Agliati, A., Vescovo, A., Anolli, L.: Conversation patterns in Icelandic and Italian people: Similarities and differences in rhythm and accomodation. In Anolli, L., Jr., S.D., Magnusson, M., Riva, G., eds.: The hidden structure of interaction. From neurons to culture patterns. Amsterdam: IOS Press. (2005) 223–236

2. Labrou, Y.: Semantics for an Agent Communication Language. PhD thesis, Computer Science and Electrical Engineering Department (CSEE), University of Maryland Graduate School (1997)

3. Mullender, S.: Distributed Systems. Addison Wesley (1993)

4. Foundation for Intelligent Physical Agents: FIPA Communicative Act Library Specification. (2002) Document number: SC00037J, document status: standard.

5. Dragoni, N., Gaspari, M., Guidi, D.: An ACL for Specifying Fault-Tolerant Protocols. In: Proceedings of AIIA Conference. Volume 3673 of Lecture Notes in Artificial Intelligence., Springer Verlag (2005) 237–248

6. Dragoni, N., Gaspari, M.: Crash Failure Detection in Asynchronous Agent Communication Languages. To appear in *Journal of Autonomous Agents and Multi-Agent Systems*, Springer Verlag, DOI 10.1007/s10458-006-0006-y (2006)

7. Dragoni, N., Gaspari, M., Guidi, D.: A Reasoning Infrastructure to Support Cooperation of Intelligent Agents on the Semantic Grid. International Journal of Applied Intelligence **25** (2006) 159–180 (In Press).

8. Smith, R.G.: The Contract Net Protocol: High Level Communication and Control in a Distributed Problem Solver. IEEE Transactions on Computers **29**(12) (1980) 1104–1113

9. Gaspari, M.: Concurrency and Knowledge-Level Communication in Agent Languages. Artificial Intelligence **105**(1-2) (1998) 1–45

10. Wooldridge, M.: Semantic Issues in the Verification of Agent Communication Languages. Autonomous Agents and Multi-Agent Systems **3**(1) (2000) 9–31

11. Finin, T., Labrou, Y., Mayfield, J.: KQML as an Agent Communication Language. In: Software Agents. MIT Press (1997) 291–316

12. Fan, X., Yen, J.: Conversation Pattern-based Anticipation of Teammates? Information Needs Via Overhearing. In: Proceedings of the IEEE/WIC Intelligent Agent Technology conference (IAT-05), IEEE Computer Society (2005) 316–322

13. Rovatsos, M., Fischer, F., Weiss, G.: An integrated framework for adaptive reasoning about conversation patterns. In: AAMAS '05: Proceedings of the fourth international joint conference on Autonomous agents and multiagent systems, New York, NY, USA, ACM Press (2005) 1123–1124

14. Stergiou, C., Arys, G., Wooldridge, M.: A policy based framework for agents: on the specification of an agent policy language including roles, relationships, conversation patterns and co-operation patterns. In: AAMAS '03: Proceedings of the second international joint conference on Autonomous agents and multiagent systems, New York, NY, USA, ACM Press (2003) 1126–1127

Enabling Mobile Agents Interoperability Through FIPA Standards

Joan Ametller-Esquerra, Jordi Cucurull-Juan, Ramon Martí,
Guillermo Navarro, and Sergi Robles

Department of Information and Communications Engineering,
Autonomous University of Barcelona,
08193 Bellaterra - Spain
{jametller, jcucurull, rmarti, gnavarro, sergi}@deic.uab.cat

Abstract. Mobility offers important advantages to information agent applications, specially those related to information retrieval. However, problems like security and interoperability are important barriers to the adoption of this technology. This paper focuses its attention to interoperability. Over the years, several solutions for mobile agents have been proposed, but each one covering specific problems leaving others unsolved. In this paper we analyse the problem of interoperability of mobile agents as a whole. We present an approach based on the use of FIPA ACL as the foundations to reach interoperability between different mobile agent system implementations at different levels. The implementation of the proposed solution has been adopted by JADE as the default mechanism to move agents among platforms and it has been widely used by its community.

Keywords: Mobile Agents, Interoperability, FIPA, JADE, Code Mobility.

1 Introduction

Mobility is a feature from which information agents can get a lot of benefits. For instance, information retrieval applications [5] show that agent mobility enables a uniform, distributed, autonomous and efficient way to process vast and heterogeneous amounts of information at Internet scale.

However, mobile agent technology seems not to be mature enough, having a set of core problems braking its adoption [21]. While great part of the community tends to think that mobile agent-based infrastructures could help building powerful and flexible distributed applications, everybody concludes that current knowledge is not mature enough to solve some of the main challenges presented by this technology.

In the development of mobile agent-based applications we are facing two main problems: security and interoperability. Security is mandatory in any reliable application based on mobile agents. No commercial application will be built until security in mobile agents can be assured. However, the lack of applications also causes a lack of security requirements, which forces researchers to build holistic security models trying to cover all security threats.

Interoperability is also an important problem for this technology. Since the initial proposals of mobile agent systems, a wide number of platforms have been implemented.

M. Klusch, M. Rovatsos, and T. Payne (Eds.): CIA 2006, LNAI 4149, pp. 388–401, 2006.

The platforms, typically developed by research groups, focus their implementation on several areas of mobile agents research. While some of the platforms focus their implementation on bringing security, others try to build high-performance mobile agents, methods to attain resource access control, communication among agents, and so on. These differences in these platforms design goals cause differences in programming languages, architectures or patterns chosen to design the frameworks and, also, the use of different communication protocols to transport agents or messages among platforms. This set of heterogeneous platforms is one of the main obstacles to agent interoperability and movement through different platform implementations. This fact is critical in some mobile agent applications, specially on the information retrieval ones, where a great number of reachable platforms are supposed to be present, each one with several resources for agents.

These interoperability problems also concern security because there is no standard set of protection mechanisms for mobile agents. Moreover, some of these protection mechanisms proposed in the literature, restrict the possibilities of interoperability among agent systems, as we showed in [2].

In the security area, several issues are well known and there are some protection mechanisms to face them. Other problems have no solutions yet, but a clear scenario of threats and possible vulnerabilities has been defined [14]. Probably, security in mobile agents has reached a limit where it needs more inputs from application requirements in order to produce effective protection mechanisms. In contrast, the case of interoperability is not like this.

Although several proposals have been presented to provide interoperability among mobile agent systems, this is not an area with as much maturity as in security. In the following sections different research works trying to cover interoperability are discussed. Most of these works are focused in software engineering techniques to provide portability of agents between platforms. However, these works often suppose a common programming language and a common communications infrastructure. Others like IEEE FIPA [10] (Foundation for Intelligent and Physical Agents), try to standarize some aspects of communication between mobile agent platforms to provide a minimum degree of interoperability to those systems implementing this standard. Finally, standarisation efforts also come from OMG with MASIF [17] (Mobile Agent System Interoperability Facility). This is an specification based on CORBA (Common Object Request Broker Architecture), which uses a standard communications and distributed objects infrastructure to attain interoperability.

From all reviewed works, there is no aim to properly define mobile agents interoperability, a complex capability affecting the different levels at which mobile agents can interact, and at which different degrees of interoperability can be reached using current techniques. Moreover, most of the research works provide partial solutions to specific problems, sometimes leaving others aside.

Our goal in this paper is to present all the issues related to interoperability of mobile agents, defining it, reviewing proposed solutions and presenting a global approach to the interoperability problem based on the use of FIPA standards. The main reason presented for such an approach is that important interoperability problems solved by FIPA specifications are isomorphic to mobile agents interoperability problems, what justifies as we will see, the use of FIPA solutions to make mobile agent systems interoperable.

The rest of the paper is structured as follows. Firstly, in section 2, we will define interoperability in mobile agent systems not as a whole, but through the different levels at which mobile agents must be able to interact with a host system. After that, in section 3 we analyse the related work done in FIPA about mobile agents, and in section 4 an approach to attain interoperability based on FIPA specifications is proposed. Section 5 presents experimental results extracted from the implementation over JADE [13] of preliminary work. The paper finishes with conclusions about the work done and results obtained from the implementation.

2   Interoperability

Interoperability is one of the most desirable capabilities of any software component. Software agents are probably the best programming paradigm to ease the creation of distributed applications with the ability to interoperate with others. However, agent systems need to set a first substrate for enabling its capacity to interoperate on higher levels. This initial layer has been set by efforts like FIPA [10] specifications or KSE (Knowledge Sharing Effort) defining the KQML language [7]. The main goal of both has been the definition of standard ways to communicate agents of different agent system implementations. In the case of FIPA this effort has been presented as a set of specifications offering standardisation on different levels of the agent-to-agent communication. For instance, communication protocols, message format, content languages, ontologies and interaction protocols.

Mobile agents are a special case of software agents in which interoperability is really critical. In contrast to static agents, mobile agent systems interaction with other implementations is not only restricted to send, receive and interpret messages, but also to interact with unknown environments. Moreover, this is not the only new challenge of mobile agents in front of static ones. Code mobility protocols used to transport agents through different platforms, are additional barriers to interoperability, because they are often built taking into account different design goals (performance, security, fault-tolerance and others) or data formats used to encode transmitted information.

In order to propose effective mechanisms for a better interoperability of mobile agents, it is needed to study the different levels of interaction and the different interoperability problems which may arise on them. Secondly, a study of which degrees of interoperability can be achieved on each level, depending on the conditions imposed by the desired interaction, is needed too. Finally, it is obvious that some aspects must be standardised in order to get the basis for interoperability, but such standardisation must not be restrictive to differential aspects of each implementation.

In the following lines we will define the mobile agents interoperability levels that can be considered. Each level presents several problems and solutions to allow different implemented mobile agents to interact. The whole mobile agent's interoperability will be threaten if all of them cannot be guaranteed.

Executable Code Level. This first level shows a common problem not only present in mobile agents, but also in software deployment in general. The existing architectures and operating systems make impossible a unique executable code format. Moreover, each operating system has its own system calls, libraries and so on, making also difficult a unique source code distribution. Interpreted or intermediate languages have been the most widely used approach to overcome this problem. This is probably one of the main reasons for which Java has become a *de facto* standard to write mobile agent systems. Its support to several architectures and operating systems and its abstraction of the underlying operating system resources has been, together with the portability of its bytecode, one of the reasons to choice it. Despite these reasons, probably it is not the best suited language to implement mobile systems with strong migration support, mainly because its poor management on handling threads state. Research works like [22] or [3] illustrate how difficult it can be.

Platform Level. When interoperability at previous level is guaranteed, for example because both are build using Java, we may face the problem of fitting agents from different platform implementations. In the existing ones, agents are heavily linked to the platform. Libraries and interfaces (agent and platform) are directly used by each other in order to facilitate internal platform operations management. Futher-more, agent interfaces are very diffrent from a system to another. If agent interfaces were more general and the interactions with the platform were done through less-restrictive interfaces (CORBA or Web Services) this problem would be less sig-nificant. However, most of the platforms have focused its design in efficiency and simplicity instead of interoperability. The reality is that different platforms have different interfaces, different toolkits and different implementations of the same concepts. Several works exist addressing interoperability at this level, tipically pro-viding solutions based on software engineering patterns to adapt different interfaces or encapsulating agent implementations inside other agents. For instance, [4], [18], [16], [20] or [12] are clear samples of this kind of solutions. It is interesting to note that most of interoperability work in mobile agents has been done at this level.

Communication Protocol Level. Within the communication level we can identify several critical points directly related to data exchange between agent systems. To make this interaction possible, agent systems involved in the communication must agree on several layers:
- Underlying data transfer network protocols
- Syntactical Level (Data format)
- Semantic Level (Data interpretation)
- High Level Protocols

Without agreement, at least at the first three levels, information exchange between different implementations is not possible. The efforts of FIPA have been focused on setting specifications to cover these four levels by means of MTP (Message Transport Protocols), ACL (Agent Communication Language) Messages definition and content languages, ontologies to structure message information, and Interaction Protocols to build complex agent interactions.

The most interesting feature is that current standardisation permits that agents with different ontologies may attempt to interact. Of course, if they do not share the same ontology, one will not "understand" messages sent by the other but they will be always able to interact at some degree, at least, to communicate to the other part its inability to understand the message. This is possible due the specifications provided by FIPA, and permits the sender to initiate alternative ways of communication, in order to be understood.

It is interesting to note the rapid analogy we can make between the problem of transferring mobile agents and transferring messages. In both cases, we must agree in some data transfer protocols, data must be written in a common agreed language, we must be able to, at least, attempt to interpret transmitted data. Furthermore, both need some kind of high level protocols providing the foundations for sophisticated ways of interaction in one case, and efficient, fault-tolerant and secure ways of transmitting agents in the other.

To conclude, it is clear that several solutions exist to provide some kind of interoperability at each of the levels we have seen. The only problem, when interoperability solutions exist, is to establish a process by which interested parts on interoperating decide which mechanisms to use and how to use them.

This reason and the fact that FIPA standards are a good solution, and also the most accepted ones, to attain interoperability on communications and information interchange level, clearly suggests defining mobility in terms of FIPA specifications. The flexibility in interchange of knowledge with different implementations and negotiation capabilities perfectly enables expressing mobility protocols with a high level of interoperation.

3   FIPA-Based Mobility: Related Work

In the previous section an analogy between sending messages and sending agents has been presented as the main reason to build a FIPA-based agent mobility. We stated that benefits in terms of interoperability given by FIPA specifications in message sending, may give also benefits to agent mobility.

In that sense, the FIPA Agent Management support for Agent Mobility specification [8] was proposed several years ago, but it was deprecated due to the lack of implementations. Our aim in this paper is to continue with that work. More precisely, our work has started with the study of the deprecated specification, trying to redefine those issues that were more poorly handled and implementing a proof of concept over JADE.

3.1   The Old Specification

The basic idea behind the FIPA specification about agent mobility is sending agents with their characteristics inside ACL Messages using a given ontology. Two types of protocols are presented:

Simple Migration Protocol. This protocol delegates the conversation necessary to exchange agent data to the local platform. Basically, the agent sends a request to the local platform by means of an ACL message and the platform is responsible of locating the agent's code and data, and forwarding agent's request to the destination platform.

Full Migration Protocol. In this case, the whole protocol is driven by the agent itself, which contacts the remote platform to recreate itself on it, transfering its identity to destination at the end of the process.

It is assumed that messages based on the presented ontology provide enough information to decide whether is possible to execute an incoming agent to the destination platform.

The proposed ontology defines two actions, *move* and *transfer* and several concepts like *mobile-agent-description* which contain all agent information, including its code, data, and its *mobile-agent-profile*. This last one defines agent characteristics to assure compatibility with the receiver platform, like the name of its native agent system, language in which it has been written and operating system in which it was running.

This ontology is presented as the basis to gain interoperability in the sense we have expressed in the previous section. By means of *mobile-agent-description* and *mobile-agent-profile* the ontology transmits the characteristics of the environment for which the moving agent has been built. It permits to set up interoperability mechanisms according to the received agent thanks to this specification. When not all mechanisms do not exist, mobility cannot be done but both platforms have been able to interoperate, although in a low degree. The idea is transmitting all the needed knowledge to trigger, when they are present, the necessary mechanisms to adapt both systems, allowing always a minimum degree of interaction.

3.2   Specification Drawbacks

Although the specification goals are quite interesting its scope is very limited and it has been written very ambiguously. This is not surprising taking into account that it was a first version which fell in deprecated state. Nevertheless, the philosophy it suggests, consisting in using the standardised ACL level as a base layer to gain in interoperability for mobile agents, is probably the most logical way to operate. Some lacks of this specification are, for instance, the following ones.

First, no interaction protocols are used at all. FIPA-request interaction protocol can be perfectly used as a building block to define both proposed protocols for mobility. It would help to handle special cases and situations where interoperability cannot be assured. Inform messages, not present in the simple protocol, would help, for instance, the local platform on deciding whether an outgoing agent has been restarted correctly or not in the destination one, avoiding agent duplicates. Agree messages of this protocol can be used isomorphically to access control directives from destination platform.

Secondly, code migration is not only a matter of shipping code and agent data from origin to destination. For instance, works like [19] show how complex can be mobile agent mobility protocols in order to get an acceptable performance in different environments and circumstances. The fixed behaviour of the proposed protocols, having no possibility of negotiating protocol type or configuration parameters, vastly simplifies agent mobility despite ACL and FIPA are providing necessary foundations for this kind of negotiations.

If we look at performance issues, maybe protocols based on ACL messages are not the best suited for this matter. Nevertheless standardisation of some other MTP (Message Transport Protocols) designed to improve performance in sending/receiving messages, and using for instance, light and fast Content Encodings like [9], may significantly improve efficiency keeping interoperability goals.

Moreover, sending agent code and data in the first protocol message, the same that contains the agent description, will not allow devices with limited resources to decide whether they have enough storage capabilities to store the transmitted agent.

Finally, it is not clear how the protocol operates with a single message sent from the source to the destination platform. For example, it is not clear what happens if the agent's restarting process fails at the destination. There is no message informing about the result of that process. On the other hand, the phrase *"...the AP upon which the agent is executing will have to implement the necessary protocol to realise the entire migration operation"* does not clarify whether this protocol implies another communication process not described here.

4   FIPA-Based Mobility: Our Proposal

Instead of starting a new specification from scratch, we have used the groundwork provided by the FIPA specification on Agent Management support for Mobility. Our proposal wipes out the main drawbacks shown in the obsoleted specification, and described in section 3. Moreover, it enhances mobility by conceiving migration between different types of platforms, provided they all observe the FIPA standards.

One of the main drawbacks of the old specification, which restricts the possibilities for interoperability if used, is its lack on performing negotiation. The agent is sent on the first message of the migration, excluding any possibility to negotiate mobility parameters. This lack of negotiation is also noted in the protocol part, totally imposed by the sender part, and giving to the destination no possibility to configure nor impose any parameter to it.

We propose to redefine the specification by designing, instead of a protocol, a framework protocol to negotiate specific mobility parameters and configuration. This will enable migration between different types of platforms. The framework protocol is defined in three phases:

Negotiation Phase. Using a FIPA-Proposal Interaction protocol, the origin platform can propose a set of mobility protocols to use with the destination platform. These sub-protocols must be also standardised by FIPA and their negotiation can be performed exchanging a set of standard names. This operation also enables the possibility of negotiate sub-protocols, even if they are not standard, provided they are known by the communicating platforms.

Configuration Phase. Once the two parts have agreed the mobility protocol to use, they must negotiate a set of protocol parameters in order to enhance interoperability, efficiency, fault-tolerance, security and other issues, depending on the requirements of both.

Execution Phase. By using the agreed protocols and their parameters an agent is transfered from source to destination.

The specification must be concluded by defining a minimal subset of basic protocols, which, for instance, can be the presented in the old specification with its corresponding ontologies and parametrisation capabilities. The power of this new approach does not lie in standardised sub-protocols but in the possibility to express new protocols following the main framework proposed. Like ontologies, giving the ability to express relations about concepts which are not standardised in any specification, the framework would allow to specify and negotiate a rich set of user-defined protocols.

4.1 Preliminary Proposal

In the time of writing, our experimental work has not produced a whole implementation of the previous framework protocol. Although the roadmap is clear, we have started by overcoming some of the worst drawbacks of the specification to make its implementation easier. This implementation, done using one of the most widely used FIPA-compliant Agent Platforms, JADE, follows previous works of our group on this topic [1].

Basically, we have extended the simple mobility protocol proposed in the FIPA specification, enforcing it to follow the FIPA-Request Interaction Protocol [11] which we call Power-Up protocol. Figure 1 illustrates the sequence of messages.

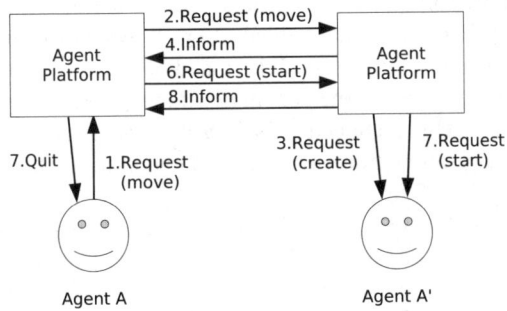

Fig. 1. FIPA-based mobility protocol

Basically, the agent is sent in the request message to the destination platform, as described in current FIPA specification. Destination platform tries then to extract it from the ACL message, taking into account the parameters sent within the message. If this operation can be performed, an inform message is sent to the home platform, which definitively kills the requesting agent. Then, the home platform sends a second request (Power Up request) to the destination platform, which starts the agent.

The purpose of this first implementation has been to experiment with the old FIPA specification, to identify drawbacks, to evaluate performance of an ACL-based mobility with respect to others, and to evaluate its flexibility to interoperate with different types of platforms and how it could be implemented. In the next section these results are described in more detail.

5   Implementation

As we have previously said we have implemented a preliminary proposal based on the FIPA mobility specifications. In this section we describe the structure of our mobility service, its integration with the intra-platform mobility service provided by JADE, and the tests used to evaluate its performance.

5.1 Mobility Service Structure

Our implementation is built on top of the JADE agent platform. This platform already had a mobility service, but it only supported intra-platform migration among containers. A container is a non standard abstraction defined in JADE to support distributed computing and consisting in an agent execution environment. Every container usually runs on an independent Java virtual machine, and it communicates via RMI with the rest of containers belonging to the same platform.

Despite having already a basic mobility service in JADE, we have implemented a new one based on our preliminary proposal, which adds new functionalities and improvements to this service. Firstly, our service allows agents to migrate between different platforms, whereas the former service only permits to migrate between containers in the same platform. Secondly, our service takes advantage of the preliminary interoperable protocol proposed on section 4, that is the first step to allow, in the future, applications exploiting the mobility between many heterogeneous platforms.

Since we have chosen JADE, we have made our service in accordance with its services architecture [6]. This architecture, thanks to its flexible structure based on vertical and horizontal commands, makes it possible to add new services to the platform without modifying it. Moreover, it has the benefit of allowing interaction and collaboration between other services. This architecture is very flexible, but it is also quite complex, because it has to manage all platform services and to coordinate their instances over all platform containers.

The inter-platform mobility service in JADE is a complex piece of software, specially taking into account that it coexists with the existing intra-platform mobility service built into the platform, as we explain in section 5.2. In order to simplify the service organization and its tasks it has been structured into these parts: main service, code analyser, class analyser and packer, code warehouse, and migration protocol. As we can see in figure 2 each one of these service parts has an instance in each container, except for the migration protocol. This protocol only resides in the platform main container, which is the only one visible according to FIPA specifications.

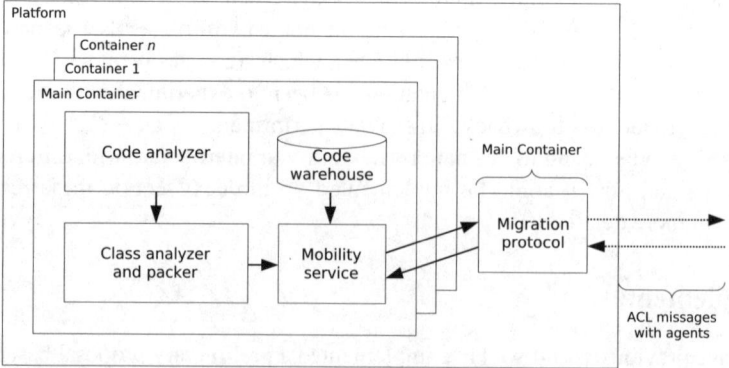

Fig. 2. Inter-Platform mobility service parts

The main component offers a JADE service image of our migration software. It deals with the coordination of all service parts over one or more containers, with the intra-platform mobility service integration and with agent interactions. In short, it is the inter-platform migration manager.

The class analyser, implemented as a standalone library called Class Analysis Library (CAL), is a key component to ease the agent dependant classes collection. As JADE does not have class spaces differentiated for agents, a search of the dependant classes has to be done in order to decide which classes must be packed to be sent to the destination platform. The CAL recursively searches dependencies for a given class by including them on the agent's code package.

To analyze each class the code analyser component is used. It loads the constant pool [15] table of a Java class in memory, being able to easily access to it. This table shows the relationships between the analysed class and the dependant ones.

The CAL, by using the code analyser, first gets the direct dependencies of the agent class, then it searches for the dependencies of these direct dependencies, and so on. It is easy to see the enormous amount of classes that can finally be found. This is a problem, because most of the classes will be in the mobile agent target platform, and it is not needed to transfer so much data. In order to fit the classes transferred to the real needed, we have made a filter based on the class package names to exclude some of them from the analysis. Finally, with the dependency list, all needed classes are packed into a JAR file (known as a JAR agent) ready to be got and sent by the migration protocol component to the destination platform.

Another important component of the service is the code warehouse. It is implemented by a class called CodeLocator that is placed inside the JADE Agent Management Service. This component is used to maintain a binding between all mobile agents of the platform and their code (the JAR files). Has to be noted that the first time a mobile agent is executed, previously to migrate, it is not generally packed in a JAR file and, because of that, it is not registered in the code warehouse. It is from the first migration that, by using the code analyser component, the JAR file is made and registered.

Furthermore, a method preventing from duplicated JARs, in case of the existence of many equal code agents, has been implemented. A unique identifier is included in each one according to the code inside them. Together with the code warehouse, a specific ClassLoader to dynamically load classes from the JAR files has been developed. It allows to have a separated class space for every JAR agent avoiding class conflicts.

And the last component, the migration protocol, is in charge of running the dialogue between platforms involved in an agent migration. It defines the steps needed for a successful migration and the data structures used in them.

To exchange messages the interaction protocols proposed by FIPA have been used, which contribute to standarize communications. More precisely, the chosen one has been the FIPA Request Interaction Protocol [11], as it has previously said at section 4, that allows to make a request to an agent and to be answered accordingly to the result (with an inform or a failure message).

Basically two steps have been defined, each one implemented with one instance of the FIPA Request Interaction Protocol with an action associated. The first step sends a "move" action with the agent code and instance and waits for the success. Then, the second step only sends a "power-up" action to start the agent previously sent (the messages exchanged can be seen in figure 1):

1. A "move" request message with the agent code and data is sent.
2. An acknowledge of the agent creation is received from the target platform.
3. The receiver is requested with a "power-up" message to start the agent sent.
4. An acknowledge of the agent startup is received from the target platform.

A migration ontology similar to the one proposed by FIPA [8] has been used for data structure. The ontology used includes code and data of the agent and, moreover, information about the agent platform, the language of the agent, and the migration protocol used. This prevents the platform to execute an agent incompatible with some of the mentioned characteristics.

5.2 Integration with JADE Mobility Service

The mobility service currently presented has been integrated with the Intra-Platform Mobility Service of JADE, allowing an agent to migrate between containers and platforms by using the same methods.

In JADE the destination of an agent migration is indicated by using an object implementing the Location interface. With the intra-platform migration service the ContainerID class, implementing the Location interface, is used as agent container destination representation. Then, with the inter-platform migration service a PlatformID class has been implemented to represent the destination platform. That's the fact that allows the user to use the same methods to start a migration. When an agent needs to migrate, it just has to call the *doMove* method with a ContainerID or a PlatformID depending on the desired kind of migration (inside or outside of the agent platform).

Moreover in current service special attention has to be paid to the agent's code location among the platform's containers. When an agent decides to migrate to another platform its code could be in another container because an older intra-platform migration of the agent. On this kind of migration, the agent's code is not pushed to the destination container. Instead of that, the code is requested on demand, remaining the original code all the time in the same container. For this reason a service horizontal command has been implemented to ask the source agent container to generate a JAR with the agent code.

5.3 Performance Tests

Reaching the end of the implementation we have made tests to evaluate our service performance in comparison with the non interoperable Intra-Platform Mobility Service provided by JADE. Our efforts have been focused on testing the time spent by migrating agents under different conditions. In order to do that a test agent in charge of launching other migration agents has started and time measures have been done.

The agents launched migrate from one site to another and then come back to the first one, in what it is called a round trip. This has been done a fixed number of times (1, 10, 100, and 1000 times), called from now on iterations. Moreover, these agents have launched concurrently, with 1, 10, and 100 instances running simultaneously.

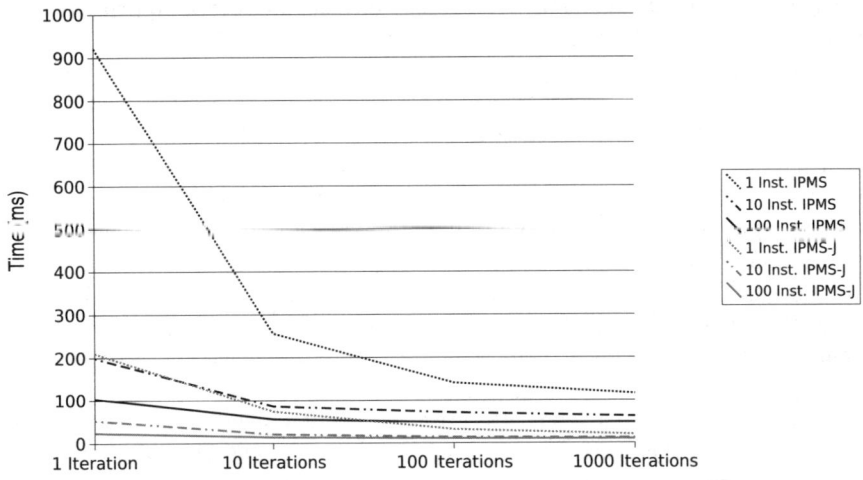

Fig. 3. Performance test of two migration services

These tests have been done with the Intra-Platform Mobility Service and with the Inter-Platform Mobility Service, where a site respectively is a container or a platform.

The results are shown in figure 3. We have used two Pentium IV at 2 GHz, with 256 MB of RAM, 40 GB on an ATA 100 hard disk, and a GNU/Linux based operating system (Fedora Core 2 distribution) with kernel version 2.6.10 each, both using a 100 Mbps switched Ethernet network. We used JADE Snapshot few days before it was released as JADE 3.4. The tests with our Inter-Platform Mobility Service (IPMS) use a Message Transport Protocol based on HTTP, while the tests based on the Intra-Platform Mobility Service of JADE (IPMS-J) use an Internal Message Transport Protocol based on RMI.

As it can be appreciated in the figure, performance increases with the number of agent instances. This is because moving an agent is a process that implies many steps. If there are many agents migrating concurrently, these steps can be parallelised and a lower average time per migration can be got.

But the most noticeable issue is the performance variation between inter-platform migration and the JADE intra-platform migration as can be appreciated in figure 3. From such result it can be seen that inter-platform mobility service is not as efficient as Intra-Platform Mobility Service provided by JADE. However, the new service has an important advantage: it follows standard FIPA methods for communication and a protocol that is a standard proposal. Interoperability has an inherent cost due to the required mechanisms, as it has been seen. Albeit of this, this cost is affordable and not as expensive as it could seem in advance. Moreover, as has previously been said, performance can be improved by defining new MTPs and content encodings.

6   Conclusions

This paper studies the problem of interoperability in mobile agent systems, probably, one of the main obstacles to the deployment of this technology. Despite that, several research works on interoperability exist, most of them are focused on specific levels and a few of them tackle the problem as a whole.

In this paper we define interoperability in mobile agent systems at three different levels, reviewing existing solutions proposed for each level. Through this work we show that mobile agents mobility and static agents communication have analogous problems. For this reason we have adopted one of the most widely extended interoperability models (FIPA specifications) for communicating static agents as foundations proposing a solution to mobile agents interoperability.

This solution sets a first layer of interoperability in communications level. Moreover, the expressivity of ACL Messages and protocols can be used, not only to build extensible, negotiable and highly configurable mobility protocols but to set the basis to attain interoperability at other levels, at least to express the conditions to reach it, in a powerful way.

In this directions went a deprecated FIPA specification (due to a lack of implementation) that we, in this work, try to extend and discuss about. From the study of the drawbacks of this specification, and following the same philosophy, we propose the standardisation of a framework protocol, rather than a specific protocol which enables the possibility of handling several mobility protocols based on ACL and enhance interoperability capabilities of the platforms.

An experimental work has also been done, implementing preliminary ideas enhancing some present specification and evaluating some performance results. This work has been implemented over the JADE platform and its community is starting to exploit it in order to build mobile agent based applications.

The performance results show that a lot of work must be done in the transport area, defining fast MTPs, and using lightweight content languages in order to make ACL based migration more competitive in terms of performance.

Acknowledgments

This work has been partially funded by the Spanish Ministry of Science and Technology (MCYT) though the project TIC2003-02041.Also with the support of the *Departament d'Universitats, Recerca i Societat de la Informació de la Generalitat de Catalunya* and of the European Social Fund (ESF).

We want also to give special thanks to Fabio Bellifemine and Giovanni Caire from the JADE Team for their invaluable help and contributions to the development.

References

1. J. Ametller, S. Robles, and J. Borrell. Agent Migration over FIPA ACL Messages. In *Mobile Agents for Telecomunication Applications (MATA*, volume 2881 of *Lecture Notes in Computer Science*, pages 210–219. Springer Verlag, 2003.
2. J. Ametller, S. Robles, and J. A. Ortega-Ruiz. Self-protected mobile agents. In *AAMAS '04: Proceedings of the Third International Joint Conference on Autonomous Agents and Multiagent Systems*, pages 362–367, Washington, DC, USA, 2004. IEEE Computer Society.
3. S. Bouchenak. Pickling threads state in the java system. In *Third European Research Seminar on Advances in Distributed Systems (ERSADS'99)*, 1999.

4. F.M.T. Brazier, V.J. Overeinder, M. van Steen, and N.J.E. Wijngaards. Agent factory: Generative migration of mobile agents in heterogeneous environments. In *Proceedings of the 2002 ACM Symposium on Applied Computing (SAC 2002)*, pages 101–106, Madrid, Spain, March 2002.

5. B. Brewington, R. Gray, K. Moizumi, D. Kotz, G. Cybenko, and D. Rus. Mobile agents for distributed information retrieval. In Matthias Klusch, editor, *Intelligent Information Agents*, chapter 15, pages 355–395. Springer-Verlag, 1999.

6. G. Caire. Jade: The new kernel and last developments. Technical report, Telecom Italia, 2004. http://jade.tilab.com/papers/Jade-the-services-architecture.pdf.

7. T. Finin, R. Fritzson, D. McKay, and R. McEntire. KQML as an Agent Communication Language. In N. Adam, B. Bhargava, and Y. Yesha, editors, *Proceedings of the 3rd International Conference on Information and Knowledge Management (CIKM'94)*, pages 456–463, Gaithersburg, MD, USA, 1994. ACM Press.

8. FIPA. Agent management support for mobility specification. Technical report, Foundation for Intelligent and Phisical Agents, 2002.

9. FIPA. Fipa agent message transport envelope representation in bit efficient specification. Technical report, Foundation for Intelligent and Phisical Agents, 2002.

10. FIPA: Foundation for Intelligent and Physical Agents. http://www.fipa.org, 2002.

11. FIPA. Fipa request interaction protocol specification. Technical report, Foundation for Intelligent and Phisical Agents, 2002.

12. A. Grimstrup, R. Gray, D. Kotz, M. Breedy, M. Carcalho, T. Cowin, D. Chacón, J. Barton, C. Garrett, and M. Hofmann. Toward interoperability of mobile-agent systems. In *6th International Conference on Mobile Agents*, volume 2535 of *Lecture Notes on Computer Science*, pages 106–120. Springer Verlag, October 2002.

13. JADE, Java Agent DEvelopment Framework. http://jade.cselt.it, 2004.

14. W. Jansen and T. Karygiannis. Nist special publication 800-19 - mobile agent security, 2000.

15. Tim Lindholm and Frank Yellin. *Java Virtual Machine Specification*. Addison-Wesley Longman Publishing Co., Inc., Boston, MA, USA, 1999.

16. L. Magnin, T. Viet Pham, A. Dury, N. Besson, and A. Thiefaine. Our guest agents are welcome to your agent platforms. In *Seventeenth ACM Symposium on Applied Computing (SAC)*, 2002.

17. OMG Mobile Agent Systems Interoperability Facilities Specification (MASIF), OMG TC Document ORBOS/97-10-05 .

18. P. Misikangas and K. Raatikainen. Agent migration between incompatible agent platforms. In *Twentieth International Conference on Distributed Computer Systems*. IEEE Computer Society Press, April 2000.

19. W. Rossak P. Braun. *Mobile Agents. Basic Concepts, mobility models & the tracy tookit*. Morgan Kaufmann, Elsevier, 2005.

20. U. Pinsdorf. A formal approach for interoperability between mobile agent systems and component based architectures. In *11th IEEE International Conference and Workshop on the Engineering of Computer-Based Systems*, pages 536–542, 2004.

21. V. Roth. Obstacles to the adoption of mobile agents. In *IEEE International Conference on Mobile Data Management*, 2004.

22. E. Truyen, B. Robben, B. Vanhaute, T. Coninx an W. Joosen, and P. Verbaeten. Portable support for transparent thread migration in java. In *ASA/MA*, pages 29–43, 2000.

Characterising Agents' Behaviours: Selecting Goal Strategies Based on Attributes

José Cascalho[1], Luis Antunes[3], Milton Corrêa[2], and Helder Coelho[3]

[1] Departamento de Ciências da Educação
Universidade dos Açores
9701-801 Angra do Heroismo, Portugal
jmc@notes.uac.pt
[2] Coordenação da Ciência da Computação e Laboratório Nacional de
Computação Científica
Av. Gertúlio Vargas, 333
Petrópolis, RJ-Brasil
mcorrea@lncc.br
[3] Departamento de Informática
Faculdade de Ciências da Universidade de Lisboa
Bloco C6, Piso 3, Campo Grande
1749-016 Lisboa, Portugal
hcoelho@di.fc.ul.pt, xarax@di.fc.ul.pt

Abstract. The growth in the demand of autonomous agent systems which take decisions on behalf of other agents or human users, increases the necessity to study systems which use affective elements to manage their resources and to take decisions in order to become more efficient and to facilitate human-machine interaction. In this paper we present an architecture that allows an agent to select a sequence of actions based on a previously predefined planning structure, by using a tree of goals and a set of informational beliefs. The affective elements which we call attributes, such as urgency, insistence and intensity, have the capacity to alter the agents' behaviours, modifying their priorities with regard to resource consumption, the implicit costs of action execution and even their capabilities to execute an action. In a preliminary experiment made in a multi-agent system environment, a modified predator-prey workbench, we show how the attributes linked to these beliefs change the agents' behaviour and improve their global performance.

1 Introduction

The introduction of affective elements in an architecture has previously been discussed by Sloman [1][2], Minsky and others [3]. The need for a more effective management of resources along with mechanisms to prioritise goals are the fundamental reasons evoked by those who advocate their use and investigation [4]. In our previous investigation we worked with different affective elements, which we call attributes, and which are associated to the definition of a mental state[5]. In [6] we explained how these attributes can increase the plasticity of the agents' reasoning process. In this paper we study the role of the attributes in the selection of adequate behaviours and we show how attributes improve agents' global performance.

M. Klusch, M. Rovatsos, and T. Payne (Eds.): CIA 2006, LNAI 4149, pp. 402–415, 2006.

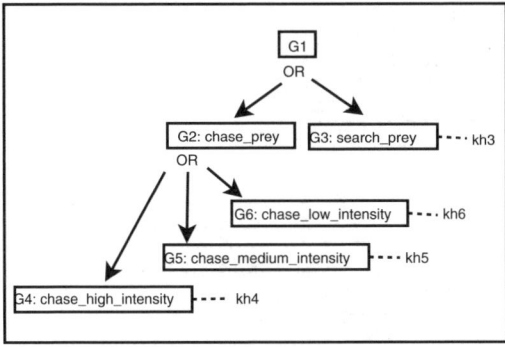

Fig. 1. The agent with CIS strategy

In the BDI-like implementation architectures, an agent commits to an intention and then selects a plan in order to satisfy a goal. The plan is usually partial, meaning that there are steps that correspond to sub-goals that must be satisfied during its execution (for a survey in programming BDI-style agents see [7]). Although the selection of several possible ways of achieve a goal is implicit in the BDI design, rarely this selection is considered (or it is only considered as a meta-reasoning process like in dMars [8]). On the other hand Castelfranchi [9] describes how after selecting a goal G_1 out of two incompatible goals, it is necessary to choose between (sub)goals G_{11} or G_{12}, using a *cost belief* (how much the agent should spend to pursue G_{11} or G_{12}), or a *convenience belief* (the value of G_1 exceeds its cost and G_{11} is better than G_{12}). And to finally arrive at the status of 'execution', an agent first should test the *conditional beliefs*. Thus, he suggests to explore more deeply the process of intention selection. This description is a source of inspiration for the model of architecture we implemented and use in the experiments we describe in this paper.

In this paper, we first succinctly describe the elements of the architecture for the agents we implemented. Then we discuss the experimental part, the pursuit domain environment we adapted to our experimentations, and the role of the intensity and urgency in the agent's architecture. Finally, we present the experimental conclusions and discuss future work.

2   The Description of the Agent's Architecture

Our agents form a goal governed-system [10], that is, the agents have goals explicitly represented which they want to satisfy. We are interested in studying the agents' inner mechanism for selecting behaviours.

The agents' mind architecture has a set of goals which are linked by an OR-connector or an AND-connector (AND/OR decomposition [11]). These connectors allow the agents' designer to create a tree (AND/OR tree) which makes possible to define 'and-goals' (the leaves of an AND-connector) or 'or-goals' (the leaves of an OR-connector). Both constitute alternative *paths* to satisfy a goal. The former means that a goal can be satisfied if all the and-goals are executed successfully, while the latter means that

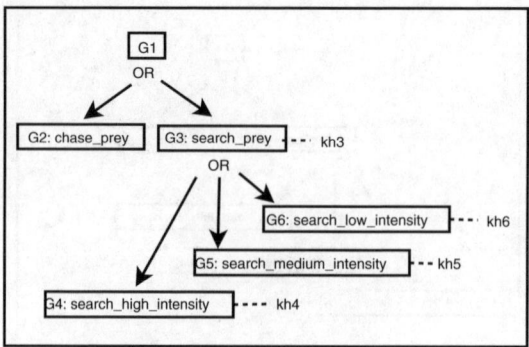

Fig. 2. The agent with SIS strategy

the goal can be satisfied, if one of the or-goals is satisfied. In figures 1 and 2 we show the two different AND/OR trees as tested in the experiments we describe in the next sections. Goals G4, G5 and G6 represent the alternative strategies to satisfy the goal G2 (for the tree in figure 1) or the goal G3 (for the tree in figure 2). The tree in figure 1 corresponds to the experiment in which agents have different strategies to chase their prey (chase intensity strategies or *CIS* experiment) while the tree in figure 2 corresponds to the experiment where agents have different strategies to search for the prey (search intensity strategies or *SIS* experiment).

In figure 3 a schematic representation of the architecture shows the different classes and their main connections. Next, we explain succinctly some of the beliefs supporting the agent's decision process:

- The **accomplishment belief** defines the conditions in which a goal is satisfied.
- The **know-how belief** links a goal to an *Action*, i.e. a *plan* to satisfy a goal. In our architecture this corresponds to a sequence of atomic actions.
- The beliefs **condition belief** defines the (pre-)conditions that support the execution of the goals and the actions of a *plan*.
- The **cando belief** evaluates the internal agents' capabilities. The difference between a *condition belief* and a *cando belief* is that the former is part of the goal (or action) external condition to the goal's (or action's) execution while the latter is an evaluation of the agents' ability (an agent can have the conditions but not the ability to reach a goal)[1]. The attribute **intensity** is evaluated with respect to the agents' ability to execute or not execute a goal.
- The **preferences belief** defines the order in which a sub-goal is chosen. The **urgency** influences this order.
- The **means-end belief** test the conditions for a goal execution (see below for a detailed explanation of the role of this belief).

Let's now describe the main cycle (*reasoning-cycle*) of the agent's mind. The agent keeps a pointer to the goal that is executing. In the **means-end belief**, a test is made to

---

[1] Both beliefs evaluate if the goal can be satisfied if the action associated to the *know-how belief* is executed.

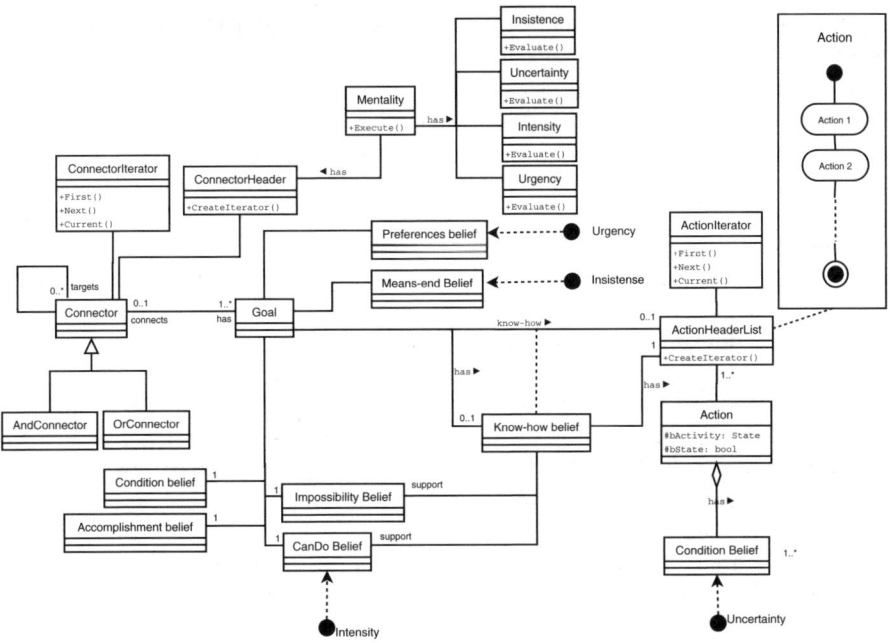

Fig. 3. The agent's architecture

evaluate whether a goal is satisfied or not by calling the **accomplishment belief**. If it is satisfied, he looks for another goal in the AND/OR tree. Otherwise, he checks if the **condition belief** is true and verifies if there is a plan to execute the goal (**know-how belief**). Finally the agent evaluates the **Impossibility belief** and the **Cando belief**. If all conditions return true, he selects an action to execute, following the plan attached to the goal. An agent search for another goal in the AND/OR tree when there is at least one condition, from the conditions enumerated above, returning false.

After each *reasoning-cycle* in which the mental state is updated, an agent will execute an action (possibly a NULL action).

Initial Energy	1000
Energy consumption per cycle (e/c)	2
e/c with movement	8
Energy gain for each prey	200

Fig. 4. Parameters related to agent's energy

3   The Experimental Setup

We adapted a pursuit simulator [12] by adding the *energy* resource to the predators. This new parameter changes the way the simulator ends a game., i.e., a game ends after the death of all predators[2] before they could catch all preys launched in the game's beginning. When a new game starts, the energy is restored to initial values.

In the original simulator, an unspecified number of predators tries to catch one or more prey agents. A game in the simulator is defined by episodes and cycles. In each cycle the simulator receives information through sockets about the moves of predator and prey agents, and messages exchanged among predators. An episode ends when all prey is caught and a new episode starts with all predator and prey agents randomly repositioned in the field. Data about how long agents take to catch all prey agents are kept as a statistical measurement of predator efficiency. We run the simulator about 40 to 80 times per experiment.

The pursuit domain was introduced in [13]. It has been widely used testbed for multiagent systems. Several variations of the original descriptions have been studied over the years (see [14] for more details). The domain we used in our experiments consists of a discrete, grid world of 20X20, in which the predators catch a prey when predator and prey share the same cell (one of the predefined capture criteria in the simulator [12]). Predators and prey can move to north, south, east and west or maintain their position. They consume more energy when they move than when they maintain their position. Moreover, their total energy is incremented by a certain predefined amount of energy after they catch a prey. In experiments we made, prey moves randomly.

In the experimental environment the density of prey agents is equal to 0.03 (12 preys per 400 places) and the number of predators corresponds to 1/4 of the total of preys (4 predators for 12 prey).

Agents tested were all included in what we called the 'obsessed type' because they persist in chasing a prey (the first they see) even if another prey comes nearer than the prey they are chasing.

An agent's decision for starting to search or to start chasing, obeys to the following strategy:

- The condition belief for *ChasePrey* returns true (*SearchPrey* returns false) if an agent sees a prey. Otherwise, *ChasePrey* returns false (*SearchPrey* returns true).
- After seeing a prey, if an agent has not yet got a fixed prey, he fixes that prey and returns *true*.
- An agent fixes a prey is removed
- The agent removes a fixed prey if he does not see the prey for a time interval longer than δt cycles,

For each experiment we recorded the following statistical measurements:

- the number of episodes the set of predators survives;
- the average and standard deviation of the number of episode cycles;
- the average energy of all the surviving predators (at the end of the episode);
- the average and standard deviation of the average energy.

---

[2] They die after their energy decreases below a survival threshold.

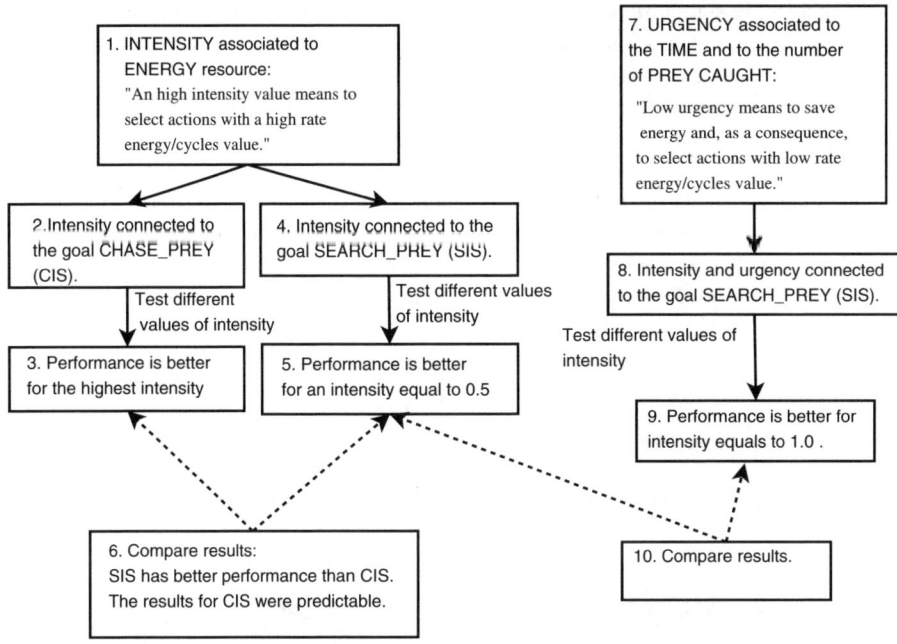

Fig. 5. The rationale in the experimental design

With this setup we had two main goals in mind:

- To measure the capacity of the survival of agents with different strategy trees;
- To test how an agent can change its behaviour by changing the attributes;
- To evaluate how the attributes can contribute to a better adaptation of the agents to the environment (improving their performance).

In the next sections we will discuss the experimental work (see the graphical representation in the figure 5). We first endowed agents with only an intensity attribute and then tested agents possessing both intensity and urgency attributes. In the former we test the agents for the *CIS* and *SIS* strategies. In the latter we test the agents while adding the urgency parameter only for the SIS strategies, and finally, we compare the results with the set of agents with the best performance in the last experiment.

3.1 The Intensity Attribute

An **intensity** measures the 'potential' an agent applies to satisfy a goal. The idea of potential comes from physics and in on our research we link this idea to the resources that an agent uses to satisfy his goals, i.e., the energy [15].

An *high intensity agent*(IA) is a predator that **selects** a strategy that corresponds to a high energy consuming behaviour. This selection is made by the 'Preference belief' following the rules:

- The agent has an initial level of intensity, the **innate_intensity level**.
- For different values of **innate_intensity level**, different goals will be selected as the total energy of the agent decreases.
- Attached to each defined goal (G4,G5 and G6) there is a different behaviour with a specific consumption of energy per step rate.
- We calculate the percentage of energy usage with respect to the total energy the agent has ($rate\%energy$), e.g., when agent's energy equals 1000 and he is executing goal G4 behaviour, the percentage of energy usage equals 1.1%.
- The agent selects a strategy that fits the interval of percentage of the total energy usage. The strategy selected is calculated using the expression:

$$0\% \leq intensity * rate\%energy < 5\% - > G4$$

$$5\% \leq intensity * rate\%energy < 10\% - > G5$$

$$10\% \leq intensity * rate\%energy < 50\% - > G6$$

$$intensity * rate\%energy \geq 50\% - > Nome$$

Total energy	Rate % Energy			Agent's intensity		
	G4(high intensity)	G5(med. intensity)	G6(low intensity)	1	0.5	0.1
1000	1	0.73	0.6	G4	G4	G5
900	1.11	0.81	0.67	G4	G4	G5
800	1.25	0.92	0.75	G4	G4	G5
700	1.43	1.05	0.86	G4	G4	G6
600	1.67	1.22	1	G4	G4	G6
500	2	1.47	1.2	G4	G4	G6
400	2.5	1.83	1.5	G4	G5	G6
300	3.33	2.44	2	G4	G5	G6
200	5	3.67	3	G5	G5	G6
100	10	7.33	6	G5	G6	-
1	1000	733.33	600	-	-	-

Strategies	G4(high intensity)	G5(med. intensity)	G6(low intensity)	Factor
Rates (energy/step)	10	7.33	6	1

Percentages Strategy change	
G4(until % total energy)	5
G5(until % total energy)	10
G6(until % total energy)	50

Fig. 6. Agent's strategy selection simulation for different values of intensity and energy

In figure 6 we present simulated results of the strategy selection for different levels of energy and intensity. Note that as the energy decreases the agent tends to choose G5 and G6, which correspond to the least energy consuming actions. The same can be observed with regard to the decreasing intensity.

3.2   Discussing the Results for the First Experiment

We compare here the results of the two approaches: CIS and SIS. As expected, for CIS experiment a high intensity gives better results, i.e., the average of survivors increments with the intensity (see the left side of figure7). With regard to the SIS, the better performance is achieved at intermediate value of intensity. This is somewhat unexpected. In

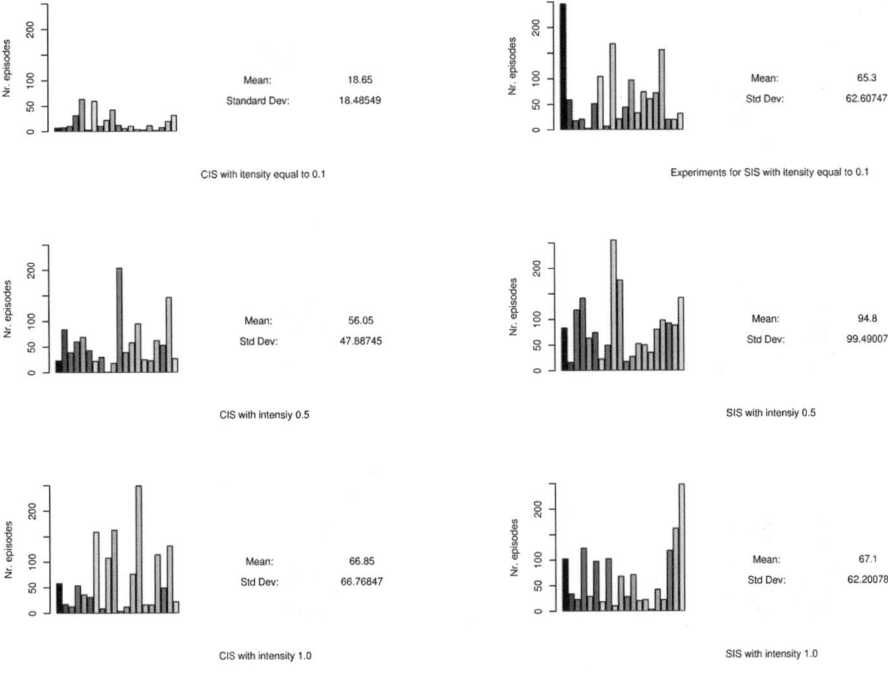

Fig. 7. Number of episodes of 20 CIS and SIS experiments

the SIS experiment an agent with the lowest level of intensity crosses the field slowly while searching for a prey and we had anticipated that this was the cleverest way of doing it because with this strategy the agent could still find a prey, while at the same time he was saving energy. Instead, we found out a trade-off between the speed with which the agent moves and the finding of the prey. If the agent moves fast, he spends too much energy, and if he moves slowly, he takes too much time in finding prey to catch. Consequently the best result lies in the medium intensity value. Figure 8 shows for each experiment the average energy of all predators at the end of each episode. This value shows the level of energy of the predators after catching all the prey. The higher levels of energy correspond to experiments in which agents 'live longer'.

3.3 The Urgency Attribute

We define **urgency** as the level of time pressure an agent has to satisfy a goal. He dynamically changes the value of urgency based on the information in the world. In the last experiment we assume that agents should always select the most expensive strategy in terms of energy rate consumption and controlled the applicability of those strategies using **intensity**. But during the experimentation we noticed that the agents could improve their energy management. For example, let us suppose that agents catch all the preys except two in the first 20 cycles (a value well above the average). The agents could now calm down and reduce the rate of energy consumption. We propose

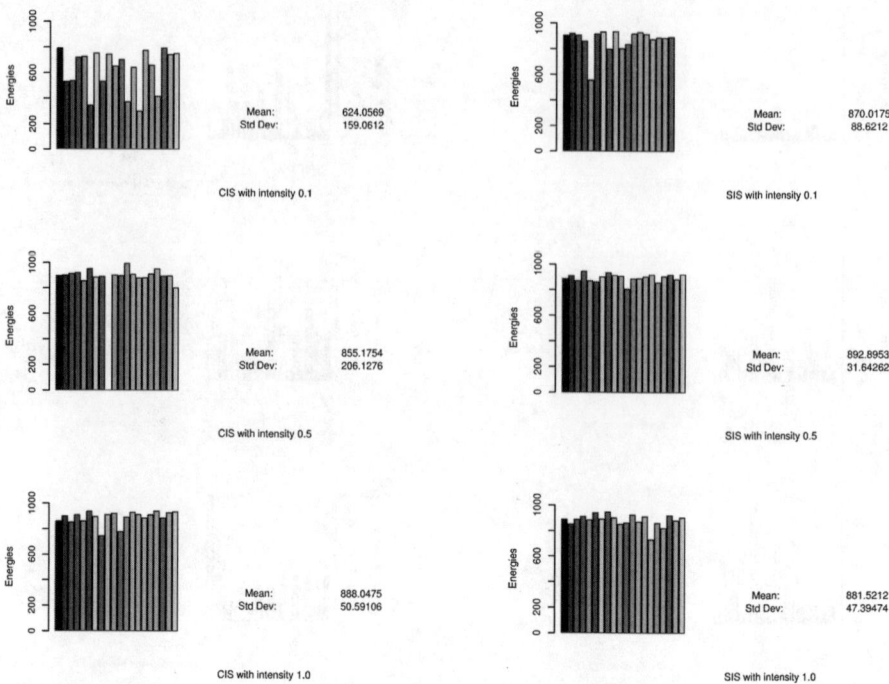

Fig. 8. Average predator energy at the end of each episode for CIS and SIS experiments

to do this with the urgency attribute. Thus, for a scenario in which predators capture quickly almost all prey, i.e., below a certain average capture time value, they should have a reduced value of urgency.

An average capture time is measured as the simulation runs. This dynamic value converges with the increment of the number of episodes. We use this value as a reference for the urgency level (the urgency to finish an episode increases as the number of cycles per episode increases as well).

We also consider the number of prey caught in a certain episode as a measure of the urgency level. We can assume two possible scenarios:

- Agents communicate to others the preys they already caught and so every predator knows how many preys are still alive in the scene.
- Agents do not communicate, but they assume an initial optimum number of prey each one should catch. This number can be fixed or can change dynamically depending on average of prey agents caught in each cycle of all the episodes.

We implemented the second scenario: the agents do not communicate and they have an optimum fixed value for the number of preys to be caught in each episode.

Using these two variables (the optimum value for the number of preys to be caught and the average capture time) we manage the value of urgency to satisfy the goal 'searching a prey'. The urgency value is calculated using the following expression:

$$urgency = weight * (bias + 1 - Nr.PreyCaught/PreyTarget)+$$

$$(1 - weight) * (bias + Nr.Cycles/CyclesAverage - 1),$$

where $bias$ gives a 'value of reference' for the urgency when the number of prey caught is equal to the value $PreyTarget$ and the the number of cycles in the episode is equal to the value $CyclesAverage$. As shown in figure 9 the reference values for $PreyTarget$ is 4 and for $CyclesAverage$ is 100 cycles. $weight$ gives the relative weight of the two dimensions in the evaluation of the final urgency value. In the simulation we used a $bias$ value of 0.45 and the $weight$ value of 0.3.

Our goal is to allow the agent to select the strategies that reveal the greatest efficacy. While applying the attribute urgency to the *preference belief* we do the following:

- If the urgency is low, the agent tends to save resources and so it will use the strategies with which the energy/steps rate is smaller.
- If the urgency is high, the agent must use all the resources he has to quickly solve the problem he has at hand, so he admits to select the best strategy even if he has to spend the rest of the resources he has got.

In figure 9 the bottom table shows the selection policy of strategies. For values higher than 0.6 the urgency will suggest the agent to select a strategy that corresponds to an action with a high energy/steps rate. For values between 0.3 and 0.6 the urgency suggests an action with a medium energy/steps rate and finally for values above 0.3, it suggests an action with low energy/steps rate.

Cycles	Preys caught					
	1	2	3	4	5	6
1	H	M	M	L	L	L
20	H	M	M	L	L	L
40	H	H	M	L	L	L
60	H	H	M	M	L	L
80	H	H	M	M	L	L
100	H	H	H	M	L	L
120	H	H	H	M	M	L
140	H	H	H	H	M	L
160	H	H	H	H	M	L
180	H	H	H	H	M	M
200	H	H	H	H	M	M
220	H	H	H	H	H	M
240	H	H	H	H	H	M

Cycles average	100
Preys target	4

	Threshold	Name
Low intensity rate (0 < u <=0.3)	0.3	L
Medium intensity rate (0.3 < u <= 0.6)	0.6	M
High intensity rate (u > 0.6)		H

Fig. 9. The different simulated urgency values (high,medium or low) for the two dependent variables, the number of cycles and the number of prey caught

Urgency	Total energy	Rate % Energy			Agent's intensity		
		G4(high intensity)	G5(med. intensity)	G6(low intensity)	1	0.5	0.1
0.4	1000	1	0.73	0.6	G5	G5	G5
0.4	900	1.11	0.81	0.67	G5	G5	G5
0.4	800	1.25	0.92	0.75	G5	G5	G5
0.4	700	1.43	1.05	0.86	G5	G5	G6
0.4	600	1.67	1.22	1	G5	G5	G6
0.4	500	2	1.47	1.2	G5	G5	G6
0.4	400	2.5	1.83	1.5	G5	G5	G6
0.4	300	3.33	2.44	2	G5	G5	G6
0.4	200	5	3.67	3	G5	G5	G6
0.4	100	10	7.33	6	G5	G6	-
0.4	1	1000	733.33	600	-	-	-

Urgency	Total energy	Rate % Energy			Agent's intensity		
		G4(high intensity)	G5(med. intensity)	G6(low intensity)	1	0.5	0.1
0.7	1000	1	0.73	0.6	G4	G4	G5
0.7	900	1.11	0.81	0.67	G4	G4	G5
0.7	800	1.25	0.92	0.75	G4	G4	G5
0.7	700	1.43	1.05	0.86	G4	G4	G6
0.7	600	1.67	1.22	1	G4	G4	G6
0.7	500	2	1.47	1.2	G4	G4	G6
0.7	400	2.5	1.83	1.5	G4	G5	G6
0.7	300	3.33	2.44	2	G4	G5	G6
0.7	200	5	3.67	3	G5	G5	G6
0.7	100	10	7.33	6	G5	G6	-
0.7	1	1000	733.33	600	-	-	-

Strategies	G4(high intensity)	G5(med. intensity)	G6(low intensity)	Factor
Rates (energy/step)	10	7.33	6	1

Percentages Strategy change	
G4(until % total energy)	5
G5(until % total energy)	10
G6(until % total energy)	50

Fig. 10. Strategy simulation decision for maximum urgency and different levels of intensity

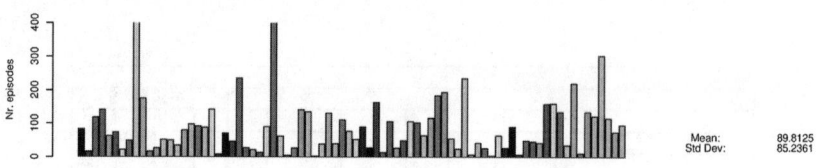

| | Mean: | 89.8125 |
| | Std Dev: | 85.2361 |

Fig. 11. Plotting the episodes per game in the IA agent

In figure 10 the policy for saving resources is simulated. When comparing figures 6 and 10 we notice that when the urgency is highest (the second table counting from the top of figure 10) the agent selects the same strategies. But for lower values of urgency the agent will select strategies with a small energy/steps rate.

With the urgency attribute we expect to manage the energy in order to surpass the critical moments, i.e. the urgency could be used as a regulator for the agent's resources (the intensity is an attribute characterising an agent's type).

3.4   Discussion of the Results of the Second Experiment

Results presented in figures 11 and 12 show that agents with mental attribute urgency and intensity (UIA) have a better performance than agents with just intensity attribute (IA). As a matter of fact, the average number of episodes per experiment for UIA predators is 140 episodes which is an improvement of about 55% when compared to experiment with IA predators. This clearly shows a better performance of UIA agents.

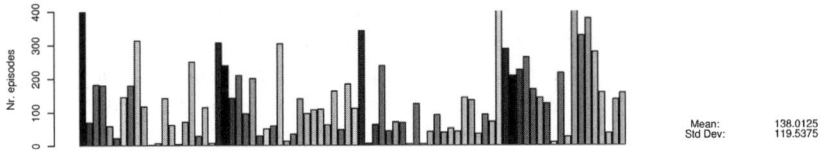

Fig. 12. Plotting the episodes per game in the UIA agent

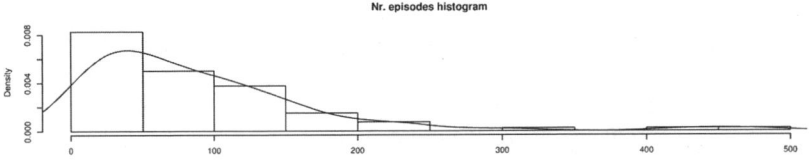

Fig. 13. Scenario with IA agents with intensity equal to 0.5

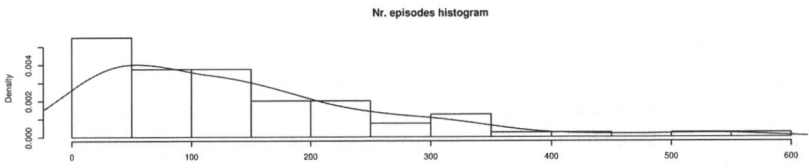

Fig. 14. Scenario with UIA agents with urgency and intensity equal to 1.0

Our guess concerning the improvement of an agent's performance was correct. Urgency attribute dominates over intensity attribute resulting in a less consuming behaviour, i.e., urgency rationalizes an energy consumption by letting agents select behaviours with higher consuming rates only in urgency situations. With this constraint imposed by the urgency attribute, we have noticed a diversity of behaviours in our game scenario. We hypothesize that this diversity of behaviours can also be responsible for the success of this approach, but this needs further investigation[3].

Density curves of figures 13 and 14 show the shift of the mean from less than 50 to a value around 100. This curve seems to fit a Poisson distribution. In the future several statistical relevance tests should be made to evaluate this conjecture.

4   Discussion

With the set of experiments presented in this paper, we tried to understand how attributes could affect the agents' behaviour. We linked the attributes to agents' context. Thus, we first looked for a connection between attributes and the environmental related variables. For intensity we chose energy resource and for urgency we selected the number of prey caught and the number of cycles average per episode. We also added two guiding principles related to the attributes definition. An agent with a high value

---

[3] Agents tend to spread over the whole game board and this helps them finding prey.

of intensity is an agent which selects the most energetic behaviours, i.e., the behaviours with the highest consuming rate energy per step, while an agent with a low value of urgency saves resources. We found that agents using both attributes, urgency and intensity, performed better. The selection of behaviours supported by the attributes urgency and intensity improved the efficacy of the agents in the tested environment.

This line of research is concerned with a deep understand of how agent behaviour can be tuned with the help of attributes. In fact, looking back to the way we operationalized the attributes insistence and urgency, we notice that both can be helpful in the definition of an agent's character. Examples of characters are, for instance, an impetuous agent, having a high value of intensity and a low sensitivity toward the parameters that increments the urgency level, or an anxious agent which has a high sensitivity to the parameters which increment the urgency level. Other researchers have been discussing the idea of type, but they use the interaction between mental components of a higher level [16].

Some of the parameters used for attributes calculation were not fixed during the experiment. Instead their values changed in each episode, allowing agents to tune their behaviour in real-time fashion [4]. This resembles the valence control model proposed in [3] connected to the idea of motives and in which the concepts of intensity and urgency have been associated to affective part of an agent's mentality [1].

Like in Tropos metamodel, our agent's architecture uses an AND/OR tree[17][11] to model agent's goals and a means-end analysis to evaluate if the plan attached to the goal can be executed. Expanding the tree corresponds to expand the possible behaviours to be used by the agent. Thus it is easy to add more goals (and consequently more behaviours) to an already tested agent. This was one of the main reasons to select this reasoning strategy.

The decision to persist or to drop a goal, the evaluation of the worth of an effort, and other measures belong to the affective part of an agent's mind mechanism. For example, in the search for information in the Internet, the affective domain has a role in the relative success of the search [18]. In our research, the study of how affective elements as uncertainty, intensity and urgency can be inserted in the agent's strategy selection mechanisms (the micro-level described in [18]) can give the agents the ability to interact with an end user, giving clues about the easiness of a task, or how long it will take or can even serve as a measure that can help the user to predict the worth of the effort to be successful.

5   Conclusion

In this paper we have drawn on our previous work with regard to applications of the Mental State Framework [5,6,19] in order to experiments in highly dynamic and complex settings, to focus on the idea of using mind attributes such as insistence and urgency to help illuminate the selection of the correct strategies for goal selection.

We have used the pursuit workbench and classical predator/prey scenario to show that the urgency attribute helps enhance the performance of the overall system by as much as 50%. In these experiments the agent mentality and decision is based on individual motivations whereas our evaluations are global, taken from the whole set of

---

[4] Actually we don't discuss in what extent this adaptation has influence in the agent's performance, this is an issue postponed for future work.

agents in the system. In the future we plan to take these social measures into the agents' minds and endow our agents with both individual and social motivations as well as a conflict management to sort out those motivations.

References

1. Sloman, A. In: Motive Mechanisms Emotions, M.A. Boden (ed), The Philososphy of Artificial Intelligence. Oxford University Press (1990) 231–247
2. Sloman, A.: Varieties of affect and the cogaff architecture schema (2001)
3. Davis, D., Lewis, S.C.: Affect and affordance: Architectures without emotion. (2004)
4. Cohn, A.C., Jennings, N.R.: Interaction, planning and motivation. In: Cognitive systems: Information processing meets brain science. Springer (2005) 163–188
5. Cascalho, J., Nobrega, L., Correa, M., Coelho, H.: Exploring the mechanisms behind a bdi-like architecture. In: Conceptual Modeling Simulation Conference. (2005) 153–158
6. Cascalho, J., Antunes, L., Coelho, H.: Toward a motivated bdi using attributes embedded in mental states. In: XI Conferencia de la Asociación Española para la Inteligencia Artificial (CAEPIA 2005). Volume 2. (2005) 215–224
7. Bordini, R., Braubach, L., Dastani, M., Seghrouchni, A.E.F., Gomez-Sanz, J., Leite, J., O'Hare, G., Pokahr, A., Ricci, A.: A survey of programming languages and platforms for multi-agent systems. In: Informatica 30. (2006) 33–44
8. D'Inverno, M., Luck, M., Georgeff, M., Kinny, D., Wooldridge, M.: The dmars architecture: A specification of the distributed multi-agent reasoning system. Autonomous Agents and Multi-Agent Systems **8** (2004) 5–53
9. Castelfranchi, C.: Reasons: Belief support and goal dynamics. Mathware and SoftComputing (1996) 233–247
10. Castelfranchi, C., Conte, R.: Cognitive and Social Action. UCL Press (1995)
11. Susi, A., Perini, A., Mylopoulos, J.: The tropos metamodel and its use. Informatica **29** (2005) 401–408
12. Kok, J., Vlassis, N.: The pursuit domain package. Technical report, Informatics Institute, University of Amsterdam, The Netherlands (2003)
13. Benda, M., Jagannathan, V., Dodhiawala, R.: On optimal cooperation of knowledge sources. Technical report, Boeing Artificial Intelligence Center, Boeing Computer Services (1985)
14. Haynes, T., Sen, S.: Evolving behavioral strategies in predators and prey. In Sen, S., ed.: IJCAI-95 Workshop on Adaptation and Learning in Multiagent Systems, Montreal, Quebec, Canada, Morgan Kaufmann (1995) 32–37
15. Morgado, L., Gaspar, G.: Emotion based adaptive reasoning for resource bounded agents. In: AAMAS '05: Proceedings of the fourth international joint conference on Autonomous agents and multiagent systems, New York, NY, USA, ACM Press (2005) 921–928
16. Dastani, M., van der Torre, L.: A classification of cognitive agents. In: Procs. of Cogsci02, Fairfax (VA). (2002)
17. Bresciani, P., Giorgini, P., Giunchiglia, F., Mylopoulos, J., Perini, A.: Tropos: An agent-oriented software development methodology. Journal od Auronomous Agents and Multi-Agent Systems **8** (2004) 203–236
18. Nahl, D.: Measuring the affective information environment of web searchers. In: Proceedings of the 67th ASSIS&T Annual Meeting. Volume 41. (2004) 191–197
19. Corrêa, M., Coelho, H.: Collective mental states in an extended mental states framework. In: International Conference on Collective Intentionality IV, Certosa di Pontignano. (2004) 13–15

A Framework of Cooperative Agents with Implicit Support for Ontologies

Riza Cenk Erdur and Inanç Seylan

Ege University, Department of Computer Engineering,
35100 Bornova, Izmir, Turkey
{cenk.erdur, inanc.seylan}@ege.edu.tr

Abstract. W3C's OWL has gained wide acceptance in the agent community and it has already been used in many agent applications which we think syntactically. By taking advantage of OWL's description logic foundation, this paper defines a hybrid description logic language which facilitates the use of ontologies as first class entities in agent communication. Using this language, we axiomatize cooperative agent behavior. Then we suggest an operational model to implement this behavior. As a case study, we present an application from software package management domain that tests the model's usability.

1 Introduction

The Semantic Web is built on the vision of giving explicit meaning to information, making it easier for machines to automatically process and integrate information available on the Web. *Ontologies* play a central role in this vision. The Semantic Web standards, especially the W3C's[1] ontology language OWL[2], have drawn the attention of many agent researchers. This is most probably the outcome of the emphasis on ontologies since the early work on agent communication languages [1] which led to the current standards[3].

OWL and its predecessor DAML+OIL has already been used in many agent applications, middleware and platforms [2,3,4]. It is a repeating pattern of these implementations to use it as a content language and/or a knowledge representation formalism thus storing agent's knowledge with it. It is generally accepted that an agent's knowledge representation language can also be the content language it uses inside an agent communication language. This decision though is not as easy as one might think because it is highly related to the formal model of agent communication.

Botelho et. al. has reviewed content languages that are suitable for agent to agent communication[5]. DAML+OIL, which OWL is based on, is among the languages that were reviewed. There are some several points that are worth to mention of the conclusion about DAML+OIL. First, DAML+OIL is good

---

[1] http://www.w3.org
[2] http://www.w3.org/TR/owl-ref/
[3] http://www.fipa.org

M. Klusch, M. Rovatsos, and T. Payne (Eds.): CIA 2006, LNAI 4149, pp. 416–430, 2006.

for expressing class and individual declarations. Since it is an ontology definition language, it is a good way to define languages. Despite this advantage, a language defined in DAML+OIL needs to have its own semantics for the new terms and operators defined. In case of the agent domain, the new language must provide semantics for *actions, beliefs, goals*, etc. It is also not clear how defined logical operators could be conveniently composed. Finally, it does not allow referential expressions. With the introduction of SWRL[6] and the standardization effort of an RDF query language SPARQL[4], the last point could be overcome. But the actual problem is bigger than that.

Carrying domain specific information with an OWL-based content language is easier compared to FIPA SL, KIF or Prolog. Nevertheless, the underlying semantic model of FIPA ACL messages, which is given in terms of the mental attitutes (belief, uncertainty, desire, goal, intention) of BDI agents, can not be used. Even if the mental attitudes can be modelled as OWL assertions, this is verbose and insufficient. It requires additional semantics as stated by the first conclusion of Botelho et. al.'s work. In [3] for example, *Belief* itself is a concept and such propositions are given inside *person (agent)* individuals. This usage is rather cumbersome and it raises questions about how multiple levels of modal operators could be applied to propositions.

Our previous work [7] contains a detailed evaluation of OWL's insufficiency to capture the ACL semantics of BDI agents and our solution to that by taking advantage of OWL's description logic foundation. We have extended OWL in order to elaborately integrate it with a formal agent communication framework. In the literature, there has been a particular effort that facilitates the programming of agents that attempt to conform to the semantics of FIPA ACL[8]. The authors come up with an operational model that allows agents to interpret messages by its semantics rather than hardcoding the agents to conform to a limited set of interaction protocols. However, this approach, being based on FIPA ACL, is geared towards the use of FIPA SL[5] which is an expressive first order modal language. The language we propose is specialized for ontology-based *information agents* on the Semantic Web. As well as the static characteristics of traditional description logic languages that represent the knowledge about an application domain, this language also represents more dynamic knowledge such as beliefs and intentions. This in turn allows to normalize agent communication to the knowledge representation level for agents that work on the Semantic Web.

In this paper, we focus on our operational model of *cooperative agent communication* which emphasizes the use of our extension to OWL, and a case study that is being developed with it. The first half of the paper is concentrated on the theory behind our work and the second half is about the application. The paper is organized as follows. In Section 2, we present a DL based language with modal operators of belief and intention. In Section 3, we discuss our operational model. In Section 4, we provide a case study using the operational model. Section 5 concludes the work.

---

[4] http://www.w3.org/TR/rdf-sparql-query/
[5] http://www.fipa.org/specs/fipa00008/

2   The $\mathcal{ALC_{BI}}$ Language

As proved by [9], the description logic $\mathcal{ALC}$ is in fact a notational variant of the propositional modal logic $K_{(m)}$. In addition to the correspondance between two logics, there have been efforts in the literature to integrate modal operators into description logic languages (see e.g. [10] and for a survey [11]). [12] lists the properties that determine the design of such a language.

The language that we'll define is an extension of $\mathcal{ALC}$ [13] that includes modal operators for belief and intention. We name it $\mathcal{ALC_{BI}}$. OWL is based on $\mathcal{SH}$ family of description logics. Our approach can be expanded to it as well. The $\mathcal{SH}$ family is basically $\mathcal{ALC}$ extended with transitive properties and a property hierarchy[14].

$\mathcal{ALC_{BI}}$ is used for defining the formal semantics of *communicative acts* (in terms of feasibility precondition and rational effect). Similar to FIPA SL, it is also designed as a content language for use in conjunction with FIPA ACL. Note that the logic under consideration has neither dynamic nor temporal characteristics (see [15] for a survey of temporal extensions of description logics and [9,16] for the correspondance between description logics and propositional dynamic logics). Being such, this might raise e.g. the question of how actions and accordingly *requests* can be modelled. We think of actions as entities in the domain of an executor (for instance a HTN [17] planner), therefore instances of an action concept are exchanged between agents in order to request for acts to be done. Accordingly, it is not a full agent programming language in the sense that it allows agent plans to be defined. Writing plans is still done with a lower level programming language.

In the rest of this section, we will first give the syntax and semantics of our hybrid language so that it's formally defined. Then we will discuss the framework of communication by listing the set of axioms between mental attitutes and for the cooperation of agents. Finally we will talk about the satisfiability.

2.1   Syntax and Semantics

First we give the syntax of this multi-dimensional DL with modal operators. The alphabet of the language is defined as follows.

Definition 1. *As for standard DL, we assume a set of concept names ($C_0, C_1, ...$), role names ($R_0, R_1, ...$), and a set of object names ($x_0, x_1, ...$) to be given. $\top$ and $\bot$ denote top and bottom concepts respectively. $\wedge$ and $\neg$ represent standard logical connectives. $C \rightarrow D$ is an abbreviation for $\neg(C \wedge \neg D)$. Let $\mathcal{AG} = \{i, j, k, ...\}$ be the set of agents. Then to every $i \in \mathcal{AG}$, the modal operators of belief B_i and intention I_i are associated.*

Concept descriptions are defined as follows.

Definition 2. *All concept names, as well as $\top$ and $\bot$ are concepts. If C and D are concepts, and R is a role name then a) $\neg C$ (concept negation), $C \sqcap D$ (concept conjunction), and $C \sqcup D$ (concept disjunction) b) $\forall R.C$ (value restriction) and $\exists R.C$ (exists restriction) are concepts.*

New formulas are introduced according to the definition below.

Definition 3. *Let C and D be concepts, R a role name, x and y object names and m a (possibly empty) sequence of modal operators from $\{B, I\} \times \mathcal{AG}$. Then axioms of the form $C = D$ (terminological), $R(x, y)$ and $C(x)$ (assertional) are atomic formulas. If φ and ψ are formulas then so are $m\varphi$, $\neg\varphi$, and $\varphi \wedge \psi$.*

A formula $B_i\varphi$ is read "agent i believes φ". The formula $I_i\varphi$ is read "agent i intends φ". The modal operators will be interpreted by "possible worlds" semantics using an extended multi-relational Kripke model.

Definition 4. *A Kripke model $M = \langle W, \Gamma, K_I \rangle$ consists of a set W of possible worlds, a set of accessibility relations on the worlds in W (in order to model beliefs and intentions), and a K-interpretation K_I over W.*

Γ contains for every $i \in \mathcal{AG}$ a) an accessibility relation γ_{B_i}, which is a function $\gamma_{B_i} : W \to 2^W$ and b) a function $\eta_{I_i} : W \to 2^{2^W}$.

The K-interpretation K_I consists of a domain Δ^{K_I} and an interpretation function $\cdot^{K_I}$. Δ^{K_I} is the union of non-empty domains $\Delta^{K_I(w)}$ for all worlds $w \in W$. The interpretation function $\cdot^{K_I}$ associates with each w a structure

$$\cdot^{K_I(w)} = \left\langle \Delta^{K_I(w)}, \mathcal{R}^{K_I(w)}, \mathcal{C}^{K_I(w)}, \mathcal{X}^{K_I(w)} \right\rangle$$

where $\Delta^{K_I(w)}$ is the domain of w, $\mathcal{R}^{K_I(w)}$ are binary relations on $\Delta^{K_I(w)}$, $\mathcal{C}^{K_I(w)}$ subsets of $\Delta^{K_I(w)}$, and $\mathcal{X}^{K_I(w)}$ are objects in $\Delta^{K_I(w)}$.

The relation γ_{B_i} is transitive, serial and Euclidean. The belief operator of FIPA SL has the same logical model[6]. In contrast to the formal model of FIPA where intention is explained in terms of the goals of an agent, here it is a primitive mental attitude. η_{I_i} is a neighborhood function of the classical modal logic E [18] with the only rule:

$$RE \ : \ \frac{\varphi \leftrightarrow \psi}{I_i\varphi \leftrightarrow I_i\psi}$$

To work in a more uniform model consisting of only accessibility relations, we use the idea of translation from minimal models into Kripke models [19]. According to this translation, the formula $I_i\varphi$ is valid in classical modal logic E if and only if the formula $\neg I_{i,1}\neg(I_{i,2}\varphi \wedge I_{i,3}\neg\varphi)$ is valid in normal multi-modal logic. Hence Γ contains the three accessibility relations for intention $\gamma_{I_{i,1}}, \gamma_{I_{i,2}}, \gamma_{I_{i,3}}$ along with γ_{B_i} for each $i \in \mathcal{AG}$. The reason behind providing such semantics for belief and intention is because of the formal framework of communication we chose that will be explained in the following two subsections.

The extension of the interpretation function for concept descriptions is as in standard DLs (see e.g. [13]). The satisfiability of a formula is defined next.

Definition 5. *For a model $M = \langle W, \Gamma, K_I \rangle$ and a world $w \in W$, a formula φ is satisfied (written as $(M, w) \models \varphi$) in the following way:*

---

[6] http://www.fipa.org/specs/fipa00037/

$$(M, w) \models C = D \text{ iff } C^{K_I(w)} = D^{K_I(w)}$$
$$(M, w) \models C(x) \text{ iff } x^{K_I(w)} \in C^{K_I(w)}$$
$$(M, w) \models R(x, y) \text{ iff } (x^{K_I(w)}, y^{K_I(w)}) \in R^{K_I(w)}$$
$$(M, w) \models B_i \varphi \text{ iff } (M, v) \models \varphi \; \forall v.(w, v) \in \gamma_{B_i}$$
$$(M, w) \models I_{i,n} \varphi \text{ iff } (M, v) \models \varphi \; \forall v.(w, v) \in \gamma_{I_{i,n}}$$
$$(M, w) \models \neg \varphi \text{ iff } (M, w) \not\models \varphi$$

2.2 Axiomatization

In this section, we define the axioms holding in the language. We adopt the work of Herzig et al. in which they try to obtain a minimal logic of intention that can be mechanized in a simple way[20]. The aim of the authors is to define the *simplest* dynamic doxastic logic. For this reason, their semantics is easier to implement than FIPA ACL's.

The FIPA ACL semantics has some severe problems which limit its practical applicability. [21] is a good discussion of these problems wherein the authors share their experience on trying to implement such semantics and examine how the semantics for some standard communicative acts can be improved. The discussion of social agency vs mental agency is out of the scope of this paper though [22].

Also in their work, Herzig et al. use *assertive speech acts* which serve to make an assertion that, in the speaker's belief, some proposition is true. They show that the request communicative act and yes-no questions can be inferred from literal communicative acts *indirectly*. In our opinion, assertive speech acts are helpful because by using them agents only *inform* each other about their mental states. They do not need to know the explicit semantic specification of all the communicative acts. Agents deduce these acts by the communication axioms. The relations between mental attitudes is given below.

$$
\begin{aligned}
B_i(\varphi \to \psi) &\to B_i \varphi \to B_i \psi & \text{(K)} \\
B_i \varphi &\to \neg B_i \neg \varphi & \text{(D)} \\
B_i \varphi &\to B_i B_i \varphi & \text{(4)} \\
\neg B_i \varphi &\to B_i \neg B_i \varphi & \text{(5)} \\
I_i \varphi &\to B_i \neg \varphi & \text{(A1)} \\
B_i \varphi &\to \neg I_i \varphi & \text{(T1)} \\
\neg B_i \varphi &\to \neg I_i \neg B_i \varphi & \text{(T2)} \\
(I_i B_i \varphi \wedge B_i \neg \varphi) &\leftrightarrow I_i \varphi & \text{(A2)} \\
I_i \varphi &\to I_i B_i \varphi & \text{(A3)} \\
B_i I_i \varphi &\leftrightarrow I_i \varphi & \text{(A4)} \\
B_i \neg I_i \varphi &\leftrightarrow \neg I_i \varphi & \text{(A5)}
\end{aligned}
$$

Axiom (A1) defines the simplest relation between intention and belief. Thus, if agent i intends φ, then it believes that $\neg \varphi$ holds. In other words, it drops its intention to achieve φ as soon as it believes that φ holds. (see [20] or [7] for the explanation of other axioms).

2.3 Cooperation Principles

Consistent with the aim of a simpler logic, the cooperation among agents is explained in terms of two principles: *belief adoption* and *intention generation*.

Belief Adoption. In order to constrain the adoption of any belief that has been uttered by another agent, Herzig et. al. use the notion of *competency*. Basically, an agent adopts i's belief if it believes that i is competent at that belief. $i \rightsquigarrow \varphi$ means that i is competent at φ. Using this relation, they formulate the following axiom:

$$B_i\varphi \rightarrow \varphi \text{ if } i \rightsquigarrow \varphi \wedge md(\varphi) = 0$$

where $md(\varphi)$, *modal depth* of a formula φ, means the maximal depth of nested modal operators in φ. If $md(\varphi) = 0$, then the formula φ is said to be *objective*.

Intention Generation. These principles explain how an agent e.g. i can adopt the intention of another agent e.g. j in order to satisfy its (j's) goals. They are related to the basic axiom, (A1), in that i should only generate the intention that φ if it believes $\neg\varphi$.

$$(B_iI_j\varphi \wedge \neg B_i\varphi \wedge \neg I_iB_i\neg\varphi) \rightarrow I_iB_i\varphi \quad (\text{G}_\text{I}1)$$
$$(B_iI_j\varphi \wedge B_i\neg\varphi) \quad \rightarrow \quad I_i\varphi \quad (\text{T}3)$$
$$B_iI_j\varphi \quad \rightarrow I_iB_j\varphi \quad (\text{T}4)$$

Axiom (G$_I$1) is the main principle of intention generation. It expresses that when i knows that j intends something i has no idea about, i should first intend to believe it.

It is then according to the result of this intention ($B_i\neg\varphi$ or $B_i\varphi$) that i can choose to intend φ (T3) or intend to make believe j about it (T4).

2.4 Testing Satisfiability of $\mathcal{ALC_{BI}}$ Formulas

We allow modal operators only in front of terminological and assertional axioms. Let $\mathcal{ALC_M}$ be the name of such an arbitrary modal extension of the DL $\mathcal{ALC}$. According to *Theorem 7* in [12], if the modal logic characterized by a class of frames $\mathcal{C}$ is decidable, then the satisfiability problem is decidable for the sets of formulas in $\mathcal{ALC_M}$ that are satisfiable in the classes of all models based on frames in $\mathcal{C}$. Thus by choosing a decidable DL component such as $\mathcal{ALC}$ (or OWL DL), the decidability of $\mathcal{ALC_M}$ depends on the decidability of the modal logic component.

A satisfiability algorithm for $\mathcal{ALC_B}$ ($\mathcal{ALC}$ augmented with only multiple belief operators) has been presented in [23]. In $\mathcal{ALC_{BI}}$, we have three more normal modal operators for each agent i. General completeness results for most of the axioms characterizing belief, intention and their interactions exist [20]. It is our goal to design a tableau algorithm that extends the one given in [23].

3 An Operational Model

The reasoning algorithm that we work on considers only the semantics that we have given up to Section 2.3. What we so call "operational model" is actually a compensation for the semantics of the terms that we won't include in this algorithm. For example, we asked ourselves how we could take into account the *competence* of an agent without representing such a notion in the knowledge base. Speech acts are another example because they are not formalized in the KB either. But their pre and post conditions are given as $\mathcal{ALC}_{BI}$ formulas which we can reason about from the KB. Therefore speech acts could be kept in an ontology as templates of actions that an agent is capable of performing.

As we have said in the introduction, this approach is similar to [8] in which we try to *approximate* the communication semantics of a framework we chose. The modal operators are used to define the rules of introspection of an agent and cooperation between agents. Inside modal operators are definitions and assertions in OWL, thus satisfying our goal of representing domain-dependent knowledge with it. The rationale for such a design is that OWL is a web standard and there are many tools (being) developed for it. Therefore we want to make use of these tools in order to reduce the development time.

Acts are defined in terms of two semantic features: feasibility precondition (FP) and rational effect (RE). The former characterizes the conditions that have to be satisfied for the act to be planned and the latter the reasons for which the act is selected[7]. This is in fact same as the FIPA semantic model. RE in FIPA's terminology also means the *effect* of the speech act on the addressee as expected by the sender. However we don't assume that kind of specialization. Here, one can also feed an $\mathcal{ALC}_{BI}$ formula to the interpretation process as shown in Figure 1 which could then lead to the planning of a local action, i.e. no speech act. Therefore, RE here means a local action's *post condition* too and intending to achieve the RE results in the execution of the local action.

An agent has to take the cooperation principles into account when it observes a communicative act. It first generates the *sincerity precondition* (corresponds to the ability precondition in FIPA terminology) of the speech act. Because our speech acts are of assertive type, the sincerity precondition describes the hearer's belief that the utterer believes what it has asserted. For example, assume that the speech act that has just been performed is $\langle i, j, \varphi \rangle$, φ being an objective formula. The sincerity condition of this act is $B_j B_i \varphi$. If $i \rightsquigarrow \varphi$, then agent j will adopt i's belief, hence we get the formula $B_j \varphi$.

To summarize, we came up with the following five types of behavior that the interpretation process exerts. Figure 1 depicts how communicative acts and formulas are processed.

1. Belief checking: It corresponds to $Bif_i \varphi$ and means that the agent i consults its knowledge base whether $B_i \varphi$ or $B_i \neg \varphi$.
2. Rational behavior: When the agent intends the RE of an act, then it performs the act.

---

[7] http://www.fipa.org/specs/fipa00037/

3. Sincerity condition generation: The agent i asserts $B_iB_j\varphi$ after it receives the speech act $\langle j, i, \varphi\rangle$.
4. Belief adoption: For agent i to adopt the belif of agent j at a formula, i first decides whether j is competent at that formula.
5. Intention generation: It allows an agent to decide how to adopt the intention of another agent by considering intention generation axioms.

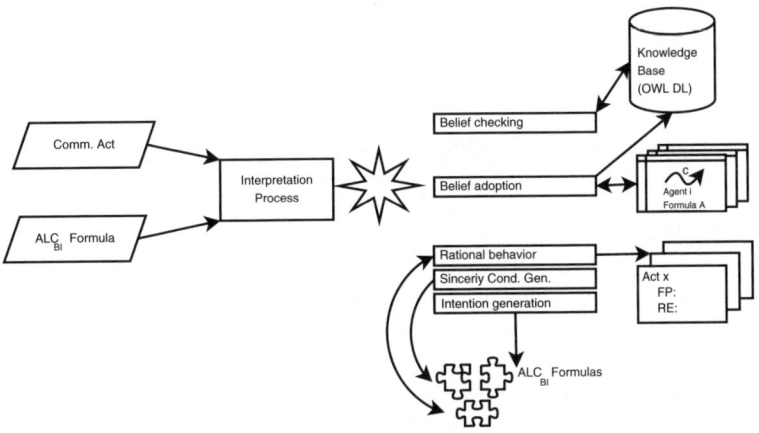

Fig. 1. An operational model for agent interaction semantics

As shown in Figure 1, the knowledge base of the agent is in OWL DL. One might ask how modal formulas are stored in the knowledge base then. The answer is that they are not. We use an approach analogous to *working memory* and *long-term memory*. The knowledge base corresponds to the long-term memory of the agent but unlike a real long-term memory is not subject to the natural forgetting process. What we mean by the working memory of an agent is a place to *temporarily* store and manipulate information. The five behaviors we have listed above correspond to the processes that manipulate information and they underlie the general intelligence of the agent. One can add more behaviors to improve an agent's "intelligence". The temporality of the working memory comes from the consumption of the formulas in the memory by these behaviors. The interaction between these two types of memory is done via the *belief checking* behavior where an assertion in the knowledge base is brought to the working memory.

At this point, we want to give some insight to the implementation. The interpretation function is a thread inside the agent. Each behavior conforms to an interface that allows the interpretation thread to check if the current formula matches with the type of formula the behavior modifies. The interface also requires the implementation of a behavior to be specified. The working memory is implemented as a FIFO queue where the behaviors have modification access. In the knowledge base we use the Jena Semantic Web Framework[8]. For

---

[8] http://jena.sourceforge.net

example, assume that agent i is processing $Bif_i\varphi$. If φ is an objective formula $(md(\varphi) = 0)$, then it is translated into a SPARQL "ask" query that returns either *true* or *false*. Otherwise it's a search in the working memory. It is determined by pattern matching whether φ is objective or not.

Pattern matching is used extensively in expressions. Another example would be its use in *rational behavior*. An agent has a table of actions defined by the FP and RE. Let the formula an agent is processing at any time t during the interpretation $\mathcal{I}$ be $I_i B_j(Colleague(mary) \wedge currentStatus(mary, onThePhone))$.

If there is an action with the RE pattern such as $B_j(Colleague(?x) \wedge currentStatus(?x, onThePhone))$ in the action table, then it would match with the formula, binding $?x$ to the *mary* individual. After that, the actual programming language code corresponding to that action will be executed.

4   Case Study

For us, the engineering point of view and applicability is top priority. Therefore we want to provide here a test application that is being developed by our framework. The aim is to implement a Linux package management system using our operational model. In this section, we will first give a very brief introduction to Linux package management. Then we will describe the abtract view of the system which will be followed by the anatomy of a package. Finally we will illustrate the coding of agents for a scenario in the system. This scenario and the application as a whole require cooperative agent behavior which is in accordance with the general agent behavior in the framework.

A Linux package is a piece of software (program, library, etc.) packed together with its related resources such as configuration files, documentation, etc in a single (and most probably compressed) file. These packages are used to install software to a Linux box by means of a package manager. Some examples of package managers are Red Hat's *rpm*, Debian's *dpkg*, Slackware's *pkgtool* and Gentoo's *portage*. We want to use the distribution specific package management on the local site as much as possible.

In fact, the local package manager can be abstracted in a way to make our system work on different Linux distributions. So the question is what the advantages of this work are in terms of the used technologies. In terms of multi-agent systems, the packages are distributed among different agents so there is no need for a central package repository. For example, the agent of a package maintainer can be responsible for the distribution of the packages of its owner. As for the semantic web point of view, the packages are categorized according to application types, dependencies, etc. This allows semantic searches on the packages, recommendation of alternatives, etc.

We distinguish two roles that can be played by agents in the system. An agent can play the role of a package maintainer, thus producing packages and sharing it with other agents. Alternatively, it can be a package user that installs/

updates/removes packages created by maintainers. A maintainer will most probably play the two roles because it must have in its system some prebuilt packages to build a package. Package users register with producers so that new packages can be notified to users immediately.

The platform services are similar to that of FIPA Abstract Architecture[9]. There is an agent communication channel that transports all the messages within the platform and an agent management system that maintains agents' lifecycles and resolves addresses. There are multiple directory facilitators (DF) to where the package provider agents register their services (in other words their roles) and the information about the packages they provide. FIPA allows the existence of multiple DFs within an agent platform and their federation[10]. In our platform, each DF represents the providers of a general software category such as *Development, Graphics & Design, Internet & Network*. All these DFs in turn register to the main DF where all the categories are managed. Assigning a DF to a general category helps balancing the search requests.

We have chosen Slackware Linux[11] to implement this system. Slackware's package management is rather simple in the sense of implemented features. For example, there is no dependency checking while installing a package unlike in *rpm*. A normal Slackware package is a compressed tar archieve that has all the binaries, documentation, etc. related to a software organized into a relative directory structure. In the standard format, a package has a directory named "install". This directory can be thought as a meta directory with package specific information. It contains a "slack-desc" file in which the package information (it's name, version, a textual description and the maintainer if it's not included in the standard distribution) is written. This information is shown when the package is being installed and doesn't have much value for the package management task. We propose not to interfere with the inner workings of the standard package manager but add the metadata about a package in a file named "metadata.owl" in the "install" directory. We give here a part of the *package management ontology* in DL syntax although it's actually in OWL because this form of syntax is less verbose. It's the responsibility of the maintainer to manage a well-defined file. Notice that the definition of Package is circular, it refers to another package for the depends role. Although this might be a problem for a restricted $\mathcal{ALC}$ TBox, it is not for a DL as expressive as OWL.

$$Package \sqsubseteq \exists hasVersion.Version \sqcap \exists category.Category \sqcap \exists hasCreator.Maintainer$$
$$\sqcap compiler.Compiler \sqcap \forall depends.Package \sqcap \forall description.String$$
$$Version \sqsubseteq \exists no.Integer \sqcap \exists arch.Architecture \sqcap \exists state.State$$
$$Maintainer \sqsubseteq \exists name.String \sqcap \forall email.EMail \sqcap \forall homepage.URL$$
$$Compiler \sqsubseteq \exists version.Version \sqcap \exists language.Language$$

---

[9] http://www.fipa.org/specs/fipa00001/
[10] http://www.fipa.org/specs/fipa00023/
[11] http://www.slackware.com

4.1 A Scenario: Installing/Updating a Package from a Known Provider

In this subsection, we describe the interaction between agents for the scenario of updating a package. We provide here a less formal and verbal description that is supported by an illustration in the end. A key point to note is that, the content of the messages exchanged between agents have instances of the concepts from the *package management ontology* we have just shown. This will be better seen in the next subsection.

Suppose that agent i is the provider of a software package named x. Agent j knows from before that i maintains x and it has registered with i to be informed about the updates on x. When there is an update on x, i notifies all its registered agents along with j about the properties of its new package. Agent j while processing this information recognizes that x depends on the package y but is unaware of its supplier. So j asks i about the supplier of package y which is most likely to be known by i. i knows this because the build process of x depends on y. Hence i informs j that package y is maintained by k.

After requesting package y from k (and assuming that there is no other dependency), j finally requests package x from i. After all packages have been downloaded, then j coordinates the local package manager of the Linux box to install/upgrade x in the dependency order. Although we exemplified here a single dependency, this scenario can be propagated to multiple dependencies.

Figure 2 shows the order of the messages sent between agents. The numbers near the acts are identifiers for the tables which will be given next.

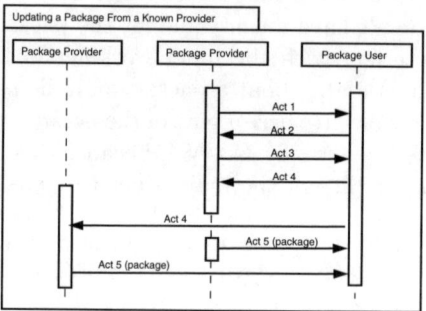

Fig. 2. Updating a package from a known provider

4.2 Coding the Agents

Here we want to give a grasp of how an agent is programmed. The programming model we chose is not as high as an agent programming language such as AgentSpeak(L) [24] and a popular (extended) implementation of it, Jason[12]. It is neither pure Java code such as in Jade [25] or SEAGENT [4]. Actions are programmed in Java, but the interpreter decides on which action to execute based

---

[12] http://jason.sourceforge.net

on its FP and RE. These are encapsulated in the definition of an action. An agent can be customized to adopt a specific type of belief from a given agent but the use of patterns allows flexibility in this. All knowledge at any level is represented with a description logic foundation, thus allowing a tight integration between the execution model and the knowledge representation formalism.

For the sake of clarity, we explain each communicative act with two tables. This first table is related to the planning of an act. We give a *sequence number* to the act regarding when it is performed during the protocol. *Role* defines the producer of the act. *Description* is a textual explanation in natural language. *FP* and *RE* are similar to FIPA ACL semantics. The second table is for showing the steps in the consumption of the act on the receiver side. It is not related to the programming of agents; it is only given to explain the interaction axioms better.

Act (1):	$\langle i, j, \varphi_1 \rangle$
	$\varphi_1 = Package(?p) \wedge Version(?v) \wedge hasVersion(?p, ?v) \wedge no(?v, ?n)$
Role:	Package provider
Desc.:	Agent i's intention to make j believe about a newer version of a package results in this speech act.
FP:	$RegisteredUser(j)$
RE:	$B_j \varphi_1$

Operation	Explanation
1. $B_j B_i \varphi_1$	1. Sincerity condition
2. $i \rightsquigarrow \varphi_1$?	2. Check if i is competent.
3. $B_j \varphi_1$	3. i is competent so adopt i's belief.
4. $+I_j Bref_j \varphi_2$	4. Assert that j wants to know the creator of the package that is depended on.

Comp. Formula	$i \rightsquigarrow \varphi_1$	Execute:	$+I_j Bref_j \varphi_2$

Act (2):	$\langle j, i, I_j Bref_j \varphi_2 \rangle$
	$\varphi_2 = Package(?p2) \wedge hasCreator(?p2, ?m)$
Role:	Package user
Desc.:	Agent j intends to know the creator of package $?p2$. Informing i about this intention will be indirectly interpreted by i as "tell me the creator".
FP:	$hasCreator(?p1, i) \wedge depends(?p1, ?p2) \wedge installed(?p2, false) \wedge \neg B_j hasCreator(?p2, ?m)$
RE:	$Bref_j \varphi_2$

Operation	Explanation
1. $B_i B_j I_j Bref_j \varphi_2$	1. Sincerity condition
2. $B_i I_j Bref_j \varphi_2$	2. (A4)
3. $B_i B_j \neg Bref_j \varphi_2$	3. (A1)
4. $B_i \neg Bref_j \varphi_2$	4. (5)
5. $B_i I_j Bref_j \varphi_2 \wedge B_i \neg Bref_j \varphi_2 \rightarrow I_i Bref_j \varphi_2$	5. By 3, 4 and (T3)

Act (3):	$\langle i, j, \varphi_2 \rangle$
Role:	Package provider
Desc.:	Agent i's intention to make j believe about the maintainer of the package that is depended on results in this speech act.
FP:	φ_2
RE:	$Bref_j \varphi_2$

The consumption of this act is similar to *Act 1*.

Act (4):	$\langle j, i, I_j \varphi_3 \rangle$
	$\varphi_3 \quad = \quad Action(download) \quad \wedge$ $package(download, ?p) \quad \wedge$ $done(download, true)$
Role:	Package user
Desc.:	Agent j's intention to do the download action results in an indirect request to the maintainer of the package .
FP:	$hasCreator(?p, k) \wedge installed(?p, false)$
RE:	φ_3

Operation	Explanation
1. $B_i B_j I_j \varphi_3$	1. Sincerity condition
2. $B_i I_j \varphi_3$	2. (A4)
3. $(B_i \varphi_3 \quad \vee$ $B_i \neg \varphi_3 \quad \vee$ $\neg B_i \varphi_3)?$	3. Check which formula is satisfied.
4. $B_i I_j \varphi_3 \quad \wedge$ $B_i \neg \varphi_3 \quad \rightarrow$ $I_i \varphi_3$	4. By 2, 3 and (T3)

The expressions in the tables above contain variables (e.g. *?p*) for individual names and property values. It would be unreasonable to specify concrete values (unless needed) because these acts are generic. The variables would bind to values during execution.

One can customize the adoption process of a formula and define a piece of code to be executed when the formula is adopted. The fourth step in the second table for *Act 1* above is the execution of the code specified in the customization table shown beneath it.

After *Act 3*, it's time for the agent to download the packages since it knows the maintainer of all the dependencies. This will result in a request (*Act 4*) to all the maintainers collected so far, plus the maintainer of the goal package (agents i and k in our scenario).

Unfortunately, because of the space limitation we could only show *a part* of *a* scenario here. But we think that it gives an understanding of how agents are programmed.

5   Concluding Remarks

We believe that it is not a trivial claim when one says that he uses OWL in a BDI style of multi-agent system. Therefore, the first half of the paper focused on the reasons for that and the theory behind our framework. In general though, we did not want to lose the application oriented view. Nevertheless, we are investigating a formal satisfiability decision algorithm for our logic that has a termination property.

The Linux package management case study will provide us a testbed for this cooperative agent framework. We are currently implementing services from the FIPA Abstract Architecture such as message transport service, agent management system and directory facilitator as agents upon which we will build the actual system. The implementation model is similar to the one presented in Section 4.2.

Acknowledgements

This work has been financially supported in part by Netsis Software. It is gratefully acknowledged. We also thank Jean-Philippe Bürckert for providing us a resource from the DFKI Library.

References

1. Finin, T., Fritzson, R., McKay, D., McEntire, R.: KQML as an Agent Communication Language. In Adam, N., Bhargava, B., Yesha, Y., eds.: Proceedings of the 3rd International Conference on Information and Knowledge Management (CIKM'94), Gaithersburg, MD, USA, ACM Press (1994) 456–463

2. Chen, H., Perich, F., Chakraborty, D., Finin, T., Joshi, A.: Intelligent agents meet semantic web in a smart meeting room. In: AAMAS '04: Proceedings of the Third International Joint Conference on Autonomous Agents and Multiagent Systems, Washington, DC, USA, IEEE Computer Society (2004) 854–861

3. Zou, Y., Finin, T., Ding, L., Chen, H., Pan, R.: Using Semantic web technology in Multi-Agent systems: a case study in the TAGA Trading agent environment. In: Proceeding of the 5th International Conference on Electronic Commerce. (2003)

4. Dikenelli, O., Erdur, R.C., Kardas, G., Gümüs, Ö., Seylan, I., Gürcan, Ö., Tiryaki, A.M., Ekinci, E.E.: Developing multi agent systems on semantic web environment using seagent platform. In Dikenelli, O., Gleizes, M.P., Ricci, A., eds.: Proceedings of ESAW'05. Volume 3963 of Lecture Notes in Computer Science., Springer Verlag (2006) 1–13

5. Botelho, L., Willmott, S., Zhang, T., Dale, J.: Review of content languages suitable for agent-agent communication. Technical Report 200233, EPFL I&C (2002)

6. Horrocks, I., Patel-Schneider, P.F., Bechhofer, S., Tsarkov, D.: OWL rules: A proposal and prototype implementation. J. of Web Semantics **3** (2005) 23–40

7. Erdur, R.C., Seylan, I.: An extended description logics approach to agent communication language semantics. In: Proceedings of the AAMAS 2006 Workshop on Agent Communication (AC2006), http://www.cs.uu.nl/people/rogier/AC2006/ (2006)

8. Louis, V., Martinez, T.: The jade semantic agent: Towards agent communication oriented middleware. AgentLink News (2005) 16–18

9. Schild, K.: A correspondence theory for terminological logics: preliminary report. In: Proceedings of IJCAI-91, 12th International Joint Conference on Artificial Intelligence, Sidney, AU (1991) 466–471

10. Baader, F., Laux, A.: Terminological logics with modal operators. Technical Report RR-94-33, Deutsches Forschungszentrum für Künstliche Intelligenz GmbH, Erwin-Schrödinger Strasse, Postfach 2080, 67608 Kaiserslautern, Germany (1994)

11. Baader, F., Küsters, R., Wolter, F.: Extensions to description logics. [26] 219–261

12. Wolter, F., Zakharyaschev, M.: Satisfiability problem in description logics with modal operators. In A.G. Cohn, L. Schubert, S.S., ed.: Proceedings of the 6th International Conference on Principles of Knowledge Representation and Reasoning (KR'98), Montreal, Canada, Morgan Kaufman (1998) 512–523

13. Baader, F., Nutt, W.: Basic description logics. [26] 43–95

14. Horrocks, I., Patel-Schneider, P.F., van Harmelen, F.: From $\mathcal{SHIQ}$ and RDF to OWL: The making of a web ontology language. J. of Web Semantics **1** (2003) 7–26

15. Artale, A., Franconi, E.: A survey of temporal extensions of description logics. Annals of Mathematics and Artificial Intelligence **30** (2000) 171–210
16. Calvanese, D., Giacomo, G.D.: Expressive description logics. [26] 178–218
17. Sycara, K., Williamson, M., Decker, K.: Unified information and control flow in hierarchical task networks. In: Working Notes of the AAAI-96 workshop "Theories of Action, Planning, and Control. (1996)
18. Chellas, B.F.: Modal Logic: An Introduction. Cambridge University Press, Cambridge (1980)
19. Gasquet, O., Herzig, A.: From classical to normal modal logics. In Wansing, H., ed.: Proof Theory of Modal Logics. Number 2 in Applied Logic Series. Kluwer Academic Publishers (1996) 293–311
20. Herzig, A., Longin, D.: A logic of intention with cooperation principles and with assertive speech acts as communication primitives. In: AAMAS '02: Proceedings of the first international joint conference on Autonomous agents and multiagent systems, New York, NY, USA, ACM Press (2002) 920–927
21. Pitt, J., Mamdani, A.: Some remarks on the semantics of fipa's agent communication language. Autonomous Agents and Multi-Agent Systems **2** (1999) 333–356
22. Singh, M.P.: Agent communication languages: Rethinking the principles. IEEE Computer **31** (1998) 40–47
23. Laux, A.: Representing belief in multi-agent worlds via terminological logics. Technical Report RR-93-29, DFKI, Deutsches Forschungszentrum für Künstliche Intelligenz GmbH, Erwin-Schrödinger Strasse, Postfach 2080, 67608 Kaiserslautern, Germany (1993)
24. Rao, A.S.: AgentSpeak(L): BDI agents speak out in a logical computable language. In van Hoe, R., ed.: Seventh European Workshop on Modelling Autonomous Agents in a Multi-Agent World, Eindhoven, The Netherlands (1996)
25. Bellifemine, F., Rimassa, G.: Developing multi-agent systems with a fipa-compliant agent framework. Softw. Pract. Exper. **31** (2001) 103–128
26. Baader, F., Calvanese, D., McGuinness, D.L., Nardi, D., Patel-Schneider, P.F., eds.: The Description Logic Handbook: Theory, Implementation, and Applications. In Baader, F., Calvanese, D., McGuinness, D.L., Nardi, D., Patel-Schneider, P.F., eds.: Description Logic Handbook, Cambridge University Press (2003)

Specifying Protocols for Knowledge Transfer and Action Restriction in Multiagent Systems

María Adela Grando[1,*] and Christopher David Walton[2,**]

[1] Research Group on Mathematical Linguistics,
Rovira i Virgili University, Tarragona, Spain
[2] Centre for Intelligent Systems and their Applications,
School of Informatics, University of Edinburgh, UK

Abstract. In this paper we present the MAP^a language for expressing knowledge transfer and action restriction between agents in multiagent systems. Our approach is founded on the definition of patterns of dialogues between groups of agents, expressed as protocols. Our protocols are flexible and directly executable. Furthermore, our language allow us to specify the connection between communication and knowledge transfer in a way that is independent of the specific reasoning techniques used.

1 Introduction

Communication in a multiagent system is necessary because agents are independent and autonomous entities. By this, we mean that an agent has the freedom to make decisions, and these decisions are not controlled externally to the agent. If the agents in a multiagent system were not autonomous, then all of the decisions could be centrally managed, and there would be no need for inter-agent communication. In order to maintain autonomy and independence, an agent is typically designed with decision-making machinery and knowledge that is local and private to the agent. For example, the local knowledge of the agent may contain the beliefs, desires, and intentions of the agent. This local knowledge allows the agent to reason in a way that is independent of the behaviour of any other agent in the system. Nonetheless, an agent will often be unable to complete certain tasks due to insufficient local knowledge or ability. To overcome this limitation, the agent must communicate with other agents in order to convey its requests, and to update its knowledge with the outcome of these requests. As a result, an autonomous agent must be equipped with a communicate ability in order to interact in a multiagent environment.

To illustrate the need for local knowledge, we may consider a pair of agents who wish to negotiate on the price of an item. In this setting, each agent is seeking to maximise the outcome of the negotiation from their own perspective.

---

* Sponsored by the Research Grant "Programa Nacional para la Formación del Profesorado Universitario" from the Ministry of Education, Culture and Sports of Spain.
** Sponsored by the Open Knowledge Project (www.openk.org), European Union Sixth Framework Programme, Information Society Technologies.

M. Klusch, M. Rovatsos, and T. Payne (Eds.): CIA 2006, LNAI 4149, pp. 431–445, 2006.

If the decision making processes and local knowledge of each agent were freely available, then the negotiation process could be readily subverted. Therefore, in this situation, each agent will keep its knowledge private, and only release parts of this knowledge as necessary during the negotiation process. There is clearly a close relationship between the knowledge of an agent, and any communication that it performs. In effect, when a pair of agents communicate, they are effectively exchanging knowledge. In performing a communicative act, and agent may be revealing part of its own local knowledge to another, and its own local knowledge may be extended as a result of the communication.

In this paper we define a language that makes explicit the relationship between agent communication and the exchange of knowledge. In particular, our language enables us to state precisely the exchange of knowledge between one agent and another, and to define common knowledge. Our language is founded on the definition of *protocols* that express patterns of *dialogue* between groups of agents. If a group of agents follow a particular dialogue then they should reach a particular well-defined outcome. Nonetheless, our protocols contain decision points that allow the agents to behave autonomously. The protocols that we define are *executable specifications*. That is, the formalisms that we use to specify our protocols are exactly the same as those used for enactment.

Our language defines Multi-Agent Protocols, and is called MAP^a. This language is an extension of the MAP language which we previously presented in [12]. The extensions in this paper make the protocols more flexible and dynamic, but retain the lightweight nature of the previous definitions. In MAP^a, we treat protocols as first-class objects which can be passed between agents as opposed to our previous static definition. We also permit the organisation of roles in hierarchies, structuring role definitions in a modular and reusable way. Most importantly, we permit the management of knowledge to be expressed in our protocols, which enables a better connection between the protocol and the agent reasoning processes at the decision points.

There are many existing approaches to the definition of protocols for expressing dialogues in multiagent systems. Conversation policies [4] represent agent dialogues using finite-state automata. Electronic Institutions [2] are a more expressive approach, which define graphs of finite-state automata (state-charts) to express multi-agent protocols. Virtual organisations [9] are another approach to defining patterns of communication between independent agents. However, none of these approaches enable the relationship between knowledge and communication to be precisely stated. The usual approach to the formal definition of knowledge exchange in multiagent systems is the use of epistemic logics, e.g. [10]. However, while this work is very important from a theoretical perspective, it is difficult to implement these proposals in real multiagent systems. By contrast, the purpose of this work is to describe knowledge and communication in a formal and unambiguous way, which nonetheless takes into account pragmatic considerations found in real implementations. In doing so, we avoid the issues with other formal approaches, such as FIPA-ACL, which are both ambiguous and not readily implementable, i.e.

due to the sincerity assumption between agents. We are currently implementing the MAP^a language within our MagentA framework [13].

The remainder of the paper is organised as follows. In section 2 we define the abstract syntax of MAP^a. To illustrate the language, we present a detailed protocol example in section 3. We define an operational semantics of MAP^a in section 4 that may be used to implement the language. Finally, we conclude in section 5 with an overview and discussion of future work.

2 MAP^a Language Definition

MAP^a is a lightweight language-based formalism for the definition of protocols, which express social interactions between groups of agents. The language is a sugared process-calculus, which is a common approach to the formal definition of concurrent systems. In particular, MAP^a has many similarities to the π-calculus [6] though it has an asynchronous semantics. The extensions to the core calculus are designed to make the language more suited to the concepts found in multi-agent systems and dialogues.

The key concepts in MAP^a are *scenes*, *roles* and *protocols* that we now describe. A scene is conceptually a bounded space in which a group of agents interact on a single task. We assume that a scene is initialised with a set of active agents who start the dialogue and is concluded when there are no active agents remaining, i.e. when all the agents have exited the scene. The scene definition comprises a set of roles required to accomplish the task, and the set of performatives and knowledge to be shared and understood by all the agents playing a role within. An example scene is shown in Figure 2 where a buyer agent interacts with a set of sellers with the purpose of buying some items.

The concept of an agent *role* is also central to the definition of our protocols. Agents entering a scene assume an initial role, though this role may change during the scene. By adopting a specific role, an agent obtains the capacity to perform certain operations and to know certain facts associated with the role. For our example in Figure 2 agents with the roles of *buyer (B)* and *seller (S)* are defined. When adopting the role of buyer an agent knows the market situation and some commercial strategies that guide him in taking decisions. Roles are defined as a hierarchy, where more specialised roles appear further down in the graph of roles and inherit knowledge and decision procedures from upper roles. For example, an agent may initially assume the role *buyer* but may change to the more specialised role *car buyer* during a scene. This will allow the buyer to obtain knowledge and perform actions related specifically to the car market, which a generic buyer does not need to know.

For each role in a scene, a *protocol* is defined that describes the sequence of operations that an agent performing that role needs to follow. It is important to note that a protocol only contains operations that are specific to the mechanisms of communication and coordination between agents. This makes it straightforward to understand the operation of the protocol without extraneous details, and makes it possible to verify the protocols using automated means, e.g. model checking [11]. All of the other agent facilities, e.g. the reasoning processes, are encapsulated by *decision procedures* that are external to the protocol. In effect, the decision procedures provide an interface between the communicative and the rational process of the agent. In MAP^a we distinguish two levels of decision procedures: those private to the agent, and those shared between all of the agents in the same role.

Interaction between the agents in a scene is performed by the exchange of messages. Every message has an associated *performative* that is used to indicate the type of the message and parameters. For convenience, we do not assign any fixed semantics to these performatives. However, individual agents can agree on a semantics for a particular scene. In this way, we can readily represent FIPA-style agent communication, e.g. the contract-net protocol.

The final concept in MAP^a is the representation of *knowledge*. The language allows to define knowledge as sets of axioms at the scene level, the role level, and the level of a particular agent. In this way we can clearly establish differences between the knowledge. Scene and role knowledge is common knowledge that can be accessed by all agents in the scene or role respectively. By contrast, the private knowledge of the agent cannot be accessed externally.

We now define the syntax of MAP^a more formally. A BNF-style syntax is shown in Figure 1. Superscripts are used to indicate a set, e.g. $P^{(i)}$ is a set with elements P of size i.

$$
\begin{array}{llll}
S & ::= & \langle R^{(i)},\ P^{(i)},\ K^{(b)},\ M^{(k)} \rangle & \text{(Scene)} \\
R & ::= & \langle id,\ Proc^{(l)},\ K^{(m)},\ r^{(n)} \rangle & \text{(Role)} \\
P & ::= & \mathbf{agent}(id, r, Proc^{(l)}, K^{(m)}, \phi^{(f)}) = op. & \\
K & ::= & axiom & \text{(Knowledge)} \\
Proc & ::= & type :: id((\phi, type)^{(g)}) & \text{(Procedure)} \\
M & ::= & id((\phi, type)^{(h)}) & \text{(Performative)} \\
op & ::= & v & \text{(Variable)} \\
  & | & op_1 \ \mathbf{then} \ op_2 & \text{(Sequence)} \\
  & | & op_1 \ \mathbf{or} \ op_2 & \text{(Choice)} \\
  & | & op_1 \ \mathbf{par} \ op_2 & \text{(Parallel)} \\
  & | & (op) & \text{(Precedence)} \\
  & | & \alpha & \text{(Action)} \\
\alpha & ::= & \mathbf{null} & \text{(No Action)} \\
  & | & v = p(\phi^{(g)}) & \text{(Decision)} \\
  & | & id(\phi^{(x)}) \Longleftarrow \mathbf{agent}(id,\ r) & \text{(Receive)} \\
  & | & id(\phi^{(y)}) \Longrightarrow \mathbf{agent}(id,\ r) & \text{(Send)} \\
  & | & \mathbf{agent}(id,\ r,\ Proc^{(w)},\ K^{(v)},\ \phi^{(d)}) & \text{(Invocation)} \\
\phi & ::= & c \mid \_ \mid v & \text{(Term)}
\end{array}
$$

Fig. 1. MAP^a Language Syntax

A conversational environment, called a scene, comprises a *role hierarchy* $R^{(i)}$, a set of protocols $P^{(i)}$ that are parameterised on these roles, a set of axioms $K^{(b)}$ that is the *common knowledge* in the scene, and finally a set of performatives $M^{(k)}$ which defines the *dialogic structure* (i.e. all of the allowed performatives) for the scene. The role hierarchy is defined as a set of role definitions. Each of these definitions R has a unique identifier id, a set of decision procedures $Proc^{(l)}$ which are shared within the role, a set of axioms $K^{(m)}$ which are common to the role, and lastly a set of upper roles identifiers $r^{(n)}$, which appear above the role in the hierarchy. This set will be empty for a top-level role.

A protocol P is defined by a set of parameters and a body op. The parameters comprise a unique identifier for the protocol id, a role r, a set of procedures $Proc^{(l)}$ and axioms $K^{(m)}$ which are private to the agent. The remaining parameters $\phi^{(f)}$ are terms ϕ, which are constants c, variables v, or wild-cards _.

As previously noted, knowledge K is represented by axioms within a protocol. These axioms represent facts which are believed to be true. The reasoning over this knowledge is performed by decision procedures $Proc$ which are formally defined giving the type of their incoming an outgoing parameters. Decision procedures are external to the protocol and have full access to the scene knowledge, the knowledge of the played role and upper roles, and the agent private knowledge. The result of the procedure evaluation is bound to a variable v.

The core of the protocols are constructed from operations op which control the flow of execution, and actions α which have side-effects and can fail. The operations can be defined by a variable or by a sequence **then**, choice **or** or parallel composition **par** of operations, and parenthesis can be used to enforce precedence. It is possible to introduce operational variables during design time, which are replaced during run-time by operations. This feature provides MAP^a protocols with dynamism and with the possibility of defining protocols where part of the behaviour is not known beforehand but depends on agents interaction during the scene execution. With respect to the other operations, they have a standard interpretation. A sequence means that the first operation op_1 is evaluated before the second operation op_2. The non-deterministic choice means that either op_1 or op_2 is evaluated. Finally, parallel composition means that both operations are evaluated at the same time.

The actions an agent can perform are: null action, invocation of decision procedures, receiving and sending messages, and introducing agent invocations. A null action is included which is convenient for protocol termination. Decision procedures are interfaces between the dialogue protocol and the rational processes of the agent. The interchange of messages requires the indication of the identifier id and the role r of the agents that sends or receives the message, respectively. It also requires the content or performative $id(\phi^{(x)})$. With respect to the action of introducing agent definitions is a very powerful mechanism that can be used for creating new agent instances, changing the agent role or keeping the current role for simulating recursive calls.

3   A Protocol Example

To illustrate the use of MAP^a we define in Figure 2 two protocols for the description of a selling scene. One protocol definition corresponds to the *Buyer (B)* role and the other to the *Seller (S)* role. The buyer needs to buy products satisfying the conditions stated in Bc. He has to choose the best offer from a set of bids *Bids*, each bid introduced by a seller with selling conditions Sc. If a bid is chosen the interchange of products take place.

$agent(\mathbf{id}, \mathbf{B}, \mathbf{P_b}, \mathbf{Bids} \cup \mathbf{Bc} \cup \mathbf{R}) ::=$
$(id_1, Sc) = choose(Bids \cup Bc \cup R)$ then
$(accept(Sc) \Longrightarrow agent(id_1, S)$ then
$sold(Sc) \Longleftarrow agent(id_1, S)$ then
$R = add(R, buy(Bids, Bc) = (id_1, Sc))$
$(prot_r, prot_s) = getprot(buy, Sc, P_b)$ then
$protocol(prot_s) \Longrightarrow agent(id_1, S)$ then
$(prot_r$ par $agent(id, B, P_{nb}, Bids \cup Bc \cup R))$
or
$(R = add(R, buy(Bids, Bc) = failed)$ then
$nconds = getnewcond(Bids \cup Bc \cup R)$ then
$Bc = add(Bc, ncond)$ then
$agent(id, B, P_{nb}, Bids \cup Bc \cup R))$.

$agent(\mathbf{id}, \mathbf{S}, \mathbf{P_s}, \mathbf{Sells} \cup \mathbf{Sc}) ::=$
$(accept(Sc) \Longleftarrow agent(id_1, B)$ then
$sold(Sc) \Longrightarrow agent(id_1, B)$ then
$Sells = add(Sells, sold(id_1, Sc) = T)$
then $protocol(prot_s) \Longleftarrow agent(id_1, B)$
then
$prot_s$ par $agent(id, S, \emptyset, Sells \cup Sc))$
or
$(Sells = add(Sells, sold(id_1, Sc) = F)$
then $agent(id, S, \emptyset, Sells \cup Sc))$.

Fig. 2. Example Negotiation Protocol

In Figure 2, the buyer (B) is defined with a private set of decision procedures P_b and a set of facts that correspond to its private knowledge. These facts have been classified in three sets. A set of conditions Bc that the buyer expects the products to have in order to buy them, a set of offers $Bids$ received from sellers before adopting buyer role, and a set of results R that record the history of his commercial transactions.

According to the result of the rational procedure *choose*, the buyer has two options. In the first option, the buyer has to find a suitable bid with conditions Sc from a seller with identifier id_1. The buyer then communicates acceptance to the selected seller. After receiving a confirmation from the seller, the buyer actualises his record R of transactions. Finally, according to the agreed conditions Sc and his private decision procedures P_b the buyer decides (by *getprot*) the way to perform the interchange of products. The buyer communicates to the seller the operational description $prot_s$ of what to do to deliver the products and get the payment. The buyer then fulfils the commitments in the transaction by behaving in the way described by $prot_r$, and restarts the protocol. The second option means that the buyer has not found any bid that fulfils his buying conditions. In this case the buyer records in R that the transaction failed and then tries again with more relaxed conditions Bc.

The seller (S) protocol is defined with a set of decision procedures P_s. The sellers' private knowledge is the union of two sets: a record $Sells$ of the results of his participation in selling transactions and a set Sc of conditions over the products offered for sale.

The seller protocol is a choice between two options. In the first case, the seller receives a notification of acceptance of its bid. After sending to the buyer a message of confirmation he actualises his record of operations $Sells$. Finally he receives from the buyer a description $prot_s$ of the operations to perform in order to deliver and receive the payment for the products. Simultaneously, while behaving as described by $prot_s$ he restarts his participation in the scene as a buyer. The second case is performed by the seller when a decision is made not to wait more for a bid acceptance from the buyer. He records in $Sells$ that the selling process failed and then restarts the protocol.

To illustrate the selling protocol in operation we present an example instantiation in Figure 3. The scene starts with a factory F as a buyer and two chemistry

$agent(\mathbf{F}, \mathbf{B}, \mathbf{P_{Spain}}, \mathbf{Bids} \cup \mathbf{Bc} \cup \mathbf{R_1}) ::=$
$(M, ScM) = choose(Bids \cup Bc \cup R_1)$ then
$accept(ScM) \Longrightarrow agent(M, S)$ then
$sold(ScM) \Longleftarrow agent(M, S)$ then
$R_1 = add(R_1, result(Bids, Bc) = (M, ScM))$
$(eprot_b, eprot_s) = getprot(buy, ScM, P_{Spain})$
then $protocol(eprot_s) \Longrightarrow agent(M, S)$ then
par $eprot_b$ par
$agent(F, B, P_{Spain}, Bids \cup Bc \cup R_1) \dots$

$agent(\mathbf{M}, \mathbf{S}, \emptyset, \mathbf{T_M} \cup \mathbf{ScM}) ::=$
$accept(ScM) \Longleftarrow agent(F, B)$ then
$sold(ScM) \Longrightarrow agent(F, B)$ then
$T_M = add(T_M, sold(ScM, F) = T)$ then
$protocol(eprot_s) \Longleftarrow agent(F, B)$ then
$eprot_s$ par $agent(M, S, \emptyset, T_M \cup ScM) \dots$

$agent(\mathbf{N}, \mathbf{S}, \emptyset, \mathbf{T_N} \cup \mathbf{ScN}) ::=$
$T_N = add(T_N, sold(ScN, F) = F)$
then $agent(N, S, \emptyset, T_N \cup ScN) \dots$

Fig. 3. Example Protocol Instance

industries N and M as sellers. Factory F wants to buy a formula fla to get a chemical component Q from substances S_1, ..., S_n. The conditions under which F starts the buying process are $Bc = \{delivery \leq 15\ days, cash = 800,\ checks = 1000,\ item = fla,\ country = Spain\}$. F gets bids from chemistry industries M and N, $Bids = \{M, N\}$, and has a record of transactions $R = R_1$. Because factory F is in Spain and performs transactions with sellers from European Union, it needs to know how to perform buying and selling processes that respect Spanish commerce and security laws. For this purpose F is defined with a set of private decision procedures P_{Spain}. Industry M offers to provide the formula under the conditions $ScM = \{delivery = [10 \dots 13\ days],\ price = 1000,\ payment = (cash50\%, check50\%),\ item = fla,\ country = Scotland\}$, and has already performed transactions with F according to $T_M = \{sold((cond_t, F)) = true\}$. While the conditions of chemistry N are $ScN = \{delivery = [7 \dots 10\ days],\ price = 900,\ payment = (cash100\%),\ item = fla,\ country = Italy\}$ and it has not performed any transaction with F according to $T_N = \{sold((cond_y, Y)) = true\}$. It is not required for M or N to know Spanish commercial laws, because the factory F will provide them with the protocol in case of successful transaction, for this reason $P_N = \emptyset$ and $P_M = \emptyset$. Finally, factory F decides to buy from industry M because it offers better payment conditions.

The example that we have presented shows the practical importance of the new features that we have included in MAP^a. The formalisation of the concepts of knowledge and decision procedures clarify the protocol definitions. Now we can define explicitly the influence of certain facts or decision procedures over agent rational processes. Also the effects that agent action have over the sets of agent beliefs and presuppositions.

In the example we have shown the use of protocols as first-order objects. The buyer can decide (through rational procedure $getprot$ depending on current condition ScM) the next actions to perform to complete the transaction. In this case the buyer decides to perform the executable protocol $eprot_b = agent(F, Mana, \emptyset, Bc)$ and to communicate to the seller the executable protocol $eprot_s = delivery(v^{(w)}) \Longleftarrow agent(F, Manager)$ then $r = deliver(v^{(w)})$. This means that he chooses to change to $Manager$ role in order to select the best way to perform delivery process. And he asks the seller to wait for the delivery details $v^{(w)}$ like day, transport company, etcetera and perform the delivery. From this example it is clear that the use of protocols as first order objects allows to define dialogues highly flexible and adaptable. In MAP^a it is not necessary

$$
\begin{array}{lll}
\text{Scene Environment} & \Theta & ::= s \overset{map}{\mapsto} (R^{(i)},\, K^{(e)},\, M^{(t)},\, OP) \\
& OP & ::= (a,\, r,\, \phi^{(k)}) \overset{map}{\mapsto} op \\[2ex]
\text{Role Environment} & \Upsilon & ::= r \overset{map}{\mapsto} (Proc^{(u)},\, K^{(q)},\, r^{(g)}) \\[2ex]
\text{Agent Environment} & \Delta & ::= a \overset{map}{\mapsto} (r,\, s,\, V,\, K^{(o)},\, IM^{(j)},\, OC) \\
& V & ::= (v,\, c)^{(w)} \\
& IM & ::= (a',\, r',\, M) \\
& OC & ::= op
\end{array}
$$

Fig. 4. MAP^a Execution Environments

to contemplate all the possible scenarios in advance, but agents can rationally choose during run time what to do next, according to current conditions. This new feature of MAP^a provides agents with the capacity to react better to open and non-deterministic environments and to deal with more realistic situations. And the use of roles and change of roles allow to get simple, modular and reusable behavioural descriptions.

4 MAP^a Operational Semantics

The provision of a clean and unambiguous semantics for our MAP^a language was a primary consideration in the design process. The purpose of the semantics is to formally describe the meaning of the different language constructs, such that protocols expressed in the language can be interpreted in a consistent manner. We consider this to be a failing of the formal semantics of FIPA-ACL [3], which is expressed in a BDI-like logic. The FIPA semantics is an abstract description, which neglects practical aspects such as a definition of the communication primitives. Furthermore, the BDI modalities can be interpreted in a number of different ways, e.g. [5,7,8], meaning that implementations of BDI agents have typically been *ad-hoc* in nature.

To define the MAP^a semantics, we capture the state of a scene definition by a number of structures called *environments*. We define the evaluation environments for MAP^a in Figure 4. There are three kinds of environment which track the state of evaluation at a scene, role, and individual agent level respectively. During evaluation, there will be a single scene environment which is shared between all agents in the scene, and a role environment for each role which is shared between agents of that role. By contrast, the agent environment is private to each agent in the scene. Thus, each environment tracks the evaluation at a different level of detail. While scene and role environment remain unchangeable during execution time, agent environments change with the execution of every operation that define their behaviour. We define a *transition function* to specify the changes produced in agent environments by the execution of operations. But before we introduce in Figure 4 the formal definitions of scene, role and agent environments.

The scene environment is a function that given a scene s returns its set of roles $R^{(i)}$, the scene knowledge $K^{(e)}$, the dialogic structure $M^{(t)}$ and a function OP. Function OP takes as argument an agent identifier a, a role r and parameters $\phi^{(k)}$ and returns the corresponding operational clause op.

A role environment is a function that provided a role identifier returns the set of role decision procedures $Proc^{(u)}$, the common knowledge for the role $K^{(q)}$, and a set of upper roles identifiers $r^{(g)}$.

The agent environment is an function that given the agent identifier returns the state specific to that agent. This environment records the role r and the scene s in which the agent is present. The values of the bound variables are in V. The decision procedures which are local to the agent are referenced in the set $Proc^{(j)}$, and the private knowledge of the agent is recorded in the set $K^{(o)}$. Any incoming messages are stored in $IM^{(j)}$, where a' and r' identify the sender identifier and role and M is the actual message. Finally, the current operation under evaluation is recorded in OC.

To describe the effect that the execution of MAP^a operations and actions have over the agent environment we define a transition function. This function takes as argument an agent environment and an operation or action and returns the agent environment resulting after the performance of the corresponding operation or action. We divide the definition of the transition function in evaluation rules for the operations, and rules for actions. These evaluation rules are presented in a standard proof-rule style with the premises above the line, and the conclusions below the line. The premises must be satisfied before the conclusion may hold. Satisfying the premises may involve the evaluation of further rules. Thus, applying these rules to an entire protocol will result in a proof tree.

Before we define the rules, it is necessary to explain the workings of a number of auxiliary functions which we use in these rules. These functions are defined in Figure 5. Function $getProced$ in Rule 1 retrieves the procedures accessible by a role through a recursive traversal of the hierarchy of roles. The base case applies when there is no upper role. In this case, the procedures are simply retrieved from the role environment. When the recursive case happens the procedures are retrieved from all of the upper roles. Function $getKnowledge$ defined in Rule 2 behaves like function $getProced$ but retrieves all the knowledge accessible by a role.

The $unify$ function, defined in Rule 3, performs pattern matching, and binds matching variables to values. This function is evaluated against an environment V, and the result is a new environment containing V and any newly bound variables. The arguments of this function are a pair of terms, or a pair of sets of terms. There are four cases in this definition. The first case states that the wild-card _ matches any term. The second case states that two identical terms match together. The third term states that a variable v will be bound to the term ϕ in the current environment V, provided that the types match. The final case breaks a set of terms into individual matches which are then composed to produce the resulting environment. The final $subst$ function from Rule 4 is

$$getProced(r) = \begin{cases} Proc^{(l)}, \text{ if } \Upsilon(r) = (Proc^{(l)}, \_, \emptyset) \\ Proc^{(l)} \cup getProced(ur^{(1)}) \cup \ldots \cup getProced(ur^{(k)}), \\ \text{if } \Upsilon(r) = (Proc^{(l)}, \_, ur^{(1)} \cup \ldots \cup ur^{(k)}) \end{cases} \tag{1}$$

$$getKnowledge(r) = \begin{cases} K^{(l)}, \text{ if } \Upsilon(r) = (\_, K^{(l)}, \emptyset) \\ K^{(l)} \cup getKnowledge(ur^{(1)}) \cup \ldots \cup getKnowledge(ur^{(k)}), \\ \text{if } \Upsilon(r) = (\_, K^{(l)}, ur^{(1)} \cup \ldots \cup ur^{(k)}) \end{cases}$$
$$\tag{2}$$

$$unify(\phi_1, \phi_2, V) = V \cup \{(\phi_1, \phi_2)\}, \text{ if } type(\phi_1) = type(\phi_2) \tag{3}$$
$$unify(\phi_1^{(k)}, \phi_2^{(k)}, V) = unify(\phi_1^1, \phi_2^1, V) \cup \cdots \cup unify(\phi_1^k, \phi_2^k, V)$$

$$subst(\phi_1, V) = \phi_2, \text{ if } (\phi_1, \phi_2) \in V \tag{4}$$

Fig. 5. Auxiliary Execution Functions

defined similarly to $unify$, but substitutes variables for their values from the environment V.

We also consider functions $rewrite$ and $eval$ whose definitions we do not give but whose behaviour we explain. Function $Rewrite(v, op_1, op_2) = op_3$ returns the operational expression op_2 resulting of rewriting each occurrence of variable v by the operational expression op_1 in op_2. Function $eval(proc, values, vble, V, K) = (newV, newK)$ returns a tuple. First component of the tuple is the set $newV$ resulting of adding to the set of matching pairs V the pair $(vble, proc(values))$. This new pair represents the association to the variable $vble$ of the value obtained from applying procedure $proc$ to the parameter values $values$. The second component of the tuple is the set $newK$ resulting of modifying the set of axioms K after the evaluation of $proc$.

Now we can introduce the rules that define the transition function for MAP^a operations. There is a separate rule for each of the different kinds of operation in the language.

According to Rule 5 the sequential execution of operations produces the sequential composition of agent environment. The operation op_1 is evaluated followed by op_2, unless op_1 involves an action which fails.

Rules 6 and 7 state that any of the operational component of an or-expression can be chosen for its execution. Action failures are handled by the or operator. Such that if one operator fails then the other operator is evaluated, otherwise it is ignored.

Rule 8 says that if two agent environments $\Delta(a)$ and Δ' are equivalent, any agent environment Δ'' that can be reached from one of them can be also reached from the other.

Rule 9 states that the effect of the execution of an operational variable v is the replacement in the agent operational clause OC of all the occurrences of that variable v for its bounded operational expression value op, according to the agent set of matching pairs V. We use the notation $\Delta_{\sigma_1, \ldots, \sigma_n}^{\phi_1, \ldots, \phi_n}$ to mean the state

$$\frac{\Delta(a) \xrightarrow{op_1} \Delta' \quad \Delta' \xrightarrow{op_2} \Delta''}{\Delta(a) \xrightarrow{op_1 \text{ then } op_2} \Delta''} \tag{5}$$

$$\frac{\Delta(a) \xrightarrow{op_1} \Delta'}{\Delta(a) \xrightarrow{op_1 \text{ or } op_2} \Delta'} \tag{6}$$

$$\frac{\Delta(a) \xrightarrow{op_2} \Delta'}{\Delta(a) \xrightarrow{op_1 \text{ or } op_2} \Delta'} \tag{7}$$

$$\frac{\Delta(a) \equiv \Delta' \quad \Delta' \xrightarrow{op} \Delta''}{\Delta(a) \xrightarrow{op} \Delta''} \tag{8}$$

$$\frac{\Delta(a) = (\_, \_, V, \_, \_, \_, OC) \quad subst(v, V) = op' \quad rewrite(v, op', OC) = OC'}{\Delta(a) \xrightarrow{v} \Delta(a)_{OC'}^{OC}} \tag{9}$$

resulting of the simultaneous substitution in Δ of each of the terms ϕ_i for the corresponding term σ_i.

We now turn our attention to the evaluation of the actions. According to Rule 10, the null action introduces no change in the agent environment. Rule 11 explains the effects that the adoption of a new role by an agent has over its environmental state. When an agent playing role r adopts a new role r_1 it keeps its set of matching pairs V, the set of role decision procedures $Proc_{ur}^{(x)}$ and the set of private decision procedures $Proc_p^{(u)}$. It also keeps the knowledge associated to role r, $K_{ur}^{(y)}$, and the agent set of input messages $IM^{(g)}$. And it incorporates the set of decision procedures associated to new role r_1, $Proc_{ur_1}^{(t)}$, and a set of new decision procedures, $Proc_q^{(h)}$. Besides it incorporates a set of axioms K_{ur_1} corresponding to the knowledge associated to role r_1.

Rule 12 explains the effects of the introduction of a new agent instance with a role different from the role of the agent that makes the invocation. The new agent instance playing role r_1 is assigned an initial environmental state composed by the set of decision procedures of role r_1, $Proc_{ur_1}^{(t)}$, plus the set of decision procedures assigned in the invocation, $Proc_q^{(h)}$. Analogously it adopts the knowledge of role r_1, $K_{ur_1}^{(z)}$, and private knowledge $K_q^{(i)}$. The created agent instance participates in the dialogue through the execution of the operational clause associated to the role it adopts, $OP(b, r_1, \phi_1^{(k)})$.

Rule 13 explains the effect that the execution of a decision procedure p belonging to the agent set of decision procedures $Proc^{(q)}$ has over the set of matching pairs V and set of agent private knowledge $K_p^{(i)}$. The procedure p is evaluated with the arguments $\phi_1^{(h)}$ replaced by the matching values subtracted from V by

$$\overline{\Delta(a) \xrightarrow{\text{null}} \Delta(a)} \qquad (10)$$

$$\Theta = (R^{(i)}, OP, \_, \_)$$
$$\Delta(a) = (r, s, V, Proc_{ur}^{(x)} \cup Proc_p^{(u)}, K_{ur}^{(y)} \cup K_p^{(o)}, IM^{(g)}, OC)$$
$$\exists r_1 \in R^{(i)} \mid$$

$$\left. \begin{cases} \Upsilon(r_1) = (Proc_{r_1}^{(t)}, K_{r_1}^{(\tilde{n})}, ur^{(v)}) \\ V' = \{(r_1, subst(r_1, V)\} \\ \phi_2^{(k)} = subst(\phi_1^{(k)}, V) \\ V'' = unify(\phi_1^{(k)}, \phi_2^{(k)}, V') \\ getProced(r_1) = Proc_{ur_1}^{(t)} \\ getKnowledge(r_1) = K_{ur_1}^{(z)} \\ Proc_{ur}^{(x)} \cup Proc_{ur_1}^{(t)} \cup Proc_p^{(u)} \cup Proc_q^{(h)} = Proc_d^{(x+t+u+h)} \\ K_{ur}^{(y)} \cup K_{ur_1}^{(z)} = K_r^{(y+z)} \\ \Delta(a) \xrightarrow{\text{null}} \Delta(a)^{(r,V,Proc_{ur}^{(x)} \cup Proc_p^{(u)}, K_{ur}^{(y)} \cup K_p^{(s)}, IM^g, OC)}_{(r_1,V'',Proc_d^{(x+t+u+h)}, K_{ur}^{(y)} \cup K_p^{(s)} \cup K_q^{(i)} \cup K_{ur_1}^{(z)}, OP(a,r_1,Proc_q^{(h)}, K_q^{(i)}, \phi_1^{(k)}))} \\ OP(a,r_1,Proc_q^{(h)}, K_q^{(i)}, \phi_1^{(k)}) \\ \xrightarrow{\qquad} \left(r_1, \ s, \ Q, Proc_d^{(x+t+u+h)}, \ K_{ur}^{(y)} \cup K_{ur_1}^{(z)} \cup NK_p^{(f)}, IM'^{(j)}, null \right) \end{cases} \right\}$$

$$\overline{\Delta(a) \xrightarrow{\text{agent}(a,r_1,Proc_q^{(h)}, K_q^{(i)}, \phi_1^{(k)})} \Delta(a)^{V,K_{ur}^{(y)} \cup K_p^{(s)}, IM(g)}_{Q, K_{ur}^{(y)} \cup NK_p^{(s)}, IM'(j)}} \qquad (11)$$

$$\Theta(s) = (R^{(i)}, OP, \_, \_) \qquad (12)$$
$$\Delta_{(a)} = (\_, \_, V, \_, \_, \_, \_)$$
$$\exists r_1 \in R^{(i)} \mid$$

$$\left. \begin{cases} \Upsilon(r_1) = (Proc_{r_1}^{(t)}, K_{r_1}^{(\tilde{n})}, ur^{(v)}) \\ V' = \{(b, subs(b, V)), (r_1, subst(r_1, V)\} \\ \phi_2^{(k)} = subst(\phi_1^{(k)}, V) \\ V'' = unify(\phi_1^{(k)}, \phi_2^{(k)}, V') \\ getProced(r_1) = Proc_{ur_1}^{(t)} \\ getKnowledge(r_1) = K_{ur_1}^{(z)} \\ \Delta(b) \xrightarrow{\text{null}} \left(\begin{matrix} r_1, \ s, \ V'', Proc_{ur_1}^{(t)} \cup Proc_q^{(h)} \\ K_{ur_1}^{(z)} \cup K_q^{(i)}, \ \emptyset, OP(b,r_1,Proc_q^{(h)}, K_q^{(i)}, \phi_1^{(k)}) \end{matrix} \right) \\ OP(b,r_1,Proc_q^{(h)}, K_q^{(i)}, \phi_1^{(k)}) \\ \xrightarrow{\qquad} \Delta' \end{cases} \right\}$$

$$\overline{\Delta(a) \xrightarrow{\text{agent}(b,r_1,Proc_q^{(h)}, K_q^{(i)}, \phi_1^{(k)})} \Delta(a)^V_{V''}}$$

invocation of operation $subst(\phi_1^{(h)}, V)$. The result of the evaluation of p is the inclusion in V of the pair that bounds the variable v with the value resulting of performing p. In case v includes an axiom, the agent knowledge set $K_p^{(i)}$ is modified getting a new knowledge set $NewK_p$.

Rule 14 explains the conditions under with an agent simulates the reception of a message m that it is in his set of agent input messages $IM^{(l)}$. In case the received message is a proper performative, it means it belongs to the set of scene performatives $M^{(t)}$, it is checked whether the sender is already known by the agent or not. In the first case the agent subtracts from the set of matching pairs V the identifier and role of the sender. If they are the same as the sender identifier id and role r, the message reception is simulated. While in the second case no substitution of terms is possible because the message is sent by an unknown agent. In this case a unification of terms is performed $(unify(id, a', V) = V' \wedge$

$$\Theta(s) = (\_, \_, \_) \tag{13}$$
$$\Delta(a) = (\_, \_, V, Proc^{(q)}, K_p^{(i)}, \_, \_)$$
$$\exists rtype :: p((\phi_1, type)^{(h)}) \in Proc^{(q)} \mid$$
$$\left\{ eval(p, subst(\phi_1^{(h)}, V), v, V, K_p^{(i)}) = (V', NewK_p^{(t)}) \right\}$$
$$\frac{}{\Delta(a) \xrightarrow{v = p(\phi_1^{(h)})} \Delta(a)^{V, K_r^{(x)} \cup K_p^{(i)}}_{V', K_r^{(x)} \cup NewK_p^{(t)}}}$$

$$\Theta(s) = (\_, \_, M^{(t)}) \tag{14}$$
$$\Delta(a) = (\_, \_, V, \_, \_, IM^{(l)}, \_)$$
$$\exists \rho((\phi_1, type)^{(h)}) \in M^{(t)} \mid$$
$$\left\{ \begin{array}{l} \exists m = (a', \ r', \rho(\phi_3^{(h)})) \in IM^{(l)} \mid \\ \left\{ \begin{array}{l} (subst(id, V) = a' \wedge subst(r, V) = r' \wedge V = V'') \vee \\ (unify(id, a', V) = V' \wedge unify(r, r', V') = V'') \end{array} \right\} \\ unify(\phi_1^{(h)}, \phi_3^{(h)}, V'') = Q \end{array} \right\}$$
$$\frac{}{\Delta(a) \xrightarrow{\rho(\phi_1^{(h)}) \Leftarrow \mathbf{agent}(id, r)} \Delta(a)^{V, IM^{(l)}}_{Q, IM^{(l)} - m}}$$

$$\Theta(s) = (\_, \_, M^{(t)}) \tag{15}$$
$$\Delta(a) = (t, \_, V, \_, \_, \_, \_)$$
$$\exists \rho((\phi_1, type)^{(k)}) \in M^{(t)} \mid$$
$$\left\{ \begin{array}{l} subst(id, V) = a' \\ subst(r, V) = r' \\ \forall (a', r') \mid \left\{ \begin{array}{l} subst(a, V) = b \\ subst(t, V) = q \\ subst(\phi_1^{(h)}, V) = \phi_3^{(h)} \\ \Delta(a') \xrightarrow{null} \Delta(a')^{IM^{(l)}}_{IM^{(l)} \cup (b, q, \rho(\phi_3^{(h)}))} \end{array} \right. \end{array} \right\}$$
$$\frac{}{\Delta(a) \xrightarrow{\rho(\phi_1^{(h)}) \Rightarrow \mathbf{agent}(id, r)} \Delta(a)}$$

$unify(r, r', V') = V'')$. In both cases the message reception is completed by deleting the incoming message m from $IM^{(l)}$.

Finally, Rule 15 explains the effect of sending a message over the recipients. We check that the outgoing message m is a proper message, i.e. it belongs to the scene set of performatives $M^{(t)}$. The message terms a, t and $\phi_1^{(h)}$ are replaced by the corresponding values b, q and $\phi_3^{(h)}$ obtained by substitution from the set of matching pairs V. The resulting message is included into the set of input messages $IM^{(l)}$ of all the agents to whom the message is destined. The semantics of message passing corresponds to reliable, buffered, non-blocking communication. Broadcast and multi-cast communication modes are possible when the result of the substitution of recipient agent identifier or role is the wild-card value.

5   Conclusions

In this paper we have presented an overview of our MAP^a language. The purpose of this language is the specification of the communication and transfer of knowledge between groups of agents in a multi-agent system. This is accomplished by the definition of protocols which express social behaviours between the agents. In particular, these protocols define social norms which agents must observe if they are to participate in, and benefit from, the society. The use of protocols ensures that the interactions between agents in the society happen in a controlled and predictable manner. Nonetheless, these protocols do not overly restrict the individual autonomy of the agents.

Our approach differs from previous work on multi-agent protocols in a number of important ways. Our protocols are executable specifications, and we have constructed a meta-interpreter for our protocols in Java. This direct execution eliminates a potentially error-prone refinement task between the specification and implementation. Our protocols are defined separately from the reasoning processes. This enables our protocols to be independently examined and verified before an agent subscribes to the society. Furthermore, it permits a range of reasoning strategies to be adopted, e.g. reactive or planning systems, rather than restricting us to a single rational model. We have noted that MAP^a is an extension of our previous MAP language. The first of these extensions is the ability to express knowledge management within protocols. This gives us the ability to state precisely the exchange of knowledge between one agent and another, and to define different levels of shared (i.e. common) and private knowledge. The second extension is the ability to define restrictions on the actions that an agent can perform according to their role or private capacities. Ours is a simple alternative for defining agent authorisations to perform tasks. Finally, the ability to pass protocol fragments between agents. Previously our protocols were statically defined. This allows an agent to inform another "what to do" in a given situation, as illustrated in our worked example.

The semantics of MAP^a in this paper are defined in the operational style. This style is appropriate as it states precisely how the language should be implemented. It is a straightforward process to take these rules and evaluate them in a meta-interpreter, or refine them into a full implementation. At the present time, we are involved in extending our previous implementation [13] with the new facilities of MAP^a. With regard to future work, we plan to use MAP^a in conjunction with Web Services, to perform service composition on the Semantic Web. We also plan to use the language with eco-grammars [1] to perform automatic agent-based grammar generation. Our future plans for extensions to the language include facilities for constraint satisfaction and the inclusion of deontic relationships between agents.

References

1. A. H. Dediu and M. A. Grando. Simulating evolutionary algorithms with eco-grammar systems. In *Proceedings of the First International Work-Conference on the Interplay Between Natural and Artificial Computation (IWINAC05)*, number 3562 in Lecture Notes in Computer Science, pages 112–121, Las Palmas, Spain, June 2005. Springer Verlag.
2. M. Esteva, J. A. Rodríguez, C. Sierra, P. Garcia, and J. L. Arcos. On the Formal Specification of Electronic Institutions. In *Agent-mediated Electronic Commerce (The European AgentLink Perspective)*, number 1991 in Lecture Notes in Artificial Intelligence, pages 126–147, 2001.
3. Foundation for Intelligent Physical Agents. Fipa specification part 2 - agent communication language. Available at: www.fipa.org, April 1999.

4. M. Greaves, H. Holmback, and J. Bradshaw. What is a Conversation Policy? In *Proceedings of the Workshop on Specifying and Implementing Conversation Policies, Autonomous Agents '99*, Seattle, Washington, May 1999.

5. N. R. Jennings. Specification and Implementation of a Belief-Desire-Joint-Intention Architecture for Collaborative Problem Solving. *Journal of Intelligent and Cooperative Information Systems*, 2(3):289–318, 1993.

6. R. Milner, J. Parrow, and D. Walker. A Calculus of Mobile Processes (Part 1/2). *Information and Computation*, 100(1):1–77, September 1992.

7. A. S. Rao and M. P. Georgeff. BDI-agents: from theory to practise. In *Proceedings of the First International Conference on Multiagent Systems (ICMAS-95)*, pages 312–319, San Francisco, USA, June 1995. AAAI Press.

8. M. D. Sadek. A Study in the Logic of Intention. In *Proceedings of the 3rd Conference on Principles of Knowledge Representation and Reasoning (KR92)*, pages 462–473, Cambridge, MA, 1992.

9. Y. B. Udupi and M. P. Singh. Contract Enactment in Virtual Organizations: A Commitment-Based Approach. In *Proceedings of the 21st National Conference on Artificial Intelligence (AAAI-06)*, Boston, USA, July 2006.

10. W. van der Hoeck and M. Wooldridge. Cooperation, Knowledge, and Time: Alternating-time Temporal Epistemic Logic and its Applications. *Studia Logica*, 75(1):125–157, October 2003.

11. C. Walton. Model Checking Multi-Agent Web Services. In *Proceedings of the 2004 AAAI Spring Symposium on Semantic Web Services*, Stanford, California, March 2004. AAAI.

12. C. Walton. Multi-Agent Dialogue Protocols. In *Proceedings of the Eighth International Symposium on Artificial Intelligence and Mathematics*, Fort Lauderdale, Florida, January 2004.

13. C. Walton and A. Barker. An Agent-based e-Science Experiment Builder. In *Proceedings of the 1st International Workshop on Semantic Intelligent Middleware for the Web and the Grid*, Valencia, Spain, August 2004.

Flexible Service Composition

Adam Barker[1] and Robert G. Mann[2]

[1] Centre for Intelligent Systems and their Applications (CISA)
School of Informatics, University of Edinburgh, UK
`a.d.barker@ed.ac.uk`
[2] Institute for Astronomy, University of Edinburgh, UK

Abstract. Both the agent and Grid communities develop concepts for
distributed computing, however they do so with different motivations.
This paper demonstrates how the flexible coordination technique of interaction protocols, from the field of multiagent communication, can be
used to model the processes found in scientific workflow, a typical composition problem faced by the Grid community. Our approach is founded on
the adaptation of the MultiAgent Protocol (MAP) language to perform
web service composition. A definition of the language and framework
is presented, in order to solve a detailed scientific workflow taken from
the field of time-domain astronomy. MAP offers a flexible, adaptable
approach, allowing the typical features and requirements of a scientific
workflow, to be understood in terms of pure coordination and executed
in an agent-based, decentralised, peer-to-peer architecture.

1 Introduction

Scientists are increasingly sharing their data and computational resources, as a
direct result of this, new knowledge is acquired from analysing existing data;
which would not have been previously so readily available. This information explosion has helped to shape new multi-disciplinary fields such as bio-informatics,
geo-informatics and neuro-informatics [10]. The term *'Grid'* refers to the infrastructure that builds on today's Internet and Web to enable and exploit large-
scale sharing of resources within distributed, often loosely coordinated groups,
commonly termed *Virtual Organisations* [4]. The Grid is the machinery which
enables e-Science. Grid computing has attracted a great deal of interest and
funding firstly from the computer science community, but also from the application of this computing research to problems in the engineering and the physical
sciences.

Both the agent and Grid communities develop concepts for distributed computing, however they do so from differing points of view. The agent community's
focus lies with creating autonomous, flexible software components. Agents are
designed to operate in dynamic and uncertain environments, making decisions at
run-time. Communities of agents exhibit flexible cooperation and coordination
through techniques such argumentation and social laws. The Grid community
however, has focused on the development of middleware, which provides reliable, scalable and secure access to distributed resources. It is clear that these

M. Klusch, M. Rovatsos, and T. Payne (Eds.): CIA 2006, LNAI 4149, pp. 446–460, 2006.

two communities of research are starting to see a convergence of interests. The typical features of each community are illustrated by figure 1. In practise however, the application of techniques from the multiagent systems community to the Grid is a relatively new research area, as highlighted in [7]. Although the field is starting to see an increased level of interest, demonstrated by the recent series of workshops [3], [2] and new journal publication [9].

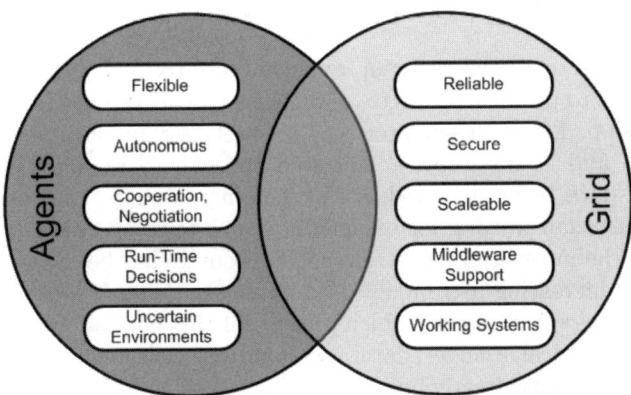

Fig. 1. A Convergence of Interests

The research presented in this paper addresses the problem of composing multiple services to form an e-Science experiment, or workflow [8]. There are a plethora of organisations creating Business Process Modelling languages. The current front runner is BPEL (Business Process Execution Language) [1] for web services, but there are many competing standards which occupy the same space [16]. Although scientific and business workflows have an overlapping set of requirements, it is also true that they each have their own domain specific requirements, and therefore need consideration separately. There are however, very few languages which deal with the flexible *knowledge acquisition* and *discovery processes* found in the sciences. Kepler [5], ICENI [11] and myGrid [14] are the current state of the art in scientific workflow composition, all using a dataflow modelling paradigm in order to capture the series of steps required to describe a distributed e-Science experiment.

This paper aims to demonstrate how the flexible coordination technique of interaction protocols, from the field of multiagent communication, can be used to model the processes found in scientific workflow, a problem from the Grid community. Allowing the typical features and requirements of a scientific workflow, to be understood in terms of pure coordination and executed in an agent-based, decentralised, peer-to-peer architecture.

The remainder of this paper is structured as follows. Sections 2 and 3 introduce a motivating scientific workflow, taken from the Large Synoptic Survey Telescope (LSST). This scenario demonstrates the need for of agent-based techniques, as the systems which perform this computation need to be reactive, collaborative and flexible systems. In section 4 a proposed framework and interaction protocol language is discussed, as a way to address the requirements laid down by the scenario. This language and framework is then applied to the motivating scenario in section 5, demonstrating the use of interaction protocols to model scientific workflow. Conclusions and current implementation work are then discussed in section 6.

2   Virtual Observatory Technology

Breakthroughs in telescope, detector, and computer technology allow astronomical instruments to produce terabytes of images and catalogs; astronomy is facing a data explosion. The data sets produced cover the sky in multiple band widths, from gamma and X Ray, optical, infrared through to radio. With such vast quantities of data being archived, it is becoming easier to 'dial up' a piece of the sky, rather than waiting for expensive, scarce telescope time. The software which allows the integration of astronomical resources has been slow to catch up with the ever increasing astronomy data volumes. *Virtual Observatories (VO)* are the technology frameworks which aim to fill this gap, allowing transparent access to astronomical archives, databases, analysis tools and computational services. Real science has already been demonstrated using VO technologies, and as the middleware develops it will give astronomers seamless access to image and catalogue data on remote computer networks.

2.1   Change in the Universe

Observations of change in the universe are difficult to obtain. Most change in the universe is so slow, that it can never be directly observed, taking place over millions of years; much like the evolutionary processes taking place on Earth. However many of the most remarkable astronomical events occur on human, and even daily, time scales; these changes have proven the most difficult to observe. Current observatories are able to look very deeply at very small parts of the sky. This small field of view means that any one observation is not likely to catch a transient event in the act, as the observatories are always looking somewhere else. A small field of vision means that an impractically large number of separate observations are required to map the entire night sky. Observational facilities are also in great demand, astronomers must apply for scarce telescope time, with the assignment of only a few nights per year to each astronomer. This means that with the lack of continuous observatory access and a global view, astronomers are almost certainly missing out on what's going on in the universe.

3   Time-Domain Astronomy Scenario

The Large Synoptic Survey Telescope (LSST) [15] has been proposed to address many of these difficulties and open up 'time domain' astronomy, the telescope will be able to tile the entire night sky over a three night period, generating 36 gigabytes of data every 30 seconds. This section introduces a motivating scenario taken from the LSST science use cases, an influential factor behind the development of the LSST program. The data reduction and analysis in LSST will be done in a way unlike that of most observing programmes. The data from each image will be analysed and new sources detected before the exposure for the next tile is ready. This means that if anything unusual is detected, normal observation can be interrupted, in order to follow up any new or rapidly varying events. Other observing resources can then be queried instantly, providing a different perspective on the event. As data is collected it will be added to all the data previously detected from the same location of sky to create a very deep *master image.*

Fig. 2. An example of a Subtracted Image

Every time a new image of the sky is obtained, the master image will be subtracted from it. The result is an image which only contains the difference between the sky at that time and its average state; in other words a picture of what has changed, this image is known as the *subtracted image.* Figure 2 illustrates two images of a cluster of galaxies, taken three weeks apart, the far right plate is the subtracted image, revealing that a supernova has exploded in one of the galaxies. This subtracted image is then processed by a cluster of computers. The first task involves computing which objects are expected to appear in the subtracted image, given the area of sky, time of day, and the current state of knowledge of known orbits. A query is made to the *orbit catalogue,* which contains data about all known orbits. The results of this query are then cross matched with the subtracted image, leaving only objects which cannot be classified, and hence may be a new object discovery, or orbit. Further processing is performed, to try and compute smaller sections of orbit, known as a *tracklets.* If these smaller sections of orbits can be extrapolated (by cross referencing them with observations at earlier points in time), these new orbits, along with re-detections of known objects are updated in the orbit catalogue. With each re-detection of a known object, more information is provided, increasing the accuracy and further constraining the orbit. This process allows an accurate map of the sky to be built up, catching transient events in the act.

3.1   An Agent-Oriented Approach

The classification process described in section 3 is for known classes of object, but the hope is that, since LSST will provide a first attempt at time domain astronomy, it will discover new classes of object, previously undetected. Once the initial processing has finished, there will be some data which is left over. This data includes objects and orbits which can't be classified by the processing software. Typically, most of these objects will simply be junk, but this may only be revealed on the basis of comparison with other detections made from the same night. The systems which attempt to classify this data need to be reactive, collaborative, intelligent systems. On this basis, agent based techniques have been applied to the classification problem. It is important to note that certain details are left intentionally abstract, the moving objects scenario serves as a motivating factor, illustrating the kinds of features that our interaction protocol language and framework are required to model.

It is intended that agents will take over where the subtracted image processing left off. Groups of agents form a multiagent system, working on behalf of an observatory, in an attempt to classify whatever data is left over from the automated processing stage. Agents are initially set up with a certain amount of knowledge about properties of the data, and a number of statistical tests to perform. Agents need to cooperate and coordinate with one another, hence they are also set up with some rules about when and how to share information. Engineers can focus on developing individual, intelligent agents which are specialised in their own right. For example certain agents will have expertise on pixel failures on the camera, others contain data and a hypothesis about a certain kind of unclassified object. Figure 3 is an overview of the example scenario. Observatories are defined within the dotted circle, inside each observatory is a certain amount of local data (illustrated by databases), and a group of agents (illustrated by the square). Web services are shown as rounded rectangles. Communication between agents is shown by arrowed solid lines, web service invocations are shown as single arrowed dotted lines. An example interaction between a group of agents could be viewed as the following.

Agents at observatory A are attempting to classify objects left over from the image processing, one of the agents has located an item which cannot be classified locally. This anomaly appears on several plates of the sky on the subtracted image, so it wasn't present on the master image. The object and orbit classification algorithms cannot identify the anomaly, so it could potentially be a new species of object, or some kind of equipment failure. The agent has exhausted the possibility of solving the problem locally and needs to compare similar observations made on the same night with distributed observatories, databases and repositories. It wants to ask a question equivalent to 'has anybody else found anything strange in this particular area of sky, at time t, which could solve this possible anomaly?'.

In order to discover which observatories can offer the required data, the contract net protocol [13] is executed over a group of observatory agents known to have possible data about the area of sky we are interested in, at time t. This is illustrated by steps 1 to 4 of figure 3. A contract net agent (on behalf of the observatory) issues a call for participation over the set of possible observatory agents. The call for participation contains a proposal, defining the terms of agreement.

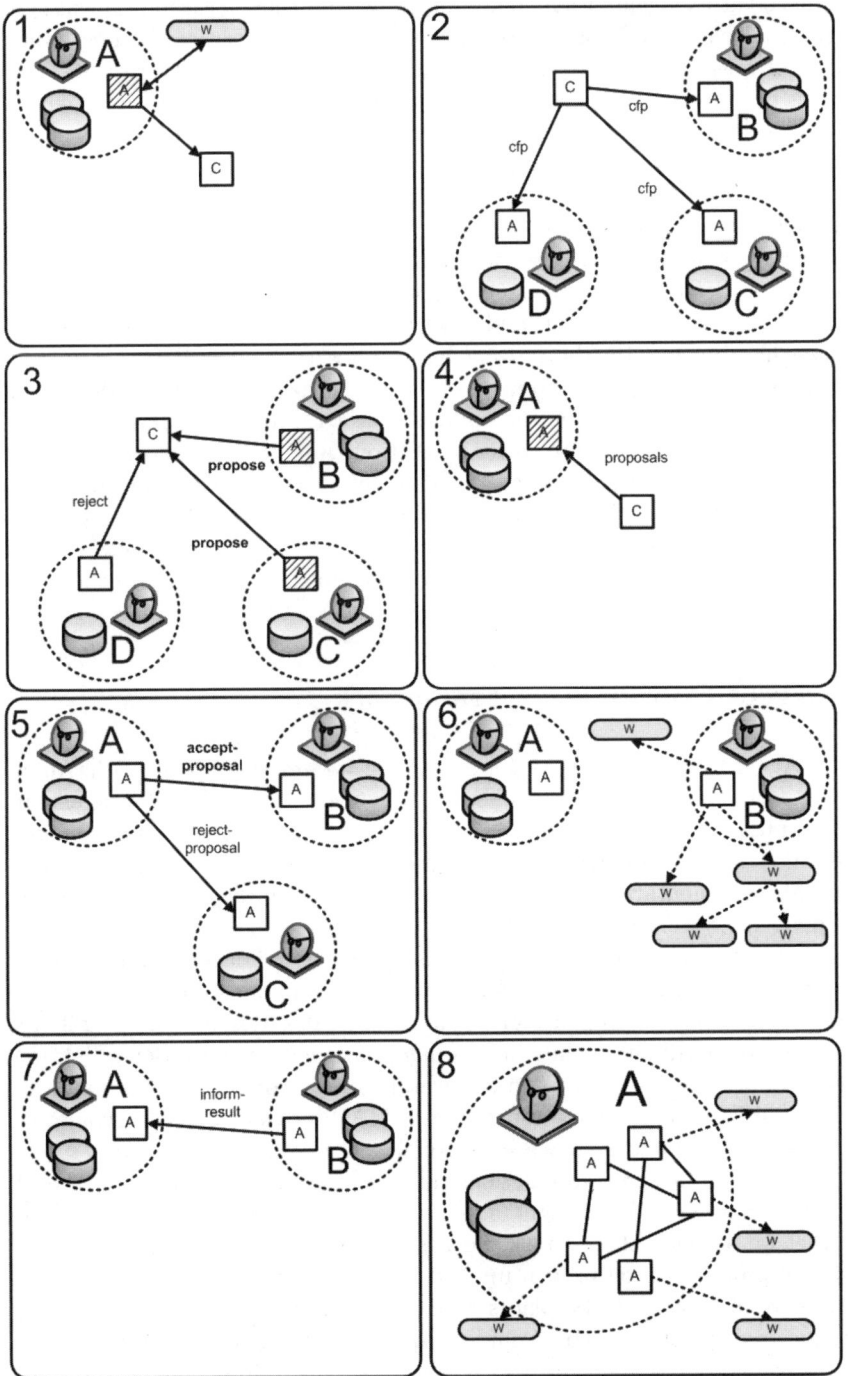

Fig. 3. Overview of LSST Scenario

The observatory agents then communicate within their local multiagent system to try and reach some form of conclusion about participation, issuing either an accept or reject message to the proposal. The set of agents who returned accept (in this case observatories B and C) are returned to the classification agent, who locally decides (based on some internal local knowledge and runtime conditions) which agent to obtain the data from. Step 5 of figure 3 shows an accept-proposal message being issued to the selected observatory (in this case B) and the remaining observatories are issued a reject-proposal message. It is then up to the observatory agent to locally retrieve and process the data in accordance to the agreed contract net proposal (step 6 of figure 3), this will involve negotiation of agents local to observatory B and a set of external web service calls. Once this process has finished, the data is sent back to observatory A. Here the agents can use the evidence gathered from the distributed observatories and databases to reach a conclusion regarding the unknown object, reporting anything to human scientists which may require closer inspection. Agents then continue to process the remainder of the junk data, following the same process again if an object cannot be classified locally. The paper now proposes an Agent Coordination Framework to address the problem of communication and web service invocation by agents in a distributed open, environment in order to solve the scenario detailed in this section.

4   Agent Coordination Framework

Multi Agent Protocols or MAP for short is an *interaction protocol* [12]. An interaction protocol is essentially a collection of conventions which allow agents in an open multiagent system to interact with one another. The term *open multiagent* system means that any agent can take part in the interaction, regardless of their internal implementation details; such as the language they are programmed in, or operating system they are run on.

The work of the MAP language builds upon the foundations laid down by the Electronic Institutions [6] framework; a popular technique for providing structure and organisation in an open multiagent system. It is designed as a light weight language to coordinate agents in an open multiagent system. Being lightweight it is therefore relatively sparse in features, however more complex semantics can, if required be layered on top of the basic MAP language. The abstract syntax of the MAP language is shown in figure 4.

The division of agent interactions into *scenes* is a key concept in the MAP language. Scenes can be thought of as a bounded space in which a group of agents interact on a single shared task. Scenes also allow the division of a large and complex protocol to be broken up into more manageable chunks. Scenes allow a measure of security to be places on a protocol, allowing agents which are not relevant to the protocol to be excluded from the scene. The most basic component in this framework is an agent, which is defined by a unique name:n and a role:r. The *role* of an agent is fixed until the end of the scene and determines which parts of the protocol code an agent can execute. Roles allow agents to be grouped together, many agents can share the same role, which means the agents have the same capabilities. Roles also allow us to specify multicast communication in MAP. For example, we can broadcast messages to all agents of a specific role.

An Agent's behaviour is defined by a set of Methods {M}, which can optionally take a list of Terms as arguments $\phi^{(k)}$. Methods are constructed from an Operation Set op, which enforce control flow in the agent and a set of actions α, which allow the agent to communicate and interact with a reasoning layer.

$$
\begin{array}{lll}
P \in \text{Protocol} & ::= n \ (r\{M\})^{+} & \text{(Protocol)} \\[2mm]
M \in \text{Method} & ::= \text{method}(\phi^{(k)}) = \text{op} & \text{(Method)} \\[2mm]
op \in \text{Operation} & ::= \alpha & \text{(Action)} \\
& \mid \ op_1 \ \text{then} \ op_2 & \text{(Sequence)} \\
& \mid \ op_1 \ \text{or} \ op_2 & \text{(Choice)} \\
& \mid \ op_1 \ \text{par} \ op_2 & \text{(Parallel Composition)} \\
& \mid \ \text{waitfor} \ op_1 \ \text{timeout} \ op_2 & \text{(Iteration)} \\
& \mid \ \text{invoke}(\phi^{(k)}) & \text{(Recursion)} \\[2mm]
\alpha \in \text{Action} & ::= \epsilon & \text{(No Action)} \\
& \mid \ \phi^{(k)} = p(\phi^{(l)}) \ \text{fault} \ \phi^{(m)} & \text{(Decision Procedure)} \\
& \mid \ p(\phi^{(k)}) \ \texttt{=>} \ \text{agent}(\phi^{(1)}, \phi^{(2)}) & \text{(Send)} \\
& \mid \ p(\phi^{(k)}) \ \texttt{<=} \ \text{agent}(\phi^{(1)}, \phi^{(2)}) & \text{(Receive)} \\
\phi \in \text{Term} & ::= v \mid a \mid r \mid c \mid \_ & \text{(Terms)}
\end{array}
$$

Fig. 4. MAP Abstract Syntax

Actions α, can have side-effects and fail. Failure of actions causes backtracking of the protocol. The action set firstly consists of the decision procedure. The decision procedure set is implemented as a set of methods, exposed as a *reasoning web service*. When an agent needs to make an internal decision, it invokes methods on this web service; for example the logic deciding which observatory agent to choose after the initial round of the contract net protocol. Given a list of input Terms $\phi^{(l)}$, a procedure will invoke the required method on the reasoning web service p, using the terms as input. If required it will produce a list of output terms $\phi^{(k)}$ (results from the procedure) which can be referenced throughout the duration of the agents execution cycle. A procedure can raise an exception, in which case the fault terms $\phi^{(m)}$ are bound to the exception parameters and backtracking of the protocol occurs.

The remaining two actions that an agent can reference are the send and receive actions. Interaction between the agents is performed by the exchange of messages, defined as performatives ρ , ie. message types. Messages take a list of terms as input $\phi^{(k)}$. Terms are defined as either a wildcard (_) , an agent name (a), a role type (r), a constant (c), or a variable (v). The send and receive actions contain two arguments $\phi_{(1)}$ and $\phi_{(2)}$. Agents can send a message to a specific agent (if $\phi_{(1)}$ contains an agent name), to any agent which is subscribed to a particular role (if $\phi_{(1)}$ is a wildcard and $\phi_{(2)}$ contains a role type), or simply send a message to any agent (if $\phi_{(1)}$ and $\phi_{(2)}$ are both wildcard types). Message passing between agents is assumed to be reliable, non blocking, buffered communication.

Control-flow in the protocol can be enforced in three ways. Firstly the sequence operator op_1 then op_2, evaluates op_2 only if op_1 did not contain an action that failed, otherwise it is ignored. The choice operator op_1 or op_2, handles failure in the protocol and evaluates op_2 only if op_1 contained an action that failed. The parallel operator op_1 par op_2, executes op_1 and op_2 in parallel. A waitfor loop allows repetition of parts of the protocol. If any action inside the loop body fails or the loops times out then the actions contained within the timeout body will be executed.

4.1   Protocol Execution

The MAP language is a specification designed to be directly executed by a group of agents. The typical process of executing a MAP interaction protocol is illustrated by figure 5.

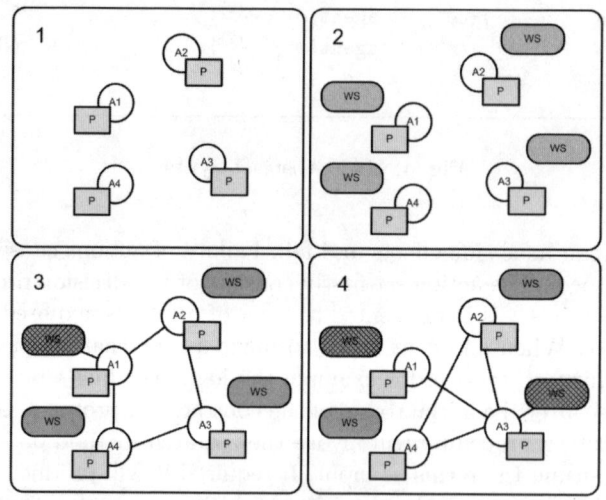

Fig. 5. MAP Protocol Execution

Once an engineer has designed a MAP interaction protocol, each agent taking part in the coordination must obtain a copy. This copy is stored locally to each agent, illustrated by step 1 of figure 5. Agents are represented as a circle with (A) inside and the interaction protocol as a grey rectangle with (P) inside. The only requirement on an engineer designing an agent is a layer of software which can translate and execute the steps in the protocol, and a reasoning web service which implements the decision procedures of a particular role type. Each agent maintains its own internal state. This internal state records which steps of the protocol it is currently executing and any variables which may be needed for sending/receiving messages and decision procedures.

Each agent taking part in the interaction must adopt a role, by adopting a role the agent must reference a reasoning web service which implements all the decision procedures required for that role type. This concept is illustrated by step 2 on figure 5: the reasoning web services are represented as a rounded rectangle containing (WS). This reasoning web service can be different for each agent. Once agents have obtained a copy of the protocol and have reference to a reasoning web service, enactment of the interaction protocol can begin. Agents follow the protocol as a script, calling the web services if and when required. Step 3 on figure 5 shows a pattern of interaction taking place, with the agent in the top left invoking its web service (hashed out on the diagram). A further pattern of interaction takes place, resulting in the agent on the bottom right invoking a method on its reasoning web service, illustrated by step 4 of figure 5. Execution terminates when all the protocol steps have been enacted, or the protocol fails. Failures can be classified as *external failures*, due to faulty web services invocations; or *internal failures*, due to a badly written protocol.

5   Application of Framework to Scenario

This section further illustrates the MAP protocol language by applying it to the motivating scenario presented in section 3. Figure 6 is a MAP protocol definition of an agent attempting to classify some of the left over data from the subtracted image processing. For simplicity the protocol contains just one agent definition, the role of classification, however it interacts with agents who have adopted the scientist, contractnet and observatory roles. Firstly it is important to note that different types of term are represented by prefixing variable names with $, role names with % and agent names with !

The classification protocol, shown in figure 6 implements the classification agent process described in section 3.1 and proceeds as follows. A list of un-classified objects ($junk) is received from a scientist agent (line 3). This list contains pointers to objects which cannot be classified by the automated algorithms discussed in the scenario. The agent then recursively traverses the list, attempting to classify the items locally. If at any time the agent cannot classify an object, calls to distributed observatories need to be made (line 14). This is achieved by making a request to an agent who has adopted the con-tractnet (line 21) role, supplying as parameters to the message: a list of suit-able agents ($potential_agents, line 18) and a proposal ($proposal, line 19). The contractnet agent (not described in this example) executes the contract net protocol, contacting all observatory agents in the list $potential_agents. When finished the contractnet agent returns a list of observatory agents (line 23) who returned propose to the protocol. The list of open proposals is then

```
%classification{
1  method() =
2    waitfor
3      (request($junk) <= agent($scientist, %scientist)
4        then invoke (localanalysis, $junk)
5        then invoke())
6    timeout (e)
7
8  method(localanalysis, $junk) =
9    (($head, $tail) = ExtractNext($junk)
10     then $result = StatTest($head)
11     then UpdateKnowledge($result)
12     then (QueryKnowledge($head)
13     then invoke(localanalysis, $tail)
14   or invoke(contractnetsend, $head, $tail))
15   or e)
16
17 method(contractnetsend, $unknown, $objects) =
18   $potential_agents = LookUp(%observatory, $unknown)
19   then $proposal = GenerateProposal($unknown)
20   then $cn = LookUp(%contractnet)
21   then request($potential_agents, $proposal) => agent($cn, %contractnet)
22   then waitfor
23     (response($open_proposals) <= agent($cn, %contractnet)
24       then ($accept, $reject) = Evaluate($open_proposals)
25       then invoke(contractaccept($accept, $objects, $unknown))
26          par invoke(contractreject($reject, $objects)))
27   timeout(e)
28
29 method(contractaccept, $accept, $objects, $unknown) =
30   ($observatory, $proposal) = ExtractProposal($accept)
31     then accept-proposal($proposal) => agent($observatory, %observatory)
32     then waitfor
33       (inform-result($opinion) <= agent($observatory, %observatory)
34         then $combined_opinion = GenerateOpinion($opinion)
35         then inform($combined_opinion) => (_, %scientist)
36         then invoke(localanalysis, $objects))
37       or (inform-failure() <= agent($observatory, %observatory)
38         then invoke(contractnetsend, $unknown, $objects))
39     timeout(e)
40
41 method(contractreject, $reject) =
42   ($head, $tail) = ExtractNext($reject)
43   ($observatory, $proposal) = ExtractProposal($head)
44     then reject-proposal($proposal) => agent($observatory, %observatory)
45     then invoke(contractreject, $tail)}.
```

Fig. 6. LSST Agent Protocol

evaluated locally (line 24), generating a list of rejected agents: $reject and a single suitable agent: $accept. An accept-proposal message is sent to the selected agent. If the observatory agent completes the tasks specified in the proposal an inform-result message is received (line 33). The data $opinion is used to generate a combined_opinion which is forwarded to the original scientist agent; informing a human scientist if anything unusual has occurred. A recursive call is then made, in an attempt to classify the remaining objects (line 36). However, if the observatory agent has been unsuccessful in completing its task, an inform-failure message is received (line 37). In this case, another attempt must be made to find suitable data from distributed observatories (line 38). In parallel to this task taking place, the agents who were unsuccessful in the proposal bid are rejected by the reject-proposal message (line 44).

The classification protocol is a straight forward implementation of the required functionality of the scenario, however there are some subtle issues in the protocol which require explanation. Role definitions can be divided up into a set of methods, allowing protocol code to be separated into smaller, manageable code chunks. Our protocol contains five method declarations. Protocols always begin execution with the default method, which is shown in this example from lines 1-6. Methods can be called by using the invoke operator, passing the necessary set of Terms as parameters to the method. For example, line 4 of the role definition shows an agent invoking the localanalysis method, using the list of unclassified objects, stored in the variable $junk as a parameter. An empty invoke() operation (line 5) will restart the default method when the protocol execution has terminated, effectively restarting the agent.

Agents connect to their internal reasoning layer by making invocations to a set of functions exposed as a reasoning web service. This set of functionss implements a given role definition, so for our classification agent the web service contains the following functions: ExtractNext, StatTest, UpdateKnowledge, QueryKnowledge, LookUp, GenerateProposal, Evaluate, ExtractProposal and GenerateOpinion. Line 12 shows the QueryKnowledge function being invoked, using the $head variable as a parameter. As discussed briefly in section 4, control flow is enforced by the sequence (then), choice (or) or parallel (par) operators. The use of the sequence and choice operators is illustrated in the localanalysis method. The agent extracts the head: $head and tail: $tail of the list and attempts to classify the head of the list locally, by invoking the StatTest function (line 10). It then proceeds to query its local knowledge based on the updated information (line 12). If the QueryKnowledge function fails, the or branch of the protocol is executed, invoking the contractnetsend method, which begins to seek assistance from distributed observatory agents. However, if the QueryKnowledge function succeeds (the agent can classify the data) a recursive call invoke(localanalysis, $tail) is made, using the tail of the list as input. If the function ExtractNext fails, meaning that the list is now empty the second or branch will be executed, in this case the empty action: e. The parallel operator is used in lines 25 and 26, in order to execute the contractaccept and contractreject methods.

The semantics of message passing corresponds to non-blocking, reliable and buffered communication. Sending a message succeeds immediately if an agent matches the definition, and the message will be stored in a buffer on the recipient. Receiving a message involves an additional unification step. The message supplied in the protocol definition is treated as a template to be matched against a message in the buffer. A unification of terms against the definition $\texttt{agent}(\phi_{(1)}, \phi_{(2)})$ is performed, where $\phi_{(1)}$ is matched against an agent name and $\phi_{(2)}$ to the agent role. For example, in line 3 of the protocol, the agent will receive the list of unclassified objects from any agent whose role is %scientist, and the name of this agent will be bound to the variable $scientist, for later reference. However in line 23, the classification agent will only receive the response from an agent of role observatory and in particular, the agent we sent the original request to, which is bound to the variable $cn. If the unification is successful, variables are bound based on the content of the message. For example, $open_proposals is stored locally upon receiving the message response($open_proposals), shown in line 23. This unification is particulary useful when we do not know the exact name of the agent in question and simply want to receive a message from a particular role type.

Sending will fail if no agent matches the supplied terms, and receiving will fail if no message matches the template defined in the protocol. Send and receive actions complete immediately (i.e. non blocking) and do not delay the agent. Race conditions are avoided by wrapping all receive actions in waitfor loops. For example in line 3, the agent will continue to loop until a request message is received. If this loop was not present the agent may fail to receive the reply and the protocol would terminate prematurely. A further advantage of using non blocking communication is that we can check for a number of different messages. Inside the waitfor loop (lines 32-39) the agent waits for either an inform-result message, indicating the observatory agent has fulfilled the original proposal, or an inform-failure message. The flow of the protocol is very different, depending on which message is received. Timeouts, which have not been used in this protocol implementation, specify what to do if a timeout (specified by a time limit) is reached.

6 Conclusions and Further Work

This paper has demonstrated how scientific workflow, a problem from the Grid community can be elegantly modelled with the use of interaction protocols, a technique from the multiagent systems community. Our scenario demonstrates a number of runtime decisions which need to be taken, highlighting why a predefined static workflow cannot solve the service composition problem. Interaction protocols offer a flexible, adaptable solution to scientific workflow modelling.

In particular, the MAP language and framework allows complex multiagent interactions and web service invocations through the use of a relatively simple formalism. It offers a number of advantages over the coordination techniques used by existing projects focused at scientific workflow composition:

- **Reasoning Models:** The MAP approach allows the rules of interaction to be explicitly expressed, while allowing individual agents to subscribe to their own reasoning models. MAP protocols do not sacrifice the self interest and autonomy of individual agents, although agents follow the protocol as a script each agent can adopt their own personalised strategy within the protocol. Reasoning web services can be mapped on an individual agent basis (providing personalised behaviour) or on role type (providing generic role behaviour). It is up to the engineer of the agent to provide the set of methods which form this reasoning web service.
- **Inter-operability:** Agents built by different organisations, using different software systems, written in different languages are able to communicate with one another in a common language with agreed semantics. The only requirement on an engineer wanting to build an agent that can coordinate within an open system, is a layer of software which can translate the protocol and a set of methods which make up the agents reasoning web service.
- **Layered Structure:** This model of interaction fills the gap between the low level transport issues of an agent and its high level rational processes. This layering removes some of the complications of designing large multiagent systems; ultimately helping in the design process.
- **Abstraction:** Agents add an extra level of abstraction, acting as stubs or proxies to the web services which are taking part in the coordination. This means that the agents can use their rational layer to make decisions at run-time when the web service coordination is actually taking place. Decisions can be taken for example about: which services to call, what to do if a particular service is down, how to react if an expected message is not received etc. This approach offers more than 'just coordination', provided by most web service composition frameworks and languages.
- **Rapid Prototyping:** As the protocols provide an executable specification of the coordination, they serve as an excellent mechanism for rapidly prototyping a sequence of interaction. Protocols can be used to engineer a prototype system from a scenario, even if the services or interaction model, or even both are undefined at the design stage. Services can be stubbed.
- **Compatibility:** The coordination mechanism defined using the MAP language is entirely external to the web services which are being coordinated. The web services themselves need no alteration or knowledge that they are even taking part in coordination. Therefore no modification of web services needs to take place and the protocol does not need to be disseminated between the web services themselves.

This work forms part of an on going research and implementation process. Many enhancements to the language are in the process of being made that make it more suited to e-Science computation. These enhancements include: support for large datasets through an extension of the type language; support for long-lived computation, e.g. by allowing break-points in the protocols; database integration for better handling of experiment data; and support for the composition of protocols into larger experiments at the scene level.

References

1. Business Process Execution Language for Web Services Specification, Version 1.1. Technical report, BEA Systems and IBM Corporation and Microsoft Corporation and SAP AG and Siebel Systems, July 2002.
2. Smart Grid Technologies Workshop. In *Fourth International Joint Conference on Autonomous Agents and Multiagent Systems*, Utrecht, The Netherlands, July 2005.
3. Agent-Based Grid Computing Workshop. In *6th IEEE International Symposium on Cluster Computing and the Grid*, Singapore, May 2006.
4. *The Grid 2: Blueprint for a New Computing Infrastructure*. Morgan Kaufmann Publishers, November 2004.
5. I. Altintas, C. Berkley, E. Jaeger, M. Jones, B. Ludaescher, and S. Mock. Kepler: An Extensible System for Design and Execution of Scientific Workflows. In *16th International Conference on Scientific and Statistical Database Management*, June 2004.
6. M. Esteva, J. Rodriguez, J. Arcos, C. Sierra, and P. Garcia. Formalising Agent Mediated Electronic Institutions. In *Catalan Congres on AI (CCIA'00)*, pages 29–38, 2000.
7. I. Foster, N. R. Jennings, and C. Kesselman. Brain meets Brawn: Why Grid and Agents Need Each Other. In *Proc. 3rd Int. Conf. on Autonomous Agents and Multi-Agent Systems*, New York, USA, 2004.
8. David Hollingsworth. *The Workflow Reference Model*. Workflow Management Coalition, Document Number tc00-1003 edition, January 1995.
9. Professor Dr. Huaglory and Dr. Rainer Unland, editors. *Multiagent and Grid Systems*. IOS Press.
10. B. Ludäscher, I. Altintas, and E. Jaeger-Frank M. Jones E. Lee J. Tao Y. Zhao C. Berkley, D. Higgins. Scientific Workflow Management and the Kepler System. *Concurrency and Computation: Practice & Experience*, Special Issue on Scientific Workflows, 2005.
11. A. Mayer, S. McGough, M. Gulamali, L. Young, J. Stanton, S. Newhouse, and J. Darlington. Meaning and Behaviour in Grid Oriented Components. In *Lecture Notes in Computer Science*, volume 2536, pages 100–111. Springer-Verlag Berlin Heidelberg, 2002.
12. Interaction Protocol Specifications. http://www.fipa.org/repository/ips.php3. Technical report, Foundation for Intelligent Physical Agents, 2002.
13. R. Smith. The Contract Net Protocol: High-level Communication and Control in a Distributed Problem Solver. *IEEE Transactions on Computers*, C-29(12):1104–1113, 1980.
14. Robert Stevens, Robin McEntire, Carole Goble, Mark Greenwood, Jun Zhao, Anil Wipat, and Peter Li. ^{my}Grid and the Drug Discovery Process. *Drug Discovery Today: BIOSILICO*, 4(2):140–148, 2004.
15. Large Synoptic Survey Telescope. http://www.lsst.org.
16. W.M.P. van der Aalst, A.H.M. ter Hofstede, B. Kiepuszewski, and A.P. Barros. Workflow Patterns. In *Distributed and Parallel Databases*, pages 5–51, July 2003.

Using Electronic Institutions to Secure Grid Environments

Ronald Ashri[1], Terry R. Payne[1], Michael Luck[1], Mike Surridge[2], Carles Sierra[3],
Juan Antonio Rodriguez Aguilar[3], and Pablo Noriega[3]

[1] University of Southampton, UK
{ra, trp, mml}@ecs.soton.ac.uk
[2] IT Innovation, Southampton, UK
ms@it-innovation.soton.ac.uk
[3] IIIA-CSIC, Spain
{sierra, jar, pablo}@iiia.csic.es

Abstract. As the technical infrastructure to support Grid environments matures, attention must be focused on integrating such technical infrastructure with technologies to support more dynamic access to services, and ensuring that such access is appropriately monitored and secured. Such capabilities will be key in providing a safe environment that allow the creation of virtual organisations at run-time. This paper addresses this issue by analysing how work from within the field of Electronic Institutions (EIs) can be employed to provide security support for Grid environments, and introduces the notion of a Semantic Firewall (SFW) responsible for mediating interactions with protected services given a set of access policies. An overarching guideline is that such integration should be pragmatic, taking into account the real-life lessons learned whilst developing, deploying and using the GRIA infrastructure for Grid environments.

1 Introduction

The Grid Computing paradigm [8] is aimed at supporting access to a variety of computing and data resources across geographical and organisational boundaries, to enable users to achieve (typically) complex and computationally intensive tasks. More specifically, the "Grid Problem" has been articulated as providing the means to support virtual organisations that can draw together different capabilities from across the Grid domain, to deliver services that might not otherwise be possible [6]. In attempting to realise this vision, research and development over recent years has focussed on directing Grid environments towards establishing the fundamentals of the *technical infrastructure* required, as represented by infrastructure development efforts such as the Globus toolkit [9], and standardisation efforts such as OGSA [16] and WS-Resource [2].

However, while such technical infrastructure is necessary in providing an effective platform to support robust and secure communication, this largely omits consideration of the other *higher-level* issues that need to be addressed before we can achieve the goal of formation and operation of virtual organisations at run-time based on a dynamic selection of services [8]. In particular, whilst low-level security concerns (including encryption, authentication, etc) are addressed, the problems of describing authorised

M. Klusch, M. Rovatsos, and T. Payne (Eds.): CIA 2006, LNAI 4149, pp. 461–475, 2006.

processes and the policies that are associated with those processes is largely ignored at this level. The requirement here is to specify which services are allowed to participate in the virtual organisation and what they are permitted to do.

If we consider virtual organisations in the context of agent-based computing, we can regard this problem as analogous to that of defining an *Electronic Institution (EI)*. Electronic Institutions, as defined in [3], can provide the necessary conceptual framework for describing the allowed participants in a virtual organisation as well as the permitted interactions in any given state. As such, they have proven useful in providing structured regulatory environments for heterogeneous external agents or users (in a broader sense). Furthermore, they are supported by tools such as ISLANDER [4], which can facilitated the process of defining an institution.

In this paper, we present a way of making use of such technologies in response to a specific set of needs for Grid applications, identified following practical experience gained through the development of the *GRIA (Grid Resources for Industrial Applications)* infrastructure [14]. Unlike Globus, GRIA was designed to support business interactions, and although it does not currently make explicit use of agent technologies, some of its underlying concepts resonate well with an agent approach. As such, it provides an ideal and flexible framework that could exploit agent technology to provide effective solutions for some of its current limitations.

In particular, we describe how EIs can be applied within the context of a Grid security device, and introduce the notion of a *Semantic Firewall*. The purpose of the Semantic Firewall is to protect Grid services by monitoring all external interactions with those services. Its key functionality is to ensure that all interactions with protected services fulfil the following criteria:

- The encountered interactions are those *expected*, given the agreed aims of the interaction and the current state of execution of a defined interaction protocol [1];
- The interactions must satisfy any security requirements associated with the interaction protocol.

The application of EIs for describing and subsequently monitoring interactions within the context of a Grid application represents one of the primary efforts in demonstrating (in practical terms) how agent technologies can be used in Grid environments. Whilst the perceived benefit of doing so has already been argued by Foster et al [7], this work represents a tangible example that realises this vision. In addition, it also demonstrates how such technologies can be *pragmatically* applied without requiring a drastic reconfiguration of existing Grid infrastructure, or the way in which Grid-developers design services. This is a significant issue since uptake of agent technologies is notoriously hard to achieve in new environments [17]. Thus, the ability to introduce agent-based principles without a significant shift in the status quo, whilst adding value within a Grid Infrastructure is a key contribution.

The paper is structured as follows. In the next section we briefly describe the GRIA infrastructure and provide an example of its operation (section 3) that we use throughout the paper. Subsequently, in sections 4 and 5 we introduce the notion of the Semantic Firewall, and briefly describe Electronic Institutions. We then discuss in section 6 how we map GRIA concepts on to EI concepts and provide a concrete example of that mapping (section 7). The paper concludes in section 8.

2 The GRIA Framework

The GRIA framework is a Grid infrastructure developed using just the basic web service specifications, as part of the EC IST GRIA project [14]. It provides the necessary infrastructure for exposing computationally intensive applications across the Grid, with ancillary facilities for data staging and quality of service negotiation. A Grid service within GRIA can be considered as a *contextualised* web service, which exposes its functionality through a well-defined interface. It is contextualised since interactions with the web service are based on a well-defined process, with a context that is maintained throughout the lifetime of the process. It is the interaction protocols associated with these long-lived processes that we aim to make explicit through an appropriate formal description, so that they can be specified to an external access control and monitoring system.

In GRIA, a number of services and systems, both external and internal, are used. Internal systems and services include resource schedulers, accounting systems and databases, while external services include data staging services, certification authorities, and so forth. GRIA also provides features such as negotiation over the quality of service and long-term accounts with service providers. We do not discuss these issues in detail here, but the interested reader is referred to [14], in which a more complete description of the GRIA system is available.

Rather, what we present here is a simplified example of the operation of GRIA, and a description of how these concepts are mapped to an electronic institution. Our example is based on a straightforward usage scenario for Grid applications that is supported by GRIA. It involves a *client* that submits a computation job (such as rendering a short, animated video clip) to a *job service*, where the computation job specifies a particular application to execute, such as a renderer. Now, in order for a client to be able to submit a computation job it must first have an *account* open where the computation job is able to bill for services. Furthermore, it must have the resources of the computation job allocated to it via a *resource allocator*.

In typical Grid scenarios, accounts are opened by *Budget Holders* (e.g. the manager of a research group), who then allow *Account Users* (e.g. the individual researchers planning and running jobs) access to the account so that they can allocate resources and run jobs charged to the account, etc.

The main limitations of the current GRIA implementation are as follows:

- Currently, the service interaction model is fixed as a static factory pattern. The business processes linking the *Account Service*, *Resource Allocation* and *Job Service* cannot be changed to fit local policies or business models.
- The interactions between services are encoded through a shared state held within the services themselves. This means that services cannot exist in different domains. While it is entirely reasonable for the *Resource Allocation* service to be collocated with the *Job Service* that uses its resources, it should not be necessary for the *Account Service* also to be operated by the same domain.
- There is no explicit description of the service interactions. This means that one cannot provide any external monitoring to detect any corruption of the services, which might become evident through some change in the interaction with them.

3   A Desired Scenario

Consider the collection of services and service clients shown in Figure 1, which illustrates the example described above. In this figure, we represent the different web services involved, whereas the functional statements positioned above the arrows represent the methods that could be used to interact with the services on the right of the organisational boundary.

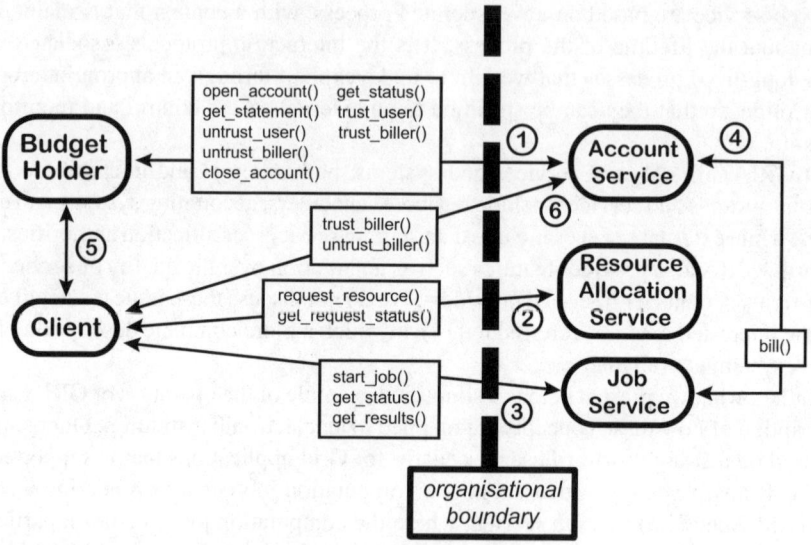

Fig. 1. Grid Interaction Example

This scenario is based heavily on GRIA, but significantly simplified to make it clear and tractable enough for our purposes. However, in one way, Figure 1 is more sophisticated than the current GRIA implementation: some interactions that would be hidden in the "back office" within a GRIA deployment have been included in the service interfaces, so that we can construct a scenario in which the *Account Service* is not collocated with the *Resource Allocation Service* and the *Job Service*.

The interactions between clients and services are as follows:

- A *Budget Holder* is able to interact with the *Account Service* (1). It first requests the account to be opened and, once the account is active it can, amongst other actions, delegate or revoke access to the account by account users and allow billers to charge for their services to the account.
- A *Client* is able to interact with the *Resource Allocation* service (2) so as to request access to a computation services.
- Once a resource has been allocated, the *Client* can interact with the *Job Service* (3), requesting the computation to be run.
- Before starting to run a job, the *Job Service* must be able to charge, or bill some entity for performing the job. The *Job Service* does this by getting a contextualised

endpoint for the *Account Service* (4) representing an Account, and billing the Account for the job using an operation of the specified *Account Service* in the specified context.

- The contextualised endpoint for billing the Account must be obtained from the *Account Service*. To get one, the *Client* must be authorised by the *Budget Holder* (5), who must call an operation of the *Account Service* (6) to inform it of the *Client's* trusted status.
- In the case where the account credit has run out, or the account has been closed, all *Account Users* should not be allowed to initiate any further resource allocations or jobs. However, it should still be possible for *Billers* to bill for any outstanding jobs remaining until the account has been properly cleared.

In trying to describe these interactions, we must also take note of other more practical challenges.

- Some interactions, such as the opening of an account, are lengthy processes that necessarily involve both online and offline actions. For example, an *Account Manager* may need to perform credit checks offline before approving a *Budget Holder's* account.
- It is likely that the *Budget Holder* and *Client* are behind opposed conventional firewalls. Bearing in mind that on the Grid, interactions may persist for a long time, this means all interactions must be initiated by clients, because if the services try to do so, their attempt may be blocked by the client-organisation's firewall.

This second point means that the interactions are one-sided, with clients polling services for the current status of the interaction where necessary. For example, a *Budget Holder* should be able to poll the *Account Service* to find out when their account has been approved, and the *Client* must poll the *Job Service* to find out when a job starts or terminates. In the context of an agent-oriented approach to modelling this scenario, we note that there are services that cannot initiate interactions. This is different to the more general agent models, in which agents are both proactive and reactive.

4   Semantic Firewall

Our goal is to enhance security in a services-oriented environment whilst addressing the challenges and limitations described above. We aim to decouple services by providing well-defined interaction protocols, and eliminating the need for the services to deal with undesired messages by filtering out such messages at the organisational level. Furthermore, we want to provide network administrators with the ability both to allow flexible interaction with Grid services (something not possible using conventional firewall technologies) and to maintain careful control over those interactions.

To achieve these goals, we introduce the notion of a security device which is able to reason about the current state of interaction between external services, and those services protected by the security device, and also to ensure that all messages sent to these services are consistent with the current state. We use the term *Semantic Firewall* *(SFW)* to describe the device since, as opposed to a normal firewall, it monitors traffic at the level of messages exchanged between web services and takes into account the context of interaction. It is important to emphasise that the SFW is only concerned with, and protects, the *interests* of the protected service, and thus does not require a *global view* of all the interactions taking place within the context of a client attempting to achieve a task in which the protected service is also involved. For example, in the above example, the SFW does not need to be aware of the interactions between the *Budget Holder* and the *Client*.

The requirements for the SFW are divided into *description and reasoning*, and *infrastructure* requirements. The former refers to what we should be able to describe about the services and interactions between them and what type of reasoning we should be able to perform, while the latter refers to what the infrastructure should be able to do given the descriptions and reasoning over them.

1) Description and Reasoning Requirements

Allowed Participants: The first step is for the SFW to have an appropriate set of descriptions of what entities are allowed to interact with protected services, and for the SFW to be able to appropriately identify the services attempting to communicate with protected services. In part, the solution involves the use of "conventional" security technologies such as PKI and X.509 for user authentication. However, beyond such technologies we must also look at the *context* of interaction and the intent of the interaction, which is an issue that the SFW, rather than lower-level security technologies, will handle.

Allowed Interactions: Subsequently, based on who is attempting to interact, we require a description of a currently permissible interaction protocol. The possible interactions in a web services environment are based on the methods described within the WSDL (Web Services Definition Language)[1] interfaces for each service. However, WSDL interfaces do not provide any information about permitted processes for any given instant. Instead, developers typically rely on documentation associated with the services to determine the appropriate process through which methods in the WSDL interface should be called. Our aim is to ensure that this process is adhered to, by providing the SFW with the descriptions of the process.

Dependencies between parties: The SFW must be aware of the dependencies between interaction protocols for different parties. This includes both the manner in which actions from one party can *limit* what another party can do, and how actions from one party can *enable* another to interact with a protected service.

2) Infrastructure Requirements

Transparent protection: The infrastructure should take into account the fact that the SFW should be invisible to services outside the protected domain. Whilst we may foresee a future situation in which several SFWs, each operating within a different organisational domain, play an active part in defining and supporting the context through which services from those domains can interact, we must begin with the assumption that external services are not aware of the existence of such a device.

Informing users on reasons for failure: In order for both system administrators and users to accept any actions taken by the SFW (such as rejecting messages, etc), the

---

[1] http://www.w3.org/TR/wsdl

device should be able provide justifications about its actions, such as why an interaction was accepted or rejected. A clear trace of the reasoning of the device is necessary to achieve this requirement.

5   Electronic Institutions

Given the set of requirements described in the previous section, an essential component is the existence of an interaction protocol and a means of defining the protocol and its dependencies. Although there are a variety of technologies that enable us to define interaction protocols (e.g. [11,1]), as well as a significant amount of work on describing appropriate policies [15], what we require is something that take a more integrated view of the situation. In this regard, EIs are able to address several of the concerns raised above. Below we provide a brief overview of this work before moving on to describe how the concepts of Electronic Institutions can be mapped to those in GRIA, so as to provide appropriate descriptions that the SFW can use to monitor interactions.

To define an EI, it is necessary first to define a common language to allow agents to exchange information, the activities that agents may perform within the institution, and the consequences of their actions. Our model of electronic institutions is thus based on four principal elements: a dialogical framework, a set of scenes, a performative structure and a set of normative rules [3,10,12].

The *dialogical framework* defines the valid illocutions that agents can exchange, and the participant roles and relationships. In the most general case, each agent that exists within in a multi-agent environment is endowed with its own inner language and ontology. In order to allow agents to successfully interact with others we must address the fundamental issue of relating their languages and ontologies to each other. EIs solve this problem simply by establishing acceptable illocutions, communication primitives and knowledge representation concepts through a common, well defined ontology (vocabulary) — the common language to represent the "world" — that all the agents adhere to. Moreover, the dialogical framework defines the participant roles within the EI and the relationships among them. Each role defines a pattern of behaviour within the institution, and any agent within an institution is required to adopt a subset of them. In the context of an EI, we distinguish between two types of roles, *internal* and *external* roles. The internal roles can only be played by what we call *staff* agents which are those pertaining to the institution. These are analogous to workers within human institutions. Since an institution delegates their services and duties to the internal roles, an external agent can never play an internal role. By sharing a dialogical framework, we enable the heterogeneous community of agents to exchange knowledge with each other.

The set of possible activities within an electronic institution is defined by the composition of multiple, distinct, and possibly concurrent dialogic activities, where each activity involves different groups of agents playing different roles. For each activity, interactions between agents are articulated through agent-group meetings, which follow well-defined communication protocols; we refer to such meetings as *scenes*. Thus, all agent interactions that take place within an EI exist within the context of a scene. In addition, the protocols for each scene model the possible dialogic interactions between *roles* instead of *agents*; thus, scene protocols define patterns of multi-role conversation, and hence can be multiply instantiated by different groups of agents. A distinguishing feature of scenes is that they allow agents either to enter or to leave a scene at certain particular moments (states) of an ongoing conversation depending on their role.

A scene protocol is specified by a directed graph, where the nodes represent the different states of the conversation, and the arcs are labelled with illocution schemes or timeouts that allow the conversation state evolve. Thus, at each point of the conversation, the EI defines what can be said, by whom and to whom. As we want the protocol to be generic, state transitions cannot be labelled by grounded illocutions. Instead, illocution schemes have to be used where, at least, the terms referring to agents and time must be variables, whilst other terms may be either variables or constants. Thus, the protocol is independent of concrete agents and time instants. Moreover, arcs labelled with illocution schemes can have some associated constraints which impose restrictions on the valid illocutions, and on the paths that the conversation can follow.

While a scene models a particular multi-agent dialogic activity, more complex activities can be specified by establishing relationships among scenes, captured in the *performative structure*. In general, the activity represented by a performative structure can be depicted as a collection of multiple, concurrent scenes. Agents navigate from scene to scene, constrained by the rules defining the relationships among scenes. In order to capture the relationships between scenes, we use a special type of scene, known as *transitions*. Transitions allow the expression of agent synchronisation points (i.e. selection points where agents can decide which path to follow), or parallelisation points (i.e. where agents are sent to more than one scene). They can be seen as a type of router in the context of a performative structure. Moreover, the very same agent can possibly participate in multiple scenes at the same time. Likewise, there may be multiple concurrent instantiations of a scene, so we must also consider: 1) whether the agents following the arcs from one scene to another are allowed to start a new scene execution; 2) whether they can choose to join just one or a subset of the active scenes; or 3) whether they can choose to join all active scenes.

A performative structure can be seen as a network of scenes in which their connections are mediated by transitions that determine the role flow policy. Finally, from the set of scenes, the initial and final scenes determine the entry and exit points of the institution respectively.

In the context of an institution, agent actions have consequences, usually in the shape of compromises which impose obligations or restrictions on dialogic actions of agents in scenes in which they are acting (or will be acting in the future). Normative rules affect the behaviour of agents by imposing obligations or prohibitions.

Note that we are considering dialogic institutions, and the only actions considered are the utterance of illocutions. Therefore, we can refer to the utterance of an illocution within a scene or when a scene execution is at a concrete state. The intuitive meaning of normative rules is that if illocutions are uttered in the corresponding scene states (and some predefined expressions are satisfied), then other illocutions satisfying other expressions must be uttered in the corresponding scene states.

To summarise, the notions presented above define the regulatory structure of an EI as a "workflow" (i.e. performative structure) of multi-agent protocols (scenes) along with a collection of (normative) rules that can be triggered off by an agent's actions (speech acts).

Note also that the formalisation of an EI focuses on macro-level (societal) aspects, instead of on micro-level (internal) aspects of agents. This allows us to more easily map the concepts between Grid environments and EIs. Since no assumptions are made about internal aspects of agents, it is possible to define one-to-one mappings between actions (or services) provided by each agent, and web services defined within a Grid environment.

6   Using Electronic Institutions in GRIA

Given the descriptions of the requirements for the Semantic Firewall in section 4 and the overview of the main Electronic Institution concepts in section 5, it is now possible to investigate how such concepts can be applied within the SFW. This is achieved by defining each *scenario* of interaction with the protected domain as an Electronic Institution. A scenario will typically be associated with a specific business model, such as described in Section 3.

6.1   Mapping GRIA Models to Electronic Institutions

Services: Each service that is expected to interact in a well-defined scenario with a protected service is associated with a role within the electronic institution. *External roles* are used to represent services that are not protected by the SFW, whereas *internal roles* are used for the protected services. This allows us to clearly distinguish between those services that perform institutional services and that the SFW has a responsibility of protecting, and external services that may be providing the client with a service but do not form part of the institution. In our running example, the *Account Service*, *Resource Allocation* and *Job Service* occupy internal roles, whereas the *Budget Holder* and *Client* occupy external roles.

Interactions and Business Process: The allowed interactions between services and the entire business process can be encoded as individual scenes within an EI. The participants in the scene are the relevant services, whilst the illocutions being uttered are mapped to the corresponding WSDL methods. In addition, in those situations where the SFW itself needs to be made aware of events that occur within protected services, it appears as a participant within a scene. To illustrate this, consider the case where a request is sent by a *Budget Holder* to close the account. In this case, the *Account Service* may still allow *Billers* to bill the account up to the point where the account has been settled (which may involve offline actions). When the account is finally closed, the SFW needs to informed about this closure explicitly by the *Account Service*, since there is no illocution that will enable it to understand that. In this case the SFW is an active participant in the scene.

The wider business process, with regards to a particular task and the protected services, is described by the performative structure of the electronic institution. This allows

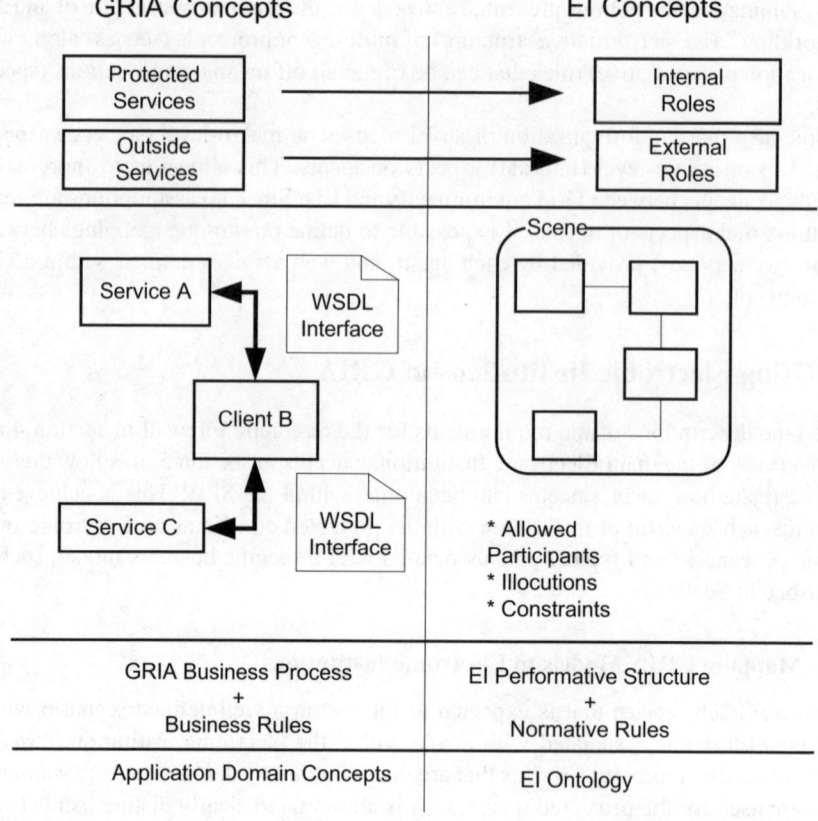

Fig. 2. Mapping GRIA concepts to EIs

us to define the appropriate flow of roles between scenes as well as impose a particular process or workflow to the entire set of interactions with different parties.

Cross-party dependencies: We have already mentioned that an important goal of the SFW is that of managing the dependencies between interacting parties. Returning to the example mentioned above, once a *Budget Holder* has requested that an account should be closed, access should be restricted to all clients associated with the closed account to prevent them from assigning other billers. Thus, an action within a scene that involves both the *Budget Holder* and the *Account Service* also has an implication on the permissible actions within scenes involving the *Account Service* and *Clients*. Within an EI, this can be modelled by defining a set of norms, to ensure that specific actions can hold only as long as some constraints hold true.

Domain Ontology: The application domain concepts that are relevant to the interactions between protected and external services are encoded within the EI ontology. The ISLANDER editor supports the management of such ontologies, thereby facilitating the creation of mappings between the datatypes used within the EI definition and the datatypes used by the web service interface.

6.2   Semantic Firewall Core Modules

Given the discussion of the mapping between the EI concepts and SFW concepts in the previous section, it is now proceed to address the structure of the SFW itself, illustrated in Figure 3.

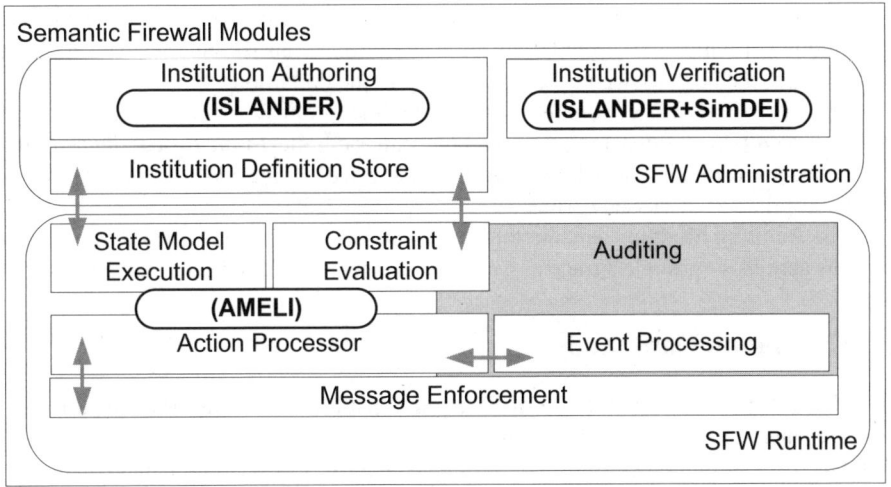

Fig. 3. Semantic Firewall Core Modules

The SFW has two main components: the *Administration* and the *Runtime Environment*. The SFW Administration deals tasks such as authoring, verification and storage of electronic institutions, whereas the SFW Runtime Environment is responsible for the verification of messages based on the electronic institution definitions. We discuss each of these in more detail below.

Semantic Firewall Administration: SFW Administration is divided into three different modules:

- *Authoring:* The ISLANDER tool provides a graphical interface to facilitate the definition of an institution. It allows for the definition of a common ontology, the performative structure and related scenes, as well as related norms.
- *Verification:* For verification of the electronic institution, ISLANDER can provide verification of the *structural properties* while verification of the dynamic behaviour can be achieved through simulation in the SIMDEI tool [13].
- *Storage:* A verified definition of the SWF is stored in the *Institution Definition Store* for use by the SFW Runtime.

Semantic Firewall Runtime: The SFW Runtime consists of several modules, and is primarily concerned with the verification of each message passing to protected services.

- *The Message Enforcement Module:* This is responsible for receiving messages and dealing with all lower level issues, such as parsing the SOAP structure of messages and providing the relevant part of the message to the *Action Processor*, which performs the mapping between the WSDL message and the definition within the electronic institution.
- *The State Model Execution and Constraint Evaluation Modules:* These modules are queried to determine whether the message is a valid one based on the electronic institution definition. This functionality can be provided by the AMELI run-time engine [5] which can directly accept a definition of an EI and can reason about what are the next allowable steps according to the definition.
- *The Event Processing Module:* At the same time as the *State Model Execution* and *Constraint Evaluation* modules are being queried, the *Event Processing* module collects information sent by the protected services to the SFW, whenever that is appropriate as discussed earlier.
- The Auditing Module: This module is responsible for keeping a record of the various actions so provide a trace as to why messages may have been rejected.

7 Evaluation Case Study

In order to better illustrate the use of Electronic Institutions within the SFW, this section presents a case study which includes a description of the performative structure, followed by a simplified definition of the scene dealing with account management.

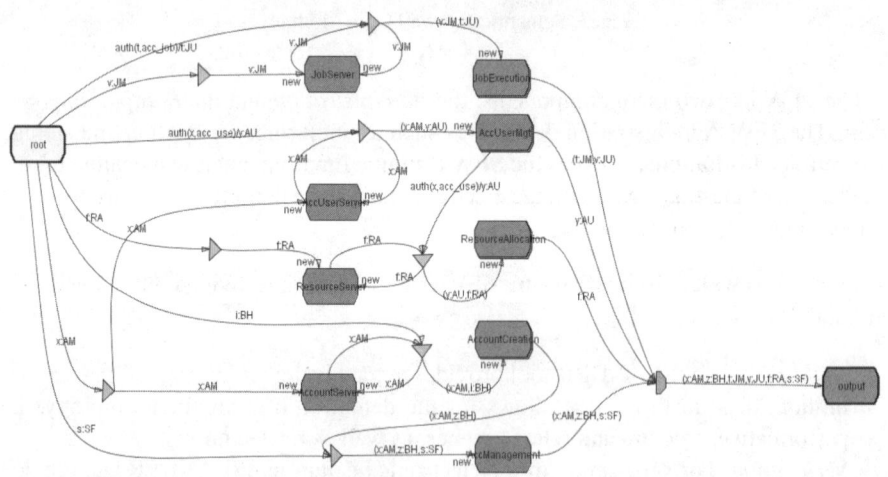

Fig. 4. GRIA Performative Structure

Figure 4 illustrates the GRIA business process as an electronic institution's performative structure. It contains a collection of scenes (represented as boxes) relating to each of the GRIA services[2]. We differentiate between *internal roles* representing the GRIA protected services; in this case the services behind the organisation boundary as depicted in Figure 1, *Account Manager* (AM), *Job Manager* (JM), *Resource Manager* (RM), and *Semantic firewall* (SF); and *external roles* representing the GRIA external users, which include the *Budget Holder* (BH), *Account User* (AU), and *Job User* (JU). Agents playing these roles migrate from service to service after synchronising at transitions (represented by triangles).

Access to services is controlled through several scenes (see Table 1). All these scenes are specified to realise a client-server model. Thus, for instance, when a *JU* agent requires a job execution, it first synchronises with a *JM* agent that is continuously listening to agents' requests at the `JobServer` scene. Thereafter, the two agents progress together through the transition to create a new execution of the `JobExecution` scene. Note that the scenes offering the GRIA protected services are specified so that they can be multiply instantiated, and thus serve multiple agents' requests simultaneously. Note also that there are scenes (`JobServer`, `ResourceServer`, `AccountServer`, and `AccUserServer` particularly devoted to the listening functions of the agents playing the internal roles.

Table 1. Various services offered through different scenes

Service	Offered through Scene
Resource Allocation Service	`ResourceAllocation` Scene
Job Service	`JobExecution` Scene
Accounting Service Service	`AccountCreation` Scene
	`AccUserMgt` Scene
	`AccManagement` Scene

Next, we examine the `AccManagement` scene, illustrating how the specific interactions with services are managed. There are three participant roles in this scene, the *Account Manager (AM)* represented by the *Account Service*, the *Budget Holder (BH)* and the *Semantic Firewall (SF)*. The boxes represent different states of the dialog, while the arcs between them represent possible illocutions.

At `W0` all roles are allowed to enter the scene. At this state the *BH* is allowed to request a statement of the account (`arc 0`), to which the *AM* can reply with a statement. In addition, the *BH* can request for the *AM* to trust a biller (`arc 1`), which the AM can either acknowledge positively (`arc 2`) or refuse (`arc 5`). If the request is accepted this will enable a *Client*, matching the criteria of the user that should be trusted to enter the institution and also assign billers to this account, as we discussed in Section 3. The *BH* can also request for an account to be closed (`arc 4`). This lead the scene to a state where the only thing the *BH* can do is request the status of the account and once the account has been closed, which as we already mentioned may involve offline actions,

---

[2] Note that the connections between scenes are labelled with the roles migrating from service to service along with agent variables that are expected to be bound to actual agent identifiers at run-time.

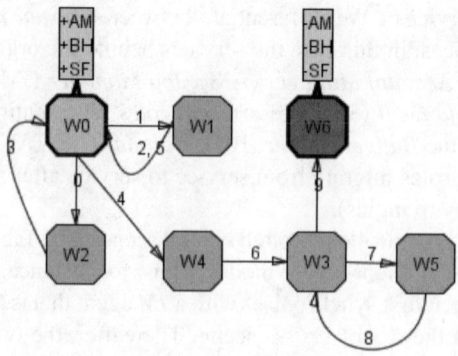

Fig. 5. Account Management Scene

the *SF* is informed of this so that is can reflect this change on the allowed actions of other interested parties such as billers.

8   Conclusion

In this paper we proposed a method for enhancing security within Grid environments by making use of Electronic Institutions to support the specification, verification and monitoring of permissible interactions within a protected (i.e. firewalled) environment. This is achieved though a dedicated device, the *Semantic Firewall*, which maintains a set of mappings between entities within Electronic Institutions and Grid Services. The Semantic Firewall facilitates the integration of agent technologies within a Grid environment, without requiring radical changes to the infrastructure or the way developers build Grid services. As such, this work represents a pragmatic example of how the worlds of Grid infrastructure and agent research can come together to provide effective solutions to the existing limitations for Grid infrastructure.

The work described in this paper provides several avenues for further development. In the short-term, we can begin to define more flexible business models within GRIA, since we can take advantage of the flexible description and monitoring capabilities to ensure that they are adhered to. Subsequently, we can begin to examine how such institutions can be agreed upon at run-time between different organisations, where each protected by a Semantic Firewall. Finally, we must also begin to investigate the possibility of making *deployment* of services within a Grid environment more flexible by providing high-level definition of allowed processes (as EIs) which developers can then ensure they adhere to.

Acknowledgements

This work was supported by the Engineering and Physical Sciences Research Council (EPSRC) Semantic Firewall project (ref. GR/S45744/01).

References

1. R. Ashri, G. Denker, D. Marvin, M. Surrdige, and T. R. Payne. Semantic Web Service Interaction Protocols: An Ontological Approach. In S. A. McIlraith, D. Plexousakis, and F. van Harmelen, editors, *Int. Semantic Web Conference*, volume 3298 of *LNCS*, pages 304–319. Springer, 2004.
2. K. Czajkowski, D. F. Ferguson, Foster I, J. Frey, S. Graham, I. Sedukhin, D. Snelling, S. Tuecke, and W. Vambenepe. The WS-Resource Framework. Technical report, The Globus Alliance, 2004.
3. M. Esteva. *Electronic Institutions: from specification to development. PhD Thesis Universitat Politècnica de Catalunya (UPC), 2003*. Number 19 in IIIA Monograph Series. IIIA, 2003.
4. M. Esteva, D. de la Cruz, and C. Sierra. ISLANDER: an electronic institutions editor. In *The First Int. Joint Conf. on Autonomous Agents and Multiagent Systems*, pages 1045–1052. ACM Press, 2002.
5. M. Esteva, J. A. Rodriguez-Aguilar, B. Rosell, and J. L. Arcos. AMELI: An agent-based middleware for electronic institutions pages 236-243, new york, usa, july 19-23 2004. In N. R. Jennings, C. Sierra, L. Sonenberg, and M. Tambe, editors, *3rd Int. Conf. on Autonomous Agents and Multi-Agent Systems*, pages 236–243. ACM Press, 2004.
6. I. Foster. The Anatomy of the Grid: Enabling Scalable Virtual Organisations. In R. Sakellariou, J. Keane, J.R. Gurd, and L. Freeman, editors, *7th International Euro-Par Conference*, volume 2150 of *LNCS*. Springer, 2001.
7. I. Foster, N. R. Jennings, and C. Kesselman. Brain meets Brawn: Why Grid and Agents need each other. In N. R. Jennings, C. Sierra, L. Sonenberg, and M. Tambe, editors, *3rd Int. Conf. on Autonomous Agents and Multi-Agent Systems*, pages 8–15. ACM Press, 2004.
8. I. Foster and C. Kesselman. *The Grid 2: Blueprint for a New Computing Infrastructure*. Morgan Kaufmann, 2003.
9. I. Foster, C. Kesselman, J. M. Nick, and S. Tuecke. Grid Services for Distributed System Integration. *IEEE Computer*, 35(6):37–46, June 2002.
10. P. Noriega. *Agent-Mediated Auctions: The Fishmarket Metaphor. PhD Thesis Universitat Autònoma de Barcelona (UAB), 1997*. Number 8 in IIIA Monograph Series. IIIA, 1999.
11. S. Paurobally, J. Cunningham, and N. R. Jennings. Developing Agent Interaction Protocols Using Graphical and Logical Methodologies. In M. Dastani, J. Dix, and A. El Fallah-Segrouchni, editors, *PROMAS*, volume 3067 of *LNCS*, pages 149–168. Springer, 2003.
12. J. A. Rodriguez-Aguilar. *On the Design and Construction of Agent-mediated Electronic Institutions, PhD Thesis, Universitat Autònoma de Barcelona (2001), 2001*. Number 14 in IIIA Monograph Series. IIIA, 2003.
13. Carles Sierra, Juan Antonio Rodriguez-Aguilar, Pablo Noriega, Marc Esteva, and Josep Lluis Arcos. Engineering multi-agent systems as electronic institutions. *European Journal for the Informatics Professional*, V(4):33–39, August 2004.
14. S. Taylor, M. Surridge, and D. Marvin. Grid Resources for Industrial Applications. In *2004 IEEE Int. Conf. on Web Services (ICWS'2004)*, 2004.
15. G. Tonti, J. M. Bradshaw, R. Jeffers, R. Montanari, N. Suri, and A. Uszok. Semantic web languages for polic representation and reasoning: A comparison of kaos, rei and ponder. In D. Fensel, K. Sycara, and J. Mylopoulos, editors, *Proceedings of the 2nd International Semantic Web Conference*, volume 2870 of *LNCS*, pages 419–437. Springer, 2003.
16. S. Tuecke, K. Czajkowski, I. Foster, J. Frey, S. Graham, C. Kesselman, T. Maguire, T. Sandholm, D. Snelling, and P. Vanderbilt. Open grid services infrastructure. Technical report, Global Grid Forum, 2003.
17. M. J. Wooldridge and N. R. Jennigns. Software engineering with agents: Pitfalls and pratfalls. *IEEE Internet Computing*, 3(3):20–27, 1999.

Author Index

Lecture Notes in Artificial Intelligence (LNAI)

Vol. 3946: T.R. Roth-Berghofer, S. Schulz, D.B. Leake (Eds.), Modeling and Retrieval of Context. XI, 149 pages. 2006.

Vol. 3944: J. Quiñonero-Candela, I. Dagan, B. Magnini, F. d'Alché-Buc (Eds.), Machine Learning Challenges. XIII, 462 pages. 2006.

Vol. 3930: D.S. Yeung, Z.-Q. Liu, X.-Z. Wang, H. Yan (Eds.), Advances in Machine Learning and Cybernetics. XXI, 1110 pages. 2006.

Vol. 3918: W.K. Ng, M. Kitsuregawa, J. Li, K. Chang (Eds.), Advances in Knowledge Discovery and Data Mining. XXIV, 879 pages. 2006.

Vol. 3913: O. Boissier, J. Padget, V. Dignum, G. Lindemann, E. Matson, S. Ossowski, J.S. Sichman, J. Vázquez-Salceda (Eds.), Coordination, Organizations, Institutions, and Norms in Multi-Agent Systems. XII, 259 pages. 2006.

Vol. 3910: S.A. Brueckner, G.D.M. Serugendo, D. Hales, F. Zambonelli (Eds.), Engineering Self-Organising Systems. XII, 245 pages. 2006.

Vol. 3904: M. Baldoni, U. Endriss, A. Omicini, P. Torroni (Eds.), Declarative Agent Languages and Technologies III. XII, 245 pages. 2006.

Vol. 3900: F. Toni, P. Torroni (Eds.), Computational Logic in Multi-Agent Systems. XVII, 427 pages. 2006.

Vol. 3899: S. Frintrop, VOCUS: A Visual Attention System for Object Detection and Goal-Directed Search. XIV, 216 pages. 2006.

Vol. 3898: K. Tuyls, P.J. 't Hoen, K. Verbeeck, S. Sen (Eds.), Learning and Adaption in Multi-Agent Systems. X, 217 pages. 2006.

Vol. 3891: J.S. Sichman, L. Antunes (Eds.), Multi-Agent-Based Simulation VI. X, 191 pages. 2006.

Vol. 3890: S.G. Thompson, R. Ghanea-Hercock (Eds.), Defence Applications of Multi-Agent Systems. XII, 141 pages. 2006.

Vol. 3885: V. Torra, Y. Narukawa, A. Valls, J. Domingo-Ferrer (Eds.), Modeling Decisions for Artificial Intelligence. XII, 374 pages. 2006.

Vol. 3881: S. Gibet, N. Courty, J.-F. Kamp (Eds.), Gesture in Human-Computer Interaction and Simulation. XIII, 344 pages. 2006.

Vol. 3874: R. Missaoui, J. Schmidt (Eds.), Formal Concept Analysis. X, 309 pages. 2006.

Vol. 3873: L. Maicher, J. Park (Eds.), Charting the Topic Maps Research and Applications Landscape. VIII, 281 pages. 2006.

Vol. 3864: Y. Cai, J. Abascal (Eds.), Ambient Intelligence in Everyday Life. XII, 323 pages. 2006.

Vol. 3863: M. Kohlhase (Ed.), Mathematical Knowledge Management. XI, 405 pages. 2006.

Vol. 3862: R.H. Bordini, M. Dastani, J. Dix, A.E.F. Seghrouchni (Eds.), Programming Multi-Agent Systems. XIV, 267 pages. 2006.

Vol. 3849: I. Bloch, A. Petrosino, A.G.B. Tettamanzi (Eds.), Fuzzy Logic and Applications. XIV, 438 pages. 2006.

Vol. 3848: J.-F. Boulicaut, L. De Raedt, H. Mannila (Eds.), Constraint-Based Mining and Inductive Databases. X, 401 pages. 2006.

Vol. 3847: K.P. Jantke, A. Lunzer, N. Spyratos, Y. Tanaka (Eds.), Federation over the Web. X, 215 pages. 2006.

Vol. 3835: G. Sutcliffe, A. Voronkov (Eds.), Logic for Programming, Artificial Intelligence, and Reasoning. XIV, 744 pages. 2005.

Vol. 3830: D. Weyns, H. V.D. Parunak, F. Michel (Eds.), Environments for Multi-Agent Systems II. VIII, 291 pages. 2006.

Vol. 3817: M. Faundez-Zanuy, L. Janer, A. Esposito, A. Satue-Villar, J. Roure, V. Espinosa-Duro (Eds.), Nonlinear Analyses and Algorithms for Speech Processing. XII, 380 pages. 2006.

Vol. 3814: M. Maybury, O. Stock, W. Wahlster (Eds.), Intelligent Technologies for Interactive Entertainment. XV, 342 pages. 2005.

Vol. 3809: S. Zhang, R. Jarvis (Eds.), AI 2005: Advances in Artificial Intelligence. XXVII, 1344 pages. 2005.

Vol. 3808: C. Bento, A. Cardoso, G. Dias (Eds.), Progress in Artificial Intelligence. XVIII, 704 pages. 2005.

Vol. 3802: Y. Hao, J. Liu, Y.-P. Wang, Y.-m. Cheung, H. Yin, L. Jiao, J. Ma, Y.-C. Jiao (Eds.), Computational Intelligence and Security, Part II. XLII, 1166 pages. 2005.

Vol. 3801: Y. Hao, J. Liu, Y.-P. Wang, Y.-m. Cheung, H. Yin, L. Jiao, J. Ma, Y.-C. Jiao (Eds.), Computational Intelligence and Security, Part I. XLI, 1122 pages. 2005.

Vol. 3789: A. Gelbukh, Á. de Albornoz, H. Terashima-Marín (Eds.), MICAI 2005: Advances in Artificial Intelligence. XXVI, 1198 pages. 2005.

Vol. 3782: K.-D. Althoff, A. Dengel, R. Bergmann, M. Nick, T.R. Roth-Berghofer (Eds.), Professional Knowledge Management. XXIII, 739 pages. 2005.

Vol. 3763: H. Hong, D. Wang (Eds.), Automated Deduction in Geometry. X, 213 pages. 2006.

Vol. 3755: G.J. Williams, S.J. Simoff (Eds.), Data Mining. XI, 331 pages. 2006.

Vol. 3735: A. Hoffmann, H. Motoda, T. Scheffer (Eds.), Discovery Science. XVI, 400 pages. 2005.

Vol. 3734: S. Jain, H.U. Simon, E. Tomita (Eds.), Algorithmic Learning Theory. XII, 490 pages. 2005.

Vol. 3721: A.M. Jorge, L. Torgo, P.B. Brazdil, R. Camacho, J. Gama (Eds.), Knowledge Discovery in Databases: PKDD 2005. XXIII, 719 pages. 2005.

Vol. 3720: J. Gama, R. Camacho, P.B. Brazdil, A.M. Jorge, L. Torgo (Eds.), Machine Learning: ECML 2005. XXIII, 769 pages. 2005.

Vol. 3717: B. Gramlich (Ed.), Frontiers of Combining Systems. X, 321 pages. 2005.

Vol. 3702: B. Beckert (Ed.), Automated Reasoning with Analytic Tableaux and Related Methods. XIII, 343 pages. 2005.

Vol. 3698: U. Furbach (Ed.), KI 2005: Advances in Artificial Intelligence. XIII, 409 pages. 2005.

Vol. 3690: M. Pěchouček, P. Petta, L.Z. Varga (Eds.), Multi-Agent Systems and Applications IV. XVII, 667 pages. 2005.